Rural Unrest during
the First Russian Revolution

Historical Studies in Eastern Europe and Eurasia

Volume I

Series editors:

Alexei Miller, Alfred Rieber, Marsha Siefert

Rural Unrest during the First Russian Revolution

Kursk Province, 1905–1906

Burton Richard Miller

Central European University Press
Budapest–New York

© 2013 by

Published in 2013 by

Central European University Press

An imprint of the
Central European University Limited Liability Company
Nádor utca 11, H-1051 Budapest, Hungary
Tel: +36-1-327-3138 or 327-3000
Fax: +36-1-327-3183
E-mail: ceupress@ceu.hu
Website: www.ceupress.com

400 West 59th Street, New York NY 10019, USA
Tel: +1-212-547-6932
Fax: +1-646-557-2416
E-mail: martin.greenwald@opensocietyfoundations.org

ISBN 978-615-5225-17-8

Library of Congress Cataloging-in-Publication Data

Miller, Burton Richard.
 Rural unrest during the first Russian Revolution : Kursk Province, 1905-1906
/ Burton Richard Miller.
    pages cm. -- (Historical studies in Eastern Europe and Eurasia ; volume 1)
 Includes bibliographical references and index.
 ISBN 978-6155225178 (hardbound)
 1. Russia--History--Revolution, 1905-1907--Social aspects--Russia (Federation)--
Kurskaia oblast'. 2. Peasants--Russia (Federation)--Kurskaia oblast'--History--
20th century. 3. Villages--Russia (Federation)--Kurskaia oblast'--History--20th
century. 4. Social conflict--Russia (Federation)--Kurskaia oblast'--History--20th
century. 5. Government, Resistance to--Russia (Federation)--Kurskaia oblast'--
History--20th century. 6. Social change--Russia (Federation)--Kurskaia oblast'--
History--20th century. 7. Kurskaia oblast' (Russia)--History--20th century. 8.
Kurskaia oblast' (Russia)--Rural conditions. I. Title.

 DK264.2.K78M55 2013
 947'.35--dc23

                    2012047916

Printed in Hungary by
Prime Rate Kft., Budapest

Dedicated to the memory of
IRINA ANATOL'EVNA MILLER
1954–2001

Contents

List of Maps, Tables and Figures

Acknowledgments

At one point in its life cycle in the second half of the twentieth century, a part of my generation of Americans was closely concerned with the question of social and political change, the transitional processes by which the mythologies and traditions that define a known societal present move into an unknown future. The manuscript that is presented in the following pages is a legacy of that brief era of intellectual ferment, an expression of my abiding interest in the character and pre-history of the "revolutionary situation"—that most extreme expression of these tectonic movements— that develops within the vast, dense and infinitely intricate architecture of customs, interrelationships, transactions, interests, expectations and perceptions, all shaped by the past, that identify a social order, render it cohesive, serve as the matrix within which individual members orient their lives, and invest its arrangements of power, authority and obedience with the vital measure of legitimacy. In the course of the extended research and writing that is presented to the reader in this volume, the author has come to the view that the keystone in this complex architecture is and remains the essential aspiration of individuals or groups of individuals toward that sense of justice that resides in the moral, material and institutional recognition by the larger society of their right to subsistence and survival, however true it is that the material requirements of "subsistence" and "survival" come to be defined very differently in different epochs and different societies.

That the history of the Russian Empire during its twilight decades provided an appropriate framework for this inquiry was a conviction that derived from my earliest work with Professors Richard G. Robbins and Byron T. Lindsey during the waning years of a long undergraduate sojourn at the University of New Mexico. To these I am obliged not only for this grand initial impetus, but also for imparting to me for the first time a profound sense of this history as a matter to be approached strictly on its own terms, shorn of the overarching preconceptions and expectations engendered by my specifically American heritage and prejudices.

The monograph that follows, however, is principally the product of an extended professional preparation at Columbia University under the direction of the late Professor Leopold Henri Haimson (1927–2010). This collaboration incorporated my participation in Professor Haimson's justly celebrated cycle of colloquia in which the asynchronous historical movement of the constituent elements of Imperial Russian society toward the shattering events of the early twentieth century were reconstructed against the backdrop of those transformative social, economic and cultural forces that gradually crystallized into a spectrum of unprecedented challenges to the existing order toward the end of the nineteenth century. It was in the course of this intensive exercise that my interest in the themes that I present in the following pages emerged and evolved. My apprenticeship also included a three-year internship under Leo's stewardship in the international Project of Labor History and its processing and analysis of primary statistical materials drawn from sources on industrial structures and labor unrest generated by various instances of the Imperial bureaucracy; the reader will have occasion to observe that this experience has exerted a powerful influence, for better or for worse, on the present work. The manuscript itself has been resurrected out of the author's dissertation, written during his tenure as a Whiting Fellow (1990–1991) and as a fellow at the Harriman Institute for the Advanced Study of the Soviet Union (1991–1992, 1992–1993), and submitted in partial fulfillment of the doctoral requirements at Columbia University at the end of 1992. The thesis was directly inspired by the fertile and profound sense of historical development that Professor Haimson propounded and under his close supervision. Even after those eleven years of direct collaboration came to a close, Leo nevertheless kept a close watch over his former student and spared no opportunity to militate for a return to a revision of that initial and rather chaotic composition, first in the form of a short summary précis, written in Paris during 2002–2004, and then in a reworking of the entire manuscript upon my return to New York. These writings were reviewed with pleasure by my former boss, until such time as the state of his health no longer permitted him to take on such tasks. In the truest of senses, this work is as much Leo's as it is mine, though any lapses in the analysis and failings of the ultimate conclusions are strictly those of the author. It is my hope that the scholarly contribution made by this effort to an understanding of the events that foretold the looming end of the *ancien régime* in Russia will be sufficient measure of my gratitude and esteem for a human being that I regarded as a mentor, a figure larger than life, but also as a friend, wise in the ways of the world.

The initial archival research from which central elements of the monograph was drawn was performed under the auspices of a grant from the International Research and Exchanges Board (IREX) during 1988–1989, in accordance with a plan developed under the supervision of Professor Ivan Dmitrievich Koval'chenko (1923–1995) of the Faculty of History of Moscow State University and facilitated by the willing aid of his assistant and collaborator, the then *dotsent* Leonid Iosifovich Borodkin in the Department of Sources and Historiography of the USSR. On both this occasion and on my irregular, unannounced appearances in Moscow over the ensuing years, Leonid Iosifovich played a decisive role both in suggesting and ensuring my access to libraries and archival institutions that would prove useful in assembling materials. Not surprising in a person in whom natural human warmth and an eagerness to impart to others from his own store of knowledge make of him a natural teacher and leader, Leonid always strove to keep me abreast of the latest developments in Russian historical writing, and in particular those that involved the application of quantitative methods to primary historical sources, an area in which he is today a leading specialist in the Russian academic establishment and continues the pioneering work of his late mentor.

The iterations of the manuscript were read at different stages of its development and in its various forms, from a short summary to a full-blown manuscript, by Professor Gerald M. Easter (Boston College), Dr. Alessandro Stanziani (Directeur d'études, École des hautes études en sciences sociales), Professor William G. Rosenberg (University of Michigan) and Professor Alfred J. Rieber (Central European University), all of whose comments and encouragement are deeply appreciated and contributed crucially in one way or another to the progress of the book.

This work would have been impossible without the active assistance of the archivists of the old Central State Archive of the October Revolution in Moscow and Central State Historical Archive in Leningrad, and the staffs of the Russian State Library (the *Leninka*), the library at the Institute of Scientific Information for the Social Sciences of the Russian Academy of Sciences (INION RAN), the Bibliothèque Nationale de France, the Bibliothèque de Documentation Internationale Contemporaine (Nanterre), the Library of Congress, the Joseph Regenstein Library at the University of Chicago, the Columbia University system of libraries and the Slavonic Division of the New York Public Library in New York.

Lastly, I would also like to express my gratitude to my wife, Maryna Aleksandrovna Miller, and to my daughter, Maria Sergeevna Savrasova, who have patiently endured the author's long preoccupation with Russian peasants and the several years of its monopoly over a good part of his free time. The area maps in this volume are the result of daughter Maria's steady hand over the old military maps and her skill and dexterity at employing the latest Adobe software suites, a facility that I was never fated to master.

Map 1. Kursk Province

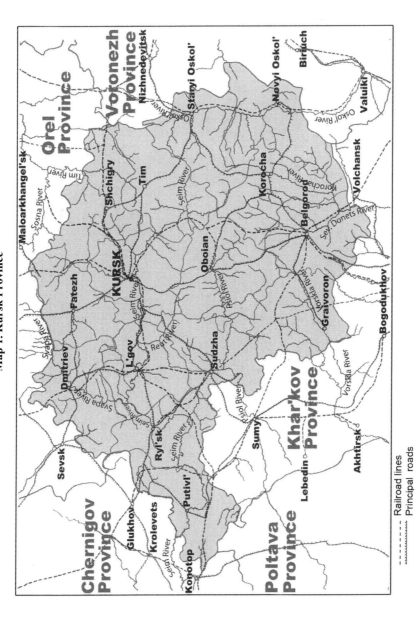

-·-·-·- Railroad lines
˙˙˙˙˙˙˙˙ Principal roads

Introduction

The events to which I shall devote my attention in this study, even at the remove of a century, retain immense interest for historians of revolutionary processes that shook the *ancien régime* in Russia in the first decade of the twentieth century. The "dress rehearsal" for the larger cataclysms of 1917 from which Soviet power emerged triumphant, the First Russian Revolution of 1905–1907 occupies a significant place in this historiography. Among the tumultuous events of these years, the waves of unrest that engulfed many rural districts of the Empire during 1905–1907, particularly in the Baltic, Central Agricultural and Mid-Volga Regions, have rightly attracted special attention. Indeed, these events are now often viewed as the opening phase in a period of rural unrest that, prefigured already in the disturbances in Poltava and Khar'kov Provinces in 1902, ended only with the Red Army's ultimately successful campaign to put down peasant revolts against Soviet power during 1920–1922.[1]

Parallels drawn between the intensification of the "peasant movement" during 1905–1906 and again in 1917–1918 derive in part from larger historical contexts: disastrous military defeats suffered by Russian armies in wartime, acute political turmoil and economic dislocation, and a paralysis of the ruling elites in the face of the ensuing crises, leading—although only for a short interval in 1905—to an eclipse of state authority. In both periods, a political crisis forced to the surface increasingly bitter conflicts between the autocratic state and those powerful cross-currents of opposi-

---

[1] T. Shanin and V. Danilov, "Nauchno-issledovatel'nyi proekt... (Vmesto vvedeniia)," in Danilov and Shanin, eds., *Krest'ianskaia*, 5–6; V. V. Kondrashin, "Krest'ianskaia revoliutsiia na Povol'zhe," *Istoricheskie zapiski* (Penza), 179–186.

tion that expressed the aspirations of disparate and competing elements within Russia's "census society" toward a decisive voice in the affairs of the nation. These extraordinary confrontations were both framed and profoundly shaped by irruptions of revolutionary unrest in the urban centers and rural districts of unprecedented scale that dictated in the most essential way the correlation of forces in the political arena and the evolving calculations of all political actors. Mass revolutionary and counter-revolutionary violence in 1905–1907, which brought Russia to the brink of civil war, the duration and ferocity of state-organized repression, and the strident, super-heated passions that colored the political struggle were, seen together, symptomatic of the larger crisis and of those social fears and hatreds tearing at the fabric of Imperial society.

The direct result of the rising revolutionary tide of 1905, the institution of a nationally elected legislature, declaration of civic freedoms of conscience, of speech, of assembly and of person, and an unprecedented proliferation of political parties and organizations inaugurated the short-lived experiment in constitutional government that was to be swept aside in 1917.[2] The Manifesto of 17 October 1905 and subsequent legislative acts, culminating in the proclamation of the Fundamental Laws of the Russian Empire of 23 April 1906, however, set out only a rudimentary and ambiguous framework for grafting "alien" legislative principles onto the old edifice of bureaucratic government that had historically derived its sense of mission and legitimacy from the unlimited personal political authority of the Russian autocrat. To be sure, the very survival of the Duma as an institution would henceforth reflect the tense and fragile consensus that the *status quo ante* could now not be restored, that the Manifesto had set down a historical boundary line that could not now be recrossed.[3] The unrestrained acrimony between Tsarist ministers and majorities of the people's deputies during sessions of the first two ("revolutionary") Dumas nevertheless expressed the central tensions inherent in the structure of "constitutional autocracy": the bitter, seemingly existential contest between the state power (*vlast'*) and that vital element of the Empire's public-minded elite (*obshchestvennost'*) that had come to see itself as representative of the nation, and the deep hostility with which the Duma was

---

[2] From an extensive literature surrounding proclamation of the Manifesto of 17 October 1905, see especially Anan'ich, Ganelin, Dubentsov, Diakin and Potolov, *Krizis samoderzhaviia v Rossii, 1894–1917*, 157–323; Verner, *The Crisis of Russian Autocracy*; Ganelin, *Rossiiskoe samoderzhevie v 1905 godu*; Malysheva, *Dumskaia monarkhiia*.
[3] G. M. Kropotkin, "Praviashchaia biurokratiia," *OI*, 2006, No. 1, 24–42.

viewed both by Russia's revolutionary parties and by reactionary circles both inside and outside government. Moreover, the single-minded insistence of peasant deputies in both the First and Second Dumas on versions of land reform that demanded expropriation of private estates without compensation was not just a most powerful challenge to the established order. It also placed in the harshest light the painful dilemmas of the moderate "constitutionalist" majorities, which relied upon the continued intensity of revolutionary violence—their "wager on *Acheron*"[4]—to extract further political concessions from the autocracy.

Extralegal enactment of the electoral statute of 3 June 1907 illustrated the fact that the government had now lost any illusions about the strength of monarchist sympathies among Russian peasants. With restoration of order by armed force in the country districts well under way,[5] the Stolypin ministry thus acted unilaterally to minimize the role of the vast majority of Russian subjects in the "political nation" at precisely that historical moment at which fundamental reforms of peasant landholding practice and rural institutions were to be debated, enacted and carried out. For even as repression mounted in intensity with redeployment of Russian armed forces from the Far East to the affected rural districts and introduction of field courts-martial, disorders in the countryside during 1905–1906 had forced a critical moment in the evolution of official attitudes on the "agrarian question." The object of debates in Imperial commissions and at ministerial levels of state bureaucracy on and off for more than three decades (most intensely in the later years of Witte's tenure as Minister of Finance[6]), reform of the civil status of the peasant *soslovie*, its juridical

---

[4] The phrase recurs in Vasilii Alekseevich Maklakov's account, *Pervaia gosudarstvennaia duma: vospominaniia sovremennika*, a memoir bitterly critical of the "theoreticians" (Miliukov) who came to dominate the direction of the Constitutional Democratic Party at the expense of the more pragmatic elements of public activism, and drove the party toward a political posture that foreclosed any real possibility of cooperation with the existing order, which, in this view, would have laid the groundwork for an alternative to the revolutionary solution.

[5] For the full range of measures to be taken to combat revolutionary sedition in the countryside that included some palliative initiatives (hastening processes of land transfers through the Peasant Bank; informal conversations between local officials and landowners and administrators known for the most egregious abuses of peasant rights), but was principally concerned with the organization and execution of police repression, see "Tsirkuliar' predsedatelia Soveta ministrov P. A. Stolypina ot 15 sentiabria 1906 g. general-gubernatoram, gubernatoram i gradonachal'nikam," in *KA*, 1929, t. 32(1), 162–182.

[6] Simonova, *Krizis agrarnoi politiki tsarizma*; Macey, *Government and Peasant in Russia*.

status, its institutions and its land use patterns, were now invested with the greatest urgency. The package of legislation proposed by the Stolypin ministry (1906–1911) incorporated, of course, land reform measures that marked the end of acrimonious debates in government circles over the fate of the peasant land commune. Yet in tandem with the Law of 9 November 1906 and related acts that were to follow, the reforms also envisioned an even more far-reaching judicial and administrative reorganization that aimed at completing the work of the Great Reforms of the 1860s by at last integrating the peasantry into the life of the nation on an equal juridical footing with other Russian citizens.[7]

The successful opposition to these reforms in the broader sense in which they were conceived must be ascribed in part to reactions to the unrest in the countryside during 1905–1906 among Imperial elites and much of "census society." Rural revolutionary violence both fed and "confirmed" those enduring social prejudices and paternalistic stereotypes of Russian peasants as a "dark" and "savage" mass, benighted by grinding poverty and low levels of cultural development, and characterized by a lack of respect for civil order or property rights, a penchant for gratuitous violence and a willing credulity before the blandishments of revolutionary propaganda. Closely interwoven both with the very *raison d'être* of the state bureaucracy, its civilizing mission, and with self-serving justifications advanced by the landed nobility for its privilege and power in rural society, such attitudes were, of course, hardly novel at the time of the revolution. They had been a dominant *leitmotiv* that surfaced and resurfaced as a sort of reflexive limit to official policy discourse on "the agrarian question" both before and after 1861, and drove a fusion of "counter-reform" and noble self-interest on rural affairs that marked the reign of

---

[7] The *ukaz* of 5 October 1906 ("Ob obmene nekotorykh ogranichenii v pravakh sel'skikh obyvatelei i lits drugikh podatnykh sostoianii," *PSZ* III, v. 26, No. 28392, 891–893), equalized peasant rights to enter state service or centers of higher learning with those of other Imperial subjects. An affidavit of exit from the commune was no longer required for these purposes or for joining the clergy. It granted peasants the right to choose their place of residence and to obtain and renew a passport (the residence permit continued to be obligatory) without consent of the head of household or the commune, the latter losing their right to recall absent members. The rule that the governor confirm all peasant *zemstvo* deputies was abolished. The *ukaz* thus went some way toward easing the juridical disabilities of the peasantry, but the segregated structures of administration and justice remained unchanged down to 1917. Diakin, "Stolypin i dvorianstvo (proval mestnoi reformy)" in Nosov, ed., *Problemy krest'ianskogo zemlevladeniia*, 231–274; Wisclo, *Reforming Rural Russia*, passim (but especially on the Stolypin ministry, 195–304).

Alexander III (1881–1894).[8] Indeed, such prejudices were more or less common to educated society as a whole, often existing incoherently with exaltation of the peasant (*muzhik*) as the very incarnation of the Russian people (*narod*).[9] Yet they most significantly reflected central preoccupations of those at the center of power, influential elements at Court, in the ruling bureaucracy and among the landed nobility, that remained viscerally unreconciled to and fearful of the socio-economic and cultural changes that were remaking Russian society after the era of the Great Reforms of the 1860s.

It is therefore not surprising that the abrupt and aggressive intrusion of the masses into political contests between Imperial elites during 1905–1907 and an unprecedented emergence of organized expressions of popular will and action should have exerted great influence on the unfolding of events. Failure of the "all-nation movement of liberation" to achieve any more than a fleeting unity at the very moment of its triumph in October 1905 reflected contradictory and competing political visions, tactical calculations and the multiple social and regional interests within the opposition itself. Yet it also fractured because these divisions were compounded and embittered by the shattering experience of mass revolutionary violence and the deep-seated social fears that it served to accentuate across the political spectrum of responses, both official and non-official, to the long-prophesied, long-dreaded spectacle of Russia's lower classes (*nizy*) in full revolt.[10] In particular, the provincial landed nobility's experience of peasant disorders in 1905–1906 and of the complete breakdown of authority in the rural districts in which they took place considerably dampened the ardor of much of "liberal" *zemstvo* opinion for changes in the existing order that might deliver the country to "troubles and turmoil." For conservatives among the landed gentry, moreover, the shocks of 1905–1906 (including the government's own brief dalliance with the idea of compulsory alienation of private property[11]) provoked a sustained and vitupera-

---

[8] Zakharova, *Zemskaia kontrreforma 1890 g.*; Whelan, *Alexander III and the State Council*; Tvardovskaia, "Tsarstvovanie Aleksandra III," in Grosul, ed., *Russkii konservatizm*, 276–360.

[9] Cathy A. Frierson, *Peasant Icons*; Stephen P. Frank, "Confronting the Domestic Other," in Steinberg and Frank, eds., *Cultures in Flux*, 74–107.

[10] Galai, *The Liberation Movement in Russia, 1900–1905*.

[11] I refer here to the so-called Kutler plan, which proposed the compulsory alienation in favor of land-poor peasants of those private lands usually leased out to peasant tenants. The plan was sponsored by Nikolai Nikolaevich Kutler during his brief tenure (1905–1906) as director of the newly created Department of Land Use and Agriculture before

tive hostility toward any reform that might compromise the primacy of its political influence and economic interests in the countryside in any way. Conservative gentry activism struggled to evolve its own national organizations[12] and aimed at erasing liberal influence in the *zemstvos*[13] during the caucuses of 1906, but also promptly came to stand as a base of support for right-wing parties that sought election or appointment of their nominees to the reformed State Council, now renovated as the upper chamber of the new national legislature. Along with the restrictive electoral criteria enacted by the Stolypin ministry, the mobilization of opinion in defense of gentry privilege played a large part in giving the "political nation" that took its seats in the Third Duma itself a markedly more conservative cast. Tacitly supported by Nicholas II, abetted in a common cause by like-minded allies entrenched at Court or in the state apparatus and seconded by influential elements of elite society, conservative reaction was to set formidable obstacles to the more comprehensive reforms for which the new electoral law was to have built a constituency.[14] Able to muster sufficient unity to bar the road to a gradual democratic integration of Russian society, the fragile and divided conservative coalition was to provide far too narrow a social base to sustain the autocracy during the final catastrophe ten years later, in February 1917.

Mass revolutionary unrest within the Empire during the First Russian Revolution, the rural "anarchy" of 1905–1906, bloody working-class insurrections in Moscow and other cities in December 1905, and the great intensity of the campaign of repression that ensued, thus provoked reactions that combined to exert a fatal influence on the fortunes of the

---

being forced to resign as a result of the uproar that the proposal provoked. He subsequently became active in the Constitutional-Democratic Party.

[12] A short review of the evolution of national gentry organizations is Hosking and Manning, "What Was the United Nobility?" in Haimson, ed., *The Politics of Rural Russia, 1905–1914*, 142–183.

[13] The *zemstvo* was an elective body instituted in 34 provinces with European Russia in 1864, empowered with certain local administrative responsibilities and assigned limited taxing authority. The populace as a whole elected deputies to provincial and district *zemstvo* assemblies, but weighting of the franchise so heavily favored noble landowners with medium-sized and large estates—these participated directly in elections rather than through delegates (*upolnomochennye*)—that these latter effectively controlled both the Assemblies and the Boards charged with executive functions.

[14] On the political struggles in the Stolypin era, see Hosking, *The Russian Constitutional Experiment*; Diakin, *Samoderzhavie, burzhuaziia i dvorianstvo v 1907–1911 gg.*; essays in Haimson, ed., *The Politics of Rural Russia, 1905–1914*; Manning, *The Crisis of the Old Order in Russia*; Koroleva, *Zemstvo na perelome, 1905–1907 gg.*

ancien régime in Russia. Paradoxically or not, assessments regarding the origin, character and direction of the "peasant movement" during 1905–1906 have been less revealing. The recurring image in official and non-official correspondence was of a *Pugachevshchina*, which recalled not only the devastation wrought by peasant "*bunty*" (revolts) of the seventeenth and eighteenth centuries, Pushkin's image of the "Russian *bunt*— senseless and merciless," but also the fearsome intensity of social grievances that were now clearly exposed. Be they representatives of officialdom or exponents of "census society" of all political stripes, contemporary observers of the Russian peasantry generally held deeply ambivalent, if not always hostile, views of peasant society. Such biases were particularly evident in the corpus of administrative, police and judicial documents that have come to form the main source foundation for most analyses of the events in the countryside during the revolutionary period, including this one. Moreover, it goes almost without saying that the "peasant question" touched upon the most crucial interests of state and society in the late Imperial era and that discussions and scholarly exchange on the issue were thus among the most politically charged. The seismic events of 1917 did little to change the stakes of these debates, which became, if anything, even more vituperative, urgent and, in the end, potentially fatal for participants.

1. Peasant Societies, Peasant Revolts

The present study is offered principally as a contribution to the monographic literature treating the "peasant question" and rural unrest in Russia at the dawn of the twentieth century. It will nevertheless touch upon some of the themes at the heart of the larger debates that grew out of the emergence of rural militancy or revolutionary movements that drew upon peasant support in the era after 1945 and their origins in traditional rural societies that did not exhibit the cultural preconditions for models of socioeconomic development prescribed by theories of "modernization," defined as such theories have been more or less entirely by the Western experience and assumed as they are today in the structural adjustment prescriptions of the International Monetary Fund. The general contours of the narrative and analysis that follow will thus be familiar to those who have grappled with the changes that "development" has produced within the structure of "pre-modern" or traditional societies. In their broad outlines, such debates center on the nature and cohesion of the "little communities" in which the peasantry lived, worked and died—the "ecology" of rural life—and those factors, both exogenous and endogenous, that acted to move rural populations toward organizing and expressing their political will on the national stage.

Although this is not a comparative study, there are certain controversies in the vast scholarly literature on the question of protest and revolt in peasant societies that will be germane to my analyses. A particularly enduring and fruitful discussion has both enriched and polarized this field of inquiry since the publication of James C. Scott's seminal 1976 study *The Moral Economy of the Peasant: Rebellion and Subsistence in Southeast Asia*, which was followed by several additional works that supplement and broaden central themes of the 1976 work.[15] Scott's contribution appeared almost as a culminating point to an era of extraordinary scholarly interest in issues of rural revolt and the role of the peasantry, an era that featured publication of "foundational" works that brought the peasantry more fully into historical analyses as a central actor.[16] The recognition that a "moral economy of the poor" acted as the touchstone of social justice that drove urban food riots in eighteenth-century England, borrowed first by Edward P. Thompson from Chartist literatures for his influential 1971 essay,[17] was adapted by Scott both to the findings of many of these scholars and to his studies of Southeast Asian rural society to produce analyses of traditional peasant communities in the throes of those most profound changes brought about by the invasion of market capitalism and the expansion of a centralized state apparatus.

The "peasant" is defined first "as a rural cultivator whose production is largely oriented toward family consumption needs; this defines his central economic goal. Second, he is part of a larger society (including non-peasant elites and the state) that makes claims upon him, and this, in a sense, defines his potential human antagonists (or collaborators) in attain-

---

[15] James C. Scott, *The Moral Economy of the Peasant: Rebellion and Subsistence in Southeast Asia*, "Protest and Profanation," *Theory and Society*, IV (1977), No. 1, 1–38, No. 2, 211–246, "Hegemony," in *Politics and Society*, 7: 3 (1977), 267–296, "Revolution in the Revolution," *Theory and Society*, VII (1979), No. 1–2, 97–134, (with Benedict J. Tria Kerkvliet, eds.), *Weapons of the Weak*; and *Domination and the Arts of Resistance*.

[16] Hobsbawn, *Primitive Rebels*; Hobsbawn and George Rudé, *Captain Swing*; Moore, *Social Origins*; Moore, *Injustice*; Wolf, *Peasant Wars*; Migdal, *Peasants, Politics and Revolution*; see also essays assembled under the editorship of Henry A. Landsberger, *Latin American Peasant Movements*; *Rural Protest*.

[17] E. P. Thompson, "The Moral Economy," *Past and Present*, v. 50 (1971), No. 1, 76–136.

ing that goal."[18] A peasantry is thus a discrete socio-economic formation profoundly marked, first and foremost, by its eternal struggle with nature for subsistence on the land, which forged, over the *longue durée*, a "little tradition": an ethos of community membership rooted in shared historical memory and expressed in the operation of collectively accepted concepts of moral rights, reciprocal obligations, norms of behavior and attitudes toward processes of cultivation ("safety first"). Any claim that its functions in the rural setting were egalitarian in any strict sense was denied, yet this normative apparatus was nonetheless held to have strongly influenced interpersonal relationships among villagers and regulated the interfamily interactions of stronger and weaker households within village communities, thus providing a sort of subsistence insurance for all members in time of need.

Secondly, the long history of the peasant's subordination to the exactions of powerful external forces compelled rural communities over time to adopt certain assumptions and expectations in dealings with non-peasant milieux. In opposition to the force of law or the law of force by which "outsiders" imposed their demands for tribute on the exceedingly tenuous resources with which village communities struggled for survival, peasants set the inviolability of their right to subsistence. The justice or legitimacy of their exchanges with landlords, state tax officials or local notables was assessed in the final analysis by judging the degree to which such exchanges remained sensitive to their subsistence requirements and hewed to norms of reciprocity between social unequals in which measures of social and economic protection are afforded by elite patrons in exchange for the fulfillment of demands made on the human and material resources of peasant clients. This equilibrium, in the view of specialists who adhere to this general schema, is progressively vitiated, first, by inroads of market capitalism and those concurrent alterations it worked on older relationships, especially between the dominant class of landowners and their peasant clients, and, second, by a growing appetite of state structures for tax revenue, labor dues and military recruits. Systemic violation and/or devaluation of the subsistence schemes of the masses of peasants that such larger trends brought in their train gradually prepared both the revolutionary situation, in which peasants rose in an armed struggle for a restoration of the old order of social arrangements, and the solidarity with which they pursued these aims.

While this representation of operative systems of culturally defined collective rights, mutual obligations and reciprocities between individual

---

[18] Scott, *The Moral Economy*, 157.

householders in village communities and between villagers and powerful patrons outside the village as the touchstone of peasant views of justice that drive rural protest remains enormously influential in scholarly treatments, it has also been subject to some serious criticism. Alternative views have generally echoed Mancur Olson's oft-quoted dictum that "unless there is coercion or some other special device to make individuals act in their common interest, rational, self-interested individuals will not act to achieve their common or group interests."[19] Samuel L. Popkin agreed that the aim of subsistence security in both the long and the short term was the central struggle for all householders in the village setting, but held that interests of separate households could be conflated with those of a larger community only with great difficulty. In contrast, Popkin's view of peasant solidarity stressed the degree to which all actors in the village viewed participation in collective action strictly in terms of a calculation of risk and gain in their own narrow interest and especially avoided contributions to schemes that would "set a banquet for a neighbor to eat," whether these involved supporting subsistence insurance (subsidizing poorer villagers), initiatives to implement improvements in regimes of cultivation or the much riskier participation in acts of revolt. Indeed, if individual householders were to benefit from collective actions without any personal participation, such individuals were seen to be entirely rational in riding on the backs of those who risked all ("free riders"). To the extent that individual householders could realize personal advantages in alliances with powerful patrons, either vertically (extra-village) or horizontally (intra-village) or in the very opportunities presented by market capitalism, such advantages are pursued regardless of and even at the expense of community interests. A revolutionary movement succeeded only when peasants were organized to resist *from without*, by parties or movements that not only appealed to the peasant's sense of injustice and oppression, but also enacted measures (e.g. land reform, distribution of confiscated grain, and shares in landlords' livestock and inventory) that promised immediate, concrete benefits only to those who adhered as active members, reducing, in this manner, the "free rider" phenomenon.[20]

---

[19] From his *The Logic of Collective Action*, 2. Olson went on (Chapter I), however, to stress that smaller groups characterized by "face-to-face" intimacy are generally more successful in producing consensus, even if this consensus is "sub-optimal" and evidences a surprising capacity of the weaker members to dictate to the stronger.

[20] Popkin, *The Rational Peasant*.

These seemingly divergent perspectives on peasant community and rural protest generated important debates among specialists in various academic disciplines, which, even if they tended to focus on Southeast Asia, had larger implications for the study of peasant societies generally.[21] Popkin's central idea that individualistic economic pragmatism (investment logic, cost-benefit analysis) drove peasant attitudes toward collective action was largely found to be at odds with the accumulated findings of ethnologies and anthropologies of village life that emphasized the central role played by shared local heritages of historical memory, cultural knowledge, ritual observance and concepts of the sacred in the formation of self in rural settings. Nevertheless, the locus of viewpoints tended to fracture on the extent to which the subsistence ethic alone defined these domains of knowledge in rural society and the degree to which the normative prescriptions drawn from them retained a capacity to regulate behaviors of individual actors even in the precapitalist epoch.[22]

Yet the two points of view were not always considered to be mutually exclusive,[23] and efforts to find a synthesis have persisted. Interviews conducted by Anderson in three villages of Costa Rica and three Nicaraguan settlements in the aftermath of the Sandinista revolution are instructive in this sense. The narrative is situated against the backdrop of rapid expansion of heavily capitalized agriculture and animal husbandry tied to export markets and its deleterious effects on rural communities. Though these communities are described by peasant interviewees in terms that conform easily to criteria of village solidarity set out by Eric Wolf and James Scott, interaction between strong (landholding) and weak (landless) households, and their interdependence, even as purely individualistic expressions of

---

[21] For example: Adas, "'Moral Economy' or 'Contest State?'," *JSH*, 13: 4 (1980), 521–546; Moise, "The Moral Economy Dispute," *Bulletin of Concerned Asian Scholars*, 14 (1982), 72–77; Jane Haggis *et al.*, "By the Teeth," *World Development*, 14: 12 (1986), 1435–1455; Evans, "Sources of Peasant Consciousness," *Social History*, 12: 2 (1987), 193–211; Marcel Fafchamps, "Networks in Pre-Industrial Societies," *Economic Development and Social Change*, 41: 1 (1992), 147–174; Booth, "A Note on the Idea of the Moral Economy," *APSR*, 87: 4 (1993), 949–954; Booth, "On the Idea of the Moral Economy," *APSR*, 88: 3 (September, 1994), 653–667; Marc Edelman, "Bringing the Moral Economy back into the Study of 21st Century Transnational Peasant Movements," *American Anthropologist*, 107: 3 (2005), 331–345.

[22] Michael G. Peretz, "Moral and Political Economies," *Comparative Studies in Society and History*, 25: 4 (1983), 731–739.

[23] See Pierre Brocheux, "Moral Economy or Political Economy?," *Journal of Asian Studies*, XLII: 4 (1983), 791–803.

homo economicus in Popkin's sense, are more fully fleshed out in the villagers' descriptions (notably in labor exchange).

Anderson's critique of agrarian scholarship's focus on revolutionary unrest among the peasantry is also particularly cogent. In her findings, peasant reactions to systemic violation of subsistence rights and the deep sense of injustice that these fostered really involve a range of responses, from passivity to open revolt, but incorporating a middle register of tactics: petitions, marches, demonstrations, boycotts, road blockades and non-violent occupation of disputed lands, each entailing an increasing element of both risks and potential benefits for participants and eventually posing the problem of a need for a larger organization in pursuit of their interests. The key factors in this analysis appear to have been the degree to which state power and its armed agents operated as neutral actors, and whether a political space for the eventual success of middle-ground tactics existed. Where this political space existed, rural protest finally resulted in legalization of a Costa Rican national smallholders' union; land disputes were resolved, however grudgingly, by state mediation. Close identification of the interests of the Nicaraguan dictatorship with a clientèle of especially rapacious latifundists (of which the Somoza clan was increasingly the most prominent) and its bloody repression of middle-ground modes of peasant protest slowly created a critical mass for a revolutionary solution.[24]

When Anderson's interviewees recount the experience of systematic encroachments on their way of life and that gradual process by which the modalities of group action evolved, what emerged was the fact that movements of protest drew much more on an intense sense of injustice, which was both deeply emotional and widely shared in the community, than on any individual calculations of gain or loss. I do not now, of course, have any chance to poll villagers who took part in acts of unrest in the Russian rural districts in 1905–1906. We may safely agree, however, that in the rural districts of the Russian Empire on the eve of the events of 1905–1906, the space for middle-range forms of peasant protest set out by Anderson was so closely monitored and regulated as to render it nonexistent. The documentary materials from which I will draw an outline of rural unrest in Russia, its crescendo in the last months of 1905, and the rearguard action of 1906, will nevertheless speak directly both of this

---

[24] L. E. Anderson, *From Quiescence to Rebellion*, "Agrarian Politics and Revolution," *JTS*, 5: 4 (1993), 495–522, *The Political Ecology of the Modern Peasant*, and "Between Quiescence and Rebellion among the Peasantry," *JTS*, 9: 4 (1997), 503–532.

same deep sense of injustice that she identified and of its twin: a collective rage that was communicated in the purposefulness of peasant actions and the almost meticulous destruction visited upon the material wealth of those that were deemed to be violators of a just rural order.

2. Russia in 1900: the Marxist-Populist Debates

The "peasant question" in Russia predated the foregoing scholarly exchanges by more than a century, standing as it did near the heart of debates between "Slavophile" and "Westerner" in the first half of the nineteenth century, and surviving the intense discussions that surrounded the emancipation acts of the 1860s to remain a looming concern in public life until the collapse of the *ancien régime* and beyond. Stripped of the labels that often become attached to the contending camps, the controversies engendered by the "peasant question" in Russia prefigure, in their general outlines, the central issues that reemerge in scholarly discussions about peasant societies in the era after 1960 to which I have referred.

Of particular import for analyses of the "peasant movement" in Russia, both during 1905–1907 and during 1917–1922, are the well-known disputes that pitted those that styled themselves as "orthodox Marxists" against the spectrum of observers of rural life later to bear the pejorative sobriquet of "populists." These disputes were, at the time, only an episode in the long, painful struggle of educated society in Russia (*obshchestvo*) to fix its place in the embryonic "nation" that was slowly emerging from the older order of patriarchal hierarchies and its certainties in the post-Emancipation era. This place was to be found on the perilous terrain somewhere between a powerful autocratic state, from which it was to demand, in 1905, a vital role in the affairs of government, and the great masses of Russian peasants, who constituted four-fifths of the populace of European Russia in 1897, masses from which it was separated by a vast cultural and emotional chasm, but which it sought nevertheless to "lead" and "enlighten."

Even if most of these Russian observers at the end of the nineteenth century shared a deep antipathy to the existing order, they held sharply different views of the historical fate of Russia's rural order generally and the extent to which market forces had altered the socio-economic character of rural society at the dawn of the twentieth century in particular. Many specialists of the time insisted that the very viability of small peasant farms—and the "non-class" character of village society generally—

resided in their *essentially* non-capitalist orientation, in the central (if not exclusive) role played by subsistence security and family labor as the primary drivers of small-farm economy. Such features, along with a constant leveling of disparities of wealth and economic power among households by processes of family demography and the collectivist values of the communal culture in which they were bound, were specific to the "peasantry" as a discrete socio-economic formation.[25] That the scale of the peasant farm economy was closely associated with the size of the peasant family household (i.e. the number of workers that it could field), and that its economic activity was mainly (although not exclusively) directed at the satisfaction of household consumption needs were two of the fundamental observations drawn by *zemstvo* statistical studies after about 1885. Adherents of the "organization-production school," of which A. V. Chaianov was only the most eminent representative, devoted special attention to this problem.[26]

For these specialists, the non-capitalist character of both the "laboring" (*trudovoi*) peasantry and the family farm remained central to understanding rural life in Russia, even given the formation of a national market economy in the post-Emancipation era. Moreover, research on movement of peasant households up and down the ladder of prosperity as defined by material attributes of economic power, first observed by Chernenkov in a comparison of the changing positions of households in censuses for 1894 and 1897 in six parishes of Petrovskii District, Saratov Province, demonstrated that village society hardly resembled a static order of separate classes. Social mobility of such family units was a continuous, "molecular," and multidirectional process.[27] The ascent of some households, as

[25] Shcherbina, *Krest'ianskie biudzhety*, 205–240; Peshekhonov, "Iz teorii i praktiki krest'ianskogo khoziaistva," *Russkoe bogatstvo*, 1902, 9: 161–193, 10: 71–119; Chernenkov, *K kharakteristike krest'ianskago khoziaistva*. Treatment of peasant economy as a non-capitalist enterprise *par excellence* in Kosinskii, *K agrarnomu voprosu*, especially 161–198, and Oganovskii, *Ocherki*, 586–598.

[26] Chaianov, *Biudzhety krest'ian Starobel'skago uyezda*; Chelintsev, *Opyt izucheniia krest'ianskago sel'skago khoziaistva*; Makarov, *Krest'ianskoe khoziaistvo*. Chaianov's synthetic work, *Organizatsiia krest'ianskogo khoziaistva*, was the ultimate statement of this "school" on this issue, since it combined findings drawn from studies of peasant budgets (with which Chaianov had been directly associated from at least 1910) and schemes of "multi-directional" mobility examined by Chernenkov, Makarov, Khriashcheva and others.

[27] Chernenkov, *ibid.*, 26–54. In his understanding of this "molecular" process (based on comparison of two card files for households in Saratov Province compiled in 1894 and 1897), he noted the following: 1) extinction (*vymiranie*) of households (quite often

measured by expansion of the scale of economy (by number of horses, by total area of sowings or of allotment, leased or purchased land, by budget income and expenses)—and the decline (by these same measures), extinction, migration or emigration of others—were only the external aspects of the position of individual households at any given point in this fluid process. In its main outlines, this mobility was, if not precisely "cyclical,"[28] then in principle "two-sided." From a small nuclear family unit—a young married couple of working age with minor dependents and limited means of production—the household as a unit of labor grew apace. Male children reached working age, allowing an expanded scale of farming as measured by sown area, work stock, year-end surplus, maintenance costs, product *en nature* (from their plots) and so on. Conversely, big wealthy households, especially those housing three generations and numerous married males of working age and their wives, tended to fissure into their constituent nuclear units. *Post-mortem* partition had always been a customary option upon the death or incapacitation of the head of the household (*bolshak*), but *pre-mortem* fission now occurred with increasing frequency as the issue of endemic conflicts between members to which big complex households were especially prone.[29] Material differences among households (accumulation of advantages and surpluses among higher cohorts, concentration of disadvantages and deficits among the lower) at a given

---

already distinguished in 1894 by an unusual preponderance of females of working age in the household over males), 2) the union of the remainder of such households with another, 3) out-migration and return and 4) family partitions, which affected larger family household units most of all (percentage-wise).

[28] The longest interval for which the phenomenon was studied appears in a study of 1,477 households in seven villages registered in the 1882 census of Surazh District, Chernigov Province, 29 years later (1911). The study showed that among households sowing up to 3 *desiatiny* in 1882 that had not partitioned, 28.2% remained in this same cohort, 43.3% had moved up to the cohort of households sowing 3.1 to 6 *desiatiny*, 22.3% appear in the group sowing 6.1 to 9 *desiatiny*, 3% were registered as sowing 9.1 to 12 *desiatiny* and 3% had moved into the group of households sowing over 12 *desiatiny*. Kushchenko, *Krest'ianskoe khoziaistvo.* The movement was thus entirely cyclical for only a very small minority of the 1882 households.

[29] The conception of a complex mobility of peasant households, which appeared first in the work of N. N. Chernenkov at the end of the 1890s, was also employed by others. See Rumiantsev, "K voprosu ob evoliutsii," in Dorovatorskii and Chausnikov, eds., *Ocherki*, 453–547, which treated 12,520 households polled in 1884 in Viazemskii District, Smolensk Province, comparing their position in 1900; G. A. Kushchenko, *Krest'ianskoe khoziaistvo*, the sample of 7 villages (1,477 households); A. I. Khriashcheva, ed., *Materialy... Epifanskii uyezd*, treating 12,285 households surveyed in 1899 as they appeared eleven years later.

moment only screened the action of opposing tendencies—at once leveling and differentiating—in the long-term lifespan of any sample of peasant households. These ideas arrived in the West with exiled specialists
during the 1920s (while their colleagues, who remained active in Soviet
agrarian debates,[30] were later repressed), and were later adopted by Western historians and broadly employed in efforts to view the history of rural
Russia of the pre-revolutionary era independently of the rigid class typologies and theories of static class differentiation of Soviet historical
orthodoxy.[31] Core elements of this general perspective form a vital reference for James C. Scott and adherents to the view that a "moral economy"
in village life, rooted in a right to subsistence security, acted as a decisive
factor in peasant views of justice.[32]

In his early analyses, Lenin departed from assumptions of the defining
role of market capitalism and wage labor in agricultural production both
on private estates and in peasant economies *already* at the end of the nineteenth century, highlighting a steep expansion of commercial agriculture
and its regional specialization. Moreover, he posed these trends against
data selected from *zemstvo* statistical work in several provinces that he
used to show that expropriation of the mass of peasant householders and
their "proletarianization" by processes of concentration of means of production in the hands of an emergent rural bourgeoisie was well advanced.[33] Consequently, he considered evident, as the twin sources of
social discord in rural society, not only the historic conflict between the

---

[30] We do not take up here a review of the vast literature on this subject, which has been
ably conducted by Alessandro Stanziani in his *L'Economie en révolution*.

[31] Particularly notable in this regard, of course, are the works of Teodor Shanin, *The Awk-
ward Class*, and *The Roots of Otherness* (volume 1). See also, in this connection,
Wilbur, "Peasant Poverty in Theory and Practice," in Kingston-Mann and Mixter, eds.,
Peasant Economy, 101–127; Worobec, *Peasant Russia*, 76–117 (Chapter III).

[32] Scott, *The Moral Economy*, 13–15.

[33] *Razvitie kapitalizma v Rossii: Protsess obrazovaniia vnutrennego rynka dlia krupnoi
promyshlen-nosti*, as *PSS*, t. 3 (5th ed.) Notably, the data that Lenin used in 1899 did not
suggest a *process*: they were selected for a given year in a given county (*uyezd*) and did
not make use of repeated polls of the same locality. Indeed, he dismissed in the most
cursory manner the importance of family size (i.e. its labor component) to which material differences between households was correlated to the scale of farm economy even in
the data that he used. He did not engage with the implications for this issue of
Chernenkov's work (*K kharakteristike krest'ianskago khoziaistva*), in circulation at the
time, on its merits. See also *Agrarnyi vopros i "kritiki Marksa"* (1901–1907) *PSS*, t. 5.
From this era also, see the articles "K derevenskoi bednote" (1903), t. 6, 363–430, and
"Proletariat i krest'ianstvo," (1905), t. 8, 231–236.

landed nobility and peasantry, but also the growing stratification of the village itself into hostile classes, born of the capitalist transformation of rural Russia's socio-economic life, and presaging an inevitable dissolution of the peasantry as a whole.[34] Analyzing these larger developments, the future leader of the Bol'shevik faction lost no opportunity to pour scorn on Populist attempts to depict village society generally, and the Russian land commune in particular, as a sort of rural socialism in embryo. Lenin's accusations that the *narodniki* "romanticized" rural life, "idealized" intra-village relationships and ignored the evidence of the centrality of class struggle in the countryside retain a curious echo in Western scholarly discussions in our era. In Soviet Russia after 1917, however, Lenin's early views formed a principal pole in the contest of opposing views of the peasantry and rural development, and stood at the center of the fateful struggle to identify the primary elements of a master narrative not only for the collapse of the *ancien régime* but, by extension, for the outcomes of the revolution of October and the evolution of Soviet agrarian policies.[35] From the late 1920s onwards, in its resolve to shape a heroic account of October 1917, around Leninist conceptions of *socialist* revolution—driven by the Russian working class in alliance with its clearly junior partners among "proletarianized" and "semi-proletarianized" elements of rural society against a fully formed "bourgeois" order—Soviet analyses turned decisively toward a liquidation of all historical nuances and to insist, likewise, on categorical affirmation of the maturation of rural capitalism and emergence of a powerful village bourgeoisie in the two decades that preceded the Great War.[36]

Lenin's own views on the degree and tempo of modernization of rural life, however, remained fluid and tended to evolve over time. Analyzing

[34] Also Plekhanov, "Nashi raznoglasiia," *Sochineniia*, II, 199–232; Struve, *Kriticheskie zametki*, 239–240; Maslov, *Agrarnyi vopros v Rossii*, I: 285–316.

[35] The debates are treated in Solomon, *The Soviet Agrarian Debate*; Cox, *Peasants, Class and Capitalism*; Stanziani, *op. cit.*; Tarnovskii, "Problemy agrarnoi istorii Rossii perioda imperializma v sovetskoi istoriografii (1917-nachalo 1930-x godov)," in *IZ*, 78: 31–62; Tarnovskii, "Problemy agrarnoi istorii Rossii perioda imperializma v sovetskoi istoriografii (konets 1930-x—pervaia polovina 1950-x godov)," in *IZ*, 83: 196–221; Savel'ev, "Put' agrarnogo razvitiia Rossii," in A. P. Korelin, ed., *Rossiia sel'skaia*, 25–53.

[36] Shestakov, *Kapitalizatsiia sel'skogo khoziaistva*; Gaister, *Sel'skoe khoziaistvo kapitalisticheskoi Rossii*; Liashchenko, *Istoriia narodnogo khoziaistvo SSSR*, II, 60–94; Liuboshits, *Voprosy marksistsko-leninskoi teorii*; Khromov, *Ekonomicheskoe razvitie Rossii*, 154–172; Karnaukhova, *Razmeshchenie sel'skogo khoziaista Rossii*; Dubrovskii, *Sel'skoe khoziaistvo i krest'ianstvo*.

events in the countryside in 1905–1907, the leader of the Bol'shevik faction drew two principal conclusions. First, it had to be admitted that "feudal survivals" in the countryside—especially in the Central Agricultural Region—acted as a far more powerful brake on reorganization of productive relations and its attendant social transformations than had been anticipated before the revolution.[37] From this conclusion, it was wholly evident that the central conflict in rural life, "saturated to its core by survivals of the era of serfdom," would remain the historic antagonism between large-scale, mostly noble, landowners and the peasantry *as a whole*; differentiation of the peasantry itself into warring classes was judged now to be rather far from complete.

Why was this so? After 1905, Lenin was often to attribute this peculiarity to the bitter competition of "models" of capitalist development in Russia's countryside as the generator of the central tensions in rural society: the "Prussian" model (based in the large landed estates of the nobility and backed by state policies, including, in his view, the Stolypin land reform) and the "American" model (of peasant farmers).[38] It flowed from

---

[37] Analyzing in 1908 the modesty of the agrarian program of Social Democracy on the eve of the events of 1905–1907, Lenin wrote (undoubtedly in part with reference to his own positions in his 1899 work *The Development of Capitalism in Russia*): "That mistake was due to the fact that, while we correctly defined the *trend* of development, we did not correctly define the *moment* of that development. We assumed that the elements of capitalist agriculture had already taken full shape in Russia, both in landowner farming (minus the cut-off lands and their conditions of bondage—hence the demand that cut-off lands be returned to the peasants) and in peasant farming, which seemed to have given rise to a strong peasant bourgeoisie and thus incapable of generating 'peasant agrarian revolution.' The erroneous program was not the result of 'fear' of peasant agrarian revolution, but of *an over-estimation of the degree* of capitalist development in Russian agriculture. Survivals of serfdom appeared to us then to be a minor detail, whereas capitalist agriculture on the peasant allotments and on the proprietors' estates seemed to be quite mature and well established. The revolution has exposed that mistake; it has confirmed the trend of development as we defined it... But the survivals of serfdom in the countryside proved to be much stronger than we thought: they have given rise to a nationwide peasant movement and they have made *that* the touchstone of the bourgeois revolution as a whole." V. I. Lenin, *Agrarnaia programma sotsial-demokratii v pervoi russkoi revoliutsii 1905–1907 godov* (1908), *PSS*, 16: 268–269.

[38] The model dates to the post-1905 era. *Ibid.*, 219–231; see also letter of 16 December 1909 to Ivan Ivanovich Skvortsov-Stepanov, *PSS*, 47: 226–232. On the shift in Lenin's view of the peasant unrest after 1905, Tarnovskii, "Problemy agrarnoi istorii Rossii period imperializma v sovetskoi istoriografii (1917-nachalo 1930-x godov)," *IZ*, 78:31–32; Gefter, "Stranitsa iz istorii marksizma nachala XX veka," in Gefter, ed., *Istoricheskaia nauka*, 13–44.

this that, as in 1905, the events of 1917 *in the countryside* could only signal a "bourgeois-democratic" phase of the revolution, aimed at the expropriation of "feudal latifundia" and the "clearing of the ground" for unfet-
tered growth of small peasant capitalism,[39] a development that the famous
Decree on Land (1917) would (reluctantly) sanction.[40] Further, the entirely spontaneous revolutionary upheavals in the countryside in 1917–
1918 and their broadly leveling effects on peasant economies (*oserednia-
chinanie*) made it less than ever possible to speak of capitalist dominance
of social relations in the village. Rather, Lenin chose to describe the new
Soviet state as necessarily passing through a difficult transitional stage in
which competing "orders" (*uklady*)—patriarchal, small-commodity-
producing, private capitalist, state capitalist and socialist—struggled to
gain the upper hand. In this schema, patriarchal and small-commodity-
producing orders that characterized the peasantry stand clearly apart from
those deemed to be "capitalist."[41]

3. The "New Direction" in Soviet Historiography: 1956–1974

After the 20th Party Congress of the CPSU in 1956, the older disagree-
ments over the nature of pre-revolutionary agrarian society and economy
resurfaced. Their reemergence was itself part of a larger (albeit short-

---

[39] Nationalization of the land, in the "peasant agrarian program" in the First and Second
Dumas (i.e. the "Project of the 104"), for Lenin, "is the peasant 'clearing of the land' for
capitalism," *op. cit.* (*Agrarnaia programma...*), 244–264 et seq.

[40] Lenin's analysis of the two stages of the October Revolution (i.e. the proletariat with the
peasantry *as a whole* against the "military-feudal" autocratic state and the "medieval"
edifice of the old order in the countryside—the consummation of the "bourgeois-
democratic" revolution—and, from the autumn of 1918, the forging of the alliance of the
proletariat and *the poor and the "semi-proletarian" elements within the peasantry*
against village capitalism) in *Proletarskaia revoliutsiia i renegat Kautskii* (1918), in
PSS, 37, especially 305 and following. See also "Rech' o godovshchine revoliutsii 9-go
noiabria 1918 g." at the VI All-Russian Extraordinary Congress of Soviets of Workers',
Peasants', Cossack and Red Army Deputies (6–9 November 1918), 37: 141–144; "Doklad o rabote v derevne 23-go marta 1919 g.," at Eighth Congress of the RKP(b) 18–23
March 1919, 38: 192–205; "Rech' na soedinennom zasedanii VTsIK, Moskovskogo
Soveta rabochikh i krest'ianskikh delegatov i fabrichno-zavodskikh komitetov, posvia-
shchennom dvukhletnei godovshchine Oktiabr'skoi revoliutsii 7-go noiabr 1919 g.," 39:
292–303.

[41] In particular, "O 'levom' rebiachestve i o melkoburzhuaznosti," (1918) in *PSS*, 36: 285–
314, and "O prodovol'stvennom naloge: znachenie novoi politiki i ee usloviia (1921),
PSS, 43: 205–245.

lived) effort of a new generation of Soviet specialists to break with the "*Short Course* paradigm" of historical causality and to fashion, out of the Marxist-Leninist heritage, new tools and understandings of historical processes.[42] This effort (which, as we have seen, had its parallels in the West) seemed all the more significant in the light of the emergence in the 1950s of national revolutionary movements in the "third-world" agrarian societies of North Africa, Southeast Asia and Latin America that drew heavily on Marxist-Leninist teachings, but surfaced in socio-economic contexts quite different from that in which the Russian revolutions of 1917 unfolded, to say nothing of Europe in the era of the *Communist Manifesto*. The "new direction" in Soviet historical writing, in particular, sought to "re-read" the Leninist *œuvre* with regard to the "preconditions for the Great October Socialist Revolution," and it provided a natural haven for those Soviet historians who had grown skeptical of the Stalinist establishment's canonical insistence on *definitive* maturation of capitalist modes of production and social relations as the dominant socio-economic context that defined Russian society by 1917 and, *ipso facto*, made it "ripe" for the "socialist" transformations that ensued.

The "new direction" historians took up detailed studies of specific socio-economic structures of the late Imperial era, aided by a sustained, systematic effort to employ the broad range of archival materials of the pre-revolutionary era.[43] New treatments of interactions between "monopoly capitalism," the Russian commercial-industrial elite, the autocratic "military-feudal" state and its bureaucratic machine,[44] interrelationships of lord

---

[42] See the introduction to the collection of essays edited by M. Ia. Gefter *et al.*, *Istoricheskaia nauka*, 5–10. Also Sidorova, "Innovatsiia v otechestvennoi istorigrafii," in Karpov, ed., *Problemy*, 401–410; Markwick, "Catalyst of Historiography, Marxism and Dissidence," *Europe-Asia Studies*, 46: 4, 579–596.

[43] The cataloguing and publication of new multi-volume collections of official documents from the archives of the Tsarist ministries was a hallmark of the era. Among these were *Revoliutsiia 1905–1907 gg. v Rossii: dokumenty i materialy*; *Krest'ianskoe dvizhenie v Rossii: sbornik dokumentov*, for the years 1796–1917; *Rabochee dvizhenie v Rossii v XIX veke: sbornik dokumentov i materialov* (8 volumes, Moscow, Izdatel'stvo sotsial'no-ekonomicheskoi literatury, 1955–1960). A fifth, expanded edition of Lenin's collected works was also compiled and published between 1958 and 1965.

[44] Iosif Frolovich Gindin (1900–1980) was a leading proponent of a new view of the pre-revolutionary context. His work after 1956 focused mainly on the uneven and contradictory development of advanced forms of financial and industrial organization, but reached out for a broader view: *Gosudarstvennyi bank*, "Russkaia burzhuaziia," *ISSSR*, 1963, 2: 57–80, 3: 37–60; with L. M. Ivanov, "O neravnomernosti razvitiia," *VI*, 1965, 9: 125–135, "O nekotorykh osobennostiiakh," *ISSSR*, 1966, 3: 48–66, "Sotsial'no-

and peasant in the Russian countryside after Emancipation, or the historical development of ancient societies,[45] did not, however, emerge fully formed, but were implicitly or explicitly a renewal of the intense debates in the social sciences over many of the same themes during the 1920s.[46]

Results of the new research fostered a growing awareness of the simultaneous co-existence, interaction, interweaving and competition of pre-capitalist, proto-capitalist and fully capitalist forms of economic organization and production—and their reflection in the increasing complexity of the fabric of social relations—that defined Russia's national profile on the very eve of the October Revolution. The profoundly composite quality of socio-economic structures (*mnogoukladnost'*) on the eve of the October Revolution not only testified to their transitional, unconsummated status, but also implied "peculiarities" specific to Russia's path to modernization as opposed to the "classic" patterns of historical development in the West laid out by Marx and Engels. The very distinctiveness of Russia's experience told, moreover, on the overall array and character of social forces in Russia's towns and rural districts at the beginning of the twentieth century, and thus on the nature of the revolutionary processes itself. Indeed, some historians went so far as to assert that—*at least initially*—the staying power of the autocracy (the "state capitalist" sector) and an aristocratic elite of estate owners (the "Prussian model") after 1861 rested in great part on their very success in *adapting new economic forces to older "feudal" structures.*[47]

As these matters were debated among Soviet historians from the late 1950s to the early 1970s, issues associated with rural development after

---

ekonomicheskie itogi," in I. I. Mints *et al.*, eds., *Sverzhenie samoderzhaviia*, 39–88; with V. V. Timoshenko, "Mnogoukladnost'," in *Ekonomicheskie nauki*, 1962, 2: 61–68. His paper from the fourth session (Leningrad, 1961) of the Academy of Science's Scholarly Council on the issue of historical preconditions for the October Revolution, "Politika tsarskogo pravitel'stva v otnoshenii promyshlennykh monopolii," appears in Sidorov, ed., *Ob osobennostiakh*, 86–123. Among the papers in the collection, Sidorov's own contribution, "V. I. Lenin o russkom voenno-feodal'nom imperializme" (11–52), treating the autocracy and its military-bureaucratic machine as an autonomous historical actor, is also of considerable interest.

[45] Review of newer views and a frank critique of the five-stage model (*piatichlenka*) of historical evolution and its narrow focus on ownership of the means of production as the determining criteria for all other socio-economic phenomena at any given stage of development in Danilova, "Diskussionye problemy," in Danilova *et al.*, eds., *Problemy*, Book 1, 27–66.

[46] Gefter, "Mnogoukladnost'—kharakteristike tselogo," in Adamov, ed., *Voprosy istorii kapitalisticheskoi Rossii*, 85.

[47] *Ibid.*, 93–97; Krasin, *Lenin, revoliutsiia, sovremennost'*, 308–374.

Emancipation and the role of the peasant in the Russian Revolution were among the most bitterly contested. The degree to which rural society had engaged its expected transformation—whether "the glass was half full or half empty"—was not merely an academic question. Implicitly or explicitly, the core issue involved the character, direction and political significance of those explosive social conflicts that generated mass revolutionary movements in the country districts in 1902, 1905–1906 and 1917–1922, and thus the very legitimacy of master narratives of the emergence of Soviet power that had defined the parameters of historical writing generally and during the Stalin era in particular.

The defects in these narratives and their incapacity to explain the complexities of rural socio-economic relationships before October were drawn with particular force in the work of Andrei Matveevich Anfimov (1916–1995). For Anfimov, the study of peasant and estate economies and their interactions at the dawn of the twentieth century revealed the extent to which habits, usages and practices drawn from the experience of serfdom exerted a decisive influence over rural socio-economic relationships throughout the era before 1917. "One should not understand semi-servile relationships as an equivalent to 'semi-bourgeois,'" he wrote in 1956. "These were the very same servile relationships modified, it is true, by capitalism."[48] When debates surfaced in leading historical journals in the early 1960s over the nature of the small-commodity producer culture (*melkotovarnyi uklad*) of peasant family farms that Lenin saw as dominant in Russia in the revolutionary era, Anfimov was uncompromising in affirming the non-capitalist sense that the Bol'shevik leader had attached to this mode of production.[49] The findings of Anfimov and his

---

[48] From his extensive bibliography, we will cite only a few of his works. In its capacity almost as a programmatic statement for what came later, see his "K voprosu o kharaktere agrarnogo stroia," *IZ*, 65: 119–162, followed by *Zemel'naia arenda* and *Krupnoe pomeshchich'e khoziaistvo*. The two works *Krest'ianskoe khoziaistvo* and *Ekonomicheskoe polozhenie* were published after his censure; the first contains his recanting of earlier positions, "which covered the author of these lines with disgrace, particularly in his own eyes," as he was later to state. An important posthumously published work treating these issues in the context of the Stolypin land reform is *P. A. Stolypin i rossiiskoe krest'ianstvo*, parts of which had been published as "Neokonchennye spory," in *VI*, 1997, 5: 49–72; 6: 41–84; 7: 81–99; 9: 82–113. A full listing of his publications follows the editor's foreword in A. P. Korelin, ed., *Rossiia sel'skaia*.

[49] Ryndziunskii, "O melkotovarnom uklade," *ISSSR*, 1961, 2: 48–69; Koval'chenko, "Ob izuchenii melkotovarnogo uklada," *ISSSR*, 1962, 1: 74–93; Rubenshtein, "O melkotovarnom proizvodstve," *ISSSR*, 1962, 4: 66–86; Anfimov, "O melkom tovarnom proizvodstve," *ISSSR*, 1963, 2: 141–159; Ryndziunskii, "Voprosy izucheniia melkotovarnogo

associates[50] and their implications for the old orthodoxies drew heated reaction from adherents of the traditional view.[51]

The most interesting and innovate efforts at defending the older paradigm were organized by Ivan Dmitrievich Koval'chenko (1923–1995), whose research is justly celebrated for pioneering multivariate statistical analyses of quantitative historical data in Soviet historiography. Econometric studies conducted by Koval'chenko and his "school" in the early 1970s document the maturation and accelerating integration of a national agrarian market at the dawn of the twentieth century and its rapidly growing capacity to impose a uniform price structure on both production and means of production, despite clearly anachronistic or transitional features that continued to characterize Russia's economic structure in this era. During the 1980s, the school's analyses of factor components drawn from census data and budget materials, and their interaction in estate and peasant economies, tried to test the extent to which competing "Prussian" and "American" models showed sufficient maturity to drive a capitalist reorientation of rural landscapes, even while recognizing that "semi-servile" and "feudal" practices continued to restrain this development.[52]

---

uklada," *ISSSR*, 1963, 4: 95–119. Also essays in Ivanov and Tarnovskii, eds., *Obshchestvenno-ekonomicheskaia struktura Rossii*, and V. V. Adamov, ed., *Voprosy istorii kapitalisticheskoi Rossii.*

[50] Most notably Liudmila Petrovna Minarik (1925–1993), long associated with the State Historical Museum in Moscow. See "Sistema pomeshchich'ego," in Novosel'skii, ed., *Materialy,* 377–397, "Kharakteristika krupneishikh zemlevladel'tsev," in *EAIVE. 1963 g.,* 693–708, "Ob urovne razvitiia," in *EAIVE. 1964 g.,* 615–626, *Ekonomicheskaia kharakteristika,* and "O sviaziakh," in *EAIVE. 1971 g.,* 307–318.

[51] Anfimov's exchange with S. M. Dubrovskii at a scholarly conference on the peculiarities of Russia's agrarian order on the eve of the 1917 revolution (in the series of conferences dedicated to "The Historical Preconditions for the Great October Socialist Revolution") in May 1960 was justly celebrated in this connection. K. N. Tarnovskii's commentary: "Problemy agrarnoi istorii Rossii perioda imperializma v sovetskoi istoriografii (diskussiia nachala 1960-kh godov)," in Ivanov, ed., *Problemy,* 264–311. Dubrovskii's view remained stubbornly "orthodox."

[52] Koval'chenko, "V. I. Lenin o kharaktere," *VI,* 1970, 3: 30–51 (containing his declaration that "the [class] division of the village, the bourgeois order and the new social structure become an accomplished fact from the 1880s of the past century." 39), with Milov, *Vserossiiskii agrarnyi rynok,* with Selunskaia and Litvakov, *Sotsial'no-ekonomicheskii stroi pomeshchich'ego,* "O burzhuaznom kharaktere krest'ianskogo khoziaistva," *ISSSR,* 1983, 5: 50–81, and with Moiseenko and Selunskaia, *Sotsial'no-ekonomicheskii stroi krest'ianskogo khoziaistva.* For Anfimov's generally accurate assessment of the main thrust of this body of work, see Anfimov, "Neokonchennye spory."

By the end of the 1960s, however, the drift of discussions over preconditions for the October Revolution toward very significant revision of traditional canons provoked administrative reprisals from the guardians of ideological orthodoxy. Even after the 20th Party Congress, close ideological supervision of historical writing remained ever present, as the "Burdzhalov affair" (1957) and the closing of the journal *Istoricheskii arkhiv* (1962) showed, but the situation worsened with Khrushchev's ouster in 1964 and the appointment of Brezhnev's longtime crony S. P. Trapeznikov as head of the CPSU Central Committee's Department of Science and Educational Establishments in late 1965. The persecution of Nekrich over his work on the invasion of 22 June 1941, followed (1966–1967)[53] and attacks on the new generation of Soviet historians in the party press multiplied. After heated public exchanges between Soviet specialists at a conference of Soviet and Italian historians in April 1968,[54] the Institute of History was reorganized, its "revisionist" party committee (headed by V. P. Danilov) dissolved and the Section of Methodology closed. Both the increasingly public impatience of the revisionists with ideological controls and the great interest that the debates had begun to arouse among foreign specialists, however, drove the Central Committee's Department of Science to harsher measures. Publication of the papers of the 1969 Sverdlovsk conference on preconditions for the October Revolution in 1972[55] served as a pretext for imposing heavy sanctions against the known adherents of the "new direction" within the academic establishment in historical writing and research, which sanctions included forced retirements or reassignments, demotions, travel bans, and long official "delays" for publication of completed manuscripts.[56] A sharp anathema on the mat-

---

[53] On the poisonous atmosphere that persisted in the social sciences even after the 20th Party Congress, see Nekrich, *Otreshis' ot strakha*, and Donald J. Raleigh's preface to his translation of Burdzhalov, *Vtoraia russkaia revoliutsiia. Vosstanie v Petrograde* (published in Moscow in 1966) as *Russia's Second Revolution*, ix–xxii.

[54] *Dokumenty sovetsko-ital'ianskoi konferentsii.* Avrekh had publicly declared at this conference the heretical notion (from the point of view of accepted "class" analysis) that the Russian peasantry had always acted—along with the landowning nobility—as the main social bulwark of the autocracy.

[55] V. V. Adamov, ed., *Voprosy istorii kapitalisticheskoi Rossii.*

[56] During 1973–1974, Pavel Vasilievich Volobuev (head of the Institute) and K. N. Tarnovskii were transferred out of the Institute of History, I. F. Gindin and M. Ia. Gefter were "retired," M. S. Simonova and A. M. Anfimov demoted. The latter was forced out of his post as head of the Sector of Capitalism at the Institute, banned from travel abroad and later forced to publicly recant his views. Major works in manuscript authored by figures associated with the "new direction—Danilov, Gindin, Tarnovskii, Shatsillo,

ter of composite socio-economic structures pronounced by a party hack for *Problems of History* during 1974 appeared almost as an anticlimax.[57]

4. Western Treatments of the "Crisis of the Rural Economy"

Echoes of these debates also reverberated widely in scholarly discussions among historians in the West, where, at the same time, an older consensus on the background of agrarian unrest in Russia during the twentieth century was also beginning to be reexamined. For until relatively recently, even contending assessments, both in Russia and in the West, tended to agree that it was a *systemic* crisis of the rural economy in Russia that generated the larger tensions in the rural social order, expressed in revolutionary impulses on a large scale in Russia's country districts in 1905–1906. The elements of this crisis were said to be several. First, the Emancipation statutes of 1861 reduced the amount of land available to former serfs in favor of the old serf-owners, vesting title to these lands in the land commune (*obshchina, mir*), which was invested with the power to distribute rights to use these lands to member households. The commune—acting through the village assembly (*skhod*) of male heads of household—and its elected officials were charged with enforcing the regime of collective responsibility (*krugovia poruka*) of member households for taxes, redemption dues, conscripts for the armed forces and performance of unremunerated public services (road repair, convoying of convicts, fire-fighting, police duty), which saddled the household units with heavy financial burdens in exchange for the undersized allotments that they received.

Second, the Imperial legislation also codified a strict juridical and administrative segregation of the peasant *soslovie* from the rest of the populace, mandating a close supervision of peasant affairs by a host of local officials and provincial bureaus (the institution of the Land Captain was an innovation of the reign of Alexander III), a structure in which the old serf-owning gentry

---

Simonova, and Aron Iakovlevich Avrekh—never appeared or were published only after long delays or after 1991. Polikarpov, "'Novoe napravlenie' 50–70-kh gg.," in Afanas'ev, ed., *Sovetskaia istoriografiia*, 349–400; Sidorova, *Ottepel' v istoricheskoi nauke*; Markwick, *Rewriting History in Soviet Russia*; Anfimov, *P. A. Stolypin*, 186–236; Ganelin, "Tvorcheskii put' A. Ia. Avrekha," *ISSSR*, 1990, 4: 102–112; Ganelin, *Sovetskie istoriki*, 109–201. Also Emets and Shelokhaev, "Tvorcheskii put' K. N. Tarnovskogo," *IZ*, 118 (1990), 202–231; Tsamutali, ed., *Konstantin Nikolaevich Tarnovskii*; Sevost'ianov, *Akademik P.V. Volobuev*.

[57] I. V. Kuznetsov, "Ob ukladakh," *VI*, 1974, 7: 20–32.

retained key roles. The rural populace was granted rights to elect its own administrative and police officials, whose meager salaries were borne by their electors, but these nonetheless sooner acted as the lower links in the state apparatus. Legal disputes among peasants were adjudicated in special class courts, which tried their cases on the basis of customary law, quite apart and separate from the Imperial system of jurisprudence and its law codes. The subaltern social status and economic dependency of Russian peasants on the former masters and its conspicuous lack of rights before its local "superiors" (*nachal'stvo*) thus continued to typify rural society even after 1861. This close control of village life "from above" was thought to have restricted peasant mobility and to have erected—in the land commune and the village assembly as custodians of peasant land rights—insurmountable barriers to the technical modernization of peasant agriculture.

Third, massive natural increase in the population of country districts in the second half of the century, given the static technologies of peasant cultivation, steadily reduced man: land ratios in the countryside, promoted overpopulation and pauperized growing segments of the rural population. The condition of the peasantry, in addition, tended to perpetuate the dependency of the old masters on the old ways. For most owners, the known advantages (and disadvantages) of lease and labor contracts with neighboring villagers outweighed the unknown costs and risks of adjusting estate cultivation to new economic realities by expanding demesne cultivation, undertaking its technical improvement or maintaining work stock. The decline of the landed nobility's economic fortunes, hastened by falling grain prices during the era 1875–1895, was thus equally indicative of the crisis of the rural economy.

Fourthly, the consequent low level of rural consumption that this state of affairs assumed acted as a powerful brake on national economic growth and made necessary—in its place—massive state intervention to foster broader and more rapid expansion of Russia's industrial sector. Monetary, tax, tariff and spending policies pursued by the state to such ends sharply disadvantaged the agricultural sector, further depressing rural consumption. Various indices—shrinking man:land ratios, rising tax arrears, the growing frequency of harvest failures between 1890 and 1905, the multiplication of incidents of rural unrest—all were used to paint a picture of an increasingly critical situation in the rural districts, particularly in the provinces of the Central Agricultural Region.[58]

---

[58] Robinson, *Rural Russia*, 129–137; Gerschenkron, "Russia: Patterns and Problems of Economic Development, 1861–1958," in his *Economic Backwardness*, 119–151; Gerschenkron, "Agrarian Policies and Industrialization: Russia, 1861–1917," in Habakkuk

Key aspects of this view of a *general* crisis of the rural economy have increasingly been subjected to revision. Headlong growth in indirect tax receipts on consumer goods, even accounting for a growing share of urban populations (for which estimates vary), indicated that consumption in the rural districts grew uninterruptedly during the second half of the nineteenth century.[59] An influential study of Russia's national economy as a whole during 1885–1913 made by Paul Gregory held that, far from stagnation or decline, the agricultural sector—as measured by grain output, buildings and equipment, livestock herds or rural wages—had made significant advances.[60] The studies of Nifontov and Gregory refocused attention on the growth of both net and *per capita* grain production in the era after 1861; Gregory's study on grain marketing[61] pointed to expansion of the portion that was actually retained in the village. Seen in this light, the long-established fact that steadily falling mortality rates drove accelerated natural increase of Russia's rural population after 1880 took on new significance.[62] Attributed to a diminishing incidence of infectious disease, more recent scholarship has treated that decline as due, not to improvements in medical services or sanitation practices, comparatively limited in rural Russia, but to enhancement of the quantity, if not the variety, of nutrition.[63] These studies

---

and Postan, eds., *The Cambridge Economic History of Europe*, VI: Part II: 706–800; Von Laue, *Sergei Witte*; Kahan, "Government Policies," *Journal of Economic History*, 27: 4 (1967), 460–477; Pavlovsky, *Agricultural Russia*; Volin, *A Century*, 40–93; Shanin, *The Roots*, I: 133–149.

[59] Simms, "The Crisis of Russian Agriculture," *SR*, 36: 3 (1977), 377–398.

[60] Nifontov, *Zernovoe proizvodstvo Rossii*; Gregory, *Russian National Income, 1885–1913* and *Before Command*, especially, Ch. 3; Gatrell, *The Tsarist Economy*, 98–140. For a more recent analysis that makes similar conclusions, see Leonard, *Agrarian Reform in Russia*, 189–205, 225–243.

[61] Gregory, "Grain Marketings," in *Explorations in Economic History*, 17: 2 (1979), 135–164. Davydov's more recent exhaustive examination of grain shipments (external/internal) as a portion of net grain production in each province confirmed Gregory's view. By accepted *per capita* consumption norms, images of the Russian countryside as chronically on the brink of starvation were inaccurate. Davydov, "Vnutrennii i vneshnii khlebnyi rynok," in his *Ocherki*, 81–239.

[62] In his writings from the pre-1917 era, Sergei Aleksandrovich Novosel'skii (1872–1953) had already posited the general decline of mortality rates in European Russia at least from the beginning of the 1880s: "K voprosu," *Vestnik obshchestvennoi gigieni, sudebnoi i prakticheskoi meditsiny*, 1914, 4: 339–352, and *Smertnost'*. See also Rashin, *Naselenie*, 152–256; Urlanis, *Rozhdaemost'*; Herr, "The Demographic Transition," *JSH*, 1: 3 (1968): 193–240; Chertova, "Smertnost' naseleniia," in A.G. Vishnevskii, ed., *Brachnost'*, 154–166.

[63] Gatrell, *The Tsarist Economy*, 59–60; Hoch, "On Good Numbers and Bad," *SR*, 53: 1 (1994), 41–75; Hoch, "Famines," *Population Studies*, 52 (1998), 357–368.

have mostly worked with national trends. Where analysis accounts for regional variations in production, differences of scale are more apparent.[64] Indicative as a measure of national consumption, state indirect tax receipts become less helpful for local studies, since they were taxes on production and not a sales tax.[65] Moreover, budget studies of peasant economies of different sizes made by *zemstvo* statisticians from the 1870s onward, whatever their defects, have consistently shown that different levels of consumption among various strata of villagers were a normal occurrence. The great value of recent historical studies on this issue has nonetheless been to modify in important ways our assumptions regarding the economic backdrop against which rural unrest during 1905–1906 took place. It has been duly noted that many portrayals of a "crisis of the rural economy," both official and non-official, drew upon the situation of the Central Agricultural Region, where (with the Baltic region) rural unrest was to be far more extensive and destructive in 1905–1907 than elsewhere, but which made up, after all, only a small part of the Empire.[66]

One must also be less inclined to accept the view of an all-powerful state presence in the countryside or of the effectiveness of its prohibitions and prescriptions. The growing mobility of a ceaselessly expanding number of rural inhabitants in search of wage work outside their provinces of residence, and for longer and longer terms, fits poorly with the view that state restrictions, enforced by communal and township officials, acted to keep the peasant populace down on the farm.[67] The failure of late nineteenth-century state administrative structures to provide for even the most basic requirements of rural inhabitants for justice and security[68] or to oversee such matters as communal land repartition, family partitions or fire codes were well known at the time.[69] For many educated Russians, these very failures accentuated a pervasive sense of insecurity about the chasm

---

[64] Wheatcroft, "Crises," in Kingston-Mann and Mixter, eds., *Peasant Economy*, 128–172.

[65] *Ministerstvo finansov 1802–1902*.

[66] Bushnell, "Peasant Economy," *RR*, 46: 1 (1987), 75–88.

[67] Tikhonov, *Pereselenie*. Passport data assembled for the Commission on the Center was quite illustrative on this point, not only in terms of numbers of passports, but also with regard to the prevalence of one-year issues after 1890. *Materialy Vysochaishe utverzhdennoi 9-go noiabria 1901 g. kommissii*, Table XX.

[68] Frank, *Crime*.

[69] These latter issues were commonly taken up in proceedings of the local committees of the Special Conference on the Needs of Rural Economy. The committees were officially barred from addressing legal and administrative matters, but commentary on such themes was nevertheless widespread and bore a sense of real urgency. An overview is Rittikh, ed., *Svod trudov... Krest'ianskii pravoporiadok, passim*.

that they perceived between their own "cultured" milieux and those defined by the poverty, domestic and community violence and cultural ignorance in which Russian peasants were perceived to live and labor, a perception that was in part true, and in part the product of the social isolation of the educated Russian. The state's lack of control over processes of change in the country districts—and rural revolt during 1905–1906 would confirm the worst fears of Imperial elites on this score—could not but provoke growing alarm among members of the Russian public who might have hoped for an orderly resolution of the "peasant question."

5. Peasant Unrest in 1905–1906: The "Two Social Wars" Doctrine and Its Fate

Differences of opinion in the literature on general conditions of rural society at the end of the nineteenth century were reflected, in turn, in analyses of the character and causes of peasant unrest during the First Russian Revolution. Already in the wake of extensive unrest in Khar'kov and Poltava Provinces in the spring of 1902, the Socialist Revolutionary organ *Revoliutsionnaia Rossiia* hailed the long-awaited stirring of the peasant masses as the action of a united and independent contingent of the toilers, "the working class of the countryside." This movement was viewed by the Socialist Revolutionaries as standing solidly against the institution of private property (either of the estate owner or of the rich peasant) and for transfer of all land to those who worked it by their own labor and was thus "semi-socialist" in character.[70] Conversely, while the peasantry's revolutionary potential could no longer be denied after 1905, Marxists of a more orthodox stripe, for whom the ambivalent "petit-bourgeois" motivations of the *muzhik* were axiomatic, emphasized the narrowly anti-feudal, bourgeois-democratic essence of the rural unrest of 1905–1906, in which only a struggle for the renewal, reinforcement and extension of peasant smallholding economies at the expense of the private estates was in evidence.[71]

---

[70] *Revoliutsionnaia Rossiia*, No. 8 (June 1902): 3–4 ("Krest'ianskoe dvizhenie"), 5–14 ("Ot krest'ianskago soiuza Partii Sotsialistov-revoliutsionerov ko vsem rabotnikam revoliutsionnago sotsializma"); *ibid.*, No. 11, September 1902 ("Klassovaia bor'ba v derevne"); *ibid.*, No. 12, October 1902 ("Proletarii-batraki v russkoi derevne"), 5–7; *ibid.*, No. 13, November 1902 ("Kharakter sovremennago krest'ianskago dvizheniia"), 4–6; in this same vein, see A. V. Peshekhonov, *Agrarnaia problema v sviazi s krest'ianskim dvizheniem*, 5–71.

[71] Lenin, *op. cit.* (*Agrarnaia programma*), 272: "The peasant mass lays claim to the land spontaneously, because they are oppressed by the feudal latifundia and do not associate

Only Russia's industrial working class and its junior allies among "proletarianized" elements of an increasingly stratified village society remained the true bearers of revolutionary socialist values. This view was to exert broad influence on Soviet historiography, and was responsible, by the late 1920s, for a significant departure from earlier analyses. If the undoubted main thrust of agrarian unrest during 1905–1907 was against estates of the nobility and representatives of the established authorities (a "first, anti-feudal social war"), assertions began to appear with growing frequency in the historical literature of the late 1920s that the struggle had begun a transition (*"pererastanie"*) to a "second, anti-capitalist (and in essence intra-peasant) war" *already* during the First Russian Revolution, a transition driven by the village poor (*nizy*), under the "hegemony" of Russia's proletariat and its *avant-garde*—the Russian Social Democratic Workers' Party, small "b." This conception, associated in particular with the writing of Sergei Mitrofanovich Dubrovskii (1900–1970)[72] and reproduced in one

---

transfer of the land to the people with any defined economic ideas at all. Among peasants, there is only a very urgent demand, born, so to speak, from suffering and hardened by long years of oppression—a demand for the revival, strengthening, consolidation and expansion of small farming, a demand that the latter be made predominant and nothing more. All that the peasant visualizes is transfer of landowner latifundia into his own hands. In this struggle, the peasant clothes his own hazy idea of the solidarity of all peasants, as a mass, in the phrase 'ownership of the land by the people.' The peasant is guided by the instinct of the property owner, who is thwarted by the endless fragmentation of current forms of land ownership and by the impossibility, should all this motley medieval system of landowner-ship be perpetuated, of organizing the cultivation of the soil in a manner that fully corresponds to 'property-owning' requirements. The economic necessity of abolishing landlord-ism, of casting off the 'fetters' of allotment ownership, these are the negative concepts that exhaust peasant ideas of nationalization. What forms of landownership may eventually be needed to renovate small farming, which will have digested, so to speak, the landowner latifundia, the peasant does not think about."

[72] See his well-known *Krest'ianskoe dvizhenie*, published soon after his rehabilitation and return from exile (1936–1954). Before 1925, the views of Dubrovskii (he was a student of M. N. Pokrovskii) on rural unrest during 1905–1907 differed little from monographic treatments before 1917 in its identification of the "middle" peasant as the most consistently active stratum in collective actions against the private estates. At this juncture (1923), his identification of the onset of the "second social war" with formation of the *kombedy* during the Civil War echoed the Leninist chronology: *Ocherki russkoi revoliutsii*. In this same vein will be Kots, *Krest'ianskie dvizheniia*, 148–201. In 1925, though, Dubrovskii inserted the new paradigm into several articles in the Communist Academy's journal for agrarian issues, *Na agrarnom fronte* (*NAF*): "Krest'ianskoe dvizhenie v gody Stolypinshchina," 1: 99–115; "Krest'ianskoe dvizhenie nakanune revoliutsii 1905 goda," *NAF*, 1925, 10: 99–112; 11–12: 107–122; and in the journal *Istorik-Marksist*: "Krest'ianstvo v revoliutsii 1905 goda," 1 (1926): 256–279. By 1935, Dubrovskii's

form or another in most Soviet treatments from the end of the 1920s,[73] nevertheless failed even to account for contradictions within the data on which it was based, which themselves indicated only very limited incidence of intra-peasant conflict. It is not surprising that the evidentiary bases of the theory of the "second social war" in the countryside during 1905–1906 were subjected to withering criticism for the first time in 1956 against the backdrop of a renewal of the general debate on the character of rural society and economy in pre-revolutionary Russia. Not least of all, Lenin's own repeated observations after 1905 that peasant revolution in Russia would inevitably be "bourgeois-democratic" (aimed mainly at expropriation of the estate owners and nationalization of the land as a "clearing of the ground" for small-peasant capitalism)—*and his frequent depiction of the October Revolution in the countryside in this vein*—provided fertile ground for a critique of the fundaments of the orthodox paradigm. The challenge was famously taken up by A. M. Anfimov in the course of one of the first conferences "On the Preconditions for the October Revolution" in May 1960 during his exchange with Dubrovskii: even if the canon remained officially obligatory largely down to the end of the Soviet era, its legitimacy had now been compromised. [74]

---

views were fully formed, as shown, in this connection, by his 1935 pamphlet, *Partiia bol'shevikov v rukovodstve*. The model emerged alongside L. N. Kritsman's work on class differentiation in the NEP countryside: "K voprosu," *NAF*, 1925, 2: 47–55; 7–8: 3–37; 9: 23–32; 10: 17–46. By the late 1920s, this formula—and reemphasis on the definitive maturation of capitalism in the countryside before 1917 and the final breakdown of the peasantry into warring classes—had become fixed in historical writing on the rural revolution. See K. A. Popov and Ia. Razvushkin, *O pererastanie*, 3–65 and 71–127, Morokhovets, *Krest'ianskoe dvizhenie*, and Shestakov, *Krest'ianstvo*.

[73] Piaskovskii, *Revoliutsiia 1905–1907 gg.*, 47–49, 143–154, 264–270; Pershin, *Agrarnaia revoliutsiia*, 226–271; Tropin, *Bor'ba bol'shevikov*; Tiukavkin and Shchagin, *Krest'ianstvo Rossii*, 64–92; Senchakova, *Krest'ianskoe dvizhenie*.

[74] Anfimov, "K voprosu." Sharply opposing views advanced at a scholarly conference at the USSR Institute of History in 1960 on the issue are preserved in the conference reports. S. M. Dubrovskii, "K voprosu ob urovne razvitiia kapitalizma v sel'skom khoziaistve Rossii i kharaktere klassovoi bor'be v derevne v period imperializma (dve sotsial'nye voiny)," 5–44; Anfimov, "V. I. Lenin o kharaktere agrarnykh otnoshenii v Rossii v nachale XX-go veka," 64–85, in *Osobennosti agrarnogo stroia Rossii*. An analysis of revolutionary events in the Central Black Earth countryside published at this time that is rather free of *a priori* constructs is Abramov, "Iz istorii krest'ianskogo dvizheniia," *IZ*, 57 (1956), 293–311.

6. Contemporary Russian Historians on Rural Unrest, 1905–1906

The disintegration of the USSR and the eclipse of official canons govern-
ing the social sciences has in part revealed and in part promoted a deep
ambivalence in Russian historical writing regarding the idealized master
narrative of the "great seismic events" of the first decades of Russia's
twentieth century, which opened with the First Russian Revolution. The
overarching conceptual framework for events in the countryside—the
"crisis of the rural order"—has now taken on considerable nuance.[75] Although the Russian working class is still seen as the mainspring of the
revolutionary process in 1905, older assertions of its "hegemony" over
rural protest have all but disappeared from the newer literature. Recent
Russian histories depict the revolution itself as a complex series of asynchronous reactions to the collapse of authority at the center, understood in
the localities through local events or reports of events elsewhere in the
Empire. Indeed, some Russian scholars have treated these upheavals not
simply as revolutionary, but as the opening installment of the civil war
that would reach its dénouement in Russia during 1918–1922.[76] Thirdly,
the new monographic literature reflects a broad revival of interest in "non-
proletarian" political figures, movements and party organizations that
contributed to shaping the events of 1905–1907, and has amply confirmed
a view that Bol'shevik activists could not and did not manage to play the
role attributed to them by Soviet hagiography.[77] Fourthly, along with "de-
idealization" of revolutionary events and processes generally, a de-
emphasizing of intra-peasant class conflict in historical writing on agrarian unrest has been of particular note, reflecting, in turn, a larger reluc-

---

[75] See, for example, Korelin, "Rossiia sel'skaia," in Iakovlev, ed., *Rossiia v nachale*, 224–
233, and Korelin, "Istoki," in Korelin and Tiutiukin, eds., *Pervaia revoliutsiia v Rossii*,
21–76. Korelin accepts the "new economic history" in its *overall* implications for agriculture (expansion of grain production, growth of consumption), but beyond these aggregates, he continues to value indices associated with "crisis": tax arrears, shrinkage of
average acreage per household, growing unprofitability of household economy, multiplication of poor harvest years, and rural unrest (1902).

[76] Iu. A. Petrov, "1905 god: Prolog grazhdanskoi voiny," in *ibid.* (*Rossiia v nachale*), 354–
395.

[77] This more realistic view applies even to the general political strike of October 1905. See
the comments of Irina Mikhailovna Pushkareva in her chapter (Chapter 5: "Pervaia pobeda revoliutsii") in Korelin and Tiutiukin, eds., *Pervaia revoliutsiia v Rossii*, 342–345,
and in her "1905 god: revoliutsionnyi shturm ili 'perestroika' gosudarstvennoi vlasti?"
in Golikov and Korelin, eds., *Rossiia v XIX-XX vekakh*, 276–289.

tance to apply class analysis to Russia's peasantry as a whole.[78] In rural conditions in Russia at the dawn of the twentieth century, one historian writes thus: "Any talk of a sharp division of the peasantry into 'kulaks,' 'middle peasants' and 'poor'—the essence of the Leninist conception of the development of the Russian village and foundation for the future so-called socialist revolution in the countryside and the socialist reorganization of the rural economy—is absolutely far-fetched and utopian... All discussion of class struggle in the village, of the *kulak* as the focus of capitalist tendencies, today seem not merely wholly driven by ideology and politicized, but simply naïve. The Russian village continued its retarded and difficult transition from the medieval epoch to the new era: it was the transitional, contradictory and dramatic nature of this evolution, a struggle of communal collectivism and bourgeois pragmatism and individualism that was the essential feature of Russia's rural life."[79]

The affirmation of the essential solidarity of Russian peasants in their quest to enact the age-old dream of a Black Repartition has received a new twist in recent writings of O. G. Vronskii on the *cul-de-sac* into which the communal order of peasant life was mired. Vronskii concluded that peasant collective actions during 1905–1907, in their single-minded pursuit of a resolution to the land question—and with little abiding interest in fateful national political debates—were hardly revolutionary. "The effort to 'revolutionize' the peasant movement of 1905–1907 and to make it 'heroic'—and in that connection to view its actions at the same time in a very negative light—has long dominated historical science... *The struggle of peasant land communes to maintain traditional ways of village life and to extend them outward* (by means of swallowing up private, state, appanage and monastery lands, by means of installing on these their own archaic techniques of agricultural production, landed relations and juridical

---

[78] Rehabilitation of views of the pre-revolutionary Russian peasantry and peasant economy that had previously been considered anathema—i.e. "populist" or "neo-populist"—was a prominent feature of the era following "perestroika." Several of Chaianov's writings, for example, have been republished in whole or in part: his 1919 *Osnovnye idei i formy sel'skokhoziaistvennoi kooperatsii* (Moscow, Nauka, 1991); A. A. Nikonov *et al.*, eds., *Krest'ianskoe khoziaistvo. Izbrannye trudy* (Moscow, Ekonomika, 1989), including the reprint of his classic 1925 work, *Organizatsiia krest'ianskogo khoziaistva*, 194–442; I. I. Eliseeva, ed., *Izbrannye trudy* (Moscow, Finansy i statistike, 1991); *A. V. Chaianov: chelovek, uchenyi, grazhdanin* (Moscow, Dashkov i Ko., 2000). An even-handed 1987 review of theories of the peasant economy—including those of populist and neo-populist specialists—appears in Savel'ev, *Agrarnye otnosheniia*.

[79] Sakharov, "Vvedenie," in A. N. Iakovlev, ed., *Rossiia v nachale*, 28.

norms), *given the peasantry's adherence to an autocratic-monarchist state ideal, cannot be considered revolutionary.*"[80]

It is hard to understand how the fundamental revision of landed relations at which peasant militants aimed could not be considered revolutionary, but such views are not unusual, given the current climate of ambivalence toward or minimization of the progressive sides of Russia's revolutionary past.[81] Yet Vronskii tries here to get at the inward-looking aspect of Russia's peasant movements during the first decades of the twentieth century, their close preoccupation with local concerns and conflicts, and their propensity to define and justify revolutionary acts in the language of traditional, even conservative understandings of the movement's broader aims.

7. Western Analyses of Rural Unrest during the First Russian Revolution

The first monographic works on rural unrest during 1905–1906, based principally upon responses to a 1907 survey conducted by the Imperial Free Economic Society,[82] newspaper reports and documents surfacing randomly in the press, appeared directly in the wake of the events themselves. Written by specialists close to Russia's radical parties, such works tended markedly toward a "heroic" view of their subject, which, by comparison with what was to follow, was nevertheless less overtly ideological. Peasant disorders were described as local in nature, flowing from the crisis of the rural economy, in which land hunger (*malozemel'e*) occupied a crucial place among all motives—the character of the crisis itself varying considerably by region and between the center and the "peripheries" of the Empire. Peasant communities are commonly depicted as acting with high degrees of solidarity—the "middle peasants" playing the most reliably militant role—and village assemblies everywhere functioned as the main organizer. An immediate *organizing* role of political forces outside the village was noted only in isolated events, thus denying the validity of

---

[80] Vronskii, *Gosudarstvennaia vlast'*, 122. Italics in original. Vronskii considers the conduct of peasant deputies both in the All-Russian Peasant Union and in the first two Dumas as testimony to this thesis. See also his *Krest'ianskaia obshchina*.

[81] See also in this connection Buldakov, *Krasnaia smuta*.

[82] Survey results appeared as *Agrarnaia dvizhenie*, in *Trudy IVEO*, 1908, 3, 4–5, in essay form, by region, drawing on 1,400 answers obtained to 10,800 questionnaires sent out in 1907.

conservative representations current both inside and outside government[83]—and, ironically, the thrust of much of later Soviet portrayals. Yet
the frequent participation of migrant industrial laborers or demobilized
soldiers as the "brains" or "ferment" in rural unrest suggested a certain
heterogeneity in the spectrum of social elements that participated in the
disorders. The emergence of the All-Russian Peasant Union and organization of its local chapters, in which various social groups in the country
took part, speaks of the same heterogeneity. While the later emphases on
intra-peasant conflict, its origins in class stratification of village society
and the role of the "rural proletariat" were significantly absent, both in
early monographs and in the IFES survey's responses, the "spontaneity"
and "unorganized character" of rural disorders in 1905–1906 were repeatedly stressed.[84]

This earlier approach to analysis of the rural disorders of 1905–1906
has been largely characteristic of Western treatments, which have also
stressed the leading role of the "middle peasant," the primacy of local
concerns, village solidarity as the typical aspect of collective action, and
the limited influence of external political actors.[85] Although the identity of
the "middle peasant" remains somewhat nebulous, Wolf's conception of a
middle peasantry as "a peasant population which has secure access to land
of its own and cultivates it with family labor"[86]—that is, the peasant population that Chaianov described—seems appropriate to this conception.
Since the 1960s, however, Western histories of rural unrest in Russia during 1905–1906 have begun to make important observations with regard to
the influence of the sea change in the cultural framework of rural life. The
effect of the development of means of communication within the Empire,
an expanding migration of labor that retained ties to the land while mov-

---

[83] The fact that the majority of the provincial governors polled by Minister of the Interior
P. N. Durnovo in January 1906 considered "revolutionary propaganda" as the prime
cause of peasant unrest is shown by a reading of the collection of responses to the government's request for analysis in N. Karpov, ed., *Krest'ianskskoe dvizhenie*, and
Durnovo's report to Nicholas II stressing this general opinion at 94–98.

[84] Veselovskii, *Krest'ianskii vopros*; V. Gorn, Mech and Chervanin, eds., *Bor'ba... III.
Krest'ianstvo v revoliutsii*; Maslov, *Agrarnyi vopros*, II; Maslov, "Krest'ianskoe dvizhenie 1905–1907 gg.," in Martov, Maslov and Potresov, eds., *Obshchestvennoe* II: 2,
201–282; Prokopovich, *Agrarnyi krizis*, 64, 94, 108 and 112–148. Most of the writers
had written parts of the IFES report.

[85] Alavi, "Peasants and Revolution," *The Socialist Register*, 1965, 241–277; Wolf, *Peasant
Wars*, 291–292; Shanin, *The Roots of Otherness*, Vol. 2; Edelman, *Proletarian Peasants*.

[86] Wolf, *Peasant Wars,* 291.

ing into diverse occupations, rising literacy and the formation of a rural intelligentsia out of a mélange of social elements, the growing inroads of urban culture even if refracted through prisms of rural understandings—all such influences breached the isolation of Russia's country districts. In relating such broader changes to rural unrest in 1905–1906—and noting the direct effect of national events in triggering peasant protest—both Maureen Perrie and David A. J. Macey suggested further avenues of inquiry.[87]

Such work appeared in an era of new interest in "peasantries" as discrete socio-cultural phenomena generally and of a reassessment, in that light, of the rich and varied body of sources and theoretical postulates that Russian and Soviet scholars had brought to bear on the "peasant question," drawing in particular on the research of specialists working in *zemstvo* organizations after about 1885. Analyses of peasant budgets and studies of household mobility over time during this era were crucial to formulation of the theories of Aleksandr Vasilievich Chaianov[88] and other exponents of the "organization-production school" on the peasant economy and its refinements and syntheses of the household budget and mobility studies conducted by a generation of *zemstvo* specialists. These works, in turn, played a central role in the seminal analyses of Teodor Shanin that treated rural society in the Imperial era and sought to assess why Russian peasants so commonly displayed great solidarity against external forces during the upheavals of the early twentieth century. The claiming of an exemption for Russian village communities in this era from processes of "class" stratification and for its "low classness"—due to the *essentially* non-capitalist, subsistence character of small family farming and to demographic processes of household mobility that acted to minimize the impact of material differences between households—has not suited all historians.[89] In addition, however, Shanin sought to more explicitly couch the

---

[87] Macey, "The Peasantry," *Columbia Essays in International Affairs*, VII (1971), 1–35; Perrie, "The Russian Peasant Movement," *Past & Present*, 57 (1972), 123–155.

[88] It is of note in this connection, of course, that Chaianov's influential synthetic work, *Organizatsiia krest'ianskogo khoziaistva* (1925) was made available in English for the first time in 1966 as *The Theory of Peasant Economy* (Homewood, IL: American Economic Association, 1966), translated and introduced by Basile Kerblay, Daniel Thorner and R. E. F. Smith. The work was reprinted in 1986 with introduction by Teodor Shanin (Madison, Wisconsin University Press).

[89] Gary Littlejohn, "The Peasantry," *Economy and Society*, Vol. 2, No. 1 (February 1973), 112–125; Gatrell, *The Tsarist Economy*, 70–83. In particular, Mark Harrison, "Chayanov and the Economics," *JPS*, 1974, 1: 389–417, "Resource Allocation," *JPS*,

findings of Chaianov and his associates within the larger literature on peasantries and peasant protest that appeared during this era. Even four years before the publication of Scott's work, he depicted the Russian village community as follows:

> ... a territorially-based human group united by ties of social interaction and interdependence, by an integrated system of accepted norms and values and by a consciousness of being distinct from other groups delineated along similar lines. High self-sufficiency should be added as a major characteristic of a traditional peasant community. Pitt-Rivers' description of a "closed community" as based on habitual contact, wide endogamy, homogeneity of values, emphasis on strict conformity, intense group solidarity, marked ideological egalitarianism, etc., is a fair generalization of the cultural traits of peasant communities. Community of descent and relatively low territorial mobility, primary personal contact and lack of anonymity, low division of labor and simple cooperation seem to underlie the high cultural cohesion of rural communities. Common political and economic interests find their expression in at least some rudimentary elements of local authority, administering common affairs and representing the village to outside authorities.[90]

This application of the subsistence ethic paradigm at its most rigorous and of the conception of the solidarity of the "little community" in the frame that Redfield gave to it[91] has thus had a decisive influence on the manner in which Russia's rural life and its discontents at the dawn of the twentieth century are now viewed.[92] Newer studies have buttressed this central canon with findings of ethnography and anthropology that fix the sharp divide in rural socio-political perspectives between matters and persons that are "one's own" (*svoi*) and those that are "foreign" or "alien" (*chuzhie*), pertaining to hegemonic forces beyond the horizon of a home terrain (*rodina*). This divide defined membership in the community and framed the interests and loyalties of members. Examinations of shared heritages of collective socio-historical memory associated inextricably with *rodina* (Magagna's "folklore of place") as these are preserved in rituals of ancestor worship and propitiation, animistic conceptions of natu-

---

1977, 1: 127–161, and "The Peasant Mode of Production," *JPS*, 1977, 4: 323–336. Also Rogalina and Gromova, "Kontseptsiia," *Vestnik Moskovskogo universiteta, Seriia 8: Istoriia*, 1993, 4: 35–46.

[90] Shanin, *The Awkward Class*, 32–33; see also Shanin, "Socio-Economic Mobility," *Soviet Studies*, 1971, 222–235, and "The Nature and Logic of Peasant Economy," *JPS*, 1973, 1: 63–80. See also n. 85.

[91] Redfield, *Little Community; Peasant Society and Culture*.

[92] For an engaging discussion on the conception of "community" in the rural setting that adds to this view, see Magagna, *Communities of Grain*, 1–24.

ral forces and settings, death rites and marriage ceremony, healing practice or the calendrical cycles of agricultural labor and community festivity
suggest that, if these differ in their regional inflections (even from village
to village), they exercised strong integrative influences on Russian rural
life and invested normative constructions and community sanctions with
force.[93] A picture of communal harmony and solidarity in village life,
however, has not been congenial to all elements of scholarly opinion.[94]
Rather, mutual distrust, envy, chronic generational tensions, bitter enmities between households, factional disputes and the ever-present phenomena of domestic and intra-village violence are seen as normal features of
this setting. The fact that modes of domination in archaic communities
remained intensely interpersonal, veiled or "euphemized" under the forms
and rituals of mutual responsibility, cannot deny their crucial influence in
structuring social and economic relationships between households and in
generating the potential for conflict.[95] A collectively accepted view of
moral right, reciprocal obligation and norms of behavior thus provided
only a malleable and uncertain barrier against such forces in rural life:
these could only be finally enforced by the resort to open violence.[96] A
close study of communal life in a Russian village during the servile era
made by Stephen L. Hoch and recent research on rural crime in the post-
Reform era[97] lend credibility to this view. The present work does not seek
to resolve this larger issue, yet we shall see that an acute internal discord
within subsistence communities generated both by growing demographic
and economic burdens and by deepening cultural dissonances will stand
among the primary factors driving the emergence of a revolutionary situa-

---

[93] Perrie, "Folklore," *RR*, 48: 2 (1989), 119–143; Worobec, "Death Ritual," in Frank and
Steinberg, eds., *Cultures in Flux*, 11–33; Chulos, *Converging Worlds*, and essays in
Balzer, ed., *Russian Traditional Culture*. A document attesting to the continued vitality
of this heritage in the modern Russian village and its interweaving with both Orthodoxy
and Soviet-era mythologies is Paxson, *Solovyovo: The Story of Memory in a Russian
Village*. I am indebted to Natasha Haimson for directing my attention to this latter work
and the line of thought contained therein.

[94] Oscar M. Lewis, *Life in a Mexican Village*; Banfield, *The Moral Basis*; Foster, "Interpersonal Relations," *Human Organization*, 19: 4 (1961), 174–178; Foster, "Peasant Society," *American Anthropology*, 67: 2 (1965), 293–315.

[95] The process of "veiling" modes of domination in archaic communities—the obligation
of wealthy householders to their poorer neighbors through the giving of gifts, sponsorship of community feasts, and similar ritual responsibilities are presented as elements—
is closely examined in Bourdieu, *Le sens pratique*, Book 1, especially 87–232.

[96] Frank, "Popular Justice," *RR*, 46: 3 (July 1987), 239–265.

[97] Steven L. Hoch, *Serfdom*; Frank, *Crime*; Frierson, *All Russia Is Burning!*

tion at the dawn of the twentieth century. I also note that the model of the "little community" assumes a society in which primary, "face-to-face" contact between members is the rule ("everyone knows everyone else"): what is the effect on the integrative force of tradition where, as in larger, densely populated rural settlements, this vital element is significantly impaired?

8. The Case Study: Kursk Province, 1905–1906

Rural unrest in Russia during the First Russian Revolution is commonly treated and interpreted within large geographical frames, by region or by closely analogous groups of provinces that echo conventions in official reporting and scholarly practice of the time. Aggregation of data from IFES surveys by month and numbers of districts (*uyezdy*) in each province seized by unrest, published by S. N. Prokopovich in 1912 and later revised at intervals by Soviet historians, remained the standard tool for assessing chronology or scale thereafter.[98] The painstaking archival work of Soviet archivists and historians in the 1920s laid the foundations not only for the subsequent development of source materials on a major scale in the era after 1953, but also for the first sustained efforts to present major documentation for individual incidents themselves. The fruits of these efforts were soon evident in a proliferation of publications devoted to the rural unrest of 1905–1907: multi-volume compilations of official documents from Imperial administrative bodies in both central and regional archival repositories and provincial anniversary chronologies or monographs that narrate events from a provincial viewpoint.[99] Yet scholarly *analysis* continued to present new materials in large units of aggregation and to employ them anecdotally as elements illustrating accepted master narratives. A consistent effort to review, *on the level of events themselves*, concrete local conditions and conflicts associated with single incidents of rural

---

[98] Prokopovich's "by county" schema was progressively updated, first, by E. A. Morokhovets, who added data for the Baltic counties, then by Pershin and lastly by V. I. Tropin, who added figures for the provinces of the Caucasus. The general effect of these revisions, all the same, has been to accentuate the "supremacy" of the peak of October–December 1905—i.e. following the general strike of October 1905, as opposed to the peak of May–July 1906. See Morokhovets, *Krest'ianskoe dvizhenie*, and Tropin, *Bor'ba bol'shevikov*.

[99] For an overview, see Simonova, "Krest'ianskoe dvizhenie 1905–1907 gg.," *IZ*, 95 (1975), 204–253, and Senchakova, "Opublikovannye dokumenty," *ISSSR*, 1979, 2: 68–86.

unrest was still largely absent. This framing resulted in depictions of the actors that drove events in Russia's rural districts in 1905–1907 as a homogeneous mass of "peasants," as ideological stereotypes in close accordance with a master narrative (*kulak-seredniak-bedniak*) or as "middle peasants." Non-actors—those that took no part in acts of protest, whatever their sympathies—remain entirely invisible. Lastly, the panoramic perspective tended to promote a picture of the great scale of rural protest during 1905–1906, despite the real absence of any consistent analyses of local events.

It was this convention in the literature on rural collective actions in Russia during 1905–1906 that prompted the author to design the research of those events around a single province in the agricultural center of European Russia.[100] The device of the "case study" is chosen in order to offer a scale of observation somewhat narrower than the "all-Russian" frame of reference that typifies historical literature on the peasant disorders of 1905–1906, in both Russia and the West. To be sure, the principal resources have been in scholarly circulation for almost a century—fragments of official reporting on the events themselves since the 1920s and the vast corpus of materials (both statistical and descriptive) treating multiple facets of rural life in the provinces of the Empire (gathered both by state agents and by local specialists in the employ of the *zemstvo*) from the 1870s onwards. The study thus seeks to replicate some of the advantages of micro-history as Jacques Revel has described them.[101] The selection, employment and interaction of these source materials in a closely limited geographical focus, it was hoped, would magnify their explanatory power not only for describing the context of revolutionary unrest in the rural districts in a concrete fashion, but also for teasing out the immediate background both for specific acts of protest and, just as importantly, for non-participation in such acts. In this circumscribed geographical setting, the analysis will demonstrate that "context" was not at all uniform, but multiple: differences in access to material resources, survival of social interactions between lord and peasant on the ground and contending elements of socio-historical memory among diverse peasant cohorts will be

---

[100] To my knowledge, the only relatively recent efforts to take an entirely local view of the causes of revolutionary unrest in the countryside during and after 1905, based on the close study of a single province, are Wilbur, "The Peasant Economy," Ph.D dissertation, University of Michigan, 1977, and Mixter, "Peasant Collective Action," in Wade and Seregny, eds., *Politics and Society*, 191–232.

[101] Jacques Revel, "Microanalysis," in Revel and Hunt, eds., *Histories*, 492–502.

shown in unexpected relief, not only between communities of former state peasants and those of ex-serfs, but also between rural dwellers in big settlements and those of the many small villages and hamlets that dominated the provincial landscape.

From this more local perspective, I will attempt to close in on tentative answers to several questions that have long stood at issue in the literature on rural unrest in 1905–1906 and animated the disputes that we reviewed in the foregoing sections. What was the general character and scale of revolutionary processes at work in the outbreak of peasant unrest in the localities themselves? How can we more closely identify the milieux from which unrest first emerged? Were there identifiable actors who played key roles, who served as initiators or catalysts for larger events, whether from within, from outside or from somewhere astride criteria usual to definitions of "peasantries?" Is it possible, on a level of aggregation closer to events themselves, to approximate more precisely specific *local* factors that distinguished villages involved in peasant unrest—by the nature of their interaction with nearby landowners or of their particular occupational orientations? One best approaches answers to such questions by close analysis of peasant unrest in the narrow confines of the localities in which they occur, and by an effort to acquaint oneself, as far as the sources permit, with the character of the villages identified with incidents of disorder. Such an approach, it seemed to me, could shed further light on the nature and scale of the peasant movement during 1905–1906, on its intensity and typological and chronological "architecture," *but already in local contexts*. Using a large sample of villages associated by documentary sources with incidents of unrest, one may then erect a socio-economic profile of the "milieu" from which the key actors of the movement emerged and with which those detachments of the peasantry that took part in these events were associated.

The selection of the provincial setting for the case study, however, was admittedly driven by the author's own initial expectations that a study of peasant unrest during the First Russian Revolution could be conducted within the context of a "traditional" rural order, still remote from those economic, social and cultural influences that had transformed the face not only of Russia's urban and industrial centers, but also of the provinces that lay within their orbit. Within the central region of European Russia during the Imperial period, Kursk Province was bounded by Orel and Chernigov Provinces to the north and west (respectively), by Khar'kov and part of Poltava *guberniia* along its southern border and by Voronezh *guberniia* to the east, and formed part of a group of provinces known conventionally as the Central Agricultural Region (CAR). In government reports of the era and in scholarly works, then and subsequently, the provinces of the old agricultural heartland were often held out as the epitome of the larger "crisis" of the rural economy and society, commonly treated as the most backward and impoverished region in European Russia. Lacking the dynamism in its systems of cultivation that marked the territories on the peripheries of the Empire (New Russia, the Northern Caucasus or Western Siberia), the CAR had also been bypassed by the industrial and commercial development that had inspired important changes in the rural economy and village society of provinces in the vicinity of Moscow, Saint Petersburg and other rapidly growing urban centers.[102] As was typical for CAR provinces, farming was the main (stated) occupation of the vast majority of Kursk Province's residents at the end of the nineteenth century; agriculture was dominated by the family household economies of a small-holding peasantry.[103]

Of the total area of acreage allotted to the peasantry under the land settlements of the 1860s, 57 percent was held under communal tenure by just over two-thirds (68.3 percent) of all households. At the dawn of the twentieth century, on both peasant allotments and most privately held lands of the former serf-owners, the annual cycles of agricultural work were performed within the regime of the three-field system of crop rotation with obligatory fallow, grain crops remained vastly predominant and tools and techniques employed were largely those perfected in the eighteenth century. For this reason, if harvests on private lands in the province were generally recorded as higher than those on peasant allotments, variations in quantities of grain harvested in any given year from a *desiatina* (2.7 acres) of sown land in both the private and the allotment sector mirrored each other closely. As was the case in the CAR as a whole, Kursk Prov-

---

[102] See Burds, *Peasant Dreams and Market Politics: Labor Migration and the Russian Village, 1861–1905*, for an exhaustive treatment of these transformations in the Central Industrial Region around Moscow, where the entire movement predated the Emancipation.

[103] Out of a population of 2,371,012 persons of both sexes residing permanently in the province as of 28 January 1897, persons engaged in agriculture and their dependents made up 1,953,763 (82%). *Pervaia vseobshchaia perepis'. XX. Kurskaia guberniia*, table XXI, 176–177. Of 3,964,632 *desiatiny* of land counted in the province for 1905, 2,830,020 (71.4%) were controlled by peasant communes, partnerships or individuals (of these, 2,455,363 lay under peasant allotments, 374,657 in private ownership). In contrast, the gentry share stood at 859,331 *desiatiny* (21.7%). Tsentra'nyi statisticheskii komitet, *Statistika zemlevladeniia 1905 g. Vyp. 37 (Kurskaia guberniia)*, Tables I–II, 10–11.

ince experienced considerable growth (+47 percent) in its rural population after 1861 despite massive emigration, and remained among the most densely populated provinces in European Russia.[104] Located at a distance of hundreds of miles from Russia's big commercial-industrial markets, the province had no urban centers of significant size, and the district "towns" were often quite a bit smaller in size than the larger peasant villages.[105] A quite modest complex of industrial enterprises was directed mainly to processing the produce of local farming, operating for perhaps four to five months and then closing to await the end of the next agricultural cycle. Permanent cadres of local industrial labor in the usual sense were thus very limited in number.

Rural unrest in Kursk Province in 1905–1906 attained very intense levels: material losses inflicted on the private landowners alone—in both real and personal property—reached 2,973,934 rubles for 1905 alone, second only to the sum for Chernigov *guberniia* among the provinces of the CAR.[106] This sum rose to 3,291,893 rubles when the peasant actions of 1906 were included. Selection of Kursk Province as the object of a case study—and as representative of the region—thus promised to provide a good sample of incidents of agrarian revolt during these years. It seemed also to present that setting in which the traditional agricultural orientations of peasant life, communal organization in closed villages and a high degree of cultural insularity could be expected to produce a context in which the "little community" model and conceptions associ-

---

[104] At 58.06 persons per square *versta* in 1897, Kursk Province stood behind only Moscow Province (83.14), Podol' Province (81.85), Kiev Province (79.71) and Poltava Province (63.36). Tsentra'nyi statisticheskii komitet, *Obshchii svod po Imperii resul'tatov.* Tom I, 2.

[105] Population classed as "urban"—221,349 persons of both sexes—made up 9.3% of the provincial populace in 1897. The provincial seat (75,721 persons resided in the town of Kursk and its suburbs in 1897) was the province's largest center; a few district seats were of modest size (Belgorod: 25,564; Staryi Oskol': 15,617; Ryl'sk: 11,549; Oboian: 11,251; Miropol': 10,100; Korocha: 10,093). All these figures include largely peasant suburbs in which the populations held their lands in communal tenure.

[106] RGIA, f. 1291, op. 122, 1905 g., d. 34a, Ch. I, l. 284. Kursk Province was seventh among all 49 provinces of European Russia; Saratov Province led with 10,541,402 rubles' worth of damage. Assessments for Chernigov Province (4,900,006 rubles) will also have included the destruction of the big Tereshchenko sugar-beet processing facility at *khutor* Mikhailovskii, Glukhov District, 23 February 1905, an action directly inspired and led by peasants from the zone of unrest in Dmitriev District: a memo in the police file bearing the date 10 March 1905, put losses at 6,445,000 rubles. GARF, f. 102, DPOO, op. 5, 1905 g., d. 2550 (obshchaia perepiska), l. 135. The sum was obviously reduced upon later inspections at the site.

ated with the "moral economy" frame of analysis adapted by Scott from the work of E. P. Thompson and employed by him so powerfully in his work on peasant protest in Southeast Asian rural society could be successfully deployed.

The effort to arrive at my conclusions that follows is organized in five chapters. It begins with an assessment of the setting of the events of 1905–1906 in Chapter I: an account of the condition of the rural economy in Kursk Province and its demographic profile. The chapter rests heavily on analysis of the household surveys conducted by the Statistical Bureau of the Kursk Provincial Zemstvo in the fifteen districts (*uyezdy*) of the province during the mid-1880s, supplemented by statistical materials collected by the central bureaucracies (principally the Central Statistical Committee of the Ministry of Internal Affairs) for the years 1885–1913: land surveys, annual accounting of grain harvests and livestock, yearly incidence of births and deaths, descriptions of "model" economies among private estates and so on. Chapter II and III will narrate elements of a large sample of peasant collective actions during the two years, drawn from archives of the Ministries of the Internal Affairs (Department of Police) and of Justice and the Chancellery of the Governor of Kursk Province. In order to fix the scale, character and targets of these collective actions, the sample will be reviewed in Chapter IV with regard to "ignition points," chronology, typology and geographical distribution. In Chapter V, we will return to the census materials collected under the auspices of the *zemstvo*, now to build a profile of that subset of individual settlements reported in the archival materials in connection with incidents of unrest, and to offer a statistical analysis and descriptive sketches of their status at the end of the nineteenth century that will relate to the association of their populations to revolutionary unrest.

9. Summary Results of the Study: Kursk Province in 1905–1906

The results of the study, it must be said here, failed to justify the framing of the problem as constructed to the degree that was expected. On closer inspection of the major incidents of unrest—those that required deployment of troops or police units to the scene—the scale of the movement affected a little less than 10 percent of all peasant villages in the province. Considered against the background of the juridical status of various peasant communities on the land, the milieux from which agrarian disorders in Kursk Province emerged during 1905–1906 were in many ways hardly "typical." The predominance of villages of former private serfs and their descendants (roughly 40 percent of the rural population according to *zemstvo* surveys of the mid-1880s) among those associated with incidents of unrest, and the geographical distribution of such incidents in zones of influence of larger "modernizing" latifundia marked one pole of my findings. These spoke directly, *for the affected localities*, not only of the survival of a deep sense of grievance engendered by implementation of the Emancipation on the ground, but also of a breakdown of the web of exchanges between patron-lords and peasant-clients—which legitimized the character of their interactions in the eyes of both parties—that had papered over the resulting tensions and cemented a fragile social peace in the era after 1861. Much of what has been suggested in the literature about the effects of market capitalism in promoting systemic violation of norms of reciprocity that governed relationships between social unequals in rural society was thus borne out in the study. Peasant discontent with the existing order in the country was widespread. Yet while we are painfully mindful of the limits of our sample, it seems that the very ubiquity of "feudal survivals" (*perezhitki*) in the social fabric of rural life in the province—that is, the remaining vitality of such norms of reciprocity rooted in the past—in interactions between lord and peasant, their *personal, "face-to-face"* component, and the *predictability* in the concrete benefits that they ensured for both parties, moved a majority of peasant communities in Kursk Province to refrain from direct acts of violence in 1905–1906.

In particular, settlements of the old state peasantry that made up the larger part of the rural population in Kursk Province remained outside the movement. Here, the matter took on different overtones. The ancestors of these rural communities in Kursk Province had garrisoned the chain of forts that had defended contested borderlands of the Muscovite state in the sixteenth and seventeenth centuries, making up the soldiery of the various Muscovite military formations (artillerymen, musketeers or mounted infantry) or the clans of the minor nobility (known as *deti boiarskie*) that served as a frontier officer corps and had received their lands in service tenure (*pomest'e*). This finding not only places in a certain relief the centrality of the quite different historical experience of the two larger communities to their participation (or non-participation) in collective acts of revolt, and the origin and content of their grievances and perceptions of justice, but also begins to speak to the fact that a "peasantry" in Kursk Province was not at all the homogeneous mass that appears in official reporting of the time.

Outbreaks of intense and destructive unrest were recorded in sub-regions of the province that were notably more prosperous and those that were measurably less so: a "crisis of the rural economy" was thus decidedly more local than systemic. Yet it was the leading role of the more heavily populated, crowded country towns and *slobody* in the revolutionary events of 1905–1906 in Kursk Province that marked the other side of the matter. The more critical limitations of the land fund (quantity *and* location) available to farming families in bigger rural settlements had long promoted the attenuation of ties to agriculture and reorientation toward non-agricultural occupations: significant elements among the populations of the larger of such villages were only nominally "peasants." Administrative, market-commercial and small-industrial centers, located on the main road, post-and-telegraph and/or rail networks (commonly sites of the parish's only schools), these big villages had evolved a cultural face distinct from that of the more numerous smaller, outlying hamlets in their immediate orbits.[107] We will also see that an unusually high proportion of small nuclear family households was a distinguishing feature of their populations. Budget and mobility studies of peasant households had always identified the nuclear family household with younger age cohorts, limited economic assets and the prominent role of wage employment in their budgets. Given this material weakness in terms of inventory, labor power, product *en nature* (from their plots) and cash income, the lot of such households will have been, undoubtedly, most unstable, even in more varied occupational settings of larger villages. Yet the purely demographic and economic facets of changes in the character of rural life hardly exhaust the matter. First, in these settings, it is plausible to posit that subsistence insurance schemes and intra-village customs of reciprocity that may have remained operative in smaller settlements that dominate the provincial landscape (and that approximate the criteria that scholars have attributed to "little communities"), predicated as they were in part on the lack of anonymity of residents one to another, will have functioned in the big rural towns only with the greatest difficulty, if at all. Second, these demographic and economic features evolve within and interact with a slow but steady alteration of rural cultural contexts. It was natural that the younger age cohorts in the countryside, and especially in the bigger country "towns," will have been the most intensely affected, producing what

---

[107] In recent treatments of rural unrest in this era on the level of *villages*, the role of large settlements has been of special note. See Mixter, "Peasant Collective Action," and Bukhovets, *Sotsial'nye konflikty*, 174–205.

Brocheux called "a restless class of young people who found it difficult to find a place in society."[108]

For it has grown more and more evident that profound changes in Russia's rural society advanced apace, despite the regimes of civil and juridical segregation by means of which emancipated peasants were held in a subaltern, tributary position in Russian society. Under growing demographic and economic tension, the collectivist cultures that rural communities struggled to maintain in response to the vicissitudes of nature, the constant depredations of outsiders and their own powerful internal dissensions appear to have encountered ever-steeper obstacles in the effort to secure those forms of "subsistence insurance" that remained a vital anchor of village societies. Acceleration of the tempo of socio-economic change in the latter half of the century also promoted what Freeze has written of as "a high degree of ambiguity and flux" in social identities in Russian society, "oscillating between legal estate, economic status and occupation."[109]

Surely, the criteria that Wolf saw as defining "peasants"—"populations that are existentially involved in cultivation and make autonomous decisions with respect to the processes of cultivation," for whom the major aim "is subsistence and social status gained within a narrow range of social relationships"[110]—will have remained broadly applicable to most of Kursk Province's rural inhabitants at the end of the nineteenth century. Yet the grand expansion of the Empire's means of communication after 1890 brought many country districts into national rail and telegraph networks for the first time, a feat no less significant for accelerating the erosion of the cultural isolation of village life than for its impact on local markets. Moreover, by 1900, hundreds of thousands of working-age peasants were leaving Kursk Province each year, and for more extended terms, in search of wages as field hands or workers in South Russia's booming

---

[108] Brocheux, "Moral Economy or Political Economy?," 801. The reference here, as I read it, was to the neglect of the generational factor by both Scott and Popkin: "Increased education, though still limited, generated seeds of unrest, discontent and agitation... The efforts of the authorities [in Southeast Asia] to revitalize Confucianism and to restore family cohesion in the 1930s stemmed primarily from an awareness of the political and moral crisis." One thinks, in this same vein, of the slogan *Pravoslavie, samoderzhavie i narodnost'* (Orthodoxy, Autocracy and Nationality) and its longevity at the center of conservative parlance in Russia.

[109] Freeze, "The *Soslovie* (Estate) Paradigm," *American Historical Review*, 91 (1986), 11–33; Haimson, "The Problem of Social Identities," *SR*, 47: 1 (1988), 1–29.

[110] Wolf, *Peasant Wars*, xiv.

industrial, mining, transport, construction, trade or service sectors—while maintaining their ties to the home villages. Abbreviated terms of military service after 1874 meant that conscripts drafted for stints in Russia's armed forces were no longer lost to the village, but returned after demobilization, bearing with them at least the impressions of events and places beyond the horizons of village life. Among younger cohorts of the province's rural population, basic literacy began to assume a truly mass character in an era in which popular literature and cheap newspapers were beginning to make their way into the countryside. A peasant reading public had emerged, at first noted in locales associated with skilled trades, highly developed craft traditions and/or out-migration in non-agricultural employment and growing gradually more pervasive with the expansion of a provincial network of elementary schools. The rapid development of *zemstvo* services during the decade 1892–1902 (of which elementary education was a major component), won by progressives in the teeth of conservative resistance in the Zemstvo Assemblies, multiplied interactions between the villagers and "outsiders" of various social origins (teachers, doctors, agronomists and other specialists that made up the so-called third element) who occupied an anomalous and embattled position in rural society and were viewed with suspicion by both peasants and noblemen alike.

Under the influence of intensifying interaction with the larger society that changes of this sort entailed, village culture was itself pushed onto the path of change, in terms of occupational heterogeneity, relations between elders and juniors within both the household and the commune, and patterns of consumption, leisure and festivity. The oft-denounced erosion of patriarchal authority over younger peasants also spoke of a growing impatience among the latter with the habits of self-effacement and of deference, and with patterns and customs of servility that had continued to mark social relations between peasants and their "social betters." On the other side of the social divide, Russia's nobility, members of its government apparatus and much of the educated public continued to define "consciousness" among peasants in accordance with highly negative images that Stephen P. Frank has likened to colonial stereotypes. Even among such observers, however deeply "tainted" their attitudes, there *were* those who were willing to acknowledge the sea change that was taking place in the peasant milieu:

> Everyone understands that in forty years, the liberated peasant has taken an enormous step in his cultural development, but not everyone draws from this the necessary practical conclusions. They fear the "thick skull" of the peasant almost as much as they did

twenty years ago after the unsuccessful "going to the people." Nevertheless, in these twenty years, in which a generation has come into being that has never known serfdom and that has, in part, passed through the *zemstvo* schools, a broad chasm now separates us from those times of unkind memory and from the possibility of such failures as those of that time. Twenty years ago, it was very often useless to distribute books among the people, since there were no literate people to read them. Now, books find themselves readers even in the remotest village. Formerly, the ignorant *muzhik* never even saw the district town and, understandably, was unable to comprehend the simplest words, to draw the most elementary conclusions. Now almost all of peasant Russia is in motion: no fewer than ten million adult peasants annually migrate hither and thither. They change a multitude of attitudes; they encounter a mass of the most various people and phenomena; they are struck by the contrasts between luxury and poverty, between the miracles of science and their own ignorance. And this wave of need, these millions of the working peasantry thrown across all of Russia from one exploiter to another, reveals to them, from all sides, the social pyramid that crushes them, strikes them with its sharp corners. Here life teaches the illiterate better than any book. And all this great stream of impressions, feelings and knowledge flows uninterruptedly back into the country districts, constantly broadening the horizons of even those who have never left the land. It is obvious that these ten million peasants, in the hunt for earnings, become more and more energetic, more stubborn, more independent, more daring and ever angrier, that in this school of life, the personality develops quickly and a critical spirit awakens.[111]

Rural unrest in Kursk Province during 1905–1906 undeniably derived from local conflicts, and there is very little evidence that its *concrete* aims ever transcended the "estate" interests of local communities as these engaged in a final settling of scores with the neighboring landowners. Far from being an attempt at a "restoration" of the *status quo ante* ("bargaining by riot"), the record of rural disorders in the province, especially in 1905, shows that peasant militants were driven by a desire to *obliterate* the material bases of the older order. Involving as they did specific subregions (even a single village and the nearby estate) in the province at various time intervals across almost two years of unrest, peasant actions appear "spontaneous" and "unorganized" only to those who followed them from a distance. From the local viewpoint that I will attempt to fix, however, peasants proved themselves entirely capable of organizing various phases of offensive or defensive acts using their own institutions: scouting the objective, warning the landowner in advance, carrying out the looting and destruction of the estate, expelling its work force or negotiating under pressure, and refraining, with notable exceptions, from physical

---

[111] "Ot krest'ianskago soiuza Partii Sotsialistov-Revoliutsionerov ko vsem rabotnikam revoliutsionnago sotsializma v Rossii," *Revoliutsionnaia Rossiia*, No. 8, 25 iiun' 1902, 8 (col. 2).

violence against the owners.[112] Villagers made common cause with non-peasant allies and adapted novel organizational instruments (*ad hoc* peasant councils, chapters of the short-lived Peasant Union, peasant electoral curia for the Duma elections) to pursue their aims and make their views known. The emergence and rhythm of unrest and its variations over time evidence a keen awareness of national events, even if their significance was adapted to peasants' own political mythologies or was used simply to gauge the ability of local authorities to decisively confront actions, whether taken or contemplated. Lastly, our study of peasant unrest in Kursk Province during 1905–1906 gave us an awareness of the catalytic and mediating roles of groups of villagers that stand at a certain distance from Wolf's image of "middle peasantry": those associated with the labor migration and/or urban residence, the literate element among the rural populace, village youth and those residents of the big country towns whose experience of rural life partook of a measurably more variegated economic and cultural setting that colored its interactions with the outside world.

Certainly, the documentary evidence stressed, in one way or another, the centrality of the land issue in local conflicts and the importance, within this frame of reference, of a local deterioration—even the rupture—of the efficacy of those older norms of reciprocity between lord and peasant that, being closely associated with subsistence strategies of the peasant communities and rooted in socio-historical memory, shaped villagers' conceptions of justice and injustice. Yet the frequent association of villages noted in connection with incidents of unrest with traditions of labor migration and the leading role in the disorders of large rural "towns," as well as their more literate populations and small-industrial occupational profiles, show that the events in the country districts of Kursk Province in 1905–1906 could not be linked unambiguously with a "peasantry." More precisely, agrarian unrest during the First Russian Revolution displays the degree to which, even in the allegedly "backward" agricultural heartland of *fin-de-siècle* Russia, rural society had become exuberantly heterogeneous in character, a reality that defied both the persistent view, fostered by official reporting (and much of elite opinion), of the peasantry as an undifferentiated "gray" mass, and the "class" categories of Marxist social science. Indeed, the rallying cry of "land and

---

[112] If physical assaults against policemen, soldiers or estate employees were common, attacks on the persons of landowners were exceedingly rare and never fatal. This was to change in 1917.

freedom" served to unite ever-more distinct and contentious elements within the generational structure of village society and to paper over such tensions and dissonances in a collective pursuit of the millennial vision of "Black Repartition." That said, it bears repeating that, though the stresses and strain on the fabric of rural society that I will identify were widespread, both the distinctive historical experience of populations of former serfs and the site-specific parameters in which the breakdown of older social relationships took place will simultaneously define and substantially limit the locus of mass collective actions in Kursk Province during 1905–1906.

CHAPTER I

Kursk Province on the Eve
of the Revolution

Before proceeding to a narrative of peasant collective action in Kursk Province during 1905–1906, a review of the general context in which these disturbances took place is indispensable. By almost all accounts, rural unrest in the heavily agricultural provinces of the Black Earth belt had its origins in the "land question" and scholarly treatments of peasant actions in Kursk Province are no exception in this regard.[1] Yet even a cursory review of the literature suggests that this issue cannot be understood only within the framework of peasant land hunger (*malozemel'e*) to which it is often reduced. Rather, one must account for the ways in which both peasants and private landowners strove to adjust to economic and demographic trends that acted broadly upon the agrarian sector in the second half of the nineteenth century, a struggle that drove the interests of lords and peasants into increasing conflict. Among contemporary observers, and for much of the historiography that followed, verdicts on this process are rendered in conceptions of a "crisis of the rural economy," marked by a decline in the fortunes of the landed nobility and impoverishment of the peasantry, as the main background to agrarian disorders.

Certainly, within the limits of the land settlements that accompanied the major acts of the Great Reforms of the 1860s that regularized the status of the peasantry as "free rural inhabitants," the natural increase in the population of Kursk Province's country districts during the second half of the nineteenth century was to drive unfavorable trends in man:land ratios. Against the background of demographic increase, peasant agriculture in Kursk Province remained wholly extensive in character: by the mid-

---

[1] Maliavskii, "Krest'ianskoe dvizhenie," *Kraevedcheskie zapiski*, I: 3–69; Stepynin, *Krest'ianstvo*; Prilutskii, *Istoricheskii opyt*, 25–108.

1880s, between eight and nine out of every ten acres of allotment land had already been plowed under. Predominant tools and implements were outmoded, but had sure advantages in that they were cheap, light and durable, required a minimum of draught power and were easily repaired with locally available materials. The old short fallow system and the relationships of areas sown with various crops remained mostly unchanged. In the "classic" three-field regime of crop rotation, around a third of the arable land sown was seeded in autumn with winter crops (*ozimoe pole*), a third reserved for spring plantings (*iarovoe pole*) and a third left fallow for the whole cycle to "rest" the soil. In the succeeding year, fields sown in the previous cycle with winter crops (wheat and rye) were sown with spring grain (oats, barley, millet and buckwheat), the fallow was "raised" for winter sowings, and fields that had yielded the previous year's spring crop were left fallow. In a survey of these practices in Tambov Province, David Kerans showed that each household was, in principle (if not in practice), free to sow what it wished and was responsible for all agricultural operations on its own strips. Yet because each household had numerous strips in each field—and in each subsection of any given field in terms of soil quality and distance from the house plots—decisions with regard to the fallow field and the timing of its raising were made collectively and were obligatory for all members. Faced with ever-more acute deficits of livestock feed, with the progressive disappearance of pasture and meadow before the plow, fodder crops nevertheless played almost no role in fallow or rotation. This circumstance greatly accentuated the obligatory character of collective decisions concerning the fallow—especially in light of a growing dearth of pastures and meadow in peasant holdings—by its increasingly central role as a first source of fodder after winter's meager stall feeding.[2]

Contemporary agronomy condemned peasant techniques and methods of cultivation as perilously archaic, but they rested on the sanction of tradition and enjoyed the benefits of simplicity, predictability and community-wide acceptance. These critics also tended to forget that short fallow regimes represented a major advance over long fallow systems and the ancient slash-and-burn methods. Peasant cultivation was, moreover, by no means static. Steady expansion of potato crops after 1891 made a crucial

---

[2] Confino, *Systèmes agraires*; Kerans, *Mind and Labor*. See in this same connection Bloch, *Les Caractères*, Chapter II, 21–65. Ester Boserup's view that the issue of grazing rights on the fallow commonly acted as a powerful brake on agricultural innovation is to be found in *The Conditions of Agricultural Growth*, 85–86.

contribution to food production. Extension of the area under hemp (and in eastern districts, spring wheat and barley) diversified the spectrum of cash crops. In *uyezdy* most disadvantaged by the size of peasant allotments, one notes, in the first decade of the new century, both the signs and the effects of more intensive cultivation, with a more modern inventory that suggests that peasant farmers were achieving a new virtuosity within existing rotation schemes. Nonetheless, in his report on the state of the province for 1897, reviewing the factors responsible for the poor harvests of that year, the Governor of Kursk Province observed the following:

> The cultivated stratum of the soil of the province is composed of black earth [*chernozem*] between 7 inches and four and a half feet in depth with substratum of clays, sand, sand-clay mixtures, marl and limestone, but the clay-black earth mix that possesses all the characteristics favorable to agriculture predominates. Thanks to substantial admixtures of sand, the soil is not especially viscous, permitting moisture and air to penetrate to root systems. The clay substrata, at the same time, retain moisture and act as a significant reservoir of water. All these advantageous characteristics of the soil have facilitated conversion of the land everywhere to sowings of grain. All of Kursk Province has now become one large plowed field; agriculture is thus the principal productive force and the basis for the prosperity of the populace. However, despite all the favorable natural conditions for agriculture in the province, it is impossible not to observe that, with few exceptions, it is conducted in the most primitive manner and finds itself completely dependent on the random nature of meteorological conditions.[3]

This commentary was hardly directed at peasant cultivators alone. For the most part without capital and deprived of serf labor in the face of increasingly complex economic uncertainties, the vast majority of noble landowners were hardly very progressive in their approach to estate operations, and the poorest of them inspired only pity among peasants in their localities. These were holders of smaller estates dependent on the rents or labor dues of peasant tenants and exploitation of peasant labor and inventory, and in no way distinct from adjoining villagers in terms of technical level of tillage, crop rotation regimes on the demesne, the mix of sowings, their lack of capital or a certain aversion to risk.

The assessment of rural standards of living for Kursk Province before 1905 offered in the following pages reveals a rather contradictory picture. The decline of crude mortality rates for the province during 1867–1910, expansion of agricultural production between 1885 and 1913, improvement in wages for field labor and incomes reported from crafts or the labor migration, and growth of fixed assets (including privately held acre-

---

[3] *Obzor Kurskoi gubernii za 1897 god*, 1.

age) all suggest positive developments in the material basis of rural life. Such evidence, however, did not and could not do much to describe the *distribution* of the benefits of improvements within the peasantry itself. Steady deterioration of man:land ratios in the face of natural population increase (mirrored by inflation of land prices and rents) exerted unambiguously negative influences on peasant economies. The anaemic growth in livestock holdings (such as can be measured) continued to portend serious problems associated with the fodder base. Positing an expansion in provincial agricultural output depended on including the five-year period 1909–1913: the 1903–1908 interval was actually a mediocre one after the bumper crop of 1902. Indeed, the most striking feature of year-to-year grain production was its strong and often extreme variations. By the end of the nineteenth century, moreover, Kursk Province was annually "exporting" hundreds of thousands of persons of working age to other parts of the Empire, a sure sign that new increments of population could no longer be gainfully employed on the land. Growth in out-migration brought in its train new strains on the fabric of peasant life, expressed in the disruption of a sense of shared economic interests among household members, and contributed to a high frequency of *pre-mortem* fissions. Local observers commonly noted those "alien" cultural influences that migrant workers bore with them back to their home villages.

Lastly, Kursk Province—and indeed its peasantry—could not be treated as a single entity. Significant differences in historical experience (of former state peasants and ex-serfs), in ethnicity, settlement patterns, acreage per household or harvest performance would distinguish rural communities in the province's fifteen districts toward the end of the century. Yet, looking ahead, it would become clear that the incidence of rural unrest during 1905–1906 itself did not coincide at all precisely with any measurable "geography of misery." Violent agrarian disorders of great and destructive intensity in Novyi Oskol' and Staryi Oskol' Districts during November 1905 occur in a region in which warning signs of troubles in the agricultural sector had emerged already in the mid-1880s, in spite (or because) of the fact that villagers here were relatively better supplied with land than elsewhere. Conversely, unrest of equal intensity in the southwest crescent of districts (Sudzha, Ryl'sk, L'gov, Putivl' and Graivoron) unfolds in landscapes in which necessity had driven peasant smallholders toward improvements in cultivation that placed this subregion at the high end of agricultural production. Most specifically, it will be clear that agrarian disorders of 1905–1906 place in the highest relief the local collision of interests that issued from a struggle to adjust to new economic realities, and its corrosive effects on interactions between land-owners and peasant communities that had fostered a fragile social peace after 1861. In the analysis of these events and of the villages that partici-pated in them, we shall be reminded that while one may posit a general improvement in rural life on the basis of large aggregates, the underpin-nings of that prosperity, viewed on the local level, often appear tenuous and unstable.

1. The Land Settlements of the 1860s in Kursk Province Twenty Years Later

The number of detailed treatments of the Emancipation settlements in the literature[4] relieves us of the need for all but the briefest review of their specific features as these pertained to Kursk Province. According to the research of Boris Grigor'evich Litvak, the former bound peasants in Kursk Province went onto redemption at a loss of 15.7 percent of the land they had cultivated before 1861[5] and were compelled to acquiesce, some-times after considerable resistance,[6] in the systematic efforts of the land-owners to retain the most fertile parts of these lands. The former masters

---

[4] Zaionchkovskii, *Provedenie*, "Podgotovka," *ISSSR*, 1958, 4: 103–113, and *Otmena*; Emmons, *The Russian Landed Nobility*; Field, *The End of Serfdom*; Druzhinin, *Russkaia derevnia*; Zakharova, *Samoderzhavie*. Reforms of administration of the state peasantry in the 1830s and 1840s and their importance for the formulation of the 1861 decrees in Druzhinin, *Gosudarstvennye krest'iane*, II: 7–79, 525–570. See also Koval'chenko, *Russkoe krepostnoe krest'ianstvo*.

[5] Litvak, *Russkaia derevnia*. According to Litvak, allotments of ex-serfs went from 805,670 *desiatiny* before the Emancipation to 678,757 *desiatiny* as a result of the land settlement, a loss of 126,913 *desiatiny*. "Cut-offs" were most severe in Graivoron (101,239 to 75,499 *desiatiny* or 25.4%) and Fatezh (26,412 to 20,238 *desiatiny* or 23.3%) Districts, least severe in Tim (32,809 to 30,423 *desiatiny* or 7.2%) and Putivl' Districts (78,239 to 71,894 *desiatiny* or 8.1%). Of 272,324 peasant allotments 134,476 (49.3%) were reduced, 8,164 (3.0%) were augmented and 129,634 remained unchanged in size, if not in location. The Local Ordinance provided for lower norms for the districts of Kursk Province than for elsewhere in the CAR (only parts of Riazan and Tula Provinces were similarly disadvantaged). Ex-serfs in Oboian District were allowed allotments of up to a maximum of 3 *desiatiny* per male revision soul and those in Tim District 3 *desiatiny* 600 *sazhen* (2,400 *sazhen* = 1 *desiatina*) Dmitriev District alone received the norm of 3 *desiatiny* 1,800 *sazhen*. In all other districts, the maximum allotment norm for revision soul was set at 2 *desiatiny* 1,800 *sazhen*, the lowest established for the CAR.

[6] Tankov, "Krest'ianskiia volneniia v Kurskoi gubernii v 1862 godu," *Istoricheskii vestnik*, XLI (1890), 343–379; Ivanov, ed., *Krest'ianskoe dvizhenie*, 189–190 (No. 62), 349–354 (Nos. 132–133), 470–472 (No. 178), 601 ff.

now held, as private property, large tracts of woodlands, meadows and pastures, access to which had previously been open to peasant use by custom; final partition commonly built real inconveniences into peasant use of the allotments that they had accepted. Strategies of former serf owners in relation to settlements were thus to allow above all, as before, for preserving an uninterrupted supply of labor or—failing this—to recover as much equity as possible in land. The process of bringing ex-serfs to redemption was long and drawn out: twenty years after Emancipation, just over a quarter remained in the state of temporary obligation to their former masters.[7] The Emancipation preserved the nobility's possession of a substantial and diversified area of the province's most fertile lands. Of a total area of 3,993,890 *desiatiny* under the ownership of various social estates in 1877, the nobility retained within its estates 1,165,444 *desiatiny* (29.2 percent) and the peasantry (state peasants and ex-serfs) controlled 2,600,980 (65.1 percent). Peasant landholdings included both allotments (2,457,032 *desiatiny*) and 143,948 *desiatiny* in non-allotment acreage (135,733 in private ownership and 8,215 in communal ownership).[8]

The influence of the nobility in implementing the emancipation of former serfs was far less at play in regularization of the civil and landed status of state peasants. In Kursk Province, these latter not only received all the lands at that time in their use, but also received certain additional acreage.[9] No juridical or economic disabilities attached to the two-year

---

[7] Of the 268,752 "revision souls" that concluded contracts (*vykupnye sdelki*) with their former masters, either by mutual agreement or by the unilateral petition of the landowner, 155,367 (57.8%) had gone onto redemption by 1870 and 203.502 (75.7%) by 1881. Even after publication of the Law of 28 December 1881 mandating, from 1 January 1883, transfer of all temporarily obligated peasants onto the redemption regime, it was not until 1898 that the charters of the last of this number had been confirmed and the loans granted. Even so, some 50 or 60 contracts (of 2,834) appeared not to have gained the necessary confirmation even at the end of the century. See annual data in the section "On the Redemption Operation," in *Ezhegodnik Ministerstva finansov*. Vyp. I–XXIV (1869–1899) and Vyp. 1899 goda (1900).

[8] Ministerstvo vnutrennikh del. *Statistika pozemel'noi sobstvennosti naselennykh mest*, 206–233.

[9] Lands under the control of state peasants in Kursk Province increased from 1,728,881 *desiatiny* in 1858 to 1,812,084 *desiatiny* after 1866. Druzhinin, *Russkaia derevnia*, 109, Table 7. The considerable intermixing of lands of state peasants with those of private landowners continued as before. For communities of *odnodvortsy*, though, this intermixing had much to do with their genealogical ties to an ancestral clan among the soldiery posted to the Muscovite frontier in the sixteenth and seventeenth centuries, elements of which made up much of the minor Russian gentry north of the River Seim.

term granted for partitioning lands to remain in the state domain from peasant allotments and compilation of land rolls (*vladennye spiski*). The state's financial interests were, of course, evident: quit-rent payments (*obrochnaia podat'*) increased by 5–12 percent, and although the head tax was abolished in 1886, both assessments were combined when state peasants were moved onto the redemption regime in 1887. There was not the kind of venue for protracted wrangling that took place between former serfs and the masters (who held veto power in their dealings) over terms of agreement. Nonetheless, conflicts over results of the partitions and over composition of communal land rolls (which included, *inter alia*, fixed tax obligations) were often protracted and acrimonious.[10] Marked differences in conditions of emancipation for the two groups were nevertheless to have significant effects, both on their material position in the second half of the nineteenth century and, as we will see in the chapters below, on the state of attitudes on the eve of the 1905 unrest. Communities of distinct juridical standings were distributed unevenly within the province (Table 1.1[11]). Patterns of dispersion relate to the early history of the state peasantry in Kursk Province and its origins in the corps of minor nobles (*deti boiarskie*) and rank-and-file soldiery settled by the Muscovite state along the River Seim and the Belgorod Line to defend its contested southerly frontier during the sixteenth and seventeenth centuries.

In the course of its household polls of 1882–1885, the Statistical Bureau of the Kursk Provincial Zemstvo collected data on landholding, leasehold and incidence of taxation. The data illustrate the considerable material differences that resulted from the emancipation of former serfs under the General Statute of 19 February 1861, and the acts regularizing the status of state peasants in 1866, which continued to exert a defining influence on the position of various elements of the peasantry almost a

---

[10] Origins and history of the state peasantry in M. N. Druzhinin, *Gosudarstvennye krest'iane*; Semevskii, *Krest'iane*, II, 721–803; Lappo-Danilevskii, "Ocherk," in Kornilov, Lappo-Danilevskii, Semevskii and Strakhovskii, eds., *Krest'ianskii stroi*, 1–156; Bogoslovskii, "Gosudarstvennye krest'iane," in *Istoriia Rossii v XIX veke*, 1, 236–260. An abbreviated history of state peasants in Kursk Province and its distinctive tenure practices appears in Kurskoe gubernskoe *zemstvo*, SSSKG, *Vyp. I (Kurskii uyezd)*, 31–71. See also Melton, "Serfdom," Ph.D. dissertation, Columbia University, 1984, which traces the process of estate formation and enserfment of the peasant population in Kursk Province.

[11] Kurskoe gubernskoe *zemstvo*. Statisticheskoe biuro. *SSSKG. I–XIV*; Oboianskoe uyezdnoe *zemstvo*. *Sbornik statisticheskikh svedenii po Oboianskomu uyezdu (Kurskoi guberniia)*; I. A. Verner, ed., *Kurskaia guberniia. Itogi statisticheskago issledovaniia*.

Table 1.1 Distribution of the Peasant Population in Kursk Province in the Mid-1880s, by District and Juridical Standing

| Districts | Former state peasants | | | Former private serfs | | | | Other | Total peasant population, both sexes |
| | State peasants, household tenure (odnodvortsy) | State peasants, communal tenure (dushevye) | State peasants, as a % of peasant population | Emancipated after 1861 | | Emancipated before 1861 | Former private serfs as a % of peasant population | | |
				On redemption	On "beggar's" allotments				
Ryl'sk	17 079	7 864	19,9%	94 113	5 964	193	80,0%	163	125 376
Putivl'	13 824	17 636	24,9%	89 234	4 099	138	74,1%	1 173	126 104
Dmitriev	9 047	17 077	26,6%	67 338	2 339	2 358	73,4%	0	98 159
L'gov	19 816	15 086	33,3%	63 353	6 136	268	66,6%	22	104 681
Graivoron	18 116	45 710	44,8%	77 874	123	0	54,8%	492	142 315
Novyi Oskol'	35 870	42 543	59,1%	48 134	5 704	197	40,7%	185	132 633
Shchigrov	59 806	20 714	60,5%	50 406	493	550	38,7%	1 132	133 101
Belgorod	34 052	51 857	66,0%	35 947	7 165	459	33,5%	774	130 254
Staryi Oskol'	76 439	8 825	67,4%	34 629	4 756	785	31,8%	1 049	126 483
Sudzha	52 360	35 248	70,7%	31 888	4 374	60	29,3%	0	123 930
Tim	90 410	1 127	72,4%	32 094	859	123	26,1%	1 904	126 517
Fatezh	61 084	19 857	76,6%	20 017	4 037	566	23,3%	61	105 622
Kursk	56 929	50 417	77,4%	30 541	871	0	22,6%	0	138 758
Oboian	11 062	106 325	79,3%	28 329	2 364	0	20,7%	0	148 080
Korocha	55 876	58 507	84,3%	18 008	2 751	71	15,3%	553	135 766
Province	**611 770**	**498 793**	**58,5%**	**721 905**	**52 035**	**5 768**	**41,1%**	**7 508**	**1 897 779**

quarter of a century later. Lands at the disposal of 162,820 households of allotment-holding state peasants (1,085,964 persons of both sexes) totaled 1,810,055 *desiatiny*, averaging 11.12 *desiatiny* per household.[12] Land in the tenure of communes in which 115,644 households of former private serfs (734,932 persons) were registered as allotment holders totaled 649,056 *desiatiny* or 5.61 *desiatiny* per household.[13] The advantages of former state peasants were evident even in the southwestern crescent of districts—most heavily settled by ex-serfs—in which the sizes of all allotments were below provincial averages.[14] In principle, these stark differences derived from very different norms developed in the legislative acts for the upper limits of an allotment. For state peasants in "land-poor" provinces like Kursk *guberniia*, eight *desiatiny* per male revision soul constituted the upper limit; for former private serfs, this upper limit was set between 2.75 (twelve districts) and 3.75 *desiatiny* (Dmitriev District) per male revision soul.

---

[12] The total area of allotments in Kursk Province (including waste) was variously defined. Ministry of Internal Affairs surveys recorded 2,457,032 *desiatiny* in 1877, 2,542,892 in 1881, 2,576,499 in 1887 and 2,455,363 *desiatiny* in 1905. The *zemstvo* surveys of the mid-1880s recorded 2,459,111 *desiatiny* and the tax rolls of the provincial office of the Treasury (*kazennaia palata*) 2,457,902 in 1906. The compilers of the Treasury office study, however, were rather skeptical of data from their own tax rolls. In comparing total acreage in peasant control (allotments and private land) registered on the tax rolls—2,863,638 *desiatiny* and 2,096 *sazhen*—with that reported in returns of the Parish Administrations (2,484,108 *desiatiny*, 1,390 *sazhen*), the compilers clearly regarded the latter as more accurate. They argued that, despite the Law of 14 December 1893, banning transfer of allotment lands to persons not of the peasant *soslovie* (*PSZ*, t. 13, No. 10151, 653–654, "O nekotorykh merakh k preduprezhdeniii otchuzhdeniia krest'ianskikh nadel'nykh zemel"), "very substantial" elements of these lands—especially acreage formerly in household tenure—had passed to other social groups. With the abolition of collective liability for taxes and obligations (*krugovaia poruka*) in 1903, the Treasury office coordinated, together with village and parish officials, transition from communal to household assessment; local data were considered more up to date for this reason as well.

[13] Among these latter, households that had accepted "beggar's allotments" (*darstvenniki*) after 1861 appear in particularly dire straits twenty years later: 7,900 households (49,199 persons of both sexes) held but 15,871 *desiatiny* (2.01 per household).

[14] The provincial average allotment size per household in the mid-1880s was 8.83 *desiatiny*. In Putivl' District, where this average calculates as 5.59 *desiatiny*, state peasant communities retained an advantage over communes of ex-serfs, 7.63 *desiatiny* to 4.89. Analogous disparities appear in other districts where the overall average was lower than 8.83 *desiatiny*: Ryl'sk District (5.83, 8.39, 5.13), L'gov District (6.78, 9.31, 5.55), Graivoron District (7.75, 10.85, 5.21), Belgorod District (8.30, 10.21, 4.21) and Sudzha District (8.67, 10.15, 4.84).

The relative importance of land lease was an expression of the comparative situations of state peasants and former private serfs with regard to the land allotment. Thus, among households of former state peasants with allotments, 43,117 (26.5 percent) rented, in addition, 151,329 *desiatiny* of non-allotment land. In relation to the area of their allotments, this acreage made up a further 8.2 percent in area. For those 115,644 households of former serfs with allotments, however, over half of all households (64,900 or 56.1 percent) leased an area of non-allotment land (224,454 *desiatiny*) that made up 34.4 percent of that area allotted to them after 1861.[15] If peasant lease of non-allotment tracts reflected roughly similar components in the area of winter and spring fields rented, a notably greater proportion of the leasehold included hay meadow among former private serfs. Data for thirteen districts for which information on *terms* of lease was available proved that state peasants much more rarely rendered labor as consideration for acreage leased from private landowners: of 100,314 *desiatiny* rented by former state peasants in these districts, only 11,763 (11.7 percent) were worked under contracts requiring labor obligations (*otrabotka*). Among ex-serfs, fully 60,813 *desiatiny* (34.3 percent) of the total area leased (177,142 *desiatiny* in the thirteen districts) required acquittal of such obligations as consideration.[16] Yet the data affirm that, even for ex-serfs, labor dues as consideration in lease had largely been ousted by fixed money rents in most eastern and northern districts by the mid-1880s, while remaining more prominent in the southwestern districts with the highest concentrations of communes of former serfs. In Putivl', Ryl'sk and Sudzha Districts, respectively, 42.1 percent, 36.8 percent and 38.5 percent of all leased acreage bore labor dues. Even in these latter, however, money rents tended to have increasingly displaced all other consideration in lease contracts by 1905. The growing prevalence of fixed money rents, of course, represented a conscious shifting of the risk for any variation in harvests from the estate owner onto the peasant tenant.

---

[15] The *zemstvo* surveys thus calculated a total area of 375,783 *desiatiny* in peasant leasehold in the mid-1880s. This area was crudely comparable to totals published by the Central Statistical Committee for 1881 (389,129 *desiatiny*) but substantially greater than official data for 1887 (311,171). *VTsSK*, Seriia III, 1884, 4 (*Raspredelenie*) and *SRI. XXII* (*Glavneishiia dannyia… XX. Kurskaia guberniia*).

[16] Kurskoe gubernskoe *zemstvo*, *SSSKG, II–XIV*. Former state peasants in these 13 districts rented 47,651.6 *desiatiny* in the winter field (47.5%), 43,209.7 *desiatiny* in the spring field (43.1%), and 9,452.8 *desiatiny* of hay meadow (9.4%). Former private serfs leased 78,745.8 *desiatiny* in the winter field (44.5%), 76,786.4 *desiatiny* in the spring field (43.3%), and 21,609.6 *desiatiny* of hay meadow (12.2%).

By means of these leasehold arrangements, usually for a single cycle, for which either cash or the application of peasant labor and inventory for a part of the harvest stood as consideration between the parties, the old dependency of local peasants on the private landowners was thus partially preserved.[17] The acreage leased was of far more critical importance in compensating for a deficit in land, although as we will note below (Chapter 5), peasant leasehold was closely related to the capacity (in terms of available labor and inventory) of households to engage in the practice.[18] Outside the strict sense of lease of plowland or hay meadow, moreover, landed relationships in Kursk Province generated a profusion of exchanges over rights or privileges (*l'goty*) that quite escaped quantification in *zemstvo* surveys. After Emancipation, the rights of way through privately held tracts, grazing rights on fallow or stubble, watering rights for cattle or permission to gather fuel in local forests, rights formerly endorsed by custom, now are commodified as sources of labor dues or cash payments in favor of the landowners or the Ministry of State Domains.

Unequal outcomes of the land settlement issuing from the legislation of the 1860s were also expressed in the weight of taxation relative to the allotment. State taxation accounted for over two thirds (67.1 percent) of total levies in the years in which the Provincial Zemstvo surveyed the

---

[17] Forms of the *corvée* system were quite various. Commentaries attached to the census data showed these to be crudely grouped in three types. 1) Mixed labor service and money rent for each *desiatina* leased, cultivation and harvesting of one *desiatina* of the lessor's land for one sowing cycle with payment of that sum of money that defined the difference between the full money rent in the locality and the market value of the labor to be invested as agreed upon beforehand. 2) Full *corvée*: the payment of the rent in various work for the landowner-lessor agreed upon beforehand. 3) Rental for an agreed upon portion of the harvest. During 1898–1906, the *zemstvo*'s correspondents frequently noted that tenants were required to provide specified quantities of manure and that landowners provided seed grain. The survey also found that agreements for a single sowing were universal: of 62,269 leasehold agreements about which canvassers collected data during 1884–1886 (Novyi Oskol', Putivl', Graivoron, Tim, Staryi Oskol', Korocha, Ryl'sk, Shchigrov and Belgorod Districts), 59,049 involved a single cycle. A significant incidence of long-term lease (over four-fifths of all contracts) was recorded only for Solokhinskaia and Vysokovskaia Parishes, Graivoron District, in which former serfs of Count D. N. Sheremet'ev benefited from a special arrangement between themselves and the former master. This arrangement was to be annulled by his heir in the 1890s, who leased the entire estate out to sugar-beet producers.

[18] Naturally, this situation was particularly noticeable among the 8,489 households of *darstvenniki*: 5,066 households (60.7%) rented an area of non-allotment lands—20,489 *desiatiny*—that constituted 130.0% of the total area of the arable land in their allotments (15,871 *desiatiny*).

districts.[19] Peasants paid a number of other taxes: *zemstvo* levies, premiums for obligatory fire insurance, taxes supporting the operation of parish administration and assessments by the village assembly. For the 14 districts for which data were collected, the annual assessment came to 7,219,320 rubles. Comparing tax liability *for each taxable soul* of the three principal taxpaying groups (*odnodvortsy*, "state souls" and ex-serfs on redemption, or 91.8 percent of persons liable to taxes), total assessments on state peasants were slightly higher: 4.38 rubles per soul, 29.76 rubles per household among state peasants as opposed to 4.05 rubles and 27.37 rubles among former serfs on full allotments.[20] The real imbalance lay in the incidence of taxation per *desiatina* of allotment land, which remained, after all, the main source of income for peasants in the province: 2.61 rubles per *desiatina* among former state peasants, 4.59 rubles among ex-serfs on redemption. The additional 2-ruble levy on each allotment *desiatina* of those liberated in 1861 illustrates the greater burden that the redemption regime laid on former private serfs. Overvaluation of the land as the basis for government calculations, capitalization of balances at 6 percent and "frontloading" incidence of redemption on the first *desiatina* redeemed meant that those emancipated under the 1861 statute received far less per ruble rendered in redemption than did state peasants.[21]

---

[19] These include 1) the head tax (*podushnaia podat'*), abolished in 1886, 2) quit-rent paid by state peasants (*obrochnaia podat'*), converted in 1886 to redemption dues, 3) redemption payments (*vykupnye platezhi*) owed by former serfs to the Treasury as repayment for the monies advanced to the masters after 1861 as compensation for the emancipation, and 4) the state land tax, apportioned to all provinces, reapportioned by the provincial Treasury Department and finally assessed on all arable lands by village authorities.

[20] Peasants on "beggar's allotments" were exempt from redemption payments, but even so, the size of the allotment in relation to all other assessments produced an incidence per *desiatina* of 4.12 rubles.

[21] Lositskii, *Vykupnaia operatsiia*. For Kursk Province, Lositskii's data showed that loans to the total amount of 26.9 million rubles made to former private serfs at 5% interest (together with ½% for amortization and ½% for reserve capital) were based on an overvaluation of land values current at the time when the legislation was drawn up. Redemption of allotment lands in Kursk Province at 1854–1858 prices would have cost, at most, 17.4 million rubles. Evsey Domar speculated that redemption payments in the Central Agricultural Region were actually four times the value of the land. See "Were Russian Serfs Overcharged?" in Evsey Domar, *Capitalism, Socialism and Serfdom*, 280–288. The operation folded into the redemption paid by ex-serfs the prior indebtedness of the owners' estates, which for Kursk Province (1859) totaled 13,987,214 rubles. *VTsSK,* 1888, 2 (*O zadolzhennosti*). Stephen L. Hoch, in contrast, held that there was no overvaluation and that emancipated serfs probably received "viable subsistence plot" at close to market value. "Did Russia's Emancipated Serfs Really Pay Too Much?" *SR,* 63: 2

Dependence of large numbers of ex-serf households on leasing estate lands—at rents that rose with inflation of land values—made this imbalance even more visible.

The Statistical Bureau published uniform information on the composition of peasant allotments—total area, area of plowland, pasture, meadow, forest and waste—for only fourteen districts.[22] In reviewing these data, one is struck by the degree to which figures for distribution of types of arable—plowland, meadow, pasture, forest—confirm the Governor's 1897 report cited above regarding the extent to which the area given to the plow (together with house plot and garden) had displaced all other arable lands vital to the functioning of the rural economy already by the mid-1880s. The disproportion of forest, pasture and meadow to lands given to the plow was typical of both peasant communities. Among communes of state peasants, of a total area of 1,663,608 *desiatiny* of allotment land, 1,382,453 (83.1 percent) stood under house plots and plowland, 68,302 (4.1 percent) under meadow, 52,660 (3.2 percent) in pasture, 103,597 (6.2 percent) in forest and 59,596 under waste. Among communes of ex-serfs, of 633,971 *desiatiny* in allotment lands, 554,736 *desiatiny* (87.5 percent) stood under house plots and plowland, 40,992 (6.5 percent) under meadow, 20,407 (3.2 percent) in pasture, 6,934 (1.1 percent) in forest, 10,902 (1.7 percent) as waste. Evolution of land use trends in this direction was not just a matter of rising man:land ratios. Implementation of the emancipation acts allowed the former masters the full range of levers and veto powers necessary to retain the great bulk of pasture, meadow and forest in estate domains. If it allowed for allotment twice the size of that which characterized allotment to former serfs, the acts of 1866 that fixed the civil status of the former state peasantry nonetheless "arranged" the retention of large tracts of forest by the Ministry of State Domains. Minute shares of forest, meadow and pasture in holdings of peasant communities are particularly illustrative in comparison with the far larger shares of arable still under forest, pasture or meadow on the private estates, which yet retained a certain balance in land use.[23] If the wholesale disappearance

---

(2004). 247–274. It was, of course, not only the quantity of land that mattered, but also its physical disposition.

[22] The survey for Oboian District polled for total acreage and area under plowland and forest only.

[23] Kurskoe gubernskoe *zemstvo, SSSKG, I–XIV*. According to the MVD study for 1887, private estates held 1,420,192 *desiatiny* in all, within which 1,366,236 *desiatiny* were shown as arable land (96.2%). Assuming 53,956 *desiatiny* devoted to residence and other non-agricultural uses, we find 998,645 *desiatiny* under plowland (69.6%), 123,000

of forest, meadow and pasture before the plow marked the rural landscape of Kursk Province as a whole (house plots and plowland making up 87 percent of available arable), this process was most visible in the northern and eastern districts. In the mid-1880s, plowland and house plot composed 94 percent of the allotment area in Shchigrov District, 92.6 percent in Tim District, 90.4 percent in Korocha District, 87.6 percent in Fatezh District and 87.4 percent in Novyi Oskol' District. Verner observed that Kursk *guberniia* had the highest percentage of plowland within the allotment for all of the Central Agricultural Region:

> It seems clear that population density and, later, the insufficiency of land have brought about conversion of almost all land into plowland. At first, when the natural fertility of the soil was considerably higher, such a system of economy brought no negative consequences—there was no need for manuring the soil, one might maintain a small herd of cattle and take in the whole harvest from the field for free. Afterward, the increase in the population, already precluding reduction in the area of plowland, and an exorbitant growth in rents, provoked a drive to convert all land possible to the plow. This explains why even large landowners have plowed under such a significant area of their lands. The height of rents, that unmistakable index of land hunger, serves as a solid guarantee that the area of plowland in Kursk Province will not be reduced in the future.[24]

Likewise, if the area devoted to plowland by *private owners* in Kursk Province averaged 73.1 percent among different components (plowland, meadow, pasture, forest and waste), districts with the highest percentage shares of plowland in estate arable lands were all located in eastern and northern *uyezdy*: Shchigrov (82.6 percent), Tim (82.4 percent), Fatezh (81.0 percent), Staryi Oskol' (80.1 percent), Novyi Oskol' (79.9 percent), Belgorod (79.1 percent) and Korocha (78.0 percent).

2. Population and Its Effects on the Land Settlement

Employing the official digests of the Imperial Central Statistical Committee (CSC), I have calculated that the population of Kursk Province grew from 1,756,154 persons of both sexes in 1862 to 2,387,157 at the end of 1896.[25] According to these calculations, the overall population had grown

---

under meadow and pasture (8.7%), 171,432 in forest (12.1%) and 73,159 as waste (5.2%). Tsentral'nyi statisticheskii komitet, *Glavneishie dannyia.*

[24] I. A. Verner, ed., *Kurskaia guberniia*, 110–111.

[25] Tsentral'nyi statisticheskii komitet, *Spiski naselennykh mest Rossiiskoi imperii. Vyp. 20. Kurskaia guberniia*; and the 1897 census *Pervaia vseobshchaia perepis'. Vyp. XX. Kurskaia guberniia.* To arrive at the 1896 figure, we used the 1897 data, from which we have backed out the births (12,346; 11,363 in the rural districts) and added those de-

to 2.6 million persons by the end of 1904, an increase over 1862 of 49 percent.[26] Rural population[27] was the principal motor of this movement: from 1,639,983 persons of both sexes in 1862 to 2,166,113 at the end of 1896 to 2.4 million persons (again, my estimate) on the eve of the events of 1905 (+46.9 percent).[28] Mechanically adding the difference between births and deaths recorded for each year in the province after the end of 1867—the CSC began to publish materials on birth and deaths regularly only in 1867—and the end of 1904, the total would have been even more imposing. From 1,740,120 persons at the end of 1867,[29] the rural population would have grown to 2,512,674 at the end of 1896 and to 2,877,501 persons at the end of 1904—an increase of 65.4 percent! We will return to this point in a moment.

---

ceased (8,412; 7,734 in the rural districts) during January 1897, data that were published in *Dvizhenie naseleniia... za 1897 god. SRI. Vyp. L* (1900).

[26] For calculations for provincial population and crude demographic indices I used the data on births, deaths and marriages for Kursk Province from *Dvizhenie naseleniia v Evropeiskoi Rossii za... god*), published by the CSC annually between 1872 and 1916 and covering the years 1868–1910, and overall population data from Tsentral'nyi statisticheskii komitet Ministerstva vnutrennikh del, *ibid.* (*Spiski naselennykh mest*), and the CSC's digests, *SVRI*, Seriia II, 1875, Vyp. 10; *SVRI*, Seriia III, 1886, Vyp. 8 (*Sbornik svedenii po Rossii za 1883 god*); *SRI*, Vyp. I (1887), subtitled *Sbornik svedenii po Rossii za 1884–1885 gg.*; *SRI*, Vyp. XL (1897), subtitled *Sbornik svedenii po Rossii. 1896 god.*

[27] The CSC consistently defined "urban population" as residents of 15 district seats (the town of Kursk being both district seat and provincial capital) and three former administrative centers (*zashtatnye goroda*): Khotmyzhsk (Graivoron District), Miropol' (Sudzha District) and Bogatyi (Oboian District), even though many of these towns were smaller than the bigger peasant villages. The total urban population so defined was given as 116,171 persons in 1862, 221,349 in 1897 and 220,731 in 1910. For 1910, see Tsentral'nyi statisticheskii komitet, *Goroda Rossii v 1910 godu*. CSC compilers seem nonetheless to have been inconsistent in treatment of suburbs, especially for the city of Kursk and its outlying *slobody* Iamskaia, Kazatskaia, Streletskaia and Pushkarskaia. On these issues, see Fedor, *Patterns of Urban Growth*, 1–17.

[28] Disclaimers accompanied the publication of population figures for 1862: "The number of inhabitants set forth in the columns does not represent a revision or numbers of persons registered [*pripisnoe*], but the present [*nalichnoe*] population in each place according to data and evidence submitted by local officials... Taking into consideration the fact that the lower ranks of the town and rural police were by necessity made responsible for the original compilation of the lists, it is impossible to demand or to expect that all of these persons, in number more than two thousand throughout the Empire, would have been sufficiently prepared and of an ability for statistical work of this sort. Even for those in the provinces who were entrusted with verification of the lists, it is hard to assume that these were completely up to fulfilling this task."

[29] *SVRI*. Seriia II, vyp. I, 16–17.

Table 1.2 Rural Population and Its Density per Square *Versta*, by District, Kursk Province, 1862–1897

DISTRICTS	Land area (in square *versta*)	1862		1897		% increase in population
		Population, both sexes	Population, per square *versta*	Population, both sexes	Population, per square *versta*	
Putivl'	2 518,5	96 454	38,3	154 609	61,7	60,3%
Ryl'sk	2 494,3	99 717	40,0	153 959	61,0	54,4%
Graivoron	2 692,2	121 340	45,1	169 372	63,2	39,6%
Sudzha	2 461,9	97 493	39,6	134 212	58,4	37,7%
Belgorod	2 625,5	109 612	41,7	150 807	59,7	37,6%
Oboian	3 394,4	125 550	37,0	170 440	50,8	35,8%
L'gov	2 372,3	95 390	40,2	127 125	52,4	33,3%
Korocha	2 665,5	113 882	42,7	150 075	57,1	31,8%
Novyi Oskol'	2 810,8	119 306	42,4	156 383	53,8	31,1%
Tim	3 016,9	107 199	35,5	134 607	45,0	25,6%
Dmitriev	2 789,3	97 312	34,9	121 911	43,1	25,3%
Shchigrov	2 902,6	119 280	41,1	144 710	49,0	21,3%
Staryi Oskol'	2 735,0	108 890	39,8	131 950	50,5	21,2%
Kursk	2 969,5	124 272	41,8	148 477	61,4	19,5%
Fatezh	2 371,4	104 286	44,0	121 105	50,7	16,1%
TOTALS	**40 820,1**	**1 639 983**	**40,2**	**2 169 742**	**54,3**	**32,3%**

Table 1.2 shows that the natural increase in the rural population registered by the First General Census of 1897 was unevenly distributed within the province in terms of the degree to which this increase was retained in each district. Individuals born in other districts of Kursk Province and other provinces of the Empire averaged 6,385 persons of both sexes per district (4.5 percent of the permanently resident rural population as defined by the census of 1897). Since these were evenly distributed in rural districts (town centers excluded), in-migration could thus be largely dismissed as the decisive factor here. The larger question thus concerns out-migration, for which only indirect data (numbers of persons born in the province permanently residing elsewhere) were registered.

The census of 1897, fixing the population *permanently* (*postoianno*) residing in the countryside, counted 2,169,742 persons of both sexes "in the districts without towns" of Kursk Province. Accounting for births and deaths in January of 1897,[30] rural inhabitants totaled 2,166,113 on 31 De-

---

[30] Tsentral'nyi statisticheskii komitet, *Pervaia vseobshchaia perepis'*. The General Census of 1897 struggled to be more precise with regard to actual residence than many of the "enumerations" of population that preceded it. For Kursk Province, it counted 2,371,012 persons overall. Of those "in the district without the towns,"

cember 1896, a substantially lower figure than the 2,535,971 obtained by mechanically adding the natural increase from 1867 onward. Yet the census also registered an additional 408,259 persons born in Kursk Province residing permanently in other provinces, large clusters in South Russia (143,371 persons of both sexes), Siberia (86,006 persons),[31] the Northern Caucasus (78,394) and Ufa and Orenburg Provinces in the Urals (15,008).[32] We do not know, of course, how many of these native *kur'iane* were in fact permanent emigrants. Many long-term passport holders— officials issued 201,713 passports to individuals and families (6,444) for one-year absences from Kursk Province in the year following the census (close to the annual average of 211,506 for 1898–1905, including 8,919 for families)—would often have been registered as residing elsewhere.[33] It

---

2,053,707 persons were born in their districts and 59,387 persons came from other districts in the province. Persons from other provinces totaled 36,177, from other countries 214. There were 17,958 persons temporarily present at the time of the Census—subtracted from the total and ascribed to a place of residence elsewhere—and 38,215 persons temporarily absent, these latter added to the total. Permanent population "in the districts" thus totaled 2,169,742.

[31] The "Commission on the Center" put numbers of emigrants from Kursk Province to Siberia during 1885–1901 at 147,888. *Materialy Vysochaishe utverzhdennoi 16-go noiabria 1901 g. kommissii*, Table II, 17. Data compiled by the Resettlement Administration measuring emigration during 1896–1914 through ports of registration at Cheliabinsk and Syzransk, counted 231,709 documented settlers (33,316 families and 7,563 single persons) on their way to Siberian sites from Kursk Province and 32,058 (4,757 families, 7,337 single persons) returning. In addition, 90,671 *khodoki* from Kursk Province register as entering Siberia in these years and 35,890 returning. In 1907–1909 alone, 150,242 emigrants were recorded, the result of easing of restrictions in the first years of Stolypin's tenure. Pereselencheskoe upravlenie, *Itogi... c 1896 po 1909 gg.*, 2–3 and *Itogi... za vremia c 1910 po 1914 gg. vkliuchitel'no*, 2–3.

[32] See B. V. Tikhonov, *Pereselenie*, prilozhenie I. In his study of emigration within the Empire as reflected in the General Census of 1897, Tikhonov noted that the bulk of these (331,067 or 82%) now resided in provinces at the peripheries of the Empire or in those most frequented by migrant workers from Kursk Province in South Russia: Tomsk 67,421 persons; the Kuban 64,898; Khar'kov 47,598; Don Oblast' 32,140; Ekaterinoslav 25,868; Tauride 17,886; Stavropol' 13,496; Tobol'sk 11,801; Kiev 10,588; Kherson 9,291; Orenburg 9.232; Samara 8,288; Eniseisk 6,784; Ufa 5,776. Of interest as an analysis of patterns and motivations that destinations suggest is B. A. Anderson, *Internal Migration*.

[33] The less than certain situation of persons living outside the province—while still registered in their home communes—was one of the main sources of inaccuracy in all of the population materials. Commentary on data for Kursk Province for 1897 itself drew attention to a noticeable imbalance between males and females in the age group for 20–29 years (1,193 females for every 1,000 males) that it attributed to out-migration.

is nevertheless clear that the natural increase in the rural districts of Kursk Province was tempered—to varying degrees in different districts—by out-migration.

At the time of this writing, I had no serial data for emigration for administrative subdivisions of Kursk Province, and the published volumes of the First General Census, of course, made no note of the *district* within provinces of origin for individuals in a given population who were not locally born. In the course of their work in thirteen districts (out of fifteen) during 1883–1885, however, *zemstvo* polls counted 18,182 peasant households that had legally emigrated from Kursk Province during 1825–1884: two-thirds (11,698) emigrated from the eastern and northeastern *uyezdy*; the southwestern districts were least of all affected.[34] This was also the broad impression gained from comparing projected totals from natural increase for 1867–1896 and the 1897 data. From a hypothetical population "observed" for the end of 1896 (2,750,836 persons of both sexes)—i.e. not accounting for emigration—by compounding annual natural increase from 1867, and numbers of residents recorded by the 1897 census (adjusted to the end of 1896)—2,387,157 persons—363,679 persons are missing. Taken together with persons resident in Kursk Province but born elsewhere, this is a magnitude close to the figure (408,259) for emigration.[35] That most of those born in Kursk Province living "abroad" in 1897 emigrated after 1867 is inferable from this result. The numbers of those "missing" (the difference between the hypothetical and the 1897 count) vary strongly by district: larger proportions were noted for eastern

---

[34] Verner included an article on emigration (by Dobrotvorskii) in his 1887 volume reporting the results of the 1882–1884 surveys, using data for 18,182 families ("approximately" 125,880 persons of both sexes) that had legally cut their ties with their villages and moved out of the province between 1825 and 1884. In order to measure the scale of emigration in the thirteen districts for which data had been collected, he compared current numbers of households with the total of emigrating households. Fatezh District led with 2,682 families (16.7% of current), Novyi Oskol' District was second with 2,560 families (12.4%), Staryi Oskol' third with 2,017 families (10.8%), Dmitriev District fourth with 1,564 families (10.4%), Shchigrov District fifth with 1,603 families (8.2%) and Korocha District sixth with 1,533 families (7.8%). At the other end of the scale: Putivl' District (497 families, 2.4% of current), Ryl'sk District (511 families, 2.5%), Graivoron District (881 families, 3.7%), L'gov District (639 families, 3.8%), Sudzha District (948 families (4.8%). An average of 191 families per year emigrated during the 1860s, 591 families in the 1870s, and for 1880–1884 alone, 1,307 families per year had emigrated. Verner, ed., *Kurskaia guberniia*, Chapter X, 1–54.

[35] Residents of Kursk Province in 1897 who were born in other provinces or countries totaled 59,248 persons of both sexes, 22,857 (38.6%) living in the towns.

and northern districts; considerably fewer are observed for the southwestern and central districts.[36]

Table 1.3 Percentage Change in Average Area of Allotment per Household in Kursk Province between 1877 and 1905

DISTRICTS	1877			1905			% change in area
	households	area (*desiatiny*)	area per household	households	area (*desiatiny*)	area per household	
Novyi Oskol'	20 081	170 125	8,5	24 783	180 959	7,3	-13,8%
Fatezh	16 255	163 870	10,1	18 782	156 632	8,3	-17,3%
Staryi Oskol'	16 347	168 473	10,3	20 779	176 324	8,5	-17,7%
Tim	15 302	204 672	13,4	18 592	203 866	11,0	-18,0%
Sudzha	17 683	164 664	9,3	21 343	158 482	7,4	-20,3%
Oboian	19 402	251 863	13,0	25 727	260 342	10,1	-22,0%
Korocha	17 166	188 398	11,0	22 742	194 400	8,5	-22,1%
Shchigrov	16 309	162 411	10,0	21 268	163 578	7,7	-22,8%
Kursk	19 407	184 900	9,5	25 686	187 755	7,3	-23,3%
Belgorod	18 321	159 597	8,7	24 404	161 097	6,6	-24,2%
L'gov	14 630	109 002	7,5	19 441	107 886	5,5	-25,5%
Graivoron	20 960	175 443	8,4	27 406	169 897	6,2	-25,9%
Dmitriev	13 162	135 922	10,3	17 718	133 290	7,5	-27,2%
Ryl'sk	16 187	108 466	6,7	21 489	94 272	4,4	-34,5%
Putivl'	16 698	109 226	6,5	25 111	106 583	4,2	-35,1%
TOTALS	**257 910**	**2 457 032**	**9,5**	**335 271**	**2 455 363**	**7,3**	**-23,1%**

The natural increase in the rural population in Kursk Province led to a significant reduction in land available per household. This trend had a particular effect on those households of ex-serfs for whom the land settlement had already reduced the acreage and the quality of that acreage in terms of disposition and kind. Dilution of allotment area closely followed

---

[36] High proportions of absentees are noted for the districts of Staryi Oskol' (39,853, 21.3%), Fatezh (32,990, 20.6%), Shchigrov (38,568, 20.4%), Dmitriev (30,144, 19.1%), Korocha (36,941, 18.7%) and Tim (29,363, 17.2%). Kursk District (with the city of Kursk) was lowest at 1.9% (4,383 absentees) and Belgorod District (with the town of Belgorod), second at 5.5% (10,380). Sudzha (14,286, 8.6%), Oboian (19,515, 9.7%), Putivl' (18,367, 10.1%) and Ryl'sk (19,085, 10.4%) followed in order. Novyi Oskol' District, which had occupied the second position behind Fatezh District in the study of emigration that resulted from the surveys of 1883–1885, was now squarely in the middle (23,509 absentees, 12.9%) with Graivoron (28,808, 13.9%) and L'gov Districts (23,666, 15.3%).

the degree to which a natural increase in the population remained on the land (Table 1.3[37]).

Its effects were least evident in eastern and northern districts from which emigration had been most intense and more conspicuous in those of the southwest corner of the province that retained the natural increase in the population in the locality. Reduction of the average area of allotment per household was felt equally among state peasants and ex-serfs, but in all districts the land settlements of the 1860s left their mark in larger average acreages held by households of state peasants. Even more pessimistic conclusions were reached in a 1906 study published by the provincial office of the Treasury (*kazennaia palata*), based on analysis of the assessment rolls and a survey of parish administrative officials and tax records, the latter being laboriously recalculated for individual households after abolition of collective liability for taxes in 1903.[38] Using as a standard for a subsistence allotment the maximum allotment norms for a male "revision soul" established by Local Ordinance of 1861 for Kursk Province—a criterion unacceptable to many contemporary agrarian special-

---

[37] Data from Tsentra'nyi statisticheskii komitet, *Statistika zemlevladeniia, vyp. 37*, Table 1, 10–11. State peasants and ex-serfs were both affected, but with the initial disproportion created during the 1860s wholly in evidence. Average allotment area among state peasants decreased from 11.9 *desiatiny* per household in 1877 to 9.3 per household in 1905 (low of 5.7 in Putivl' District; high of 12.9 among Tim District's *odnodvortsy*). For ex-serfs average allotment area declined from 6.1 *desiatiny* per household in 1877 to 4.8 in 1905 (lows in districts of Putivl': 3.8, and Belgorod: 3.9; high in Korocha District: 6.9 *desiatiny*). In Korocha District, ex-serfs had managed to *increase* allotment acreage by 9,434 *desiatiny*.

[38] Kurskaia kazennaia palata. *Materialy po krest'ianskomu i chastnomu zemlevladeniiu Kurskoi gubernii*. See note 5 above for these norms. The survey was ordered in September 1906 by then Governor V. M. Borzenko. The compilers treated the data as valid for the year 1905. The questionnaire asked the 195 Parish Administrations to submit, for each commune, data on 1) number of *registered* (*pripisnye*) households and the number of persons registered to them, 2) area of their allotment holdings and acreage purchased, 3) acreage leased (both of allotment land and of private land), 4) number of cattle and 5) principal occupations (agricultural, non-agricultural). These data were checked against the tax rolls (*okladnye knigi*) and verified by local inspectors in cases of contradiction or conflicts. In addition, all private owners with holdings in excess of 100 *desiatiny* (1,952 estates) were called upon to return information on 1) total acreage and distribution of plowland, pasture, meadow and forest, 2) acreage cultivated by the estate itself, both with its own and—inexplicably—with peasant inventory and land leased out, 3) systems of crop rotation and acreage in each system, 4) numbers of cattle, and 5) information on hired labor. On the latter point, returns were so poor that no attempt was made to analyze them.

ists—the authors estimated that three of every four peasant households in the province disposed of land (*including acreage purchased*) that did not meet these norms.[39]

All surmises regarding population increase must also take note of the movement of those demographic indices that accompanied growth of the provincial population after 1861. Between 1868 and 1910, the natural population increase for Kursk Province balanced crude birth rates (51.7 births per 1,000 residents) and crude death rates (36.0 deaths per 1,000) that were high even by Russian standards of the time, yielding an average natural increase of 1.57 percent *per annum*. Marriage in village society was universal and, until the first years of the twentieth century, early, especially for women (the cohort of brides aged 20 or less consistently hovered between 65–70 percent of all females entering matrimony each year[40]), so that the interval of female fertility was extended.[41] Infant mortality was an especially enduring component in high death rates: decedents of up to 1 year of age hovered at between 200 and 250 per 1,000 recorded live births until 1890, went to 300–350 in the era of famine and epidemic of 1892–1894. After 1897, infant mortality relapsed into the former range until 1907, when it again spiked upward, ending at around 300 per 1,000

---

[39] Of 369,267 registered (*pripisnye*) households with 1,284,276 male souls on the rolls, 280,131 (75.9%) with 1,053,657 male souls (82.1%) held allotment *and purchased* acreage less than the maximum norms established in 1861 for their districts. Among 148,493 households of ex-serfs with 510,673 male souls, 122,291 (82.5%) of households with 495,034 male souls (89.3%) were so classed. Among the 209,365 households of former state peasants (738,646 male souls), the group of households with lands less than the 1861 norms was typically smaller: 146,751 households (70.1%) and 563,689 (76.3%) male souls. Of these, 14,734 households had no allotments (4.0%), 90,386 had allotments of less than 1 *desiatina* per male soul (24.5%), and 117,502 of between 1 and 2 *desiatiny* (31.8%) per male soul.

[40] Very considerable downward inflections in this percentage followed periods of short-term crisis: poor harvests and epidemics of 1879–1884, crop failures in 1891–1892 and the events of 1905–1907. As an average for 1876–1910, this percentage was highest in the rural districts (64.6%) and in the district centers (57%), and lowest in the town of Kursk (48.7%).

[41] Mironov, "Traditsionnoe demograficheskoe povedenie," in Vishnevskii, ed., *Brachnost'*, 83–104. The study made by A. J. Coale and associates on the demographic transition in Russia concerned mainly the era after 1897, but it posited that changes in fertility patterns had begun to appear after 1881, most visibly after 1900. At .797, the rural marital fertility rate calculated by Coale and his team for Kursk Province against the most prolific known natural fertility rate (among Hutterites) at 1, showed that natural fertility was the norm and did not decline much even by 1926. Coale, Anderson, and Härm, *Human Fertility*.

in 1910.[42] Figure 1.1 following,[43] however, tracks the general decline in crude death rates for the populace—90 percent resident in the rural districts—as the motor generating a sustained natural increase in the province, especially from about the mid-1890s onward. The graph tracks a much slower decline in crude birth rates over the era measured and an even less perceptible decline in incidence of marriage. These general trends are replicated in almost all district profiles for the years 1871–1910, and functioned equally in *uyezdy* dominated by communal tenure (Ryl'sk District) or household land tenure (Tim District). Decline in mortality began to register in the mid-1880s following the period 1879–1884 and accelerated after the interval of high death rates in 1889–1894.[44]

---

[42] It was observed that if Great Russians had higher birth rates than Ukrainians, infant mortality was higher among the former. To the population of Great Russians, the Census registered 40 infants to 1 year of age per 1,000 persons; for the Ukrainian population 39.2. Children of 1 to 9 years, however, made up 263.3 per 1,000 among Ukrainians, 243.5 for Great Russians. Tsentral'nyi statisticheskii komitet, *Pervaia vseobshchaia perepis'*, Table XV, 124–157. Yet poor harvests in 1889, crop failures in 1891–1892 that struck most seriously in the eastern and northern *uyezdy*, and the spread of disease—even to districts that had not suffered the effects of poor harvests—meant that Kursk Province experienced the years 1889–1894 with great difficulty. From 73,352 deaths in 1888, mortality climbed to 80,062 in 1889, to 89,245 in 1890, to 90,317 in 1891, to 97,024 in 1892 and to 100,843 in 1893, before beginning to recede, falling to 94,093 decedents in 1894 and 88,322 in 1895. Infant mortality rose substantially: most of the heavily Great Russian districts—which bore the brunt of the harvest failures of 1891–1892—experienced two to four years of rates well over 300 per 1,000 live births.

[43] Data points on the graph are calculated from the CSC's series entitled *Dvizhenie naseleniia v Evropeiskoi Rossii za... god*, based on the clergy's notations of births, deaths and marriages. The R^2 index calculates "goodness of fit" of the curve to the data, where a perfect linear fit would yield an R^2 of 1.000. Given year-to-year variation, these are not particular impressive.

[44] Intervals of crisis mortality during 1867–1910 followed upon sharply reduced harvests in 1872–1873, 1880–1881, 1889, 1891–1892; however, no demographic "event" followed crop failures in 1885–1886, 1896–1897 or 1908. Where it could be observed, moreover, its *incidence by district* did not match up well at all to the geography or even timing of crop failure. In 1889 and 1891–1892, the most damaging and sustained declines in grain harvests occur in the eastern part of the province, together with Oboian District in the center; the western districts were less affected. The interval of crisis mortality, however, ranged from 1889 to 1895, well after general recovery. Death rates spiked over 45 per 1,000 inhabitants not only in Novyi Oskol' and Oboian Districts—*in 1890*—but also in L'gov District in 1891, Putivl' and Sudzha Districts in 1892 and L'gov and Ryl'sk Districts in 1893. Kursk District, with the city of Kursk, registered over 50 deaths per 1,000 residents during 1892–1894. From a close study of clerical records for Borshevka Parish, Tambov District, between 1830 and 1912, Stephen L. Hoch determined that crisis mortality of this sort was *not* associated with harvest failure, but

Figure 1.1 Crude Demographic Indices, Kursk Province, 1868–1910

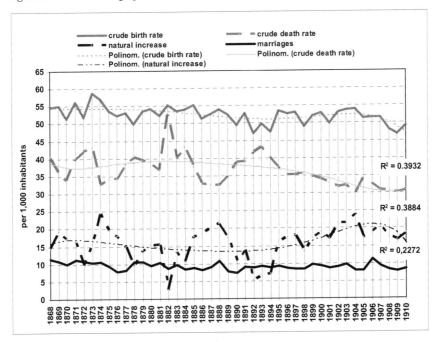

Diminution of the land fund available to peasant farmers in Kursk Province against the backdrop of a substantial natural increase in the population appears therefore to have been driven in great part by the *overall* tendency for crude death rates to fall faster than the slower decline in birth rates. It has been argued that this broader demographic tendency reflected a general improvement in conditions of rural life, and in particular, of levels of nutrition, based on both growth of grain production and retention of a greater component of production in the village.[45] Published material on births and deaths had major limitations in this regard. Not only were

---

with "exaggeration of the effects of normally recurrent epidemics." Hoch, "Famines," 357–368. Various views on "synergy" between nutrition/malnutrition and disease are in Rotberg and Rabb, eds., *Hunger and History*.

[45] Reconstructions of rural diets in the second half of the nineteenth century may be drawn from Smith and Christian, *Bread and Salt*, 263 (estimates), 328–331; Maress, "Pishcha," *Russkaia mysl'*, 1893, X: 45–67 and XI: 60–75; Maress, "Proizvodstvo," in Chuprov and Posnikov, eds., *Vliianie urozhaev*, I: 1–96; Klepikov, *Pitanie russkogo krest'ianstva*; Kerblay, "L'évolution," *Annales. Economies, Sociétés, Civilisations*, 17: 3 (1962), 885–913. The mid-nineteenth-century peasant diet in Kursk Province, reflecting the central role of grain, is in Mashkin, "Byt krest'ian," *Etnograficheskii sbornik*, vyp. V, otd. I (6th essay), 13–19.

the data themselves often hard to parse into rural and town populations by district, but they also did not permit any analysis of differential mortality for various groups within the populace. Studies of peasant budgets undertaken by *zemstvo* statisticians after 1870 tended to show substantive differences in the material condition of different strata of the peasantry. Did the poorer strata of the rural population benefit from the decline in mortality as much as more prosperous elements? Were similar trends observed among noble families, who presumably enjoyed better access to a variety of nutrition? These problems are quite beyond the capacity of the published data to resolve and remain unanswered questions of some importance.[46] It is, nevertheless, necessary to review the materials for harvests in Kursk Province, in order to ascertain whether a general trend toward greater abundance moved in tandem with the engine that drove natural increase.

3. Field Cultures and Harvests, 1885–1913

Harvest data drawn from the Central Statistical Committee's annual digests, despite gaps in their coverage and questions of method that provoked serious criticism from some scholars,[47] give grounds for a more optimistic picture of the progress of grain production—and for levels of consumption—than is usual for a province of the Central Agricultural Region. Despite the many well-known defects of agricultural practice associated with the three-field system, almost everywhere the organizing principle for cultivation in Kursk Province, the harvest data illustrate the

---

[46] Based on data for Voronezh Province, F. A. Shcherbina showed that among poorer groups (by sown area per household), mortality (of children and adults) and incidence of disease were measurably higher than among groups that were more prosperous. Shcherbina, *Svodnyi sbornik*, 352–361, and *Krest'ianskie biudzhety*, 176–177. Anfimov reached similar conclusions in reviewing data for Kaluga Province: Anfimov, *Ekonomicheskoe polozhenie*, 164. Conscription in Kursk Province had increasingly to contend with growing percentages of conscripts who were physically unfit for service, even when standards were eased. Of 90,732 conscripts in 1874–1878, 8,221 (9.1%) were rejected for insufficient height or other physical defects, or got deferments for insufficient physical maturity (*nevozmuzhalost'*). For the period 1879–1883 (98,113 conscripts), 12,587 (12.8%) were so classified, for 1884–1888 (103,366 recruits), 13,798 (13.3%), for 1889–1893 (90,338 draftees), 13,596 (13.7%) for 1894–1898 (114,373), 17,999 (15.7%) and for the three years 1899–1901 (74,150 conscripts), 13,495 (18.2%) were rejected by such criteria. *Materialy Vysochaishe utverzhdennoi 16-go noiabria 1901 g. kommissii*, Table III, 27–33. We note, however, that percentages for the Empire as a whole are even higher.

[47] See in particular Ivantsov, *K kritike russkoi urozhainoi statistiki*.

fact that *overall* production during 1885–1913 advanced measurably, in terms of both overall output and output per *desiatina* sown.

Table 1.4 Grain Production in Kursk Province, 1885–1913

Year	Winter sowings			Spring sowings		
	Sown area (desiatiny)	Net harvest (poods)	per 1 desiatina	Sown area (desiatiny)	Net harvest (poods)	per 1 desiatina
1885–1889						
allotment lands	647 816	21 980 808	33,9	627 431	12 197 870	19,4
private holdings	322 373	13 820 888	42,9	302 338	8 180 968	27,1
1890–1894						
allotment lands	635 577	20 798 099	32,7	624 279	15 219 970	24,4
private holdings	322 373	13 820 888	42,9	302 338	8 180 968	27,1
1895–1899						
allotment lands	625 413	24 026 698	38,4	606 306	15 931 089	26,3
private holdings	291 056	13 701 463	47,1	286 438	10 681 466	37,3
1900–1904						
allotment lands	645 926	32 228 514	49,9	615 156	21 425 714	34,8
private holdings	275 052	16 793 552	61,1	249 872	12 263 624	49,1
1905–1909						
allotment lands	609 436	23 658 409	38,8	593 299	17 796 673	30,0
private holdings	255 214	15 328 881	60,1	255 155	12 874 753	50,5
1910–1913						
allotment lands	618 048	28 361 924	45,9	597 611	27 447 445	45,9
private holdings	240 253	18 012 959	75,0	249 529	17 137 608	68,7

Gains were most notable for spring sowings (particularly oats) and most definitive for 1910–1913. Winter sowings did less impressively, harvests were subject to more extreme variation, and what was more, these latter regressed in the years 1905–1909, punctuated by a serious crop failure in 1908 that struck winter sowings especially. Leaving aside the issue of variations in harvests for the moment, the record nonetheless suggests, in concert with the decline in mortality, that, generally speaking, *total* grain production kept pace with the consumption needs of the local populace, including residents of the town centers. The addition to diet indicated by massive increases in potato harvests after the crisis of 1891–1892 was especially crucial in this respect.[48] Using the CSC's harvest data for 1885–

---

[48] According to the CSC digests, net harvests of potatoes on peasant allotments in Kursk Province averaged 4,487,633 *poods* on 17,180 *desiatiny* (261.2 *poods* per *desiatina* sown) in 1885–1889, 13,045,051 *poods* on 34,875 *desiatiny* (374.0) during 1890–1894,

1913 *for both peasant and private producers* and accounting, even crudely, for both grain export and provincial distillery, we calculate that during 1885–1910, a provincial supply of grain and potatoes adequate to annual *per capita* consumption norms of 300 kg (*not accounting for cattle*) was perilously breached in 1889, 1891 and 1897 (less than 65 percent). Supplies retained in the province also contracted seriously in 1908 (less than 75 percent), and in some years (1885–1886, 1892, 1896, 1901, 1903 and 1905) stood at 80–90 percent of this norm. In intervening years, a small surplus was the rule even after export, and in good years (1887, 1894–1895, 1899–1900, 1902 and 1909) the surplus could be very substantial.[49] Using total production (all producers) for the estimate, it was clear that production on allotments *by itself* did not cover the consumption needs of the population: recourse to the market was essential for large numbers of peasant households. Despite a decline in the area sown on privately held acreage (from 629,573 *desiatiny* in 1885–1889 to 505,234 in 1910–1913 *for crops measured by the CSC*), this sector contributed 38–40 percent of total grain production over the entire period. More broadly, improvement in grain yields moved within different limits among districts. Figure 1.2 shows average yields net of seed on allotment lands for the two most prominent grains in rotation.[50]

20,284,369 *poods* on 51,460 *desiatiny* (394.2) for 1895–1899, 22,004,460 on 55,175 *desiatiny* (398.8) for 1900–1904, 23,281,489 *poods* on 59,089 *desiatiny* (394.0) for 1905–1909, and 32,594,295 *poods* on 65,545 *desiatiny* (497.3) for the years 1910–1913.

[49] Our calculations are drawn from a comparison of the annual grain statistics for Kursk Province and the record of grain traffic in and out of the province for the railway stations within its borders: 31 in 1885–1889 on three lines, Kursk-Khar'kov-Sevastopol', Moscow-Kursk and Moscow-Kiev-Voronezh, 67 in 1911 on six lines, adding the South-eastern (Elets-Valuiki, 1897), Belgorod-Sumy (1901), and Northern Don (1911) lines. Data for these appear in the annual, Ministerstvo putei soobshcheniia, *Sbornik statisticheskikh svedenii Ministerstva putei soobshcheniia*. Where possible, we used several official publications to verify that our results were roughly analogous for almost all years compared: for 1893–1895, Obshchii tarifnyi s"ezd predstavitelei russkikh zheleznykh dorog, *Statisticheskiia dannyia*; for 1909–1913, Upravlenie delami Osobogo soveshchaniia dlia obsuzhdeniia i ob"edineniia meropriatii po prodovol'stvennomu delu. *Proizvodstvo;* for 1901–1903 and 1908–1911, Departament zhelezno-dorozhykh del Ministerstva Finansov, *Materialy k peresmotru*, 265–289; for 1912–1914, *and Statisticheskiia dannyia ob otpravlenii i pribytii prodovol'stvennykh gruzov po russkim zheleznym dorogam s raspredeleniem po guberniiam i oblastiam za 1912, 1913 i 1914 gg.* Railway Affairs Department data are also cited in M. V. Komarinets, "Vyvoz khlebov," *TS-KhSKGZ. 1903 g.*, I: 34–49, II: 15–24.

[50] As an average characterization for all years in which the CSC published sown area estimates (1881, 1887 and 1893–1913) for various grains in Kursk Province on allot-

Figure 1.2 Average Net Yields on Allotments, Kursk Province, 1885–1913 (by District)

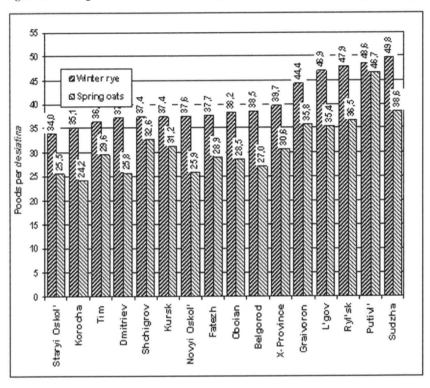

These data make it clear that yields were most favorable for that group of adjacent districts in the southwest part of the province that posted the

ment lands (1,354,033 *desiatiny* in total acreage sown) and private holdings (567,588 *desiatiny*) testify to the weight of rye among all other sowings. On allotment lands, 593,800 *desiatiny* were sown with rye—43.9% of total sowings in both winter and spring fields—as opposed to 32,277 with winter wheat. On private holdings, rye was sown in 208,301 *desiatiny* (36.7% of total sowings) and winter wheat in 63,309 (11.2%). For the same period, spring sowings of oats (327,743 *desiatiny*: 24.2%), buckwheat (134,918 *desiatiny*: 10.0%) and millet (96,176: 7.1%) combined to make 558,837 *desiatiny* (41.3% of total sowings), dominating spring plantings on allotments; even in private cultivation, the three grains, planted respectively in 165,510, 39,718 and 30,474 *desiatiny*, made up 41.5% of all sown area. Peasants in Graivoron, Belgorod, Korocha and Novyi Oskol' Districts, forming a contiguous *massif* in the southeastern part of the province, nevertheless developed a greater diversification in their choice of sowings. Winter wheat, spring wheat and barley played greater roles here than elsewhere in peasant cultivation, and the predominance of other grains was correspondingly somewhat less imposing.

highest averages—including Sudzha and L'gov Districts, in which disorders during 1905–1906 were to be quite intense. Conversely, Novyi Oskol' and Staryi Oskol' Districts, in which unrest during November 1905 was to wreak great destruction, belonged to that group of *uyezdy* (including Tim, Shchigrov, Belgorod and Fatezh Districts) in the northeastern and eastern portions of Kursk Province in which agriculture was measurably less productive.[51] Low yields were recurring phenomena even aside from crop failures in 1885–1886, 1889, 1891–1892[52] and 1896–1897, these being unusual only in their severity: average harvests per *desiatina* sown over the 29-year period 1885–1913 show that these same six districts (and Dmitriev District) harvested less per *desiatina* sown than in the center and west.[53] Low overall yields concealed the greater frequency

---

[51] Table data based on my calculations, drawn from the serial digests of harvest statistics for 1888–1913 put out by the CSC under the title *Urozhai... goda* as a part of its series *Statistika Rossiiskoi imperii*. Data for 1885–1887 are drawn from the preceding standalone series, *Urozhai (1885–1887) goda v Evropeiskoi Rossii* (Sankt Peterburg, 1886–1887).

[52] For the province as a whole, the harvests of winter crops for 1891 (rye, winter wheat) came in at 43.1% of average net yield per *desiatina* for 1885–1913, for spring sowings (spring wheat, oats, millet, barley, buckwheat) at 40.5%. Shortfalls were most severe in the eastern half of the province. Harvests of winter sowings fell below 30% of average in the districts of Shchigrov (26.8%), Graivoron (24.1%), Oboian (22.8%), Belgorod (20.5%), Tim (20.4%), Korocha (17.5%), Staryi Oskol' (10.3%) and Novyi Oskol' (2.5%). Harvests of spring grain fell below 30% of average in the districts of Tim (21%), Korocha (19%), Oboian (9.8%), Novyi Oskol' (4.4%) and Staryi Oskol' (0.2%). In the most westerly districts, shortfalls were less severe: winter sowings escaped without serious damage in Dmitriev, Putivl', Ryl'sk and Fatezh Districts, but in L'gov, Sudzha and Kursk Districts, harvests of winter grains fell, respectively, to 76.9%, 51.3% and 43.5% of average. In all the western districts, harvest of spring sowings came in at 40–60% of average. In 1892, harvests of spring crops everywhere showed improvement (78.6% of provincial average). But harvests of winter sowings suffered a second disastrous year in a row (for the province 48.4% of the average for 1885–1913). The eastern districts were once again the most seriously affected: except for Novyi Oskol' District at 56.3% and Shchigrov District at 67.6%, harvests in the rest of aforementioned eight districts remained below 40% of average. Significant shortfalls now struck the districts of Sudzha (65.1%), L'gov (61.3%), Putivl' (58.8%), Ryl'sk (58.1%) and Fatezh (48.0%) that had largely escaped the worst of the calamity of 1891. A grim eyewitness account of conditions in the eastern districts during 1891, and of large crowds of men, women and children wandering the roads in search of food, is in Korf, "Poezdka," in *Trudy IVEO*, 1892, tom vtoroi, razdel 1, 109–120.

[53] As a sample, the period 1885–1913 featured ten years in which harvest in one field or both were 75% or less against the provincial average: 1885 and 1905 (spring sowings), 1886, 1893, 1896 and 1908 (winter sowings), 1889, 1891–1892 and 1897 (winter and

of below-average results from either winter or spring sowings or shortfall in both in the same year. A more impressive resilience is visible in shorter terms of poor performance in the western and southwestern districts, a group for which (Dmitriev District aside) higher average yields were typical.[54]

What seemed paradoxical was that if the average allotment in Kursk Province as a whole equaled 8.83 *desiatiny* per household according to the censuses of the mid-1880s, villagers residing in the group of districts in the eastern and northern parts of the province—among whom state peasants were frequently the predominant element—were better supplied with land. In Tim District, peasant allotments averaged 12.35 *desiatiny*, in Fatezh District, 10.55 *desiatiny*, in Oboian District, 10.45 *desiatiny*, in Staryi Oskol' District, 9.82 *desiatiny*, in Shchigrov District, 9.26 *desiatiny*, in Novyi Oskol' District, 9.10 *desiatiny*. In addition to larger allotments, peasants in these districts worked consistently better soils: the black-earth topsoil layers tended to be of greater depth and quality (humus content) than those in the western half of the province. The natural fertility of these soils had long been legendary: peasant farmers, their fathers and grandfathers had been able, for as long as anyone could remember, to harvest sufficient amounts of grain and maintain livestock herds without

---

spring sowings). Of these, harvests of 1885 (spring plantings), 1889, 1891–1892 and 1897 (spring and winter sowings), and 1893, 1896 and 1908 (winter sowings) netted 50% or less of the provincial average. Conversely, the period includes the bumper crops of 1887, 1894 and 1902, and the five consecutive good harvests of 1909–1913.

[54] The high average southwestern districts generally had the fewest years of serious shortfall (less than 75% of average) in one or both fields and/or suffered poor harvest years with less severity: L'gov District: 1885–1886, 1888–1889, 1891–1892, 1896–1897, 1906 and 1908 (ten years, with only two under 50% of the district average for 1885–1913); Sudzha District: 1885–1886, 1888–1893, 1897 and 1908 (ten years, five falling under 50%): Putivl' District: 1885–1886, 1889, 1892, 1895–1897, 1907–1908 and 1911 (ten years, with six under 50%): Ryl'sk District: 1885–1886, 1888–1893, 1896–1897, 1901, 1908 and 1911 (thirteen years, four of them with harvests under 50% of district average), and so on. Conversely, peasant farmers in Korocha District suffered seventeen harvest seasons of serious shortfall in one or both fields during 1885–1913—1885–1886, 1890–1893, 1895–1901, 1903, 1905 and 1908—and ten fell below 50% of the district average. Novyi Oskol' harvested less than 75% of its district average in fifteen years—1885–1886, 1889, 1895–1897, 1899–1901, 1903, 1905 and 1907–1908—among which eight fell below half the average. Staryi Oskol' District went through fourteen poor harvests (1885–1886, 1889, 1891–1893, 1896–1897, 1900–1901, 1903, 1905–1906 and 1908), among which six underperformed the average for the *uyezd* by half. Dmitriev District witnessed shortfalls in 1885–1886, 1889, 1891–1892, 1896–1897, 1901 and 1906–1908, among which eight of the eleven years fell below the average by 50%.

manuring, repeat plowing and careful seeding. *The benefits of these latter methods had always been known, but only the most conscientious tillers employed them.* When polled in 1885, for example, villagers in the eastern districts gave various reasons for a general failure to fertilize their grain fields and, in the best case, reserved manure for their gardens and hemp patches. The most common observation of those interviewed concerned a lack of livestock in sufficient numbers to practice such fertilization more widely. Then, transporting manure for distances over three *versta* was thought too onerous. Repartition or the threat of repartition was also very often cited as an impediment: to invest labor in improving one's strips, only to see them pass to another household, hardly motivated consistent practice. Households reported undertaking more systematic efforts at manuring only upon cessation of repartition. Furthermore, manure, mixed with straw, had long ago become a principal fuel in the largely deforested landscape of the eastern districts. Lastly, private landowners sometimes demanded delivery of a specified quantity of manure as part of lease agreements. Yet many respondents declared that the soil itself needed no special treatment, that crops would grow anyway.[55]

Yet a system relying so heavily on the natural fertility of the soil had perhaps for too long accustomed plowmen to disregard the need for even these rudimentary technical adjustments: by the mid-1880s, there were already signs that the usual modes of cultivation were under growing pressure. Canvassers polling the region in 1884 noted that extension of plowland at the expense of all other types of arable (forest, meadow or pasture), well advanced in Kursk Province as a whole, had proceeded furthest in the eastern districts. Even if it was true that in several of them spring sowings were notably more diversified than in the western part of the province, continuous cropping without any fallowing at all, once reserved for fields farthest from house plots, had invaded a considerable area of arable land in peasant cultivation.[56] In contrast, peasants in south-

---

[55] *SSSKG. Vyp. X* (Belgorod District), Chast' I ("Opisanie volostei i obshchin"), 1–180; *Vyp. XI* (Novyi Oskol' District), Otd. B ("Opisanie volostei Novooskol'skago Uyezda"), 1–163; *Vyp. XII* (Tim District), Otd. B ("Opisanie volostei Timskogo uyezda"), 1–110; *Vyp. XIII* (Korocha District), Chast' I-B ("Opisanie otdel'nykh volostei Korochanskago Uyezda"), 1–95.

[56] Employment of this method (*zapol'e, raznopol'e or pestropol'e*) had spread already in the 1880s to ever-larger areas of arable lands, notably in Tim District (40,500 *desiatiny*, or 21% of all allotment land), Staryi Oskol' District (22,650, 15%), Korocha District (15,500, 8.8%), Novyi Oskol' District (15,000, 8%) and Belgorod District (9,000, 6%). Local peasants themselves were well aware of the consequences for future harvests of

western parts of the province, with significantly smaller plots—ex-serfs predominated here—and somewhat poorer soils, began to adopt, even within the traditional tillage and rotation regimes, more intensive methods of field cultivation that resulted in consistently higher yields.[57] Observers here noted that peasants far more commonly followed a practice of regular manuring fallow fields in preparation for winter sowing, at least on those fields within reasonable distance of the settlement.[58] By 1910, this part of the province had also opted for a more modern inventory: in Putivl' and Ryl'sk Districts, the wooden *sokha* and *borona* had been mostly replaced by the iron-shared plow (*plug*) and iron-shod harrow, these also making up about three-quarters of peasant inventory in L'gov District. In Sudzha District, the old wooden plow (56.5 percent of plowing instruments) and harrow (18.2 percent of harrowing tools) was clearly on the way out. The trend was also far advanced in Dmitriev District, where the *sokha* made up 13.2 percent of plows and the old-style *borona* about a third of harrowing inventory. Elsewhere, the traditional tools remained far more predominant.[59] Thus the response of peasant cultivators in Kursk Province to

---

continuous cropping, but told interviewers that for poorer villages "there is nothing else to do; they are almost dying of hunger." Verner, ed., *Kurskaia guberniia*, 113–114.

[57] The value in higher yields of adjusting tillage regimes for more careful preparation of soils before sowing was the subject of local agronomists' repeated exhortations in the provincial agricultural digest. After harvest of winter crops, while draught power was still at strength from regular feeding, plowing under the stubble followed immediately by harrowing in autumn already set up soils for spring plantings in April, which then needed a second pass in soil that was already loose. A second adjustment involved early raising of the fallow—in April after spring sowings—to aerate soil and preserve its nutrients. Repeat harrowing before sowing of winter crops helped to control weeds and broke up crusts caused by rainfall, a second shallower plowing and harrowing to precede seeding. G. A. Ganevich, "Ob obrabotke zelenago i zaniatogo para," *TS-KhSKGZ. 1900 g.*, V, otd. III: 33–38; "Otvet Korochanskago uyezdnago agronoma I. V. Ianovskogo," *ibid., 1905 g.*, I: 88–89. On these methods, more broadly adopted by peasants in Tambov Province, see Kerans, *Mind and Labor*, 46–66. They are noted in sporadic use in Oboian District in the 1860s (Mashkin, "Byt krest'ian") and by a limited number of "more conscientious" tillers in the eastern districts surveyed by the *zemstvo* in the 1880s.

[58] Ministerstvo zemledeliia i gosudarstvennykh imushchestv. Departament Zemledeliia. *Sel'skokhoziaist-vennyia statisticheskiia svedeniia... Vyp. X. (Rasprostranennost')*, Otdel II, 1–5. The province had large local sources of phosphates (called *samorod*), but only a single small operation (north of Kursk in Fatezh District) was at work in mining this material at the beginning of the 1890s.

[59] Tsentral'nyi statisticheskii komitet. *SRI*. Vyp. LXXIX (1913): *Sel'skokhoziaistvenniia mashiny*, 34–35.

an acceleration of the natural increase in the population living on the land was everywhere an "intensification" of production, but the modalities employed in this latter process, comparing the eastern and western sub-regions of the province, were strikingly different.[60]

If the *overall* trend in agricultural production was toward improvement—especially if the data for 1909–1913 are included—the trend moved across devastating oscillations in output, punctuated by the disastrous harvests of 1889, 1891–1892, 1897 and 1908. "King Hunger" (*Tsar'-golod*) remained an ominous and ever-present figure in the background of rural life, sustaining historical memories of scarcity and the peasant's consciousness of the tenuous character of any subsistence arrangements.[61] Major variations in yields also impaired the capacity of villages to maintain livestock. Insufficient acreage in meadow and pasture made animal husbandry heavily dependent on good harvests, since oat or rye straw, often mixed with grain, remained the staple feed for livestock during the winter months.[62] The fodder problem, moreover, increasingly burdened the fallow field with the irreplaceable role of providing the first spring grazing for villagers' livestock after a long winter of stall-feeding, at that moment before any fodder became available. This crucial function acted, in turn, as a powerful deterrent to any decision for an early raising of the fallow (a matter that could only be approved by the commune as a whole) and more careful preparation of soil for winter sowings that it afforded the tiller, and may well have played a role in retarding improvement in yields of winter sowings over time.[63] The consequence of poor

---

[60] Ester Boserup treated these developments as a normal consequence of demographic pressure in the long-term life of agrarian communities, and the specific modalities employed—or not employed—in response as the result not of ignorance, but of the rural cultivator's rational calculation of likely return on the necessary added increments of labor. See her 1965 essay *The Conditions of Agricultural Growth*.

[61] V. V. Kondrashin, "Golod," in Danilov and Milov, eds., *Mentalitet*, 115–123.

[62] The amount of straw expended as the main winter fodder, which, given a normal harvest, was mixed with rye flour or a mix of rye, oats and millet ground together, depended on the demand on the supply of straw for heating and roof thatch. One local agronomist, basing his estimate on opinions of the *zemstvo*'s local correspondents, estimated that in the *uyezdy* of the east and northeast, 40–50% of all straw was used as a fuel or for roof repair. This share was smaller (20–30%) in the central and western districts. Mikhailov, "K voprosu o prokormlenii skota," in Kurskoe gubernskoe *zemstvo* (Statisticheskoe biuro), *Kurskaia guberniia. Statisticheskii obzor, 1896 g.*, 273–283.

[63] David Kerans has shown convincingly that this function was a powerful impediment not only to sowing fodder crops but also to adjustment of tillage regimes for increasing harvests of winter sowings—i.e. early raising of fallow and double plowing (*dvoenie*). The

harvests on livestock appears in stark terms in the Governor's report on conditions in Kursk Province for 1897.

> The grim results of the harvest in the reported year reflected disastrously, first and foremost, on the main source of economic prosperity of the populace, on the cattle, particularly in peasant economies. Thanks to the poor harvest of grasses and the shortage of other fodder sources, the prices of which grew to vast sums, a broad sell-off of peasant livestock began already in early autumn of last year and that stock that remains in peasant households wintered with difficulty, lost much weight and in places was so weakened that it had become unable to fulfill various kinds of agricultural work.[64]

In the following year (1898), the situation continued to worsen:

> Animal husbandry in the province during the reported year, following hard upon a year distinguished by an especially poor harvest of fodder, has suffered a considerable decline. Despite a warm winter, livestock bore it with difficulty because of shortages of feedstock, which has been clearly more significant this year than in 1891, when rye straw was mixed with grass, an incomparably better fodder than this year, and there was more straw from the spring crop. Private estates in preceding years have sold or granted to the peasants (in exchange for labor obligations) their surpluses of straw, but this year even the estate owners are buying fodder and at year's end even resorted to cutting up rye straw and mixing it with a bit of flour. The peasants, foreseeing shortages of fodder and having insufficient means to purchase it, began already in the fall to sell a major part of their livestock for a pittance, but even that number that remains will be difficult to feed through the spring. So intense was the demand for fodder at the end of the winter that the price of oat and rye straw in places went to 40–65 kopecks a *pood*. All such difficult circumstances could not but tell upon the state of livestock holdings, which, especially in localities in the province where losses had already been quite severe, will undoubtedly undermine the productivity of household economies for some time to come.[65]

The censuses of horses conducted by the Ministry of War in Kursk Province in 1888, 1893, 1900 and 1912 illustrated the stark truth of such an assessment, revealing that after the famine of 1891–1892, especially in the

---

toll taken on nutrients by proliferation of weeds and the packing down of soils caused by extended grazing of herds of cattle had strongly negative effects. Kerans, *op. cit.*, 234–247. Fodder crops in Kursk Province were poorly developed: according to the CSC, peasants sowed clover, timothy, lucerne or other grasses in just 1,074 *desiatiny* in 1901; private landowners did only a bit better, planting 13,225 *desiatiny* under grasses. Tsentral'nyi statisticheskii komitet, *SRI. LIII* (1902): *Urozhai 1901 goda. III. Posevnye kormovye travy, len i konoplia*, 32–33; Ministerstvo zemledeliia i gosudarstvennykh imushchestv. Departament Zemledeliia, *Sel'skokhoziaistvennyia statisticheskiia... XII: Sostoianie travoseianiia*, Otdel, II, 1–12.

[64] *Obzor Kurskoi gubernii za 1897 god* (1898), 6. Such outcomes hardly spared the landowners: most also found themselves in highly unenviable positions.

[65] *Obzor Kurskoi gubernii za 1898 god* (1899), 7.

eastern and northern districts, the number of peasant horses declined by some 16 percent.[66] Eight years later peasant holdings of horses were recorded at levels well below those of 1888 in nine of Kursk Province's fifteen districts. Undoubtedly, crop failures in 1896–1897 and their after-effects in a number of localities had much to do with matters as they stood at the turn of the century. Yet the surveys also indicated considerable losses in numbers of horses in peasant communities in districts (Putivl', L'gov, Ryl'sk and Sudzha) in which, despite comparatively higher yields and lesser durations of periods of poor harvests, an increase in the population may have posed the dilemma of extending plowland at the expense of other types of arable land much more sharply. Likewise, the Ministry of War censuses revealed that decline in horse ownership throughout the province recorded in this era had the effect of raising shares of horseless and one-horse households (*malomoshchnye*) in the populace at the expense of cohorts with larger herds.[67] By 1912, twelve out of fifteen districts had fewer horses than in 1900 (Shchigrov, Kursk and L'gov Districts being exceptions), and only for Shchigrov District did the total actually exceed that of 1888. Although far less reliable, published materials on livestock holdings suggest a largely analogous picture: at best, these data point to the deleterious influence exerted by variations in harvests and fragility of fodder supplies from year to year in severely limiting the growth of herds in Kursk Province.[68] However, indices for livestock own-

---

[66] The largest declines in numbers of horses between 1888 and 1893 as recorded in these surveys occur in the eastern districts. Materials for Kursk Province in Tentral'nyi statisticheskii komitet, *SRI, XX* (1891): *Voenno-konskaia perepis' 1888 goda*, table IX, 192; *XXXVII* (1896): *Voenno-konskaia perepis' 1893 goda*, table IX, 208; and *LV* (1902): *Voenno-konskaia perepis' 1900 goda*, table IX, 209.

[67] The effects of the famine of years of 1891–1892 were naturally most notable in the areas that suffered most. The census of 1893 showed that the group of households with no horses or one horse reached 55% to 65% of all households in the eastern region of the province (the districts of Korocha: 56.8%, Staryi Oskol': 58.7%, Novyi Oskol': 64.7%, Fatezh: 57.1 % and Belgorod: 63.0%). In all districts, a third census in 1900 showed that this cohort remained larger in terms of its share of all households than in 1888.

[68] I arrived at this conclusion by an examination of three data sets collected for 1) horses, 2) large horned cattle, 3) sheep and goats and 4) pigs for yearbooks of the Veterinary Administration (1887–1912), the Central Statistical Committee (1900–1912), both housed in the Ministry of Internal Affairs, and the annual figures assembled by the Chancellery of the Governor of Kursk Province (1891–1912) appearing in *Obzor Kurskoi guberniia za...god*. The sometimes very substantial variation between the figures published by these instances in any given year indicates the degree of their overall unreliability, but the general trend in each set of materials showed that the size of provincial herds grew very little over the period 1887–1912.

ership also intersect, as we will see, with a movement of growing elements of working-age persons to off-farm work, not only in handicraft and industrial occupations in the locality, but also, and even more strongly, in long-term wage-earning activities outside the province.

4. The Private Estates

The land question in Kursk Province in its larger sense can hardly be addressed without reference to the evolving situation of the private landowners. The solvency of peasant economies depended not only on harvest performance, but also on movements of wages, rents and prices. Local labor markets and land lease continued to be the crucial economic nexus of the relationship between the province's private estate owners—dominated by the provincial nobility—and neighboring peasants that recalled much of their interaction during the servile era. Materials collected for 1,344 private estates (over 50 *desiatiny*) in eight districts by the Statistical Bureau of the Kursk Provincial Zemstvo in the course of the surveys in 1882–1883[69] show demonstrably the pervasiveness of interaction between estate economies and adjoining peasant communities that led Lenin, at the close of the 1890s, to include Kursk Province among those typified by "feudal survivals" in agrarian relations.[70] Quite visible in these data is the prominent place of leasehold for estates in all districts polled: of 369,474 *desiatiny* of arable land (of a total area of 547,544), fully 164,242 (44.5 percent) was let out to peasant lessees. Moreover, on demesne plowland directly exploited by estate owners (100,290 *desiatiny*), peasant labor and inventory played an important role, especially for those districts in which the weight of smaller estates defined average size in the surveys (Shchigrov, Sudzha, Fatezh and L'gov Districts) as opposed to those in which large latifundia made their weight felt.

---

[69] The sample of 1,344 estates, excluding those under 50 *desiatiny*, had an average total area of 407 *desiatiny*, twice the provincial average of 204 *desiatiny* shown by CSC surveys of 1877. The samples for Shchigrov (310 estates, average of 251 *desiatiny* in size), Sudzha (150 estates, average 283 *desiatiny*), Fatezh (132, average 292 *desiatiny*) and L'gov Districts (195, average 338 *desiatiny*), however, show the same weight of smaller estates as in those reported in 1877 (133, 166, 138 and 349 *desiatiny*, respectively). The greater weight of larger units is measurable for Dmitriev (205 estates, average size of 475 *desiatiny*), Ryl'sk (137 estates, average size 548 *desiatiny*), Putivl' (134 estates, averaging 567 *desiatiny*) and Graivoron Districts (81 estates with an average size of 981 *desiatiny*).

[70] Lenin, *Razvitie kapitalizma*, *PSS*, 3, chart and note on 188, discussion, 185–204.

The dependency was, therefore, a mutual one. Deficits of various types of arable land in allotments ensured an enduring dependence of thousands of households—particularly among communes of ex-serfs—on the former serf-owners for land lease or for wage work. Conversely, estate economies in both large and small units all relied on both strategies of leasehold and a mix of small numbers of employees hired for extended terms and on the labor and inventory of neighboring villagers, hired for sowing operations, hay mowing or the frenetic harvest period on estate lands cultivated by the owner himself. The surveys show that such methods were particularly vital for owners of the smaller estates, who made up the majority of Kursk Province's landowners: in 1905, 70 percent of gentry estates measured 100 *desiatin* or less in size and 57 percent of holdings less than 50 *desiatin*.[71] Even acreage under estate exploitation could not be worked without peasant inventory.

> However favorable the soil and climatic conditions in Kursk Province for agriculture, owners of private land here, with their own resources, cultivate far from all the lands belonging to them. Right after the Emancipation, the estate owners could not adapt to the new conditions of conducting economy with the aid of hired labor. In the majority of cases, they exploited only that part of estate lands that could be worked by means of the labor dues of temporarily obligated peasants, leaving to the use of these latter the better part of the non-allotment demesne. Yet as peasants went over to the redemption regime these relations—labor dues of the peasants in exchange for land leased from the estate owner—became the usual, customary means of estate economy. Thus, on the majority of estates, as in former times, the demesne arable occupied only a part of the land, the rest rented to the peasants in exchange for their obligation to work the demesne. With the passage of time, private estates began little by little to put in practice the use of hired labor [*batrachnaia sistema*] in their economies. Nevertheless, a new condition emerged that motivated landowners to return to leasing out the greater or lesser part of their lands—exorbitantly high rents at which land produced good income without any personal efforts and without any risk of loss from a poor harvest.[72]

This same consideration—income to be drawn from leasing land to peasants living in the environs of the estate in an era of rapidly rising land values—drove that broad trend toward short-term leases and the growing weight of

---

[71] Tsentral'nyi statisticheskii komitet, *Statistika zemlevladeniia*. Of 4,533 noble landowners registered by the land census of 1905 in Kursk Province, 2,577 (56.9%) owned estates with an area of less than 50 *desiatiny*; the combined acreage (43,373 *desiatiny*) of these estates made up about 5% of the 859,331 in gentry ownership. An additional 563 owners (12.4%) held estates between 50 and 100 *desiatiny*, the total area of which (40,094 *desiatiny*) constituted an additional 4.7% of all such lands.

[72] Verner, ed., *Kurskaia guberniia*, 119–120.

money rents that is already visible in the data for the mid-1880s. The great majority of owners possessed little capital (gains from the redemption regime were relatively modest for smaller owners) and had felt no need to develop broad entrepreneurial outlooks or expertise. It is not surprising then that the majority of estates surveyed in the 1880s retained the three-field system and the field cultures of neighboring peasant communities.[73] For the post-Emancipation attitude among noblemen toward estate economy often reflected outlooks and attitudes formed in the era of serfdom and described by Confino as indifference to the benefits of investment, capital improvement or transition to a more modern approach to cultivation.[74]

These aspects of estate economy drew critical comment from a number of specialists in the subsequent period. Relying on various forms of short-term lease, increasingly for cash, but also for labor dues or for parts of the harvest, the majority of landowners simply drew profits from the land with little or no reinvestment, not always maintaining even a minimal inventory of estate work stock or implements, since these were to be supplied by peasant tenants.[75] An analyst of the Ministry of Agriculture and

---

[73] M. Confino, *Systèmes agraires*. An observer from the Moscow Agricultural Society noted retention of the three-field system on the great majority of estates in Kursk Province in 1893. Chuikov, *Kurskaia guberniia*, passim. *Zemstvo* census material for the eight districts in which private estates were surveyed—showing the size of the fallow component—confirmed this impression. When the Treasury's provincial office (*kazennaia palata*) polled 1,952 estate owners of Kursk Province with holdings in excess of 100 *desiatiny* during late 1906, 975 of the 1,328 estates that reported demesne sowings retained three-field rotations (73.4%), 200 had moved to four-field rotations and 153 to multiple rotations. Three-field rotation dominated sown acreage on private estates in the northeast: Novyi Oskol' (88.0%), Shchigrov (75.2%), Staryi Oskol' (71.6%), and Tim (67.2%). Nonetheless, by 1906, the general abandonment of the old rotation in western and southern districts in favor of four-field or multiple rotations was clearly under way. Taken together, newer rotation regimes encompassed 95.3% of sown area on private estates in Graivoron District, 78.9% in Belgorod District, 74.4% in Oboian District, 71.5% in Putivl' District, 68.8% in Sudzha District, 50.3% in Ryl'sk District and 50.2% in Kursk District. Kurskaia kazennaia palata, *op. cit.*, summary table.

[74] Confino, *Domaines et seigneurs*. The author cogently argued that serfdom, granting a free and elastic supply of labor to serf owners, produced in these latter a general reluctance to think in categories of profit, investment and technological improvement, since income could be augmented merely by increasing labor input. He noted, too, that the very fact of physical intermixing of peasant allotments and the demesne (*cherespolositsa*), all cultivated by peasants, using their own inventory and technique, made possibilities for such strategies quite difficult to implement. Obviously, the terms of emancipation in the CAR acted to preserve many of the same conditions after 1861.

[75] Chuikov, *Kurskaia guberniia*, 12–14.

State Properties decried (1897) the very detrimental effects of extensive conversion of forest to plowland—and of the almost universal resort of private landowners to short-term leases to extract income from the land— in advancing erosion and exhaustion of the soil on Kursk estates, writing that "despite favorable external factors, however, private estate economies (in Kursk Province) do not stand on the proper level and, alongside isolated signs of progress in rural economy, we sooner encounter general backwardness. Of course, this latter circumstance is conditioned not solely on the lack of ability (of the owner) to conduct affairs, but nevertheless, hardly a small share of the blame lies with the master himself: living in the present, he never looks ahead and, striving to extract large incomes, in the end reduces the capacity of the land to produce income."[76]

As the late Andrei Matveevich Anfimov long ago observed, even the owners of large latifundia, who in the era of low grain prices forged ahead with technical improvements and heavy investment in plant and equipment, frequently employed variants of the *corvée* system to gain the service of peasant labor and inventory in cultivating demesne lands.[77] Administrators of Princess Iusupova's estate in Graivoron District, one of the largest and most advanced in the province, pursued such practices on a large scale regularly, not only during spring and fall plantings, but also, and especially, at harvest, when peasant inventory clearly appeared as the dominant element.[78]

Throughout the post-Emancipation era, private (mainly gentry) landowners in Kursk Province remained largely dependent on cash rents, rents *en nature*, labor obligations and a plethora of fees and fines extracted from their peasant neighbors, the latter continuing to provide a ready supply of laborers and lessors.[79] That these villagers were commonly the former serfs or their descendants of these selfsame owners or *their* descen-

---

[76] Ministerstvo zemledeliia i gosudarstvennykh imushchestv. Departament Zemledeliia. *Opisaniia*, 40; the compilers of the Treasury study of Kursk Province of late 1906 largely concur. Kurskaia kazennaia palata, *op. cit.*, 37.

[77] Anfimov, *Krupnoe*, 125–127.

[78] Minarik, "Sistema"; Anfimov, "Karlovskoe imenie Meklenburg–Sterlitskikh," in Novosel'skii, ed., *Materialy*, 348–376; Emel'ianov, "Pomeshchich'e khoziaistvo kniazei," in V. V. Adamov, ed., *Voprosy istorii kapitalisticheskoi Rossii*, 325–352.

[79] According to the local Treasury office study (1906) of returns from 1,952 private owners with holdings exceeding 100 *desiatiny*, three out of every four (1,458) were engaged in leasing away part of their arable lands: 377 leased up to a quarter, 273 between 25% and 50%, 210 between 50% and 75%, and 598 between 75 and 100% of the demesne. Kurskaia kazennaia palata, *op. cit.*, summary table.

dants also suggests that the interpersonal character of these interactions had a long history. After an inspection tour of the province undertaken on behalf of the Moscow Imperial Agricultural Society in 1893, N. A. Chuikov recorded the testimony of landowners themselves that "servile dependency still exists, only now it is no longer juridical right that serves as its basis, but the economic power of the landowners on the one hand, and the insecurity of the peasant estate on the other."[80] The parlous financial condition of many small- and medium-sized estates and their dependency on lease and labor strategies designed to replicate the older arrangements, however, suggests that this view told only part of the story.

The more lucrative branches of provincial agro-industrial enterprise, in contrast, fully evidence sustained efforts mounted by an elite of absentee owners of large latifundia to escape the iron embrace of this system. Linked to the decline of grain prices on European and Russian markets during 1885–1895, this shift was typified by capital investment in new agricultural technology, imported livestock and on-site processing capacity, cadres of full-time and seasonal laborers and diversified sowings realizable in cash in raw or processed form. If this advanced sector, too, continued to rely partly on leases to attract the services of peasant labor and draft power at critical moments in the agricultural cycle, its achievement in evolving a new freedom of action in estate economy was quite striking. Yet if the old system of "patron-client" relationships, with its roots firmly in the servile era, was undoubtedly highly exploitative and kept alive a background of bitter tension in rural social relations, it also had the most significant advantage of *a certain history of personal interaction and predictability for both lord and peasant alike.* The very success of Kursk Province's landowning elite in instituting significant changes to estate operations, reacting to the economic trends of the 1880s and 1890s, brought about a complete rupture of this interchange in locales later to be

---

[80] "Thanks to the insufficiency of peasant allotments and their commonly inconvenient physical dispersion, a mass of labor dues in favor of the estates is levied on the peasants. For the lease of land, he works. For the lease of pasture, in most cases, he works, less often paying cash. For use of the estate's oxen he works, and even for the right to wash his clothes on the estate's side of the brook, he works... We are inclined to think that evolution of [demesne] agricultural technique meets a powerful brake in such local conditions—mainly the high rents in by-*desiatina* leaseholds, but also in the vast development of the profitable system of extracting labor dues from the peasants [*otrabotochnaia sistema*]. Estate economy cannot move forward when it is simply more profitable to rent land to the peasants than to undertake sowings at one's own risk." Chuikov, *op. cit.*, 96–97.

venues for revolutionary unrest during 1905–1906. We will return to a detailed treatment of this issue in Chapter IV.

The struggle to boost revenues in the context of a long price depression and periodic crop failure, however, proved a crushing burden for land-owners without the financial resources of the magnates. Increasing debt loads of mortgagors to the State Bank of the Nobility was a clear sign of trouble. The Governor's report for 1898 noted the following:

> Last year's harvest, which reflected extremely unfavorably on the prosperity of the majority of peasant economies in the province, was no less disastrous for the econo-mies of the private estate owners. The heady rise of prices for grain and fodder might have improved the material position of only those landowners who had husbanded supplies from previous years' harvests, but such owners in the province were very few in number. The majority of estates, burdened with debts, have been compelled at some time to sell such reserves at very low prices and, given this year's harvest, it is a rare one among the estate owners who has wrested enough income from his affairs to cover the estate's expenses, not to speak of the payment of interest on his loans. Growth of the capital debt of just the [Kursk office of the] Bank of the Nobility by 3,782,600 ru-bles in the current year alone, loaned out on almost 60,000 *desiatiny* of land, is obvious proof of the declining situation of estate economies.[81]

As of 1 January 1889, the State Bank of the Nobility carried 442 loans on estate lands of the nobility in Kursk Province totaling 164,901 *desiat-iny* for face values of 12,143,417 rubles. By 1 January 1893, the number of loans had grown to 781, on 672 estates with an area of 282,450 *desiat-iny*, at a face value of 19,439,800 rubles; the Bank carried 854,817 rubles in arrears. On 1 January 1905, bank digests count 1,360 outstanding loans on 1,342 estates totaling an area of 445,868 *desiatiny*—or 51.8 percent of all lands under noble ownership—for a total face value of 30,391,700 rubles. Furthermore, the Bank's reportage on dispersion of money loaned showed that only a little over a third (34.3 percent) of the face value amounts ever reached borrowers, the rest being withheld for extinguishing outstanding tax arrears and private debts.[82] Total indebtedness of private holdings was far higher: at the end of 1903, the Ministry of Finance esti-mated the capital debt of 4,267 private estates in Kursk Province (754,950 *desiatiny* or 54.2 percent area in private ownership) mortgaged to indi-viduals or various state or private banks at 57,780,994 rubles.[83] Chronic

---

[81] *Obzor Kurskoi gubernii za 1897 god* (1898), 8.

[82] Calculated from the published annual report, Gosudarstvennyi dvorianskii zemel'nyi bank, *Otchet.*

[83] Ministerstvo finansov. *Ezhegodnik Ministerstvo Finansov za 1906–1907 god,* 282.

tax arrears, often cited with regard to the state of peasant fortunes, were comparatively worse in the private sector. Arrears of private landowners in Kursk Province of 556,824 rubles (67.2 percent) of average annual state and local assessments of 828,530 rubles over the period 1891–1906 show the mounting financial pressures on the private estates, even given rates of assessment that blatantly favored them at the expense of the mass of peasant smallholders.[84]

Land censuses for Kursk Province from the period reveal that a considerable number of gentry landowners (who in 1877 owned 1,165,444 *desiatiny* or 82.3 percent of the total area of privately held lands) were losing the battle to hang on to their estates. A substantial loss of a fifth of the estates (from 5,712 estates in 1877 to 4,533 estates in 1905) and over a quarter of the total area held by the nobility (the area declined from 1,165,444 *desiatiny* in 1877 to 859,311 *desiatiny* in 1905—a loss of 26.3 percent) echoed trends in the Central Agricultural Region generally.[85] The average size of estates in the province also grew smaller, a process in which the failure of traditions of primogeniture in inheritance to take hold among Russian noble families played no small role. The decline appears broadly distributed throughout Kursk Province. Most notable on the somewhat poorer soils of Dmitriev District (where the total area declined by almost 38 percent), the contraction in noble landholding most affected—once again—the eastern districts (Novyi Oskol' by 29.8 percent, Tim by 31.3 percent, Belgorod by 35.2 percent, and Korocha by 36.1 percent). Losses were least notable in Graivoron and Putivl' Districts, where a tiny cohort of owners of huge estates (Iusupov, Kharitonenko, Khorvat, Bariatinskii, Tereshchenko and Sheremet'ev) maintained their positions either by means of strategies of capital investment or by leasing large tracts of demesne lands to operations of others. Data for the province illustrate the fact that the trend advanced generally regardless of the size of estates, but that the extremes were least affected.[86]

---

[84] Ministerstvo finansov (Departament okladnykh sborov), *Svod svedenii... za (1891–1906) god.*

[85] But Kursk estate owners might have considered themselves relatively lucky. In the eight CAR *gubernii* (Chernigov, -41.6%; Riazan, -35.2%; Orel, -31.4%; Tambov, -30.1%; Voronezh, -27.8%; Penza, -26.9%; Kursk, -26.3%; Tula, -22.3%;), noble landholding declined from 9,878,178 *desiatiny* in 1877 to 6,871,130 in 1905, losing 31% of the 1877 area. Tsentral'nyi statisticheskii komitet, *Statistika zemlevladeniia*, Table II, 12–17.

[86] Tsentral'nyi statisticheskii komitet, *ibid.* In the category of owners of holdings from 1 to 50 *desiatiny* between 1877 and 1905, holdings declined from 2,845 to 2,577 (-9.4%) and the acreage decreased from 57,254 *desiatiny* to 43,373 (-24.2%). In the category of own-

5. Land Lease, Rural Wages and Grain Prices

Not surprisingly, faced by such financial pressures, landowners availed themselves of the potential for raising rents in order to squeeze as much income as possible from their estates. A. M. Anfimov observed that with the end of the 1880s (when average rents in 46 provinces of European Russia stood at 6.9 rubles for 1 *desiatina*), land rents tended to fall through the 1890s, but to rise sharply in the 1900s.[87] Kursk Province was no exception here, but data from the *zemstvo* surveys make it clear that average land rents in the mid-1880s in this very densely populated province were three times Anfimov's average.[88] The whole movement was thus to be played out on much more inflated levels. If land rents in Kursk Province appear to have languished throughout the 1890s, they are substantially above levels measured by the *zemstvo* surveys by 1902. The very speed of this process is quite striking: between 1898 and conclusion of contracts in 1905, rents rose 38.1 percent for lease of 1 *desiatina* of plowland to be sown with winter crops and 57.8 percent for land to be sown in spring. Especially sharp rates of increase in land rents were recorded for Novyi Oskol', Staryi Oskol', Sudzha, L'gov and Oboian Districts—in which peasant unrest was to be particularly intense during 1905–1906.[89] Conversely, in districts in which rents ran up less sharply,

---

ers of 51 to 500 *desiatiny*, the number of holdings shrank from 2,371 to 1,612 (-32%), while total acreage shrank from 412,008 *desiatiny* to 289,267 (-29.8%). Holders of 501 to 5,000 *desiatiny* went from 476 owners in 1877 to 325 (-31.7%) in 1905; acreage decreased from 510,767 *desiatiny* to 340,259 (-33.4%). Estates over 5,000 hardly changed their position: 20 owners to 19 (-5%); acreage from 185,415 to 186,432 *desiatiny* (+0.5%).

[87] Anfimov, *Zemel'naia arenda*, 164–166.

[88] The surveys conducted by the Statistical Bureau of the Kursk Provincial Zemstvo during the mid-1880s recorded rents for 1 *desiatina* under winter plantings that average 20.10 rubles for the province (range: 27.30 rubles in Shchigrov District to 15 in Novyi Oskol' District) and 13.10 rubles for acreage rented under spring sowings (range: 17.70 in Shchigrov District to 6.80 in Dmitriev District). When the Bureau returned to work in 1897 and collected leasehold data for 1898, it found rents to have fallen to 17.10 rubles for 1 *desiatina* in the winter field and to 10.70 for 1 *desiatina* in the spring field. For contracts concluded in 1905, however, rents for acreage in the winter field stood at 23.60 rubles for 1 *desiatina* (+38.1% against 1898 contracts) and 16.70 for 1 *desiatina* sown under spring crops (+56.8% against 1898 contracts).

[89] *TS-KhSKGZ za (1898, 1902, 1905) god*. The largest rent increases between 1898 and 1905 were as follows: Novyi Oskol' District: 14 rubles to 22.10 (+57.9%) for 1 *desiatina* of land under winter sowings, 10.70 rubles to 20 rubles (+88.7%) for 1 *desiatina* of land under spring sowings; Staryi Oskol' District, 15.80 rubles to 24.20 rubles (+57.6%)

staying fairly close to the levels of the late 1880s (Tim, Fatezh, Shchigrov), unrest was to be relatively limited. The CSC's study of 1881 had fixed 389,129 *desiatiny* of non-allotment land in peasant leasehold, *zemstvo* surveys of the mid-1880s 375,783,[90] but data for the area of non-allotment land leased by peasants afterwards are fragmentary and contradictory. According to figures used by the "Commission on the Center," the area of non-allotment land leased had grown to 512,400 *desiatiny* by 1901.[91] Compiled returns of parish officials to a poll organized by the provincial Treasury office in 1906 put this area at 244,345 *desiatiny*. Labor dues or portions of the harvest as consideration in leasehold retained a foothold in the southwestern districts most heavily settled by ex-serfs, yet even here money rents had clearly begun to crowd out rents *en nature*.[92]

---

in the winter field and 10.80 rubles to 17 rubles (+57.6%) in the spring field. Analogous increases appear for Oboian District (+50.0% and +71.2%), for L'gov District (+40.5% and +57.1%) and for Sudzha District (+46.9%, +58.7%). Belgorod District also registered substantial increases, +59.1 % for land in the winter field and +71.7% for land in the spring field.

[90] *VTsSK*, Seriia III, 1884, vyp. 4 (*Raspredelenie*). The *zemstvo* surveys of 1882–1885 counted 151,329 *desiatiny* of non-allotment land leased by state peasants and 224,454 by ex-serfs. The CSC study of 1887 gave a smaller area: 311,135 *desiatiny*. Tsentral'nyi statisticheskii komitet, *Glavneishiia dannyia*, Table V, 16–23.

[91] *Materialy Vysochaishe utverzhdennoi 16-go noiabria 1901 g. kommissii*, Table XIV, 114–153 (and supplements). The figure is from supplementary table VI ("Total Area of Non-Allotment Land Leased by Peasants at the Present Time,"), 148, and is without any source reference. A partial sample of 115,970 *desiatiny* reported by parish administrations in the same time frame showed 14.6% of area leased by communes, 58.8% by peasant partnerships, and 26.6% by individual householders. Glavnoe Upravlenie Zemleustroistva i Zemledeliia, Otdel Sel'skoi Ekonomii i Sel'skokhoziaistvennoi Statistiki. *Statisticheskiia svedeniia po zemel'nomu voprosu*, 53.

[92] The study organized by the provincial Treasury office at the end of 1906 estimated, based on responses of owners of estates of over 100 *desiatiny* with a total area of 951,864 *desiatiny*, private acreage leased at 350,671 *desiatiny* (36.8%). Of this acreage, peasants leased 244,345 *desiatiny* (and an additional 127,823 of allotment land from their fellow villagers). Kurskaia kazennaia palata, *op. cit.*, 35–49, tables. The same study also showed that within the leased acreage (350,671 *desiatiny*), labor dues were consideration in the lease of 6,278 *desiatiny* and portions of the harvest (*po ispolu*) for 25,713, or 31,993 *desiatiny* (9.1% of total area leased). Compare this to surveys of the mid-1880s: of 375,783 *desiatiny* leased by both state peasants and ex-serfs, fully half (188,905 *desiatiny*) were leased under one of these two forms of agreement. The validity of the figure for non-allotment lease, unfortunately, is open to doubt. For *sloboda* Rakitnaia, for example, the 1906 study put non-allotment acreage leased by villagers at 273.5 *desiatiny*. Reporting in police files for this village, though, show peasants of Rakitnaia leasing, from the Iusupova estate alone, 3,069 *desiatiny* under winter crops and 2,054

Note that adoption of money rents by the landowners now constituted a fixed charge on the peasant's "take" from the leased acreage, irrespective of the abundance or penury of the harvest, and thus shifted the consequences for any shortfall onto the shoulders of their tenants.

Sharp increases in land rents took place in tandem with the general recovery of grain prices in the province after the long twenty-year downward spiral, aided by a superb local harvest in 1894, had reached its nadir in 1894–1895. The crop failures of 1889 and 1891–1892 imposed their own logic on local prices of all major grains, trebling rye prices by November 1891, and maintaining them at well over 1 ruble per *pood* during spring and summer of 1892.[93] Similar distortions appear in the wake of poor harvests in 1896–1897. Short-term trends aside, however, the general movement of all grain prices, propelled by domestic and foreign demand, was clearly in the ascendant after 1895: the price series assembled by B. N. Mironov reveals that between 1895 and 1905 aggregate grain prices in Kursk Province (wheat, rye, barley, oats, buckwheat) rose by some 77 percent.[94]

Data for agricultural wages submitted annually by provincial correspondents—mainly landowners—to the Department of Agriculture and Rural Industry and published with the returns for other provinces suggest modest increases in pay for that segment of the rural population that worked on the estates on day wages.[95] Consistently among the lowest in

---

desiatiny under spring crops for 1906. GARF, f. 102 (Departament Politsii), 4-e delo-proisvodstvo, 1907 g., ch. 34.1, ll. 48–50 (Governor V. M. Borzenko to the Department of Police, No. 8783, 5 July 1907).

[93] My sense of this trend gathered from the month-by-month variations in grain prices for Kursk Province between January 1889 and the end of October 1902, recorded in *TS-KhSKGZ za (1898–1902) god* and Ministerstvo finansov (Departament torgovli i manu-faktur), *Materialy po statistike khlebnoi torgovli* that preserved provincial aggregates for 1889–1898. On this level of aggregation—and given the obvious effects of the crop failures of 1891–1892 and 1896–1897—a regular seasonal local price fluctuation was not consistently evident. Depression of prices in the wake of the harvest, when peasants sold their grain *en masse* to realize sums needed to meet obligations to the tax collector and their landlords, and inflation of prices during spring, when supplies ran short and villagers entered the market as buyers of grain are only occasionally evident. On this phenomenon in the mix of factors that define a "small commodity producing milieu," Anfimov, "O melkom tovarnom proizvodstve," *ISSSR*, 1963, 2: 141–160.

[94] Mironov, *Khlebnye tseny*, Prilozhenie, Tables 11–17. On the grain trade in Russia, see Kitanina, *Khlebnaia torgovlia*, ch. IV, 121–170; Izmest'eva, *Rossiia v sisteme*, ch. II, 38–118. The growing role of domestic demand for grain has been emphasized in a recent work by Davydov, *Ocherki*, 81–205.

[95] Shanin estimated agricultural laborers ("rural proletarians") *per se* to have made up 6–8% of households in rural Russia, plus perhaps an additional 2% of households that di-

the Central Agricultural Region,[96] wages tended to decline in the years 1882–1892, and to have risen throughout subsequent years up until the harvest of 1902, after which wages at harvest declined sharply. Yet the five-year periods mask great instability in the year-to-year data, especially when measured in rye equivalents. Aggregate wages by this measure tended naturally enough to depend on the size of the harvests, being most meager during 1881–1882, 1891–1892 and 1897–1898 and most generous during good harvest years, 1888, 1894–1895 and for the period 1900–1903, after which, during 1904–1905, wages in rye equivalents fall measurably. Nonetheless, in aggregate, average day wages during 1902–1906 stood 22 percent higher than during 1882–1886.[97] Reports on handicraft industries and rural trades during the years after 1892 (see below) also point to similar expansion of incomes in the non-agricultural sector.

6. Tax Arrears and Other Indices of Rural Prosperity

In sum, the rural community in Kursk Province—both peasants and landowners—in the era immediately before the events of 1905–1906 was experiencing an accumulation of demographic and financial pressures on its capacities to produce and on the means at the disposal of households to

---

vided their time between the allotment and wage work on holdings of private landowners. Shanin, *The Roots of Otherness*, v. 1, 93–102. Naturally, this share would have varied fairly substantially on the local level, in dependence on the local land fund and the availability of other employment.

[96] *Materialy Vysochaishe utverzhdennoi 16-go noiabria 1901 g. kommissii*, table XXII, 233–245.

[97] Calculations from data assembled from the annual published by the Departament zemledeliia i sel'skoi promyshlennosti, ... *god v sel'skokhoziaistvennom otnoshenii*. Correspondents provided data for three intervals: on work performed during spring plantings (invariably the lowest paid and the most stable), during hay mowing, and for wages contracted for harvesting grain, the latter being the highest paid, but subject to considerable (and at times extreme) variations from year to year. These data were provided for male and female laborers (on their own or on the estate's provisions) and for a worker with his own horse. Large added increments were paid to workers with work stock. The local *zemstvo* statistical bureau registered data on wages for longer contract laborers (year, month, seasonal) only for 1898–1906, too short a period to make broad judgments. *TS-KhSKGZ za (1898–1906) god*. Reviews undertaken by the Ministry of Agriculture and State Properties of "leading estates" during the 1890s show that contract workers remained a distinct minority in the estate labor forces even in the 1890s. They fared relatively well during the years prior to 1905, with the exception of 1902, when their pay fell sharply.

meet vital expenditures. Traditional assessments of the condition of the Russian peasantry at the end of the nineteenth century have referred repeatedly to the data on tax arrears as an index of well-being, and we will not miss the opportunity to review these here. Bulletins posted in the yearbooks of the Ministry of Finance show that provincial peasant taxpayers acquitted their obligations to the state more or less correctly right up to 1891–1894.[98] This dutifulness meant that reductions in redemption payments for Kursk Province under implementation of the *ukaz* of 12 December 1881 were to be relatively modest.[99] After the crises of 1891–1892, however, substantial arrears went on the books. Out of a total average annual assessment of 6,939,397 rubles (1891–1906), the average year-end arrears equaled 4,474,467 rubles (64.5 percent). The assessment included direct state taxes (a state land tax and redemption dues), *zemstvo*, parish and village levies and premiums for obligatory fire insurance. If some level of non-payment was everywhere in evidence in Kursk Province subsequent to 1891 (the obligatory fire insurance program was everywhere deeply in the red), the highest levels of tax arrears for 1891–1906 were concentrated mainly in eastern and northern districts in which the effects of poor harvest performance had been especially severe.[100] Con-

---

[98] This conclusion was suggested by a review of materials on the soul tax (abolished at the end of the 1886 tax year), quit-rent payments paid by former state peasants (converted to redemption payments beginning in 1888), redemption dues of ex-serfs and the state land tax contained in the annual, *Ezhegodnik Ministerstva finansov*, which posted bulletins from 1870 onwards. According to this source, arrears between 1870 and 1891 rarely rose above 3% of assessments; only during 1882–1886 (in the wake of crop failures in 1880–1881 and 1885–1886) did sums owed reach 9%, but they declined to 0.7% in 1888.

[99] Kovan'ko, *Reforma 19 fevralia 1861*, 387–414.

[100] The eastern districts formed the high end of the ranking by arrears: on an average annual assessment of 473,639 rubles, peasants in Tim District owed 675,300 rubles (142.6%). On an average annual assessment of 446,439 rubles, communes in Staryi Oskol' District owed 508,964 rubles (114%). Peasant communes in Oboian District owed a full year's assessment (on an average annual assessment of 629,309 rubles, arrears averaged 635,048) and data for Shchigrov (annual assessment 484,090 rubles, average arrears 461,144 or 95.3%) and Fatezh Districts (annual assessment 432,089 rubles, average arrears 386,491 or 89.4%) were over the provincial average. Arrears for Belgorod (annual assessment 477,758 rubles, average arrears 299,052 or 62.6%) and Novyi Oskol' Districts (annual assessment 515,031 rubles, average assessment 301,897 or 58.6%) were also substantial. Once again, it should be noted that as a percentage arrears in the private sector were even larger: on an average annual combined levy for 1891–1906 of 828,530 rubles, private owners owed 556,824 rubles or 67.2%. Calculated from Ministerstvo finansov (Departament okladnykh sborov), *Svod svedenii... za (1891–1906) god*.

versely, published tax records reveal that the western districts, with better yields and fewer years of poor harvest performance, were less impaired in comparison.[101] The portion of direct state taxes declines steadily;[102] rising annual assessments sooner reflect growth of *zemstvo* and local taxes that expanded provincial tax bills from 6,589,661 rubles in 1891 to 7,905,000 in 1905. The expression of a new wave of local activism in this era, *zemstvo* levies were among those issues that provoked bitter clashes between the state bureaucracy and the local organizations.[103]

---

[101] In Graivoron District, the majority of its arrears were recorded in assessments in favor of organs of peasant self-government at the village level, carrying a deficit of 216,000 rubles (over four times the annual assessments) from the mid-1890s down to the beginning of 1906. This anomaly (quite by itself within the tax records for the province) suggests that peasant taxpayers in delinquent settlements bore a particularly bitter view of their "own" officials. Even in 1906, this refusal to advance tax money to village officialdom continued: on 1 January 1907, arrears still stood at 183,000 rubles.

[102] The Law of 28 December 1881 (*PSZ*, III, t. 1, 376, at No. 576, entitled "O ponizhenii vykupnykh platezhei") prescribed reductions in redemption payments for communes of ex-serfs throughout the Empire. These tended to be least of all favorable for the CAR provinces (20–21%) in which redemption payments were highest. For Kursk Province, reductions were on the order of 19%. *SVRI*, Seriia III, 1885, vyp. 5 (*Ponizhenie*), and *SVRI*, Seriia III, 1886, vyp. 11 (*Materialy... po spetsial'nomu ponizheniiu*). For Kursk Province (on 1 January 1906), the Ministry of Finance calculated that the original amortized redemption debt of 83,371,846 rubles had been reduced by close to 10%: by 5,094,700 rubles in reductions mandated by the state, 1,288,940 in prolongations and annulments and 1,551,077 in delayed payments.

[103] That the tax question was a bone of contention between the *zemstvo* and the central bureaucracy throughout the 1890s was evident in repeated efforts by the central bodies to enact limits to *zemstvo* taxing authority or to mandate certain spending. Property evaluation and proposal for the annual levy were made the competence of District Committees in which state officials sat after 1893 (*Sobranie uzakonenii i rasporiazhenii pravitel'stva, izdavaemoe pri Pravitel'stvuiushem Senate*, II, 1893 g., 17 iiulia, No. 856). In 1895, the state agreed to fund local institutions of justice, but the funds—previously extracted for this purpose from *zemstvo* levies—were "returned" to the local organs, provided that they be used only for road maintenance. Any other use required the permission of the Minister of Finance and involved lowering of annual levies by the same sum (*Sobranie uzakonenii*, II, 1895 g., 19 iiulia, No. 899). Limits legislated on the right of the *zemstvo* to levy fees on commercial paper in the Law of 8 June 1898 on the state industrial tax (*PSZ*, III, v.18, No. 15601, "Vysochaishe utverzhdennoe Polozhenie o gosudarstvennom promyslennom naloge," 489–515, preamble). Transfer of control over famine relief to the Ministry of Internal Affairs in *PSZ*, III, t. 20, No. 18855 (12 June 1900), "Vysochaishe utverzhdennyia Vremennyia Pravila po obespecheniiu prodovol'stvennykh potrebnostei sel'skikh obyvatelei," 764–778. The cap on tax levies was enacted on the same day at No. 18862, "Vysochaishe utverzhdennoe mnenie Gosudarstvennago Soveta ob ustanovlenii pre-

During the 1890s, the tax inspectorate, backed by rural police and local administrative bodies, struggled to force delinquent peasant taxpayers to remit arrears. The Department of Direct Taxation ceased publishing material on measures employed in this effort after 1895, but one notes that even in this short period thousands of peasant households in Kursk Province had property inventoried, confiscated and sold at local auctions. It is also evident that the villagers began to organize collective resistance: peasant communities ordered their elders to refuse to pay, forcibly disrupted inventories and confiscations and engineered boycotts of auctions. Arrests and fines grew with each recorded year.[104] By the end of the 1890s, however, the state had embarked on a series of reforms. During 1899–1903, various schedules of arrears within the overall menu of taxes were put in abatement or postponed: arrears in redemption dues in 1899, delinquencies in *zemstvo* levies in 1901, overdue premiums for obligatory fire insurance in 1903. In 1903, the institution of joint responsibility of all householders—via the peasant commune—for payment of taxes (*krugovaia poruka*) was abolished. In honor of the Tsarevich's birth in August 1904, an Imperial Manifesto ordered all state tax arrears struck from the rolls and use of corporal punishment in its last civil venue—parish courts—forbidden.[105] On 3 November 1905, redemption assess-

---

del'nosti zemskago oblozheniia v guberniiakh, v koikh vvedeno v deistvie Polozhenie o gubernsklkh i uyezdnikh zemskikh uchrezhdeniiakh i ob osvobozhdenii zemstv ot nekotorykh raskhodov" (790–792). As part of a broad review of *zemstvo* activity after 1890, see in this connection S. Iu. Witte's memorandum, *Zemstvo i samoderzhavie*, 157–162.

[104] Ministerstvo finansov (Department okladnykh sborov), *Svod svedenii… za (1891–1899) god.* In just four years 1891–1894, inventories were conducted in 118 villages in 1891, 66 in 1892, 530 in 1893 and 735 in 1894—1,449 villages in all. Actual auctions numbered 170, although the numbers of households involved were not noted. Sixty-six parish elders were arrested, 552 village elders, 54 tax collectors and 238 of the delinquents themselves, presumably for resistance of some sort. After 1894, data on arrests disappear, and the materials were divided between communal and household tenure peasants. Altogether, between 1895 and 1899, 17,515 households were subjected to tax sales of their property. Among communal peasants, these operations were conducted in 505 villages in 1895, 429 in 1896, 183 in 1897 (the year of especially poor harvests), 470 in 1898 and 207 in 1899, or 1,794 villages for 1895–1899.

[105] "Ob otmene krugovoi poruki krest'ian po oplate okladnykh sborov v mestnostiakh, v koikh vvedeno v deistvie Polozheniia 23 iiunia 1899 goda o poriadke vzimaniia sikh sborov s nadel'nykh zemel' sel'skikh obshchestv," *PSZ*, III, v. 23 (No. 22629, 12 March 1903), 134–138; "O milostiakh darovannykh v den Sviatago Kreshcheniia Naslednika i Tsarevicha Alekseia Nikolaevicha"), *PSZ*, III, v. 24 (No. 25014, 11 August 1904), 856–857.

ments were cut in half for 1906 and eliminated in 1907.[106] Commenting on retreat of state policy on this front some years ago, Stephen Wheatcroft wrote that it signified a victory for peasant collective resistance and a sign of the state's weakness that "may well have contributed to peasants' psychological readiness for revolt."[107] For the concessions of 1903–1904, in particular, are also enacted in the shadow of ominous omens: mass rural revolt in Khar'kov and Poltava Provinces in March–April 1902 and sustained labor unrest throughout South Russia from November 1902 to August 1903. In the autumn of 1903, as a sense of alarm in ruling circles grew, police forces in several *gubernii* (Kursk Province included) received substantial reinforcements (see below).

Nonetheless, tax arrears borne by peasants in Kursk Province— actually amounting to less than a single year's assessment—were really rather modest relative to those recorded elsewhere.[108] Second, their meaning as an index of economic vigor is also not without interest, for higher concentrations of arrears in the northeastern and eastern *uyezdy* of the province reflect more than just the geography of harvest performance. Published digests of the Department of Direct Taxation confirm that it was mainly *state peasants* (the dominant element in these localities)— those most favored by the land settlements of the 1860s—that ran up provincial arrears. In contrast, arrears carried by communes of ex-serfs most heavily settled in western and southwestern *uyezdy*—plainly the more disadvantaged in terms of land allotments—were far more limited. In 1893, for the state's assessment of 2,815,069 rubles (redemption payments and state land tax), state peasants failed to pay 1,995,022 (70.9 percent); ex-serfs on an assessment of 1,290,387 rubles for that year registered arrears of 448,115 (34.7 percent). By 1901, despite reductions in the assessments, arrears for former state peasants (2,751,855 rubles) already exceeded the annual levy (2,671,535 rubles); for ex-serfs, arrears were

---

[106] On tax arrears, see M. V. Komarinets, "Okladnye sbory," *TS-KhSKGZ. 1904 god*, III: 34–41.

[107] Wheatcroft, "Crises," in Kingston-Mann and Mixter, eds., *Peasant Economy*, 128–172.

[108] Thus by the end of 1901 arrears in state taxes (redemption dues and the land tax) for Kursk Province stood at 3,299,751 rubles, 83.7% of the 1901 assessments (3,941,132) for both state peasants and ex-serfs. Compare this to those run up in provinces with over five times the annual levy: Nizhegorod (8,749,445 rubles on assessments of 1,457,669), Kazan (16,062,292 on assessments of 3,084,628) and Orenburg (3,810,268 on assessments of 709,870). Saratov, Voronezh, Riazan, Penza and Orel Province carried between two and three times annual assessments, Tula and Samara Provinces between three and four times.

comparatively modest: 547,896 rubles—43.2 percent of 1901 assessments (1,269,597 rubles).[109]

The use of tax arrears as a measure of economic conditions in the Russian countryside clearly derived from a dearth of other sources that would measure disposable income, and the newer surrogates are even harder to apply in a *provincial* setting. Indirect taxes were a levy on production and not a sales tax: an examination of provincial indirect tax receipts with an eye to assessing local consumption would conclude erroneously that matches or kerosene were unknown to Kursk peasants, or that sugar consumption in Kiev Province was 40 times higher than in Kursk Province.[110] There are, however, other indicators of the condition of the rural economy that fly in the face of the picture often drawn from the tax data. Peasant farm structures covered by the obligatory fire insurance program administered by the *zemstvo* grew from 895,618 structures at an estimated value of 58 million rubles in 1889 to 1,283,427 structures valued at 86,446,618 rubles in 1905, and to 1,456,191 structures at a value of 118 million rubles in 1913.[111] Although admittedly representing a tiny minority of peasant households, persons "engaged in agriculture and village industry" ("landowners" appear separately) were the fastest-growing group of clients for provincial savings banks. Just for the period from 1 January 1898 to 1 January 1906, passbook holders registering such occupations grew from 8,584 persons to 20,925 persons, and monies on deposit from 1,668,000 rubles to 4,768,800 rubles.[112] When the state liquor monopoly became fully opera-

---

[109] Calculated from Ministerstvo finansov, Department okladnykh sborov, *Svod svedenii... za (1891–1906) god.*

[110] Kerosene lamps began to replace other forms of lighting in peasant houses in the 1870s. The process sped up after national refineries drove more expensive American imports off the market and reduced prices from 20 rubles per *funt* to 6 rubles. Use tended to dwindle, however, with increasing distance from a local center of supply. S. Ia. Moiseev, "Kerosin," in *TS-KhSKGZ za 1904 god*, II, otd. 1, 23–60.

[111] "Vzaimnoe strakhovanie ot ognia gubernskoe, zemskoe i gorodskoe, 1889–1892 gg.," in *VTsSK*, Vyp. 27 (1893), 18–33, and the annual issues of Kurskaia gubernskaia zemskaia uprava, *Otchet... po vzaimnomu strakhovaniiu ot ognia za (1893–1913) god* held by the Russian State Library. Discounting for inflation in construction costs during 1889–1913, this represents an even larger investment. For comparison, I note that during 1867–1876, structures covered under the program grew from 665,890 valued at 17,497,972 rubles to 675,553 valued at 27,901,166. Tsentral'nyi statisticheskii komitet, *Vzaimnoe zemskoe strakhovanie, 1866–1876*, Razdel XIII, "Kurskaia guberniia," 106–107.

[112] "Ocherk deiatel'nosti gos. sberegatel'nykh kass v Kurskoi gubernii," from *TS-KhSKGZ za 1904 god*, I, otd. 1, 9–24. Data for 1906 from *Ezhegodnik Ministerstva finansov*. De-

tional in Kursk Province (1901), the Ministry of Finance recorded provincial sales of 10,055,315 rubles for the year; in 1905, sales totaled 13,169,370 rubles.[113] Even as some branches succumbed to cheaper manufactures, growth in provincial handicraft employment and incomes (see below) suggests that demand for locally produced goods and services was increasingly lively. Even against steeply rising land prices and rents, peasant purchase and lease of land continued apace.[114] From such indices, the disposable incomes of the population appear not to have shrunk, but to have grown, even if distribution of the benefits of this trend were undoubtedly skewed toward its more prosperous strata among provincial peasants.

7. Peasant Land Purchases in Kursk Province: 1877–1905

Between 1877 and 1905, the main group of private landowners—the Kursk provincial gentry—had suffered a measurable decline in its fortunes: 1,179 estates (20.6 percent) of some 306,113 *desiatiny* (26.3 percent) of its lands

---

posits held by 6,399 passbook holders on 31 December 1888 totaled 1,645,097 rubles in 15 state savings banks. By 1 January 1906, there were 69,949 passbook holders with deposits of 18,288,200 rubles in 18 "central" state savings banks and 55 branches in local post and telegraph offices (authorized to open in 1889). Among patrons in 1906, we find 5,141 members of the clergy (deposits of 2,237,200 rubles), 6,583 persons engaged in trade (2,037,600 rubles), 9,348 persons (2,303,900 rubles) in "private service" (*sluzhba chastnaia*) and 7,004 "juridical persons" (2,750,200 rubles). Persons listing themselves as "landowners" number 1,757 depositors (680,400 rubles).

[113] *Ezhegodnik Ministerstva finansov* for relevant years. Kursk Province appears in the *vedomost'* for state sales for the first time in 1900 with receipts of 4,744,050 rubles from 701 liquor outlets (*vinnye lavki*). The five state outlets (*sklady*) opened only in 1901. During the phase-in of the monopoly, the usual excise taxes were exacted (in 1900, 5,839,425 rubles; in 1901, 5,481,524) but in 1902 became nominal (149,584 rubles).

[114] At land rents prevailing in the mid-1880s (average 16 rubles, 60 kopecks for 1 *desiatina*), the total amount paid by peasant lessors for 375,782 desiatiny arrives at around 6 million rubles. By 1901 (average 18 rubles, 5 kopecks)—assuming an area of non-allotment lease cited in the data assembled for use of the "Commission on the Center" (512,400 *desiatiny*)—this bill had climbed to over 9 million rubles. Purchases of 135,586 *desiatiny* through the Peasant Land Bank during 1885–1907 were of the following magnitudes: 1884–1887, 12,819 *desiatiny* at 105 rubles per *desiatina* (1,345,995 rubles); 1888–1891, 2,311 *desiatiny* at 107 rubles per *desiatina* (247,277 rubles); 1892–1895, 2,283 *desiatiny* for 113 rubles per *desiatina* (257,979 rubles); 1896–1899, 22,311 *desiatiny* at 130 rubles per *desiatina* (2,900,430 rubles); 1900–1903, 79,485 *desiatiny* for 166 rubles per *desiatina* (13,194,150 rubles); 1904–1907: 16,377 *desiatiny* at 194 rubles per *desiatina* (3,177,138 rubles). By 1914, purchases through the Bank averaged 297 rubles per *desiatina*.

had been liquidated and sold off to various local and sometimes non-local proprietors. Three quarters of this acreage (the CSC estimated 230,709 *desiatiny*) passed to peasant owners: 39,383 *desiatiny* to communes, 69,065 to peasant partnerships, 122,261 to individual households.[115] This accumulation of private lands, however, did not greatly alter the land situation for the peasant community as a whole. If the total acreage under the control of communes made advances during 1877–1905, only 4.1 percent of the province's 4,314 communes managed to get a share. Among individual owners, private lands were held among a minority of villagers (6 percent of all households) that had scarcely grown in size since 1877, although it tended to be larger in the western districts. Three out of every four owners bought lots averaging 3.86 *desiatiny* (10.5 acres) per holding, hardly qualifying them as members of a rural bourgeoisie. The remaining group (25.2 percent) of owners, however, controlled just under 75 percent of all private, non-allotment land held by individual peasants, and from these there had indeed emerged a tiny number of large farm operators with tracts of more than 100 *desiatiny* (the average for these 264 holdings was 208 *desiatiny*). Their weight was most evident in Graivoron and Dmitriev Districts in the south and west, and in Shchigrov, Tim, Staryi Oskol', Novyi Oskol' and Korocha Districts in the east, where 1.6 percent to 3.0 percent of all owners held 23–33 percent of private lands. The process of transfer thus favored a minority of households that disposed of funds to take on more acreage. Since credit institutions were poorly developed in Kursk Province even at the dawn of the twentieth century[116] and in light of a rapid inflation of land values (three times the average for the Empire in this era), these most prosperous peasants must have had clear prior advantages before entering the land market.[117]

---

[115] Just between 1906 and 1914, the landed nobility in Kursk Province will sell off an additional 172,736 *desiatiny*, of which the lion's share (168,533) went to individual peasants, communes and partnerships. Ivanov, "Nekotorye itogi," in *Vekhi minuvshego*, 170; Anfimov and Makarov, *Dinamika zemlevladeniia.*

[116] Sazonov, "O kreditnikh tovarishchestvakh" in *TS-KhSKGZ. 1903 g.*, I: 59–71.

[117] According to the study organized by the provincial office of the State Treasury in late 1906, land prices, as reflected in the purchases underwritten by the Peasant Land Bank, had almost doubled between 1884 and 1907. The average price per *desiatina* registered for purchases of 12,819 *desiatiny* made during 1884–1887 cost 105 rubles per *desiatina*, between 1888 and 1891 (2,311 *desiatiny*) 107 rubles, during 1892–1895 (2,283 *desiatiny*) 113 rubles, for 1896–1899 (22,311 *desiatiny*) 130 rubles, during 1900–1903 (79,485 *desiatiny*) 166 rubles, and between 1904 and 1907 (16,377 *desiatiny*) 194 rubles. Kurskaia kazennaia palata, *op. cit.*, 69–70. These data were roughly similar to central ministry figures (Department of Direct Taxation), which showed that 1 *desiatina* of

The opening of a Peasant Land Bank branch in Kursk in 1884 for extending credit to peasant buyers for land acquisitions—during 1885–1907, it facilitated the purchase of 135,586 *desiatiny* valued at over 21 million rubles—had only a modest impact on this trend. Conservative credit policies of the Bank, which required substantial down payments from prospective purchasers—beyond the means of most households—tended to reinforce the direction of land transfers toward a minority. The Bank's clientèle did include large numbers of peasant partnerships (three or more households) within which various strata of the peasantry were represented. Between 1892 and 1901, of 826 closings (58,839 *desiatiny*) funded by the Bank through loans in total amounting to 6,757,001 rubles, 503 transactions (45,948 *desiatiny*, 5,218,416 rubles) involved partnerships. Analysis of the transactions, though, demonstrated that the Bank insisted on a "creditworthy" clientèle. Prospective buyers had to be able to afford plowland at prices *averaging* 136 rubles per *desiatina* (1885–1907), to lay out the substantial down payments demanded by the Bank in order to obtain loans, and to pay fees for drafting and filing documents, and for the services of the notary, jurist and witnesses.[118] It is not surprising, then, that allotment holders with work stock made up the majority of partnership members; large numbers of potential loan recipients owned private land already at the moment of application. Communes were last on the Bank's list of priorities and appear to have been the object of discriminatory loan

---

land in Kursk Province cost 52 rubles in 1868–1877, 74 rubles in 1878–1887, 110 rubles in 1888–1897. Lands purchased with the aid of the Peasant Land Bank cost 104 rubles between 1883 and 1885, 107 rubles during 1886–1890, 119 rubles during 1891–1895 and 131 rubles during 1896–1900. Glavnoe Upravlenie Zemleustroistva i Zemledeliia, Otdel Sel'skoi Ekonomiki i Sel'skokhoziaistvennoi Statistiki, *op. cit.*, table III, 37. The data, of course, were averaged and concealed very substantial variations. State peasants were by far the leading element in peasant private landownership (77.3% of area) according to materials of the *zemstvo* censuses. The Land Census of 1905 failed to make any distinction between old juridical categories for private lands.

[118] The Tax Inspector for Sudzha District, P. P. Pustovitov, calculated that fees for buying one *desiatina* of land (150 rubles) amounted to about 35 rubles, a full fifth of the price of the land. The burden of such fees grew, of course, for the buyer who could afford only a smaller parcel. ("Doklad Podatnago Inspektora P. P. Pustovitov o polozhenii krest'ianskago khoziaistva v sviazi s lezhashchim na nikh platezhami"), *Trudy mestnykh komitetov*, 619–620. Pustovitov also made interesting observations in this context with respect to the growing importance of written law in peasant life—especially as this concerned transfers (deeds of sale and exchange, testamentary documents) of communal or household acreage. Such observations, which advanced a view that peasants were very conversant with statutory law when it came to their own property, are once again at odds with much of official reporting on peasant "backwardness."

ceilings.[119] As a result of all purchases, land under peasant control in Kursk Province grew from 2,600,980 *desiatiny* in 1877 to 2,830,020 in 1905—a net gain of 8.8 percent.[120] By our estimate, however, the rural population of Kursk Province during this same period (1877–1905) grew by around 29 percent. With steady growth of the population in the rural districts, pressures on resources vital to the subsistence of peasant communities in Kursk Province began to intensify rapidly. These tensions were alleviated to a certain extent by the evolution of "off-farm" wage labor occupations as the crucial outlet for surplus working hands.

8. "Off-Farm" Employment

Reports of the Governor's chancellery demonstrate that Kursk Province experienced a modest restructuring of its industrial plant during 1892–1904: from 22,745 employees in 8,586 enterprises in 1892 (with ruble output 16,696,629), the workforce rose to 27,672 in 5,081 enterprises.

---

[119] Bakhirev and Komarinets, "Obzor deiatel'nosti krest'ianskago banka," in *TS-KhSKGZ. 1903 god*, IV: 15–36. Failure of the Bank to meet the needs of the most hard-pressed peasants—landless and land-poor—is a common theme in the literature and was conceded by state officials. See *Zhurnal Vysochaishe uchrezhdennoi 16-go noiabria 1901 g. Kommissii*, 48–57. This was also to be Governor V. M. Borzenko's verdict in his report on the 1905 unrest. RGIA, f. 1291, op. 122, 1906 g., d. 123 ("Doneseniia gubernatorov o prichinakh agrarnykh besporiadkov"), ll. 43–43 ob. Indeed, the Peasant Land Bank is at times viewed as a state "program" for allowing landowners to liquidate heavily indebted estates at very generous prices, recouping this largesse at the expense of peasant buyers and borrowers. Zak, *Krest'ianskii Pozemel'nyi Bank, 1883–1910*; Vdovin, *Krest'ianskii Pozemel'nyi Bank: 1883–1895 gg.*; Simonova, "Krest'ianskii Pozemel'nyi Bank v sisteme," in *EAIVE. 1966 g.*, 471–484.

[120] Tsentral'nyi statisticheskii komitet, *Statistika zemlevladeniia*, Table I, 10–12. That this estimate may have been optimistic was suggested by the study made by the Kursk *kazennaia palata*. According to the *assessment rolls*, the combined area of allotment and purchased land at the disposal of peasant communities made 2,863,639 *desiatiny* (405,737 in private tenure), while the poll of *volost'* administrations of the winter of 1906 put the total at 2,484,108 *desiatiny*. The compilers contended that the difference was the result of undocumented sale (particularly by *odnodvortsy*) of allotment lands to persons outside the peasant *soslovie*—despite the Law of 14 December 1893, prohibiting this practice. For this reason, and in light of the close collaboration (after abolition of *krugovaia poruka* in 1903) between the Treasury office and village and parish officials in collecting and notating land per household, the study treated the parish responses as more accurate. Kurskaia kazennaia palata, *op. cit.*, 16–17. Peasant proclivities for deliberately understating their assets in these kinds of surveys (and this poll was conducted by tax officials!) were well known to *zemstvo* statisticians (see Verner's observation in Chapter V). Treasury commentators had nothing to say on this issue.

Output doubled to 32,538,794 rubles, driven mainly by new capacity in sugar refining, distillery and processing of grain,[121] but also in the manufacture of bricks, lime and chalk, and in small spinning and wool-washing enterprises that prepared raw materials and engaged in the production of thread.[122] Small units typified industrial plant in the first years of the century, but larger units appeared in sugar and flour processing. This development unfolded in tandem with an extension of railways in the province from 312 track miles in 1892 to 713 miles in 1905, which tied many districts into the national rail network for the first time and generated employment for large numbers of local peasant laborers.[123] For a rural population of about 2.2 million persons (1897), of course, the contingent of workers engaged in industry remained a tiny minority. Industry retained its status as a subordinate branch of agriculture, almost exclusively engaged in processing the produce of the harvest: grain, potatoes, sugarbeets, seed crops and hemp. Increase in annual output in rubles in the province's sugar-refining operations points to an expansion in capacity during this period, in terms of both the number of existing plants and the addition of large new units, as these are shown in Ministry of Finance data.[124] The steady disappearance of windmills in flour production (typically these survived in the eastern districts) symbolized the advance of this industry in Kursk Province and its restructuring on more efficient lines.[125] Data from the Governor's reports on the annual ruble product of

---

[121] *Obzor Kurskoi gubernii. Prilozhenie... za 1892 god* (1893), Vedomost' No. 2; *Obzor Kurskoi gubernii za 1904 god* (1905), Vedomost' No. 2.

[122] The Glushkovskaia (Ryl'sk District) Cloth Factory was founded in the reign of Peter I in 1719 (owned by Tereshchenko in 1905), but there was no further expansion of the industry. Home spinning industries, although they grew in number, became smaller, and Komarinets noted that the increase in the numbers of women in the migrant labor force was associated with the inability of home spinning to compete with Moscow-manufactured cloth. Komarinets, "Otkhozhie promysly," *TS-KhSKGZ. 1903 g.*, II: 48.

[123] Kurskoe gubernskoe *zemstvo. Kurskaia guberniia. Statisticheskii obzor. 1896 g.*, 330. Mileage for 1905 in *Obzor Kurskoi gubernii za 1905 god*, 54.

[124] Ministry of Finance materials for 1880–1881 record 12 refineries with plantings of 8,370 *desiatiny* and a general output of 241,146 tons of sugar, molasses and other products. By 1905–1906, 21 operations with plantations of 53,932 *desiatiny* had elevated output to 970,994 tons (from the annual, *Ezhegodnik Ministerstva finansov* for the relevant years). The plantation area, reported by excise inspectors, would not have included all areas under sugar-beet cultivation on neighboring estates and peasant lands. The governor's reports cited showed increase in ruble output from 7,044,931 rubles in 1892 to 18,940,796 rubles in 1904.

[125] On the major role of flour export in the provincial grain trade, see Lositskii, "Proizvod-stvo khlebov," Kurskoe gubernskoe *zemstvo, Kurskaia guberniia. Statisticheskii obzor, 1896 g.*, 300–367; Komarinets, "Vyvoz khlebov," I: 34–49, II: 15–24.

industry for 1892, 1904 and 1906, however, illustrate the fact that the eastern part of the province—Tim, Fatezh, Shchigrov, Novyi Oskol', Staryi Oskol' and Korocha Districts—lagged far behind central and western districts, especially those in which sugar refiners had organized large-scale production (Putivl', L'gov, Ryl'sk and Belgorod Districts).[126]

Gubernatorial reporting on industry in the province did not refer to ownership, but the Factory Inspectorate regularly recorded this information for plants under its supervision. A 1908 sample, which omits thousands of small peasant enterprises, nonetheless accounts for the major part of the provincial workforce and annual production. From this sample, it is possible to shed some light on the "class" profile of leading elements of Kursk industry in the era of the revolution. Of 173 enterprises listed by the Ministry of Industry and Trade for Kursk Province in 1908 (47,793,454 rubles output), 135 of these (88 percent) were owned or controlled by nobles (60), members of the elite urban estates (53) or corporate interests (22). With a ruble product of 38,195,041 rubles (80 percent of the provincial total), these enterprises dominated the local economic landscapes. Of 129 enterprises for which founding dates could be fixed, over half (66) were founded after 1890, precisely in that era in which grain prices reached their nadir.[127] Even in these larger enterprises, however, the availability of industrial employment was seasonal in character: operations followed the agricultural calendar. Tied closely to the processing of agricultural produce, the mills, refineries and distilleries that produced over 90 percent of Kursk Province's gross annual ruble product and employed 71 percent of its industrial labor operated for four to five months then closed to await start-up at the end of the following agricultural year.

More extended in terms of time was employment in handicrafts, which underwent an impressive growth (55.2 percent) in the 1890s[128] and continued to expand thereafter. The numbers of persons engaged full time in handicraft pursuits grew from 15,451 persons with total annual incomes of

---

[126] *Obzor Kurskoi gubernii. Prilozhenie... za 1892 god* (1893), Vedomost' No. 2; *Obzor Kurskoi gubernii za 1904 god* (1905), Vedomost' No. 2; *Obzor Kurskoi gubernii za 1906 god* (1907).

[127] Ministerstvo Torgovli i Promyshlennosti (V. E. Varzar, ed.), *Spisok*, I: 46, 80, 111, 158, 222–223, 285; II: 73–75, 178–179.

[128] The Governor's report for 1892 noted 15,451 persons registered as engaged in handicraft industries, with total incomes of 852,960 rubles. In the report of 1897, the number had risen to 19,556 persons with total wages of 1,062,106 rubles, and for 1899, 23,017 persons with total wages of 1,285,221 rubles. *Obzor Kurskoi gubernii za (1892, 1897, 1899) god*).

852,960 rubles in 1892 to 38,258 with annual incomes of 2,643,000 rubles by 1905.[129] Average incomes were lowest in the eastern and northern (Shchigrov, Tim and Fatezh) districts (except for Novyi Oskol' District, where incomes were highest in the province) and generally higher in the west and south.[130] *Zemstvo* surveys of 1882–1884 found the highest percentages of "households with members engaged in industrial occupations" in Novyi Oskol' (734 per 1,000 families), Belgorod (756) and Graivoron (759) Districts, which appear to have held the principal place in the province's handicraft production.[131] Often depicted as symptomatic of the decline of agriculture—and we will see that in significant cases there was much truth to this view—expansion in handicraft employment must also testify to the growth of local demand for goods and services.

Small crafts had always existed as a supplement to agriculture in the off-season and were oriented mainly toward production for household use. In the late nineteenth century, full-time handicraft employment in Kursk Province attained a semi-industrial status in various branches of production. According to the Governor's reports, its largest branch (8,576 persons in 1905) prepared hides and put out an array of boots, shoes, belts, harnesses, sheepskin coats and other items. Woodworking (carpenters of various specialties, makers of sleds and carts, wheelwrights, coopers) followed with 5,760 workers and, though ever-more restricted by advancing deforestation of the province, retained centers near the larger state forests: Nekliudovskaia Parish (Korocha District) and the big villages of Novyi Oskol' District. Some 4,000 persons were noted in the report as engaged in the making of garments of various kinds in 1905, mainly near the district seats and the town of Kursk. The province still boasted some

---

[129] *Obzor Kurskoi gubernii za 1905 god*, 18–31.

[130] From the Governor's report for 1899, average annual wage per worker was lowest in Belgorod District at 21 rubles 53 kopecks, in Korocha District at 31 rubles 10 kopecks, in Staryi Oskol' District at 38 rubles 59 kopecks, in Shchigrov District at 39 rubles 18 kopecks in Oboian District, at 39 rubles 38 kopecks, and in Fatezh District at 40 rubles 18 kopecks. Substantially larger annual incomes appear for Dmitriev District (64 rubles 41 kopecks), L'gov District (67 rubles 18 kopecks) and Sudzha District (70 rubles 15 kopecks). The average annual wage for a handicraftsman in Novyi Oskol' District stood at 91 rubles 81 kopecks for 1899. In the same year, however, the average annual wage for persons engaged in handicraft industries in the city of Kursk—quite obviously full-time—stood at 247 rubles 62 kopecks.

[131] In 1892, 10,956 (70.9%) of the total number of 15,451 handicraftsmen recorded in the Governor's report for that year were concentrated in these three districts. Even if this preeminence had eroded by 1899, it was imposing: of 23,017 handicraftsmen counted in that year, 12,990 (56.4%) were based here.

2,644 blacksmiths, but smithing retained the status of an independent profession in very few districts. Local ceramics had benefited from the easy availability of clays of good plasticity and composition since the sixteenth century, but with inflation of prices for wood, exhaustion of easily accessible clays and an influx of cheaper imports at the bazaars, the craft had experienced a steady decline. Some 1,500 potters remained active in 1905 in many of the bigger rural villages. Less numerous were those artisans that made wooden agricultural tools, baskets, woven rugs, tablecloths, rope, string, fishing nets—the standard product of household fabrication. Other crafts bore uniquely local characters. At Borisovka, icon painting engaged 900 masters (the craft was hereditary) and some 450 framers and finishers. In the southeastern corner of Ryl'sk District, at Snagost', peasant artisans specialized in producing felt goods, and in Blagodatenskaia Parish rural craftsmen made scythes that were prized throughout Russia.[132] Notwithstanding its growth as a branch of labor, numbers of workers and income, the fortunes of the handicraft industry closely mirrored the levels of peasant demand and revealed a marked tendency to expand and contract in relation to harvests.[133] Furthermore, the industry was beset by numerous handicaps:

> The negative aspects of the handicraft industry are bound up with insufficiency of knowledge among craftsmen, the imperfections in their tools and methods of production, in the lack of minor credit and its great expense, in the difficulties experienced in procur-

---

[132] *Obzor Kurskoi gubernii za 1904 god*, 13–26; *Obzor Kurskoi gubernii za 1905 god*, 18–31. Processes in handicraft manufacture in Dobrotvorskii, *SSSKG. Otdel obshchii. Ch. II. Promysly*, 124–213, and the detailed descriptions, by district, in the 1904 *zemstvo* publication, *Materialy po issledovaniiu kustarnoi promyshlennosti v Kurskoi gubernii*. Legends among the icon painters in Borisovka held that the art had come to the village from St. Petersburg when, in 1710, Field Marshal Count B. P. Sheremet'ev founded the nearby Bogoroditsa-Tikhvinskii Convent in honor of Peter's victory at Poltava and had invited the icon painter Ignat'ev to adorn the chapel.

[133] The Governor's reports discontinued district breakdowns in the *Obzory* after 1899, so distributions of the benefits in the expansion of handicraft industries, actively encouraged by state and *zemstvo* institutions, are not known. The data on handicraft earnings in Kursk Province do tend to show that, if the average for the province tended to improve only slightly during the 1890s, variations by district meant that some localities did better than others did. The materials assembled by the Governor's chancellery showed a decline in the earnings of *kustarniki* in Novyi Oskol' District's big villages (even though they retained larger incomes than elsewhere) and substantial losses among Shchigrov District's handicraftsmen. The gross figure for 1905, averaging to 95.22 rubles per worker, implies a real jump in compensation—and perhaps, as well, that handicraft occupations were beginning to evolve toward something more than auxiliary employment.

ing raw materials and the sale of finished products, and in the harmful interference of middlemen. It is thus only in certain branches—namely in those directly serving peasant needs or in those based on the easy availability of the necessary materials—that production has exhibited a certain development and expansion. For these reasons, handicrafts that are motivated by peasant demand (and not relying on sale) very often border upon fully formed industrial trades and undoubtedly bear such a character.[134]

The chronic problems of handicraftsmen drew much public attention and became a special object of *zemstvo* expenditures: subsidies or micro-credit, sponsorship of shops, small-scale plants, special schools and programs to promote sales and educate the artisans on sanitation.[135] Nevertheless, one *zemstvo* specialist wrote the following, in 1903:

> First, craftsmen rarely possess good machines, tools, lathes and instruments with which they ought to work, and this circumstance causes them to lose time, to produce less of a product and a product of poorer quality at that. Second, there are often difficulties in purchasing raw material at the right price and, lastly, wares often do not find buyers, not because the goods are poor, but because the craftsmen themselves are unable to or cannot disseminate them, not knowing how to attract customers. Quite a great difficulty for the craftsman (almost the most critical) lies in shortages of circulating capital, precisely at the moment when it is necessary to buy materials. Not possessing such capital, they are obliged to borrow money—using the goods to be produced as collateral—and rapidly fall into the hands of intermediaries and usurers, whose services are more expensive than those of any other sort of agent. Paying off their debts with their wares, the craftsmen are often forced to give up such goods at a price considerably lower than that at which these middlemen later sell them, and as such, the handicraftsmen are deprived of a large part of their incomes.[136]

By and large, despite expansion of numbers of workers and of incomes over time, handicraft employment thus retained an unstable, poorly organized and under-equipped aspect. It is not be without interest even here to stress that handicraft industries were most closely associated with big rural centers in which, more than elsewhere, they attained the status of year-round rural industries.[137] In analyses of the subset of villages associ-

---

[134] *Obzor Kurskoi guberniia. Prilozhenie... za 1892 g.*, 19.

[135] *Zemstvo* programs to improve this sector described in *Obzor Kurskoi gubernii za (1899, 1900, 1902) god*, in section V ("Promysly sel'skago i gorodskogo naseleniia"); Anisimov, "Svedeniia," *TS-KhSKGZ. 1903 g.*, I: 78–84; *Ocherk deiatel'nosti Sudzhanskago uyezdnago zemstvo*, passim.

[136] V. I. Anisimov, "O kustarnoi vystavke," *TS-KhSKGZ. 1903 g.*, I: 48–49.

[137] In particular, Veliko-Mikhailovka, Chernianka, Ol'shanka, Slonovka, Khalan, Pokrovskoe and Ninovka in Novyi Oskol' District; Orlik, Obukhovka, Kazatskaia, Ezdotskoe and Iamskaia in Staryi Oskol' District; Zimoven'ka, Korenek-Alekseevka, and Strelitsa in Korocha District; Tomarovka, Shopino, Plosskoe, Temovka and Pokrovka

ated in the documentary record with rural disorders during 1905–1906, we will have occasion to see that these big country "towns" often stood at the center of peasant unrest.

9. Labor Migration: *"Otkhod na storonu"*

Industrial and handicraft employments, taken together, were not sufficient to provide off-farm work in the measure that natural increase in the population demanded. It is thus not surprising that Kursk Province, by the late 1890s, became the largest net exporter of labor in the Empire when a balance of in-migration and out-migration is calculated.[138] The peasant-workers leaving the village in search of wage employment followed in the footsteps of those who had resettled permanently outside the province, principally going to the fields, factories, mines and construction sites of South Russia, New Russia and east to the Black Sea ports as far as Batumi. Already in the mid-1880s, the *zemstvo* household censuses of Kursk Province recorded 130,055 male migrant workers (*otkhodniki*) in all fifteen districts, constituting 27.5 percent of all 473,098 males of working age (aged 18 to 60 years). Particularly high rates of migration were noted for Graivoron District and those in the eastern part of the province.[139] Passport data from the parish administrative archives, published by the

---

in Belgorod District; Goncharnaia, Zaoleshanka and Miropol' in Sudzha District; Mikhailovka and Kutka in Dmitriev District; Melekhino and Velikii Ol'khovat in Shchigrov District; Kozhlia and Droniaevo in L'gov District; Apalkovaia and Zvegintsevo-Kamyshevka in Kursk District; Linovo in Putivl' District; Borisovka in Graivoron District; Snagost' in Ryl'sk District.

[138] Tikhonov, *op, cit.*, 93–94.

[139] For Graivoron District, the census recorded 16,657 of 36,005 working-age males (46.3%) as *otkhodniki*. Analogous numbers were collected for Belgorod District: 14,506 of 32,943 (44.0%). Novyi Oskol' District (10,966 of 32,062 or 34.2%) and Staryi Oskol' District (10,253 of 30,821 or 33.3%) released around a third of their working-age population. Three other districts—Korocha (10,851 of 33,963: 31.9%), Ryl'sk (9,444 of 30,743: 30.7%) and Oboian (10,750 of 36,005: 29.9%) exported just under a third. The census for Kursk District, with the province's largest town, listed only 2,209 migrant workers for its population of 35,196 males of working age (5.8%). The Statistical Bureau's teams went to great lengths to register these persons as part of the local populace (*nalichnoe naselenie*) by reviewing all the passport data in the parish records prior to visiting the villages, at which time they tried to verify their findings. For obvious reasons—migrant workers did not always apply for papers—this method was not entirely accurate.

zemstvo in numbers of its annual agricultural digest between 1899 and 1906,[140] illustrate the fact that out-migration from the province had grown noticeably since the census.[141] Excluding one-month or five-year passes and counting only three-month, six-month and one-year passports, annual issue for 1898–1905 averages 235,160 documents: 195,174 to males (86.3 percent), 30,903 to females and 9,082 to families. Papers granting absence for one year (211,506) dominate all issues (87.4 percent), a development that dates to the 1890s.[142] In the sample of one-year passports for 1898–

---

[140] *TS-KhSKGZ za (1898–1905) gg.* Use of passport data raises certain questions, since the activities—and *de facto* residential status—of those who got papers and left the province are not indicated. For this reason, I have excluded five-year passports, which most of all seem to resemble permanent settlement, and one-month documents. The relationship of passport data to out-migration is subject to various evaluations. Based on examination of data from the central districts of Kursk Province (Dmitriev, Kursk, L'gov, Sudzha and Fatezh), N. A. Dobrotvorskii felt that the relationship between numbers of passports and numbers of migrant laborers was a close one. Dobrotvorskii, *Promysly*, 52–55. Editors of the provincial agricultural journal treated them as synonymous. B. V. Tikhonov (*op. cit.*, 104–147), conversely, opined that passport data really underestimated migration: the undocumented migrant was common. In all probability, a sort of *de facto* emigration complicates the problem. Annual *Reports* (*Obzory*) of the provincial Governor contain data—collected and sent in by District Police Commandants—on numbers of persons leaving the province for wage earnings (*dal'nie zarabotki*) that are considerably lower than passport issues. For the same years (1898–1905), numbers of *otkhodniki* in the Reports average 127,793 persons, average numbers of passports 235,160. I assume that local police accounted only for those who departed and *returned* in the reporting year. Large numbers of the remainder are simply renewing their passports through the mails.

[141] From passport data for five districts surveyed during 1882–1883 (Dmitriev, L'gov, Sudzha, Fatezh and Kursk Districts) that he used for his 1884 study, Dobrotvorskii counted 34,518 total issues for various terms. In addition, the Tim and Graivoron District volumes (1884) show, respectively, 6,556 and 10,783 issues. Of 51,857 issues, 7,149 (13.8%) were for one-year absences, which Dobrotvorskii characterized as "sent mainly to peasants who live continually, for several years, on earnings in far-off locales, but who have not yet re-registered out of their communes." *Promysly*, 53. Annual issue for these same districts during 1898–1905 averages 100,395 passports for various terms. One-year passports account for 89,703 (89.3%).

[142] According to data collected by the "Commission on the Center," this phenomenon was general typical of the Central Agricultural Region. During 1861–1870, six-month passports made up 47.1% of all issues (1,436,000), passports for 1–3 months 14.6% (443,900), one-year passports 38.1% (1,160,900). During the 1870s and 1880s, three-month passports grew in importance, to 4,650,500 or 49.7% of all passports issued in 1871–1880, and to 6,512,300 or 50.7% of issues during 1881–1890. At the same time, all other types receded in relative importance even while registering substantial gains: six-month documents to 2,741,300 (29.3% of all issues) and 3,681,500 (28.7%); one-

1905, Belgorod District led all *uyezdy* with 19,580 passports issued annually, Kursk District was second with 19,317, Ryl'sk District third with 17,415, Oboian District fourth with 16,370, and Fatezh District fifth with 16,261.[143] Aligned closely to the agricultural calendar, issuance grew consecutively from September to March and reached its peak in April, the low points coinciding with harvest and winter plantings during June, July and August.

According to local observers, factors of population density, *per capita* allotment area, yield at harvest, the province's historically low wages, and the degree to which off-farm employment in specific localities had developed sufficiently to retain labor all conspired in this equation. M. V. Komarinets wrote in the *zemstvo*'s agricultural digest for 1903:

> The population of Kursk Province, occupying an area of 780 square miles [*German geographical mile, 24,500 ft.—BRM*], totals over 2,600,000 persons. In other words, about 3,330 persons populate 1 square mile, although in agricultural regions with the three-field system of farming (to which Kursk Province belongs), the greatest density of population, according to observations of economists, never reaches even 3,000. In such conditions, naturally, not all of the population of Kursk Province is able to find the means to satisfy its needs within the *guberniia*: a part of it must search out places for applying its labor in other more sparsely settled regions or go over to non-agricultural occupations at home or outside the province. The peasants' agricultural labor, given contemporary modes of cultivation in their economies and the agricultural economy of the province generally, is not sufficiently productive to cover all their economic requirements. Given average conditions, the land in their possession yields harvests that are insufficient for the consumption needs of the families of a significant majority of the populace. Here, a bit worse or a slightly better quality of land plays a negligible role: in Kursk Province, there are no lands that justify the weight of taxes and obligations attached to them and if such exist, they are a rare exception, since broadly speaking, yields in the province are fairly uniform. Given his relative lack of sufficient land [*malozemel'e*], the peasant's "take" from his farming activities only very rarely covers, apart from consumption needs, the financial demands of taxation, acquisition of necessary inventory and purchases of consumer goods available only on the market (tea, kerosene, sugar, and so on).[144]

---

year passports to 1,965,300 (21% of all issues) and 2,632,000 (20.5%). During 1891–1900, these proportions changed completely: the number of passports for one to three months and for six months decreased, respectively, to 5,801,300 (30.9% of all issues) and 3,239,600 (17.2%); numbers of one-year passports exploded from 2,632,000 in 1881–1890 to 9,448,100—50.3% of all issues. *Materialy Vysochaishe utverzhdennoi 16-go noiabria 1901 g. kommissii*, Table XX.

[143] *TS-KhSKGZ za (1898–1905) goda.* Shchigrov District averaged 15,438 one-year passports, Korocha District 13,666, Staryi Oskol' District 13,648, Dmitriev District 12,853, Putivl' District 11,806, Novyi Oskol' District 11,761, Tim District 11,753, L'gov District 11,457, Sudzha District 10,446 and Graivoron District, 9,634.

[144] Komarinets, "Otkhozhie promysly," II: 42–57.

Exact proportions of agricultural and non-agricultural workers within the annual labor migration are impossible to determine. The Governor's annual report for 1906 gave an impressionistic picture of these occupations in which agricultural labor and unskilled workers of all sorts (*chernorabochie*) made up six out of every ten migrants.[145] N. A. Dobrotvorskii, an associate of the Statistical Bureau, published a study based on census interviews from 1882–1883 in the central part of the province (Kursk, L'gov, Sudzha, Fatezh and Dmitriev Districts), which revealed that of the 58,775 males registered as engaging in 122 different occupations (*promysly*), 29,245 left the province for earnings. Of these, 12,564 (43 percent) worked in agriculture-related employment (11,660 field hands) and 16,681 in non-agricultural occupations.[146] Of special note were those employed in what peasants themselves called *mastershchina*: Dobrotvorskii counted 12,004 skilled tradesmen, mainly in construction (carpenters, sawyers, stone and brick masons, roofers, stovemakers), but in wood- or metalworking, carriage making and other trades as well.[147]

---

[145] The Governor's report estimated, quite generally (no figures), that agricultural laborers made up 32% of labor migrants and unskilled workers of all sorts 29%. Of the rest, carpenters, furniture makers and coopers made up 9%, stone and brick masons 9%, miners 9%, railway workers 3%, traders and middlemen 2%, plasterers, carters, leatherworkers and servants each 1%, and "other" 12%. The latter included sawyers, stove makers, roofers, blacksmiths, metalworkers, woodworkers, sailors, skilled factory workers. *Obzor Kurskoi gubernii za 1906 god*, 40.

[146] These included the following: 1) 1,480 workers in industry and transport (including 604 railway workers and 802 factory workers), 2) 633 small traders, 3) 294 handicraftsmen (including 107 coopers), 4) 1,924 persons of various "professions" (among them 671 bakers, 414 domestics, 279 watchmen, 199 woodcutters, 49 policemen, 48 waiters and 85 sailors, these latter all from Zamostianskaia and Krinichanskaia Parishes adjacent to the town of Sudzha), 5) 346 persons of the "literate" professions (scribes, teachers, nurses, administrative personnel), and 12,004 skilled tradesmen. Dobrotvorskii, *Promysly*, chart, II: 60–69.

[147] These trades differed from handicraft in that all work was performed only for hire or by order. In order to gain mastery and reputation, they required a long and careful apprenticeship, during which the novice accumulated the tools and experience in their use that qualified him and won him sufficient respect. Wages for a master "of the first hand" (150–200 rubles for a seven-month tour) were quite commonly two or three times those for a worker "of the third hand" or a novice. Tradesmen arranged for work outside the province through contractors—preferring "their own" locals to outsiders for obvious reasons. The contractors commonly made much-needed cash advances (*zadatki*) to hard-pressed tradesmen in winter and thus had at their call up to 200 carpenters and stonemasons for a given project when the construction season opened in spring. With experience of working abroad (and of contractors' manipulations), however, many tradesmen formed their own associations of 12–18 members, electing their own fore-

In preparing the annual reports, District Police Commandants were ordered to submit data on numbers of migrants—presumably those that left *and returned*—and their earnings. Both indices rose: from 1892 (103,259 workers) to 1904 (133,113 workers), reported earnings more than doubled from 2,207,820 to 5,813,075 rubles.[148] The surveys of the 1880s presented data only for male *otkhodniki*: the female component among the migrants was considered negligible.[149] Passport data for 1898–1905 revealed a changed picture. Female recipients of one-year issues rose from 27,812 in 1898 (11.9 percent of issues) to 33,061 in 1904 (14.3 percent): "in other words, every fourteenth female of working age is forced by conditions of life to look for earnings at a distance from her home."[150] Families taking out one-year passports climbed from 6,637 in 1898 to 11,067 in 1904. To some extent, then, one must see in this movement a sort of *de facto* emigration to new places of residence, keeping in mind the fact that the vast majority of all passports were for one year.

Even in the short interval of eight years for which district data were available, annual passport issuance in Kursk Province showed itself to be sensitive to the crisis of 1899 and its effect on South Russian industry.[151] The Bureau also polled its correspondents each year to assess whether, on balance, local *otkhodniki* had had success or failure in actually finding work. Out of 100 correspondents, 36 noted failure in 1898, 28 in 1899, 23 in 1900, 57 in 1901 and 35 in 1902. For 1905, 596 of 1,000 correspondents reported that local migrant workers had generally failed to find work during sojourns in the South.[152] Even if it did not affect all districts

---

men and treasurers, who were charged with the business of the group. These traveled to South Russia in the company of one or two other members to make contracts over terms of hire and to arrange travel, living quarters and board. *Ibid.*, 39–44.

[148] In 1912, local officials counted 148,964 workers reporting 8,852,368 rubles in earnings.

[149] Verner, ed., *Kurskaia guberniia*, 178.

[150] Komarinets, "Otkhozhie promysly," 44.

[151] *TS-KhSKGZ za... god* (Kursk, 1899–1906). For most districts, 1898 remained the high point of issuance of passports for males (three-month, six-month and one-year terms) in the data set for 1898–1905. Sudzha, Tim, L'gov, Putivl', Staryi Oskol' and Oboian Districts registered consecutive annual declines during 1899–1903. Data for 1903 showed contraction in all districts (save for Ryl'sk District) in comparison to the preceding year. Contraction of issuance for 1905 relative to the previous year was noted in ten districts, but was significant only in Novyi Oskol' (from 11,181 issues to 10,053; -10.1%) and Dmitriev (12,040 to 10,577; -12.1%) districts.

[152] This poll was a regular feature in the section on labor migration in *TS-KhSKGZ za... god* for 1898 to 1902 and 1905. For reasons unknown, it was not included for 1903 and

equally, the capacity of labor migration to remove excess labor from rural districts was increasingly hampered. This trend reflected two larger historical contexts. As has been noted elsewhere, the growing mechanization of agriculture in the southern and southeastern provinces of New Russia (to which the vast majority of itinerant agricultural workers from Kursk migrated) had shortened terms of hire, extended periods of idleness and made work more dangerous.[153]

> Twenty years ago, when the harvests were taken in by hand all over the South, rural entrepreneurs from New Russia often turned to the services of various agents, who concluded agreements with the workers and made cash advances [*zadatki*] to them. But after a time, when agricultural machines came into wide use in all of New Russia (especially harvesters), demand for labor in the South was sharply reduced. Not only did the usual tide of laborers not recede but, under the influence of increasingly unfavorable conditions of agricultural production in Central Black Earth and Southwestern *gubernii*, it began to grow progressively. South Russian farmers ceased to avail themselves of workers by summons—the flood of labor exceeded all demand even without this measure. The value of labor fell, wages were cut, but every year hundreds and even thousands of workers from Kursk, Orel, Chernigov, Mogilev and Kiev Provinces failed to find work even at these reduced wages.[154]

These observations found their way into official reports as well, in exactly the same terms. For the year 1897, when Kursk Province (and most of the CAR) was in the throes of crop failure, the annex to the governor's report described a grim situation:

> It is necessary to attest the fact that the agricultural character of these pursuits in the places to which the workers migrate are identical in character with those in Kursk and the other Central Black Earth provinces, causes a uniformity in the supply of migrant

---

1904. Correspondents answering numbered 398 in 1898, 466 in 1899, 321 in 1900, 313 in 1901, 435 in 1902 and 1,000 in 1905.

[153] Mixter, "The Hiring Market" in E. Kingston-Mann and T. R. Mixter, eds., *op. cit.,* 312.

[154] Komarinets, "Otkhozhie promysly," 52–53. The author noted that more expensive machines had become increasingly common among peasant proprietors in the South Russian provinces. "Application of improved agricultural machines speeds up work on the peasant's own economy and gives him the possibility of hiring himself out for field work not with empty hands or with just the traditional scythe, but with a single-share, iron plow (*plug*), with a seeder, with a harvester, with a thresher. Four years ago, when the Falts-Fein estate, famous throughout the South, applied to nearby villages with a summons to work with their harvesters, word of the estate's request quickly spread through the surrounding countryside and at the appointed time, peasants with 2,000 harvesters appeared on the premises, though only a tenth of that number was needed. This fact shows how much conditions of work in all of New Russia have deteriorated for migrant labor." (53)

workers and thus promotes a strong competition between them. The interests of the laborers come into mutual confrontation, especially in periods of crop failure, when the supply of working hands far exceeds demand. But given the simultaneous decline of harvests and the contraction of demand for hands due to the employment of agricultural machinery on the (southern) estates that spreads more and more with each passing year, the saddest of all is that this flood of workers grows. Thus many migrant workers return with empty pockets, having expended the monies taken for the road in feeding themselves.[155]

The industrial crisis of 1900–1903 vastly compounded the unstable situation of Kursk Province's migrant workforce, since it sorely affected industry-related and construction occupations. A consequence of a severe credit crunch in European financial institutions, upon which both Russian industry and state budgets were highly dependent, the financial crisis of 1899 had the effect of suddenly starving overextended industrial structures of operating capital at low interest rates, caused a hiatus in lucrative government orders and disrupted operations in the market as a whole. Industrial stocks plunged and inventories began to accumulate, provoking a steep fall in prices. Production in the heavy industrial sectors fell dramatically; factories and mines shut down in many localities. South Russian industry, closely linked to European capital, was particularly devastated.[156] Komarinets pointed to plant closures and cutbacks in production at iron ore pits and coal mines, strongly depressing the demand for labor, as a major factor in decline of the male component of labor migration down to the end of 1902. The industrial crisis had serious effects on construction activity as well, since big projects were very much tied to the fortunes of industry.[157] Hopeful signs of recovery in 1903 were overshadowed by the outbreak of the Russo-Japanese war in 1904. Rising state military expenditures, financed in part by resort to capital markets, reignited the credit problem; stocks on the Bourse fell precipitously. Railway construction, one of the great engines for output of ferrous metals and a steady source of off-farm employment in Kursk Province during the 1890s, greatly reduced in 1900–1903, ground to a halt. Locomotives and rolling stock,

---

[155] *Obzor Kurskoi gubernii za 1897 god*, 22.

[156] Anan'ich, *Rossiia i mezhdunarodnyi kapital*; Liashchenko, *Istoriia narodnogo khoziaistvo SSSR*, II: 230–261. Bovykin, "Dinamika," *ISSSR*, 1983, 3: 20–52; Rashin, *Formirovanie*, 40–72.

[157] On South Russian industry and its capital foundations, see Rieber, *Merchants and Entrepreneurs*, 219–255; McKay, *Pioneers for Profit*; Gefter, "Iz istorii monopolisticheskogo kapitalizma," *IZ*, 38 (1951), 104–153, Gefter, "Tsarizm i monopolisticheskii kapital," *IZ*, 43 (1953), 70–130; Shpolianskii, *Monopolii*.

drawn into deployments of men and ordinance to the Far East, became less available for the use of civilian industry. Military orders generated some advances in metallurgical and mining branches of South Russian industry in 1904, but these were achieved by intensifying work schedules at a reduced number of installations. These were not sufficient to elevate prices and did not extend much benefit to the plummeting fortunes of industry and construction in the region as a whole. Labor unrest throughout the South disrupted industrial operations in early 1905 and industry came to a standstill during the weeks of the national rail strike.[158]

To the extent to which resettlement to the peripheries of the Empire continued and South Russian industry and agriculture acted as venues for soaking up annual migrations of increasing numbers of working-age persons, a considerable portion of natural increase in the rural population of Kursk Province was removed from the rural districts. Variations in the numbers of those leaving the province to find work and unfavorable estimates of their success or failure in finding jobs, however, show that the years preceding the events of 1905–1906 witnessed instability or contraction in the availability of work in these locales.[159] Interruption in patterns of labor migration meant the enforced presence in the village of a social element that was often more literate, diverse in life experience and occupations and commonly at odds with traditional rural familial and social hierarchies. Official reporting, assessments of *zemstvo* specialists and monographic literature on *pre-mortem* household partitions have repeatedly referred to young migrant workers as an irritant in the family and communal order. For the issue relates not simply to tensions within

---

[158] Even these general indices (drawn from the relevant years of *Ezhegodnik Ministerstva Finansov*) suggest that, especially in 1904, recovery had involved increases of production at a reduced number of facilities. These data showed that in 1899, 747 coal pits in Ekaterinoslav Province and the Don Region produced 499,233,078 *poods* of coal, 63,405,657 *poods* of anthracite and 103,623,431 *poods* of coking coal. In 1904, 640 operations mined 714,579,949 *poods* of coal, 82,555,966 *poods* of anthracite and 146,092,557 *poods* of coking coal. In 1899, 92 iron ore pits (35 smelters) had an output of 170,542,708 *poods* of ore, 147,356,279 *poods* of smelted iron and 82,044,832 *poods* of pig iron. In 1904, at 61 pits (44 smelters), production had risen to 205,258,562 *poods* of ore, 176,652,972 *poods* of smelted iron and 106,356,457 *poods* of pig iron.

[159] Observations on the labor migration from the Governor's reports for 1892, 1897, 1898, 1899, 1902 and 1904–1906 attest that migrant earnings were notably higher in the first years of the new century. Dmitriev District, with its high share of laborers in non-agricultural occupations, reported the highest annual average at 61 rubles 31 kopecks; Korocha District the lowest at 21 rubles 58 kopecks. Provincial average for the eight years for which these observations were made public was 37 rubles 66 kopecks.

households. Even in the mid-1880s, Dobrotvorskii found that, among the thousands of skilled tradesmen who regularly left the province for work, the experience of migration correlated with considerable differences in literacy, styles of dress and intellectual interests. On village streets, peasant-workers were readily distinguishable by their citified clothing and leather boots, "which moved and quickened the heartbeats of all the village beauties":

> Their houses are always neat, high-ceilinged and well illuminated. Inside, one finds that wonderful cleanliness and tidiness that recalls Little Russia. You will always see some pictures on the wall, depicting both religious and secular figures. Here one will find the life of Saint Barbara the Martyr in pictures, and Il'ia Muromets killing the infamous Solovei the Bandit, who had settled in the twelve oaks on the great highway. Here also is Anika the Warrior conversing with Death, and Bova the Prince, attacking a whole army with his whip. Yet here you also find the heroes of the last Russo-Turkish War, Gurko, Skobelev and others, and even a picture of Bismarck, torn from some illustrated magazine. If we should direct a question on this last, we would be politely told that all they do, this Bismarck and that Englishwoman, is to plot against Russia. It is an evident fact that in this advanced, more cultured mass of peasants among this type of tradesman, who has "descended from" and taken the measure of almost the whole of Russia, an interest in public affairs and politics has begun to awaken... Migration to far-off places has accustomed him to generalizing facts and has given him understandings—even if rather peculiar, *"na svoi saltyk"*—of larger world events taking place somewhere out there, far away, which sometimes have neither the slightest connection with the village nor the capacity to interest it. Together with the widening of his geographical horizon, so to speak, his intellectual horizon has also expanded. The sum of his knowledge has grown and his thinking has acquired a capacity to draw conclusions and make generalizations that already transcend the sphere of village life. Observe with what interest they follow the newspapers, to which the local parish administrations subscribe in localities with highly developed migrant trades. The parish scribes often complained to us: "You can't keep newspapers in supply, they pass them from hand to hand and read them, and there are never any left for us to paper the walls and ceilings. But you can't keep them, because nowadays they get abusive: 'You subscribe to the papers with our money, with our public funds! It's not for you alone to use them!'" Many tradesmen themselves subscribe to newspapers, among which *The Light* and *Village Herald* are especially popular, because they are cheap.[160]

That events that took place in regions traditionally frequented by migrant laborers from Kursk Province should influence the moods of such peas-

---

[160] Dobrotvorskii, *Promysly*, 226–227. For the larger implications of this growing mobility of peasant labor out of the villages, the ties that bound them to their homes and the tensions that arose out of this ambiguous status, see the excellent analysis produced by Jeffrey Burds, *Peasant Dreams and Market Politics: Labor Migration and the Russian Village, 1861–1905.*

ant-workers in the period immediately preceding the outbreaks of 1905–1906 should therefore not be surprising. The critical situation of South Russian industry, as is well known, sparked a period of intense labor unrest among the industrial workers of the region's principal urban centers. It began with strikes in the main shops of the Vladikavkaz Railway in Rostov-on-Don that rapidly drew in a large proportion of the city's workforce during 4–26 November 1902—after which the strikes were suppressed by military force—and attracted national attention. The ensuing labor movement in South Russia reached a peak in July–August 1903, when strikes of an extended and general (across branches) character spread to major centers in South Russia (Kherson, Tauride, Ekaterinoslav, Kiev, Poltava and Chernigov Provinces) and the Caucasus (Tiflis, Batum, Baku and Kutais Provinces).[161] It is to stretch the point too far, in my view, to say that peasant migrants formed enduring party affiliations or adopted ideological views often ascribed to them in the Soviet historical literature.

Yet there is truth to the proposition that such events laid a militant veneer on the sense drawn by the itinerant laborer from his position somewhat apart from the peasant "fold" and his more unstable fortunes in the years immediately preceding the outbreak of peasant unrest in 1905. Investigators were later to point to politicization of local migrant workers as a factor in separate cases of rural protest in Kursk Province during the revolution. In addition, the employment of heads of household in the migrant labor force—and such cases were not unusual for small families units still heavily dependent on cash income—was commonly associated with *de facto* abandonment of allotment economy, either by letting out the strips or by contracting for its cultivation with a fellow villager, a reshuffling of land resources that benefited those who remained behind. Close association of some villages with highly developed trades or out-migration at times even led to the adoption of collective cultivation (*pomoshch'*) as a usual practice.[162] The *zemstvo*'s local correspondents often

---

[161] Balabanov, *Ocherki*, III: 265–346; Chugaev, ed., *Vseobshchaia stachka*; Bortnikov, *Iiul'skie dni*; Kir'ianov, *Perekhod*, 63–110. Descriptions of separate strike actions in L. M. Ivanov, ed., *Rabochee dvizhenie v Rossii v 1901–1904 gg.*, and articles in Gessen, ed., *Arkhiv istorii truda v Rossii*, by I. Bender, "Zlatoustovskaia zabastovka," Book IV (1922), Ch. 2, 50–53; "Iz stachechnogo dvizheniia na Kavkaze v 1903 g.," in Book V (1922): 23–27; and "K stachechnomu dvizheniiu na Iuge Rossii v 1903 g.," in Book VI–VII (1923): 183–187 (Kiev, Ekaterinoslav).

[162] N. A. Dobrotvorskii, "Saiany," *Vestnik Evropy*, 133: 1 (1888), 197–213. Dobrotvorskii considered the Saiany to be survivors of the ancient *Severiane*, the aboriginal residents

identified how the scale of labor migration in a given locality acted as a factor in holding up wage levels. Termination of such arrangements in event of a sustained economic downturn in South Russian industry or disruption of activity during intervals of social turmoil, when many migrant workers returned to their homes, must also have fostered tensions in the home villages. It was precisely this "unruly"—and unemployed—element that was to be circulating within peasant communities in Kursk Province at the worst possible moment.

The foregoing broad sketch of the background to the disorders in the country districts of Kursk Province during 1905–1906 highlights the problems encountered in any attempt to assess the conditions of the rural economy in Russia in the pre-revolutionary era. Movements of the crude demographic indices, and especially of the decline in mortality, together with data that demonstrate that *per capita* availability of grain kept pace with natural increase in the population, plainly make it less plausible to speak of a "crisis" of the rural order in the sense in which the term has often been applied. The evidence is extremely fragmentary, but there is also some indication that disposable income among peasants in Kursk Province expanded in the period under review. In contrast, there can be no question that substantial reduction of quantities of arable allotment land available for peasant cultivation, driven by population increase, was only partially offset by land purchase and expansion in the area of non-allotment lands leased. If agricultural production *generally* tended to rise—and in our series, this trend was most definitive after 1908—extreme fluctuations in harvests periodically exhausted available reserves and placed great strains on household budgets. Judging by numbers of farm animals, livestock holdings between 1887 and 1914 remained largely without major expansion (presumably reducing the proportion of meat in peasant diets). Larger movements in both national (grain prices, industrial employment) and local (land prices and land rents) markets generated great challenges for both peasant communities and private landowners. One would also do well to keep it in mind that distribution of the benefits and disadvantages generated by these general trends varied strongly among different strata of peasant households and even between different villages.

The less enviable position of communities of ex-serfs is of particular significance: it will figure heavily in incidence of unrest during 1905–

---

of the region identified in the monk Nestor's "Tale of Bygone Years" (*Povest' vremennikh let*), which dates to the early eleventh century.

1906. *By this same token, however, we have noted that districts dominated by populations of ex-serfs tended to be visibly more prosperous if measured by overall harvest performance, levels of tax arrears or technical approach to cultivation.* Conversely, conditions of agriculture in the eastern and northeastern districts of Kursk Province, for both private landowners and villagers (in spite of the fact that average allotments were larger), appear to have been less promising. More severe experience of crop failures, greater frequency of major shortfalls in harvests of winter and/or spring sowings and, during the 1890s, far higher concentrations of tax arrears were all more typical of the eastern and northeastern districts. Disappearance of forest, meadow and pasture before the plow had proceeded farther here than elsewhere on both private estates and peasant allotments. On peasant lands, abandonment of fallow for continuous sowing, once reserved for the far fields, had gained a significant area even in the mid-1880s. These *uyezdy* also lagged far behind the western districts in the development of agro-industrial plant and the local off-farm employment that these generated. In comparison to those in the western and southwestern parts of the province, these districts retained a notably lower portion of natural population increase between 1867 and 1897, a trend that we have attributed to higher rates of permanent emigration, *de facto* or *de jure*.

Thus performance of provincial agriculture *per se* (and its relationship to the decline in mortality) was hardly the only issue. The optimal functioning of the arrangements by which peasant communities sought to guarantee subsistence for their members had been closely tied both to the entire web of interrelationships between villagers and between the villagers and neighboring private landowners and to the capacity of migration to draw off excess labor. These functioned to ameliorate the effects of growth of the rural population and the peasantry's expanding appetite for land and incomes. To be sure, the substantial growth in the flight of labor to other parts of the Empire already signaled that these arrangements were unable to offer a place at the table for many of its working-age members. Precisely in this connection, though, both the steady retrenchment of estate economies in Kursk Province—and most certainly those of the magnates—and the troubles of South Russian industry after 1899 made for less predictable conditions even in the more prosperous western and southwestern regions of the province. In our narrative of agrarian disorders in Kursk Province during 1905–1906, we will see that in distributions of unrest, both these larger contexts stood in the immediate background.

10. State Policy in the Locality: Peasant Views in the Local Committees (1902)

A review of the fabric of state policy towards the peasant estate in the pre-revolutionary era is outside the scope of this work, and the issue has drawn much attention elsewhere.[163] Some accounting of the local situation is necessary, however. The land issue was ever to be present in peasant perspectives during the events of 1905–1906 in Kursk Province. Yet the chaotic state of local administration and justice, its often parasitic and predatory character, and the complete lack of rights of peasants subject to their depredations, were also to be framed, in the course of the rural unrest, by repeated acts of unusual violence against local officials and by a deep general hostility toward the constituted authorities. Peasant participants in the work of Local Committees on the Needs of Rural Industry in Kursk Province that convened during 1902 had publicly expressed this hostility in bitter criticisms during sessions of the committees.

Peasant rapporteurs from Kursk Province were under no illusions whatsoever that the structure of elected parish and village offices constituted in any real sense what official parlance referred to as "organs of peasant self-administration": complete subservience to various provincial bodies of the Imperial administration (and most directly to the Land Captains instituted in 1889) made them merely the lowest links in the state's bureaucratic edifice. Commonly distrusted by their own electorate, officials from among the peasants were at the same time charged with crucial administrative functions and the enforcement of collective decisions on taxation, land use, reapportionment of land or family partition, passports, guardianship over the property of orphans, candidacies and elections to office and so on. Despite their subordination to state officials, such officers bore the burden of representing concerns of peasant constituents before their "superiors," an unmanageable duality that forever compromised their acts and made them the focus of discontent.[164] Formally enjoined to

---

[163] Zaionchkovskii, *Rossiiskoe samoderzhavie* and *Pravitel'stvennyi apparat*; Anan'ich, "Politika tsarizma v krest'ianskom voprose," in *Krizis samoderzhaviia v Rossii, 1895–1917*, Pt. 1, ch. 3, 46–69; M. S. Simonova, *Krizis agrarnoi politiki*; Yaney, *The Systematization of Russian Government*; Macey, *Government and Peasant*; Wcislo, *Reforming Rural Russia*; Gaudin, *Ruling Peasants*.

[164] On the duties of village and parish elders as set forth in the original statutes, see *PSZ*, II, v. 36, at No. 36652 (19 February 1861) "Obshchee Polozhenie o krest'ianakh vyshedshikh iz krepostnoi zavisimosti," Section II ("Ob ustroistve sel'skikh obshchestv i volostei i obshchestvennago ikh upravleniia"), 147–165.

adjudicate criminal matters according to the Rural Judicial Code, parish courts had broader latitude in civil cases, their decisions and fines based on local customs, folk perceptions of justice and the reputations of litigants. If the peasant milieu had slowly grown familiar with both rural codes and regulations and concepts from the general legislation, parish venues applied these unevenly or inconsistently. State officials, armed with broad review power, could interfere at any point and abrogate any decision. Appeals were problematic, for here, peasant appellants found themselves in another judicial world entirely. In this context, real dissonances ensued, since provincial instances—randomly endowed with personnel with training or knowledge of jurisprudence—tried all the same to square up appeals of decisions rooted in customary law to the framework of Imperial codes. This collision of cultures was made even more onerous by the cost of all ventures into the judicial thicket beyond parish venues. Widespread corruption, blatant conflicts of interest, the arbitrary nature of decisions at all levels, the ubiquitous influence of the local estate owners and the clash of customary and written law were endemic.[165]

Rural police forces in each county, partly appointed and salaried (the county police chief and his assistant, four precinct captains and between 10 and 18 constables), and partly elected by peasants as hundredsmen and tensmen (*sotskie, desiatskie*) for three-year terms, were likewise held in very low esteem. Up until 1903, the former never numbered more than 273 officers to patrol an area of 17,937 square miles with a rural population ("counties minus the towns") of 2.5 million.[166] The latter—there were

---

[165] *Trudy mestnykh komitetov*: 160–161 ("Zapiska krest'ianina Alekseia Kirillovicha Kozakova v iuridichesko-pravovuiu kommissiiu Dmitrievskago Uyezdnago Komiteta o nuzhdakh sel'skokhoziaistvennoi promyshlennosti"); 329–330 ("Doklad Troitskago volostnogo starshiny V. E. Besedina ob izmenenii poriadka naznacheniia i zhalovan'ia sel'skim i volostnym dolzhnostnym litsam i o zamene vyborov ikh naznacheniem"); 650 ("Zapiska krest'ianina N. T. Volkova o reorganizatsii krest'ianskago opekunskago dela i v sviazi s etim o reorganizatsii voobshche krest'ianskikh upravlenii"); 685–688 ("Zapiska krest'ianina F. S. Koroleva o neobkhodimosti korennogo izmenenii krest'ianskoi iustitsii i ob organizatsii iuridicheskoi pomoshchi krest'ianskomu naseleniiu"); 707–708 ("Doklad krest'ianina T. Saburova o krest'ianskom sude"). The work of parish courts is reviewed in Leont'ev, *Volostnoi sud* and recently, Czap, "Peasant-Class Courts," *JSH*, 1: 2 (1967), 149–178; Lewin, "Customary Law and Russian Rural Society in the Post-Reform Era," *RR*, 44: 2 (1985), 1–19 (and following); Frank, *Crime*; Shatkovskaia, *Pravovaia mental'nost'*.

[166] Each county had a chief officer (*ispravnik*), his assistant and a small bureau quartered in the county seat. All fifteen counties were divided into four precincts (*stan'*) directed by a precinct captain (*stanovoi pristav*) assisted by two to four constables (*uriadniki*).

1,996 hundredsmen and 8,430 tensmen according to a Ministry of Internal Affairs survey of 1888—were in their vast majority unpaid and illiterate,[167] and since all self-respecting peasant householders did (or paid) all they could to avoid such onerous offices—which demanded in practice the interruption of the household economy—and the community often used the winter elections to rid themselves of troublemakers, chronic tax delinquents, drunkards or those incapable of running their household conscientiously, the quality of these rural officers, as a rule, never inspired respect among fellow villagers.[168] Indeed, the verdict of peasant rapporteurs at local committees on the needs of the local economy in 1902 was unambiguous: assiduous in collecting taxes and dues or rounding up recruits, the rural police force appeared helpless or lethargic in the struggle against crime that increasingly plagued rural society, not to speak of more mundane matters, such as ensuring observance of fire codes, monitoring weights and measures, or differentiating toxic from non-toxic goods at bazaars.[169] Lack of zeal, rampant corruption and favoritism toward in-

---

Before the reform of 1903, these latter numbered 180 for the province as a whole. From S. N. Glavinskaia, "Organizatsionno-pravovaia sistema," in G. A. Saltyk *et al.*, *Politsiia Kurskoi gubernii*, 143. Similarly, Stephen P. Frank calculates that for Riazan District in 1888, a force of four captains and eleven constables patrolled 3,719 square kilometers with 174,790 inhabitants; in Kazimov District, three captains and ten constables served 150,908 inhabitants within an area of 4,743 square kilometers. Frank, *Crime*, 30–36.

[167] Of 1,996 hundredsmen in Kursk Province recorded by the survey in 1888, 1,419 (71.1%) served without any compensation at all; fully 1,745 (87.4%) were illiterate. Among tensmen—8,430 in that year—this situation was even worse: 8,009 served without pay. Of their number, only 580 (6.8%) were registered as literate. To be sure, in many cases (roughly a third of hundredsmen and perhaps half of the corpus of tensmen), these officers gained some exemption from communal obligations for roadwork, convoy and/or guard duty or from parish and/or communal taxes. *VTsSK, Vyp. 9* (1889): *Svedeniia o chisle sotskikh i desiatskikh v 1888 godu.* Under the legislation introducing the units of police patrolmen in 1903 (*PSZ*, III, t. 23, otd. I, at No. 22906, 5 May 1903, 477–481: "Ob uchrezhdenii v 46-ti guberniiakh Evropeiskoi Rossii politseiskoi strazhi"), the *sotskie* were abolished and the tensmen placed in the service of the parish and communal administrative organs (VII: 1).

[168] N. I. Gorlova, "Osnovy organizatsii i deiatel'nost'," in G. A. Saltyk *et al.*, *Politsiia Kurskoi gubernii*, 27–31. Gorlova notes that the resort of communal officials in weaker communities to imposing a rotation of the duties among all householders, and in stronger ones to hiring outsiders using public funds, was not uncommon. The latter practice was eventually adopted by the Ministry of Internal Affairs (*ibid.*, No. 22906, VII: 2).

[169] On the truly vast responsibilities laid upon the police structures in Kursk Province, see Gorlova, "Osnovy organizatsii," 82–119. Beyond the immediate struggle with crime, members of the rural police were tasked with facilitating the collection of taxes and labor obligations, monitoring Kursk Province's religious dissident communities, control-

laws, relatives or powerful village cliques were commonplace. Precinct captains and the constabulary were viewed as an alien element, too often in the pockets of local noble landowners or village cabals. Even their simplest duties (recruiting peasants for road work, convoy duty or firefighting, for example) were carried out with a customary brutality and arbitrariness. Watch duty (*dezhurstvo*) for hundredsmen and tensmen and at the precinct captain's quarters (the captains were recruited almost entirely from the local minor nobility) meant not police work, but turning up the captain's garden, sowing his potatoes, cutting firewood, hauling water, mowing hay and so on.[170] We will see further on that peasant hostility toward the rural police and units of patrolmen (*strazhniki*), deployed in 1903[171] in the wake of agrarian disorders in adjacent Khar'kov and Poltava Provinces the previous year, ran particularly deep.

The key officers in the countryside after 1889, the Land Captains were recruited from the local hereditary nobility and wielded (individually or jointly in District Conferences) unlimited administrative, judicial and police powers within their precincts (three of four in each district) over the persons of peasants and over their institutions. The Land Captain confirmed all village and parish officials, could freely veto their acts or those of village and parish assemblies, and was generally responsible for enforcing order, stability and moral rectitude in village life. With broad discretionary authority, this officer personified the autocracy in the locality, but his powers were also rooted in the political prerogatives and alleged virtues and paternal selflessness of the landed nobility *vis-à-vis* the peasantry, and to degrees that often disturbed leading figures in St. Petersburg, acted independently of the control of the constituted hierarchy of authority.[172] It was to become clear during the revolution, however, that the

---

ling mendicancy and public drunkenness, reporting on the condition of county public buildings, roads and bridges, assisting during the call-up of military recruits and maintaining registries of reservists, mobilization of the populace in the struggle against fires or epidemics, and so on.

[170] *Trudy mestnykh komitetov,* 680–682 ("Zapiska krest'ianina E. P. Kolesnikova o natural'nykh povinnostiakh"); 705–706 ("Doklad A. N. Shchegoleva o sel'skoi politsii"), 706 ("Doklad krest'ianina L. Petrenko o sel'skoi politsii").

[171] *PSZ*, III, t. 23, otd. I, No. 22906. Late in 1903, the Ministry of Internal Affairs announced that Kursk Province was to get an additional contingent of constables (34) and 878 new patrolmen (*strazhniki*). *Kurskie Gubernskie Vedomosti*, No. 208, 30 September 1903. By the end of 1906, the force of *strazhniki* had been reinforced to number 1,259, organized in 15 mounted units and 60 units of foot patrolmen.

[172] "Polozhenie o zemskikh uchastkovykh nachal'nikakh," *PSZ*, III, v. 9, at No. 6196, 12 July 1889, 508–535. Mandel, "Paternalistic Authority in the Russian Countryside,

Land Captains remained at too great a distance from the affairs of the villages in their precincts, choosing to rely instead almost entirely on reports and recommendations of subordinate village and parish officials. In recruitment of these officers, judicial experience or education was not in practice obligatory, even though they wielded broad judicial authority, and family "connections" sometimes had great weight in their selection.[173] What little can be gleaned about their activities in Kursk Province from the inquests ordered by the Minister of Internal Affairs (their nominal superior) in the wake of disorders in February 1905 does not suggest that they pursued their duties with any particular energy. Most inspected villages within their jurisdictions once or twice a year, kept little track of the actions of peasant officials and were often quite badly informed as to the true state of affairs in their departments.[174] In part as a result of this very lack of zeal, their irregular and arbitrary intrusions into village life made them the most hated of officials: during unrest in November 1905, peasants rarely failed to single out the estates of former or serving Land Captains for arson and looting. The Governor himself was forced to admit, in 1906, that "the existing peasant administration, the corpus of peasant institutions, in many cases proved to be wholly incapable by their own authority of halting the revolutionary movement among the peasants. In part, this is explainable by the fact that the institution of Land Captains was drawn from an element that was not always prepared by its education and service experience. As before, administration of the peasantry remained in reality in the hands of parish officials, terribly inferior in terms of their moral development, lethargic and bribed, and not infrequently, thanks to the Land Captains, undesirable for the population. Often, unfortunately, the Land Captains' secretarial personnel (*pismovoditeli*) emerged to stand

---

1856–1906" (Ph.D. diss., Columbia University, 1978); Wcislo, "The Land Captain Reform," *Russian History*, 15: 2–4 (1988), 285–326.

[173] In his discussion of the activity of the Land Section in connection with the institution of the Land Captain, Gurko recounted, as an example, how K. P. Beliaev was nominated by Governor N. N. Gordeev for the post in Staryi Oskol' District in 1903. His appointment was rejected by the MVD because the candidate, a former nurse in an insane asylum, was wholly unqualified for the post, an impression confirmed when the nominee himself appeared for interviews in St. Petersburg. Beliaev, however, was the son-in-law of Prince N. F. Kasatkin-Rostovskii, Marshal of the Nobility in neighboring Novyi Oskol' District. This was enough to set in motion a long and ultimately successful campaign by local notables to secure the appointment over the objections of the government. Gurko, *Chertyi i siluety proshlogo*, 179–182.

[174] GARF, f. 102, DP OO, op. 233, 1905 g., d. 2550 (Obshchaia perepiska), ll. 53–54 (18 March 1905), RGIA, f. 1291, op. 122, 1905 g. d. 34-b, ch. I, l. 188.

between them and the populace. All of this had as its result the growth of dissatisfaction and distrust of the local population toward local agents of state power and the decline of their authority."[175]

The system of bureaucratic tutelage over peasant life, enacted by the Emancipation and amended in subsequent legislation, did thus fail to provide for the elemental needs of the rural populace for justice and security. The dysfunction of local administration in the area of security in Russia's countryside has been treated elsewhere: analyzing Imperial crime statistics, their lacunae (gross underreporting of rural property crime) and conceptual bias ("crime" itself being defined by elite fears and preconceptions), Stephen P. Frank has shown that the data nonetheless "demonstrate a significant rise in the number of criminal cases and convictions from the late 1880s on and a veritable explosion during the years 1903–1913," against which undermanned agencies of law enforcement and justice were plainly failing to cope.[176] The incapacity of local administration on this score would grow ever more evident against a background of just such an explosion of lawlessness (in particular of property crimes) in the rural districts of Kursk Province that followed the crisis of 1891–1892 (Fig. 1.3).[177]

---

[175] RGIA, f. 1291, op. 122, 1906 g., d. 123, l. 44. Such criticisms typified views of members of the central bureaucracy (e.g. Witte), who felt that the Land Captains' freedom of action (especially in their judicial functions), uncoordinated with other administrative bodies, made them a loose cannon in the countryside.

[176] Frank, *Crime*, 80.

[177] Table data from the annual compilation, Ministerstvo iustitsii, *Svod statisticheskikh dannykh* published between 1876 and 1916. The Kursk Regional Court was, of course, only *one* of the province's judicial instances and treated felony cases meriting prison terms or exile: the vast number of more petty crimes and misdemeanors are not represented. Thus the Governor's chancellery, in the annex to its annual report for 1892, broke down 25,992 cases *in which verdicts had been reached in that year* by the Sumy and Kursk Regional Courts (816), their district members (1,239), town courts (4,005), Land Captains (6,864) and parish courts (12,998). The Sumy Region had jurisdiction over cases arising in Putivl' and Ryl'sk Districts. *Prilozhenie k vsepoddaneishemu otchetu… za 1892 god* (1893), Vedomost' No. 5, Lit. A-D. The same report for 1899 (the last year in which bulletins appeared) detailed venues for 27,540 cases so decided: the Regional Courts (768), their district members (1,649), town courts (3,841), Land Captains (4,886) and parish courts (16,396). *Obzor Kurskoi gubernii za 1899 god* (1900), Vedomost' No. 5, Lit. A-D. It is evident that the Land Captains and the *volost'* courts did much of the heavy lifting in these arrangements.

Figure 1.3 Distribution (by Year) of Criminal Cases Docketed in the Kursk Regional Court, 1876–1913

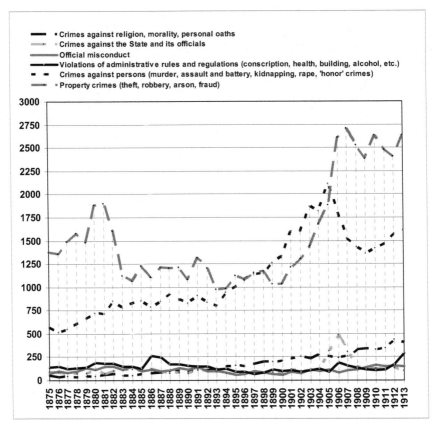

Peasant communities were thus at the mercy not only of meteorological factors as they affected harvests, but also of the equally unpredictable, predatory depredations of local officials, who so often proved indifferent to, uncomprehending of or openly hostile to village interests. Imbued with deeply patriarchal, condescending and even contemptuous views of their peasant "charges," this local bureaucratic machinery, however corruptly and inefficiently it functioned in providing for the most essential of government services, was nonetheless strong enough to hamstring peasants' own efforts to order their own affairs. One of the local peasants invited to participate in the work of the Sudzha District Local Committee on the Needs of Rural Industry put the problem in the following words:

Independence of action and innovation in the peasantry will never develop when, even in the ordering of affairs of the commune, in disposal of monies, in the matter of his own personal property, and so on, even in the use of his allotment land, the peasant is bound hand and foot by administrative tutelage [*opeka*]. Official persons have even been appointed to occupy themselves with peasant morality—not to speak of the problem of whether matters like family partition or departure of members of the commune for other places need to be controlled or not. In other words, the peasant cannot utter any word or take any step without permission and direction from administrative warders. Given such conditions, it is impossible even to conceive of a free development of the peasant as a person or of an enhancement of his economic activity that is related to it. Freedom of action, innovation, a broad horizon, daring initiative and certainty in one's strength—all these being conditions so necessary for the development of economic life—have no place in the present order of things, a state of affairs thanks to which the countryside stands on the road to complete impoverishment and ruin. The flight of the countryside's best elements into other social groups symbolizes the impossible situation created by such administration, the result, mainly, of the heavy tutelage that weighs upon peasant life. In sum, it is necessary to raise village life in all its facets to the general level and to grant it the means to do so: education, independence, equality with all other social estates, the possibility of a lowering and equalization of tax burdens, and so on.[178]

The animus of peasants against their "superiors" that was to so anger and frighten the provincial gentry thus spoke of the failure of both the system of state administration and the local elites to respond adequately, be it institutionally, materially or morally, to vital needs of the peasant community, which these same elites stigmatized as ignorant, morally backward and savage. For its part, the local gentry as a body never tired of shifting the onus elsewhere. It regularly repeated the old canard about the peasant's "complete disregard for private property rights"—evidenced in daily trespass and theft from the landowners' fields, forests and gardens— and stigmatized the ineffective response of local authorities in order to blame the government for giving every villager to understand that he or she could so act with impunity. Land Captain of Korocha District Popov, in his report to the District Committee on the Needs of Rural Industry, opined in just this sense: "Our peasants themselves do not care to adopt a concept of the inviolability of private property. As a result, willful seizure of someone else's land, timbering of another's forest, horse-theft, gathering fruits or vegetables in neighboring orchards, gardens and fields, vandalizing trees, pasturing of livestock in someone else's orchards, meadows and fields and short-cutting through other folk's yards, orchards, woods

---

[178] *Trudy mestnykh komitetov*, 706: "Doklad krest'ianina L. Petrenko o sel'skoi politsii" (Sudzha District).

and gardens are quite usual phenomena."[179] L'gov District Marshal of the
Nobility Stremoukhov offered an analogous observation:

> Considering it superfluous to elaborate on the damage done to any rural owner by vio-
> lation of the right of private property, I will note those measures that will, in my view,
> if not root out, then at least reduce this terrible evil. It is very hard to fight against such
> villainy, thanks to the fact that our populace has no conception whatsoever of respect
> for private property rights and as a result of the notion, long ago established, that to
> steal something or seize a thing from a prosperous person isn't a sin—[the victim] is
> rich anyway. If the same [acts] are noted in the peasant milieu, this happens—
> professional theft aside—out of a desire, out of ill will, to do damage to one's fellow
> villager. Although our laws anticipate such violations of right and punish them, these
> punishments are too weak and soft, and it would be worth enacting tougher and more
> energetic measures.[180]

Second, impoverishment of the rural districts (together with the troubles
of gentry agriculture) was blamed in large part on government tax, tariff
and rail freight policies that aimed at promoting industrial expansion by
pumping resources out of the countryside.[181] Third, mounting evidence
that local administrative bodies were failing in the face of changing conditions gave rise, it was true, to a number of declarations in the Local Committees in support of fundamental reforms. Yet here, the conviction that
peasants—not yet mature enough to be granted a juridical status equal to
other Imperial subjects—had to be guided, to be "administered" and thus
to be maintained in a subaltern position in society, with their own laws
and institutions, continued to define the views of an influential element of
local elite opinion. The deep-seated insecurity and fear of social change
that underlay such attitudes appear common both to most of the local gentry and to officialdom at all levels of Imperial administration. Within the
state apparatus, there *were* those who had come to accept that the pace of

---

[179] *Ibid*, 288.

[180] *Ibid*, 398.

[181] Bitter criticisms of state fiscal and economic policy in *ibid*, 478–483 ("Zapiska M. Ia.
Alferova o nuzhdakh sel'skokhoziaistvennoi promyshlennosti"); 495–498 ("Doklad P.
V. Orlova o zheleznodorozh-nykh tarifakh po perevozke sel'skokhoziaistvennykh pro-
izvedenii"); 507–520 ("Doklad A. E. Morokhovtsa o nuzhdakh sel'skokhoziaistvennoi
promyshlennosti"); 601–608 ("Zapiska V. V. Usova o vliianii finansovoi politiki na
polozhenie sel'skokhoziaistvennoi promyshlennosti"); 826–841 ("Doklad N. E. Markova
o perevozke i torgovle khlebom"). The critique advanced by the nobility resurfaced in less
heated tones in a report filed by the Governor during January 1906, to which we have
referred, on factors that encouraged peasant unrest in the province during 1905. RGIA,
f. 1291, op. 122, 1906 g., d. 123, 1. 40 ob.

socio-economic change inundating the Empire demanded some measured restructuring of the relationship between state and society. Even for such farsighted officials, the state and its bureaucratic instruments, allegedly standing above private, party or class interests, remained the only legitimate agent for carrying out this task. Yet when it moved to make any concessions to the growing signs of crisis, state policy did so only tactically, grudgingly, in fits and starts, in such a manner, vacillating between too humble a carrot and a heavy stick that bred both confusion and deep dissatisfaction.

Agrarian disorders in Kursk Province cannot therefore be viewed entirely from the angle of the unstable material position of peasant households that was in part the legacy of the emancipation and in part the result of demographic and economic trends that were at work in remaking rural society in the second half of the nineteenth century. There seems to us in these events to be a sense of "crisis" perhaps less of the agrarian economy *per se* (this was undeniably a *perception* driving discontent and in certain localities of the province the concern was very real) than of a profound and growing sense of insecurity and dissatisfaction with the existing order, both for thousands of small-holding peasant households and for the class of noble landowners. For many residents of the rural districts on a day-to-day basis, this deterioration was perceived in an increasing corrosion of the reciprocities that had long underwritten the deference of the young before their elders and defined relationships between the "dark" masses of peasants and their "superiors."

However, this was no longer the same generation that had personally experienced the wrenching processes of the 1860s and their immediate consequences. Among younger peasants, there had appeared an increasingly literate element, more familiar with the world outside their home villages, more conversant with its laws and its scientific and cultural attainments, with no memory of and less tolerance for the habits of servility and dissimulation, the veneer of deference and the patriarchal customs of old. In itself, the stinging critique of administrative and gentry paternalism delivered by peasant participants in Local Committees served notice that this element would no longer be content with a properly submissive role in rural society. On the other side of the divide, abolition of requirements of nobiliar service in the ever-more professionalized branches of the Imperial military and civil bureaucracies—combined with the troubles of estate agriculture—prompted many nobles to return to their home districts and to assume direct operation of their ancestral estates. To a degree unprecedented in Russian history, these nobles banded together in a provincial "civil society" that aspired to a decisive voice in the public life of their localities, free of state tutelage.[182] In claiming for itself the leading role in rural society, however, the new generation of noble landowners seemed to have had far less sensitivity—and less of a margin in the conduct of estate economy—for the web of compromises and concessions (*l'goty*) that had loosely cemented an uneasy and fragile peace between peasant "clients" and noble "patrons" after 1861. To be sure, in the brief interregnum of liberal activism's ascendancy in the *zemstvo* organizations of Kursk Province (1892–1902) that followed upon the galvanizing event of the famine years of 1891–1892, the outlooks of a part of the local gentry evolved steadily toward an "all-class" conception of this civil society. Yet the long-dominant conservative strain in the nobiliar politics of Kursk Province—men like Prince N. F. Kasatkin-Rostovskii, Count V. F. Dorrer, M. Ia. Govorukho-Otrok, G. A. Shechkov and the infamous N. E. Markov were but its most well-known spokesmen—obdurately opposed any encroachment whatsoever on the gentry's preeminence in the rural social landscape, the primacy of its economic interests and its continued political control of local *zemstvo* bodies and administrative offices (the land captaincies).[183]

Thus both the economic conjuncture and the deterioration of the political situation in the Empire, as these evolved toward 1905, framed the conflict, designated the main actors and ushered them onto the stage without a script. Historically deprived of traditions of local autonomy under the jealous eye of the autocratic state and in having thus to improvise in a crisis, these actors, for all that they represented the new generations in rural society, mostly fell back upon older concepts of justice wholly particular to the separate social estates and cultures to which they belonged. Noblemen demanded vigorous defense of the political preeminence and landed property of the "first estate," earned by dint of its long tradition of service to the state and its unwavering support of autocracy. Peasants in many localities during 1905–1906 chose to act under concepts of justice that could not have been more different: they did not seek the "restora-

---

[182] On the influence of the crisis of noble landownership—and the professionalization of state service—on the "return to the land," namely among the younger generations of nobles, during the 1880s, see Haimson, "Conclusions," in Haimson, ed., *The Politics of Rural Russia*, 261–300, and Manning, *The Crisis of the Old Order in Russia*, 3–44.

[183] A bitter critique of the *zemstvo* organs, the dominance of the noble element in them and the abnormal order of electing peasant deputies (the result of which was that peasant interests went mostly unvoiced) in *Trudy mestnykh komitetov* ("Zapiska krest'ianina Alekseia Kirillovicha Kozakova..."): 159–160.

tion" of the arrangements between peasants and lords that had been wrought by the emancipation acts of the 1860s, but now acted to enforce the right of tillers of the soil themselves to the land, long adumbrated in age-old expectations of "Black Repartition." Peasant unrest in 1905–1906 in Kursk Province was thus to illuminate in the starkest fashion, as if by a great flash of nighttime lightning, the unbridgeability of the social and cultural divisions within rural society. In January 1906, Prince Petr Dmitrievich Dolgorukov was to write bitterly of an historic opportunity that had been missed, noting "the distrust of the peasant populace toward the private landowners and even toward the intelligentsia element, thanks to the systematic widening of the chasm that still divides them and to the festering wounds of the era of serfdom that have not yet entirely healed. This is the bequest left to the gentry by the epoch of Alexander III, with its odious and corrupting estate privileges, with its institution of the hated Land Captain chosen from the 'lords,' its 'lords' *zemstvo*' and the impossibility of approaching the peasant with principled, open propaganda *that would have broadened his public outlook and taught him to move his economic wants into political channels*. And one can only regret the myopia of that certain part of our privileged estate that has surrendered to the corrupting influence of that policy."[184]

---

[184] Dolgorukov, "Agrarnaia volna," *Pravo*, 1906 g., No. 2, 91. Italics mine: the view of the power position of the lord who "taught" and the peasant who "learned" in this exchange was natural even for many liberal noblemen.

CHAPTER II

1905 in the Rural Districts
of Kursk Province

The accounts of incidents of rural unrest in 1905–1906 in Kursk Province that follow are drawn from a narrow complex of official documents, published in anniversary collections (among these documentation from the State Historical Archive of the Kursk Region)[1] or abstracted from the repositories of the Ministry of Internal Affairs (of the Department of Police, Special Section, and of the Land Section) and of the Ministry of Justice.[2] In almost all cases, the site, the nature of the incidents of unrest, the estate and the name of the owner and the immediate measures taken by the authorities were observed in these materials. Dates of incidents are either directly indicated or could be established with reasonable certainty by the date and content of the document in which they were noted. The documents were far less reliable in terms of numbers of persons taking part or of the organization of actions, especially during phases in which unrest was most intense. Information regarding local outcomes of unrest was absent or appeared randomly. Out of 403 questionnaires,[3] 332 inci-

---

[1] *Revoliutsiia 1905–1907 gg. v Rossii. Dokumenty i materialy*; *Revoliutsionnye sobytiia 1905–1907 gg. v Kurskoi gubernii. Sbornik dokumentov i materialov*, hereinafter *RSKG*.

[2] The State Archive of the Russian Federation (formerly known as the Central State Archive of the October Revolution), hereinafter rendered as GARF, fond 102 (Ministry of Internal Affairs, Department of Police), the Russian State Historical Archive (formerly the Central State Historical Archive of the USSR), hereinafter RGIA, fond 1291 (Ministry of Internal Affairs, Land Section), fond 1405 (Ministry of Justice, II Criminal Division). See the bibliographical appendix for specific folder titles.

[3] From our preliminary experience in reviewing the documents and the example of the method employed by Boris Grigor'evich Litvak (*Opyt izuchenie*), the author produced a form according to which data were abstracted from each document under the following rubrics: date of document, type of document (letter, report, telegram), site of the action described, family name and social estate of the owner who was the object of the action, possible time frame (month, date) between beginning and end of action, number of par-

dents were deemed to have been distinguished with that sufficient clarity by time, site and nature that gave them an individual character: 195 in the calendar year 1905, 128 in 1906 and 9 in 1907. We define actions as "single" incidents even when "objects" were multiple at identical times or could not be "parsed" into separate sites. Thus in the course of 19 February 1905, villagers of Romanovo, Glamazdinskaia Parish, Dmitriev District, set upon three noble estates, the holding of a peasant and the property of a local priest. On 4 November 1905, at the settlement of Kon'shino, Ol'shanskaia Parish, in Novyi Oskol' District, parties of villagers attacked the estates of nine local landowners. Conversely, during the events of December 1905 in Putivl' District, a cable from General N. P. Rudov (chief of the provincial gendarmerie in Chernigov Province) was to note that "many villages of Putivl' District, in particular those that border on Konotop District, have been seized by unrest." Further reporting will note specific settlements in this locale that played a part in events, but the sense from documents pertaining to this group of incidents is that the movement was broader in its scale. Disorders at the same site, involving the same object, might appear as separate incidents: holdings of Marshal of the Nobility of Novyi Oskol' District Vladimir Petrovich Miatlev at Golubina (Prigorodniaia Parish) were attacked on both the 2nd and the 5th of November 1905, each incident made separate by a clear hiatus in time.

Materials in this body of sources reflect the obligation of local authorities on several levels to keep central institutions abreast of major events taking place in their jurisdictions, especially those demanding police and military operations. Originating for the most part in a narrow circle of officials in the police and judicial bureaucracies, these documents were also distinctive in employing a certain uniformity of language with regard to incidents of unrest—something that was itself useful to our analysis. Yet reliance on central ministerial instances, even supplemented by published local sources, had several problematic aspects. First, our collection must be seen as a sample and cannot be considered to be complete. Specific forms of peasant collective actions, particularly tax boycotts and official efforts to enforce payment during 1906, for example, are perhaps poorly represented.[4]

---

ticipating persons, names of participating villages, type of incident (arson, timbering, cattle trespass, and so on), reason for incident, signs of organization, measures taken by the authorities, results. The full range of information was very rarely encountered.

[4] The first attempt to quantify numbers of incidents of peasant unrest in Kursk Province during 1905–1907 was made in a long article published in a local anthology in 1959 by Maliavskii,

Secondly, the documents in this corpus, both by their form (telegrams appear with the greatest frequency in all *dela*) and by their very nature as police reporting, are generally limited to a laconic recounting of events, in which the descriptive language employed was fairly standard. Furthermore, only in exceptional cases (reports filed by the Governor or by emissaries of the central bureaucracy) were official commentators empowered to offer more far-reaching analyses. Even in these rare instances, reporting was deeply saturated by a profoundly patriarchal view of the peasantry and an *idée fixe* regarding the "dark" consciousness of the rural population and the allegedly "thick peasant skull." Repeated references to the role of "criminal agitation of outsiders," which occurs as a central leitmotif in reportage, assume a peasant mass normally docile, obedient to its "superiors," and quite incapable of autonomously acting on its own. Incongruously, such reports ignore the very real complexity of rural society, which was evidenced—often in the very same account—by allusions to the scale of labor migration or to the influence of the national and local press, which implicitly acknowledged the role of literacy. The Governor's report (January 1906) on causes of rural unrest in Kursk Province during 1905, for example, contains the assertion, itself quite rare in official reporting, that land hunger was a principal motivating factor in the disorders, and one that had to be considered legitimate. Yet this admission is prefaced— quite in tune with changes in official views of the matter—with a spirited indictment of the technical level of peasant cultivation generally and of both the economic and "moral" consequences ("disrespect for private property rights") of communal tenure in particular.

"Krest'ianskoe dvizhenie." Making extensive use of the State Historical Archive for the Kursk Region, Maliavskii counted 624 incidents in all: 274 in 1905, 343 in 1906 and 7 in the first half of 1907, but of these, only 596 were located geographically: 262 incidents in 1905, 327 in 1906 and 7 in 1907. In his later study of unrest in Voronezh, Kursk, Tambov and Orel Provinces during 1905–1907, V. A. Stepynin based his recital of events in Kursk Province largely on the Maliavskii sample. Stepynin, *Krest'ianstvo chernozemnogo tsentra*. An inspection of the appendix to Maliavskii's article makes it clear, however, that a number (88) of incidents involved "demands," which may or may not have been related to other acts. Moreover, among the incidents for 1906, both Maliavskii and Stepynin listed 110 incidents of "resistance to tax collection," concentrated entirely in L'gov District, and drawn from a single, verbatim recital of a 16 June 1906 item in the newspaper *Die Zeit*, the clipping pasted directly into the police case file in GARF (discussed below). Yet the folder also contained the Governor's reply to the Police Department's inquiry on the matter in which he stated simply that tax apportionments had "not been done" in several parishes. A lack of concern is very evident: the issue is not recalled at all in the subsequent bi-weekly cable to the Department and disappears from correspondence thereafter.

Thirdly, the presence in police *dela* of personal petitions, letters and cables sent by provincial landowners—these quite dominated by communications of a well-connected noble elite with St. Petersburg addresses and by a tone of familiarity toward the officials to whom they are writing that is quite striking—shows that the gentry (and the magnates in particular) enjoyed direct access to the highest reaches of central government and that the state, in turn, had unofficial channels for keeping itself informed about local events. This combination of official and non-official reporting and its social profile leaves no doubt that the angle of view of the interests of the landed nobility, and the state's identification with these interests in its overriding concern to preserve order, served as one of the principal filters for reportage reaching the center. The mass character of collective acts directed by peasants against noble estates therefore occupied center stage and endemic peasant-on-peasant violence—evidently thought of as "normal" and deemed to be of lesser importance for the preservation of that which the state considered to be "order"—appear only episodically in the records of the central ministries.[5]

Lastly, reporting left entirely unaddressed large areas of analytical interest. In a province in which a substantial Ukrainian minority in that half of the province that lay south of the River Seim had lived uneasily under the sway of Great Russian overlords for two centuries, the whole corpus of documents incorporates only two significant references to the issue of ethnic conflict. Likewise, readers interested in evidence of the role of gender in the disorders or of the contribution of specific elements of village society (the *kulak-seredniak-bedniak* formula) to the events will come away disappointed: in treating the peasantry of the province as an essentially undifferentiated mass, official *rapporteurs*, even the most authoritative among them, touched only very anecdotally on the gender or "class" identities of participants in incidents of unrest.

---

[5] Cases arising out of the agrarian disorders of 1905–1906 were tried mostly during 1906–1907 and mainly in the Kursk Regional Court, which had jurisdiction over thirteen of the province's districts (crimes in Putivl' and Ryl'sk District were adjudicated in the Sumy Regional Court). It gives some perspective on our 323 incidents that during these two years the Kursk Regional Court's docket recorded the largest influx of criminal cases in its history: 5,398 in 1906 and 5,058 in 1907. Adjudication of arson cases alone account for 970 matters in 1906 and 1,045 in 1907, theft and violent seizure of property for 1,461 and 1,499, state crimes and crimes against the authorities, 485 and 311. Of 4,822 persons convicted over the two years in both the Regional Court and the "peace courts," 4,011 (83.2%) were sentenced for crimes committed in the country districts; over three quarters (76.3%) were sowing peasants (2,832) or hired agricultural laborers (846). Ministerstvo iustitsii, *Svod*, Otd. II and III.

Limitations of space and the patience of the reader will not permit a full treatment of every incident of unrest for which evidence was collected from the sources consulted for this work. I have therefore chosen, in both the present and following chapters, to include accounts of those events that were the most heavily documented, those that had highly unusual features or were of particularly massive scale, and those at sites that were "repeated" in both 1905 and 1906. In Chapter IV, I will have occasion to drawn broader summary conclusions about various aspects of the general movement, which will, it is hoped, make up for these omissions.

1. The First Outbreaks: February 1905

Rural unrest in Kursk Province—and indeed in European Russia as a whole—began in adjacent Glamazdinskaia, Prilepovskaia and Ol'khovskaia Parishes in the western part of Dmitriev District in February 1905. Despite their scale and intensity, these incidents had no immediate resonance elsewhere in the province, generating instead unrest in the adjacent parishes of Chernigov (Glukhov District) and Orel (Sevsk District) Provinces. Yet precisely because of the hiatus in time between this first outbreak and those that were to wrack the province in November and December 1905, the reconstructions of events in Dmitriev District are perhaps the best documented and most detailed of all. They provoked two separate official investigations during March and April,[6] and prompted the

---

[6] There were two reports specifically on the unrest of February. The first, composed by Privy Councilor I. A. Zvegintsev, Ministry of Internal Affairs, on 18 March 1905 (hereinafter Zvegintsev), in GARF, f. 102, DP OO, op. 233 (II), 1905 g., d. 2550 ("Po krest'ianskim bezporiadkam: obshchaia perepiska"), ll. 53–57 ob. A second, more detailed and reflective report, from the assistant superintendent of the Land Section of the Ministry of Internal Affairs Iakov Iakovlevich Litvinov to Minister of Internal Affairs A. G. Bulygin, dated 12 July 1905, in RGIA, f. 1291, op. 122, 1905 g., d. 34-b ("Materialy otnosiashchiesia do poezdki Ego Prevoskhoditel'stva Ia. Ia. Litvinov dlia rukovodstva deistviami vremennykh uyezdnykh kommissii, uchrezhdennykh na osnovaniiakh Ukaza 10 Aprelia 1905 g."), ll. 162–190 (hereinafter Litvinov), reprinted in *Revoliutsiia 1905– 1907 gg. v Rossii. Dokumenty i materialy. Nachalo pervoi russkoi revoliutsii, ianvar'– mart, 1905 g.*, No. 415, 627–630. Accounts of operations of military units sent to suppress the unrest in Dmitriev District (two squadrons of the 28th Novgorodian Dragoon Regiment) are available from Vice-Governor Kurlov for 3 March 1905 (*RSKG*, No. 24. at pp. 33–36.) and by the Governor of Kursk Province Nikolai Nikolaevich Gordeev on 15 March 1905 (GARF, f. 1291, op. 122, 1905 g., d. 34-b (II), ll. 39–45 (hereafter Gordeev). Kurlov left a description in his memoirs: Kurlov, *Konets russkogo tsarizma*, 16–

anxious authorities to order the convening of the district conferences of Land Captains to report on the situation in their jurisdictions. The mechanisms set up for compensating landowners who had been victimized in the unrest—from which chronologies of unrest can be reconstructed even today—also emerged from the February events.[7]

The disturbances began as a case of large-scale timbering. On the night of 6 February, peasants from the villages of Sal'noe and Kholzovka (Glamazdinskaia Parish) entered the forest on the estate of one of the neighboring landowners, the merchant Nikifor Pavlovich Popov, and cut down and carted off 415 trees. The village police at first attributed little significance to the incident, since the landowner and the local peasantry had long had a history of bad relations due to unauthorized timbering on his wood lots. But when, on the 8th, Popov and the police arrived in Sal'noe to conduct a search for the timbered lumber, the peasants decided to resist. Popov, the local constable and the police deputies were beaten up and ejected from the village, without ever having managed even to draw up the usual protocols. When Precinct Police Captain Vinogradskii visited Sal'noe on February 10, he too was unceremoniously expelled, having tried vainly to tear down a proclamation of inflammatory content that had been pasted to a post above the village well. On the snow-covered track

---

22. All measures of estate size drawn from list of persons eligible to participate in Dmitriev District *zemstvo* elections in the first and second electoral curia in *Kurskie Gubernskie Vedomosti* (hereinafter *KGV*), ofitsial'naia chart' No. 16, vtornik, 2 March 1904.

[7] These were the Temporary Commissions that were established to estimate damage caused by disorders and apportion this damage on the property (including allotments) of villages with members found to have taken part in acts of looting and arson. Yet the latter aspect of the committees' competence met with the resistance of the Council of Ministers, *inter alia*, on the grounds that such a step would be tantamount to further pauperizing populations in localities in which unrest had emerged. In the end, the government was forced to compensate landowners out of the Treasury, but sums in compensation were nowhere close to the actual cost of the damage. See documents in "K istorii bor'by," *Krasnyi arkhiv*, 1936 5 (78): 128–160. An extremely detailed inventory (undated) of sites and damage at RGIA, f. 1291, op. 122, 1905 g., d. 34-b, ll. 47–71 ("Podrobnaia opis' razgrablennogo i sozhzhennogo imushchestva vo vremia besporiadkov, byvshchikh v Fevrale mesiatse 1905 goda v Dmitrievskom uyezde, Kurskoi gubernii") and 83–86 ("Dopolnitel'naia podrobnaia opis'"). These inventories will be compiled for all the later centers of disorders, and served the author as a major source both for verification of specific aspects of the events and for filling in gaps in the reporting. These data can be found in the Land Section files, RGIA, f. 1291, op. 122, 1905 g., d. 112 ("So svedeniiami, donesennymi Gubernatorami o razmerakh ubytkov, prichinennykh agramymi besporiadkami"), and were updated through 1906.

from Sal'noe, Vinogradskii came upon Land Captain A. A. Kusakov, who had learned of events and had resolved to visit the scene. Taking Vinogradskii in his sled, the two officers reentered the settlement, vowing to summon the village assembly (*skhod*), but peasant officials had made themselves scarce. Leaving for the neighboring settlement of Dubrovitsy, Kusakov left orders at Sal'noe that village elder Demidov and those eight peasants identified by Vinogradskii as having obstructed his work present themselves at Dubrovitsy the following day. Demidov did appear in Dubrovitsy on the next day, but alone and without his badge of office, explaining that the peasants had torn it from him and discarded it: "If the Land Captain wants to see us," they declared, "then let him come to us in Sal'noe."[8]

Kusakov smelled trouble. No longer a simple matter of the theft of some lumber or of drunken resistance, the repeated flouting and public humiliation of lawful authorities by Sal'noe peasants appeared to constitute a more serious challenge, one to which the local police were not numerous enough to respond. At Dubrovitsy, the Land Captain composed a telegram to the attention of the Governor of Kursk Province, N. N. Gordeev, reporting on the tense situation at Sal'noe and requesting the dispatch of troops. Vinogradskii set off at once for the district seat at Dmitriev with the drafted telegram blank and made his report to District Police Commandant Ivanovskii upon arriving. Ignoring the Land Captain's sense of the situation, however, Ivanovskii wired his own report to Kursk, omitting Kusakov's request for troops, and himself left for Sal'noe on the 12th with a small band of police officers, reaching Dubrovitsy on the 13th. From Dubrovitsy, Kusakov ordered the village assembly at Sal'noe convened on the morning of the 14th, but when Ivanovskii and his party of police officers entered the village after dawn, Kusakov was forced to convoke the assembly himself. The assembled peasants allowed Kusakov to speak, but for their part blamed the police for the "misunderstanding" of the past days. The villagers promised that there would be no more trouble and permitted police officials to conduct a search for the wood cut from Popov's forests. The incident thus appearing to have ended, the Police Commandant set off for Dmitriev with his little force, perhaps congratulating himself for pocketing Kusakov's unnecessarily alarming cable.[9] On the same night, however, peasants from Sal'noe raided the farm of merchant Pavel Ivanovich Cherninin, cleaned out his

---

[8] Litvinov, 631.
[9] Litvinov, 631–632; Gordeev, 1. 39.

granaries and carted the grain back to the village. On the 15th, Kusakov this time personally telegraphed the Governor, once again pleading for dispatch of military units. However, Kusakov did not enjoy favor in Kursk—he had been slated for retirement—and once again, no urgency was attached to his request: 15 police guards were ordered from other sites to beef up local forces.[10] Only on 18 February did the Governor receive, now from Ivanovskii, requests for troop support in terms that prompted immediate action. Two squadrons of the 28th Novgorodian Dragoon Regiment, under the command of Vice-Governor P. G. Kurlov, departed from Kursk for the western parishes on the 19th, and three companies of infantry were readied for deployment to the area.

By the time the dragoons arrived in the area in the half-light of the dawn of the next day, they were greeted by the glow of great fires on the horizon. Later reconstruction of events attests that disorders spread rapidly from the 15th onward. On successive nights between 15 and 20 February, local peasants organized a series of actions against estate installations of Barons Kondrat and Aleksandr Egorovich Meiendorf (the heirs of Egor Fedorovich Meiendorf jointly held an estate of 5,288 *desiatiny* in Prilepovskaia Parish, on which they operated the province's oldest sugar refinery and a distillery), progressing from setting fire to two barns near Prilepy (on the main Sevsk-Glukhov highway) and timbering the estate's wooded tracts, to a systematic looting of all grain stores and estate property that could be carted off the estate's farmsteads and a second holding in Pogreby, just across the provincial border in Orel Province.[11] Baron Bogdan (Feofil) Egorovich Meiendorf's domains at Dobroe Pole (Prilepovskaia Parish) were invested on the night of the 20th, and grain and various goods were looted. On the same night, peasants took possession of similar stores and property from the Baron's main installation at Prilepy; looting of the sugar refinery and distillery was forestalled by the timely arrival of troops.[12]

The large estate of *general'sha* Ol'ga Alekseevna Levshina-Shaufus, at Khomutovka in Glamazdinskaia Parish (3,179 *desiatiny*), was also singled out for particular attention, beginning with outlying farmsteads on 18 February and ending with the remaining farmstead and the main estate instal-

---

[10] Litvinov, 632; Zvegintsev, l. 55 ob., Gordeev, l. 39 ob.

[11] Zvegintsev, l. 40, 55–56; Litvinov, 632; GARF, f. 102, DP OO, op. 233 (II), 1905 g., d. 2550, l. 116–116 ob. ("Kopiia s otnosheniia Orlovskago gubernatora ot 19 Fevralia 1905 goda za No. 776 na imia Departamenta Politsii").

[12] Litvinov, 633; Zvegintsev, l. 56.

lations at Khomutovka, invested in broad daylight on the 20th: in every instance, grain stores and moveable property of every sort were seized and carted back to the villages. At Khomutovka, however, the proceedings were cut short by the arrival of Land Captain Kusakov with a small company of police deputies. In the ensuing confrontation, the deputies fled without firing a shot and Kusakov was left to face an enraged crowd alone. The peasants gave way only after the Land Captain drew his pistol and opened fire, killing one person and wounding another. Fleeing the scene, peasant wagons piled high with booty unexpectedly encountered advance detachments of dragoons that arrived in Khomutovka at precisely this moment: the looters were promptly seized.[13] In six separate incidents, the estate suffered damage in the amount of 38,825.60 rubles.[14]

Participants had resorted to arson only exceptionally during the early stages of the unrest: peasants broke into granaries, removed grain and ransacked property that might be easily taken. On 19–20 February, at Romanovo and Glamazdino (Glamazdinskaia Parish), peasant rebels began to vandalize beyond repair or simply burn what they had looted. At Romanovo on 19 February, five private holdings were relieved of all of their grain supplies and property, and heavy damage inflicted on the structures: on the estate of Aleksandr Vasilievich Mytarskii (534 *desiatiny*), the *romanovtsy* not only led away the cattle, looted the granaries and carried off moveable property, but also set the dwelling house and outbuildings on fire.[15] On 19 February, at Glamazdino, the villagers began the destruction of the estate of State Councilor and Shtalmeister of His Imperial Majesty's Court Petr Petrovich Volkov (2,072 *desiatiny*), which lasted into the morning hours of the 20th. All buildings on the estate and its farmsteads, as well as a large distillery operation and a state liquor outlet, were burned to the ground after being thoroughly looted. The damage (costing 271,935.25 rubles) evidently proved too much for Volkov, who sold the estate to a German-born entrepreneur, Vitol'd Fadeevich Zablotsky, later in the year.[16]

As was to be the case in every subsequent outbreak of disturbances concentrated, at first, in and around a geographically limited core, a ripple

---

[13] Litvinov, 632–633; Zvegintsev, l. 55 ob. (Zvegintsev's dating is used.)

[14] RGIA, f. 1291, op. 122, 1905 g., d. 34-b, 11. 83–86 (#25).

[15] Litvinov, 633; Zvegintsev, l. 56 ob.

[16] Litvinov, 633; Zvegintsev, ll. 55–56 ob.; GARF, f. 1291, op. 122, 1905 g., d. 34-b, ll. 83–86. Petr Petrovich Volkov was the son of Liubov' Arkadeevna Nelidova, whose grandfather Arkadii Ivanovich Nelidov (1773–1834) had received the estate from Emperor Paul I.

effect of sorts was produced in incidents at some distance from the venue in which the outbreak began, this effect carried by the outward movement of tidings and rumor. Thus in Berezovskaia and Staro-Belitskaia Parishes to the east and Ol'khovskaia Parish to the immediate south, individual incidents of mass timbering of private forests or of the looting and burning of the holdings of several smaller landowners were reported from widely dispersed sites.[17]

Map 2. Dmitriev District, 6–22 February, 1905

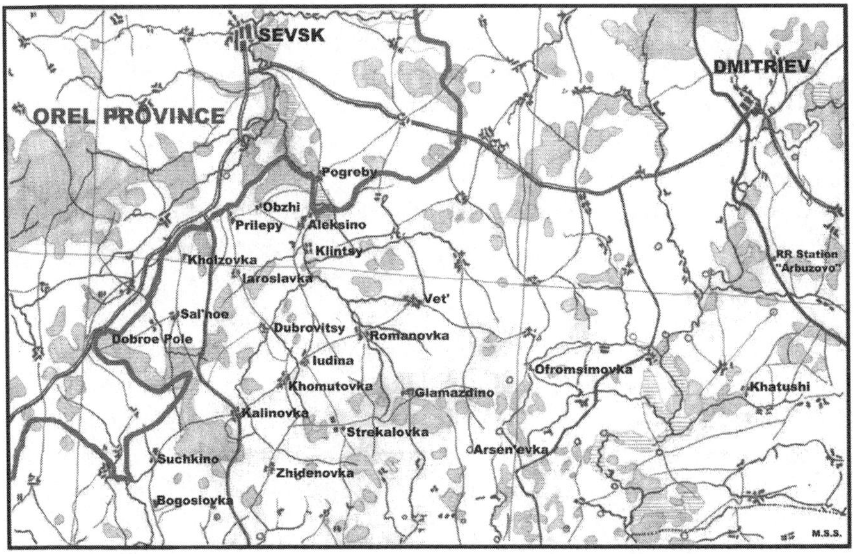

With the arrival of Vice-Governor Kurlov and the dragoons, unrest in Glamazdinskaia and Prilepovskaia Parishes ended, even though individual acts continued to be reported at some distance from the original centers up to 22 February. Under cover of this force, the Vice-Governor, together with Kusakov, Ivanovskii, judicial investigators and a host of minor police officials, began what was to become a familiar process in later events. House-to-house searches were conducted in all settlements thought to have participated, witnesses were summoned and deposed, and suspects arrested based on the depositions or apprehension of looted goods in their possession. The operation was carried out with no bloodshed: the appearance of troops itself created the desired impression. Resistance to the work

---

[17] Litvinov, 632–633; Zvegintsev, ll. 55 ob.–56 ob.; RGIA, f. 1291, op.122, 1905 g., d.34-b, ll.83–86 (#24).

of dragoons, police and investigators surfaced initially at Sal'noe, Kholzovka, Iaroslavka and Prilepy. Defiance collapsed, however, after a peasant was publicly flogged in each village as an example to their fellows. Estate property, if uncovered, was returned to the owners, but accounts of this aspect of the operation during investigations later in the summer made it clear that much of the loot had been successfully hidden.[18]

2. Interregnum: Spring and Summer 1905

After the extremity of the situation as it appeared to provincial officials in February, spring and summer were periods of relative calm. To be sure, disorders continued to be recorded in various districts, but unlike the events of February, these were primarily local affairs that had no further development in the larger locality and did not seem to have required any exceptionally large movement of troops. Despite outward calm, the February disturbances had deeply shaken the landowners of the province and produced among the peasants an enduring mood of tension and expectation. As if grudgingly acknowledging criticism leveled against it concerning the abject performance of local officials during the February events, the provincial administration conducted a purge of the corps of Land Captains and District Police Commandants.[19] Immediately following the end of the unrest, the Ministry of Internal Affairs ordered the convocation of District Conferences (on which all Land Captains sat). These were to offer detailed comment on indications of discontent in their precincts and their cause. The observations of the participants, broadly speaking, laid special emphasis on tensions between the larger estates (often specifically referenced in their reports) and the adjoining villages. Precisely this tension, of course, had defined a central aspect of the February unrest. Acute land hunger, high rents (or refusal of estates to rent), quarrels over boundaries and the often high-handed, unjust behavior of absentee owners' estate administrators (not infrequently Germans or Poles) toward the peasants figured prominently. Peasant resentments were expressed on the usual level of small acts (petty theft, small-scale timbering, minor arson or refusal to pay rent) and in those rumors of an impending "black repartition" that "have circulated widely in the country districts for as long as anyone can remember." Several troubling notes were struck, however: some Land

---

[18] *RSKG*, No. 24, pp. 33–36 (GAKO, f. 1, op. 15, d. 11, ll. 241–243).

[19] RGIA, f. 1291, op. 122, 1905 g., d. 34-b, l. 71. Kusakov, however, survived the purge.

Captains spoke of the steady increase, from about 1904, in the circulation of illegal literature among the peasants, while others noted a new frequency and intensity of "small misunderstandings" and an unprecedented persistence in peasant demands of all sorts:[20] "Since the beginning of 1905, a particular stubbornness has appeared among the peasants in making even illegal demands, such as, for example, a full and equal share-out of the public grain reserve, and obstruction of the annual accounts of peasant officials. Recently, there has emerged a mass of requests from families of lower-ranking reservists serving in the east for exemption of their lands from all taxes: they base these requests on letters from the soldiers at the front."[21]

Land Captains in Putivl' District agreed that "from the time of the unrest in Khar'kov and Poltava Provinces (1902), a powerful ferment has existed among the peasant populace of Putivl' District, expressed at present only in conversations, in illegal meetings of peasants, often at night, in a more impudent and defiant attitude of the lower classes to their superiors, and so on. In the current year, this ferment sharpened, but presently, thanks to the deployment of troops at various points in the district, it has receded."[22]

Moreover, both in the March conferences and in the dispatches of Governor Gordeev to the Ministry of Internal Affairs, a degree of anxiety was registered concerning persistent rumors of peasant plans to make trouble during the spring months. Reporting on his plan for deployment of troops in the vicinity of the town of Kursk (the most advantageous site in light of its central position within the province's road and rail networks), Gordeev reported to the Ministry on 18 March: "Even though unrest in the province has ceased at present, there are serious grounds to suppose that, with the onset of spring, peasants in various localities will be making attempts to forcibly seize private landowners' arable lands and maybe even to begin a new wave of attacks on the estates... Such an opinion rests on the persistent rumors, verified by the Land Captains and police officials, that the peasantry awaits only the removal of troops now deployed (in these localities) to set in motion their plans for land seizure, in the certainty that, in light of the continuation of military activity in the Far East, troops will be insufficient."[23]

---

[20] RGIA, f. 1291, op. 30, 1905 g., d. 4-b, ll. 176–198.

[21] *Ibid.* (*Zhurnal Starooskol'skago uyezdnago soveshchaniia, 10-go marta 1905 g.*), l. 190 ob.

[22] *Ibid.* (*Zhurnal Putivl'skago uyezdnago soveshchaniia, 10-go marta 1905 g.*), l. 195.

[23] GARF, f. 102, DPOO, op. 233 (II), 1905 g., d. 2550, ch. 44, ll. 2–3 ob.

The observations of the March conferees, to which we will return below, turned out to be actually prophetic in many specific cases, particularly with regard to the bigger estates in their jurisdictions. Land Captain
P. V. Orlov noted at the conference for Novyi Oskol' District the persistent expectation among peasants in his precinct that unrest on agrarian
grounds would take place in the spring: "There is even a rumor that students and other persons will arrive at the settlement of Chernianka to begin the partition of land and other property."[24] Fears with regard to a wave
of unrest in the spring, however, proved to be groundless. The record of
incidents during the period from March to September 1905 suggests a
reversion among the peasant populace to a tactic of "small acts": timbering, livestock trespass and minor arson. These incidents occurred in geographically disparate locales, generally pitting one village against a nearby
landowner or estate administration—in almost every case, the target was
the largest of the estates in the immediate vicinity, required troop movements to the sites during or after the event, but aroused no broader unrest
in the immediate region. Intimately concerned with local discontent over
the land and labor issues that had always stood at the heart of socio-
economic relations between peasants and former masters, the large numbers of persons involved and the increasing frequency with which even
"usual" forms of harassment were now accompanied by resort to growing
resistance "in word or deed" to the representatives of authority gave peasant collective actions a new militant tenor. In June, provincial officials
experienced great anxiety over the dangers posed by the situation in
Khar'kov Province, where peasants had gone on the offensive against the
large landowners at the height of the agricultural season. In Kursk Province, however, the situation remained generally without incident.

Certain of these incidents, however, already bore the most ominous
portents for the future. Invasion of the forests on the main Bariatinskii
estate in L'gov District (11,428 *desiatiny*) from 27 February by peasant
axemen from the big settlement of Bol'shie Ugony (on the Moscow–
Kiev–Voronezh Railway in Ugonskaia Parish),[25] an incident involving the
villagers of Kuflievka (Khalanskaia Parish) who let their herds wander
onto the meadows of the estate of Prince Ivan Iur'evich Trubetskoi (5,098

---

[24] RGIA, f. 1291, op. 30, 1905 g., d. 4-b, l. 185 (*Zhurnal Novooskol'skago soveshchaniia
zemskikh nachal'nikov, 11-go marta 1905 g.*)

[25] *RSKG*, No. 23, p. 33 (report, L'gov District Police Commandant to Kursk Governor, 1
March 1905). Size of A. V. Bariatinskii's estate from *KGV*, prilozhenie k ofitsial'noi
chasti, No. 1, 4 January 1901.

desiatiny) in Novyi Oskol' District,[26] and the heavy damage inflicted on the (vacant) manor house and administrative offices on the Sheremet'ev estate (17,303 *desiatiny*) in Graivoron District by a crowd of some 400 peasants from the adjoining settlement of Borisovka (Borisovskaia Parish)[27] all were to be followed, in the course of subsequent events, by far more serious unrest at these sites.

Similarly, in late August, police informants in Putivl' District began to report with particular concern on well-attended gatherings of peasants in Gruzchanskaia Parish, on the Moscow–Kiev–Voronezh Railway at the provincial border with Konotop District, Chernigov Province. On August 30, three unknown persons jumped off a train moving from Konotop station to Gruzskoe station and set off on horseback to the village of Viazovoe. They drew up at a deep ravine a mile from the village, where 100 local peasants awaited them. The strangers handed out proclamations to those in attendance and spoke about raising demands with the *pomeshchiki* about land, recommending, in the case of refusal to honor such demands, that peasants should set about the destruction of the estates. The report laid special stress on the influence on growing ferment in the parish exerted by those large numbers of peasants from Gruzskoe and Viazovoe who worked in the rail facilities at Konotop Depot and its freight yards. After this meeting, two more gatherings were organized in Savinki, a suburb of Viazovoe in Konotop District, at which Viazovoe peasants were in attendance. With the mood of the Viazovoe peasants in mind, and anticipating possible trouble on the Tereshchenkos' Belousov estate, the Governor ordered Cossacks deployed to the site: their "arrival produced a notable change in the mood of the villagers in the direction of public calm."[28] This "public calm" was not, however, fated to last: we will have the opportunity to review events in Putivl' District as they unfolded at this site in the following period and their close connection with the big villages that lay astride the Moscow–Kiev–Voronezh Railway.

Despite such omens (in retrospect, of course) of more serious events over the horizon, provincial authorities might well have congratulated themselves on surviving the spring and summer months that, in the provinces just south, had been full of unrest and alarums. Incidents in various

---

[26] *RSKG*, No. 46, p. 62; Size of estate at *KGV*, prilozhenie k ofitsial'noi chasti, No. 3, 13 January 1904.

[27] GARF, f. 102, DP OO, op. 233 (II), 1905 g., d. 2550, ch. 44, l. 62. Estate size from *SSSKG. Vyp. IX. Statisticheskiia svedeniia po Graivoronskomu uyezdu*, 276–279.

[28] *Ibid*, d. 106.5 ("Svedeniia po guberniiam i oblastiam. Po Kurskoi gubernii"), ll. 14–15.

parts of the province gave vent to the tense and expectant mood among peasants that had become palpable everywhere in the wake of the February disorders. For the time being, this ferment was still expressed in the "usual" kinds of harassment that had become characteristic of relations between private landowners and nearby peasant communities, although such offenses had always provoked demands among landowners that provincial administrators do more to protect their property. By the same token, even if sporadic, outbreaks of unrest during the spring and summer months now displayed a "mass" and premeditated character, frequently produced violence between participants and estate employees or local representatives of authority, and necessitated the dispatch of troop detachments, if only for "demonstrative purposes."

What was more, the period of spring and summer witnessed the emergence of two other unprecedented phenomena that were to have an important influence on the mood of the rural districts in Kursk Province on the eve of the October–December period. The first concerned the effect of the Manifesto of 18 February 1905, which, among other things, invited the Empire's subjects to advise the government on local needs and problems: "In tireless concern for the perfection of the State's good order and the improvement of the national prosperity of the Russian Empire, We deem it right to facilitate for all Our true subjects who care for the general good and the needs of the State, the possibility of being directly heard by Us. In light of this, We order that in addition to the matters already within its jurisdiction at the present time, the Council of Ministers, under Our chairmanship, will undertake a review and discussion of views and proposals addressed in Our Name from private persons and institutions on questions concerning the perfection of the state order and the improvement of national prosperity."[29]

The act provoked a wave of petitions and resolutions, forwarded to a variety of provincial and central institutions, in which peasant communities in various parts of the province not only listed their grievances over the land issue, but also advanced demands that bore a political character as well.[30]

---

[29] *PSZ*, III: 25, No. 25852, 18 February 1905 ("O prizyve vlastei i naseleniia k sodeistviiu Samoderzhavnoi Vlasti v odolenii vraga vneshniago, v iskorenenii kramoly i v protivodeistvii smute vnutrennei") and *ukaz* of even date at No. 25853, 132–133.

[30] Analysis of the mass of peasant petitions generated in response to the Manifesto of 18 February 1905 in O. G. Bukhovets, *Sotsial'nye konflikty*. In the view of some historians, however, efforts to give the peasant movement a political cast, by reference to the "petition movement" of February–August 1905, ignored both the influence of the local intel-

Secondly, in the months after the February disorders, peasant unions began—in the teeth of police actions to disrupt these efforts[31]—to organize in several districts in Kursk Province; delegates from the province took part in the July ("constituent") congress of the All-Russian Peasant Union in Moscow.[32] Sources consulted in connection with this work made few references to these aspects of the situation, but some general impressions may be offered. The union movement among peasants emerged in tandem with (if not always under the direct influence of) analogous initiatives undertaken by the local intelligentsia, and in particular by activist elements among *zemstvo* employees, after late May 1905. Rural teachers in Kursk Province (who organized their own unions in this period) were evidently most active in the efforts of "third element" collectives to participate in mobilizing peasant opinion in the province.[33] In L'gov and Sudzha Districts, however, the petition drive and the formation of peasant unions were actively supported by the local intelligentsia, led by two of the leading gentry liberals associated with the brief heyday of *zemstvo* activism in Kursk Province during 1892–1902.

Prince Petr Dmitrievich Dolgorukov (1866–1951) was already a leading personality on the national political scene: a participant of the *Beseda* Circle from its first meeting in November 1899, founder (with P. B. Struve) of the underground journal *Osvobozhdenie* ("Liberation"), published in Stuttgart from 1902 (he served as treasurer), an original member of both the Union of Liberation at its 1903 Schaffhausen congress and the Union of Zemstvo Constitutionalists in 1904, and a tireless organizer and participant in national *zemstvo* congresses in Russia and abroad during 1904–1905. An early

---

ligentsia on their composition and the dissonance of the detailed "political" articles with traditions of rural life. Vronskii, *Gosudarstvennaia vlast'*, 100–108.

[31] On the planned provincial caucus of delegates in Kursk prior to their departure for the "constituent" congress of the All-Russian Peasant Union in Moscow (31 July–1 August), and reference to the send-off of at least two of those delegates (the caucus was broken up by the police), see GARF, f. 102, DP OO, op. 233 (II), 1905 g., d. 999 ("O Krest'ianskom Soiuze"), ch. 45, t. II, ll. 49–49 ob.

[32] Speeches of delegates from Kursk Province in *Protokoly delegatskago soveshchaniia*. On the history of the VKS generally, see the somewhat tendentious treatments of E. I. Kiriukhina, "Vserossiiskii Krest'ianskii soiuz," *IZ*, 50: 95–141, and "Mestnye organizatsii," *Uchenye zapiski*. 10: 83–157; Garmiza, "Rost politicheskogo soznaniia," *ISSSR*, 1986, 6: 135–141. A recent and judicious review is Kurenyshev, *Vserossiiskii Krest'ianskii soiuz*.

[33] On the already lively organizational tradition among teachers in Kursk Province in a monograph that otherwise richly documents the foregoing, see Seregny, *Russian Teachers*, 65–67.

member of the Party of National Freedom, he was one of the organizers of the first congress of the Constitutional Democratic Party in October 1905. While nationally prominent, Dolgorukov nevertheless pursued an active regime of public service in Kursk Province over the course of many years: Deputy to the Sudzha District Zemstvo, District Deputy to the Provincial Zemstvo Assembly and Chairman of the Sudzha District Zemstvo Board during 1892–1902—the "Grand Prince of All Sudzha," as his conservative foes acidly referred to him. During these terms, he devoted special energy to the development of popular education and *zemstvo* agronomy. For the unusually open and wide-ranging discussions that took place under Dolgorukov's leadership during sessions of the Sudzha District Committee on the Needs of Rural Industry (1902) and in which peasant views were given a thorough airing (see Chapter I)—and for the content of his own public statements during the proceedings, the Prince was deprived of his eligibility to serve in *zemstvo* organs by Imperial order for a term of five years and received a personal rebuke from the Emperor himself.[34] His active engagement both in the petition drive in response to the Manifesto of 18 February 1905 and in the organizational work of the Peasant Union intensified the enmity with which he was regarded by many members of the provincial gentry and brought threats of arrest. Countermanding an order from the Sudzha District Police Commandant to the Moscow City Commandant Trepov for the Prince's arrest, the Governor noted that "information on the activity of Dolgorukov in the organization of the Peasant Union in Sudzha District does not give grounds for summoning him to legal responsibility. Personally he is a convinced partisan of the union [*splochenie*] of peasants [as a means toward] avoiding anarchy and troubles, but does not share the extreme views of the Union. However, those who are grouped around Dolgorukov in his political activities, in their majority *zemstvo* employees, are persons of extreme views. The damaging actions of several of these persons, among them Dolgorukov's steward Reizin, have been observed and they have been arrested."[35]

---

[34] *Al'bom portretov*, 37; Shelokhaev and Kanishcheva, "Dolgorukov, Petr Dmitrievich (1866–1951)," in Kara-Murza, ed., *Pervodumtsy*, 99–117; Shelokhaev and Kanishcheva, eds., *Gosudarsvennia Duma Rossiiskoi imperii, 1906–1917 gg.*, 170–171; Barinova, *Rossiiskoe dvorianstvo*, 284–292.

[35] GARF, f. 102, DP OO, op. 233 (II), 1905 g., d. 999 ("O Krest'ianskom Soiuze"), ch. 45, t. II, l. 62. It is uncertain whether the arrest order of 18 January 1906 was ever carried out. Dolgorukov confirmed the essence of these particulars concerning his own role during discussion of the Duma's interpellation (No. 153) before the MVD with regard to police persecution of the Peasant Union. He sharply defended the character and intentions of his col-

Nikolai Vladimirovich Shirkov (born 1862, Dresden) from L'gov District, even if he stated his occupation as "farmer" (*zemledelets*), had finished Moscow High School and had studied at the Mining Institute and the Petrovskii Academy. He had served as Deputy to the L'gov District Zemstvo since 1892, as Deputy for his District in the Provincial Zemstvo from 1895, and had chaired the L'gov District Zemstvo Board from 1898.[36] Here, the police dossier was categorical: on 24 June, under the pretext of conferring on issues connected with credit associations, a large gathering of peasants, personally invited by Shirkov by sealed invitation, took up a discussion (Shirkov chaired the meeting) of the formation of Peasant Union affiliates. Strategies for opposing the constitutional formulae of the Bulygin Duma, the question of peasant land hunger, seizure of private lands, and the uselessness of the police were debated. "In the end, the peasants Erokhin and Kuz'min were elected to go to Moscow for the general congress [of the Peasant Union], to stop in Kursk, however, on 30 July, for a conference with delegates from other districts at the quarters of the supervisor of the Medical Bureau of the Provincial Zemstvo, the doctor V. I. Dolzhenkov. Thanks to timely measures, we succeeded in preventing and upsetting the planned conference, but there is no doubt that its participants left for Moscow. Regarding the aforesaid peasants from L'gov District, this is known for a fact, since they were seen at Ivanino station, accompanied by Shirkov, who gave them tickets and parted from them with the words 'Remember what I said to you and don't forget what you are to ask for.'" The report observed that on the same day as the gathering of peasants (24 June), the L'gov District Zemstvo Board Chairman had scheduled a conference of the district's rural teachers at which the question of forming a chapter of the All-Russian Teachers' Union was debated and instructions were given by the Chairman regarding dissemination of "anti-government" propaganda among the peasants. Such facts in Shirkov's police dossier, attesting his very active support of the organizational activities of the Peasant Union, were enough to earn him a brief period of incarceration in Moscow's Butyrski Prison in December 1905, from which he was freed at the insistent demand of fellow members of the L'gov district nobility.[37]

---

leagues (including Reizin) who had been exiled by administrative order. *Stenograficheskii otchet. Gosudarstvennaia Duma. Pervyi sozyv*. I: 27, 15 June 1906, 1365–1367.

[36] *Al'bom portretov*, 38.

[37] GARF, f. 102, DP OO, op. 233 (II), 1905 g., d. 999 ("O Krest'ianskom Soiuze"), ch. 45: II, ll. 49–49 ob.

One of the Peasant Union's activities was to promote the dissemination of "model" petitions.[38] Dolgorukov himself observed that the petition campaign unleashed by the Manifesto of 18 February and the emergence of the peasant unions were closely associated:

[The union movement] began with the composition of petitions on general questions. The population began to take a lively interest in the fate of these petitions, often inquiring whether or not they had reached the central instances or had been read out in the Zemstvo Assembly. But a special effect was produced when local petitions appeared in the newspapers. This motivated other villages to compose their own, using as a model those that had been reprinted in the newspapers, but always bearing distinctive aspects, which were in accordance with local conditions, and traces of real creativity. Yet it was the newspaper stories that ran throughout the summer of 1905 concerning the formation of local unions or on their affiliation with the All-Russian Peasant Union that provided the point of departure for the union movement. The embryos of the new unions emerged either on the initiative of the peasants themselves, the impetus coming from the more developed [razvitoi] group among them or from those who had spent time in other locales, or at the urging of representatives of the local intelligentsia.[39]

Police documents directly report chapters of the Peasant Union at Kobylka (Ryl'sk District), Dar'ino (Sudzha District), at Golovchino and Borisovka (Graivoron District) and Fitizh (L'gov District). Its appeal was evidently far broader.[40] The chief of the Kursk Provincial Gendarmerie observed that, "thanks to the work of many employees of the zemstvo," the Peasant Union enjoyed great success in the province, and that, in particular, due largely to the efforts of Dolgorukov and Shirkov, "almost all of the peasants [of Sudzha and L'gov Districts] have joined the Peasant Union."[41] In Dmitriev District, representatives of at least six parishes met in late October to form a district organization and request its affiliation with the All-

---

[38] See Bukhovets, op. cit., 146–148.

[39] Dolgorukov, "Agrarnaia volna," No. 1, column 25.

[40] Specific references to these settlements in GARF, f. 102, DP OO, op. 233 (II), 1905 g., d. 999, ch. 45, t. II, l. 104 (Borisovka); op. 236 (II), 1906 g., d. 700, ch. 58, ll. 12–12 ob (Fitizh); ll. 17–17 ob. (Kobylka); l. 21 (Dar'ino). In Graivoron District, a chapter also existed at Golovchino (Lisichanskaia Parish): M. K. Gudilin, the rural teacher from Graivoron District later elected as a Deputy of the First State Duma from Kursk Province, was chairman (Al'bom portretov, 38). E. I. Kiriukhina ("Mestnye organizatsii," 84–156) claimed to have identified 57 village chapters and 12 village committees organized in 1905, second only to the Don Region (70).

[41] GARF, f. 102, DP OO, op. 233 (II), 1905 g., d. 1800, ch. 53 ("O predstavlenii otchetov o sostoianii revoliutsionnago dvizheniia v Imperii i spiskov anarkhistov, sotsialistov-revoliutsionerov, boevykh druzhin, a takzhe nabliudenie za litsami etikh kategorii. Po Kurskoi gubernii"), ll. 17 ob.–18.

Russian Union.[42] References to the formation of local chapters of the Union in Putivl' District date to November.[43] As late as December 1905, when the assault on Union affiliates began in earnest, an official in Graivoron District noted the following: "Throughout the whole district the rush of villagers to organize peasant unions is being observed. In several communes, 50 kopecks are being collected from each household to benefit them. A leading role of the teachers is suspected in the matter."[44] A number of militant chapters stayed active in Shchigrov District even after 1906–1907.[45]

The provincial administration's first efforts to try those accused of participation in the February unrest were also organized during the summer of 1905. The cases were heard in June–August in a series of public trials before the Kursk Regional Court, sitting at Sevsk. High numbers of convictions (108 of 134 defendants) were obtained, but the publicity of the trials—in which prominent members of the Russian Bar spared no effort in picturing the peasants in the dock as the real victims[46]—must have been deemed dangerous enough to warrant postponement of further hearings. Sentences for the July–August defendants were harsher than for those tried when hearings resumed in April 1906. Of 134 accused, 28 were acquitted, 74 ordered to serve 1–2 years under strict regime at the provincial correctional facility and 32 persons (including six minors) sentenced to

---

[42] An account of the representative from Dmitriev District on the early discussions among peasants and the final decision to send delegates to the November congress is in *Protokoly delegatskogo soveshchaniia*, 37.

[43] On November 9, the assembly of Gruzchanskaia Parish, Putivl' District, voted to join the VKS and adopted its published resolutions. Three days later, the assembly hosted a general meeting of some 1,000 local peasants, at which eight Union representatives (from nearby Konotop, Viazovoe and Zemlianka) appeared as speakers. Komissiia pri Kurskom gubispolkome po organizatsii prazdnovaniia 20-letiia revoliutsii 1905 goda, *1905 god v Kurskoi gubernii*, 53.

[44] *RSKG*, No. 168, p. 136 (telegram, Graivoron District Police Commandant T. A. Chudnovskii to Governor V. M. Borzenko, 20 December 1905).

[45] *Iz istorii Kurskogo kraia*, No. 278, 354–357 (report, 1910 [no date], Governor of Kursk Province), from GAKO, f. 1, op. 20, 1910 g., d. 8073, ll. 28–31). The report gave details on a campaign of arson and assassination during 1907–1908 that prosecutors associated with the Shchigrov District affiliate of the Peasant Union and thirty-seven local organizations, which seem from the document to have been organized between July and December 1906 (see below).

[46] Peasant defendants were represented by the dean of the Moscow Bar, Fedor Nikiforovich Plevako (1843–1909), and his associates (Roop, Orlov, Staal, Zhdanov). *Russkiia Vedomosti*, 3 July 1905, 2, col. 4.

jail terms of 8 months or less.[47] In later cases, longer terms in the correctional facility were exceptional; eight-month sentences were the rule. Yet it was entirely clear to all that the great majority of offenders were not even apprehended. The seeming leniency of courts in sentencing and the small numbers of persons actually brought to trial greatly enraged both the local nobility and the provincial authorities, who opined that the insignificance of punishments promoted among peasants the sense that one could act against one's enemies with impunity. Governor Borzenko observed tartly that "besides the aforesaid factors, the emergence of agrarian disorders in the province was undoubtedly influenced by the weakness of criminal repression and the complete material immunity [of the participants] for the damage and losses borne by the landowners. The riots that took place in 1905 in Dmitriev District ended for the guilty peasants in very insignificant punishment, and those who carried out the looting and destruction of the estates bore no material responsibility whatsoever. Moreover, at the trial in this case, thanks to the participation of several members of the Bar, the accused were held more to be the victims of violence and arbitrariness than entirely guilty thieves. All of this, of course, could not remain without influence, and acted in a demoralizing manner on the peasants, who came to believe in their full immunity from punishment."[48]

Furthermore, the severe strictures of the *ukaz* of 10 April, authorizing temporary District Committees to impose heavy reparations on communes whose members had taken part in attacks on estates, were left without action in the Council of Ministers, where it was thought that measures that further impoverished peasants would not improve matters.[49]

During the spring and summer months, ominous portents began to gather with concerning prospects for the harvest. The 1904 harvest had not nearly equaled the bumper crops of 1902, but they were judged successful when measured against yields for 1903. All winter sowings were completed on time and under good conditions: when the fields "went away under the snow," hopes were high for a repetition of the previous year's yields. Moderate and consistent winter temperatures (without sharp movement, frost to thaw) and the good condition of the crops as they emerged from under the blanket of snow encouraged such expectations.

---

[47] RGIA, f. 1405, op. 108, 1906 g., d. 6805, ll. 70, 87–88, d. 6806, 1. 98.

[48] RGIA, f. 1291, op. 122, 1906 g., d. 123, ll. 44–44 ob.

[49] See documents and commentaries in "Iz istorii bor'by," *Krasnyi arkhiv*, 1936, 5 (78): 128–160.

The vagaries of rainfall and temperatures, however, so frequently the foe of Kursk Province's farmers, turned against the tillers. April and May were unusually hot and without rain, and spring crops had to be sown in drought conditions or sown far too late. Crops wilted dangerously in the heat. In not a few places, desperate communities plowed the winter crop under and planted millet. Complete disaster was averted when the rains came at the end of May, but the damage was done. Unusually warm weather in the spring months caused premature ripening of those grains that had survived the two-month drought. Estimates sent in by correspondents of the Statistical Bureau showed that results for spring sowings were particularly poor. In most districts, harvests of the three selected crops (rye, oats and potatoes) were not only below 1885–1913 averages, but also well below 1904 yields, especially for spring grains.[50] Shortage of fodder, felt as early as the autumn and winter months of 1904–1905, forced the massive sell-offs of peasant cattle that were so often a harbinger of crop failure.

> Turning to the question of supplies of fodder for feeding livestock in 1905, it must be said that in this matter the autumn turned out to be most unsatisfactory. As a result of an insufficient harvest of grasses and a shortened time period for pasturing, several localities have been experiencing shortages of fodder since the autumn of 1904. This shortage sharpened toward the end of winter and the beginning of spring, especially in Belgorod, Graivoron, L'gov, Sudzha and Oboian Districts. Because of a shortfall in fodder, the peasants were forced to buy rye and spring straw, the prices of which rose to unheard of sums—on average, to more than a ruble a load of rye straw and to one and a half rubles for oat straw. In places, even 3 rubles a load was paid. The shortage of fodder and its great expense—and also the financial need of households for payment of taxes—caused a broad sell-off of cattle. The same sell-off has been noted in the autumn months of 1905 as well.[51]

---

[50] Harvests of winter sowings on the allotments came in at 95% of the 1885–1913 average, spring sowings at 68%. The usual suspects in the eastern part of the province made up the bulk of those districts harvesting close to or less than 50% of their 1885–1913 averages for spring sowings: Belgorod, Graivoron, Korocha, Novyi Oskol', Oboian, Staryi Oskol', Timskoi and Shchigrov Districts. Harvests of winter sowings were also seriously under average (less than 80%) for Belgorod, Graivoron, Oboian, Timskoi and Shchigrov Districts. Potato crops (15,302,292 *poods*) gave almost 7 million *poods* less than in 1904 and for the province as a whole brought in 81.3% of the 1885–1913 average. Commentary in *Obzor Kurskoi gubernii za 1905 god*, 1–7. *TS-KhSKGZ za 1905 god*. I, II, Ill, IV (1905–1906).

[51] *Obzor Kurskoi gubernii za 1905 god*, 15. Wage indices recorded by the Statistical Bureau showed a mild decline in pay in certain districts, but as it became evident that harvests were in peril, the negative effects began to spread, depressing wages during the weeks of the hay harvest (from mid-May) by an average of 3.7% and during grain harvest by 15%. Rent contracts for spring sowings (+3.3%) and those for winter plantings (+6.1 %) continued their upward trend. *TS-KhSKGZ za 1905 god*.

While the spring and summer months after the sharp outburst of unrest in February 1905 were ones of relative calm in Kursk Province in terms of recorded incidents of open disorders, mass acts requiring the intervention of police and army units continued to take place. Such events took on a new intensity in late October. The Administration of State Properties in Kursk and Orel Provinces reported timbering in the Puzatskii State Forest by peasants from the village of Puzatskii, Verkhosemskaia Parish, Tim District, during 30 September–2 October.[52] On 6 October, the Director of the Department of Police informed the chief of the Kursk Provincial Gendarmerie of acts of a gang of arsonists preying upon the estates of the Volkonskie near Sabynino, Sabyninskaia Parish, in Belgorod District.[53] In Putivl' District on 27–28 October, peasants from Gvintovo, in Popovo-Slobodskaia Parish (4 miles from the Moscow–Kiev–Voronezh Railway line), carried out attacks on two nearby estates (owned by merchants), during which they carted off timber, grain and moveable property and took care to destroy the interiors of the dwellings. In the ensuing investigation, the situation of the residents of Gvintovo, without forest or pasture, was contrasted with the actions of the owners, who refused to rent wood lots or grazing land to villagers and charged extortionate prices for lumber.[54] On October 30, fifty peasants from Shilovka (Burynskaia Parish), enraged over the steward's refusal to lease them land in an area desired, looted the estate of Countess Maria Dmitrievna Apraksina (1,591 *desiatiny*), set fire to the estate's gristmill and smashed the interior of the offending steward's apartments. A unit of Cossacks under the command of the District Police Commandant was ordered to the scene to restore order and conduct an inquest.[55] The end of October also witnessed the

---

[52] *RSKG*, No. 135, pp. 116–117 (GAKO, f. 1, op. 15, d. 68, l. 97), report, Superintendent of the Kursk-Orel Administration of State Properties to Kursk Governor N. N. Gordeev, 14 November 1905.

[53] GARF, f. 102, DP OO, op. 233 (II), 1905 g., d. 2550, ch. 44, ll. 79–80 (telegram, Director, Department of Police Iust to Governor N. N. Gordeev, 6 October 1905).

[54] RGIA, f. 1405, op. 194, 1908 g., d. 102 ("O krest'ianskikh besporiadkakh v Kurskoi gubernii"), ll. 9–9 ob. (Copy, report of the Procurator of the Sumy Regional Court to the Procurator of the Khar'kov Judicial Chamber, No. 3358, 3 November 1905.); ll. 20–21 (estate of L. Efremov): copy, report of the Procurator of the Sumy Regional Court to the Procurator of the Khar'kov Judicial Chamber, No. 3949, 22 December 1905; ll. 22–22 ob. (estate of S. Oleinik): copy, report, the same parties, No. 3951, 23 December 1905.

[55] *Ibid.*, ll. 9–9 ob. (copy, report, Procurator of the Sumy Regional Court to Procurator of the Khar'kov Judicial Chamber, 3 November 1905.); 19–19 ob. (copy, report, same parties, 22 December 1905). Initial reference in GARF, f. 102, DP OO, op. 233 (II), 1905 g., d. 2550, ch. 44, ll. 84–85: private letter, 29 October 1905 from the Main Office of

beginning of large-scale timbering in the forests on the vast domains of Princess Zinaida Nikolaevna Iusupova at Rakitnaia (26,952 *desiatiny*), Rakitianskaia Parish, and in those on the adjoining estates of Pavel Ivano-vich Kharitonenko[56] in Graivoron District, at Sitnaia (1,200 *desiatiny*) in Viazovskaia Parish. In both cases, the incidents lasted well into November and involved villagers from several large settlements. Once again, troops had to be deployed locally to restore order.[57] On 24 October in the village of Korobkovo, Saltykovskaia Parish, Staryi Oskol' District, "60–70 young fellows" invaded the estate of landowner P. N. Korobkov, attacked the steward's quarters and the administrative offices and broke 115 windows, destroying several window frames. Attempts by the District Police Com-mandant and the Land Captain to calm the mood in the parish had no last-ing effect: the locality was to join in the unrest that was to sweep the east-ern districts after November 1.[58]

3. Rural Disturbances of November–December 1905

Since the several aspects of the context in which the November wave of disorders unfolded relate directly to the chronology of the movement as a whole, we will return to it in Chapter IV, but a summary account may be

Her Radiance Countess Maria Dmitrievna Apraksina, Petersburg, to the Ministry of In-ternal Affairs, with a telegram from the Shilovka estate's steward attached.

[56] The main Kharitonenko facility (and sugar refinery) was at Krasnaia Iaruga. Ministry officials put its size at 11,023½ *desiatiny*. Ministerstvo zemledeliia i gosudarstvennykh imushchestv, Departament zemledeliia, *Kratkiia spravochnyia svedeniia. Vyp. Pervyi*, 9–10.

[57] GARF, f. 102, DP OO, op. 233 (II), 1905 g., d. 2550, ch. 44, ll. 107–108 ob.: private memo, 5 November 1905, from Princess Iusupova to Superintendent of the Ministry of Internal Affairs P. N. Durnovo. I have dated the emergence of unrest at the Kharito-nenko estate at Sitnaia (Viazovskaia Parish)—also a timbering—at this same time. Both incidents appear together on the listing of damage (RGIA, f. 1291, op. 122, 1905 g., d. 112 ["So svedeniiami, donesennymi Gubernatorami o razmerakh ubytkov, prichinen-nykh agramymi besporiadkami"], ll. 310–310) and were heard on the same days by the Kursk Regional Court (4–6 June 1907): f. 1405, op. 194, 1908 g., d. 102, ll. 126–126 ob. (Copy, report of the Procurator of the Kursk Regional Court to the First Department, Ministry of Justice, No. 2181, 27 June 1907). The villages initially involved, Morku-shino, Dunaika, and Rakitnaia, were all located in the immediate vicinity of the Iusupov and Kharitonenko estates. RSKG, No. 116, p. 105; GAKO, f. 1, op. 15, d. 13, l. 13.

[58] GARF, f. 102, DP OO, op. 233 (II), 1905 g., d. 2550, ch. 44, ll. 104–104 ob. (extract from report, Commandant of the Kursk Provincial Gendarmerie Colonel Vel'k to the Department of Police, 6 November 1905).

advanced here. Against the background of worsening prospects for the harvest of 1905, the undercurrent of tense expectation among the peasant populace after the events of February remained, fed by external events: the debacle that struck the Russian fleet at Tsushima and the unprecedented upsurge in public activism that unfolded even in "backward" Kursk Province, in which the peasantry itself could not but be caught up. This atmosphere of crisis, however, was to gain immeasurably in intensity under the impact of the events of October, and set the stage for an extraordinarily violent series of disorders that, though similar in form to the riots in Dmitriev District, were to far surpass them in scale. At least in the initial phases, the provincial administration was for a time to find itself entirely helpless to combat them.

For the period of 1–17 November concentrated quite numerous incidents of the more extreme forms of unrest in two different areas of the province, and individual incidents of a most serious character continued to be reported in a number of locales outside these centers. In an atmosphere of panic, the Governor began to be deluged with demands from badly frightened estate owners for military protection in cases of real or imagined danger. Many such requests (outside the main centers of unrest) could be dealt with through local police structures, but in cases of well-connected absentee magnates, who applied over the heads of provincial administrators to the central ministries for troops or police actions, the Governor was duty-bound to obey orders.[59] Throughout the period, the Governor of Kursk Province (to December 1905, N. N. Gordeev; the Vice-Governor V. M. Borzenko succeeded his boss after Christmas) had to conduct a continuous struggle both to secure more troops to back up local authorities in keeping the peace and to hold on to those at hand. These aims ran up against ever-more urgent demands on the manpower

---

[59] This was to be typical of the whole period. The largest number of requests came from Princess Iusupova and her husband, Feliks Feliksovich, beginning in May 1905 with a letter directed to Minister of Finance Kokovtsev who took up their case with the MVD (GARF, f. 102, DP OO, op. 233 (II), 1905 g. d. 2550, ch. 44, ll. 9–10), and repeated in November 1905 (ll. 107–108 ob., 110, 113–115, 125–127, 134–135), June 1906 (GARF, f. 102, DP OO, op. 236 (II), 1906 g., d. 700, ch. 58, ll. 81, 94–94 ob., 105–106, 184–186, 199200) and May 1907 (GARF, f. 102, DP, 4-oe deloproizvodstvo, op. 99, 1907 g., ch. 21, ll. 28–29, 34–34 ob. (this last a tart letter of Princess Iusupova herself attempting to reject the Governor's longstanding complaint that the estate's exploitive and inconsistent policies toward local peasants was the root cause of unrest at Rakitnaia), but I also encountered numerous letters or telegrams from a whole constellation of representatives of the ultra-conservatives among the local gentry or large landowners with "access."

resources available to commanders of the Kiev Military District to meet crises simultaneously in a growing number of provinces. Multiple outbreaks of unrest in the province required measures that collided with the standing order that military units not be deployed below squad levels, an order that hampered the provincial authorities' efforts to shore up local forces in several places at once.[60] As in February, local police personnel in the principal areas of the disturbances or near the bigger rural settlements proved entirely ineffectual in suppressing disorders in their initial phases. Confronted with the ineffectiveness of the authorities in combating unrest, provincial nobles gave vent to shock, despair and panic, and personal appeals to the Emperor. Yet the spectacle of defenseless noble families leaving their estates to the depredations of militant peasants and fleeing to the district seats also provoked real anger at government weakness. One acidly worded telegram fired off to the Minister of Internal Affairs by Nikolai Petrovich Dmitriev, one of Staryi Oskol' District's large landowners, on 15 November, gave voice to what was to be a common verdict of the Kursk provincial gentry on the effectiveness of the local authorities in discharging their most elemental responsibilities: "From the 1st to the 7th of November, seventeen private estates have been looted and burned down in Staryi Oskol' District, Kursk Province. As is well known, the province was declared to be in a state of increased security. This latter is expressed in a single 'hundred' of Cossacks, which seems, naturally, to act only as witness to the destruction and violence taking place. One thinks that the government would have done better if it had declared itself powerless to protect the property and lives of those persons who have the misfortune to have put all their savings into landed property. Then, at least, each of us would know that he is outside the law, and might act in light of such circumstances."[61]

Novyi Oskol' and Staryi Oskol' Districts, on Kursk Province's eastern boundary with Voronezh Province, were the sites of the first mass outbreaks, which began (as predicted) in the big village of Chernianka on 1 November 1905. The report of the Chief of the Provincial Gendarmerie on 12 November noted the role played by young peasants:

---

[60] GARF, f. 102, DP OO, op.233 (II), 1905 g., d. 2550, ch. 44, ll.4–6, 11–13, 19–23, 29, 33, 46, 49, 140. Admiral Dubasov states in the abstract of his report (undated, probably drawn at the end of his tour of duty on 1 December 1905) that in October, 1905, the authorities had on hand 1,350 infantrymen, 376 dragoons and 474 Cossacks. "Agrarnoe dvizhenie v 1905 g. po otchetam Dubasova i Panteleeva," *KA*, 1925, No. 4–5 (11–12), 185–186.

[61] *Ibid.*, l. 150 (telegram). Dmitriev's estate was at Lukoianovka, Saltykovskaia Parish, Staryi Oskol' District.

On 1 November of the current year in the settlement of Chernianka, at the fair, even though this last was not distinguished by any special liveliness, one was particularly struck by the prevalence of local peasant youth and youths from adjacent villages. These peasant youths went about the market in small groups, obviously in a state to be easily provoked. Three constables and seven police guards [*strazhniki*], assembled in Chernianka for maintenance of order at the fair, were present on the square, watching after these groups. Around 2 o'clock in the afternoon these small knots of youths, joining together, began to form a crowd of significant size near the shop of Naidenov, making noise, taunting the shopkeeper, but also threatening members of the police as they passed. Then the crowd began to break the windows of the pharmacy of Ashman the Jew and of the merchant Markov's store, and then, with the shout, "Hurrah, freedom!" marched on the estate compound of Prince KASATKIN [*1,859.20 desiatiny—BRM*], which stood at a distance of one *versta* from the square. The estate of the Prince was looted, even if there was no attempt at arson. After this, the crowd returned to the village, looted and destroyed the interior of a state liquor shop, plundered and set fire to [Petr Vasilievich] MARKOV's store and then set off for the oil press of the SHCHEVTSOVY [*1,778.75 desiatiny—BRM*], located at the other end of the village, which was looted and set on fire. At this moment, the District Police Commandant arrived with a unit of Cossacks from Novyi Oskol'. When the Cossacks were riding through the square, shouts of "Beat the Cossacks!" issued from the crowd and several shots rang out, but no one was injured. The Cossacks were nonetheless forced to draw their sabers and disperse the mob by force. Receiving news that looting and arson had begun on the farmstead of Prince KASATKIN (whose main compound had already been looted), the Police Commandant and the Cossacks hurried to the scene, but upon arriving were met by armed resistance. Shots were fired at them, and as a result, the Cossacks fired a volley into the crowd. Three peasants were killed and several wounded. The fires were put out by the Cossacks.[62]

---

[62] *Ibid.*, l. 154. It was evident from the sources that reporting individual incidents became impossible with the onset of mass disorders. Three items, however, could be used to restore a picture of the events. 1.) Report, 12 November 1905, No. 3859, Commandant of the Kursk Provincial Gendarmerie, Colonel Vel'k, to the Department of Police (GARF, f. 102, DP OO, op. 233 (II), 1905 g., d. 2550, ch. 44, ll. 154–156 ob.), hereinafter as Vel'k; 2.) a numbered list of estates attacked between 1 and 6 November in Novyi Oskol' District, compiled by the district police commandant for use of the Temporary District Committee ("Svedeniia o kolichestve razgromlennykh i sozhzhennykh ekonomii pomeshchikov v Novooskol'skom uyezde s 1 po 6 noiabria 1905 g.," *RSKG*, prilozhenie 1, 221–225 (GAKO, f. 1, op. 15, d. 4, ll. 44–48 ob.), and 3.) a list dated 11 February 1906 of estates damaged in Kursk Province (without dates of the incidents) in RGIA, f. 1291, op. 122, 1905 g., d. 112 ("So svedeniami, donesennymi Gubernatorami o razmerakh ubytkov, prichinennykh agrarnymi besporiadkami"); for Novyi Oskol' District, ll. 311–313; for Staryi Oskol' District, ll. 314–314 ob. For Staryi Oskol' District, the absence of dates was particularly problematic and had to be estimated by geographical proximity to incidents with known dates. Estate size in Novyi Oskol' District drawn from *KGV*, prilozhenie k ofitsial'noi chasti, No. 3, 13 January 1904.

The crowd in this action was estimated at 1,000 persons.[63] Later in the day, peasants at the settlement of Okuni (Chernianskaia Parish), a few *versta* north along the railway, ransacked the state liquor shop in the settlement itself and then looted and burned the gentry estate of Sofia Fedorovna Siskevich (270 *desiatiny*).[64]

Map 3. Oskol' Valley, 1–5 November, 1905

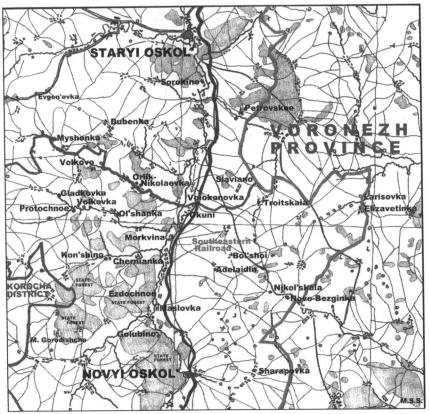

---

[63] RGIA, f. 1405, op. 108, 1906 g., d. 7006 ("O krest'ianskikh besporiadkakh v Novooskol'skom uyezde"), ll. 1–4 (copy, report of the Procurator of the Kursk Regional Court to the Procurator of the Khar'kov Judicial Chamber, No. 3233, 3 December 1905. A press account put numbers at 2,000 and reported the beating of Kasatkin-Rostovskii (in another version he was horse-whipped). In its version, the Chernianka riots had been preceded by the destruction of the parish administration and the home of parish elder Firsov at *sloboda* Slonovka. *Russkiia Vedomosti*, 10 November 1905, 4, col. 1.

[64] *RSKG*, Prilozhenie I, 221, Nos. 6–7; Vel'k, 155.

Unrest began to gather momentum with the dawn of the next day, spreading through the parish, with devastating attacks on several estates in the vicinity of the villages of Bol'shoi Khutor, just west of Chernianka, and of Maslovka, Morkvina and Ezdochnoe, moving directly south along the Southeastern Railway line. The violence struck further south along the railway into Prigorodniaia Parish, in the area of the parish center itself, when, on the night of the 2nd at the village of Golubina, the cooperage, cow barn and workers' mess on the lands of Marshal of the Nobility Vladimir Petrovich Miatlev (5,702 *desiatiny*) were burned down; the rest of the estate's installations—manor house, distillery and almost all remaining outbuildings—were sacked and burned three days later.[65]

In the course of the early stages of the disorders, local police structures appear simply to have melted away. The District Police Commandant, at the head of a unit of fifty Cossacks, appeared in Chernianka a short time after the beginning of the disorders. Aside from defending itself on the village square, however, this force seems to have confined its activity to guarding the (already looted) estate of the reactionary (former) Marshal of the Nobility of Novyi Oskol' District, Prince Nikolai Fedorovich Kasatkin-Rostovskii. Such seeming favoritism deeply embittered some members of the local community.[66]

Yet provincial authorities were already facing manpower problems on several fronts. The administration of the estate of Princess Iusupova had once again begun to importune the Governor to reinforce the unit of Kuban Cossacks already deployed on the Rakitnaia estate (Graivoron District) in order to halt massive timbering of the estate's forest tracts, which had begun at the end of October.[67] Alarming news was just beginning to flow in from the central districts (see earlier). More disturbing, though, was the speed with which the movement in the eastern districts was spreading: on 3 November, reports showed that looting and destruction of installations and inventory by fire and axe had not only become general in Chernianskaia Parish, but had also inspired a powerful wave of analogous

---

[65] RGIA, f. 1405, op. 194, 1908 g., d. 102, ll. 101–101 ob. (copy, report, Procurator of the Kursk Regional Court to Procurator of the Khar'kov Judicial Chamber, No. 4500, 28 November 1906). *RSKG*, Prilozhenie I, 221–222, Nos. 8–15; Vel'k, 155. The attacks on Miatlev's estate in GARF, f. 102, DPOO, op. 233 (II), 1905 g., d. 2550, ch. 44, ll. 98–100, and *RSKG*, Prilozhenie I, 222, No. 19.

[66] A particularly outraged telegram from the Shchevtsov brothers to the Minister of Internal Affairs dated November 5 appears in GARF, f. 102, DPOO, op. 233 (II), 1905 g., d. 2550, ch. 44, ll. 107–108 ob.

[67] GARF, f. 102, DP OO, op. 233 II), 1905 g., d. 2550, ch. 44, ll. 98–100.

acts in adjoining Khalanskaia, Ol'shanskaia and Volotovskaia Parishes, and had begun to encourage such acts at sites in Bogoslovskaia and Orlik-ovskaia Parishes in Staryi Oskol' District. A report of this date made a note of the destruction of estate installations and slaughter of cattle by neighboring peasants on the domains of the heirs of Count Kochubei at Volokonovka, Obukhovskaia Parish, Staryi Oskol' District, just off the railway line now nine miles north of Chernianka.[68] According to the testimony of a Land Captain of Korotoiak District, Voronezh Province, it was under the influence of tidings of these incidents that multiple loot-ings and burnings of estates first began in his precinct, in the small hours of 5 November, in Staro-Bezginskaia Parish, just across the provincial border.[69]

Disorders of analogous intensity and character were reported on the same day at sites clustered along the length of the River Orlik, which served as the boundary line between Novyi Oskol' and Staryi Oskol' Dis-tricts. The troubles began on the southern (Novyi Oskol') side in Ol'shanskaia Parish, at the parish center of Ol'shanka, where peasants looted and burned down the manor house, distillery, flour mills and all outbuildings on the estate of their old master, Prince Ivan Iurevich Trubet-skoi (5,098 *desiatiny*),[70] and spread quickly to smaller private holdings near the settlements of Volkovka, Gladkovo, Novomatveevka, Protochnoe and Volkovo.[71] Disorders on November 4 inflicted heavy damage on a number of estates in and around the village of Kon'shino: parties of peas-ants looted and burned the buildings on the estates of nine different pri-vate landowners.[72] On the northern side of the river in Staryi Oskol' Dis-trict, peasant crowds looted and burned a number of estates at the villages of Myshenka, Luboshev and Dubenka (Bogoslovskaia Parish).[73]

---

[68] *Ibid.*, ll. 95, 155 ob. (Vel'k).

[69] *Revoliutsionnoe dvizhenie v Voronezhskoi gubernii 1905–1907 gg.*, Nos. 204–206, pp. 290–291, No. 242, pp. 314–315. Subsequent to the events of the morning of the 5th, analogous incidents were then to be reported in Biriuch and Nizhne-Devitsk *uyezdy* at localities adjacent to the zones of disturbances in Novyi Oskol' and Staryi Oskol' Dis-tricts.

[70] *RSKG*, Prilozhenie I, 223, No. 28; Vel'k, 155. Losses at the Ol'shanka estate: 200,000 rubles.

[71] Vel'k, l. 155

[72] *RSKG*, Prilozhenie I, 224–225; Vel'k, l. 155.

[73] The Staryi Oskol' District incidents were the most problematic in terms of dating. Direct reference to the destruction of the Kochubei estate at Volokonovka was made in the Governor's coded telegram to the MVD on 3 November (GARF, f. 102, DPOO op. 233 (II), 1905 g., d. 2550, ch. 44, l. 96). Colonel Vel'k's report for events up to 7 November

The Governor's cable of November 3 noted the deployment of his last Cossack "*sotnia*": by the 6th, 200 Cossacks and a company of infantry were on the scene of unrest.[74] The arrival of troops in Chernianka on the night of 4 November began to take effect quite rapidly, and the number and concentration of disorders fell sharply. Operating at night in freezing snowy weather, parceling the available troops into smaller units, local authorities struggled mightily to gain the upper hand. District Police Commandant V. I. Uspenskii reported on the 5th from Obukhovskaia Parish on the military situation: "I have forestalled the sacking of the estate of Vsevolozhskii at Ivanovka and the Dmitriev and Slaviano farmsteads with a company of infantry. The operation at Slaviano was carried out at night: all stolen grain has been seized and 13 persons arrested. Three infantry platoons are marching on Chernianka. I have only a hundred of Cossacks: they are too few. I request another hundred. Rioting embraces a vast area: last night, a liquor store was destroyed; they burned the estate of Land Captain Starov and [an estate] at Luboshevka. It is impossible to link up with Police Commandant Ivanovskii. The area of rioting grows. The roads are out. I am going to Orlik with a half-hundred of Cossacks. A platoon is with [Land Captain] Beliaev. A platoon is at Volokonovka with the Precinct Captain and an investigator."[75]

The early centers of unrest, by now invested by considerable numbers of troops, were now without further incident. On the periphery of the original zone of disturbances, however, individual incidents continued to be recorded for 5–6 November at a distance of 25–30 miles from the original center of the outbreaks: at Sorokino in Dolgopolianskaia Parish (22 miles north of Chernianka on the railway line), in Kladovskaia Parish, on the large estate of Nikolai Petrovich Korobkov in the vicinity of

listed two more (Dubenka, Sorokino) and hinted at troubles on the estates of P. N. Korobkov (Saltykovo, Saltykovskaia Parish) and Iurkevich (ll. 255 ob., 156). Place names show two zones: Dubenka, Myshenka (Bogoslovskaia Parish), Orlik-Nikolaevka (Orlikovskaia), Volokonovka and Slaviano (Obukhovskaia) were located along the border with Novyi Oskol' District. Concerning the last two, the dates were fixed in the source. For Myshenka, Dubenka and Orlik, their very close proximity to the zone of unrest around Ol'shanka in Novyi Oskol' District suggest dating or about 4 November from incidents in adjacent locales. For Sretenka and Evgen'evka (on the post road), and Lopukhinka in the northwest corner of Kladovskaia Parish—the farthest northerly points in the unrest, I have dated them to 6 November: in accordance with a petition lodged by Madame Starova of 12 November 1907, concerning her compensation (RGIA, f. 1291, op. 50, 1906 g., d. 5, ch. X, ll. 113–113 ob.).

[74] *Ibid.*, l. 96. Troop estimates for 6 November 1905 at l. 111.

[75] *RSKG*, No. 120, p. 107 (GAKO, f 1, op. 15, d. 63, ll. 129–130).

Saltykovo Saltykovskaia, Staryi Oskol' District, and in Prigorodniaia Parish south of Chernianka in Novyi Oskol' District, these sites being now some 30 miles distant from Chernianka.[76]

Map 4. Central Districts, 3–7 November, 1905

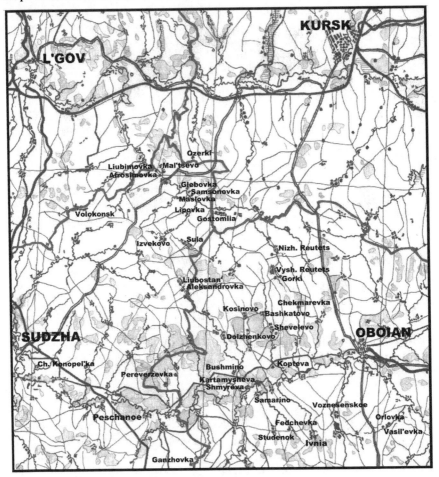

[76] RGIA, f. 1291, op. 122, 1905 g., d. 112, ll. 314–314 ob., Nos. 2, 9. Along with incident at Lopukhinka, dated to 6 November by virtue of Blanqui Starova's testimony in her petition, RGIA, f. 1291, op. 50, 1906 g., d. 5 ("O vydache po zakonu 15 marta 1906 g. ssudy postradavshim ot agrarnykh bezporiadkov zemlevladel'tsam Vitebskoi, Voronezhskoi, Ekaterinoslavskoi i Kurskoi gubernii"), ll. 113–113 ob.

The next phase of the troubles in Kursk Province, in its central districts, began at the same time that peasant disorders in the eastern districts had attained their most dangerous phase. It was in Sudzha District, at about 7 o'clock in the evening of 3 November, in Skorodenskaia Parish, that a barn on the estate of Land Captain Vladimir Aleksandrovich Rapp at Izvekova (414 *desiatiny*) was set on fire by unknown arsonists, destroying a steam thresher and other inventory valued at 9,000 rubles. Rapp and Precinct Captain Rodovich (the latter arriving on the scene to conduct the investigation) went to the nearby village of Izvekova (Nemcha) to detain two peasant suspects, but encountered resistance from the villagers. The two officers were beaten up and had to flee back to Rapp's estate, where "they defended themselves against the peasants, weapons in hand."[77] A second effort to arrest the pair and those that had participated in the beating the following day likewise failed in the face of resistance: the residents of Izvekova, now aided by villagers from nearby settlements, freed all five detainees by force. A force of Cossacks at the nearby Sabashnikov sugar-beet refinery at Liubimovka was hurriedly posted to Rapp's estate.[78] It is not without interest to note that serious outbreaks of violence were here preceded once again by narrow local acts of resistance to the representatives of authority, in which, as at Sal'noe on 8 and 10 February and at the fair in Chernianka on 1 November, these latter were publicly faced down by peasant militants. Though the 5th and the 6th passed without incident, the fact remained that peasant rebels had stood down and humiliated the Land Captain and the police. On the evening of the 7th, the disorders began in earnest, not at Izvekova (for the Cossack detachment had by this time arrived there), but at adjacent Sula, the parish's largest settlement (2,340 inhabitants in 1897). "The police captain of the 2nd Precinct on this date has informed me by telephone that in the village of Sula, Skorodenskaia Parish, on the evening of 7 November, a crowd of peasants of the said village destroyed, looted and burned down all structures on the estate of the landowner Maria Aleksandrovna Mal'tseva [*422 desiatiny—BRM*] causing damage to Mal'tseva in the sum of 70,000 rubles. The cap-

---

[77] *RSKG*, No. 134 ("Svedeniia o razgrome i podzhogakh ekonomii pomeshchikov Sudzhanskago uyezda so 2 po 14 noiabria 1905 g."), 114 (item 1), compiled by the Sudzha District Police Commandant Pozhidaev, dated November, 1905 (GAKO, f. 1, op. 15, d. 7, ll. 344–346 ob.); RGIA, f. 1405, op. 194, 1908 g., d. 137 ("O krest'ianskikh besporiadkakh v Sudzhanskom uyezde, Kurskoi gub."), l.1.

[78] *RSKG*, No. 119, p.107 (GAKO, f.1, op.15, d.7, l. 56), report, District Marshal of the Nobility Iur'evich and Acting District Police Commandant Orlovskii to Kursk Governor N. N. Gordeev, 4 November 1905.

tain is proceeding to an inquest and apprehension of the looted property and the guilty parties in the matter." The authorities were as yet badly informed: in this same action, several other estates had been heavily damaged, and the inquests, it turned out, were not to get under way for weeks, since rebels effectively sealed off the zone of unrest.[79] Well-intentioned villagers warned investigators trying to reach Sula from Sudzha that the local peasants were not allowing outsiders into the area and were threatening interlopers with beatings. Mounted armed men chased one official out of the vicinity of Sula, and by his own account, he was saved from acts of violence only by the fact that his own horse was fresh.[80]

Barring outsiders from the scene and—as had been the case in previous outbreaks—in the absence of troops or reliable police units, peasant rebels mounted devastating attacks on the private estates at several points in Skorodenskaia and adjacent Kostornianskaia Parishes. From Sula, unrest spread, the following evening, to the villages of Samsonovka and Glebovka on the Kursk-Sudzha post road and Lipovka (Lipnik) near Sula.[81]

Particular attention appears to have been paid by local peasants in Kostornianskaia Parish, during the nights of 9 and 11 November, to the estates of the Zhekulin clan, testimony to a particular animus of the surrounding communities toward this family that had long been influential in provincial affairs. The estate of Vladimir Ivanovich Zhekulin near Sula had already been destroyed by fire on the 7th. On the 9th, peasant rioters seized grain, cattle and movables at the main installations of the estate of former District Marshal of the Nobility Sergei Ivanovich Zhekulin at Belyi Kolodez (1,323 *desiatiny*) and set fire to the manor house and auxiliary structures.[82] At nearby Maslovka, on the lands of Aleksandra Ivanovna Zhekulina, already subjected to a series of minor acts of arson through the

---

[79] *Ibid.*, No. 124, p. 109 (GAKO, f. 1, op. 15, d. 7, l. 156), telegram, Acting Police Commandant Orlovskii to Governor Gordeev, 7 November 1905; full record at No. 134, p. 114 (items 2–5).

[80] RGIA, f. 1405, op. 194, 1908 g., d. 137, ll. 1 ob.-2.

[81] *RSKG*, No. 134, pp. 114–115, Items 6–12; No. 127, pp. 110–111 (GAKO, f. 1, op. 15, d. 7, ll. 128–129), report of Cornet Chekalov, 2nd Eiskii Regiment, to the Governor; No. 126, pp. 109–110 (GAKO, f. 1, op. 15, d. 7, ll. 113–119), District Police Commandant Orlovskii to the Governor. Chekalov noted that he could make no arrests; there was no one to guard detainees. Orlovskii reported that patrolmen were quitting and the constables had demanded raises. The destruction of the estate of O. K. Kologrivova at Samsonovka was undertaken at least in part by *odnodvortsy* from the big village of Gostomlia (Spasskaia Parish, Kursk District). RGIA, f. 1405, op. 194, 1908 g., d. 13 7, l. 5.

[82] *RSKG*, No. 134, p. 115 (item 13). Damage was posted at 100,000 rubles.

spring and summer months, a large haystack was set on fire.[83] On the 11th, movable property, grain and cattle were taken off the D'iakonov and Ivanov *khutora* of Sergei Ivanovich's estate and, as was now usual form, the peasants left the buildings in flames.[84] Tempers among provincial nobles were rising:

> I report to Your Excellency as follows. From 2 November, the peasants have been burning and looting the estates of the *pomeshchiki*: 30 estates have been destroyed. I have requested that the Governor save us by [sending] troops. On 3 November, [from Kursk] they promised to send us troops but sent nothing. On 9 November, 30 Cossacks arrived only after everything had been burned down. Only my estate, which is under the Cossacks' guard, remains whole. The Cossack commander has also requested help from the Governor; it was promised, but (again) nothing has been sent. The Kursk District Police Commandant, detailed to Sudzha District, is being recalled. He is sitting in Sudzha and giving completely unfulfillable orders by telephone. The landowners and estate employees are fleeing. Everything has been looted and the cost of the damage is in the millions. All is in ruins. The unrest is spreading. At the present time, the livestock and property that remain are being carried off daily, and thirty Cossacks are able to do nothing. Would that your instructions might even save peoples' lives![85]

In Skorodenskaia Parish, through the night of 10–11 November, peasants in Sula resumed their assault on Mal'tseva's ruined estate and in the days thereafter, attacks were mounted on private holdings in the parish in the vicinity of Volokonskoe, Aleksandrovka and Liubostan'; in Bol'she-Soldatskaia Parish, serious incidents of arson were reported on the Sabashnikov estates at Borshchen.[86] By November 14, however, military units—Cossacks, dragoons and infantry—had begun to arrive at Kostorna

---

[83] *Ibid.*, 115 (item 14). This estate had already been the object of a campaign of minor arson throughout the spring and summer months. GARF, f. 102, DP OO, op. 233 (II), d. 2550, ch. 44, ll.72–73 ob., 81–82 ob.

[84] *Ibid.*, 116 (items 18, 20).

[85] GARF, f. 102, DP OO, op. 233 (II), 1905 g., d. 2550, ch. 44, l. 131 (telegram, V. A. Rapp to Minister of Internal Affairs P. N. Durnovo, 11 November 1905).

[86] *RSKG*, No. 134, p. 114 (item 2); 115 (Item 17), 116 (Items 21–24). The sister of Mikhail Vasil'evich and Sergei Vasil'evich Sabashnikovy, Antonina Vasil'evna held land at Borshchen' (693 *desiatiny*) in her own right. She was also the widow of Aleksei Vladimirovich Evreinov (1853–1903), who owned a much larger estate at this site (2,230 *desiatiny*), granted to his father by Emperor Alexander I for valorous service during the campaigns of 1812–1814. Troubles on this larger estate date to 6 November, when peasants from Annina-Gusinovka (Bobrovskaia Parish, L'gov District) had driven their cattle onto the meadow land of the estate. *Ibid.*, No. 123, pp. 108–109 (GAKO, f. 1, op. 15, d. 5, l. 106).

to prepare for entry into Sula. In the northern parishes of Sudzha District, calm was to be gradually restored.[87]

According to Dolgorukov's account, "the widespread and stubborn view that the Tsar's Manifesto had granted freedom to seize landowners' wealth without punishment until 1 January" circulated widely among the peasant population of this locality. He included a description of the action:

> In the middle of November, the first blaze was lit on the estate of the aforesaid Land Captain (who had attempted to win support of the peasants for the resolutions of the Kursk Nobility on the 17 October Manifesto) and quickly the movement seized the whole region. In the course of several days, eighteen estates were more or less destroyed. Some escaped with minor damage or with the burning of individual buildings, but on other estates, absolutely everything was obliterated: stone structures taken apart brick by brick down to the very foundations, old parks and fruit orchards hacked down, apiaries destroyed, animal and inanimate inventory looted and disfigured. Steam threshers, harvesters and balers perished; pedigreed livestock, still warm, were skinned of their hides so that these might later be sold for a few kopecks. One pedigree bull, too heavy to carry across the frozen ground, was heaved onto an estate wagon, but when it failed to fit, someone took an axe and cut away from the living animal the whole hind quarters. Generally speaking, at the height of the looting, despite even the absence of troops or any measure of resistance whatever, people turned into wild beasts and the most senseless acts of vandalism were committed. In this movement, there was indeed an element of the *Pugachevshchina*. For example, a fellow from a nearby village, formerly a supervisor over the sugar-beet plantations on one of the looted estates (who had for some reason been fired and fined three rubles), appeared in a sheepskin coat over which he had donned blue and red sashes and, sitting in an armchair, directed the looting. More broadly, though, no system or premeditated plan whatever was evident in the movement. Estates were pillaged by the peasants of the nearest villages, and looted property was, in part quite openly carried back to their huts, and in part hurriedly sold somewhere for next to nothing.[88]

The outburst of violence in Skorodenskaia and Kostornianskaia Parishes had powerful echoes in the adjoining parishes of Oboian District and provoked disturbances in L'gov and Kursk Districts. To be sure, reports of troubles in Oboian District had begun to surface a week earlier, concerning a series of aggressive timberings in the forest preserves of the Ministry

---

[87] Arrival of troops on 14–15 November and the plan to utilize Kostorna as the central strongpoint in police and military operations in RGIA, f. 1405, op. 194, 1908 g., d.137,1.2 ob.

[88] Dolgorukov, "Agrarnaia volna," No. 2, column 94. The peasants called the man in the overcoat the "general with the sash," identified in later depositions as one Peter Ivanovich Makarov, against whom the police busily sought to collect evidence (RGIA, f. 1405 op. 194, 1908 g., d. 137, l. 4 ob.).

of State Domains and of various private estate owners, these limited to an area along the post road from Oboian to Sudzha at the juncture of Rybinskaia, Pavlovskaia and Dolzhenkovskaia Parishes.[89] With the onset of events in Sudzha District, however, the situation soon took a far more menacing turn. Between 12 and 16 November, peasants at various localities in Rybinskaia Parish (Kosinovo, Bashkatovo, Kopteva, Shevelevo), Medvenskaia Parish (Shelkovka-Nizhnyi Reutets, Vyshnii Reutets) and Pavlovskaia Parish (Samarino, Peschanoe) wholly or partially destroyed dwellings and outbuildings on sixteen different private holdings by fire and axe after looting the premises.[90] In reporting on disorders in localities of Oboian District adjacent to his own, the Land Captain of Kursk District's First Precinct observed that the authorities dared not appear in zones of unrest without armed convoy. "There are insults and threats at every turn and a complete non-recognition of authority"; efforts to read out the Manifesto of 3 November had no effect at all.[91] After the incidents of the 16th, however, unrest in Rybinskaia and Medvenskaia Parishes died out. The dates of the entry of troops into these parishes are not known, yet it may be assumed that the arrival of Cossack, dragoon and infantry units in the nearby parishes of Sudzha District on 14–15 November had its effect.

As in the development of events in Dmitriev District in February and in the Oskol' Valley, the concentration of acts of extreme violence in the cluster of contiguous parishes in Sudzha and Oboian Districts inspired

---

[89] *RSKG*, No. 122, p. 108 (GAKO, f. 1, op. 15, d. 6, ll. 59–61); No. 143, p. 122–123 (GAKO, f. 1, op. 15, d. 11, ll. 100–101 ob.), report, Oboian District Police Commandant Poletika to Governor N. N. Gordeev, 19 November 1905. RGIA, f. 1405, op. 194, 1908 g., d. 102, ll. 33–33 ob. (copy, report of the Procurator of the Kursk Regional Court to the Procurator of the Khar'kov Judicial Chamber, 28 February 1906, No. 740).

[90] Reconstruction of events in Oboian District began with listings of losses (RGIA, f. 1291, op. 122, 1905 g., d. 112, ll. 305–306) and the reports on prosecutions associated with disorders. These were reported in two batches in the *delo*, one for destruction of estates (*razgromy*) and the other on more minor offenses. All ministerial reporting on the former lacked any indication of dates (RGIA, f. 1405, op. 194, 1908 g., d. 102, ll. 17–18 ob., copy, report, Procurator of the Kursk Regional Court to the Procurator of the Khar'kov Judicial Chamber, 22 December 1905). All incidents were placed in the frame of 10–16 November by the report of the local Land Captain Kondrashov (*RSKG*, No. 140, pp. 119–120 [GAKO, f. 1, op. 15, d. 6, l. 142]). See Komissiia pri Kurskom gubispolkome po organizatsii prazdnovaniia 20-letiia revoliutsii 1905 goda, *op. cit.*, 13–14 ("Dnevnik politicheskikh i revoliutsionnykh sobytii po Kurskoi gubernii za 1905 god") and "Krest'ianskoe dvizhenie," 65–67.

[91] *RSKG*, No. 140, pp. 119–120 (GAKO, f. 1, op. 15, d. 6, l. 142).

similar acts at individual sites in adjoining parishes (Spasskaia, D'iakonovskaia and Rozhdestvenskaia) in Kursk District,[92] and to the west in
L'gov District (Kolpakovskaia, Penskaia and Sheptukhovskaia Parishes)
already at some distance from the initial zone of disturbances.[93] Even if
the arrival of military units at Kostorna on 14 November—accompanied
by contingents of police officials and investigators—spelled the end of
unrest in the central districts on the scale that it had assumed after 6 November, scattered clusters of more minor incidents were reported, as late
as December 4, at some distance from the early sites of the disorders, in
the southern parishes of both Sudzha and Oboian Districts; these were
expressed most frequently in acts of organized timbering of private
wooded tracts, but also in incidents of seizure of lumber, grain and sugar-
beets, and cattle trespass on private domains.[94]

The disorders at times grew to such a scale that local authorities were
simply helpless. On 30 November, landowner Kailenskii wired P. N.
Durnovo to inform the Minister on matters in adjacent Goptarovskaia Parish:

> In the course of the last week the peasants of the villages of Russkii Ilek, Koshary,
> Demidovka, Popovka and others have set willfully [*samovol'no*] to timbering the land-
> owners' forests. Provincial administration has limited itself to sending thirty soldiers
> and a police captain who has been taking depositions. The peasants of neighboring vil-
> lages, among which my estate is located, therefore assume that their superiors
> [*nachal'stvo*] have been taken with a Tolstoyan non-resistance to evil and thus have
> decided to take advantage of such a mood and for the third day, with hundreds of carts,
> are stealing the landowners' sugar-beets. I most respectfully petition Your High Excel-
> lency to command our authorities to take immediate measures in order to bring the
> population to its senses and thus to prevent this pernicious looting and disorder.[95]

Nevertheless, troops in ever-larger numbers continued to move into the
affected areas. After weeks of the most urgent demands, Governor Gordeev
won a diversion of the newly mobilized 32nd Regiment of Don Cossacks
(called up for duty in Tambov *guberniia*) to Kursk Province for reinforcement of the 2nd Eiskii Cossack Regiment, the Zaslavsk Infantry and

---

[92] *Ibid.*, No. 136, p. 117; No. 138, p. 118 (GAKO, f. 1, op. 15, d. 62, ll. 79–80); No. 140,
pp. 119–120 (GAKO, f. 1, op. 15, d. 6, l.142); RGIA, f. 1291, op. 122, 1905 g., d. 112, l.
315; RGIA, f. 1405, op. 194, 1908 g., d. 102, l. 12 (telegram, Procurator of the Khar'kov
Judicial Chamber Khrulev to Minister of Justice Shcheglovitov, 15 November 1905).

[93] *Ibid.*, No. 130, p. 112 (GAKO, f. 1, op. 15, d. 5, l. 126); No. 137, p. 118 (GAKO, f. 1, op.
15, d. 5, ll. 144–146); RGIA, f. 1291, op. 122, 1905 g., d. 112, l. 302; also *1905 god*, 14.

[94] RGIA, f. 1405, op. 194, 1908 g., d. 102, ll. 32 ob.-33 (No. 740, cases 1–3, 6, 8, 15); d.
137, ll. 5–5 ob. *RSKG*, No. 152, p. 127 (GAKO, f. 1, op. 15, d. 6, l. 268).

[95] GARF, f. 102, DP OO, op. 233 (II), 1905 g., d. 2550, ch. 44, ll. 179–180.

Graivoron and Oboian Reserve Infantry Regiments, the Akhtirsk Dragoon Regiment, and assorted artillery units already on station. Operations in the province soon came under the command of special Imperial legates, Admiral V. F. Dubasov (from 18 November 1905), later General-Governor of Moscow during the December insurrection, and General A. I. Panteleev (from about 1 December). Still, the pressure of multiple actions mounted over a large area on frozen, rutted roads covered with blowing snow, the insistent demands of well-connected estate owners for top priority in troop deployments and the necessity on occasion to dispatch troops to assist in operations in other provinces, all these factors were to place great strains on the mechanism of repression. In his cabled report of 1 December in the wake of his inspection in the field, Panteleev noted that troops were still insufficient and that, among those in the field, signs of exhaustion—even of discontent among those of the 1901 draft and those newly recruited—were evident. Yet by mid-November troop strength in the central districts was now sufficient to begin the process of inquests, house-to-house searches and arrests that acted to restrain further peasant militancy.

4. November–December Events outside the Main Centers

Even if not at all on the scale of peasant unrest in the central or eastern centers, incidents of rural unrest in November 1905 encompassed several narrower locales in Graivoron, Putivl', Ryl'sk and Korocha Districts. Scattered incidents were also recorded in Dmitriev District, despite the fact that the localities in which the February events had taken place had been "occupied" by military detachments for several months after the outbreaks at the beginning of the year.

In Graivoron District, as we have seen, disturbances began in late October and early November. On 2 November, Governor Gordeev received a telegram from Land Captain Sergeev in Graivoron District regarding "disorders" at Morkushino (Krasno-Iarushskaia Parish), Dunaika (Dorogoshchanskaia Parish), Rakitnaia (Rakitianskaia Parish) and other sites in the district.[96] Unrest on the sprawling holdings of Princess Zinaida

---

[96] Early Soviet researchers identify incidents at Morkushino, Dunaika and Rakitnaia as timbering in the Iusupov forests that begin on 17 October at various points around this huge estate. The same work notes timbering in the forests of Sheremet'ev, Kharitonenko and Golitsyn without references. A grouping of damage for Graivoron District in RGIA, f. 1291, op. 122, 1905 g., d. 112, ll. 310–310 ob. showed 30,000 rubles in damage for Sheremet'ev (the Borisovka estate), 8,000 rubles for Kharitonenko (Sitnaia) and 50,000

Nikolaevna Iusupova at Rakitnaia began toward the end of October. Extensive timbering of her vast forests and the wooded tracts on the adjacent holdings of Pavel Ivanovich Kharitonenko, despite continuous sorties of Cossack units billed on the estate, lasted into November and inflicted losses to the sum of 50,000 rubles.[97]

> *Sloboda* Rakitnaia, near which the estate of Princess Z. N. Iusupova, Countess Sumarokova-El'ston, is located, has a population of up to 10,000 and important significance for the surrounding localities. Already in the spring of this year, an agitated mood stemming from agrarian causes was observed among the peasants of Rakitnaia, but the dispatch of a squadron of dragoons, which remained until the beginning of September, prevented the emergence of unrest. Upon the removal of the dragoons from the estate and the posting of a hundred of Kuban Cossacks—this was never at full strength because of its sorties to other localities—tensions resurfaced, but now in the form of mass timbering. The importance of maintaining order at Rakitnaia—in order to forestall the spread of disorders to a considerable area—makes it necessary to recall the squadron of dragoons from Sumy, located 44 miles from Rakitnaia and connected with it by rail.[98]

In August, the central installations of the huge estate of Count Aleksandr Dmitrievich Sheremet'ev at *sloboda* Borisovka (Borisovskaia Parish) had already been assaulted by peasant crowds (see above). On 15 November, however, massive timbering began in the estate's forest preserves. The Land Captain of the Fifth Precinct reported as follows:

> At the same time that I was at Kustovo (14–17 November) for suppression of the peasant movement there, massive timbering of the forests of Count Sheremet'ev broke out on all sides [of the estate]: peasants of all five communes of Borisovskaia Parish, the Striguny commune and Porubezhnoe I and II [*Strigunovskaia Parish—BRM*] began to timber. On the 15th and 16th, some 500 peasants from each side participated (in this action), equipped with axes and saws. They carried the timbered lumber home on their shoulders in long lines with no concern at all, in broad daylight. After the 16th, crowds of 2,000 and more began to appear daily and the lumber began to be carted away. The measures and harangues of the administration accomplished nothing. Local police sought to aid matters, sending patrolmen into the woods with Count Sheremet'ev's forest guard, but the peasants put up resistance, chasing after the patrols, the forest

---

for Iusupova. Dates for these timbering incidents were verifiable elsewhere in the documents. The listing also referenced damage on the estate of the heirs of Prince Golitsyn "near the village of Orlovka" of 1,000 rubles, but no dating appears. Komissiia pri Kurskom gubispolkome po organizatsii prazdnovaniia 20-letiia revoliutsii 1905 goda, *op. cit.*, 63–65.

[97] GARF, f. 102, DP OO, op. 233 (II), 1905 g., d. 2550, ch. 44, l. 199.

[98] *Ibid.*, f. 102, 4-oe deloproizvodstvo, 1907 g., d. 34.1, ll. 49–49 ob.

guards, the village elders and the parish elder with axes, and there were several cases of severe beatings. In the end, it was impossible to enter the woods. The peasants transported the looted lumber home brazenly, in full view of all of their local officials.[99]

Cossack units had reached Borisovka by the 28th of November and timbering temporarily ceased. In December, peasants from Vasil'evka (Rakitianskaia Parish) arrived in wagons on the estate of Sergei Kirillovich Popov to carry off loads of oats and hemp.[100] On 16 December, timbering was once again to be resumed on Sheremet'ev's estate.[101]

The November events again found a resonance in Dmitriev District. In the northwestern part of the district, on or about 11 November, the elders of Berezovskaia, Fateevskaia, Selinskaia, and Popovkinskaia Parishes declared a tax strike, in which prior consultations were evident. Land Captain of the Fifth Department Bulich noted, in addition, that in several villages (Fateevka, Zveniachka and others), peasants had presented acts of the commune, uniform in text and written by a single hand, declaring abatement of all obligations for three years.[102] Tax strikes in this district were probably more widespread: there are good indications that they extended, at this time, to Glamazdinskaia Parish and the "industrial" Mikhailovskaia Parish adjacent to the Fifth Land Department parishes.[103] Troubles also emerged at sites associated with the February unrest. O. A. Shaufus wired the Governor from Petersburg on 9 November: "At Khomutovka, Glamazdinskaia Parish, disturbances have begun. I earnestly request protection"; on 11 November, Minister Durnovo sent on to Admiral Dubasov (in Chernigov) Baron Meiendorf's urgent request for

---

[99] *RSKG*, No. 149, p.126 (GAKO, f.1, op.15, d.13, ll. 132–132 ob.). The Land Captain's presence at Kustovo was associated with looting and destruction by fire of the house and granaries on the estate of A. I. Shekun (damage was estimated at 6,000 rubles) at this site, which must have taken place sometime before November 14.

[100] RGIA, f. 1405, op. 194, 1908 g., d.102, l. 24 (copy, report at No. 3472, 28 December 1905, Procurator of the Kursk Regional Court to the Procurator of Khar'kov Judicial Chamber). Disturbances took place on 14 December.

[101] *RSKG*, No. 166, pp.134–135 (GAKO, f. 1, op. 15, d. 13, l. 216), telegram, superintendent of the Sheremet'ev estate to the Governor N. N. Gordeev, 17 December 1905.

[102] *Ibid.*, No. 129, p. 111 (GAKO, f. 1, op. 15, d. 12, l. 31), report, Land Captain of the Fifth Department, Dmitrievskii District, to Governor N. N. Gordeev, 11 November 1905.

[103] Operations to recover taxes in both parishes got under way—under cover of military detachments—in 1907, at Mikhailovka in February (*ibid.*, No. 292, pp. 213–214 [GAKO, f. 1, op. 17, d. 69, ll. 11–12]) and at Vet' in Glamazdinskaia Parish in March (No. 295, pp. 216–217 [GAKO, f. 1, op. 17, d. 4529, ll. 15–16]).

military units in order to quell "open revolt" in his domains at Dobroe Pole (Prilepovskaia Parish).[104]

Echoes of the disturbances in the main centers during the November events appear in individual settlements in Ryl'sk and Korocha Districts. In Ryl'sk District, these were work stoppages. On 19 November, District Police Commandant Zarin wired the Governor to report that agricultural workers on the large estate of hereditary honorary citizen A. A. Kuznetsov (4,278 *desiatiny*) at Markovo in Markovskaia Parish had struck, demanding higher pay. The demand was quickly met, but the field workers nonetheless dispersed the laborers of the distillery and flour-mill, shutting down estate operations.[105] Later in the month, work actions broke out at Tetkino, the processing hub of the Tereshchenko estate complex in Kursk Province, despite all efforts to avoid this event. Engineer Kliucharov, the manager of the plants, cabled Governor Gordeev on 30 November: "The hidden ferment among the workers and peasants has begun to change to open violence. All economic demands were anticipated and fulfilled by the administration. Since September, all our plants have introduced the eight-hour working day and, in addition, wages have been increased. Two days ago, however, the residents of Tetkino compelled migrant [*prishlie*] laborers from Orel Province and other places to quit the sugar refinery. The peasants threaten violence and demand lumber. To prevent the events that loom over us, a squad of Cossacks must be ordered here. The District Police Commandant, upon his arrival, was also convinced of this. I urgently request appropriate action."[106]

In Korocha District, disturbances began at the very end of 1905. Disorders concerned the two big villages, Nikol'skaia and Nekliudova, in Nekliudovskaia Parish. Peasants from these adjacent villages (along with parties from Pentsovka) began to timber the extensive state forests on the eastern boundaries of their lands on or about 29 December, chasing off the forest rangers and burning down guard posts. Timbering continued well into January 1906: from January 11, parties of axemen from settlements of *odnodvortsy* on the northwest side of the forest, Nechaeva, Tiurina (Ne-

---

[104] GARF, f. 102, DP OO, op. 233 (II), 1905 g., d. 2550, ch. 44, 1.122; *RSKG*, No. 128, p. 111 (GAKO, f. 1, op. 15, d. 12, l. 13). The proximity of the two communications implies that, indeed, some actions were under way at the sites of the February events, but the documents were entirely silent on further details.

[105] *RSKG*, No. 145, p. 124 (GAKO, f. 1, op. 15, d. 64, l. 312).

[106] *Ibid.*, No. 86, p. 88 (GAKO, f. 1, op. 15, d. 64, ll. 202–204), report, superintendent of the Tetkino sugar refinery to the Governor, 30 November 1905.

chaevskaia Parish), Tsepliaeva and Repnovo (Kupinskaia Parish), joined the action.[107]

With the introduction of troops into the main centers of unrest and suppression of mass assaults on the private estates, the local authorities, smarting under the withering criticism and constant urging of the central authorities, struggled to regain the initiative. Their grudging success increasingly placed peasant militants on the defensive and gave the December incidents a different cast. A campaign of arrests was mounted, not only striking villages in troubled zones, but also reaching out to quash any sign of "ferment" and to detain "agitators" from both the peasantry and the local intelligentsia.[108] These efforts not infrequently provoked resistance. Recounting the attempts of the police to round up agitators and break up chapters of the Peasant Union—his own steward and several employees of his estate administration were arrested in December, sometime before his own brief detention in January—Dolgorukov wrote of an incident that involved the villagers adjoining his own estate.

When arrests began to grow in frequency, peasants in one village just refused to give up their teacher to the police captain who had come to make the arrest. The latter had to leave without fulfilling his task. The peasants of Guevo came to feel conscience-stricken and offended that they had failed to intercede on behalf of their own teacher. Then, during the Christmas holidays, the manager of the *zemstvo* warehouse was arrested in a suburb of Miropol' because he had quite openly taken part in a meeting of the Peasant Union on the holidays' eve. And so, at the house of the police captain, where the detainee was being held, there at first gathered a few hundred members of the Union, who were then joined by about 2,000 local peasants. They ringed the house in a circle, despite the presence of 20 soldiers with rifles at the ready, bayonets pointed at the crowd. The people, it is said, bore themselves with great restraint—no curses, no drunkenness—but remained insistent. After long negotiations with a deputation elected by the crowd and telephone calls to the authorities in Sudzha, the police captain was forced to release the detainee.[109]

---

[107] *Ibid.*, No. 178, p. 140 (GAKO, f. 1 op. 15, d. 3, l. 5), report, Korocha District Police Commandant Bogoroditskii to Governor V. M. Borzenko, 29 December 1905; No. 213, p. 171 (GAKO, f. 1, op. 15, d. 3, l. 87), report, Kursk-Orel Administration of State Properties to Governor V. M. Borzenko, 14 January 1906. GARF, f. 102, DP OO, op. 236 (II), 1906 g., d. 700, ch. 58, l. 31 ob., report, at No. 206, 18 January 1906 (Commandant, Kursk Provincial Gendarme Administration, Colonel Vel'k, to Department of Police).

[108] GARF, f. 102, DP OO, op. 236 (II), 1906 g., d. 700, ch. 58, l. 13, telegram, 6 January 1906, Minister of Internal Affairs P. N. Durnovo to Kursk Governor V. M. Borzenko. Vice-Governor Gil'khen, replying by telegram in the absence of the Governor (in the field with the troops) acknowledged receipt of a dispatch of 4 January 1906 concerning a systematic purging of *zemstvo* institutions (ll. 19–19 ob.; 9 January 1906).

[109] Dolgorukov, "Agrarnaia volna," No. 1, columns 35–36.

Such confrontations were often far less amicable. At *sloboda* Staraia Belitsa (Staro-Belitskaia Parish) on 23 December, the Dmitriev District Police Commandant with ten Cossacks tried to arrest four peasants accused by the Land Captain of being agitators. The operation provoked resistance. Not only were the Police Commandant and the Cossacks put to flight, but villagers also used the action as a pretext for immediately settling scores with the parish administration. Peasants of the first commune expelled the elder, the scribe and all the judges from the parish, emptied out the public grain reserve of its store of rye and put the building up for sale.[110]

On 28 December, at Bekhteevka (Prigorodniaia Parish), a suburb of Korocha, a squad of seven Cossacks and three mounted patrolmen came to detain one Marchenko, accused of attacking a policeman. Entering at the wrong address, the would-be arresting officers found themselves intruding on an evening *sidel'ka* attended by a good number of village youth. Admitting to no knowledge of any Marchenko, the youths began to shout the alarm and set out for the village church to sound the bell. But the bell-ropes broke and, in search of the keys to the church, the company headed first to the church watchman, then to the priest, who sent them to the church elder. At this juncture, the decision was made just to break down the doors of the church and enter, and the youths continued to sound the alarm until "all the residents of Bekhteevka, the town of Korocha, and several town suburbs were set in motion." A huge crowd gathered to confront the police and Cossacks, who, after trying to frighten the assembly with a volley fired into the air, were compelled to quit the scene.[111] Similar confrontations accompanied the efforts of police and Cossack detachments to halt the work of Peasant Union organizers in the southern parishes of Ryl'sk District. On 30 December, in the settlement of Kobylka, villagers adopted resolutions that, *inter alia*, called for affiliation with the Peasant Union, and for expelling village officials and their replacement by elected peasant delegates. The District Police Commandant, together with a unit of dragoons, succeeded in arresting "100 local peasant-leaders" and convoyed them to the nearby

---

[110] *RSKG*, No. 169, p. 136 (GAKO, f. 1, op. 15, d. 12, ll. 151–151 ob.) Report, 23 December 1905, Land Captain of the Third Land Department of Dmitriev District Vas'ianov to Governor V. M. Borzenko.

[111] GARF, f. 102, DP OO, op. 236 (11), 1906 g., d. 700, ch. 58, ll. 31–31 ob. (Report at No. 206, Commandant of the Kursk Provincial Gendarmerie, Col. Vel'k, to Department of Police, 18 January 1906).

village of Glushkovo. A large party of Kobylka peasants soon arrived in Glushkovo, intent on freeing the detainees, but the dragoons dispersed the peasants by force.[112]

Police actions provoked even more ominous consequences. On 10 December, two police officers and a squad of Cossacks attempted to arrest a "local agitator" in the big village of Banishchi in Ivanovskaia Parish, L'gov District, and were attacked by a crowd of 500 peasants. After firing five shots at the crowd, the detachment was forced to flee, but the incident evidently left local peasants in a foul mood.[113] On 28 December, a crowd of peasants from Fitizh (Nizhnederevenskaia Parish), adjacent to Banishchi, came to the estate of Marshal of the Nobility Petr Petrovich Stremoukhov and began "brazenly" to importune Stremoukhov's steward for 8 rubles for vodka. Upon receipt of this sum—the steward was forced to threaten the crowd with his revolver to get it to move on—the peasants went on to Stremoukhov's farmstead—at the time leased to the Tereshchenko clan— and replayed the same scene. When the precinct police captain and a constable arrived in Fitizh to conduct an investigation, the bell in the church began ringing and the peasants, confronting the officers, beat the captain so severely that he arrived in L'gov more dead than alive. At this juncture, some 2,000 peasants from Banishchi, alerted by the alarm, arrived in Fitizh and together the residents of the two settlements, armed with scythes, pitchforks, staves and firearms, marched on Stremoukhov's estate. There, the peasants completely destroyed the Marshal's manor house in a sort of fanatical rage: every window was shattered on all three floors and all framing, doors, fixtures and furnishings were broken, hacked apart or disfigured. All of the estate's grain stores and any moveable property that could be taken were carted off. At the farmstead, two wagons of wheat were loaded for the trip back to the village and the administrative office had all its windows broken. When word of this event reached Kursk, the Governor himself decided to pay a visit to the rebel villages, accompanied by a hundred of Cossacks, dragoon units and a squad of artillerymen with two howitzers.[114] At first residents of the two villages turned a deaf ear to the Governor's demand that those guilty in the disorders of 28–29 December be immediately

---

[112] *Ibid*, ll. 17–17 ob.

[113] *RSKG*, No. 159, pp. 130–131 (GAKO, f. 1, op. 15, d. 5, l. 274), telegram, L'gov District Police Commandant Keber to Governor N. N. Gordeev, 10 December 1905.

[114] RGIA, f. 1405, op. 194, 1908 g., d. 102, ll. 25–25 ob. The extract is from copy, report of 9 January 1906 at No. 33, Procurator of the Kursk Regional Court to Procurator of the Khar'kov Judicial Chamber.

given up, but the prospect of having cannon turned on their homes forced them to surrender some of the "ringleaders."[115] Preliminary investigation revealed intense resentment among local peasants toward Stremoukhov for the latter's spirited legal actions against peasant axemen identified in acts of timbering his forests; reference was made, as well, to the work of an active local organization of the Peasant Union.[116] In an odd coda to this episode, a breakout at the L'gov District Jail in June 1906 would free a number of those detained in connection with the incident at Fitizh to take a visible part in a new wave of unrest in the following year.

Perhaps the most dangerous explosion stemming from the effort to suppress political agitation among the peasants was to take place in Putivl' District. In spite of scattered incidents at Glushets and Cherepovka in July, at Gamaleevka, Leont'evskoe, Gvintovo and Shilovka during September–October, Putivl' District had been quiet in November. At Popovaia Sloboda (Popovo-Slobodskaia Parish), minor incidents of arson took place on the nearby estates of the Tereshchenko clan on 13 and 15 November, and at Bochechki, on the 15th, the dwelling of engineer Burnashevich, manager of the Bochechki sugar refinery, was partially damaged by a fire set by unknown arsonists.[117]

Apparently, however, the authorities were determined to root out low-level political activity that had been noted in the villages of Gruzskoe and Viazovoe (Gruzchanskaia Parish) on the Moscow–Kiev–Voronezh Railway line and its association with large numbers of peasants from these villages who were employed as railway workers in the Konotop yards and repair shops. In his report to the Governor of 3 December, Putivl' District Police Commandant Spasskii described the general atmosphere in the locality.

> I have the honor to inform Your Excellency that, according to rumors, daily meetings of workers, headed by technician Shor, are being held in the town of Konotop, at which questions concerning an all-Russian rail strike and armed revolt against the authorities are discussed. Noting the close proximity of the Konotop Railway Depot, where some 500 peasants from Putivl' District work, there is no doubt whatsoever that the agitation of the Konotop organization has freely resonated in nearby villages—

---

[115] Komissiia pri Kurskom gubispolkome po organizatsii prazdnovaniia 20-letiia revoliutsii 1905 goda, *op. cit.*, 60–61.

[116] GARF, f. 102, DP OO, op. 236 (II), 1906 g., d. 700, ch. 58, ll. 12–12 ob. Telegram, 5 January 1906, Kursk Governor V. M. Borzenko to P. N. Durnovo, Minister of Internal Affairs.

[117] *RSKG*, No. 142, pp. 120–121 (GAKO, f. 1, op. 15, d. 16, ll. 282–283), report, Land Captain of the First Land Department of Putivl' District to Kursk Governor N. N. Gordeev, 17 November 1905.

Viazovoe, Saltykovo, Gruzskoe, Popovaia Sloboda and others. In these places, one now notes an ill will and silent perturbation among the populace. It is rumored that, on 1 January, estates of the *pomeshchiki*, the parish administrative offices and the quarters of officials will be destroyed, and when all this has been done, the peasants will set about dividing the land among them.[118]

And it happened that the onset of the December disturbances in Putivl' District began almost simultaneously with the adherence of Kursk railway workers on the Moscow–Kiev–Voronezh and Southeastern lines to the strike action declared by the All-Russian Railway Workers' Union. The Kursk chapter of the Union had voted on 2 December its readiness to adhere to the strike and, during 7–16 December, the action reduced rail traffic through the province by 75 percent.[119] Four days before the strike, on December 3, the police with army units broke up a mass meeting in Gruzskoe (a station stop on the Moscow–Kiev–Voronezh main line). Then, on 10 December, the police arrested a local peasant for "criminal agitation."[120] The next day, the Governor received a telegram from Spasskii, reporting that on the previous evening, villagers from Gruzskoe, Zemlianka and Popovaia Sloboda, in a crowd of 3,000 persons, had arrived at the police station with the aim of freeing those detained. In the confrontation, the precinct captain and a patrolman were severely beaten by the crowd, and a police constable shot to death. The peasants dispersed only in the face of warning volleys fired by a half-company of infantry hastily rushed to the scene.[121] The incident was linked to serious disturbances that had begun in late November in adjacent Konotop District in Chernigov Province, Konotop itself being the center of unrest. Much influence was attributed to partisans of the Peasant Union.[122]

---

[118] *Ibid.*, No. 155, pp. 128–29 [GAKO, f. 1, op. 15, d. 16, ll. 371–371 ob.].

[119] Declaration of readiness by the Kursk Committee adopted on 1 December and cabled to Moscow on 2 December (*RSKG*, No. 87, pp. 88–89) The December rail strike is treated in "Komissiia pri Kurskom gubispolkome po organizatsii prazdnovaniia 20-letiia revoliutsii 1905 goda," *op. cit.*, 129–132; *RSKG*, Nos. 89–96, 98, 100–103, 89–95; Reichman, *Railwaymen*, 259–290.

[120] RGIA, f. 1405, op. 194, 1908 g., d. 102, ll. 15–16 (copy, report at No. 3881, Procurator of the Sumy Regional Court Gil'khen to Procurator of the Khar'kov Judicial Chamber, 21 December 1905).

[121] *RSKG*, No. 160, p. 130 (GAKO, f. 1, op. 15, d .16, ll. 377–378), telegram, Putivl' District Police Commandant Spasskii to Governor N. N. Gordeev, 11 December 1905.

[122] Reference to the influence of Peasant Union propaganda in General Panteleev's review, *Revoliutsiia 1905–1907 gg. Dokumenty i materialy. Vysshii pod'em revoliutsii (Vooruzhennye vosstaniia), noiabr'-dekabr' 1905 g.* Ch. II, No. 294, pp. 342–343.

Map 5. Putivl' District, December, 1905

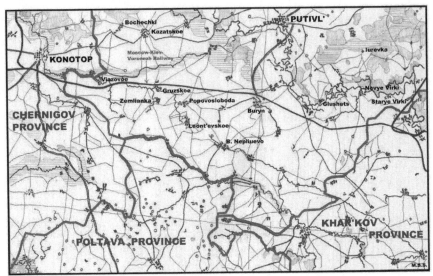

Immediately in the wake of the confrontation with the police, a new wave of daily mass meetings got under way in all settlements of Gruzchanskaia, Kazachanskaia and Popovo-Slobodskaia Parishes: at these gatherings, villagers passed resolutions calling for removal of the local authorities from office, non-payment of financial obligations, and seizure of all private lands.[123] In Bochechki on the 14th, three police officers in the village at the time were put under arrest. The village assembly was summoned "with outside agitators in attendance," and proceeded to elect a council of several peasants from Kazatskoe to wield authority in the parish. The assembly passed resolutions ordering cessation of all work for the private landowners, dispersal of workers and servants on local estates and a strict non-obedience to constituted authorities. Army recruits were not to be surrendered. Patrols were detailed to ensure that parish officials and arrested police officers remained in their homes. The next day, the assembly met again to resolve that no one would be given up for arrest and that those who tried to make arrests would be punished.[124] Workers at the Bo-

---

[123] *RSKG*, No. 162, p. 132 (GAKO, f. 1, op. 15, d. 16, ll. 435–37), telegram, Land Captain of the First Land Department Pavlov and Precinct Police Captain Novakov to Governor N. N. Gordeev, 14 December 1905.

[124] GARF, f. 102, DP OO, op. 236 (II), 1906 g., d. 700, ch. 58, ll. 3–3 ob. Report at No. 4187, 28 December 1905, Commandant of the Kursk Provincial Gendarmerie, Col. Vel'k, to Department of Police.

chechki sugar refinery went out on strike and the "surrounding peasantry" joined the action. Without even raising demands, a crowd of peasants and workers relieved the refinery's carters of 3,000 *poods* of sugar. Orators presided over non-stop meetings.[125] When a unit of Cossacks clattered through Kazatskoe on 18 November, the alarm bell was rung and the villagers poured out onto the square, armed with whatever was at hand: axes, staves, picks, rifles and revolvers. Not finding the Cossacks, the enraged crowd turned on the parish elder, accused him of calling in troops, dragged him from the parish administrative building and badly beat him.[126] Cossack units arrived in force in Gruzskoe on 20 December. Arrest of the peasant "soviet" at Kazatskoe was carried out on the 23rd. By this time, disorders of an analogous type and intensity had emerged in the big settlements of Glushets, Starye Virki and Novye Virki, Glushetskaia Parish, east of the original centers along the Moscow–Kiev–Voronezh Railway. "Propaganda is openly conducted by agitators," wrote the official correspondent, "the police and parish officials are not allowed in the villages." Rumors of joint actions against the big Tereshchenko complex at Glushets, set for the 27th, circulated wildly.[127] This picture was confirmed by General N. P. Rudov, charged with suppressing unrest in the Konotop area. In his cable of 25 December, he noted that "many villages of Putivl' District, especially those bordering on Konotop District, are seized by disturbances. The police have vanished. [Peasant] committees are replacing village authorities. I have verified this by personally visiting Kazatskoe and Bochechki. It is indispensable that rapid and energetic suppression of the revolt be undertaken jointly with my own actions in the Konotop area."[128]

Yet by 1 January 1906, the immediate crisis, at least, had passed. The new Governor, V. M. Borzenko, could report relative calm in Kursk Province in his cable to the Minister of Internal Affairs at the year's end, save for mop-up operations in a few localities.

> Concerning the situation as of 1 January, I report: in Kursk and the districts of Kursk, Belgorod, Korocha, Staryi Oskol', Oboian, Tim, Fatezh and Shchigrov, outward calm

---

[125] *RSKG*, No. 99, p. 93 (GAKO, f. 1, op. 15, d. 16, ll. 454–455), telegram (at Kiev), Gardner and Mirkin, administrators of the Bochechki sugar refinery, to Governor N. N. Gordeev, 15 December 1905.

[126] GARF, f. 102, DP OO, op. 236 (II), 1906 g., d. 700, ch. 58, l. 3 ob.

[127] *RSKG*, No. 170, pp. 136–137 (GAKO, f. 1, op. 15, d. 16, ll. 528–530), telegram, administrator of the Glushets estate (Tereshchenko) to the Governor, 24 December 1905.

[128] *Ibid*, No. 171, p. 137 (GAKO, f. 1, op. 15, d. 16, l. 534).

holds. But unrest exists in Graivoron District—a major timbering on the Sheremet'ev estate, the ringleaders have been arrested; in Dmitriev District—minor timbering, unauthorized sharing out of [public grain] stores, threats against landowners. In Novyi Oskol' District on 27 December, there was an attempt to sack the estate of Polezhaev at Bogorodskoe, but the riot was prevented. In Putivl' District, revolutionary propaganda, sending out deep roots from Konotop, produced powerful unrest on political grounds that was expressed in meetings summoned by village fire alarm, expulsion of the authorities and of workers on the estates, the beating of a police captain and elder and the killing of a police constable. Numerous arrests, including the village committees, are being made by members of the police and troops ordered to the scene. At the present time, all is calm. L'gov District had been calm up to 30 December, but despite the great number of arrests that have been made, a mass movement of peasants still made itself known: the house of Marshal Stremoukhov was destroyed and a police captain beaten. The District Police Commandant, fearing spontaneous outbreaks, requested significant reinforcement and dispatch of machine guns. I have immediately sent a hundred of Cossacks and an artillery officer recommended by military officials in order to determine actual troop requirements. This officer spoke in favor of sending artillery in light of its psychological effect. At the same time, the Police Commandant has renewed his request for machine guns and cannon. Sending a squad of artillerymen, covered by dragoons, I am setting out for L'gov myself.[129]

Durnovo's reply is preserved in the archive: "So as to finish off these disorders, take the most severe measures: the rebels' village must be wiped off the face of the earth, and they themselves destroyed without sparing the force of arms."[130]

---

[129] GARF, f. 102, DP OO, op. 236 (II), 1906 g., d. 700, ch. 58, ll. 9–9 ob.
[130] *Ibid.*, l. 10.

CHAPTER III

Rural Disorders
in Spring–Summer 1906

By the end of 1905, it must have been evident to all the protagonists that the tide had begun to turn in the local authorities' struggle to bring sufficient force to bear on the villages, both to deter new outbreaks of unrest and to speed up the work of the police and judiciary. By mid-January 1906, Governor Borzenko had at his disposal an armed force of perhaps 12,000 men: nine Cossack "hundreds" (32nd Don, 2nd Eiskii Regiments), a dragoon regiment (31st Riga; the 29th Odessa Dragoons arrived in May–June) and two squadrons of another (36th Akhtirsk) as cavalry, five infantry regiments (47th Ukrainian, 196th Zaslavskii, 123rd Kozlovskii, 203rd Graivoron Reserve, 204th Oboian Reserve) and two artillery brigades.[1] Under the cover of this force, local police officials and judicial investigators were to prepare a mass of legal actions against those suspected of taking part in the disorders.

1. Repression

The machinery of repression worked in broadly similar patterns. As in February–March 1905, police and investigators could only operate accompanied by at least platoon-sized detachments of soldiers: smaller units

---

[1] Kursk Province normally maintained three infantry regiments in its garrison around the provincial capital: 123rd Kozlovskii, 203rd Graivoron Reserve and 204th Oboian Reserve, each with a peacetime strength of 1,790 enlisted men. The 68th Reserve Artillery Brigade with 1,200 men was posted to Belgorod. (*Obzor Kurskoi gubernii za [1905, 1906] god*). That Dubasov considered the reserve regiments to be unreliable and ordered them kept out of the action is indicated in a set of notes that he had prepared for a report that appears in "Agrarnoe dvizhenie v 1905 g. po otchetam Dubasova i Panteleeva," *Krasnyi arkhiv*, 1925, No. 4–5 (11–12), 183–186.

commonly ran into real trouble. The larger the force, the more it appeared to make the necessary impression on the peasants. Floggings were employed to emphasize the determination of the authorities, or cannon or machine guns were at times dispatched with troop detachments for "psychological effect." Once a preponderance of force could be assembled in the locality, the police were able to begin taking depositions from witnesses and target suspects for searches in efforts to uncover looted property. Apprehension of such property commonly counted as *prima facie* evidence of criminal complicity, but there were extenuating circumstances:

> Up to now, the accused are being charged only on the basis of clear evidence against them. To charge the guilty only on grounds of apprehension of incriminating evidence has been made difficult in several cases, since there are clear indications that some peasants, after the riots, took estate property home in order to preserve it from looting and demolition. Estate employees, with this aim in mind, themselves turned over such property to reliable persons among the peasants, although of course each such matter is being investigated on an individual basis. For the next phase of our current investigatory tasks, aimed at apprehending the guilty parties, it has been proposed that searches be conducted in homes of those already charged or suspected in order to reveal the existence of the organization for the riots in the district, by means of apprehension and confiscation of documents—appeals, proclamations, letters—that will testify to this circumstance, should such be found.[2]

The process was thus generally the same at every site: house-to-house searches were conducted as routine procedure, hundreds of witnesses deposed, estate property retrieved and sweeping arrests organized. Severe winter weather conditions, shortages of judicial investigators and the limits of troop levels of even this magnitude slowed the process and elicited sharp expressions of Petersburg's impatience with the inertia of local officials.[3] Yet the efforts of the police and judiciary were not to be limited to peasant participants in agrarian disorders: rooting out the movement's sympathizers within educated circles of provincial society was also given priority. Many arrests had already been made among the rural intelligentsia, but communications between the Governor's Chancellery and the Ministry of Internal Affairs on preparations for a "purge of *zemstvo* insti-

---

[2] RGIA, f. 1405, op. 194, 1908 g., d. 137, l. 4 ob.

[3] GARF, f. 102, DP OO, op. 236 (II), 1906 g., d. 700, ch. 58, l. 27, telegram, Minister of Internal Affairs P. N. Durnovo to (unidentified) Akimov, 14 January 1906, on the unsatisfactory pace of investigations in Novyi Oskol' District and inaction of the district police.

tutions" date to 4 January: persecution of the specialists was to begin in earnest from this time onward.[4] Particular attention was to be paid to members and well-wishers of the Peasant Union: "to be destroyed by the arrest of all agitators," Minister of Internal Affairs P. N. Durnovo ordered, "without regard for their social standing."[5] The police offensive, along with efforts at moral persuasion aimed at "bringing peasants to their senses," extended well into the spring months, but seemed never to entirely rid itself of a certain improvisational character. At certain moments, these improvisations had rather unpredictable results.

Thus, for example, the Sudzha District Police Commandant concluded that the growing influence of the Peasant Union might be countered by the force of his own personal influence and by openly elucidating to the peasants the meaning of the October Manifesto. To this end, he invited the populace of the surrounding villages to assemble on Cathedral Square in Sudzha on 31 December and 7 January. The first gathering was poorly attended, but on 7 January several thousand peasants showed up. Among them were the fellow villagers of a man who had been arrested that day for "criminal agitation." The peasants demanded the release of this man, citing the Manifesto's declaration of freedom of person. When this demand was refused, the crowd grew increasingly insistent. Finally, the gates of the prison (also located on the square) were forced open and 38 detainees at that moment in the yard escaped and melted into the crowd. An assault on the cellblocks was abandoned only when prison supervisors threatened to fire on the crowd. The Police Commander was dismissed by the Governor for negligence.[6] In another instance, the Land Captains of L'gov District were commissioned to select "reliable" peasants to travel to the district seat on 7 December to hear General A. I. Panteleev's fatherly warnings to the populace, to be transmitted to their neighbors back home, but it turned out that the delegates had brought with them a list of their own demands: that all Russian people should be equal in their rights, that all land should be held in common and should belong to those who cultivated it by personal labor without hired workers, that the Duma elections

---

[4] *Ibid.*, ll. 19–19 ob., telegram, Vice-Governor Gil'khen for the Governor, to the Minister of Internal Affairs, 9 January 1906.

[5] *Ibid.*, l.13. Telegram, Minister of Internal Affairs P. N. Durnovo to Governor V. M. Borzenko at L'gov, 6 January 1906. This was a transparent reference to the activism of liberal noblemen like Dolgorukov and Evreinov in the union movement.

[6] RGIA, f. 1405, op. 194, 1908 g., d. 102, ll. 26–26 ob. (report, Procurator of the Kursk Regional Court V. K. Rakovskii to Procurator of the Khar'kov Judicial Chamber S. S. Khrulev, 11 January 1906).

be based on the "four-tail" suffrage, that Cossack units be recalled and emergency measures rescinded, that the police and the office of Land Captains be abolished as useless, that the death penalty be abolished and full amnesty declared for political offenses, and that the October Manifesto be enforced "in its full sense." The demands, in shortened form, were read into a telegram to the Emperor over the signatures of four plenipotentiaries (including that of future Member of the First State Duma F. G. Ovchinnikov) elected from the 220-member delegation.[7]

Moreover, as in December, the machinery of repression continued to provoke active resistance. At Dar'ino (Novo-Ivanovskaia Parish, Sudzha District), on 10 January, the efforts of the police to arrest the village teacher and members of the local Peasant Union met active resistance from residents and had to be abandoned. A squadron of dragoons was promptly sent to deal with the situation, but was met by a crowd blocking its way: one peasant was killed by gunfire in the action.[8] On January 18, a crowd of 300 villagers at Shchegolek (Cherno-Oleshanskaia Parish) in Sudzha District attempted to prevent the arrest of "ringleaders" alleged to have been involved in the November disorders. After repeated warnings, the dragoons fired on the crowd, which dispersed, taking an unknown number of dead and wounded with it.[9] Despite the campaign of repression, sporadic incidents continued to be reported. On 1 January, the Putivl' District Police Commandant reported expulsion of forest guards and renewed timbering on Tereshchenko's Glushets estate by peasants from Iur'eva (Volyntsevskaia Parish).[10] At Izvekovo (Skorodenskaia Parish), Sudzha District, the duel between local peasants and Land Captain V. A. Rapp went on. Intending to draw troops away from Rapp's estate and then attack it unimpeded, peasants of Izvekova (Nemcha) set fire to the house and outbuildings of the local priest (January 10). A unit of dragoons was deployed from another site in the vicinity; two peasants were shot to

---

[7] Komissiia pri Kurskom gubispolkome po organizatsii prazdnovaniia 20-letiia revoliutsii 1905 goda, *1905 god v Kurskoi gubernii*, 61–63. Pantaleev had replaced Admiral Dubasov as the overall commander of forces in the central provinces on December 1, 1905.

[8] GARF, f. 102, DP OO, op. 236 (II), 1906 g., d. 700, ch. 58, l. 21 (telegram; Minister of Internal Affairs P. N. Durnovo to Governor V. M. Borzenko, 10 January 1906. Governor Borzenko's replies in *Vtoroi period revoliutsii. Ch. I. Ianvar'-aprel' 1906 g., Kniga I*, No. 391, p. 549.

[9] *Ibid.* (*Vtoroi*), No. 393, p. 549 (report, Commander, 36th Akhtirsk Dragoon Regiment, Colonel E. A. Leont'evich, to Emperor Nicholas II, 27 January 1906).

[10] *RSKG*, No. 210, p. 170 (GAKO, f. 1, op. 16, d. 3, l. 10.), report, Putivl' District Police Commandant to Governor V. M. Borzenko, 1 January 1906.

death in the confrontation.[11] By January's end, in any case, unrest had almost completely ceased. Borzenko wired St. Petersburg to report an uneasy calm.

> I report to Your Excellency on the situation in the province. By February 1, considerable weakening of the activity of the revolutionary parties is noted. Agrarian disorders are limited to single incidents of timbering, cut short at their onset by the troops and police. The mood of the peasant populace is nonetheless extremely tense, expressed in threats and unfounded demands addressed to estate owners. With the aim of dispelling the perverse understanding of the peasants concerning the land, the Most Merciful words of the Sovereign Emperor to the Shchigrov deputation are being widely broadcast. The prisons are greatly overcrowded; the concentration of the most unruly element in them arouses my concern. Meetings of the Provincial Zemstvo Assembly have been proceeding peacefully up to this time. A definitely negative attitude of the rational majority toward the activities of the extreme parties and the third element is making itself known.[12]

February passed without incident; investigations and arrests continued, and the first broad application of administrative measures (deportation to distant provinces) to those detained for "anti-government propaganda and incitement to violence against officials and landowner property" was reported. The central authorities and the Governor's office strove to keep a tight rein on the zeal of the local police so as not to provoke further unrest among the peasants, while, on the other hand, extending their full approval for the use of administrative methods to remove troublemakers.[13]

In March 1906, renewed disturbances were noted at Ol'shanka, Ol'shanskaia Parish, Novyi Oskol' District, where local peasants, on or about 10 March—the opening of the agricultural season less than a month away—seized a tract of land on the ruined estate of Prince I. Iu. Trubetskoi and started to plow up the soil.[14] In April, civil calm was broken only by a few geographically isolated disturbances. From Saltykovskaia Parish, in Staryi Oskol' District, the Governor was informed on 22 April by a local landowner, Nikolai Petrovich Dmitriev, that since the onset of April, peasants from Lukoianovka had been pasturing their cattle, in numbers of

---

[11] *Vtoroi period revoliutsii, I/I*, No. 393, p. 549 (report, Commander, 36th Akhtirsk Dragoon Regiment, Colonel E. A. Leont'evich to Emperor Nicholas II, 27 January 1906).

[12] GARF, f. 102, DP OO, op. 236 (II), 1906 g., d. 700, ch. 58, ll. 37–37 ob. (telegram, No. 675, Kursk Governor V. M. Borzenko to the Minister of Internal Affairs, 1 February 1906).

[13] *Ibid.*, ll. 43–43 ob., 47–49, 50 (exchange between the Governor's chancellery and the Director of the Special Section concerning reports of "mass arrests" in the town of Miropol').

[14] *RSKG*, No. 215, p. 172 (GAKO, f. 1, op. 16, d. 19, l. 199), telegram, Governor V. M. Borzenko to Novyi Oskol' District Police Commandant, 10 March 1906.

around 2,000 head, on estate lands. Dmitriev's employees and the police repeatedly chased off the trespassing cattle; each time, village livestock was at once driven back onto the estate's fields. The incident was to escalate toward a full occupation of the estate by the peasants of Lukianovka, which was broken only at the end of May.[15]

Thus, in the wake of the events of November–December 1905, rural unrest in Kursk Province dropped off rapidly in numbers and intensity. Multiple prosecutions and police repression supported by more numerous military forces were a principal factor in this decline: for the moment, provincial authorities had recovered a capacity to inflict a sure punishment on participants in unrest. That sense, so widespread during the course of the periods of the most intense disorders in 1905, that one could act against one's social enemies with impunity, that the army was far away at the front and the local authorities weak and indecisive, was being dispelled. This sense might have gained added emphasis when, after several months, hearings on cases associated with the disorders of February 1905, together with matters of more recent date, resumed before the Kursk Regional Court. But the verdicts were mixed: of 452 accused in the 14 cases tried from 16 April to 6 June 1906, 207 (46%) were acquitted, 158 (35%) got prison terms of eight months (132) or less, 72 (20%) of 10 months to 1 year and 11 were fined and remanded to the supervision of the Land Captains. Only four defendants received longer prison sentences (1–3 years) under stricter regimes in the Provincial Detention Center.[16]

The presence of heavily tasked military units in this superheated atmosphere also held certain dangers for the apparatus of repression. A squadron of dragoons, two infantry companies and a machine-gun unit had to be sent to Belgorod in December 1905, after disorders among the garrison's enlisted men broke out on 28 November.[17] During 20–23 May, unrest took hold of the soldiery of the 123rd Kozlovsk Infantry Regiment at Kursk, only just returned from Manchuria. This took the form of mass

---

[15] *Ibid.*, No. 216, pp. 172–173 (GAKO, f. 1, op. 16, d. 19, ll. 283–286), telegram.

[16] RGIA, f. 1405, op. 108, 1906 g., d. 6806 ("O krest'ianskikh bezporiadkakh v Dmitrievskom uyezde Kurskoi gubernii," tom III), ll. 121–123, 128, 135, 137 and 138 (Reports of Procurator of the Kursk Regional Court to Procurator of the Khar'kov Judicial Chamber); RGIA, op. 194, 1908 g., d. 102 (report of Procurator of the Kursk Regional Court to the Ministry of Justice, First Department, Second Criminal Division), ll. 54–54 ob., 63, 68–68 ob.

[17] *RSKG*, Nos. 109–113, pp. 101–103; GARF, f. 102, DP OO, op. 233 (II), 1905 g., d. 2550, ch. 44, ll.183–184 (telegram, General A. I. Panteleev to the Minister of Internal Affairs, 1 December 1905).

meetings, refusals to do sentry duty or to remain in encampments, and composition of resolutions decrying poor conditions of service, but setting out, in other cases, political demands and declarations of solidarity with peasants and workers.[18] On the whole, however, military units deployed from outside the province continued to show proper obedience to the orders of the provincial authorities during 1905–1906. In contrast, disintegration of the field armies in 1917 and the return of armed veterans to the villages were to shape the reemergence of unrest in the rural districts in 1917–1918 in an entirely different manner.

2. The Duma Elections

The February–March period also coincided with the unprecedented political activities associated with upcoming elections to the First State Duma, which were to be completed in Kursk Province by 1 April. Provincial authorities reported that the comparative calm in peasant communities had much to do with high expectations for future sessions of the Duma with regard to a decisive resolution of the land question. The Governor's report to the Ministry of Internal Affairs of 16 April directly alluded to this fact: "In the past two weeks, the province has been calm. Misunderstandings emerging on agrarian grounds are cut short in their initial stages. Generally, field work proceeds peacefully. Undoubtedly, the peasant population, placing great hopes in a resolution of the agrarian question by the Duma, has adopted a wait-and-see attitude."[19] Despite the anathema on the State Duma declared by the All-Russian Peasant Union and the revolutionary parties, peasants in Kursk Province proved to be active participants in elections to the legislature summoned by the Tsar. Pre-election campaigning and the polling itself were run in an atmosphere of ongoing repression, often quite "compatible" with administrative interventions against persons whose views and activities made them politically "unreliable." Indeed, Governor Borzenko made use of the heightened atmosphere created by pre-election campaigning and elections to the State Duma as one more argument for maintenance of troop strength in the province in his ongoing negotiations with the central authorities.[20]

---

[18] *Ibid.*, Nos. 201–204, 206, pp. 160–165.

[19] GARF, f. 102, DP 00, op. 236 (II), 1906 g., d. 700, ch. 58, ll. 61–69 (telegram, No. 1989, Governor V. M. Borzenko to the Ministry of Internal Affairs, 16 April 1906.

[20] *Vtoroi period revoliutsii, I/I*, No. 396, p. 552 (memorandum, Governor V. M. Borzenko to Commander of the Kievan Military District V. A. Sukhomlinov, 4 March 1906).

The order of elections from the peasant curia was determined by the Statute of 6 August 1905: the Statute set up a four-tiered "filter" for peasant voters. First, from each 10 households, villagers sent the usual *desiatniki* to the parish assembly. Second, at the parish assembly, the *desiatniki* elected plenipotentiaries to district electoral assemblies: at district assemblies, the peasant plenipotentiaries chose their electors for the provincial congress. It was only on this final stage that the Duma deputies were elected. In contrast, landowners in Kursk Province with real property over 150 *desiatiny* or other immoveable property valued at more than 15,000 rubles caucused (with the elected plenipotentiaries of the far greater cohort of lesser landowners) in the district seat to personally choose electors to the Provincial Electoral Assembly. T. E. Emmons has calculated the deliberate slanting of the suffrage by the ratio of electors to Deputy elected: for landowners 1: 2,000; for prominent urban residents 1: 4,000; for peasants 1: 30,000; for workers 1: 90,000.[21]

Despite the blatantly discriminatory features of the election law of 1905, the efforts of the local administration to block candidatures of those judged "politically unreliable," and the presence of conservative minorities in the district peasant curia themselves, the Provincial Electoral Assembly (78 peasants, 44 landowners and 28 electors from the urban curia) came to be dominated by the alliance between a militant majority of peasant *vyborshchiki* and a cohesive group of Kadet electors that was most responsible for the fact that the Members who set out from Kursk Province for St. Petersburg had a decidedly left-leaning cast.[22] Four were members of the provincial landowning gentry with long records of public service in local and provincial *zemstvo* organizations who were or became active in the Constitutional Democratic Party (Kadets). These included Prince Petr Dmitrievich Dolgorukov (1866–1951) from Sudzha District and Nikolai Vladimirovich Shirkov (born 1862) from L'gov District, whom we have already encountered in connection with the campaign to organize chapters of the Peasant Union in their districts in 1905.

Viacheslav Evgen'evich Iakushkin (1856–1912) was the grandson of the Decembrist Ivan Dmitrievich Iakushkin (1793–1857). An historian

---

[21] Statutes in *PSZ*, III, 25: No. 26662, 6 August 1905 ("Vysochaishe utverzhdennoe Polozhenie o vyborakh v Gosudarstvennuiu dumy"), 645–651, and No. 27029, 11 December 1905 ("Ob izmenenii Polozheniia o vyborakh v Gosudarstvennoi Dume i izdaniiakh v dopolnenie k nemu uzakonenii"), 877–881. Emmons, *The Formation of Political Parties*, 239.

[22] On the Duma elections in Kursk Province, see Rexheuser, *Dumawahlen and lokale Gesellschaft*, 147–189, in which the forces arrayed in the local elections are analyzed. An account of the national elections is in Emmons, *Formation*, 238–352.

and literary scholar, he had held the post of *privat-dotsent* at Moscow University after defending his master's dissertation in 1890 (entitled "Essays on the History of Russian Land Policy during the 18th and 19th Centuries"), after which he taught Russian history and contributed numerous articles to national journals on the history of Russian literature and in particular on the *oeuvre* of A. S. Pushkin. It was in connection with the centennial of the poet's birth that Iakushkin's public presentation on Pushkin's views on the Russian state excited the disapproval of the authorities and resulted in his brief exile from Moscow to the city of Iaroslavl. Iakushkin stood in service as Deputy to both his district (Staryi Oskol') and the Provincial Zemstvo uninterruptedly from 1889 and was known for his essays on the land question, which bore a pronounced "Populist" imprint.[23]

Aleksandr Nikolaevich von Ruttsen (born 1858), by profession an engineer and a senior official (*statskii sovetnik*) in the Ministry of Ways, was nevertheless an active participant in the public life of his native province—at various times holding the elected offices of Justice of the Peace, Marshal of the Nobility from his home Fatezh District, Permanent Secretary of the Office of Civil Affairs, Chairman of his District's Zemstvo Board and Deputy from Fatezh District to the provincial *zemstvo* assembly. Along with Dolgorukov and Iakushkin, von Ruttsen took part in the work of the founding congress of the Constitutional Democratic Party in 1905.[24] His sister, Liudmila Nikolaevna, was also active in the affairs of the local *zemstvo* organs, particularly with regard to popular education, and later became a prominent advocate for women's rights in Russia and a founding member of the Women's Union at its inaugural congress of May 8–11, 1905.[25]

Vasilii Ivanovich Dolzhenkov (1842–1918), the nationally renowned physician and oculist and prominent participant in the work of the All-Russian Pirogov Congresses, acted at the same time as the longtime head of the Medical-Sanitary Bureau of the Kursk Provincial Zemstvo and leading figure and organizer of the Kursk Society of Physicians. He was a founder of the Society for the Assistance to Elementary Education in the city of Kursk, where he also served as a Deputy in the city duma. Though Dolzhenkov was also among those of noble origin who maintained close

---

[23] *Al'bom portretov*...39.). Pirumova, *Zemskoe*, 107–108. Semevskii, "Pamiati V. E. Iakushkin," *Golos minuvshego*, 1913, No. 1, 271–276. His views on agrarian issues in Iakushkin, *Krest'ianskaia reforma 1861 goda i russkoe obshchestvo*.

[24] *Ibid.*, 39.

[25] Noonan and Nechemias, eds., *Encyclopedia*, 64–65.

ties with the "*osvobozhentsy*," he was known to have rendered material aid to members of the Socialist-Revolutionary Party in the city of Kursk: police surveillance established that the SR committee in the province used Dolzhenkov's flat in the city as one of their regular meeting places.[26]

The six remaining Members that made up the provincial delegation were peasants by origin, but only two of these, Mikhail Aleksandrovich Merkulov (born 1875), owner of 60 *desiatiny* in Shchigrov District, and Illarion Grigor'evich Solomko (born 1873) of Sudzha District, actually remained at the plow; both had completed local rural primary and middle schools.[27] The other deputies were men of peasant origin whose education, training and occupations put them within the "rural intelligentsia" or "third element," and suggest the degree of esteem in such figures were held by the peasant electorate. Fedor Gerasimovich Ovchinnikov (born 1866) from the village of Ivanovskoe, L'gov District ("non-party"), and Maksim Konstantinovich Gudilin of Graivoron District (born 1865), chairman of the Peasant Union affiliate at Golovchino, "by conviction an SR," had both finished the Kursk Provincial Teacher's Seminary and had been, until the period of repression, rural teachers. Both were dismissed as "politically unreliable," Ovchinnikov in December, in the wake of his participation in the conference with General Panteleev, Gudilin in April after his election.[28]

Mikhail Danilovich Kutomanov (born 1856, Graivoron District) had been employed as secretary to the District Zemstvo Board, active in *zemstvo* statistical studies. Subjected to dismissal, blacklisted and briefly jailed for his political views, Kutomanov turned his hand to journalism and contributed articles to newspapers and journals close to public activism.[29] Grigorii Nikitich Shaposhnikov (born 1869, Novyi Oskol' District), also had a checkered résumé. At the time of his election, he worked simultaneously as director of the Kursk City Insurance Board and as accounts manager in the Veliko-Mikhailovskaia Parish Administration, and had been elected as elected representative (*glasnyi*) on the Novyi Oskol' District Zemstvo Board. He finished the Belgorod Teachers' Seminary at the

---

[26] *Al'bom portretov...*, 38; GARF, f. 102, DP, 4-oe deloproizvodstvo, 1907 g., op. 99, d. 108, ch.1, l.1.

[27] *Ibid.*, 38, 39. Solomko belonged to a local Baptist congregation.

[28] *Ibid.*, 37, 38. Gudilin had been a rural teacher for 20 years. His dismissal was the result of efforts of the clique of ultra-conservative nobles who dominated *zemstvo* organizations in Graivoron District (led by the Grigorosulo clan) to have him fired in order to deny him eligibility to stand for the elections. The order for his dismissal, however, was finalized only after the elections had taken place.

[29] *Ibid.*, 38.

end of the 1880s and secured a teaching post in the Don Region, but, like Kutomanov, lost his post after an arrest in 1890. Afterwards, he was employed as a typesetter, assistant to a parish scribe and *zemstvo* statistician. During a sabbatical in Moscow for research in the Rumiantsev Museum, Shaposhnikov got permission to attend university lectures. During the outbreaks of student unrest in Moscow in 1901, however, Shaposhnikov's flat was searched and, ordered deported from the city, he left for Paris, where he regularly attended lectures at the Sorbonne.[30] It is not surprising, then, that men of such backgrounds and views soon gravitated to the Labor Group (*Trudoviki*) in the First State Duma that was to advocate for a radical approach to land reform.[31]

Thus the delegation that left for Petersburg in April 1906 could be assumed to have had peasant interests firmly in mind, and their constituents in Kursk Province had every right to hope for a positive result from their work. On the floor of the Duma itself, Merkulov was to take note of the hopes and expectations generated by the elections:

> The Parish Assembly that elected me as plenipotentiary, and my fellow villagers, who saw me off to the District Plenum and then to the Duma, gave me an instruction. This instruction is well known to almost all of our deputies: get us land and freedom. The peasants didn't give me detailed directives; they didn't give me a sophisticated and beautifully worked-out program. They obliged me to act on my conscience, adding that they were relying on me religiously. And I swore that I would fulfill my obligation and defend the interests of those who sent me, directed by my conscience and my reason. The elections started, and then the provincial electoral assembly was convened. We were in the majority, but we understood that it was not enough to elect only peasants. We had to have the force of science. Speakers for the Party of National Freedom (Kadets) rendered themselves the closest defenders of peasant interests in their speeches, and I ardently worked for a result by which, aside from peasants, landowners would also be elected. Our triumph was brilliant and I, along with others, pronounced emotional prayers in honor of the successful elections.[32]

---

[30] *Ibid.*, 39, "V. Sh.," "Trudovaia gruppa v gosudarstvennoi Dume" (brochure, no date, probably late May, 1906), 16. Shaposhnikov was subsequently elected assistant secretary to the Duma's presidium.

[31] On the Labor Group, see Kolesnichenko, *Trudoviki*, and Sidel'nikov, *Obrazovanie*, *passim*; Chermenskii, "I i II Gosudarstvennye Dumy," in Naumov, ed., *Aktual'nye problemy*, 197–235.

[32] *Stenograficheskii otchet Gosudarstvennaia Duma Pervyi sozyv*. I: 18, 30 May 1906, 820.

3. The First State Duma and the "Land Question"

The short and tumultuous history of the First State Duma (27 April to 9 July 1906), however, was to compromise this sense of solidarity entirely. Government rejection of land reform measures that countenanced any expropriation of private land and dissension among the erstwhile electoral allies, not only within the Kursk provincial delegation but also in the Duma as a body, doomed even a unified stand in principle on the land question so eagerly awaited in the rural districts. The national press carried the Duma proceedings on a daily basis, so that, when debates began on this critical issue, Kursk peasants were quite able to follow developments. By mid-May 1906, then, the peasantry in the province must have grown increasingly aware, from the drift of debates on the agrarian question, that any hopes and expectations sustained in the rural districts for decisive action on this issue were not to be realized. The Duma's discussion of land reform began almost immediately with work on the contents of the Reply to the Throne Speech, with which certain members of the delegation from Kursk Province were not entirely satisfied. G. N. Shaposhnikov:

> In the address, the commission has tried to put that which has significance as a conquest of the Movement of Liberation, and also to indicate those first, most important measures that the Duma wishes to carry into law. From this point of view, the commission did the correct thing when it gave place to that which the peasants consider to have already been decided. The peasants have very categorically given their view that lands of appanage, ministries, the ecclesia and so on must go to the use of the land-poor and landless peasants and of the whole urban and rural population, if it takes up agriculture. As for privately held lands, the peasants consider it to be just that these be subject to compulsory alienation. These are the two positions advanced in the reply to the Throne Speech. My personal opinion is that all land should be in the hands of those who work it... My personal opinion is that compulsory alienation should be compensated, but not always; there will be those instances when alienation must be without payment.[33]

M. D. Kutomanov was less diplomatic in assessing the lacunae, the excessive modesty and respect in the Kadet version of the Reply to the Throne Speech: "I am a peasant, elected by the parish assembly. (The peasants) told me: 'Go, demand and defend the demand for land and liberty, freedom and law.' They told me that 'if the Duma will not take up resolution of this question in the near future, and doesn't resolve it in the manner that we are demanding, then we will resolve it ourselves.'"[34]

---

[33] *Ibid.,* I: 4, 4 May 1906, 207–208.
[34] *Ibid.,* 110–112. See also "Proekt otveta na tronnuiu rech, predlozhennyi komitetom trudovoi gruppy," in "V. Sh.," *op. cit.,* 3–6.

On 8 May 1906, the Kadets tabled the so-called "Project of the 42" (Dolgorukov, Iakushkin, Shirkov and Dolzhenkov were among the sponsors), a draft of principles for land reform. The draft declared it "desirable" that acreages of land in peasant use—and especially those held by the landless and land-poor—be increased to sizes that, according to local conditions, would support the consumption demands of peasant households. It proposed realizing that aim by creating a national land fund out of state, court, appanage, ministry, monastery and ecclesiastical lands (of these there was comparatively little in Kursk Province) to be made available for allotment. Privately owned lands were to be subject to compulsory alienation in pursuit of this same goal. Procedures of alienation were to be applied first to private lands "usually" granted under leasehold agreements or cultivated by peasant inventory prior to 1 January 1906. Lands of sizes in excess of norms established after analysis of various local criteria that determined the area that could be cultivated by an owner employing his own work stock and inventory (the draft said nothing about labor) were also to be subject to compulsory alienation. Private estates that had invested in technical improvements, though, were accorded a more marked solicitousness. Lands under house compounds, to be sure, but also those under gardens, orchards, nurseries, artificial forests, hemp patches, "and such of like natures," were exempted from liability, as was land under industrial or agro-industrial plant. If arable lands associated with such enterprises were declared liable, the Kadet draft nonetheless desired for their alienation "a certain order and consistency in transition." Forests that acted to slow down erosion or served to promote water conservation were also to be spared. The word "redemption" was scrupulously avoided in the text, but all private owners subject to compulsory alienation had to be compensated "at a just price" by the Treasury.[35]

This proposal and the discussions it provoked in the Duma during the second half of May enjoyed close coverage in the national press, which ran the stenographic record of speeches of the deputies in debates in the sessions on a daily basis. The Duma exchanges not only featured a full airing of these issues, but also witnessed acrimonious public clashes with representatives of the state power that immediately preceded a resurgence

---

[35] Document read out in *ibid.*, I: 6, 8 May 1906, 248–251. See Dolgorukov's contribution, the year before, to a collection of essays by the leading lights of the Constitutional Democratic Party, in which the main lines of the 1906 program are already visible: "Agrarnyi vopros s tochki zreniia krupnago zemlevladeniia," in Dolgorukov and Petrunkevich, eds., *Agrarnyi vopros: sbornik statei*, 1–10.

of unrest in Kursk Province. In particular, expectations in the rural districts for a successful result of the work of the people's elected representatives on central questions—land reform, amnesty, political freedoms and the rule of law—must have been severely shaken by the speech from the Duma tribune of Chairman of the Council of Ministers I. L. Goremykin on 13 May. In this speech, the state's intention to stand firm against the Duma's legislative agenda—and the Members' larger aspiration to play a central role in the political life of the nation—was announced in the bluntest terms.

Reviewing the programmatic declarations in the Duma's Reply to the Throne Speech, Goremykin flatly stated that the government viewed any land reform encroaching on the inviolability of private property rights as inadmissible. The Chairman also presented the political freedoms granted by the October Manifesto as "temporary regulations" that would be replaced with permanent laws, but only in such a manner that would maintain the government's broad powers in the struggle with sedition and anarchy that threatened the state and society. The Duma's urgent requests for rescinding of emergency laws, for prosecution of official persons for unlawful actions, for reform of conditions and regimes of discipline in the armed forces and democratization of the electoral franchise: these matters were within the competence of the autocrat alone and stood outside the Duma's jurisdiction. Amnesty for those detained on political, "agrarian" or religious grounds Goremykin declared the sole prerogative of the Emperor. The Chairman announced the state's intention to bring the peasantry onto an equal footing with all other members of society as juridical persons (eliminating institutions of peasant administration and justice; abolishing restrictions on sale of allotment land and personal mobility). Yet his proposals on the land question focused solely on fostering technical improvements in cultivation, expansion of peasant arable land through grants of state-owned acreage or through the activity of the Peasant Land Bank, and reform of existing policies to facilitate emigration. Members' concerns for universal compulsory education and reform of local justice had been taken under advisement and would be given attention by the proper departments.[36]

Goremykin was followed to the tribune on two separate occasions (19 and 23 May) by Superintendent of the Administration for Land Use and Agriculture A. S. Stishinskii and Deputy Minister of Internal Affairs V. I. Gurko, who addressed the narrowly agrarian aspects of the Kadet land

---

[36] *Ibid.*, I: 8, 13 May 1906, 321–324.

reform proposal. Both officials marshaled arguments against the proposal that registered the entirely negative attitude of the government toward the draft in general and toward the concept of compulsory alienation of privately owned land in particular, predicting that the proposed reforms would gain little for the peasantry at great cost to both the rural and the national economy. The first of these held that the program of obligatory alienation would do little to augment peasant holdings, especially in the more densely populated central zone, and estimated the cost of "just compensation" at four billion rubles, an amount held to be far beyond the capacity of peasant agriculture to generate, given the technical approach to cultivation that prevailed in the villages and the thicket of insurmountable obstacles that the commune posed to necessary improvements.

The second general objection departed from the state's insistence that economies of the privately held estates were typically operated at a level of agricultural technique and investment far superior to methods and tools currently in use in peasant cultivation, were measurably more productive and contributed a gross product in terms of grain and other produce quite out of proportion to their statistical weight in Russia's national economy. If the Kadet proposals were accepted and the privately held sector effectively liquidated, the national economy would lose 150 million *poods* of grain and—just as importantly—peasant households would be deprived of a very substantial portion of their off-farm revenues. Gurko asserted that both the productivity and the purchasing power of a vast rural economy dominated by tiny consumption-farming units would be very sharply reduced, leading to a contraction of industry and, in turn, migration of the working class back to the rural districts, further lowering the capacity of the land to support the populace. Imposition of norms on landholding and transfer of tracts from the land fund not on principles of property but on those of long-term use would produce not the "freedom" that the Duma deputies so often talked of, but a constant limitation on the right of an individual to use his natural talents to acquire wealth in his chosen area of endeavor. The Deputy Minister argued that indeed it was not the destruction of private landholding that would transform the rural economy, but, on the contrary, its gradual extension to all peasant lands.[37]

---

[37] Minister of Agriculture A. S. Stishinskii's observations on the Kadet draft appear in *ibid.*, I: 12, 19 May 1906, 509–517. (Deputy Minister Gurko's remarks 517–523). This view already looked toward the expanded government reform program, the drafts of which were to be submitted to the Duma on 20 June and later to gain renown as the Stolypin land reform. See Macey, *Government and Peasant*, Part Three ("The Revolution in Policy"), 121–210.

The speeches of the state's representatives before the Duma on these occasions thus made it plain, long before the formal introduction of its legislation on land reform on June 20 or the preemptory dissolution of the Duma itself on 8 July, that the state was not to allow any infringement on rights of private property or, in the larger frame of reference, on the autocracy's prerogatives to set the agenda for land reform entirely on its own, without any interference from the Duma. It must have seemed to peasants in Kursk Province as elsewhere that, even though the duly elected representatives of the people had at last been called to deliberate and act on the most critical issues facing the country, the peasant's old enemies—the officials and the landowners—had joined forces to frustrate the Duma's far-reaching plan for reform.[38]

In the course of extended debate in the Duma during 16–30 May on the land question, the Labor Group and its allies among the "non-party" peasant deputies introduced, on 23 May, a plan for land reform distinctly more radical that the Kadet scheme. The "Project of Fundamental Principles," known as the "Project of the 104," began with the statement that all land, its depths and waters must belong to all the people and that lands necessary for agriculture should be transferred into the hands of "those who cultivate it by their own labor." State, ministerial, appanage, monastery and ecclesiastical lands—and all private lands in excess of local "labor norms" (the amount of acreage that an individual and his family could cultivate on their own)—were to form a national land fund. Compensation for private lands alienated in favor of the fund were to be borne by the state, but amounts of payments and the establishment of guidelines for those cases in which alienation was to be carried out with no compensation were to be left to a time when the agrarian reform process was taken up by residents of the localities. All private transfer of land or interest in

---

[38] "We, the peasants of Melekhovskaia Parish (Belgorod District), gathering on 8 July in the number of 150 persons, and discussing the Ministry's answer to the address of the Duma and the government's declaration on land [*the 20 June program—BRM*], have found that there is nothing good to be expected from the government, that, as before, it only shows concern for those who suck our blood—the estate owners and the nobles. We do not rely on the Duma either. It has been meeting for 3 months and besides damage, it has done nothing. We shall get land and freedom only after our victory over the old government, through the Constituent Assembly, to which we will elect our representatives directly by universal, equal and secret ballot. Only such people's representatives will do the needed things. We think that at the present time it would be stupid to pay taxes, give up recruits and recognize any authorities: indeed, this will lead us only to disaster." *Vtoroi period revoliutsii, II/II*, No. 105, p. 140.

land was to cease and laws passed to prevent accumulations above the labor norm of the locality. Preparation for carrying out the envisioned land reform and management of the land fund were to be the functions of local committees elected on the basis of the four-tailed suffrage from among local residents. Allotments from the fund were in no case to exceed labor norms for each locality, and were to favor local residents over non-locals and agriculture over industry. Land in allotment was to be subject to a special tax when in use, based on location and quality, and returned to the fund in the event of cessation of use or of a desire to reduce allotment size.[39]

The "Project of the 104" expressed the increasing disenchantment of a considerable number of the peasant deputies, by the end of May, with their junior status in the alliance with the Kadets. In his speech of 30 May, the peasant Member from Kursk Province M. A. Merkulov spoke of this sense of disillusionment and increasing impatience, quite at odds with the hopes engendered by the outcome of the April elections, in his criticism both of the arguments of the government speakers and of Kadet proposals and their silences and compromises at critical points. These, in his view, scarcely concealed a shared desire to ensure the continued survival of the landed estates, at the expense of a just settlement that met the demands of his constituents.

For several days in a row, the long orations of various speakers, scholars, professors, jurists, legal experts and policy-makers have resounded from this tribune. They have been discussing the proposals and programs concerning land reform from the 42 members of the Party of National Freedom and of the 104 members of the Labor Group for transmission to the Agrarian Commission, the formation of the Commission itself and the institution of committees necessary for the collection of materials for the resolution of the land question. Along the way, these speakers have advanced views and considerations on how best to solve this problem, and two weighty concerns have been brought out: first, that the transformation should benefit the state, and second, that the prosperity of our brother, the *muzhik*, be provided for. Rest assured, on this matter, all our tastes, the objects of our affections and desires, have already been studied... Those who are most closely of all concerned with this question—the peasants themselves— have spoken more rarely and much less at length. And it is no wonder. For indeed, all the past efforts of our "fathers" and warders of various ranks and positions have consisted not only in preventing our education, but also, on the contrary, in oppressing, in throttling the spark of God [in man], [his] natural intelligence... From the speeches of our well-wishers and benefactors that I have heard, I have understood that we peasants either ought not be granted land at all or maybe not all at once, but in bits and pieces

---

[39] Text in *Stenograficheskii otchet. Gosudarstvennaia Duma Pervyi sozyv*, I: 13, 23 May 1906, 560–562.

over the course of time. With this, speakers have advanced an entire phalanx of obstacles that prevent them from rendering us their full generosity… I say firmly, once and for all: the land must go to us [peasants], all of it and without compensation.[40]

On 8 June 1906, Merkulov, with I. G. Solomko and 31 other sponsors, was to advance for transmission to the Agrarian Commission the most radical proposal yet to be tabled: for the full "socialization" of all lands without compensation. Its transmission, however, was rejected by a majority of the Duma and was never to be discussed in open session.[41] By this time, debate on the issue had moved into the Agrarian Commission, elected by the Duma in 91 members on 6 June, by an arrangement in which all factions in the assembly were allotted a roughly equal representation.[42]

4. The Resumption of Collective Actions

In Kursk Province, however, the police dispatches show that by this time peasants were already rendering their verdict on the Duma's work. For as debates dragged on in the Tauride Palace, incidents of unrest began to multiply rapidly in the last week of May. The first of these in the archival record took place at *sloboda* Golovchino (Lisichanskaia Parish) in Graivoron District, 21 May 1906, when a crowd of peasants, assembled for a well-attended village fair, suddenly confronted the police deputies (*strazhniki*) assigned to the site to maintain public order. Despite efforts to restore calm, the villagers began to shout accusations: that the deputies poorly preserved order, evidenced no zeal whatsoever in apprehending horse thieves, took bribes from the merchants at the bazaar and were too often drunk, adding that "We don't need you, and it's for nothing that we feed you out of our own pockets!" Then the peasants charged at the unarmed deputies, who fled to the constabulary to arm themselves, but the crowd, following hard behind them, seized their rifles and began to smash them. After administering beatings to both the police captain and his deputies, the peasants ordered them to clear out of town and never show their faces again. When the Assistant District Police Commander and seventy dragoons rode to Golovchino (from Rakitnaia) to demand that the

---

[40] *Ibid.*, I: 18, 30 May 1906, 819–826.
[41] *Ibid.*, I: 23, 8 June 1906, 1097–1156. Document appended to the proceedings, 1153–1156.
[42] *Ibid.*, "Spisok Chlenov Gosudarstvennoi Dumy," 3–17.

perpetrators in the incident be given up, the peasants refused. "Go ahead, arrest the whole commune!" To the admonitions of the officer, persons in the crowd replied "We don't have to talk with this guy! We have our own chiefs [*nachal'stvo*]!" and "Go take your saber and cut off your own head!" Faced down by the crowd, the dragoons bivouacked at a nearby estate for several days.[43]

On the whole, however, the resumption of peasant collective action, taking place as it did in the context of the demonstrated readiness of local authorities to react swiftly to any disturbances to public order with force, almost immediately took on a character markedly different than that which had typified unrest during 1905. On 25 May, Governor Borzenko received an urgent telegram from Graivoron District Police Commandant Chudnovskii: "The peasants of Krasnaia Iaruga, in their entire commune, have expelled [*sniali*] the laborers from the Kharitonenko estate and themselves refuse to go out to work. The estate's guards and the patrolmen of the Third Precinct have run off, announcing their unwillingness to continue serving. Half the police guards have declared they are quitting on the 1st. Under the influence of the newspapers, the peasantry has begun to close ranks. The situation everywhere is taking on a threatening character. The peasants have a terrifying animosity toward the police guards. I received telegrams from Rakitnaia and Krasnaia Iaruga just after the Vice-Governor left. Disorders are expected tomorrow."[44]

In an action that was to be broadly replicated throughout the province in the coming months, the peasants of Krasnaia Iaruga had acted evidently as the result of deliberations of the village assembly and had elected to enforce a work stoppage on the estate. This was not a work stoppage or "strike" in the usual sense, since the owner's labor force itself was *compelled* to leave the fields.

Disturbances of this same type emerged in Dmitriev District, in the same localities in which the disturbances of February 1905 had begun. Labor actions began at Glamazdino on 26 May: all estate employees and field workers were driven off (*sniaty*) the lands of the new owner of the ruined Volkov estate, V. F. Zablotsky: major adjustments to day-, term- and year-contract wages were demanded. The issue was quickly resolved when the estate administration met the demands in full. Rumors about the

---

[43] GARF, f. 102, DP OO, op. 236 (II), 1906 g., d. 700, ch. 58, ll. 88–88 ob. (report, at No. 2166, Colonel Vel'k, Commandant of the Kursk Provincial Gendarmerie, to the Department of Police, 3 June 1906).

[44] *RSKG*, No. 219, p. 174 (GAKO, f. 1, op. 16, d. 12, l. 14).

action—and its clear success—spread through Glamazdinskaia and Prilepovskaia Parishes and, "under the influence of the peasants of Glamazdino," similar actions were "organized by stages" at Kozhanovka (on the estates of merchants A. N. Zotov and L. P. Prokhorov-Birvar'), at Romanovo, on the *khutora* and main Khomutovka installation of the estate of O. A. Shaufus and on the estates of the Meiendorf heirs at Prilepy and Dubrovitsy. Efforts at persuasion by Land Captain Kusakov and the police captain were less effective than news of the arrival of a half-squadron of dragoons on 29 May, which found most laborers back at work.[45]

Reports reaching the Governor in the last days of May indicated that the unrest had spread into L'gov District, in which the movement was to have special resonance. On 27 May, in circumstances quite analogous to those at Krasnaia Iaruga and Glamazdino, the neighboring peasant communities forced a cessation of field work on the estate of Prince Ivan Viktorovich Bariatinskii at Bol'shie Ugony (4,000 *desiatiny*), and at the Mar'inskii sugar refineries at Peny (Ugonskaia Parish), on sugar-beet plantations of the huge main estate (11,428 *desiatiny*), held in 1905 by his uncle, Prince Aleksandr Vladimirovich Bariatinskii.[46] These were to be only the first of thirteen actions between 27 May and 24 June directed against the vast patchwork of estates held by the Bariatinskii *maiorat* in adjacent parishes of L'gov, Sudzha and Ryl'sk Districts. These actions were again mainly work stoppages enforced by villagers adjoining the various estates who united to chase the laborers off the fields (that is, these were not "strikes" in the classical sense) and to pose their own demands for renewal of field work. Violent clashes with police and army units often attended the dénouement of these incidents. Disorders were hardly limited to the Bariatinskii estates: on 9 June, on the domains of Princess Gagarina near Kochanovka (Iznoskovskaia Parish), taking their cue from actions on the nearby Bariatinskii estate two days earlier, local peasants drove off the estate's laborers, at the time busy sowing the fields, demanding an additional 2 rubles a day for all. Crowds appeared daily on

---

[45] *Ibid.*, No. 224, p. 177 (GAKO, f. 1, op. 16, d. 3, l. 15), report, Land Captain of the Fourth Department of Dmitrievskii District A. Kusakov to Governor V. M. Borzenko, 1 June 1906. Kusakov, considering that this quiet was only temporary, demanded permanent posting of troops in these parishes. As in February 1905, he proved to have been prescient.

[46] *RSKG*, No. 220, p. 174 (GAKO, f. 1, op. 16, d. 1, l. 10), telegram, L'gov District Police Commandant Avraamov to Governor V. M. Borzenko, 27 May 1906. Both sites were on the Moscow–Kiev–Voronezh Railway line.

the estate, threatening to go over to direct action, forbidding anyone to feed livestock, driving off even the Princess's personal servants and creating general panic. The estate's bailiff was beaten.[47] On the 13th, villagers from Fitizh went out to take in for themselves the hay on meadows of Marshal of the Nobility Petr Petrovich Stremoukhov (already victimized in December 1905 by the complete destruction of his house by persons from this same village), chased off the estate's steward, who tried to dissuade them, and set about dividing up the lands of various neighboring landowners and to preparing them for cultivation.[48]

In a private letter dated 10 June 1906 for the attention of the Department of Police, one of the local landowners, Prince Nikolai Vladimirovich Gagarin, offered a broad review of the reemergence of rural unrest, which, for all the usual overtones, seems to accurately record the chronology:

> Disturbances in L'gov District began in October of last year but were quite scattered, thanks to the competence of the Governor at the time N. N. Gordeev. Just at Christmas, Minister Witte dismissed Gordeev and appointed V. M. Borzenko, a young and energetic man. In the last days of December, the manor house of Mr. Stremoukhov at the village of Fitizh was destroyed, thanks to the inaction of the police. After this, the authorities did take action: troops arrived and the ringleaders were arrested, but no punitive measures were taken. Everyone calmed down, the voting for electors [to select the deputies] to the Duma came and went, and everyone expected something [from the Duma].
>
> Finally, the Duma convened, the press started to spread stenographic records of sessions of the Duma, and talk of amnesty and land raised the mood among the peasants. Peasants believe the printed word, but they read only "red" newspapers and no others. Duma Deputy Ovchinnikov, from the village of Ivanovskoe, the estate of Prince A. V. Bariatinskii, sent his brother a letter or a telegram: "There won't be any amnesty or any freedom. Get ready to move!" And indeed the peasants began to move. Things began at Ivanovskoe and now strikes have seized the whole District. At the very same time, persons detained for political or agrarian offenses broke down the gates of the prison and in a group of 30, went to the Administration of Police, declared to the Assistant Police Commander that they were "going back to work" and, singing revolutionary songs, marched through the whole town and went back to their villages, bringing a final measure of unrest into rural districts that were already not so calm.[49]

---

[47] GARF, f. 102, DP OO, op. 236 (II), 1906 g., d. 700, ch. 58, ll. 95–96 (telegram, Princess E. P. Gagarina to Minister of Internal Affairs P. A. Stolypin, 9 June 1906).

[48] *Ibid.*, ll. 118 ob.

[49] *Ibid.*, ll. 120 ob.-121 (private letter dated 10 June 1906, N. V. Gagarin to D. F. Trepov). The prison break is reported at l. 84 (telegram, at No. 2309, Governor V. M. Borzenko to Minister of Internal Affairs P. A. Stolypin, 2 June 1906).

Map 6. Central Districts, May–June, 1906

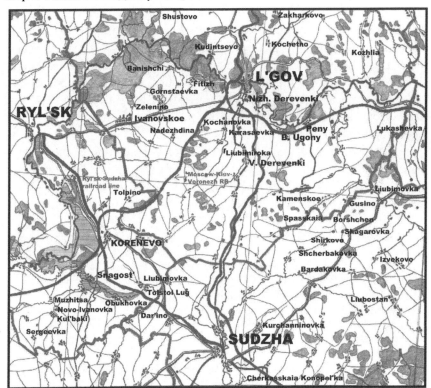

Government *rapporteurs* appear to have accepted this view of the genesis of peasant collective actions in 1906: as in 1905, it was easier to accept the idea that "outsiders" (in this case, the Duma deputies) were responsible for peasant actions, rather than to imagine that the villagers had both their own reading of the general situation and the capacity and will to organize their own responses. On 24 June, the Governor telegraphed the Ministry of Internal Affairs with a summary description of events in just such a vein:

> The movement that has seized L'gov District is inspired by Members of the Duma from Kursk Province and has erupted in the form of the mass rural strike. There is no violence or active pressure, but the movement testifies to serious organization, expressed in the stubborn refusal of peasants and laborers to perform current harvest work on agreed-upon conditions. The new conditions for supplying [their] labor are completely unacceptable to the landowners. It is impossible to foresee any amicable resolution of the question. The ringleaders and organizers are, when possible, being apprehended. The most active of these has been arrested today and another series of arrests has been scheduled. I have en-

tered into correspondence with the Department of Police concerning deportations to far provinces. I petition Your Excellency for full support in this direction, since the Department's refusal in this after my winter reports from L'gov District is one of the crucial factors at work in the present state of things. I am resorting to decisive measures, since any peaceful forms of influence are unthinkable: of this I have been convinced by conversations with the parish elders and the peasants.[50]

One of the main venues of the June events encompassed, once again, the northern parishes of Sudzha District. On 5 June, the acting District Police Commander reported that a crowd of peasants from the village of Borshchen' (Bol'she-Soldatskaia Parish) and adjacent villages had "taken over" the big estate of Aleksei Vladimirovich Evreinov: the police unit on hand—Precinct Police Captain Novikov and 15 police deputies—fled the scene after firing into the crowd, wounding one peasant.[51] District Police Commander Keber cabled the Governor on June 9 that all of the laborers on the sugar-beet plantations of hereditary honorary citizens Mikhail and Sergei Vasil'evich Sabashnikov in this same locale—at Borshchen', Shirkovo, Bardakovka, Shagarovka, Ofrosimovka, Liubimovka and Novo-Nikol'skoe and at the Liubimovka sugar refinery—had downed tools, demanding big increases in pay.[52] Despite the arrival of troops in the northern parishes in succeeding days, work had still not fully resumed on the Sabashnikov estates more than a week later, and Keber reported that local peasants at Shcherbakovka had expelled agricultural workers on the Medvedev estate.[53] The matter eventually came down to pitched battles. At Bardakovka (on the Sabashnikov estate) on 27 June, peasants armed with pitchforks and staves came out to enforce their demand that police and dragoons quit the village. In the mêlée, one peasant was killed, and two dragoons and two peasants were wounded.[54]

Demands for aid against the peasants issuing from the ranks of the provincial gentry were at times disingenuous to say the least. Such was the case in the matter of one Nikolai Vladimirovich Davydov. On 17 June

---

[50] *Ibid.*, ll. 151–151 ob. (telegram, Governor V. M. Borzenko to Minister of Internal Affairs P. A. Stolypin, 24 June 1906).

[51] *RSKG*, No. 228, p. 179 (GAKO, f. 1, op. 16, d. 7, l. 10), telegram, Acting Sudzha District Police Commandant Kolodkevich to Governor V. M. Borzenko, 5 June 1906.

[52] *Ibid.*, No. 191, p.155 (GAKO, f. 1, op. 16, d. 7, ll. 19–20), telegram, Sudzha District Police Commandant Keber to Governor V. M. Borzenko, 9 June 1906.

[53] *Ibid.*, No. 239, pp. 184–185 (GAKO, f. 1, op. 16, d. 7, ll. 24–25), telegram, Sudzha District Police Commandant Keber to Governor V. M. Borzenko, 16 June 1906.

[54] *Ibid.*, No. 259, pp. 194–195 (GAKO, f. 1, op. 16, d. 7, l. 53), telegram, "for the (Sudzha District) Police Commandant Kolodkevich" to Governor V. M. Borzenko, 27 June 1906.

in Novo-Ivanovskaia Parish near the estate of Princess Mariia Apolinar'evna Bariatinskaia, struck two days earlier, neighboring peasants appeared on Davydov's estate (442 *desiatiny*) near *khutor* Nikol'skii and began to harass Davydov's laborers and tenants ("many of whom had to pay to avoid being marked for violence"). They insisted that Davydov hire workers only from among the members of their own commune and that land in lease be rented only to their fellow villagers, setting wages and rents at levels "most unfavorable" to the landowner. On the 20th, all laborers and servants were expelled from the estate, and Davydov was forced to bow to peasant demands. This action was described in Davydov's own petition dated 30 October 1906, addressed to the Minister of Internal Affairs. The matter, apparently, dragged on. Before sowing of winter crops began, Davydov again called the authorities in to protest against conditions to which he had agreed "under duress." District Police Commandant Sabynin, accompanied by a team of constables, arrived on 6 August to try to defuse the situation. Inspecting a written copy of the conditions, turned over by "the now thoroughly cowed peasants," he stated that they could act on the basis of the agreement, since only a court could now decide on questions of its legality. Davydov:

> If he had read out to them several articles of the Statute on Punishments and explained the illegality of their actions, if he had just torn up the conditions [that would have been the end of the matter], but he spoke with the peasants in a manner that gave them to understand that they were in the right from the legal point of view. Some jurists in Sudzha District find that there was nothing illegal in the action of the peasants, because, allegedly, they threatened my property and not my person, but the acting Judicial Investigator does not agree with this and is moving the case toward a legal resolution.

Davydov went on to attack Sabynin as a sympathizer of the peasant movement and to paint the leaders of the peasant protest as dangerous revolutionaries whose acts "smelled of hard labor in exile." The whole petition, however, "smelled" of a man whose fear had prompted him to sign under those conditions—such actions were probably not uncommon in the 1905–1906 period—and now desired the authorities to assist him in their abrogation.[55]

Unrest in Sudzha and L'gov Districts was communicated to villages in the adjoining southeast corner of Ryl'sk District as well. Despite arrival of police units in the vicinity, peasants from Kul'baki (Kul'bakinskaia Par-

---

[55] GARF, f. 102, DP OO, op. 236 (II), 1906 g., d. 700, ch. 58, ll. 180a–180b ob., 344–345.

ish), on successive days (5–6 June), ran both migrant and local agricultural workers off the fields of the Olimpiadov and Kul'baki farmsteads of the nearby estate of Konstantin Semenovich Tereshchenko (6,346 *desiatiny*, formerly part of the Riboper' domains).[56] Intercession of the authorities cut short the action for a time, but on the 9th, villagers from Kul'baki, Sergeevka and Muzhitsa came back to *khutor* Kul'baki to force the workers from the estate once more.[57]

At the same time that outbreaks of unrest struck Dmitriev, Sudzha, Ryl'sk and L'gov Districts, disorders flared up again in the same localities in Graivoron District that had been sites of disturbances in 1905. At Borisovka (Borisovskaia Parish) on 4 June, a crowd of 500 peasant youths assembled to the sound of the *nabat* and, "singing revolutionary songs," set off for the nearby administrative compound on the estate of Count A. D. Sheremet'ev. The main office (with all records, bills and plats), the steward's and employees' quarters, stables, a storage shed, two granaries and the bath house were set on fire. Only a small house, reputed locally to have been built by Peter the Great with his own hands, was left unscathed. A mass of spectators gathered on the compound to watch the fires, but no effort was made to put out the flames.[58] A guard post in Sheremet'ev's forests near Borisovka burned down three days later.[59]

At *sloboda* Rakitnaia, it was not until the end of June that villagers again went over to direct action: intense efforts to adjust conflicts between the Iusupov estate and Rakitnaia communes had been under way for weeks. Attacks on police personnel at Golovchino on 21 May and expul-

---

[56] *RSKG*, No. 230, p. 180 (GAKO, f. 1, op. 16, d. 5, l. 9), telegram, Tereshchenko (no initial) to Governor V. M. Borzenko, 6 June 1906. The Ministry of Agriculture and State Domains' 1900 directory estimated this portion of the estate at 6,346 *desiatiny* and identified its owner as Konstantin Semenovich Tereshchenko. *Kratkiia spavochnyia svedeniia*, 51.

[57] *Ibid*, No. 234, pp. 181–182 (GAKO, f. 1, op. 16, d. 5, ll. 10–20), telegram, Ryl'sk District Police Commandant Zarin to Governor V. M. Borzenko, 9 June 1906, (end of report on incident at Tolpino, Korenevskaia Parish).

[58] RGIA, f. 1405, op. 194, 1908 g, d. 200 ("O krest'ianskikh bezporiadkakh v Kurskoi gubernii vesnoi 1906 g."), ll. 2–2 ob. (copy, report of 24 June 1906 at No. 2239, Procurator of the Kursk Regional Count N. M. Smirnov to the Procurator of the Khar'kov Judicial Chamber S. S. Khrulev). Detail on the house of Peter the Great (B. P. Sheremet'ev was one of the Tsar's leading *polkovodtsy*) in *Pravo*, No. 24, voskr., 18 June 1906 ("Khronika"). It was apparently built during the run-up to the battle with the Swedes at Poltava.

[59] GARF, f. 102, DP OO, op. 236 (II), 1906 g., d. 700, ch. 58, l. 91 (telegram, at No. 2429, Governor V. M. Borzenko to Director of the Department of Police E. A. Vuich, 8 June 1906).

sion of agricultural laborers on the adjoining lands of Kharitonenko at Krasnaia Iaruga on 25 May had much to do with a heightened mood among the peasants in the area. For immediately in the wake of these events, Princess Iusupova and her estate administrators began once again to put pressure on Minister Stolypin, unsparing in their efforts to depict the estate's administration as making generous concessions to peasant demands on the crucial issue of land lease and to paint the villagers' actions in the worst possible light.[60] On 11 June, Iusupova's rejection of proposals advanced by the communes was the subject of a general meeting of Rakitnaia peasants.[61] On the 14th, the Princess's steward reported that the estate's counterproposals were rejected at this meeting: "I have gone to Rakitnaia. The advantageous conditions offered by the Princess to the peasants were not accepted. Their demands would lead to the ruin of the estate. The communes are crying about the matter among themselves. They want to incite a revolutionary movement. [Peasant livestock] are trampling our grain fields, hay meadows and grassland on a daily basis. We can take just so much. The forests are being timbered and prepared lumber stolen. The Prince's property and our lives are in the hands of the mob. I consider it my duty to report to Your High Excellency that, according to information in our possession, there moves the desire, through the movement at Rakitnaia, to call forth a general revolt."[62]

This was a not-so-subtle call for a preemptive strike against the peasants of Rakitnaia, even if it was quite well known to local officials that the root cause of tensions at this locality lay in extreme forms of land hunger among peasants in this locale and the crude and tactless manner in which estate administration exploited this circumstance. In any case, it was in this context that on 26 June the stables on the Borisov farmstead of the Rakitnaia estate were set afire by unknown arsonists.[63] Much more serious disorders broke out on 29 June. The cables that follow illustrate the manner in which a steward came to "speak" to the Governor through the office of Minister of Internal Affairs Stolypin, employing all the tried-and-true tropes about "outside agitation" and the imagery of impending general revolt. The first, from Princess Iusupova (at Krasnoe Selo): "I urgently

---

[60] *Ibid.*, ll.79–80.

[61] *Ibid.*, ll. 94–94 ob. (telegram at No. 342, Minister of Internal Affairs P. A. Stolypin to Governor V. M. Borzenko, 9 June 1906).

[62] *Ibid.*, l. 105 (telegram, steward of the estate of Princess Z. N. Iusupova to Deputy Minister of Internal Affairs A. A. Makarov, 14 June 1906).

[63] *RSKG*, No. 269, p. 199 (GAKO, f. 1, op. 16, d. 12, l. 208), telegram, Graivoron District Police Commandant Maksimov to Governor V. M. Borzenko, 2 July 1906.

request that you not refuse to telegraph the Kursk Governor, asking immediate aid. I have just got the following cable from my steward at Rakitnaia: 'On our estate, mass seizures of grain have begun, in the surrounding area, there are fires. Convinced of their [ability to act with] full impunity, the peasants have simply lost their moral balance. The authorities do nothing: not one investigation has been begun even up to the present time. It is obvious that outsiders are conducting agitation. You must petition for some action. Our situation is desperate. Everything could perish.' I ask your forgiveness for the bother. My thanks in advance."[64]

Then, from Stolypin himself: "On the estate of Princess Iusupova in Rakitnaia, mass seizures of grain have begun and in the environs of the estate there are fires. Outsiders are conducting agitation. The local authorities are obviously doing nothing. Take, in person, the most energetic measures toward the cessation of the disturbances and the arrest of agitators in order in this manner to demonstrate to the local population the presence of powerful government authority. Telegraph immediately on the situation."[65]

Yet the operation was not so easy to organize quickly. Disturbances in other parts of the province had once again led to the parceling out of available troops, and the Iusupova estate was so large that the small patrols into which the dragoons had to be divided could be easily avoided. The difficulties and dangers faced by the troops were made plain by one of the reports from the scene near the village of Rakitnaia, where, in the evening of 1 July, a squad of dragoons stopped ten carts full of wheat on the road from the Iusupova estate. Rapidly a crowd gathered; some 300 peasants armed with staves, scythes and rocks began to surround the soldiers, who were hampered in their actions by the presence of women and children in the assembly. Shielded by the crowd, the carts quickly moved off to Rakitnaia to disappear among the houses.[66] Reinforced by a half-hundred of Cossacks, two companies of infantry and a squad of artillerymen with two cannons, it was still not until 7 July that the balance was to tip in favor of the local authorities and villagers were compelled to begin carting grain taken during the disturbances back to the estate. As late as 10 July, however, the Acting Governor (Borzenko had been permitted a short vacation in the Caucasus) had to report that a majority of the population

---

[64] GARF, f. 102, DP OO, op. 236 (II), 1906 g., d. 700, ch. 58, l. 185.

[65] *Ibid.,* ll. 184, 185.

[66] *RSKG,* No. 269, p. 199 (GAKO, f 1, op. 16, d. 12, 1. 208), telegram, Graivoron District Police Commandant Maksimov to Governor V. M. Borzenko, 2 July 1906.

was resisting, taking the option of just pouring sacks of grain into ra-vines.[67]

If incidents of unrest in Graivoron District in June 1906 recall the more violent strains of the "troubles" of 1905, less intense disturbances in Shchigrov, Staryi Oskol', Tim, Putivl', and Belgorod Districts were al-most entirely dominated, as elsewhere, by work stoppages collectively organized and enforced by the peasant communities that adjoined the tar-geted estates and directed toward depriving the owners of their work forces during the most intense period of the agricultural calendar. Such efforts to enforce a sort of labor boycott on the landowners, imposing such demands for the resumption of work that the aim of ruining the victim was evident, once again stands out in the documents. That this strategy had taken a step back from direct action in 1905 to the more familiar turf of the contractual relations between lord and peasant hardly diminishes the stubbornness with which peasant militancy in Kursk Province strove in the direction of its general goals. Among the reports preserved in the ar-chival sources for this period, one finds very few incidents that recall the struggle of the peasantry to "smoke out" the landowners, yet, on occasion, peasant dissatisfaction continued to resort to such acts. Thus, in Nekliu-dovskaia Parish, Korocha District, in which acts of mass timbering of state forests involving several villages had been recorded from the end of December 1905 to mid-January 1906, peasants from the big villages of Nikol'skaia, Pentsovka and Koshliakova, on the night of 25 June, ran-sacked and burned the manor house and outbuildings of the estate of Prince Iusupov after carting off the estate's grain and other property.[68]

In another singular incident, which began on June 19 on the big estate of Nikolai Petrovich Dmitriev near Lukoianovka (Saltykovskaia Parish), Staryi Oskol' District, the neighboring villagers importuned the owner to leave his estate, drove off all the estate's laborers and proceeded to effect the outright seizure of the entire holding. For the next two weeks, the peasants of Lukoianovka, led by the village assembly, divided up the Dmitriev estate among themselves and took in the harvest, ceasing pay-ment on leases: arrears mounted (Dmitriev's estimate) to 16,000 rubles.[69] On 21 July, a unit of policemen rode into Lukoianovka to begin making

---

[67] GARF, f. 102, DP OO, op. 236 (II), 1906 g, d. 700, ch. 58, ll. 196, 201, 213, 226–226 ob.

[68] *RSKG*, No. 265, p. 198 (GAKO, f. 5, op. 1, d. 1497, l. 42), telegram, *unterofitser* Romantsev, Kursk Provincial Gendarmerie, to Colonel Vel'k, Commandant, 30 June 1906.

[69] *Ibid.*, No. 272, p. 200 (GAKO, f. 1, op. 16, d. 6, ll. 47–52), telegram, landowner N. P. Dmitriev to Governor V. M. Borzenko, 4 July 1906.

arrests, but they were immediately expelled from the settlement by force. Armed with chains, scythes, pitchforks, clubs and firearms, the peasants likewise attacked a unit of Cossacks hurriedly called to the scene. The crowd dispersed only after an exchange of gunfire in which one peasant was killed and six persons (including two Cossacks) were wounded. The atmosphere remained extremely tense; residents ignored outright an order to summon the village assembly.[70] It was only in his cable of 21 July, that the Governor was able to confirm that the hold of the local peasantry on the estate had been finally broken.

Belgorod District had been almost without serious disorders in 1905, the result at least in part attributable to the united front forged by the very reactionary local gentry in its vigilance and its early and insistent campaign to secure, in addition to the garrison at Belgorod itself, a full squadron of dragoons on permanent station in the district. Unrest nevertheless emerged in June 1906 in the form of the expulsion of agricultural laborers on several estates. But on the estate of Nikolai Petrovich Volkov at Arkad'evka and Nelidovka (2,970 *desiatiny*), on 26 June, neighboring peasants, in a manner reminiscent of the 1905 unrest, burned down almost all structures, demolished the estate's inventory and carted off grain and property not given up to the flames. Police units arrived on the scene at the end of the incident and succeeded in seizing several ringleaders.[71]

Summarizing the situation at the end of June, Governor Borzenko reported the following:

With the harvest time upon us, disturbances in the province have intensified and have spread to all districts of the *guberniia*. The peasants persistently raise demands; in several places there have been incidents of violence. On 26 June, at Nikol'skoe, Korocha District, the Iusupov estate was looted and burned down; in Belgorod District, on the 25th, the farmstead of Volkov was destroyed by arson. In both cases, the attacks were completely unexpected. The principal guilty parties have been arrested and incarcerated, the looted property returned to the owners. In Sudzha District, on the 16th at *khutor* Spasskaia, [the peasants] put up resistance to the troops, and the soldiers shot [at them]: seven peasants were wounded. On the 28th, at Bardakovka on the Sabashnikov estate in the same district, the peasants, making threats, demanded departure of

---

[70] *Ibid.*, No. 275, pp. 202–203 (GAKO, f. 1, op. 16, d. 6, ll. 83–85), telegram, Staryi Oskol' District Police Commandant M. E. Pleshkov to Governor V. M. Borzenko, 22 July 1906.

[71] GARF, f. 102, DP 00, op. 236 (II), 1906 g, d. 700, ch. 58, l. 167 (telegram, Provincial Marshal of the Nobility Count V. F. Dorrer, *et al.*, to the Minister of Internal Affairs, 26 June 1906); *RSKG*, No. 261, p. 196 (GAKO, f. 1, op. 16, d. 11, l. 25), telegram, Belgorod District Police Commandant Loginov to Governor V. M. Borzenko, 27 June 1906.

dragoons and the police: in the ensuing clash, one peasant was killed and two others wounded. In L'gov District, an important agitator, who took part in the prison riot, has been arrested: Doroshev, formerly secretary to the provincial military chief Bogoduk-hovskii. Of those who fled the prison, five have been caught. In Shchigrov District, on the estate of Shchekin, about which I reported previously, the peasants have attacked the rural police. The mob was dispersed with the aid of Cossacks; one peasant was wounded. In the other districts, the movement expresses itself in the dispersing of [es-tate] laborers and the seizure of harvested grain.

Borzenko, in conclusion, took care to reflect on the local causes of the disturbances, and here we note confirmation—rather rare in official re-porting—of the influence of the economic conjuncture as it affected the relations between peasants and lords in this period:

I cannot remain silent over the fact that in many cases, the peasants are settling scores with the estate owners, [the latter] who have not always conducted themselves [toward the peasants] in an irreproachable manner. Many have ignored the growth of the price of labor, stand against a normal, moderate elevation of pay for harvest work and lease the indispensable quantity of land at very high rents. Added vacillations of wages and land rents, and the poor conditions [of work] are serving as cause for the disturbances, which have been avoided given a certain willingness to make concessions on the part of private owners.[72]

5. Decline of the Movement in 1906: July and Afterward

The July disturbances in 1906 already represent a substantial decline in the intensity of unrest after the weeks of June. Work stoppages and strike actions dominated the events in late May and June; the main aim of peas-ant militants, by means of forcing laborers off the estates and depriving private economies of a labor force precisely at harvest time, embraced, at a minimum, the possibility of radical adjustment of the terms of labor and leasehold in favor of peasant communities. But the theme that was so dominant in 1905—an elemental drive to destroy the very bases of the gentry's socio-economic hegemony in rural society—was also a common motif in the disorders of 1906, even though the incidence of *razgromy* (physical demolition of estate installations) in 1906 relative to 1905 was quite negligible. What was evident was that demands accompanying work

---

[72] GARF, f. 102, DP OO, op. 236 (II), 1906 g., d. 700, ch. 58, ll. 194–194 ob. (telegram, No. 2698, Governor V. M. Borzenko to Minister of Internal Affairs P. A. Stolypin, 31 June 1906).

stoppages were such that they seemed deliberately intended to put the landowners out of business. Second, labor actions in many cases were combined with organized acts that illustrated this larger aim (harvesting or plowing up estate fields in favor of peasant communities, cessation of rent payments, pasturing of cattle). Unrest after the month of June remained associated mainly with the same locales but the weight of labor actions began to fall.

In Dmitriev District, however, peasant militants in Prilepovskaia and Glamazdinskaia Parishes persisted. Delegates from various villages (2–3 from each) of Dmitriev, L'gov, Ryl'sk and Sevsk (Orel Province) Districts convened a mass meeting in a heavily wooded tract ("Verbnik") in the vicinity of the village of Vet' (Glamazdinskaia Parish) on 8 July. Land Captain Kusakov was unable to learn what had been discussed at this meeting, but five days later, the peasants of Khomutovka in this same parish took the initiative:

> I have the honor to inform Your Excellency that on 13 July 1906 the peasants of the settlement of Khomutovka, Glamazdinskaia Parish, Dmitriev District, on their own initiative, gathered together at the village assembly (many at several persons from a household), at which an act was adopted, which read thus: "Learning in the newspapers of the dissolution of the State Duma, on which we had placed all our hopes for an improvement of our peasant lack of rights and our extreme need as the land-poor..." and so on. In light of this, they resolved to disperse all workers on the estate of O. A. Shaufus and to provide only day labor, by turns, all to work only at an appointed wage. Special plenipotentiaries were elected to observe that these resolutions were executed.[73]

The decision of the assembly were carried into effect on 14–15 July and remained in force until the 17th, when the Second Precinct police captain and a unit of dragoons arrived and began to arrest its elected agents. With this, the incident ended,[74] but during 26–28 July, labor actions resurfaced. This time, both big estates in the area—that of Shaufus in Khomutovka and that of the Barons Meiendorf at Prilepy and Dubrovitsy in Prilepovskaia Parish—were once again subjected to the expulsion of all laborers and the same attempt on the part of the villagers

---

[73] *RSKG*, No. 276, pp. 203–204 (GAKO, f. 1, op. 16, d. 13, l. 74), report, Land Captain of the Fourth Land Department of Dmitriev District A. Kusakov to Governor V. M. Borzenko, 22 July 1906. News of the gatherings in the woods forwarded by Kusakov to the Governor by report of 15 July in *ibid.*, No. 274, p. 202 (GAKO, f. 1, op. 16, d. 13, l. 87).

[74] *Ibid.*, 202–203.

of these settlements to enforce their interests on the owners. As a result, provincial authorities transferred an entire squadron of dragoons to Khomutovka to be stationed in the locality on an extended basis,[75] bringing to a close the large-scale disturbances that had taken place here in both 1905 and 1906.

In Sudzha District, a similarly sporadic incidence of unrest after the end of June was observed. On 2 July, at Milaevka (Goptarovskaia Parish), the police captain of the Fourth Precinct and the accompanying dragoons provoked "desperate resistance" from villagers when attempting to arrest a "peasant-agitator." Armed with axes, staves and pitchforks, the peasants attacked, striking one of the dragoons a blow with a pitchfork. The crowd was dispersed with sabers and firearms. Eight peasants were "slightly" injured. The arrest was carried out.[76] On the farmstead Nikol'skii (Novo-Ivanovskaia Parish), where in June disorders had brought the landowner N. V. Davydov to appeal to the central authorities, the peasants, on or about 31 July, set about dividing and preparing Davydov's fallow field for their own winter sowing.[77] In the northern parishes, where some of the most intense mass disorders had been recorded in both 1905 and 1906, an uneasy calm was disturbed only in late September when, on the 6th of the month, barns on the estate of the merchant F. K. Fedorenko at Volokonskoe (Bol'she-Soldatskaia Parish) were burned down at the hands of unknown arsonists. Rumor had it that the act was in retribution for Fedorenko's sheltering units of dragoons and police guards under the command of the Sudzha District Police Commandant that had arrived in the parish to enforce extraction of taxes.[78]

Individual events—confiscation of grain and hay from estate fields, timbering of private forests—continued to be reported in isolated localities of L'gov District, but here too the momentum of the days of June had clearly been lost. The archival record for July, however, also contained the suggestion of a concerted effort by peasant communities to delay the process of apportioning taxes among their members. A one-line item from

[75] GARF, f. 102, DPOO, op. 236 (II), 1906 g., d. 700, ch. 58, l. 239 (telegram, 28 July 1906, No. 5202, Vice-Governor Gil'khen to Minister of Internal Affairs P. A. Stolypin).

[76] *RSKG*, No. 267, pp. 198–199 (GAKO, f. l, op. 16, d. 7, l. 62), telegram, Sudzha District Police Commandant ("for Police Commandant Kolodkevich") to Governor V. M. Borzenko, 2 July 1906.

[77] *Vtoroi period revoliutsii, II/II*, No. 101, p. 138 (telegram, landowner N. V. Davydov to Governor V. M. Borzenko, 22 June 1906).

[78] GARF, f. 102, DP OO, op. 236 (II), 1906 g., d. 700, ch. 58, ll. 289–290 (telegram, No. 3591, Governor V. M. Borzenko to the Department of Police, 13 September 1906).

the newspaper *Die Zeit* (pasted in the *delo*) contained reporting from L'gov (16 July) on 110 villages that had refused to compile apportionment acts for the payment of taxes. The Department of Police requested information on the matter, and the Governor's reply of 21 July admitted only that apportionments had not been done.[79]

For Ryl'sk and Graivoron Districts, the sources contained reports on only single incidents, but two of these were brought to a close only by armed confrontation between the forces of order and massed throngs of thousands of villagers. The more serious of these occurred at Borisovka. On July 9, a crowd of peasants had appeared at the precinct police station located in the settlement to demand a copy of the Vyborg Appeal, accusing the police captain of having concealed the Appeal from them. In spite of the officer's assurances to the contrary, the crowd invaded the police station, disarmed the captain and his constables, confiscated the station's store of sabers and rifles and then set off under red flags along the streets of Borisovka, requisitioning rifles and pistols from fellow villagers. Equipment at the telephone and telegraph post was carefully disabled and its attendant disarmed; the manor house on the Sheremet'ev estate, used to quarter troops after previous incidents at Borisovka, was burned to the ground. However, the police got word of events to a half-company of infantrymen bivouacked in the area, and this force, upon its arrival, was confronted on the public square by a crowd of "several thousand" persons. The police captain ordered the residents to disperse. The order was greeted by angry imprecations, there were scattered gunshots and the crowd began to move in the direction of the soldiers. When a volley fired into their midst had no effect in halting the rebels, who continued their advance, three more volleys were fired, and the villagers finally dispersed, taking their wounded.[80] This full-scale revolt, with all

---

[79] *Ibid.*, ll. 220–221 and 224–225: "To telegram under No. 2198 I inform: the apportionment has not been performed. For all villages in Bobrinskaia, Ivanovskaia, Iznoskovskaia, Nizhnederevenskaia and parts of Vyshnederevenskaia and Sheptukhovskaia Parishes, the Director of the Treasury Department has instructed the Tax Inspector to do the apportionment in accordance with the circular of the Department of Direct Taxation under No. 3157." No further note of this matter appears subsequently, either generally or in the Governor's bi-weekly cables to the Police Department. The provincial administration seems thus to have attached little importance to the matter, but Maliavskii and, after him, Stepynin added 110 incidents to their totals under the rubric "attacks on the tax system." Maliavskii, "Krest'ianskoe dvizhenie", 62–63; Stepynin, *Krest'ianstvo*, 113.

[80] RGIA, f. 1405, op. 108, 1906 g., d. 7011, ll. 2–2 ob. (copy, report at No. 2602, Procurator of the Kursk Regional Court Zhettsin to Procurator of the Khar'kov Judicial Chamber, 19 July 1906). Noted elsewhere: GARF, f. 102, DPOO, op. 236 (II), 1906 g., d. 700,

the signs of the effort to seal off the town and to secure its defense, occasioned a personal visit by the Governor himself. One hundred and fifty weapons were turned in during Borzenko's sojourn, but the police guards' rifles were never returned and many weapons remained in the hands of residents. Five of nine persons accused in the matter—out of a crowd of "several thousands"—escaped and were being hunted.[81]

In his cabled report to Minister of Internal Affairs P. A. Stolypin of 21 July 1906, Borzenko told of attempts by peasants of the big settlement of Snagost'e in Ryl'sk District to destroy the central installations of the estate of Prince A. V. Bariatinskii at this site. The authorities had been informed beforehand that the attack was scheduled for July 20, the day of the agricultural fair in Snagost'e, so the District Police Commandant, a detachment of police guards and a unit of dragoons were present in the village on that day. Despite the presence of police and dragoons, however, a crowd of some 3,000 peasants, "led by outside agitators," assembled and launched their attack. Shots were fired from the crowd and a hail of stones flew at the soldiers. In answer, the Police Commander ordered three volleys fired into the crowd: six peasants were killed outright and three wounded. "In all the other districts," the report continued, "the situation is very tense; there are attempts to foment disorders, seizures, which have been cut short by the police and the soldiers in a timely manner. The dissolution of the Duma has greatly agitated minds: the arrival of former Duma members and their influence may cause complications. Surveillance is being tightened. The mood in Novyi Oskol' and Staryi Oskol' Districts—I am going there now—causes concern."[82]

According to the sources consulted for this work, however, the eastern districts never again regained the revolutionary élan that had followed upon the events of 1 November 1905 in the settlements of the Oskol' Valley. True enough, the Governor's reference, as far as Staryi Oskol' District is concerned, was to the stubborn unwillingness of peasants of Lukoianovka to bow to the authorities. Police and military units

---

ch. 58, l. 213 (telegram, Acting Governor Gil'khen to Minister of Internal Affairs P. A. Stolypin, 10 July 1906); *Vtoroi period revoliutsii, II/II*) No. 106, p. 141 (telegram at No. 47, Commander of the 204th Oboian Reserve Infantry Regiment, Colonel I. V. Russiian, to Emperor Nicholas II, 16 July 1906).

[81] *Ibid.* (RGIA), l. 2 ob.

[82] GARF, f. 102, DP OO, op. 236 (II), 1906 g., d. 700, ch. 58, ll. 226–226 ob. (telegram, No. 2889, Governor V. M. Borzenko to Minister of Internal Affairs P. A. Stolypin, 21 July 1906).

had just broken the villagers' month-long occupation of the estate of N. P. Dmitriev and had begun to attempt the arrests of individuals who had led the community in the action.

Novyi Oskol' District, despite the fact that a number of incidents were registered at scattered sites here during 1906, had nevertheless been quiescent throughout the year. The old centers of unrest along the Southeastern Railway line had been quiet, and reports of unrest were sporadic. The deep hostility that persisted between the villagers of *sloboda* Ol'shanka (Ol'shanskaia Parish) and their former master Prince I. Iu. Trubetskoi—the Prince's estate had been almost entirely destroyed on the night of 4 November 1905—was reflected in additional incidents during 1906. In March, Ol'shanka peasants had seized a tract of Trubetskoi's land, divided it among themselves and set about plowing up the soil. On July 28, peasants from Ol'shanka again moved against the Trubetskoi estate, invading one of the Prince's farmsteads to cart grain directly from the fields.[83] To the south, at *sloboda* Slonovka (Slonovskaia Parish) on 15 August, on the day of the fair, a force of police guards on the scene was compelled to fire on a crowd of attackers, leaving one peasant dead and two wounded.[84] Furthermore, several state forest reservations in the central part of the district were under almost continuous besiegement by peasant axemen from at least August to mid-December. The Chief Forester for Novyi Oskol' District (Kursk-Orel Administration of State Domains) informed his superior on 1 December that after peasants of the village of Maloe Gorodishche (Khalanskaia Parish) had successfully obstructed the local police captain and his men from recovering lumber timbered in the Bubnov State Forest Reservation (August 10), the local populace had only grown bolder. Large-scale timbering in the Bubnov, Kholokov, Mikhailov and Solonetsko-Poliana State Forest Reservations continued uninterruptedly up to the time of the report. Forest rangers were not numerous enough to halt these acts, let alone to recover the lumber.[85] Finally, on 17 and 26 October, at *sloboda* Golubina (Prigorodniaia Parish), the estate of District Marshal of the Nobility V. P. Miatlev—already almost completely lev-

---

[83] *RSKG*, No. 263, p. 197 (GAKO, f. 1, op. 16, d. 2, l. 16), telegram, Governor-General of St. Petersburg D. F. Trepov to Governor V. M. Borzenko, 28 July 1906.

[84] GARF, f. 102, DP 00, op. 236 (II), 1906 g., d 700, ch. 58, l. 267 (telegram, No. 3358, Governor V. M. Borzenko to the Ministry of Internal Affairs, 16 August 1906).

[85] *RSKG*, No. 291, p. 213 (GAKO, f. 1, op. 16, d. 2, l. 210), report, Superintendent of the Kursk-Orel Administration of the Ministry of State Properties Luk'ianov to Governor V. M. Borzenko, 7 December 1906.

eled by fire during incidents on 2 and 5 November 1905—was once more a target: "Finishing the destruction of my estate and the timbering of my forests that haven't let up the whole year, they have burned down half (the structures on) my farmstead on the 17th, and on the 26th, the brick factory on the (main) estate. The distillery had only just been rebuilt. For a whole year, the police authorities have been helpless to protect me from inevitable ruin, and my case is not unique. I see the reason in the leniency of court sentences, in a dearth of real measures for (achieving) a cessation and prevention of crimes and in the immunity of the majority of the criminals from punishment. Losing any hope for succor from the local authorities, I am driven to the necessity of requesting Your High Excellency's personal protection."[86]

The archival record for the 1906 disorders came to a close with the October report of acts of arson on the Miatlev estate in Novyi Oskol' District. But it had already become clear that, with the end of the May–June work stoppages, the peasant movement in various parts of Kursk Province had entered its final phase, a phase in which such anonymous acts of arson against the landowners signaled that ongoing peasant resistance was being forced underground. Facts surrounding these incidents (dates and sites) are absent from the record, but the sources show that gangs of arsonists were at work in Vyshne-Ol'khovatskaia Parish in Shchigrov District, Fateevskaia Parish in Dmitriev District and at Borisovka. In the last two districts, the authorities broke up and arrested small groups of peasants that had stubbornly continued the struggle by means of a series of systematic, if minor, arson attacks on nearby private estates, even if the incidents themselves are not reflected in the sources.[87] More frequent were the reports of timbering, notably in Novyi Oskol' District. But obviously, the waning of the movement of labor actions that had lasted from the last days of May to early July meant the end of the "peak" of 1906, even though, in July and August, disturbing tidings continued to cross Governor Borzenko's desk. The autumn and winter of 1906 witnessed the retreat of peasant militancy in Kursk Province into individual acts—most frequently cases of nighttime arson—against the

---

[86] GARF, f. 102, DP OO, op. 236 (II), 1906 g., d. 700, ch. 58, l. 303 (telegram, District Marshal of the Nobility Miatlev to Minister of Internal Affairs P. A. Stolypin, 27 October 1906).

[87] Ibid., l. 353 (telegram, No. 4640, Commandant of the Kursk Provincial Gendarme Administration to the Director, Department of Police, 12 December 1906); ll. 360–360 ob. (telegram, Governor V. M. Borzenko to Minister of Internal Affairs P. A. Stolypin, 2 January 1907).

estates, but the powerful mass character of the rural unrest of February and November–December 1905 and of the summer of 1906 were now entirely absent.

The tempo of disorders in Kursk Province in 1907, expressed in scattered reports of timbering and arson, confirmed that the peasant movement had all but ceased. An official account (1910) of unrest in Shchigrov District noted that from February 1907 an organized, methodical campaign of acts of arson had been mounted, not only on private estates, but also on the holdings of priests and peasants considered to be politically reactionary. This campaign (in its later phases including assassination) was later to be associated with the district affiliate of the Peasant Union and a conference of 37 local committees that had been held in October 1906. The report reveals that the Shchigrov organization, unlike those in Graivoron and Dmitriev Districts that had attempted to adopt underground tactics, proved to be far more difficult to suppress. Arrests and prosecution were to be undertaken only at the end of 1908. The case was decided by the temporary section for Kursk Province of the Kievan Regional Courts-Martial: of 88 persons accused, 20 were acquitted, 34 (a former District School Board Chairman, the nobleman and *zemstvo* activist Iosif Antonov Mikhailov, was among these) sentenced to exile, 25 to hard labor of various terms and 9 persons to death by hanging, including those considered to be the leaders of the movement: M. A. Merkulov, former Member of the First Duma, and I. E. Pianykh, former Member of the Second Duma, both openly identified with the Socialist-Revolutionary (SR) Party. The death sentences were commuted to hard labor: Merkulov got ten years, Pianykh a life sentence.[88] Even in Shchigrov District, however, peasant unrest never regained the mass character that marked unrest during the labor actions of the summer of 1906. Returning from yet another in a series of inspections that occupied him in the following year, Governor Borzenko could telegraph the Minister of Internal Affairs on 26 May 1907:

---

[88] *Iz istorii Kurskogo kraia*, No. 278, pp. 354–357 (Extract, 1910 report of the Governor on peasant unrest in Shchigrov District during 1906–1908). Both Merkulov and Pianykh returned to Kursk Province after the February revolution and became active in the All-Russian Society of Former Political Prisoners and Deportees. Both participated in the work of the Democratic Assembly and the Pre-Parliament. Both were also elected as deputies to the Constituent Assembly on the SR line, which won overwhelmingly in Kursk Province (12 of 14 deputies, 869,000 of 989,000 ballots cast). Pianykh died in 1929. Merkulov was arrested and shot in 1937, to be rehabilitated only in 1989. Saltyk, "Es-Ry," *OI*, 2004, 1: 55–69.

In the course of the week, there have been no excesses on the part of the peasants. I have just returned from Graivoron District, having toured the whole region in which there was unrest in the past year. I inspected the parishes and all officials, summoned the assemblies and held long talks with the peasants. The mood is generally calm. The peasants, obviously, now view the problems of life today more reasonably and unanimously condemn the few instances of hooliganism on the part of the "conscious youth," who are quite numerous in the wealthy *slobody* and districts.[89]

---

[89] GARF, f. 102, DP, 4-oe deloproizvodstvo, 1907 g., d. 108, ch. 21, ll. 4–4 ob.

CHAPTER IV

Typology, Chronology and Geographical Distributions of Rural Disorders, 1905–1906

In the foregoing chapters, a selection from the narrative record of a large sample of incidents of peasant collective actions in Kursk Province during 1905–1906 has been presented in detail. A review of the main characteristics of these events, however, will allow us to draw out some general conclusions about the revolutionary processes at work. What does a typology of peasant unrest in the province, and its chronology and geographical distribution, tell us about the emergence of acts of revolt or protest in these localities? What do distributions by type, by time and by place suggest about the local character of disturbances and their connection to external events? What changes in tactics, if any, are notable in the course of the events described, and to what factor or factors were they due?

In the unfolding of its agrarian troubles, Kursk Province reflected the chronological characteristics long ago noted by S. M. Dubrovskii and other historians during the Soviet era, even if one is not bound to their assessments of the significance of this chronology.[1] Notable in our findings here are three principal peaks of rural unrest. In 1905, the February disorders that began in Dmitriev District and spread to parts of Chernigov and Orel Provinces (22 incidents involving strictly sites in Kursk Province

---

[1] A first effort at breakdown by district (*uyezd*) appeared in Prokopovich, *Agrarnyi krizis*. Prokopovich's schema was gradually expanded first by Evgenii Andreevich Morokhovets, who added missing data for the Baltic districts (*Krestian'skoe dvizhenie*), then by Pershin (*Agrarnaia revoliutsiia*), I: 240–245, and lastly by Tropin, who added figures for the provinces of the Caucasus (*Bor'ba bol'shevikov*). The effect of these revisions was to accentuate the "supremacy" of the peak of October–December 1905 as opposed to the peak of May–July 1906. "By-district" tabulations had been by this time discredited by the work of Dubrovskii, who founded his analysis on single incidents. *Krest'ianskoe dvizhenie*, 36–45.

constitute 11.3 percent of the total for 1905). The great burst of upheavals in November–December (139 incidents, 71.3 percent of the 1905 total) made up the second chronological cluster, and the reemergence of a wave of unrest in late May through August 1906 (114 incidents or 89.1 percent of incidents for that year) the third. In all for 1905–1906, these 275 incidents made up the vast majority (85 percent) of recorded disturbances. In general, the low points of peasant militancy in 1905 coincide with the high point of the agricultural season. By character, disturbances were dominated by seizure and looting of neighboring estates, including complete destruction of estate facilities—manor house, outbuildings, inventory—by fire and axe. Conversely, disorders during 1906 were concentrated mainly in the intervals of the heaviest fieldwork. This shift was quite marked: it indicated a marked change in peasant strategy—in the face of growing concentrations of troops in the province—toward organized disruption of labor relations at a crucial moment for the landowners. In its geographical distributions, agrarian unrest in the province displays concentrations both in districts where, on balance, peasant agriculture seems actually to have begun to prosper during the era 1888–1906 and in those in which it had long exhibited signs of particular difficulty. Rather, the common denominator in the events proved to be most evident in the character and economic orientation of the villages noted in the documents as associated with unrest, and in the state of their interactions with the estates in their vicinity.

1. Forms of Unrest: 1905 and 1906 Compared

A site and time frame for all incidents of unrest, as a rule, could be established in the archival record or be approximated by the date of the document or the close proximity of a reported incident to other analogous events dated to the same locality. The form that incidents of unrest took was usually in evidence either in the immediate reports from the scene or in materials compiled in connection with the government's effort to compensate the victims. Commentary on agrarian disorders during the 1905–1907 upheavals, dating to the era immediately in the wake of the events, have produced schematized typologies of all the forms of unrest, delineated for the purposes of a display of subtotals within the number of incidents recorded. In keeping with the traditional practice, figure 4.1 provides a breakdown of the main groupings by year. These data must be read with the caveat that grouping these data simplifies a more manifold and complex reality. Significant numbers of incidents (especially during attacks on estates) were clearly "multiple" in character, involving complex acts and several objects during a single frame of time.[2] Obviously, in such cases various forms found to occur in such single incidents, if they were continuous, had to stand as one in analysis. We may nonetheless examine these in their major groupings.[3]

Figure 4.1 Rural Disorders, Kursk Province, 1905–1906

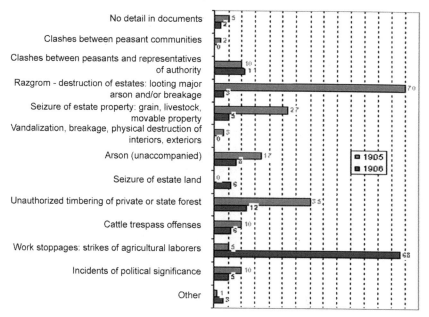

_____

Violent Clashes (stolknoveniia)

Unrest in Kursk Province, as elsewhere during 1905–1906, brought peasants into face-to-face confrontations with the forces of order, from which violence often issued. Documents on 323 incidents in the sample recorded incidents of armed clashes ("armed" here suggesting not only firearms, but also—most commonly—clubs, pitchforks, axes, sharpened staves and so on) in 61 cases (18.4 percent): only 21 (6.5 percent) stood alone as the principal form of unrest during 1905–1906. Unprovoked attacks on police units or military detachments were recorded in fifteen cases; armed clashes with the forces of order during attempts to conduct investigations or arrests in thirty-six. Attacks on estate personnel without evident provocation occur in two events; assaults on estate employees attempting to intervene in an incident were observed in eight cases. Local rapporteurs were extremely laconic about casualties in such clashes: direct actions for which documents give information counted 19 dead and 160 wounded among peasants. With their personnel often outnumbered, commanders did not always remain in place to ascertain body counts, and, in addition, peasant communities sought to hide the dead and wounded, whose injuries were proof of presence at the scene of the action. Considering the scale of repression in the aftermath of the peak periods of unrest, about which the source materials consulted provide very little information, these data must be considered as purely anecdotal. They nonetheless illustrate the fact that disorders were hardly without bloodshed: behind the terse telegram phrases—"the crowd was dispersed by military force"—lay more peasant dead and wounded.

It is difficult to arrive at a simple quantitative summary of violent clashes in the mix of incidents, since they very often marked a distinct phase in the unfolding of a single incident and most often bore a "defensive" cast. The documents reveal that participants in disturbances commonly resisted the initial efforts of local police and their deputies to put an end to unrest. When successful, such resistance, as at the village of Sal'noe (Dmitriev District) during 6–15 February, at Chernianka (Novyi Oskol' District) on 1 November and at Izvekova (Sudzha District) during 4–5 November, demonstrated to peasants the degree of weakness and indecision of the local authorities that appears to have served as an inspiration to further acts. In other contexts, when police or army units intervened at moments when an incident was in full swing, the "defensive" character of these clashes was fully in evidence. In still other cases, peasants attacked army and police units in order to free detainees or forcibly resisted the authorities during attempts to make arrests or carry out searches. If "defensive" clashes formed a distinct stage in multiple incidents, not only does the "offensive" aspect of several cases of unrest recorded in these years leave little doubt of the hatred of the population for the police and the new units of police guards (*strazhniki*) recruited largely from among the local peasantry, but all such actions also illustrate the willingness of peasant populations to go toe to toe with representatives of authority in unprovoked or premeditated assaults on police or army units.

Trespass Offenses

In this grouping of 63 incidents (19.5 percent), were those "traditional" acts that peasants in Kursk Province commonly directed against neighboring estates and that often ruptured that uneasy peace across the social divide between them, much of which recalls what James C. Scott has written about such tactics as a form of resistance.[4] Minor incidents of land seizure (*zakhvat*) by peasant communities, timbering of private forest (*porubka*), grazing of peasant livestock on estate meadows (*past'ba*) and pasturing of peasant stock on an estate's sown fields (*potrava*) to feed on—and to trample—the crops, were hardly rare occurrences even before the outbreak of disorders in 1905. Indeed, the issue of "security of private property" had been raised more than once by the landowners in the District Committees on the Needs of Rural Industry during 1902. They bemoaned the fact that such offenses were so common in rural life. This evil resulted, it was said, from both the peasant's lack of respect for private property rights and the leniency of the courts:

> At the present time, the lives of peasants and of estate owners are lived in two completely separate and special worlds replete with distinctive views and perceptions developed from childhood to old age. Within his family, the peasant boy, from early childhood, hears on a daily basis about how somewhere a bit of someone else's land had been cultivated illegally, how a shock or more of grain from someone else's field had been taken into another's granary, how an oak had been timbered in someone else's forest. The boys, who with us usually watch over the cattle, often receive direct instructions from their elders that, if field fodder is insufficient, to let the livestock out onto a neighboring owner's lands, fields and forests, so that the cattle will be fed. At night, the older peasants themselves not infrequently drive their horses onto a neighbor's fields and it is a usual occurrence that the horses "run off" and here we have a new misfortune—horse theft—so well known in every village. Normally sensitive to the accepted views and understandings of their families, it is the children who,

---

[4] Scott and Kerkvliet, eds., *Weapons of the Weak.*

at the first opportunity, sneak over ditches and through fences of neighbors' gardens for berries and fruits and, if possible, drive their beloved horse or cow into the garden to feed... In a word, the majority of peasants do not consider the violation of right as crime, although at the same time, in good peasant homes as in all noble and landowner families, special attention is directed, from earliest childhood, to inculcating a belief in the inviolability of another's property.[5]

During 1905–1906, however, the scale (in many cases of timbering, the losses to private owners ran into the thousands, and in two or three instances into the tens of thousands of rubles), mass character and duration of these incidents made them distinct from the constant pinpricks of peasant violations in more peaceful times and necessitated the movement of troops to restore order.[6]

Attacks on the Estates (razgromy)

On 10 November 1905, Kursk Governor N. N. Gordeev sent an urgent appeal to then Acting Minister of Internal Affairs P. N. Durnovo, which painted the state of affairs in the countryside in stark tones and testified to a feeling of helplessness among local officials:

> [In] Novyi Oskol' and Staryi Oskol' Districts, the *Pugachevshchina* has died down. Twenty-one estates destroyed [*razgromlennye*] in Novyi Oskol' District, in Staryi Oskol' four, in Kursk two and in Putivl' one, but in Sudzha District, the situation is critical and spreading. According to the last information, there have been sixteen estates destroyed there in three days. Forces there number 60 Cossacks and a half-company of infantry. If the troops that are expected arrive, there will be, on the morrow, another squadron of cavalry and another 160 infantrymen. I have sent Pokidaev, the Kursk District Police Commandant, to Sudzha to put down the disorders. I cannot at present vouch for the accuracy of the information on the destruction of estates. I petition for Your Excellency's aid in the reinforcement of the cavalry (at our disposal). The unrest is led by revolutionaries, the seizure of whom we are effecting only as an exception. More than 100 rioters have been arrested. [In] Oboian, Tim and Kursk Districts, rioting on the estates is expected. All measures are being taken, but troops are too few. I am working alone. Appointment of a Vice-Governor is requested.[7]

---

[5] *Trudy mestnykh komitetov*, 814–815.

[6] Losses in timber offenses in 1905 alone totaled 128,042 rubles on the private estates, not counting truly massive clear-cutting in state forests. RGIA, f. 1291, op. 122, 1905 g. d. 112, 11. 302–315 ob.; GARF, f. 102, DP 00, op. 236 (II), 1906 g., d. 700, ch. 58, 1. 31 ob.; *RSKG*, No. 213, p. 171 (GAKO, f. 1, op. 16, d. 3, 1. 87); No. 291, p. 213 (GAKO, f. 1, op. 16, d. 2, 1. 10. No. 135, pp. 116–117 [GAKO, f. 1, op. 15, d. 68, 1. 971]).

[7] GARF, f. 102, DP OO, op. 233 (II), 1905 g., d. 2550, ch. 44, 1. 129 (telegram, Governor N. N. Gordeev to Superintendent of the Ministry of Internal Affairs P. N. Durnovo, 10 November 1905).

In their mass character and scale of destructiveness, in the great strain that they put on local manpower resources, and in the sense of loss of control and panic that they aroused among provincial officials and the local gentry, it is no wonder that large-scale disorders of this sort should have brought to mind the events (1773–1774) associated with the name of Emilian Pugachev, the word *Pugachevshchina* itself recurring in various accounts and reports. To most outside observers, the attacks were distinguished by their "spontaneity" (*stikhiinost'*), lack of consciousness and senseless destruction. These characterizations appear at odds with all the signs of premeditation, organization and single-mindedness in the actions themselves. For the attacks on the private estates by crowds of peasants, more than any other form of unrest, testified to a now irresistible urge not just to test the old, contested barrier between peasants and privileged society in the rural districts or to effect a "restoration" of peasant rights in the context of existing landed relations. Rather, they sought to obliterate the very foundations upon which rural social relations rested—to "smoke out" the estate owners and divide their land among members of the peasant community, to set in motion, at last, the long-awaited Black Repartition. In this grouping (133 incidents, 40.9 percent) most of all, fragments of the typology must be aggregated, for indeed, in the great majority of cases, these are "multiple" in character: looting of estate goods, inventory and livestock being followed, particularly during the unrest of November 1905, with destruction by fire. In twenty cases, anonymous persons, without even attempting to seize property, set fire to an outbuilding or a haystack in an obvious effort to sow terror. As one frightened landowner wrote to the Minister of Internal Affairs, "Arson is a most convenient way to threaten and sow panic with impunity. There is no evidence and the apprehension of perpetrators is impossible for the police."[8]

Labor Actions

Descriptions of labor actions on private estates (73 or 22.6 percent of incidents) suggested that the main impetus in these incidents did not originate among the growing mass of full-time agricultural wage laborers. As Robert Edelman discovered in his study of unrest in Kiev, Volyn and Po-

---

[8] *Ibid.*, ll. 72–73 ob. (private letter, 18 June 1905, A. I. Zhekulina to the Minister of Internal Affairs). The common use of arson in peasant-on-peasant violence as a weapon of simple revenge or for the enforcement of social control over violators of community norms is treated at length in Frierson, *All Russia is Burning!*

dol' Provinces in the southwest, they seem to have emerged within that part of the peasant community that depended upon wages as a supplement to a meager household economy on the allotment.[9] In the majority of labor actions (58 cases), the documents state that "the peasants drove off [*sniali*] estate workers," leaving little doubt that the initiative lay in the hands of "peasants" and not "workers." In 14 cases, documents employ the word "strike" with no detail and 8 cases directly noted agricultural workers themselves calling work stoppages. One case records "peasants" refusing to honor terms contracted for rendering labor obligations.

The most salient aspect of this grouping lies in the degree to which, in 1906, labor actions against the landowners almost wholly displaced the destructive assaults on private estates as the main vehicle of peasant unrest, often in the same localities in which attacks on the estates had been most violent. This change in strategy was also expressed in their timing. If intervals of the heaviest destruction of estate property during 1905 pertained to February and November, the wave of work stoppages in 1906 began at the very end of May (the start of spring sowings), reached a peak in June (the onset of the harvest cycle) and faded in July and August. Timed to disrupt estate operations at critical moments of the agricultural calendar, labor actions struck observers as a continuation of peasant efforts to force profound changes in local economic relationships. The Governor himself noted that "the situation in the province in the last two weeks is quite serious. From 1 June, the time of the hay harvest, the peasant movement has begun and has embraced twelve districts. Peasant demands bear an economic character, but undoubtedly spring from political considerations, since they are commonly utterly unfulfillable. Obviously, they are pursuing the aim of forcing the landowners to leave their estates."[10] There is also little doubt that concentration of large numbers of soldiers, dragoons and Cossacks in the province in the aftermath of the events of November–December 1905 did much to make such a change of strategy advisable.

Incidents of Political Character

Incidents of unrest in the sample that bore a pronounced political cast (18, or 5.8 percent) embraced a variety of forms. Common to almost all of them, as their initial stage, were mass meetings associated in police

---

[9] Edelman, *Proletarian Peasants*.

[10] GARF, f. 102, DP 00, op. 233 (II), 1905 g., d. 2550, ch. 44, 1. 128 (telegram, No. 2524, Governor V. M. Borzenko to the Minister of Internal Affairs, 16 June 1906).

documents with "political" activities: dissemination of inflammatory literature, discussion of agrarian grievances, preparations for a dispatch of a delegation to the Emperor or decisions to affiliate with the All-Russian Peasant Union, and so on. If in several cases such mass meetings had no later consequences (at least, in the police sources),[11] they give evidence of a lively undercurrent of debate and discussion among villagers in many localities that characterized the whole period 1905–1906, when these meetings were often organized outside village and parish assemblies. A report from late November 1905, for example, stated that "the populace" of the adjoining villages of Liubimovka, Obukhovka (Snagostnaia Parish, Ryl'sk District), Dar'ino and Tolstoi Lug (Novo-Ivanovskaia Parish, Sudzha District) "assembled during the day on 18 November 1905 at Kolomok, posted red flags on the poles, and then, having counseled among themselves on some matter, dispersed because of the inclement weather, agreeing to meet again on Sunday the 20th." At the conclusion of the meeting, parties of peasants from Tolstoi Lug disassembled twenty stages of telegraph wire and tore down the poles, which lent an ominous cast to the whole event. Such incidents not only attracted particular official attention, but in some instances resulted in the dispatch of troops.

Such was the case in Putivl' District, where well-attended gatherings of peasants at sites outside the village proper, at which political themes of discussion and distribution of inflammatory proclamations were reported, appear in the record already for the summer months of 1905. But in December, when police and army units finally tried to put an end to such assemblies—part of a larger effort mounted by provincial authorities to suppress peasant militancy and to decapitate its leadership—such acts provoked a veritable storm of mass meetings in all of the villages of Gruzchanskaia, Popovo-Slobodskaia, Kazachanskaia and Glushetskaia Parishes. These gatherings, sometimes nominally coinciding with meetings of village and parish assemblies, passed resolutions calling for seizure of estate lands, removal of local officials, non-payment of taxes and refusal to give up recruits at call-up. Big crowds of peasants attacked a police station and parish administrative offices at Gruzskoe and Kazatskoe. If place-specific documentary evidence on the formation of committees of peasant deputies, exercising authority in the place of local officials,

---

[11] *RSKG*, No. 146, pp. 124–125 (GAKO, f. 1, op. 15, d. 62, l. 117), extract from report, Sudzha District Police Captain Pozhidaev to Governor N. N. Gordeev, 19 November 1905. These were all large villages (taken together around 8,000 persons in 1897) populated by former private serfs of the Bariatinskii clan.

pertain only to adjacent settlements of Bochechki and Kazatskoe (Ka-zachanskaia Parish), such committees were also reported to have been formed elsewhere in the western parishes of the district. Such attempts to seize political authority were, to my knowledge, limited to the December incidents in Putivl' District. In July 1906, however, a crowd of some 2,000 peasants at Borisovka, Graivoron District, attacked and destroyed the local police station, telegraph office and the manor house of Count A. D. Sheremet'ev that had served as a barracks for troops more or less per-manently stationed in the locality since the autumn of 1905. Arms were collected throughout the town and pitched battles with police and army detachments were fought before a preponderance of force could be brought to bear in the locality to put down the rising. The clear intent of the rebels was to organize and defend the village against incursions from "outsiders," but the documents gave no clear sense of the "political" cast of the rising in the form of its organization or demands raised, so the event was classed together with those under clashes with the authorities.[12] "Unlawful" replacement of village and parish officials in less dramatic fashion was apparently more common than the single incident at Staraia Belitsa (Staro-Belitskaia Parish), Dmitriev District on 23 December, but we have no other specific information on these.[13]

The deep hostility among peasants toward the rural police force, to which we have referred in our initial chapter, is evident from the narrative record of clashes that so often resulted from the attempts of the represen-tatives of authority to intervene in the course of unrest. Other means were used to express this hostility: acting through the village assembly, peas-ants sought to expel villagers in police service from the commune, depriv-ing them of house plots and allotments. On various dates in June 1906,

---

[12] RGIA, f. 1405, op. 108, 1906 g., d. 7011, ll. 2–2 ob. (copy of report, No. 2602, Procura-tor of the Kursk Regional Court Zhettsin to Procurator of the Khar'kov Judicial Cham-ber S. S. Khrulev, 19 July 1906). The attack on the station was prefaced, however, by a confrontation between the crowd and the police captain. The crowd demanded a copy of the Vyborg Appeal, which it accused him of concealing. Despite the captain's protesta-tions to the contrary, he and his patrolmen were disarmed and arms at the station seized.

[13] *RSKG*, No. 169, p. 136 (GAKO, f.1, op. 15, d. 12, ll. 151–151 ob.), report, Land Captain of the Third Land Department of Dmitriev District Vas'ianov to the Governor, 23 De-cember 1905. From the Governor's report of 15 January 1906: "In certain districts of Kursk Province, especially in Sudzha, Putivl', L'gov and in parts of Ryl'sk and Dmitriev Districts, this agitation has been expressed not only in incitement to the de-struction of landowners' estates, but also in attempts at revolt by means of (unlawfully) changing village and parish officials and an open defiance of properly constituted au-thorities." RGIA, f. 1291, op. 122, 1905 g., d. 123, 1. 43 ob.

such motions were adopted by assemblies in four big centers: Veliko-Mikhailovka and Ol'shanka in Novyi Oskol' District, Bol'shoe Nepluievo in Putivl' District and Khomutovka in Dmitriev District.[14]

The incidence of non-payment of taxes as a form of collective political action was unfortunately almost entirely absent in the police and judicial documents consulted for this study—underreported perhaps as a result of divisions in the flow of reportage to the center on such matters to the Department of Direct Taxation. In 1905, assemblies in Berezovskaia, Fateevskaia, Selinskaia and Popovkinskaia Parishes in Dmitriev District, declared a full boycott (to which Glamazdinskaia and Mikhailovskaia Parishes adhered); declarations of three-year abatement, written by a single hand, were posted in some of the larger villages (Fateevka, Zveniachka and others).[15] Resolutions in this same vein were adopted by village assemblies in the western part of Putivl' District in December.[16] The archival record made reference (reciting an item in *Die Zeit* of 16 July 1906) regarding "110 villages" in Bobrinskaia, Ivanovskaia, Iznoskovskaia, Nizhne-Derevenskaia and parts of Vyshne-Derevenskaia and Sheptukhovskaia Parishes, L'gov District, that had refused or failed to compile apportionment acts (*prigovory*) for payment of taxes.[17] There was a measurable resurgence of arrears for 1905–1906: data from the Department of Direct Taxation attest to a trebling of arrears on peasant land in Kursk Province between the end of 1904 and the end of 1906.[18] How much this

---

[14] GARF, f. 102, DP OO, op. 236 (II), 1906 g., d. 700, ch. 58, l. 270 (draft of telegram, at No. 12574, "for the Director P. Kharlamov" to Governor V. M. Borzenko, 26 August 1906); *RSKG*, No. 225, p. 178 (GAKO, f. 1, op. 16, d. 2, l. 9), report, Novyi Oskol' District Police Commandant Ivanovskii to Governor V. M. Borzenko, 2 June 1906; No. 277, p. 204 (GAKO, f. 1, op. 16, d. 2, l. 82), report of acting Novyi Oskol' District Police Commandant Bazilevich-Kniazhnikovskii to Governor V. M. Borzenko, 26 June 1906; *ibid.* (GARF), l. 270 (draft of telegram, Department of Police to Governor V. M. Borzenko, at OO No. 12574, bearing date 26 August 1906).

[15] *RSKG*, No. 129, pp. 111–112 (GAKO, f. 1, op. 15, d. 12, l. 31), report, Land Captain of the Fifth Land District Bulich to Kursk Governor N. N. Gordeev, 11 November 1905. The report carried the notation, in an unknown hand, as follows: "To the District Police Commandant: The monies must be collected as soon as troops arrive."

[16] *Ibid.*, No. 162, p. 132 (GAKO, f. 1, op. 15, d. 16, ll. 435–437), telegram, 14 December 1905, Land Captain Pavlov and Police Captain Novakov to Kursk Governor N. N. Gordeev on resolutions passed by village assemblies in Gruzchanskaia and Popovo-Slobodskaia Parishes, Putivl' District.

[17] GARF, f. 102, DP OO, op. 236 (II), 1906 g., d. 700, ch. 58, ll. 220–221 and 224–225. See discussion in Chapter III, n. 79.

[18] Arrears in Dmitriev District went from 31,100 rubles in 1904 to 138,900 in 1905 and 173,320 in 1906 (41% of 1906 assessments on peasant lands). For L'gov District, arrears

situation owed to refusals to pay and how much to conditions created by a serious shortfall in harvests and contraction in demand for migrant labor is unknown. Troop movements associated with refusals to pay taxes during 1905–1906 are indicated in a very small number of cases.[19]

"Political" incidents were not always of an anti-government character. Police reported on actions of the villagers of Arkhangel'skoe (Naprasnoe), Muromskaia Parish, Belgorod District, former serfs of Count Gendrikov settled in 1864 on "beggar's allotments." On 17 July 1905, the village *skhod* met to discuss the issue of obtaining an enlargement of their allotments and resolved to send two of their number to see the Emperor in St. Petersburg with a petition seeking his aid. Monies for the travel of these plenipotentiaries, upon whose mission the peasants of Arkhangel'skoe placed great hopes, were raised by selling rights to timber a part of their wooded lot. Passports were obtained on 28 July and the delegates left for the capital two days later. For this act of "naive monarchism," the authorities planned to have the two emissaries deported from the province.[20]

2. Other Attributes of the Unrest: Causes, Organization, Social Focus, Demands

If aspects of time, place and the typology of incidents of unrest were commonly present in the documentary record of peasant disorders in Kursk Province for 1905–1906, other criteria for assessing the attributes of these

---

rose from 71,500 rubles at the end of 1904, to 207,600 at the end of 1905 and to 194,100 at the end of 1906 (37.6%). Figures for the province as a whole suggest that the reemergence of arrears was not limited to Dmitriev and L'gov Districts alone: from 661,760 rubles in 1904, arrears stood at 2,264,580 rubles at the end of 1906 (26.7% of the provincial assessment on peasant lands for 1906). Once again, however, the eastern districts were the principal delinquents, in which arrears had been concentrated before the *ukaz* of 1904, carrying between 32.8% and 46.6% of the annual assessment of 1906. Ministerstvo finansov. Departament okladnykh sborov. *Svod svedenii... za (1904–1906) god.*

[19] Forcible extraction of taxes, backed by troops, recorded for *sloboda* Mikhailovka (Mikhailovskaia Parish) and the village of Vet' (Glamazdinskaia Parish) in Dmitriev District, *RSKG*, No. 292, pp. 213–215 (GAKO, f. 1, op. 17, d. 69, ll. 11–12), report, Dmitriev District Police Commandant K. M. Pleshkov to Governor V. M. Borzenko, 28 February 1907; GARF, f. 102, DP, 4-oe deloproizvodstvo, 1907 g., d. 34, 1. 5, (letter, peasant R. Latykin to newspaper *Kurskaia byl'*, 23 March 1907) and at Volokonsk (Bol'she-Soldatskaia Parish) and Russkoe Porechnoe (Miropol'skaia Parish) in Sudzha District: GARF, f. 102, DP OO, op. 236 (II), 1906 g., d. 700, ch. 58, ll. 279, 289–290.

[20] GARF, f. 102, DP OO, op. 233 (II), 1905 g., d. 2550, ch. 44, ll. 58–58 ob. (telegram, Colonel Vel'k, Commandant Kursk Provincial Gendarme Administration, to Department of Police, 26 August 1905).

incidents were far less regularly available on a case-by-case basis. Out of 323 recorded incidents in the sample, some reference to immediate cause was present for 132 (39.8 percent), attributes of organization of incidents in 246 (74.1 percent)—although the great majority of these latter were indicators of scale—and demands raised in the course of an incident in only 32 cases (9.6 percent). The documents did fully identify 215 (93 percent) out of the 231 estate owners whose properties were attacked; in all but 27 cases (11.7 percent), the social status of these owners could be established.

Causes (in the Documents)

Text fragments concerning the immediate causes of disorders in Kursk Province during 1905–1907 appear grouped below, together with their frequency. In their entirety, representing only 40 percent of all cases, these fragments suggest the degree to which local conditions—the difficulties in which peasant economies found themselves and the sharp tensions in relations between private estates and nearby peasant communities—defined the background to the revolutionary events.

Eighty-two cases made some reference to the concrete economic conditions of the subject peasant communities: land hunger (*malozemel'e*) generally (24) or lack of a specific arable type (forest: 1, pasture and meadow: 2). Seventeen cases, regarding the incidents in Dmitriev District during the events of 6–22 February, made note of "a lack of local wage labor employment." One case observed that the lack of fodder in householders' stores had motivated peasants to act. Thirty-seven cases directly cited the economic interrelationships of peasant communities with nearby private landowners as the cause of unrest. Discontent of peasants over terms of labor (18), usually wages, led this list (mainly from 1906), followed by dissatisfaction over issues (high rents, refusal to let land) associated with lease (8), general conduct of estate administrators (5), reduction of peasant privileges in connection with a changeover to direct demesne exploitation (3), high prices for lumber sold by the targeted estate (2), high fines levied for cattle trespass (1).

Thirty-one cases reported stubborn peasant claims to a "legal" basis for their acts, by appeals to "peasants' rights" either unspecified (5) or associated with a "manifesto" (3—these being all before 17 October 1905), also unspecified. But the bulk of such references (23) pertain to the disorders of 1–6 November 1905 in Novyi Oskol' and Staryi Oskol' Districts, for which the chief of the provincial gendarmerie laid special emphasis on rumors circulating widely among the peasants "that the Tsar has granted a Manifesto on land, but that this manifesto is being concealed from them."[21]

For twenty-seven incidents, the actions of the authorities were clearly the cause of further unrest. Sixteen of these directly associated peasant resistance with the efforts of the authorities to halt a disturbance in a given locality and to set in motion the process of house-to-house searches, confiscation of looted property and/or arrests of participants. Landowners who collaborated with these efforts—allowing troops to be quartered on their estates—faced retribution in three incidents. In five other matters, official acts sparked clashes well after the close of disturbances—either during a search for suspects ("agitators") or in the course of forcible extraction of tax arrears (1). In two other cases, bitter dissatisfaction with the performance, conduct and/or efficiency of the village police provoked attacks.

A separate set of conflicts (15) giving rise to disorders fell under disputes over claims to specific tracts of land. In a province in which physical intermixing of tracts of different owners was quite common, confrontations pitting peasant claims against those of nearby estates or against those of other villages were bound to act as a goad to discontent. As late as 1909, 439 large lots amounting to 600,000 *desiatiny* to which private owners and peasant communities had competing claims remained unsurveyed.[22] Threats from other peasants were blamed for setting one incident in motion, and dissatisfaction over the dissolution of the First State Duma was mentioned in the *prigovory* that circulated in Glamazdinskaia Parish, Dmitriev District prior to the onset of labor actions in July 1906.

Lastly, an additional 38 cases were attributed to "agitation" as a principal cause of incidents of agrarian disturbances in Kursk Province during 1905–1906. Together with a persistent effort to minimize the importance of the land question as an objective factor at the root of rural unrest (peasant views on this matter were most often pictured as simply misguided or worse), official reporting continued to insist that "outside agitation" was of central importance in explaining the disturbances. Behind this view lay

---

[21] *RSKG*, No. 54, p. 66 (GAKO, f. 1, op. 15, d. 2, l. 188), report, Kursk District Police Commandant V. L. Pozhidaev to Governor N. N. Gordeev, 22 August 1905. See comments of Colonel Vel'k, Commandant of the Kursk Provincial Gendarme Administration in his report of 12 November 1905, No. 3859, to the Department of the Police, GARF, f. 102, DPOO, op. 233 (II), 1905 g., d. 2550, ch. 44, ll. 154–156 ob.

[22] RGIA, f. 1291, op. 74, 1907 g. d. 673, l. 267 (From Anfimov, *Krest'ianskoe khoziaistvo*, 78.)

a caricature of the peasant estate that stressed its "dark" and insular character, its "normally" obedient and respectful attitude toward its "superiors" in word and deed, and its incapacity collectively to think for itself and to undertake, independently of the tutelage of its social betters, collective political action in its own interest. To be sure, peasants themselves were well aware of this condescension and made use of it in an exculpatory fashion when face to face with judicial investigators. The after-the-fact declarations of villagers that "they had acted on the teachings of bad people," that the Tsar himself had permitted seizure of the landowners' property until such-and-such a date, or that some "manifesto" or "new laws" allowed villagers to let their cattle onto the landowner's sown fields, all played at least partly on the various cultural conceits of the dominant classes.[23]

If rural society had become far more complex since the 1860s in its occupations, its literacy and its connections to the larger society outside the village, this new complexity commonly went unacknowledged in official reports and in the views of rapporteurs from the nobility in particular. Yet the record itself continuously cited facts that contravened the caricature. Official correspondence in the archival folders on peasant unrest during 1905–1906 darkly and repeatedly denounced the "deleterious influence" of the national press and its reporting of national and local news (war, strikes, peasant unrest elsewhere in the Empire), the appearance of peasant petitions in the newspapers, letters of soldiers from the eastern front, the views and influence of workers returning home from South Russia, revolutionary proclamations, transmission of the stenographic record of the Duma debates, interaction (by correspondence or during visits home) of Duma deputies with the electorate and so on. Among those accused of "agitation" one finds not "outsiders," but representatives of a more complex face of rural society. These were local "students," the same Duma deputies, rural teachers, *zemstvo* doctors, priests, demobilized soldiers, mine workers returned home from the South, parish or village elders, local peasants or those unhappy residents of the settlement of Peschanoe in Sudzha District, arrested for having read out in the village assembly, at the request of their illiterate fellow villagers, protocols of the November Congress of the All-Russian Peasant Union, reprinted in a number of *Russkoe Slovo*, which newspaper was itself later produced as material evidence.[24]

---

[23] The classic work on this phenomenon in peasant unrest has long been Field, *Rebels*.

[24] *Trudy IVEO*, 1908, No. 3 (May–June), 56.

In precisely the sense that they were acted out before an increasingly literate and interested peasant audience, the bitter divisions within the provincial nobility in Kursk Province in the latter half of the 1890s, which reached their dénouement in conservative victories during the *zemstvo* caucuses of 1906, are incontestably part of the background to the revolutionary unrest of 1905–1906. Very public splits within the provincial elite, and the state's continuous interference in the situation, culminating in the Emperor's well-publicized rebuke of A. V. Evreinov and Prince P. D. Dolgorukov (Dolgorukov was thereafter banned from participation in *zemstvo* affairs for five years), have been examined in detail elsewhere.[25] A principal bone of contention between the liberal faction (members of the Sudzha District nobility were particularly prominent) and its right-wing enemies (typically from poorer eastern districts) had always been associated not only with the scale and costs of *zemstvo* work in the village. Conservatives inveighed loudly and at length against the increasingly decisive role of the many employees hired in light of their expertise to implement—and, what was worse, to serve on boards which decided policy and directed—*zemstvo* programs in health, education, literacy, agronomy, micro-credit, statistical collection, mutual fire insurance or technical aid to agriculture, animal husbandry and handicrafts. It is hardly surprising that both reactionaries and provincial authorities were already predisposed to see these educated persons of undistinguished social pedigree not only as a threat to the preeminent place that they arrogated to themselves *vis-à-vis* the peasant mass, but also as "outsiders" or "interlopers" that posed a grave danger to public order generally. For right-wing nobles from Belgorod District, summoned by the Ministry of Internal Affairs to comment on local tensions in the wake of unrest in February 1905, the problem had long since reached a bad pass:

> Arriving at the true reasons for these phenomena, members of the conference must linger over the unfavorable influence of an unreliable element on peasants and on so-called revolutionary propaganda. Unfortunately, the progress and development of revolutionary parties in recent times is undoubted and hardly anyone will argue with that fact. Yet an understanding of revolutionary propaganda cannot include only dis-

---

[25] Ivan Petrovich Belokonskii (1855–1931), associated with *zemstvo* work in Kursk Province during the 1895–1897, left several memoirs drawing in part on his years in Kursk province. See, for example, *Zemskoe dvizhenie* or *V gody bezpraviia*. Also Boris Borisovich Veselovskii, *Zemstvo za sorok let*, t. I–IV (Sankt Peterburg, Izdatel'stva O. N. Popovoi, 1909–1911), *passim*, and R. Rexheuser, *Dumawahlen and lokale Gesellschaft*, the latter which uses Kursk Province and the *zemstvo* elections of 1906 as a test case.

semination of leaflets and the appearance of agitators. Propaganda, by the way, is the business not only of representatives of revolutionary committees, but also of persons having any kind of ties with the village, not as specialists but as amateurs and dilettantes. It is not the responsibility of the conference to name such people, but cases of "enlightening" of peasants in the sense of disobedience to the Tsar and their superiors by teachers, students, factory workers, junior employees of large estates, doctors and even some landowners are sufficiently well known. Thus the leaflets, most of them unintelligible although of clear criminal content, serve only as support and affirmation of that conveyed to peasants in the conversations and advice of the rural intelligentsia.[26]

To be sure, there is quite sufficient evidence to suggest that interaction between the liberal *zemstvo* men from the nobility in Kursk Province and the local rural intelligentsia went beyond the strict bounds of those close professional affiliations that had been forged in the wake of the galvanizing event of the crop failures of 1891–1892 and their extended aftermath. During the events of 1905–1906, they had entered into a more openly political collaboration that exhibited distinctly constitutionalist, if not revolutionary, overtones. Cooperation of these elements of rural society during the petition drive and the formation of unions—including local chapters of the All-Russian Peasant Union—during the spring and summer of 1905 has been referred to in the narrative section. The Party of Socialist-Revolutionaries appears to have enjoyed special success among persons associated with *zemstvo* work, especially teachers.[27] Several of the markedly leftist deputies sent by peasant electors to the First State Duma—Shaposhnikov, Solomko, Kutomanov, Gudilin, Merkulov and Ovchinnikov—were later jailed and tried for criminal agitation. The courts exonerated all but one of these (Merkulov), yet provincial authorities exercised their right to deport them by administrative order. Both Shirkov and Prince Dolgorukov were briefly detained in January 1906 for their roles in organizing chapters of the All-Russian Peasant Union in Kursk Province and later imprisoned for signing the Vyborg Appeal.

---

[26] RGIA, f. 1291, op. 30, 1905 g., d. 4-b, 1. 195 (*Zhurnal Belgorodskago uyezdnago soveshchaniia 9-go marta 1905 g.*).

[27] On S-R activities in Kursk Province, see GARF, f. 102, DP OO, op. 236, 1905 g., d. 1800, ch. 13 ("O predstavlenii otchetov o sostoianii revoliutsionnogo dvizheniia v Imperii. Po Kurskoi gubernii."), ll. 5–7, 17–22, and d. 80 ("Sotsialisti-revoliutsionery"), ll. 19–22. A recent evaluation of important organizational achievements for Socialist-Revolutionary activists in the province is Saltyk, "Es-Ry," 55–69. The crucial work on political activism among rural teachers in Russia during 1905 is Seregny, *Russian Teachers and Peasant Revolution*.

Undoubtedly, though, the great majority of "agitators" were peasants—but from a cohort somewhat on the margins of rural life. In his extensive review of the disturbances of 1905, Governor V. M. Borzenko, grudgingly acknowledging that grounds for the unrest had been prepared by impoverishment of the peasantry generally, nonetheless held the following view:

> The factors cited, which have brought about the impoverishment of the peasant populace and produced a feeling of dissatisfaction in peasant life, undoubtedly could not but serve as extremely fertile ground for revolutionary agitation. In this connection it must be noted that the peasantry, by the very nature of its life, has begun to separate out from its midst a significant number of persons leaving the province for wage employment, mainly in the factories and mills, an element whose household economies have already been undermined. This element, thrust into the new milieu, bears with it back to the village all of the negative facets of factory and industrial life. Frequent disturbances at the factories, unrest in the cities along with the pogroms, cannot but exert demoralizing effects on peasant-workers returning home and, in individual cases, they have been so entirely propagandized that they themselves have become organizers of revolutionary cells in the localities. In recent times, the Party of Socialist-Revolutionaries has acted with special energy here, setting itself the aim, by organization of the Peasant Union, of fomenting a peasant uprising.[28]

The effects of labor migration on village life, its close connection with phenomena associated with family partitions and formation of large cohorts of younger, economically vulnerable nuclear families, the connection of both these factors with higher rates of literacy, and the attenuation, to varying degrees, of the ties to an "agricultural" household economy—these features of the general characterization of a "revolutionary milieu" in Kursk Province will be examined below. Suffice it now to note that, even given the pejoratives that clutter the Governor's characterizations, the peasantry "by the very nature of its life" had long since begun to evolve and ramify, to enter into closer contact with the outside world.

Lastly, we should note that ethnic hostility between Great Russians and Ukrainians in Kursk Province as a cause of unrest found direct expression in only one case: in a contest over 421 *desiatiny* long used in common, Great Russian peasants settled in the villages of Novo-Slobodka, Lomovo, Zaiach'e and Mazikinaia (Novoslobodskaia Parish), Korocha District, repeatedly attempted between 30 August and 6 Septem-

---

[28] RGIA, f. 1291, op. 122, 1905 g., d. 123 ("Doneseniia gubernatorov o prichinakh agrarnykh bezporiadkov"), 1. 43 ob. (report, Governor V. M. Borzenko to the Minister of Internal Affairs, 15 January 1906). A circular requesting these reports was sent to all governors on January 7 (1. 1).

ber to divide this tract among themselves. Each effort was blocked by crowds of Ukrainian peasants from the nearby villages of Koren'ki, Plosskoe, Pestunovo and Gorodishche, armed with clubs, staves, scythes and pitchforks. Efforts to mediate an amicable end to the conflict by local authorities were without issue and, finally, a half-hundred of the 2nd Eiskii Cossack Regiment had to be deployed to the site to disperse peasant crowds.[29] There are indications, however, that this side of the question was often simply not framed in official correspondence. Acting Prosecutor Rakovskii of the Kursk Regional Court, reporting on unrest in Novyi Oskol' District during 1–6 November 1905, asserted that "disorders seized only those settlements populated by Ukrainians; the Great Russian villages took almost no part in the riots."[30] Reflecting the old settlement patterns along the contested borderlands of the Muscovite state, Graivoron District (61.1 percent), Putivl' District (56.1 percent)—particularly the parishes south of the River Seim—and Novyi Oskol' District (52.9 percent) all had especially large Ukrainian populations. Ukrainians also made up a major part of the rural populace of Sudzha (43.4 percent), Korocha (35.1 percent) and Ryl'sk Districts (34.0 percent). Ethnic composition of specific village populations could not be verified, however, since both the surveys of 1882–1885 and the published listings of villages (over 500 or 2,000 inhabitants) drawn out of the 1897 census included breakdowns by gender and religious affiliation, but failed to incorporate data on ethnicity.

Organizational Attributes

Summary data on the organizational aspects of peasant unrest suffer even more from the lack of detail in official reporting from the locality. In general, the best success was achieved in assessing the "mass" character of incidents, in which I have used the scale advanced by the late A. M. Anfimov, who identified acts of 10 or more participants with a mass incident, 3–9 participants with "group" actions and 1–2 participants with "individual acts."[31] Since the documentation provides actual police estimates for only 41 incidents (12.3 percent; average 575 participants), other criteria had to be used as a means for a characterization. The scale of 64 incidents

---

[29] GARF, f. 102, DP OO, op. 236 (II), d. 2550, ch. 44, ll. 67–69, 70–71, and 190–191 ob. (report, Kursk Governor N. N. Gordeev to the Department of Police). A similar conflict between the parties had occurred in 1882.

[30] RGIA, f. 1405, op. 108, 1906 g., d. 7006, ll. 1–4 ob.

[31] Anfimov, "O metodike," in Tikhvinskii, ed., *Sotsial'no-ekonomicheskoe razvitie*, 131–144. See also Leshchenko, "Itogi," in Ianin, ed., *Sovetskaia istoriografiia*, 47–59.

(19.2 percent) was estimated by examination of prosecutorial reports that gave the numbers of peasants convicted of participation in disorders, despite the fact that local authorities arrested only a small percentage of participants and that the acquittal rate was high (37.2 percent). An additional 141 incidents (42.5 percent) had to be characterized by textual references in archival documents to "crowds" (*tolpa, skopishche, "skopom"*) or "gangs" (*shaiki*), ascribed, respectively, to mass and small-group acts. All such references were entirely absent in texts describing 86 incidents (26 percent), including by definition anonymous acts of arson (20 incidents) in which apprehension and conviction of miscreants were virtually impossible. On the basis of these criteria, the disorders in the sample collected for Kursk Province in 1905–1907 were overwhelmingly of a mass character (perhaps not so surprising in reports reaching gubernatorial and ministerial instances): 237 of the 323 incidents (71.4 percent) present one or more relevant textual clues in the documents reviewed.[32]

The remaining attributes appear only at levels of the anecdotal. The organizing role of the village assembly in the course of events was expressly recorded in fifteen instances, but these cases were geographically widespread: the districts of Oboian, 4; Dmitriev, 2; Novyi Oskol', 2; L'gov, 2; Putivl', 1; Graivoron, 1; Fatezh, 1; Staryi Oskol', 1; Belgorod, 1. Unofficial reports of events in certain localities, however, gave the village assembly a far greater stature in the unrest. In like manner, joint actions of two or more villages were recorded in over half of the districts: Dmitriev (four times), Putivl', Graivoron, Korocha (3), Oboian (2), L'gov, Kursk, Ryl'sk (1). The materials thus at least hint at much broader dimensions of inter-village and communal cooperation in collective actions. Investigatory materials collected in the wake of the February disturbances in Dmitriev District judged this role to have been central:

---

[32] A listing of 597 persons arrested and tried in connection with incidents of unrest in February 1905 in Dmitriev District, with reference to both age and village of residence, suggest indirectly a certain solidarity in the degree to which, once the movement got under way, all age groups were represented. There were 132 arrestees between the ages of 17 and 25 (22.1%), 160 between 26 and 35 (26.8%), 179 between 36 and 45 (30.0%), 84 between the ages of 46 and 55 (14.1%) and 42 over the age of 55 (7.0%). The average age for this group was 36. RGIA, f. 1291, op. 108, 1906 g., d. 6805 ("O krest'ianskikh bezporiadkakh v Dmitrievskom uyezde, Kurskoi gubernii"), ll. 55–57, 59–61, 66–70; d. 6806 (same), ll. 4–5, 7–8 ob., 9–11 ob., 13–15, 17–18 ob., 20–21, 22–23, 59–61 ob., 63–76 ob., 80–83, 86–88 ob., 111–114 ob. It is worth noting that Land Captain Kusakov estimated the number of participants at 10,000 persons. "Krest'ianskoe dvizhenie," *Krasnyi arkhiv*, 1935, No. 6 (73), 168.

The peasants, sometimes several villages, assembled in a predetermined site in their carts, mostly at night and, at a signal (a rifle shot or a bundle of straw set afire), proceeded to the estate and carried out its sacking, not touching any of those living there and sometimes not even looting property, striving only to destroy it or make it unusable. Among the looters were observed persons that seemed to be directing matters, and there were villages that had evidenced no hostile relations to the neighboring estates until the appearance of inciters. Various relations to the landowners seem not to have played a role, and one can only note that the estates that were attacked, for the most part, were those in which the landowner was an absentee or was temporarily away. *The initial investigation has presently established that before the unrest, the organization of the attacks was discussed in the village assemblies, and eight persons from each village were elected as marshals.*[33]

The reports also reveal that in most cases, the peasants warned the owner beforehand and a small group was detailed to look at the estate and to declare that they would come back on a given day. Despite the level of violence, physical assaults on the persons of the landowners themselves were very rare. A quite similar degree of organization suggesting the same role of the village assemblies was observed in the wave of incidents in Novyi Oskol' District during the first week of November:

The planned and uniform action of the actions of these crowds during the disorders leads one to the conclusion that they had been organized, that their beginning had been designated for the fair in Chernianka. In almost all cases, several peasants appeared in the targeted estate beforehand, warning of an imminent attack and arson and demanding that the owners quit the scene. Then the peasants from the adjoining village came during the day, armed with clubs, staves and sometimes rifles and revolvers, and with huzzahs began to seize property and livestock, after which the buildings were set on fire. The appearance of members of the police in no way hindered the looters: police officials were told to "take themselves off," but cases of violence against persons were exceptional.[34]

Mass actions of entire parishes were recorded for Dmitriev District (joint tax strike of four parishes, November 1905), Graivoron (Borisovskaia Parish, all communes, mass illegal timbering, November 1905) and Putivl' Districts (four parishes, mass political meetings after the 3 De-

---

[33] GARF, f. 102, DP OO, op. 233, 1905 g., d. 2550 ("Po krest'ianskim bezporiadkam: obshchaia perepiska"), ll. 57–57 ob. (Report of Privy Councilor I. A. Zvegintsev, 18 March 1905). Italics mine.

[34] RGIA, f. 1405, op. 108, 1906 g., d. 7006, l. 1 ob. Rumors "that students and other persons will arrive at the settlement of Chernianka to begin partition of land and other property" had been reported as circulating among peasants in his precinct by the local Land Captain in March. RGIA, f. 1291, op. 30, 1905 g., d. 4-b, l. 185 (*Zhurnal Novooskol'skago uyezdnago soveshchaniia zemskikh nachal'nikov 11 go marta 1905 g.*).

cember dispersal of a large assembly of peasants at Gruzskoe by police, cut short by suppression of the Kazachanskaia Parish peasant council by force on 23 December).

Lastly, despite all the dark references to "the work of the revolutionary parties" in the official reporting, no actual record of direct participation of known representatives of any political party or faction in incidents of unrest or their organization came to light in the documents consulted in connection with this work. As has been shown, of all political formations, the Socialist-Revolutionaries succeeded best in disseminating inflammatory literature and initiating, during the spring and summer of 1905, the organization of chapters of the All-Russian Peasant Union in Kursk Province—in collaboration with sympathetic elements among the local intelligentsia and with the active encouragement of several liberal noblemen. The Union struck far deeper roots in Kursk Province than in the three villages actually named in police reports (Dar'ino in Sudzha District, Kobylka in Ryl'sk District and Fitizh in L'gov District). Fragmentary evidence from other sources (see above) suggests that affiliates had been organized in many other sites in each of these districts as well as in Graivoron (Borisovka, Golovchino), Sudzha and Dmitriev Districts, leaving one with the sense, at least, that Union organizations emerged mostly in these western (and, as we recall, more prosperous) regions of the province. It is far from certain that union affiliates were really any more revolutionary than the rather moderate national directorate: testimony from two local correspondents insisted on their tendency sooner to restrain violent peasant unrest;[35] association of the three named villages with numerous acts of unrest tends to suggest that this was not always so. The protocols and resolutions of founding (31 July–1 August 1905) and delegate (6–10 November 1905) congresses of the All-Russian Peasant Union were widely circulated in the press and gave a national voice to peasant views and demands.[36] The great novelty of the Union may indeed have resided more in the fact that for peasants the organization was quite incontestably "theirs" and served as a sounding board for their public demands, discus-

---

[35] GARF, f. 102, DP OO, op. 233 (II), 1905 g., d. 2550, ch. 44, 1. 83 (telegram, landowner I. N. Protas'ev to S. Iu. Witte, 26 October 1905); P. D. Dolgorukov, "Agrarnaia volna," No. 1 (9 January), col. 26–31. Dolgorukov later contended that the very success of Peasant Union organization tended to restrain peasant disturbances, contrasting events in the southerly parishes of Sudzha District where his estate was located with the far greater violence in the northern parishes. *Stenograficheskii otchet Gosudarstvennaia Duma. Pervyi sozyv.* I: 18, 16 June 1906, 1365–1367.

[36] Dolgorukov, "Agrarnaia volna," No. 2 (15 January), col. 96–97.

sions and aspirations, quite independent of the tutelage of their "superiors." At the very least, then, the Peasant Union and its local chapters—if
they rarely appear in archival materials in connection with specific incidents—were still part of the atmosphere of the revolutionary "moment"
that built in force throughout 1905.

Peasant Demands

Peasant demands, raised during acts of unrest, were recorded in official
documents in only 32 cases (9.7 percent). Most of these observations (23)
pertained to material for the May–August 1906 phase of the movement
during which demands associated with wages and rents were raised in the
course of labor actions. These latter, associated with incidents in 9 out of
15 districts, concern mainly wage issues and labor obligations, but were
frequently combined with demands with regard to land rents, leasing practices, exclusion of "non-local" (*prishlie*) laborers and all manner of
strictly local concerns. Four additional cases (resolutions of village or
parish assemblies) contained overtly political demands, and three mixed
demands of political and economic content—these were concentrated in
Dmitriev, L'gov, Sudzha and Putivl' Districts. The small number of cases
rules out more solid conclusions, but the general tenor of the demands
attests to peasant dissatisfaction not only with economic relationships with
the private estates, but also, in some localities, to a deep discontent with
structures of local authority. Although "contractual" demands were noted
for nine districts, political or "mixed" demands were recorded only in the
western part of the province (districts), in which the union movement
seems to have been stronger.[37]

---

[37] Rank order of frequency of demands for: increase in wages (19); the exclusion of non-
local laborers (8); reduction in rents or labor obligations under existing leases (6); exclusion from the commune of families with members serving with the local police (3);
grazing or timbering rights (3); demands raised but not specified (2); release of land into
leasehold (1); lease of land exclusively to one's own village (1); introduction of the 8-
hour work day (1); removal of police and soldiers from the village (1); release of persons detained by the police (1). Frequency of points adopted in resolutions issued by village and/or parish assemblies, which demanded: expulsion and/or election of new village and/or parish officials (4); expulsion or barring of laborers from the estates condi-
tional or unconditionally (3); non-payment of taxes (1); not to provide recruits at call-up
(1); seizure and partition of estate lands (1); to surrender no one for arrest (1); affiliation
with the All-Russian Peasant Union (1); to cease drinking vodka (1).

Targets of Peasant Disorders

Within the sample of official reporting selected—and it has been observed that such a sample is hardly unimpeachable in terms of its biases—peasant unrest in Kursk Province struck "targets" that, by their social and institutional identities, left no element of the rural order untouched. It is wholly evident that, in Kursk Province as well as elsewhere, the animus between the peasant estate and members of the local gentry was a principal social feature of agrarian disturbances in 1905–1906. Of the 251 objectives identified as subject to peasant depredations during 1905, 210 (83.7 percent) were estates belonging to the gentry (177), to prominent persons of the urban estate (16) or properties (forest preserves, liquor stalls) administered by state agencies (17). Ten direct confrontations with representatives of authority unassociated with specific incidents must be considered in addition. In 1906, for 126 identified objectives, 100 (79.4 percent) were estates of nobles (74) or of highly ranked urban dwellers (18) and 7 state properties. Eleven unassociated clashes with troops or police are also on record for 1906. The holdings of peasants (12, three stemming from inter-village quarrels[38]) and of members of the lesser urban estates (*meshchane*) made up 16 of the objectives during 1905 (6.3 percent) and two (1.6 percent) in 1906.

That victims of various social standings suffered simultaneously during incidents of unrest (peasants along with members of the gentry and a state liquor store during a single incident) hardly suggests that the actors took into consideration all the niceties of theories of "two social wars" in their acts. Rather, peasant militants used the disorders to settle a variety of scores that had local roots and histories. Indeed, peasant collective actions seemed to take a "shotgun" approach toward all its social enemies. One example here will be sufficient. On 20 February 1905 in the village of Romanovo, Glamazdinskaia Parish, Dmitriev District, in a single continuous incident, peasants looted and burned the estate of A. Mytarskii (no-

---

[38] The three: 1) on 30 June 1905 between villagers of the settlements of Gladkaia and Luboshevo, Dmitriev District, over meadows used up until that time in common (GARF, f. 102, DP 00, op. 233 [II], d. 2550, ch. 44, 11. 31–32); 2) clash between 30 August and 6 September 1905 between Great Russian and Ukrainian peasants in Novoslobodskaia Parish, Korocha District, over a tract of 421 *desiatiny* formerly used in common (GARF, f 102, DP 00, op. 236 [II], d. 2550, ch. 44,11.67–69, 70–71, and 190–191 ob.); 3) the destruction of the house plot and garden of the peasant Tutov by the entire population of Peschanoe, Pavlovskaia Parish, Oboian District, between 12 and 14 November 1905. Tutov lived in another village. RGIA, f. 1405, op. 194, 1908 g., d. 102, 1. 33 (No. 740, case 9).

bleman), broke doors and windows and destroyed the cookhouse of V. M. Shchegoleva (noblewoman), ransacked and burned down the house and buildings of Voinov, the priest, plundered the property of the peasant M. A. Kudakov and relieved the peasant Basiukov (who leased property from one D. N. Lazarevich, a nobleman) of his grain supplies.[39] Notwithstanding the fact that absentee noble owners of the larger estates were repeatedly attacked in the first instance, rank-and-file nobles were the most often victimized.

Attacks on the estates of prominent noble *functionaries* were an interesting feature of disorders in 1905. This facet of the unrest was of particular note in Novyi Oskol' District, where local peasants took out after estates of the local Land Captains and their relatives (families Arsen'ev, Starov, Beliaev and Skibin) and serving or former Marshals of the Nobility (Kasatkin-Rostovskii, Dorrer, Miatlev), the latter particularly notorious for their reactionary political leanings.[40] These attacks reflected deep peasant resentment against the concentrations of power shared out among cabals or clans of local noblemen, who used multiple posts within district administrative structures and *zemstvo* organs for extending their personal influence and lording it over the peasant population.[41]

Documentary evidence from police and judicial institutions was far less illuminating in its reflections on conceptions of "legality" with which participants in disorders attempted to clothe their actions, if only later, for the benefit of police investigators. Thus, for example, on 28 July 1905, police officials reported on an event occurring at Cherkasskaia Konopel'ka (Zamostianskaia Parish) on the estate of the nobleman M. N.

---

[39] GARF, f. 102, DP OO, op. 233, 1905 g., d. 2550, 1. 55 ob.

[40] Land Captain A. A. Kusakov in Dmitriev District; Land Captain V. A. Rapp and former Marshal of the Nobility S. I. Zhekulin in Sudzha District, Marshal of the Nobility P. P. Stremoukhov in L'gov District, the Grigorosulo clan in Graivoron District, Land Captains P. A. Lukin and N. G. Gamalei and former Marshal of the Nobility K. N. Ustimovich in Oboian District.

[41] In this regard, see the anonymous article "'Rodstvennye poriadki' v *zemstvo*: pis'mo is N-skago uyezda, Kurskoi gub.," *Russkoe bogatstvo*, 1898 g., No. 2, 212–223, in which the domination of local positions of authority in their own interest by a few local noble clans in Graivoron District is only thinly masked: the bitter denunciation of the Grigorsulo clan and its activities read out in the First State Duma by M. D. Kutomanov, Member from Graivoron District, made the identities of at least one of these clans public. *Stenograficheskii otchet. Gosudarstvennaia Duma. Pervyi Sozyv*, I: 18, 30 May 1906, 858. See also Gurko's account of the unflagging pressures brought to bear by local notables to gain the appointment of one Pavel Konstantinovich Beliaev as Land Captain in Staryi Oskol' District (Chapter I, n. 171).

Shmidt (1,000 *desiatiny*). The peasants of this village, in the full comple-
ment of their assembly (70 households), had appeared before the owner
(their former master) to demand permission to pasture their cattle along
with the estate's livestock without the usual assessment of labor dues.
The assembly further demanded lease of land for a portion of the harvest
without labor obligations (the lands for winter planting to be assessed at
15 rubles per *desiatina*) and announced their refusal to do fieldwork
under conditions set by previous agreement. The owner objected; the
peasants threatened violence. Three days later, 300 head of peasant cattle were let out onto Schmidt's meadows and forest tracts. Efforts of the
local authorities to persuade peasants to cease illegal pasturing were
answered by the latter with reference to "the new laws" that gave them
the right to graze their cattle wherever they wished.[42] Even broader
claims were made by peasants during an incident that took place on August 16 on the estate of N. S. Obidin near Tsvetovo (Ryshkovskaia Parish), Kursk District. On the 15th, a peasant from Tsvetovo II appeared
before Obidin's steward to warn him that the villagers now considered it
their right to let their cattle onto the estate's meadows and gardens, since
there had now appeared a Manifesto that granted peasants leave to graze
their cattle freely on all private lands, meadows and gardens. On the
16th, six peasants from Tsvetovo-II and Dvoretskaia Poliana let village
horses onto Obidin's meadows. When the estate's watchman sought to
chase the horses off, the peasants said to him, "Take your carcass out of
here and don't touch the horses! By the Manifesto, they now have a right
to free pasture!"[43] The frequency with which unrest in 1905 was reported in association with peasant references to "the Manifesto" or to
"new laws" as a "legal" basis for their acts reflected the manner in
which the efforts of the central government to parry mounting political

---

[42] *RSKG*, No. 52, p. 65 (GAKO, f. 1, op. 15, d. 8, ll. 1–5); GARF, f. 102, DP OO, op. 233
(II), 1905 g., d. 2550, ch. 44, ll. 47–48, 54, 63–65; *Revoliutsiia 1905–1907 gg. v Rossii.
Dokumenty i materialy. Revoliutsionnoe dvizhenie vesnoi i letom 1905 goda. Aprel'-
sentiabr'* Chast'1, No. 477, pp. 693–694.

[43] *RSKG*, No. 54, p. 66 (GAKO, f. 1, op. 15, d. 2, l. 188), report, Kursk District Police
Commandant Pozhidaev to Governor N. N. Gordeev, 22 August 1905. Peasant representation of their "right"—especially in intercourse with outsiders—commonly seized upon
and reworked available printed or oral evidence, in the event, probably the Manifesto
and Statute of 6 August 1905 regarding the form of the consultative ("Bulygin") Duma
(*PSZ*, III, 25: 637, at No. 26656 ("Ob uchrezhdenii Gosudarstvennoi Dumy") and 640–
645 at No. 26661, as proofs of the existence of rights which, in actuality, peasants held
as operating independently and in opposition to the written laws of the "lords."

ferment by piecemeal concessions were closely followed in the country-side and seized upon, particularly in November, as a cover for a far broader peasant agenda. Proclamation of the "freedoms" of 17 October, even though of critical importance, was but one of the events that took place during 1905 that transmitted to the country districts rather the sense of the weakness of the state power. In turn, this sense produced an equally powerful feeling of the possibility of action that generated attempts to destroy the old rural order in one blow.

By 1906, however, central and local authorities, backed by fresh infusions of troops, had reasserted themselves in the affected areas and began to conduct inquests, house-to-house searches and sweeping arrests. In April 1906, the circuit courts began hearing cases connected with the disorders, a process that was to last into the summer months of 1907 and to result in the imprisonment of thousands of peasant participants. Archival documents reviewed for this work recorded 1,709 prison terms handed down in cases concerning just 76 (23.5 percent) of the 323 incidents of unrest; one may assume that the true number was quite a bit higher.[44] The rural disorders of 1906, then, unfolded against the backdrop of both a stiffening of the resolve of the authorities and an improvement of their logistical capability not only to detain and prosecute peasant militants and their well-wishers among the local intelligentsia, but also to respond swiftly and forcefully to the merest sign of trouble. In such circumstances, the fact itself that, despite the campaign of repression that began in late November 1905, peasant militancy in 1906 resurfaced at many of the same sites in Kursk Province in which disorders had been recorded in 1905 testifies to the depth of social grievances that animate the history of the period.

---

[44] See reports of the Procurator of the Kursk Regional Court on these cases to the First Department, Second Criminal Division, Ministry of Justice in RGIA, f. 1405, op. 194, 1908 g., d. 102. In almost all cases when the numbers of participants were fixed by police observers (14 cases, 5,420 participants), the numbers convicted constituted a very small minority (291). This state of affairs was openly admitted by government officials. Writing of the Dmitriev District events, the composer of the draft of "temporary rules" to guide the punitive function of the County Commissions noted the following: "Very many people who have beaten, robbed and committed arson escape from punishment that they merit because of the excessive difficulty of analyzing the whole complexity of an incident of destructive riot [*razgrom*], carried out by a mob of several thousand persons, in light of an absence of incontrovertible evidence of specific actions of this or that person that conforms to the standards of the definition of crime demanded by law." RGIA, f. 1291, op. 122, 1905 g., d. 34-b, ll. 80–82, reprinted in "K istorii bor'by," *Krasnyi arkhiv*, 1936, 5 (78), 132–150.

Incidents of rural unrest in Kursk Province in the sample that we have examined were thus overwhelmingly "mass" in character, most often aimed at the gentry's estates and most commonly linked, in both causes and demands observed by local reporting, to deep-rooted peasant dissatisfaction with the erosion—or even breakdown—of older reciprocal relationships between the private landowners and neighboring peasant communities. Both lord and peasant experienced this disruption as much as a wider violation of an extant, if unwritten, social contract, and not simply as a contest over their economic interactions associated with vital issues of land and labor. If in 1905 the movement had been defined by a series of destructive attacks on private estates in which looting, arson and vandalism forced many noble families to hurriedly pack their valises and to flee their homes for the safety of the district seat, peasant militancy in 1906 made use of the agricultural calendar to force suspensions of operations on the estates at a critical juncture. In 1905, disorders expressed the elemental struggle of peasant militants to "smoke out" the estate owners—to carry out the long-awaited "Black Repartition"—and by so doing to alter the balance of social and economic relations in the most fundamental manner. In the case of Putivl' District in December 1905, this drive developed into short-lived seizures of power in certain localities, swiftly put down by the intervention of the forces of order. Disorders in 1906 surely represented a step back from a decisive break with the past that had appeared briefly possible in 1905, yet they were nevertheless played out on the plane of the crucial economic nexus between landowners and local villagers at a most critical moment. The labor actions of 1906, too, were aimed at least as much on ruining the landowner entirely as on forcing concessions on wages, rents and hire. Yet they focused, perhaps even more starkly and "programmatically" than in 1905, on those concrete issues that constituted the substance of the interaction between peasants and the *gospoda*, often in the same locales where attacks on the estates had been recorded in the previous year.

3. The Chronology of Unrest and Its Background

A chronology of peasant unrest in Kursk Province strongly suggests sufficiently close relationships between rural disorders in its country districts with events taking place in the Empire as a whole, even if the findings of this study do not support the more pointed conclusions that are sometimes drawn from observations of this sort. The disturbances unfolded against the background of a general situation in the province itself that by the spring of 1905 had begun to cause alarm. Both on peasant allotments and on private lands, harvests of spring sowings for 1905 (including one of the principal cash crops, oats) were to be drastically below the average for the period 1885–1913. Fodder supplies were particularly affected: the Governor's annual reports for both 1905 and 1906 made note of a widespread sell-off of peasant horses and livestock.[45] Land rents, their upward trend uninterrupted in the wake of the famine years of 1891–1892, continued to rise at a time when the day wage for labor at harvest time, after 1902, fell for the third straight year. Average figures for grain prices in the province's main markets show that prices for rye and oats, which had reached their lowest points during 1894–1896 had begun, year by year, to record increases: against the background of poor harvests during 1905–1906, the price of one *pood* of rye stood at its highest level since 1891–1892.[46]

In connection with the first outbreak of disorders in the province in February 1905, however, when a prognosis concerning harvests would have played no role, investigators pointed to the influence of the Russo-Japanese War in three of its most salient aspects. First, given the fact that mobilizations had taken 48,161 working-age males and 17,196 horses[47] in the course of eight call-ups for 1904–1905, it was entirely natural that news of the fortunes of Russian armies and other events taking place beyond the horizons of village life would have attracted especially intense interest. Land Captains in Staryi Oskol' District noted much discussion everywhere about military actions in the East, the land question and the state reforms promised by the Manifesto of 12 December 1904, reforms that country people awaited with great expectations and trepidation.[48] Close attention in the villages to this range of issues was fed by the national and local press. Conservatives in the Belgorod District conference of Land Captains in March 1905 warned that "the success of propaganda is served in still greater measure by the press and

---

[45] *Obzor Kurskoi gubernii za 1905 god*, 15. Peacetime conscription averaged perhaps 6,600 men.

[46] Ministerstvo finansov, Departament torgovli i manufaktur, *Materialy po statistike*. Vyp. II–III; idem, *Svod tovarnykh tsen*; Ministerstvo zemledeliia i gosudarstvennykh imushchestv. Departament Zemledeliia. *(1904–1906) god v sel'skokhoziaistvennom otnoshenii po otvetam*; *TS-KhSKGZ za (1898–1902) god*.

[47] *Obzor Kurskoi gubernii... za 1904 god*, 43–44; *Obzor Kurskoi gubernii... za 1905 god*, 50–52.

[48] RGIA, f. 1291, op. 30, 1905 g., d. 4-b, l. 189 (*Zhurnal Starooskol'skago uyezdnago soveshchaniia zemskikh nachal'nikov of 10-go marta 1905 g.*)

the newspapers permitted by the government, which are sold at every bazaar and railway station. Given the unusual interest in the country districts concerning the war, one sees newspapers on the streets of the most isolated villages and in the hands of any peasant riding by with a load of hay, and the discourse in such newspapers is hardly that typical of *Our Day*, *Our Life*, *Rus'* or other journals. Less didactic and better intentioned than the usual (revolutionary) proclamations, these nonetheless have in relation to the latter the enormous advantages of being semi-professional, permitted by law and recognized allegedly as useful."[49] The Imperial postal services, moreover, dutifully and regularly delivered to addressees in the rural districts letters from the front, newspaper and journal subscriptions of various political hues, all sorts of "red" literature and revolutionary broadsheets "of the most rabid content."[50] Once again, a sharp contradiction reappears between the characterizations of the peasantry as an ignorant mass that typify official analysis and evidence produced by the same analyses that literacy and a lively interest in matters outside the daily round of village life were at work in localities later associated with incidents of unrest.

There is thus little doubt that proclamation of the 12 December 1904 Manifesto with its vague promises of reforms, increasingly disastrous news from the East (punctuated by the surrender of the Russian garrison at Port Arthur on 2 January 1905), and the rising tide of public disgruntlement in the urban centers that gained a new and urgent intensity in the wake of the massacre of a peaceful procession of working people in St. Petersburg on 9 January 1905 all provided the immediate background to the outbreak of disorders in Dmitriev District, since reportage of such developments appeared almost everywhere in the national or local press. Peasant opinion in Kursk Province was said to have been particularly impressed, if not by news of the events of 9 January itself, then by the sense that they attributed to the speech of Nicholas II in receiving a delegation of workers ten days later, in which the Tsar absolved them of their guilt in the matter. Local peasants interpreted this event, Litvinov noted, "in the sense that the Tsar himself did not actually prohibit one

---

[49] RGIA, f. 1291, op. 30, 1905 g., d. 4-b, l. 178 (*Zhurnal Belgorodskago uyezdnago soveshchaniia*).

[50] *Revoliutsiia 1905–1907 gg v Rossii. Dokumenty i materialy. Nachalo pervoi russkoi revoliutsii, ianvar'-mart, 1905 g.*, No. 415, p. 628. Document reproduced from GARF, f. 1291, op. 122, 1905 g., d. 34-b ("Materialy otnosiashchiesia do poezdki Ego Prevoskhoditel'stva Ia.Ia. Litvinov dlia rukovodstva deistviami vremennykh uyezdnykh kommisii, uchrezhdennykh na osnovaniiakh Ukaza 10 Aprelia 1905 g."), ch. I: ll. 162–190.

from plundering the lords," thus providing their acts with a certain tincture of legality.[51] Rumors were also said to have been rife in the area of unrest, undoubtedly in reference to the future state reforms, that "the lords strive once again to restore serfdom and do not want to obey the will of the Tsar, who wishes to give land to the peasants," and people talked of the time when they would be able to settle accounts with the lords.[52]

Secondly, the presence of the great bulk of Russian armies at the eastern front created the impression of "opportunity" for direct action among more radical-minded elements of the rural population. The preceding review suggested that major outbreaks of unrest were often immediately preceded by instances in which unexpected peasant resistance and a clearly insufficient response of local officials in a purely local contest of wills led not only to the failure of these representatives of authority to impose order, but to their public humiliation as well. Such instances (as at the settlement of Sal'noe between 6 and 15 February) could only confirm the impression that—without troops at their backs— local officials were unable to mount a response at all. As if by reflex, though, official reporting initially tended to blame peasant militancy on "outside agitators." Dismissing from the outset any notion that the "land question" or "hostile relations" between villagers and the *pomeshchiki* might have "roused peasants against the landowners' estates" in Dmitriev District, the rapporteur for the Ministry of Internal Affairs, after his visit to the region in March, wrote that, in light of the "absence" of such historical hostility,

> One must seek out such motives in the influence exerted on the peasant mass from without. And in fact, from partial information gained from the police depositions to the present time and from reports of the Marshals of the Nobility, it is evident that the majority of those arrested in connection with cases of disorder stated that they had acted "on the teachings of bad people," that before the outbreak of unrest, there had appeared in the locality some unknown outsiders who had persuaded the peasants that a partition of the land was necessary, that such partitions might be easily accomplished at the present time, since the Army had left for the Far East, that nothing now prevented the peasants, looting and setting fire to the estates, from forcing the estate owners to renounce the land and themselves taking control of it as abandoned. These circumstances, along with apprehension of two proclamations of inflammatory content found in the village of Sal'noe (Dmitriev District) and evidence that such appeals or summons were widely circulated,

---

[51] *Ibid.* (*Nachalo*), 630.

[52] GARF, f. 102, DP OO, op. 233 (II), 1905 g., d. 2550, ch. 44, l. 1 (extract from the report of the Kursk Governor to the Minister of Internal Affairs, 18 February 1905, at No. 99).

establish that the unrest that occurred was the fruit of the activities of the revolutionary parties, who have made use of the constant aspiration of the peasantry toward enlargement of their lands and their sincere belief that the estate owners own the land unlawfully, that this land ought to belong entirely to the peasantry.[53]

Outright denial of any basis for grievance within the peasant community, depiction of "the peasantry" as "a dark people" naturally obedient to their "superiors" (*nachal'stvo*) and incapable of any independent action unless roused to it by "outsiders": these were the themes that recur in official reports or correspondence of noble authorship during 1905–1907. The report of General-Adjutant Litvinov to Minister of Internal Affairs Bulygin on the February events, however, contains a more careful treatment of the investigatory data. Since November 1904, Litvinov noted, *local* peasants had *themselves* begun to organize mass meetings (attended by up to 800 persons) in a wooded swampy area between the villages of Vet', Romanovo and Glamazdino.[54] "Agrarian" issues were openly discussed and debated at these *skhodki*, and the "agitators"—those who organized and spoke at the meetings—were all local residents.[55] Characterization of unrest as the direct "fruit of the activities of revolutionary parties" disappeared from conclusions of the later report, to be replaced by a more nuanced picture.

For, thirdly, the war in the East had acted to draw out the consequences of industrial depression in the South Russian provinces that had followed the financial crisis of 1899. Both the industrial depression and the nationwide strike movement that followed the events of 9 January 1905 meant that a very large contingent of Kursk Province's migrant (*otkhozhie*) laborers from the construction sites, factories and mines of South Russia now languished at home. Litvinov's report echoed the canonical denial that land issues and social tension between peasants and the local large landowners were at the root of unrest. Yet he then documented, somewhat

---

[53] GARF, f. 102, DP OO, op. 233, 1905 g., d. 2550, ll. 100–101. Zvegintsev attributed this perspective to the influence of "outside agitators," in whose work he saw the designs of revolutionary parties. Later and less hysterical reporting tended to incriminate persons from the local peasantry.

[54] This wooded area is probably called *"Verbnik,"* the same meeting place for large gatherings that preceded the outbreak of labor actions on the Shaufus and Meiendorf estate in the summer of 1906 (see Chapter III).

[55] *Nachalo pervoi russkoi revoliutsii*, 628–629. Among the several persons Litvinov indicts as being active in organizing meetings was a migrant worker, Nikolai Osipovich Ovodov (aged 52), who was later elected by the peasant curia as a Member of the Second Duma. He is identified as a Socialist-Revolutionary.

inconsistently with this premise, the fact that a large part of the local labor force was annually forced ("by lack of local wage employment") to quit the province in search of livelihoods elsewhere.[56] The report found no direct link between the "activities of revolutionary parties" and the events of February: it nonetheless highlighted the influence of these peasant-workers on the mood of their fellow villagers in terms later echoed by the Governor himself.

> All these workers have imbibed the negative sides of urban and factory life, have fallen under the sway of revolutionary-socialist propaganda so widespread in those places and become willy-nilly participants in all kinds of disorders and strikes that have been a chronic phenomenon in the southern provinces in recent years. Such workers return home already torn from the land and the peasant economy, with completely perverted views, bearing with them deep into the countryside rash rumors and ideas that, thanks to the ignorance of the peasant masses, are easily accepted. The peasant milieu, it turns out, hungrily pounces on any rumors about socio-economic movements that have emerged in various places in the Empire in recent times, and eagerly devours any source (newspapers, for example) from which news of them may be gleaned… The corrupting influence of periods of work in faraway places is evident in other regards. The investigative reports have confirmed that under the influence of factory life, atheism with political overtones has gained extraordinary development in several of the villages (Glamazdino) that took part in the unrest.[57]

Thus the wave of strikes in the wake of 9 January that had powerful echoes in South Russian urban and industrial centers (the main venues for earnings not only for local migrant laborers but also for those of the province as a whole) must have had particular local effects, in that workers returning home bore with them personal accounts of such events.[58]

It was perhaps most critical, however, that not only did local officials fail to respond effectively to mass timbering on the Popov estate after the events of the night of 6 February, but that the authorities were repeatedly and pub-

---

[56] *Ibid.*, 627–628. The view that Dmitriev District's peasants were better supplied with land, repeated in both reports, simply ignored the fact that the emancipation settlement itself had allotted a larger allotment norm per male soul (3 *desiatiny* 1,800 *sazhen*), because soils in this district had been recognized as significantly inferior in character to the *chernozem* that prevailed in Kursk Province as a whole (2 *desiatiny* 1,800 *sazhen*).

[57] *Ibid.*, 628. The correspondents from Kursk Province responding to the Imperial Free Economic Society survey also observed the leading role of migrant workers and demobilized soldiers ("*manchurtsy*") in their locales, calling these "the element of ferment" among the local populace or "the brains" of the movement. *Trudy IVEO*, 1908, No. 3, May–June, 58.

[58] In the district itself, traffic on the Moscow–Kiev–Voronezh Railway (19 miles from Glamazdino) had been halted by 10 February.

licly humiliated in the process. Able to bring force to bear only weeks after the initial incident, local authorities were helpless to prevent what must be considered successful probing actions by peasant communities in the days before the explosion of 18–20 February. The obvious incapacity of local forces to impede peasant acts—and the abject performance of the new units of mounted patrolmen (*strazhniki*) was notable in this respect—verified the sense that, with the army far away in the East or perhaps otherwise occupied, the peasant in this isolated "bear's corner" could act against his enemies with impunity. It was now not only a question of what peasants read and heard about unrest in the capitals and strike actions in the cities. The concrete experiences of their brethren "just down the road" in contests with local officials—whom peasants of Sal'noe had beaten up, expelled from the village and then, with respectful mien, simply tricked—confirmed the weakness and indecision of local authorities. Direct action, long "necessary," was now a real possibility. This was the sense that was to reemerge, although in different locales and on a far broader scale, in November 1905.

Even before the upheavals of November, the authorities in Kursk Province began to receive news of peasant unrest at scattered sites as early as the last week of October. The outbreaks were preceded by the nationwide rail strike of 10–11 October, in which local railway workers took part,[59] and by a series of short strikes over wage and hour issues in several sugar-beet refineries in the western districts (L'gov, Sudzha, Putivl' and Oboian Districts) between 12 and 16 October.[60] Such strikes were generally successful: in many plants wages were raised by 10–50 percent, hours reduced and other concessions made by the plant owners. The Governor's report on the matter, however, suggested that the temper of the movement hardly reflected the proletarian face of the labor force in the province:

> A favorable issue of the local workers' movement was facilitated, though, mainly as a result of the following circumstance. In Kursk Province, where livelihoods are secured principally by agriculture, the processing of agricultural products dominates factory

---

[59] *RSKG*, Nos. 60, 62, 66, 67, pp. 75–76, 78 (GAKO, f. 1642, op. 1, d. 236, ll. 396, 399, 401, 405); Nos. 61, 64, pp. 76–77 (GAKO, f. 1, op. 15, d. 5, ll. 1–3); No. 63, p. 77 (GAKO, f. 1, op. 15, d. 16, ll. 49–49 ob.).

[60] Strike actions recorded at the following plants: L'gov sugar-refining factory, L'gov station (Vyshne-Derevenskaia Parish), 12–13 October, at the Sabashnikov sugar refinery at Liubimovka (Kostornianskaia Parish, Sudzha District) on 13 October, at the Mar'insk sugar-refining factory at Peny (Ugonskaia Parish, L'gov District) on 13–16 October, at Buryn (Burynskaia Parish, Putivl' District) on 13–14 October, and at the Kleinmikhel' refinery at Ivnia (Kurasovskaia Parish, Oboian District) on 30 October. *RSKG*, Nos. 65, 68, 71, 72, 76, pp. 77–84 (GAKO, f. 1, op. 15, d. 5, ll. 44, 49–49 ob., 71–72).

production, and because of this, the majority of the bigger plants (distilleries, sugar refineries, starch works, oil presses and grist mills) do not work all year round, but
maybe 3–4 months a year. At such plants, the contingent of workers is not constant
and the largest part of them are from the local peasantry, who have not lost their ties to
the land and have not yet adopted the characteristics of the industrial proletariat. For
the majority of the local workers, the interests of fieldwork predominate over the needs
of factory labor. Thus those that work in the plants are not especially demanding with
regard to working conditions, which are sometimes better than the domestic circumstances of the poorer [*maloimushchie*] peasants. The predominance of local peasants
among the workers at our factories and mills is reflected, incidentally, in the fact that
at sugar refineries, workers' demands often included such items as demands for sale or
lease of meadow, for use of pasture, for release of remainders [*zhom*] and molasses for
feeding livestock, for the monopoly of one's village in the collection and carting of
sugar-beet, and so on. Demands of a purely industrial character were imposed only in
plants with constant labor forces.[61]

The resurgence of scattered disturbances in the country districts in late October also occurred in tandem with a rash of anti-Jewish pogroms in the city
of Kursk and several other district centers in the province.[62] Dolgorukov
noted that the pogroms in Kursk, in which peasants from the northern
parishes of Sudzha District took part, had the effect of arousing "the
predatory instincts" of certain elements of the population that were in
short order to be turned against the landowners.[63] In the immediate aftermath of such pogroms in Putivl' District on 23–24 October, destructive
attacks on at least three private estates were carried out by peasants in the
region.

Archival material consulted in connection with this work was far more
unambiguous in associating the November–December disturbances with
the widespread expectation among the peasants of Kursk Province that the
time was nigh for a resolution of the land question once and for all. Surfacing as early as the proclamation of the Manifesto of 12 December
1904, with its vague promises of reform, and expressed broadly in the
petition campaign in the spring of 1905, this expectation was, of course,
not to be realized. The Manifesto of 17 October 1905, appearing immediately in both the local and the national press, would have sorely disappointed peasant readers in any case. Provincial authorities in Kursk, however, evidently deeply fearful about the effects of a public reading out of
the historic document, refused to authorize its proclamation in local

---

[61] *Obzor Kurskoi gubernii za 1905 god*, 32.
[62] RGIA, f. 1405, op. 194, 1908 g., d. 70 ("O protivoevreiskikh besporiadkakh v Kurskoi
gubernii osen'iu 1905 g.").
[63] Dolgorukov, "Agrarnaia volna," No. 2, columns 92–93.

churches and parish administrative offices, as had long been customary
for acquainting the populace with important state acts. The silence of local
authorities at this critical juncture gave rise to strange scenes. Dolgorukov
described how an instance of "loyal revolt" unfolded in a village of
Sudzha District:

> The peasants had been insisting that the priest read from the pulpit the Tsar's Mani-
> festo of 17 October, about which they themselves had been reading in the newspapers
> already for two weeks. The priest continued to refuse for several days, noting the fact
> that there had been no order from the Consistory to do this. Then one fine day, the
> peasants themselves rang the church bell, assembled in full complement and then
> compelled the priest to come to the church by force, don his habit and read the Mani-
> festo from the pulpit from newspaper excerpts that they themselves provided him. Af-
> terwards, they composed a telegram of gratitude to the Sovereign and sent it off to
> [Chairman of the Council of Ministers S. Iu.] Witte. Several days later, one of the ini-
> tiators of this demonstration was arrested by the local authorities and confined in the
> District Jail on the basis of martial law statute.[64]

This was a best-case scenario, however. Official silence elsewhere created a context in which rumor, widely informed by an older and enduring aspiration of the peasantry to a share-out of lands of the private
landowners, very often won the day. In Sudzha District, for example,
peasants reported the commonly held view that the Manifesto allowed
for seizure of landowners' property until 1 January or, by other versions,
until 6 December.[65] Colonel Vel'k, the Chief of the Provincial Gendarmerie, reporting on 7 November from the scene of unrest in Novyi
Oskol' and Staryi Oskol' Districts, noted the following: "Among the
peasants there is borne the rumor that the Tsar has granted a Manifesto
on land, but that this manifesto is being concealed from them. According
to our information, in many villages and hamlets to this very day, neither
the clergy nor the local officials have read out the Manifesto of 17 October or its sequels to the peasants, and nor have they tried to explain them
to the people. This cannot but give rise to the most absurd rumors,
spread about by agitators."[66]

    Governor Borzenko summarized the provincial administration's view
(and its broader cultural caricature of peasant mentalities), writing, in

---

[64] *Ibid.*, columns 93–94.

[65] *Ibid.*, column 94.

[66] GARF, f. 102, DP OO, op. 233 (II), 1905 g., d. 2550, ch. 44, l. 155 (report, Colonel
Vel'k, Commandant of the Kursk Provincial Gendarme Administration to the Department of Police, No. 3859, 12 November 1905).

1906, that "when the Manifesto of 17 October was proclaimed, the peasantry, completely confused [*sbitoe c tolku*] and not in a condition to sort out the essence of the reform, interpreting 'freedom' in its own way and, seized by a thirst for gain and acquisition, greedily and spontaneously rushed out to seize the landowners' property and destroy their homes."[67]

This alleged "confusion" concerning the new "freedoms" was further accentuated by the fact that belated public proclamation of the October Manifesto in the first weeks of November occurred amidst a blare of official and unofficial manifestos, publication in the newspapers of the radical-sounding protocols of the November conference of the All-Russian Peasant Union and the declaration of a state of emergency in Kursk Province.[68] The Manifesto of 3 November 1905 reaffirmed the sanctity of private property and offered the Emperor's stern paternal warning on the evils of disorder for the peace and prosperity of the realm. The *ukazy* published at the same time nonetheless pledged the reduction of redemption payments in 1906 and their elimination in 1907, and dangled the prospect of expanded activity of the Peasant Land Bank as a means by which peasants might gain access to more land. The Manifesto also hinted strongly at a further resolution of the land issue when the new State Duma took up the matter.[69] Such promises had little effect at a time when the drive to "smoke out" the masters in Kursk Province was now in full swing. Belated, frantic efforts by officials to publicize Imperial pronouncements had little effect—except to prompt many peasants to quit making redemption payments immediately.[70]

Matters were little aided by the declaration of a state of "increased security" (*usilennaia okhrana*) throughout Kursk Province on 4 November.

---

[67] RGIA, f. 1284, op. 194 (1906 g.), d. 71, l. 4.

[68] GARF, f. 102, DP OO, op. 233 (II), 1905 g., d. 2550, ch. 44, l. 96. The order declaring a state of emergency arrived in Kursk 5 November. *RSKG*, No. 77, p. 84 (GAKO, f. 1, op. 15, d. 63, l. 140).

[69] The Manifesto of 3 November 1905 ("Ob uluchshenii blagosostoianiia i oblegcheniia polozheniia krest'ianskago naseleniia") in *PSZ*, III, v. 25, No. 26871, 790. The related *ukazy* with regard to redemption payments (No. 26872) and streamlining procedures at the Peasant Land Bank (No. 26875) follow (791).

[70] The Marshal of the Nobility of Sudzha District wired the Governor on 12 November: "[The Land Captain V. A.] Rapp, with 60 Cossacks, publicly read out the Manifesto of 3 November in the village of Sula. The people responded with Homeric laughter. The manifesto had been read out on the 6th without the soldiers. (Now) Rapp simply refuses to leave Izvekovo and begs to be told how he is to explain the manifesto. I am distributing copies of the manifesto that has been printed here in the thousands." *RSKG*, No. 133, p. 113 (GAKO, f. 1, op. 15, d. 7, ll. 210–211).

The statute gave local authorities broad latitude to use administrative measures against individuals, organizations or assemblies deemed to be a menace to public order. Dolgorukov pointed to the particularly damaging effect of declaring a state of emergency at the same time that the October Manifesto was finally being grudgingly read out in the churches. "In fact, the peasants were very well acquainted with the text of the Manifesto, which by this time had been solemnly read out in the cathedral church and in which had been proclaimed freedoms of speech, of union, of assembly. No one had interpreted it to them in any way to the contrary, but suddenly the authorities were dispersing assemblies, unions were being banned and one could not even speak with one's fellow villagers! ... Most damaging of all has been the application of the Statute of Increased Security, which was declared here simultaneously with the proclamation of the Manifesto of 17 October. This completed the confusion in peasants' understanding of things: on the one hand, the Tsar allegedly granted freedom, but the lords [gospoda] and the officials are opposed to this freedom."[71]

The waters were roiled still further by efforts of conservative nobles to propagandize their own point of view among the peasantry after 17 October. In an extraordinary session in the wake of the proclamation in St. Petersburg, the Assembly of the Kursk Provincial Nobility, led by Provincial Marshal V. P. Dorrer, Prince N. F. Kasatkin-Rostovskii and the soon-to-be notorious N. E. Markov, adopted a declaration that made known its displeasure at the reforms and affirmed, in the name of the Russian people, its unshakable fidelity to Orthodoxy, Autocracy and Nationality. Resolutions annexed to the document bore the pungent anti-intellectual and anti-Semitic strains that had been features of the province's particularly reactionary right-wing resurgence. Disseminated through the good offices of the Land Captains and District Marshals of the Nobility, efforts were made to get copies of these resolutions adopted by local peasant communities.[72]

Ominous portents thus began to multiply in the last week of October in a context of growing violence, the effects of poor harvests that struck particularly at the usual cash crops (it should be recalled that October was the usual month for tax collection), official confusion and a growing aggres-

---

[71] Dolgorukov, "Agrarnaia volna," No. 2, column 97.

[72] *Russkiia Vedomosti*, 8 November 1905, 3, col. 6. The effort was associated with the newly founded right-wing Kursk People's Party of Order, in which Dorrer, Kasatkin-Rostovskii, Markov, G. A. Shechkov and M. Ia. Govorukho-Otrok were leading figures. The party merged with the Union of Russian People shortly thereafter. Biographical sketches in Barinova, *Rossiiskoe dvorianstvo*, 181–193 (Markov), 198–202 (Dorrer), 202–206 (Shechkov), 207–210 (Govorukho-Otrok), 210–214 (Kasatkin-Rostovskii).

siveness of opposing sides in "census" society in publicly pushing their various agenda. The railway strike, labor actions at the sugar-refining plants and flour mills in a number of localities in the western districts and the return of numbers of migrant workers from the strike-torn southern provinces brought home to local peasants the extent to which unrest was sweeping the Empire. In such an environment, in which the sense of the authorities' indecision and loss of control was palpable, it was perhaps inevitable that proclamation of "freedom"—inseparable in peasant thinking from final settlement of the land question—should now be seized upon as cover for the now very real prospect of getting rid of the lords and sharing out their lands. The Manifesto evaded the land question entirely, of course, and government pronouncements offered only vague hints at its resolution by the Duma. The circumstances surrounding its actual proclamation in the tense atmosphere of the moment, however, put the very worst face on matters. This gave force to peasant rejection of any interpretation of "freedom" that did not address its corollary—the "return" of the land to those who cultivated it by their own labor—as an attempt by the lords to conceal its "true" nature.

These points were well understood by Admiral V. F. Dubasov, appointed as General-Adjutant to the Emperor to quell unrest in Kursk and nearby provinces (and soon to gain such notoriety in the same role during the December days in Moscow). In a cable to the Minister of Internal Affairs on November 20 (in the wake of the most serious unrest, as it turned out), he reported that "[in Kursk] it is worse than in Chernigov Province… The main reason for the disorders that have broken out here is the long-critical question of land. The peasants consider that the source of their problems lies in the acute shortage of land [*malozemel'e*]. The *pomeshchiki* have a lot of land, and the peasants have decided to squeeze them out and take over their land. Active propaganda, in part by local elements, in part by outsiders, has roused them to this. The catalyst was the Manifesto of 17 October, since the peasants expected land, but did not receive it." Dubasov went on to warn his readers of the dangers of the situation. "The movement has a character, given which a struggle against it is very much hindered. All of the disorders take place in the absence of troops and cease with their appearance, but once the soldiers are recalled or transferred, unrest is renewed. Moreover, because of the insufficiency of the number of troops, it is impossible to have them everywhere. Troops are not sufficient even in the main centers of unrest. I foresee the inevitability of turning to severe measures—the physical annihilation of one or two villages—if in spite of my warnings the peasants undertake new disorders after departure of the troops. Otherwise, the fact that peasant disorders go clearly unpunished will call forth new unrest on a scale against which it will become impossible to struggle."[73]

The incapacity of local officials, in the absence of troops, to respond immediately and effectively to peasant challenges, as was the case in the earliest moments of the February disturbances, was thus to be reproduced as a factor in encouraging rural disorders in November. At Sal'noe between 6 and 15 February, the villagers not only successfully deflected efforts to restore order, but also publicly humiliated the representatives of authority sent to investigate. The initial outbreak in Novyi Oskol' District on 1 November 1905 at the settlement of Chernianka likewise involved, in its very first phase, threats against police officials (three constables and seven police guards) on the scene, who are then notably absent from descriptions of subsequent attempts to restore order in the village. Similarly, the first disorders in Skorodenskaia Parish, Sudzha District, at the settlement of Sula on 7 November, followed within days the unsuccessful attempts of local officials to arrest arsonists in the adjacent village of Izvekovo (Nemcha)—attempts that resulted in their public humiliation (the local Land Captain and a police captain were roughed up and forced to flee) and the freeing of five detainees. The inability of local authorities to bring any force to bear at the outset of unrest emboldened peasant militants in adjacent villages.

The renewal of rural disorders in Kursk Province at the end of May 1906—and the sharp change in peasant tactics that became evident—took place in more complex local conditions. Undoubtedly, the new wave of disturbances was associated with the cul-de-sac into which the First State Duma's debates over the land question and amnesty had entered. Though dissolution of the Duma on 9 July was said to have "strongly agitated minds" in the rural districts, it provoked as few incidents of protest as would the dismal end to the Constituent Assembly in 1917. Evidently, conclusions on the Duma's likely success in resolving the critical issues of land reform and amnesty had already been drawn. It was also now obvious that local authorities were no longer without resources in combating

---

[73] GARF, f. 102, DP OO, op. 233 (II), 1905 g., d. 2550, ch. 44, ll. 160–160 ob. S. Iu. Witte recalled an interview with Dubasov before the convening of the First State Duma, during which the Admiral advised in favor of enacting a law, even before the Duma opened, that would leave in the possession of the peasant the lands that they had seized. When Witte objected, Dubasov replied thus: "You will calm the peasants [by this measure], and the landowners will be better off, since otherwise the peasants will take all the land from them." *Vospominaniia*, Tom 3, 145.

unrest. Even if troop strength in the province was still chronically insufficient, six months of the presence of more significant numbers of infantry, cavalry and Cossack detachments in the affected zones and the process of investigations and arrests that could now be pushed forward aggressively by local authorities must have exerted a certain influence on even the most militant peasants. Yet the resurgence of agrarian disorders in Kursk Province in late spring and summer owed the most to the onset of crucial stages of the agricultural calendar—hay mowing and the harvest of grains—and by itself clearly distinguishes peasant unrest during 1906 from the disturbances of 1905, even in the same localities. If the single-minded intention of the peasants to "smoke out" the lords was the most obvious motif in the movement during 1905—which led many commentators to liken it to the *Pugachevshchina*—then deprivation of the estates of their laborers at the most critical moment and the obviously unacceptable conditions put forth for renewal of work revealed that this motif remained quite alive in 1906 as well. In part because their acts concentrated on the economic links (wages and rents) between the landowners and the adjacent villagers, however, the disorders of 1906 appear to have propelled the effort to realize a more concrete local program to the forefront of direct action. After suppression of the *Pugachevshchina* of 1905 and from under the machinery of military repression, one witnesses in the late spring and summer of 1906 a resumption of the stubborn and desperate struggle of the rural population with the neighboring private landowners—but especially, once again, with the magnates—to force upon these latter essential changes in local economic conditions.

4. Geographical Distribution of Rural Disorders

As has been noted in Chapter II, our collection of the data has to be viewed to a certain extent as a sample. Moreover, it was not infrequently the case that, when events slipped out of control, reportage from the countryside—at best hardly at the level of that which one encounters in the urban centers in any case—began to lose much of its detail generally and the identity of villages participating in unrest in particular. That being said, our data nonetheless suggest the fallacy of the broad geographical frames of reference for the revolutionary events of 1905–1907 that have generally been employed in many historical treatments. What appears as a widespread wave of unrest even from the point of view of numbers of parishes "affected" turns out to concern a fairly small population of villages in each district. The usual tenor of much of the historiography has emphasized the great scale of rural disturbances during 1905–1907. One has grown accustomed to the presentation of events in highly aggregated treatments, commonly by region, by province or by district. Such analyses have depicted a truly massive wave of unrest. Details for localities appear as illustration, without reference to the particular internal dynamic at work in provincial events. This problem was succinctly stated in the short review of the 1905–1907 rural unrest in four provinces of the Central Agricultural Region (Voronezh, Tambov, Orel and Kursk) in a 1956 article by P. N. Abramov. The author noted that if all 51 districts in the four provinces reported disturbances, thus creating the impression of a movement of great scale, the picture changed when the analysis descended to the level of parishes. Of 954 parishes only 456 (47.8 percent) recorded disturbances. Of 2,509 populated points in Voronezh Province, incidents of unrest were associated with only 243 (9.7 percent) of these.[74] Abramov did not analyze the other provinces in his survey and did not offer a characterization of the villages that were swept up in the unrest. The only other extant pieces on the Kursk peasantry in the revolution, if extraordinarily rich in both narrative and archival references, failed to make any such attempt.[75]

The *zemstvo* data for Kursk Province were quite adequate to the task, although only in concert with other source materials. The major difficulty lay in following the continuing reorganization and consolidation of parishes throughout the period under review. Census data was collected in the 1880s for 216 parishes; the appendix to the 1905 gubernatorial report to the Ministry of Internal Affairs noted 195. From this beginning point, references in the archival and published documents on the unrest, a listing of parishes contained in an *Adres'-Kalendar Kurskoi gubernii* for 1912, later publications of the Statistical Bureau of the Provincial Zemstvo (an

---

[74] Abramov, "Iz istorii krest'ianskogo dvizheniia," *IZ*, 57 (1956), 300.

[75] *Ibid*, 294–311; Komissiia pri Kurskom gubispolkome po organizatsii prazdnovaniia 20-letiia revoliutsii 1905 goda, *1905 god v Kurskoi gubernii*, 41–83; A. Kazarin, "Bor'ba za zemliu," in Matusevich and Kazarin, *1905 god v Kurskoi gubernii*, 55–91; Maliavskii, "Krest'ianskoe dvizhenie," 1–69. A later Soviet specialist produced crude estimates for neighboring provinces that were somewhat higher for 1905–1906: 356 active villages for Tambov (of 3,123 villages or 11.9%) and 437 for Voronezh Province (out of 2,419 populated villages, or 18.1%): Stepynin, *Krest'ianstvo*, 61 (table 2), 102 (table 4), 133–134 (estimates for 1906). Even accepting such estimates, which left aside the issue of "repeaters" for 1905 *and* 1906, they by no means obviate our point that agrarian unrest was in fact narrowly concentrated within the peasant community as a whole.

annual agricultural review), a 1913 edition of the military-topographical atlas and a directory appended to the anniversary documentary collection (1956) allowed for the location of all place names in the 1905 parishes.[76] All 15 districts in Kursk Province reported incidents of collective actions. But the varying intensity of unrest is reflected in the ranking by total numbers of disturbances in the sample: Sudzha District (56 incidents); Novyi Oskol' (43), Dmitriev (41), L'gov (37), Oboian (27, all in 1905) and Staryi Oskol' (24) Districts, accounting for 71 percent (228) of all incidents during 1905–1906 (140 incidents in 1905, or 72 percent; 88 incidents in 1906 or 69 percent). These formed, we have seen, the three geographical centers of unrest in the western, central and eastern parts of the province.[77] Events in Putivl' District in December 1905 (18 incidents), during which disorders bore an intensely political cast, and disturbances in Graivoron and Korocha Districts, which tended to be associated with particular villages both in 1905 and in 1906—Rakitnaia and Borisovka in Graivoron District, and several settlements in Nekliudovskaia Parish, Korocha District—occupy a more specific place in this scheme. The geography of the 1906 disorders, in part, overlapped those of 1905: indeed, a number of sites in Dmitriev, Sudzha, Graivoron, Korocha and Ryl'sk Districts evidenced high degrees of militancy in both years. In L'gov District—where only scattered incidents of unrest are noted in November–December 1905—most participating settlements (those associated with

---

[76] Kurskoe gubernskoe *zemstvo*. Statisticheskoe biuro. *SSSKG. Vyp. I Kurskii uyezd; Vyp. II. Statisticheskie svedeniia po L'govskomu uyezdu; Vyp. III. Statisticheskie svedeniia po Dmitrievskomu uyezdu; Vyp. IV. Statisticheskie svedeniia po Sudzhanskomu uyezdu; Vyp. V. Statisticheskie svedeniia po Fatezhskomu uyezdu; Vyp. VI. Statisticheskie svedeniia po Ryl'skomu uyezdu; Vyp. VII. Statisticheskie svedeniia po Putivl'skomu uyezdu; Vyp. VIII. Statisticheskie svedeniia po Shchigrovskomu uyezdu; Vyp. IX. Statisticheskie svedeniia po Graivoronskomu uyezdu; Vyp. X. Statisticheskie svedeniia po Belgorodskomu uyezdu; Vyp. XI. Statisticheskie svedeniia po Novooskol'skomu uyezdu; Vyp. XII. Statisticheskie svedeniia pa Timskomu uyezdu; Vyp. XIII. Statisticheskie svedeniia po Korochanskomu uyezdu; Vyp. XIV. Statisticheskie svedeniia po Starooskol'skomu uyezdu*. The collection for Oboian District was published separately (1883). Villages in each parish were counted by hand. The 1905 listing of *volosti* appears in *Obzor Kurskoi gubernii za 1905 god* (1906), 177, the 1912 listing in *Kurskii calendar.' Spravochnaia i adresnaia kniga za 1912 g.*, 94–100. A list of populated places in the former Kursk Province is attached to *RSKG*, 231–247.

[77] Our findings for all 323 incidents grouped the 15 districts as follows: Sudzha District: 56 incidents; Novyi Oskol': 43; Dmitriev: 41; L'gov: 37; Oboian: 27 (all in 1905); Staryi Oskol': 24; Putivl': 21; Graivoron: 16; Ryl'sk: 12; Shchigrov: 11; Korocha: 9; Kursk: 9; Tim: 8; Belgorod: 6; Fatezh: 3.

the Bariatinskii estates) appear in the sample for the first time only during 1906. Conversely, after the violent revolutionary surge of November 1905 the large Oskol' Valley centers along the Southeastern Railway line in Novyi Oskol' and Staryi Oskol' Districts were mostly (Ol'shanka and Golubina aside) quiescent in 1906. The December events in Putivl' District were also to have almost no further resonance in the official record in the following year.

Inspection of the entire sample of incidents shows that only 109 (55.9 percent) of the 195 *volosti* extant in 1905 were sites of unrest. Out of 2,916 populated places noted by census takers in 1882–1885, only 289 (9.9 percent)[78] appear in official records reviewed for this work, a narrow concentration that may have been typical for other provinces in the CAR, as the work of Abramov and Stepynin has shown. The impression of a broad "mass" movement of a homogeneous peasant mass is thus not borne out from this angle of analysis. Further, even in "active" parishes, viewed as a subset, the resonance of collective acts of unrest among neighboring villagers was often not especially pronounced: the number of villages noted in connection with disturbances in any given parish very rarely rose above a fifth of the settlements within its bounds. This rule nonetheless conceals the exception: that unusual intensity that characterized disorders in locales in which they first unfolded during the three "peaks" just mentioned. In great part, this intensity reflected the degree to which large-scale incidents emerged and expanded rapidly in scope within a cluster of villages and parishes that were directly adjacent to each other, and the manner in which this intensity was diffused or lost as the distance from the original centers of outbreaks increased. In the localities in which disorders originated, participation was relatively high.

The close physical proximity of villages participating in outbreaks of unrest thus appears as a crucial aspect of the geographical distribution of unrest. Not surprisingly, the expansion of a zone of disturbances moved outward along principal local means of communication. From sites in the most westerly portion of Dmitriev District, disorders spread into both Chernigov and Orel Provinces along the axis of the main Sevsk-Glukhov highway that ran within a kilometer of Prilepy. During the first days of November 1905, the early locus of unrest in Novyi Oskol' District coin-

---

[78] This group included the district seats of L'gov and Sudzha, at which, as we have noted in the previous chapter, disturbances reported at overcrowded prison facilities led to the escape of peasant detainees arrested for participation in agrarian unrest. These were not included in our subset of villages.

cided almost exactly with the stretch of the Elets-Valuiki (Southeastern Railway) right-of-way line north and south of Chernianka station and then spread west and east along roads linking Chernianka with the adjacent parishes. The Sudzha–Kursk post road bisected the zone of the most intense disturbances that began in Skorodenskaia Parish, Sudzha District, on 7 November. Unrest in Putivl' District during December 1905 spread to the east along the Moscow–Kiev–Voronezh Railway into Glushets Parish from its origins in the "railway towns" in the western part of the district, across the provincial border from Konotop and its railhead in Chernigov Province.

Within the narrow circle of documentary evidence of principally local origin, there are few indications concerning the direct influence of peasant disorders in adjacent provinces on the movement in Kursk Province itself. Undoubtedly, unrest in the western parishes of Putivl' District in December 1905 had roots in the troubles of late November in Konotop District, Chernigov Province, and its suppression was treated as a part of the overall effort to put down revolts in the larger zone. The initial phase of these disorders was quite clearly associated with the political militancy of the large contingent of peasant-workers from villages in the affected parishes of Putivl' District who were employed in the repair shops and rail yard of the Moscow–Kiev–Voronezh Railway at Konotop.[79] Conversely, events in Kursk Province ignited disturbances in adjacent provinces. During February 1905, peasants from the zone of disturbances in Dmitriev District not only pursued their actions against the Meiendorf holdings into Sevsk District (Orel Province), but also appeared there in large numbers to incite and lead local attacks on estates elsewhere in Sevsk District and Glukhov District, Chernigov Province (among these, the Tereshchenko estate at Khinel').[80]

The wave of November disorders in Kursk Province, though, is harder to characterize in this manner. Unrest in Novyi Oskol' and Staryi Oskol' Districts began in the weeks following intense outbreaks of unrest during 22–23 October in Balashov District, Saratov Province, in which forty estates were attacked and burned, and in Gorodniansk Uyezd, Chernigov Province, where similar assaults on a number of gentry holdings are recorded during 23–30 October. In the adjacent Voronezh Province, incidents of unauthorized timbering and pasturing, of thefts of grain and fodder, multiplied throughout October. But major attacks on private estates

---

[79] Drozdov, *Agrarnye volneniia*, 75–147.
[80] *Nachalo pervoi russkoi revoliutsii*, Nos. 398–415, pp. 612–650.

began in Voronezh Province on 4 November 1905 in Staro-Bezginskaia Parish, Korotoiak Uyezd, directly adjoining Novyi Oskol' District. Reporting on a simultaneous looting and burning of four estates, the local Land Captain linked these acts to the troubles that had begun in Chernianka (30 *versta* from Staraia Bezginka) three days earlier. Large-scale outbreaks spread thereafter to nearby parishes in Korotoiak District and to parishes of Biriuch and Nizhne-Devitsk *uyezdy* contiguous to Novyi Oskol' and Staryi Oskol' Districts.[81]

Such connections are otherwise more difficult to establish with any real precision. On the basis of rumors circulating in the rural districts in the wake of the February events, provincial authorities awaited the spring and summer months of 1905 with great concern. Yet Kursk Province remained generally quiet, despite powerful unrest during these months in localities immediately to the south in Khar'kov Province. During the events of November–December 1905, the main clusters of incidents of unrest of record in Khar'kov Province are concentrated in the time period from late November 1905 and January 1906, at which juncture the movement in Kursk Province (save for Putivl' District) had already receded significantly and lapsed into a tense silence.[82]

5. Geographical Distributions and the Large Estates

That agrarian disorders in Kursk Province during 1905–1906 flowed from the "land question"—both in its very real aspect for peasant communities and in its equally potent capacity to crystallize a larger sense of peasant grievance—would seem evident from much of the foregoing analysis. The land issue itself and its relationship to the natural increase in rural population, however, cannot be viewed apart from those developments that had adversely affected the strategies that peasant households had adopted to combat this central tension: leasing non-allotment acreage, local off-farm earnings and large-scale migration of labor in search of work outside the province. Worsening of conditions in relation to local markets of land and labor appear in particular relief during the rural disorders of the late spring

---

[81] *Revoliutsionnoe dvizhenie v Voronezhskoi gubernii*, 290–293, Nos. 204–206 (Staro-Bezginskaia) and following; *Revoliutsiia 1905–1907 gg. v Rossii. Vysshii pod'em revoliutsii 1905–1907 gg. Noiabr'-dekabr' 1905 goda. Ch. II*, 319–329, Nos. 266–278; see also Stepynin, ed., *Khronika*.

[82] Astakhov, ed., *Revoliutsionnye sobytiia*.

and summer of 1906. The social face of the disturbances was associated directly with the land issue—disorders were by and large directed against noble landowners and to a lesser extent against the estates of the higher urban classes and installations of the state itself. The tense and hostile relationship of the Kursk peasantry with the class of former serf-owners is evident here, a history that is attested not only by a long record of rural disturbances before 1905,[83] but also by the deep prejudice mixed with fear regarding peasants—the "dark people"—that saturate documents of official origin or noble authorship during this era.

But it is worth repeating once again that dependency between lord and peasant was a mutual one—the position of the vast majority of privately owned estates was such that there was little alternative outside of the traditional reliance on land lease to extract cash or labor dues and a limited demesne cultivation worked with peasant labor and inventory. In this connection, the narrow concentration of rural unrest in 1905–1906 (9.9 percent of populated settlements) should give one pause. If the relationships of mutual reciprocity between representatives of socially unequal strata in this rural setting continued to retain stable measures of predictability and the older personal character of such interactions was maintained, then local peasants seem to have been less likely to consider direct action, even despite a sense of profound discontent.[84] To be sure, on both sides, interactions in the old way were more and more fraught with tension. But peasant unrest in 1905–1906 broke out—and was repeated—in those localities in Kursk Province in which older reciprocal relationships between peasant "clients" and landlord "patrons" had not only begun to be violated, but had largely ceased to operate at all. The decline in the fortunes of the noble estate forced the new generation of landowners to look more severely on violations of their "rights," to which their fathers had perhaps turned a blind eye, and to strive to sharply restrict the "privileges" that

---

[83] Nifontov and Zlatoustovskii, eds., *Krest'ianskoe dvizhenie v Rossii v 1880–1889 gg.*, No. 12, pp. 60–65; Nos. 215–217, pp. 461–469; No. 255, p. 547; No. 336, pp. 697–700. Shapkarin, ed., *Krest'ianskoe dvizhenie v Rossii v 1890–1899 gg.*, Nos. 48–50, pp. 129–137; No. 129, pp. 317–319. Anfimov, ed., *Krest'ianskoe dvizhenie v Rossii v 1900–1904 gg.*, 86–88, 151–153, 268, 271–272, 277.

[84] I am also impressed here by the image of the noble landowner (*pomeshchik*) that appears ubiquitously in peasant folk tales as reviewed in an essay by Maureen Perrie, "Folklore as Evidence," *RR*, 48 (1989), 119–143. These tales suggest that an unremitting hostility, mixed with a certain condescension, characterized peasants' attitudes toward the squires, but on occasion (*"Muzhik razgadyvaet zagadki"*), the landowner retained his old role as judge and arbiter between peasants.

their fathers had granted to their peasant neighbors in an effort to ease the tense economic situation of the villagers. The Governor himself admitted that landowners did not always behave "irreproachably" in relation to the peasants or with the necessary spirit of compromise (*ustupchivost'*). "Many of them, despite an increase in the value of labor, stood against even the most moderate elevation of wages during the grain harvest and leased lands indispensable [to the peasants] only at greatly inflated rents."[85]

Yet the attentive reader will have observed the frequency with which outbreaks of unrest were associated with larger "modernized" estates—frequently estates of *absentee* noble owners—and the zones of their influence in given geographical locales. Indeed, the inordinate influence of large estates on the situation in different locales seems to have been commonly acknowledged at the time, and appeared as a major theme of the March conferences of Land Captains convened at the behest of the Ministry of Internal Affairs in the wake of the events of February 1905.[86] Of particular note in the archival record of unrest in 1905 or 1906, the huge latifundia of Iusupov, Kharitonenko and Sheremet'ev in Graivoron District in the southern part of the province were sites of disorders in both years. In the eastern districts, peasant unrest completely destroyed the large holdings of Kasatkin-Rostovskii, Shevtsov, Trubetskoi, Orlov-Davydov and Miatlev in Novyi Oskol' District during November 1905; the large estates of Korobkov, Popov, Dmitriev and others in Staryi Oskol' District, if only a few were directly attacked in November, were all the subject of labor actions in 1906. In the western districts, unrest on the large estates of the Meiendorf heirs, Shaufus and Volkov (later Zablotsky) in Dmitriev District was to recur throughout 1905–1906, ceasing only with the billeting of an entire squadron of dragoons at Khomutovka on a permanent basis. Extensive holdings of the Zhekulin heirs and of Evreinov and the Sabashnikovy in the northern parishes of Sudzha District, along with other "modernizing" estates, attracted particular attention in November 1905; incidents of unrest were to recur in this vicinity during June 1906. Disturbances also recurred on the vast holdings of the Bariatinskii *maiorat* in L'gov, Ryl'sk and Putivl' Districts (especially in June 1906), and on those of the Kleinmikhel' in Oboian District and of the heirs of Artem Iakovlevich Tereshchenko throughout the province.

---

[85] GARF, f. 102, DP OO, op. 236, d. 700, ch. 58, ll. 194–194 ob.

[86] RGIA, f. 1291, op. 30, 1905 g., d. 4-b.

The transition of a number of the larger estates in the province to direct exploitation of demesne arable, introduction of multi-field crop rotations that evolved well outside the traditional grain culture, heavy investment in inventory and modern technology, down to construction or expansion of plant for processing the estate's own produce, could not pass without the most serious consequences for adjacent villages. The sugar-refining industry merits special attention here, not only for its rapid growth in capacity and output in these years,[87] but also for the participation of outside capital investors that was a crucial feature of its development. These outsiders include the Tereshchenko clan most notably, but also representatives of the Moscow merchant class (Botkiny, Sabashnikovy) and Kievan investors (Galperiny, Balakhovskie) that appear as owners and members of the boards of directors in industrial directories of the era.[88]

Owners of larger estates occupied a central position in the process of agro-industrial development. They possessed not only a "feudal" elite's strategic local position in terms of landholding, but also, joined to their very substantial landholdings, access to large blocks of capital. These made for an ensemble of resources that allowed them to react flexibly to changing economic conditions, and to balance wage labor and leasehold strategies in order to maximize incomes. Large estates were thus far more likely to invest heavily in plant and equipment, to introduce new crops in multiple rotations, and to absorb the freight costs of shipping large quantities of grain over the Empire's expanded railway network.[89] Such estates were better able to come up with added increments of wages in order to attract day labor during the most intense intervals of the agricultural calendar, often to the detriment of smaller owners in the vicinity. Thus, every summer, when administrators of the large latifundia owned by the Tereshchenko family in Putivl' and Ryl'sk

---

[87] See Chapter One.

[88] Of 22 agro-industrial firms registered in Kursk Province in 1908, 11 of these were joint-stock companies engaged in sugar-refining operations run out of Kiev. The rest of these plants were operated by the families (incorporated or unincorporated) of absentee owners of the large estates. Most were established in the period after 1890. Ministerstvo Torgovli i Promyshlennosti. *Spisok*, II: 178–179; S"ezd sovetov predstaviteli promyshlennosti i torgovli, *Fabrichno-zavodskaia*, vyp. II, at Nos. 7737D, 7739D, 7740D, 7747D, 7749D, 7752D, 7755D. Anfimov, *Krupnoe*. The Botkin estate at Novaia Tavolzhanka, Belgorod District, described in Ministerstvo zemledeliia i gosudarstvennykh imushchestv, *Opisaniia otdel'nykh russkikh khoziaistv* (hereinafter *Opisaniia*), 42–61.

[89] That such costs were generally considered oppressive is indicated by the complaints raised against them during sessions of local Committees on the Needs of the Rural Economy. See, for example, the report of N. E. Markov, "On Transport and Trade of Grain" (Shchigrov Committee), *Trudy mestnykh komitetov*, 826–841.

Districts hired up to 10,000 workers to tend vast sowings of sugar-beet that fed their refineries, smaller landowners complained loudly that the wages paid stripped the countryside bare of peasant laborers.[90]

The industrial aspect of estates of this sort is quite clear from the sources. Operations of the Tereshchenko clan in Kursk Province had long had its original center (since 1861) at Tetkino (Tetkinskaia Parish, Ryl'sk District), the site of the estate's two flour mills and two sugar refineries, which employed 1,328 workers and had an estimated annual output of 3,433,106 rubles. The Kursk estates of these "sugar kings" included large units purchased in the adjoining parishes of Ryl'sk and Putivl' Districts (27,586 *desiatiny*) and at Timiriazevo in Staryi Oskol' District (5,414 *desiatiny*), all estates equipped with the latest agricultural technology and running multiple rotations with sowings oriented toward both market demand and the processing plants of the owners. These holdings were but a part of a more extensive clan operation not only in Kursk Province, but also in Orel, Khar'kov, Ekaterinoslav, Kiev, Chernigov, Podol' and Volyn Provinces.[91]

On estates of the Bariatinskii *maiorat* held by Prince Aleksandr Vladimirovich Bariatinskii (1848–1910) in L'gov (11,428 *desiatiny*), Ryl'sk (11,781) and Putivl' (28,206) Districts, two flour mills, a grist mill, three distilleries and two sugar refineries (991 workers, 2,562,896 rubles annual output) processed raw produce from vast and varied sowings. Initial investment in these facilities dated to the years 1858–1864, but an additional distillery was built in 1882, a large new sugar-refining plant was added in 1899 and another distillery was opened in 1905. In the 1890s, the Bariatinskii family trust leased its holdings in Putivl' District (Krupets-Shalygino) to the Tereshchenko family partnership.[92]

---

[90] Verner, ed., *Kurskaia guberniia*, 128.

[91] *Spisok*, II: 75, 179–180. Ministerstvo zemledeliia i gosudarstvennykh imushchestv, Departament zemledeliia, *Kratkiia spravochnyia svedeniia* (hereinafter *Kratkaia*), 46–52. Also Anfimov, *Krupnoe*, 169–170.

[92] *Spisok*, I: 73: II: 178–179. Dates of founding from *Fabrichno-zavodskaia...* at Nos. 1080D, 1081D, 4514D, 4522D, 4545D, 6845D, 7746D, 7757D. The Bariatinskii clan held at least 69,159 *desiatiny* in Ryl'sk, L'gov Sudzha and Putivl' Districts, including the eighteenth-century family seat at Ivanovskoe. These included the vast Krupets-Shalygino complex (28,206 *desiatiny*) in Putivl' District, leased to the Tereshchenko family firm by 1908. Compiled from Kurskoe gubernskoe *zemstvo*, Statisticheskoe biuro, *SSSKG, Vyp. II* (L'gov District), *IV* (Sudzha), *VI* (Ryl'sk) and *VII* (Putivl'); *KGV*, "Spisok lits imeiushchikh pravo uchastiia v vyborakh glasnikh v L'govskoe Uyezdnoe Sobranie na trekhletie s 1901 g.," prilozhenie k No. 3, 4 ianvaria 1901; *Kratkaia*, 31–36. The Bariatinskii estates were held in *maiorat*—clan property indivisible in testamentary proceedings and ruled by primogeniture—by Imperial dispensation.

The Rebinder estate at Shebekino (Shebekinskaia Parish, Belgorod District) ran a sugar refinery, distillery and saw mill employing 520 workers: annual output in 1908 totaled 1,858,992 rubles. The estate itself had an area of 3,631 *desiatiny* (of which some 2,300 were in forest), but from the mid-1880s, the administration had embarked on an aggressive campaign to rent substantial acreage from nearby estate owners. Employing a multiple crop rotation, it pursued the cultivation, among other crops, of large sowings of sugar-beets (1,600 *desiatiny*) for the estate's own processing and winter wheat (1,100 *desiatiny*) for export. The estate was linked directly to the Kursk-Khar'kov-Sevastopol' Railway—Rebinderovo station—via Nezhegol to the Belgorod-Kupiansk branch. The Rebinder operation maintained 1,000 head of oxen, over 200 horses and a vast stock of improved tools and implements, including three steam threshers imported from Hungary. Experiments had been conducted in an effort to develop a motorized plow. Especially high wages were offered to graduates of the local Mariinskaia Agricultural School at Shebekino to lure them into the cadres of estate administration.[93]

The ministerial observer found that wages were often bid up by competition between Rebinder and the Botkin brothers' estate operations at nearby Novaia Tavolzhanka. In the 1890s, the Botkin estate (3,411 *desiatiny*, bought in 1883) inaugurated an aggressive policy of investment. The brothers funded construction (1890) of a large sugar refinery (911 workers, 1,582,494 rubles annual output), a water-driven mill with six stations that joined hulling, grist and flour milling capacities, three brickworks that put out 300,000 bricks a year, a repair facility that employed 27 full-time masters and a two-and-a-half-mile rail link that connected the estate with Nezhegol station. Like the adjacent Rebinder operation, Botkin administrators leased large tracts from adjacent estates: 6,701 *desiatiny* in 1896. On the demesne and the leased lands, estate administration ran a highly sophisticated multiple rotation that yearly allowed for just over 2,200 *desiatiny* in sugar-beets. The estate maintained around 600 head of work stock (oxen and horses); its steam threshers and domestic and imported plowing, seeding and harvesting technology had required capital outlay estimated at 110,000 rubles. Brick and wooden structures were valued at 220,000 rubles (excluding refinery and mill).[94]

Count Konstantin Petrovich Kleinmikhel' (1840–1912) operated sugar-beet refineries on each of his Oboian District estates: at Rzhava (2,787 *desi-*

---

[93] *Spisok*, I: 158; II: 179; *Opisaniia*, 79–81.
[94] *Spisok*, II: 178; *Fabrichno-zavodskaia*, No. 7750D; *Opisaniia*, 42–61.

atiny), Ol'shanskaia Parish, and at Ivnia (6,374 *desiatiny*), Kurasovskaia Parish, and his son and heir sat on the board of the joint-stock company that ran a plant on the Kleinmikhel' estate at Pereverzevka, Dolzhenskaia Parish, in the same district. Combined, the three estates' (13,977 *desiatiny*) sugar refineries had a total annual output of 1,770,842 rubles and a force of 1,166 workers just after the revolution. An 1882 report on the Ivnia-Troitskoe estate reveals that its operations, even at that time, had gone over to multiple rotations on lands cultivated directly, had invested heavily in imported horse-drawn inventory and had refitted the sugar refinery to work on a diffusion process rather than a simple press.[95]

On the extensive latifundium of Princess Zinaida Nikolaevna Iusupova (1861–1939), Countess Sumarokova-El'ston, at Rakitnaia, Rakitianskaia Parish, Graivoron District (26,952 *desiatiny*), a sugar refinery was opened in 1895 (777 workers, 1,351,423 rubles annual production); the estate also operated a steam-powered flourmill. L. P. Minarik, who reviewed the records of Iusupova's St. Petersburg administrative offices, saw this as only the initial stage of a vast program of capital investment. In the years before 1905, in addition to the sugar refinery, Iusupova invested heavily in inventory: during 1901–1904, the St. Petersburg office spent 12,000 rubles annually to buy steam threshers and modern tools for sowing and harvesting grain and sugar-beets sown in complex multiple rotations. In these years, estate administration laid out about 100,000 rubles on work stock. It paid 200 contract laborers to work for the five winter months and maintained 1,200 contract workers for the spring and summer months. During summer, these latter were joined by a small army of day laborers (some 5,000 in the 1900s). Total labor costs for term and day labor in 1899 stood at 118,757 rubles; in 1907, despite the disorders, the estate's wage bill stood at 225,454 rubles. The Belgorod-Sumy Railway through Graivoron District opened in 1902, linking estate production (Iusupova and Rakitnaia stations) directly to external markets. A Ministry summary (1900) noted, however, that of the 15,718 *desiatiny* of the sown area in the Rakitnaia demesne, the estate was able to cultivate only 6,400 with its own inventory (at the time, 400 work horses and 500 pairs of oxen), leasing the rest to the surrounding peasant communities.[96]

---

[95] *Spisok*, II: 74, 178; *Fabrichno-zavodskaia*, No. 7744D, 7751D, 7754D. See also "Imenie Grafa K. P. Kleinmikhel Oboianskago uyezda, pri sele Ivne" in Oboianskoe uyezdnoe zemstvo, *Sbornik statisticheskikh svedeniia po Oboianskomu uyezdu*, ch. I, No. 2, 31–61. Descriptions in *Kratkiia*, 39–44.

[96] *Spisok*, II: 180; *Fabrichno-zavodskaia*, 7753D; *Kratkiia*, 11–12. Minarik, "Sistema," in A. A. Novosel'skii, ed., *Materialy*, 377–397. The investment program of 1901–1904, however, will have substantially altered this equation.

Not all owners of such estates in Graivoron District went to all this trouble, however. Ex-serfs of Count D. N. Sheremet'ev (1803–1871) on the large estate (17,303 *desiatiny*)[97] at Borisovka, in Borisovskaia, Solokhinskaia, Vysokovskaia and Strigunovskaia Parishes, regained the use of the lands that they farmed before Emancipation on three-year-lease contracts with a closely regulated rate of increase.[98] The Count's heir (Aleksandr Dmitrievich, 1859–1931) must have found this custom confining: by 1905, the estate had been leased out to sugar-beet refiners for large-scale plantation.

Agriculture on the family estate of the widow Ol'ga Andreevna Levshina-Shaufus in Dmitriev District (acreages at Khomutovka, Glamazdinskaia Parish, and Kalinovka, Ol'khovskaia Parish,[99] making up a contiguous area of 3,179 *desiatiny* in five farmsteads) was conducted on a somewhat lesser scale. A third of the estate remained under woodlands, and demesne plowland made up about 1,900 *desiatiny*. Field culture featured 7-, 8- and 9-field rotations and an annual fertilization of the fallow. Wheat, sugar-beets and potatoes predominated in sowings. Inventory included 114 oxen, 100 horses (in addition to 120 breeding horses of mixed English and Arab lines), and 3,000 imported sheep. Some 10,000 rubles had been invested in a small but imposing array of modern agricultural implements of domestic and foreign manufacture. Ninety-eight full-time workers were employed on the estate during the mid-1890s, 134 male and female laborers were hired on seasonal contracts (1 April through 1 November), and 50–150 day hires were employed during sowing and harvest.[100]

The Shaufus estate's sugar-beet harvest was processed locally on the adjacent estate of the Barons Alexander and Kondrat Egorovich Meiendorf (5,288 *desiatiny*), site of the Georgievskii refinery (one of the province's oldest, built in 1836, rebuilt after it had been destroyed by fire in 1882) at Prilepy, Prilepovskaia Parish, that employed 261 workers. Descriptions of the Meiendorf estate leave little doubt as to its complete conversion to a business model. On seven adjacent farmsteads making up 2,503 *desiatiny*

---

[97] Lands ceded by Peter I to Field-Marshal Boris Petrovich Sheremet'ev (1652–1719) in 1706 upon granting him the title of count included those near Khotmyzhsk on which the settlement of Borisovka was built.

[98] *SSSKG. IX, Statisticheskiia svedeniia po Graivoronskomu uyezdu*: see parish tables.

[99] Birthplace of Nikita Sergeevich Krushchev (1894–1971).

[100] *Opisaniia*, 75–78; *Kratkiia*, 20–21. *General'sha* Ol'ga Andreevna was the widow of the highly decorated Major General Dmitrii Nikolaevich Schaffhausen-Schonberg-Eck-Shaufus (1842–1893).

of plowland, it ran 8-, 9-, 10-, and 11-field rotations with sugar-beet, winter wheat, oats, clover, timothy, and other grains and fodders in rotation. Heavy manuring of fallow (2,000–3,500 *poods* per *desiatina*) meant that up to 300 *desiatiny* were fully treated each year. In 1895, the estate's fund of buildings (including the Barons' two homes, sugar refinery, brick works and flourmill) made up 120 structures valued at 212,152 rubles. Inventory (56,974 rubles) included all of the latest Sack, Ekkert, Edelheim and Ransom technology and two steam-powered threshing machines. In the same year, the Prilepy operations maintained 330 horses (154 work horses), 485 large horned cattle (143 pairs of work oxen), 3,229 sheep (2,511 Merino) and 53 pigs, in all 4,097 head of livestock (64,881 rubles). One hundred agricultural and husbandry workers were employed for the whole year, together with 36 technical personnel, but during the April–November period these were joined by a like number of male workers and some 300 female workers (the latter hired every year from villages in Novgorod-Seversk District, Chernigov Province). At the height of the harvest, the Meiendorf administration availed itself of the labor of "masses" of day workers from adjacent villages and from the western part of Sevsk District, Orel Province. According to the long memorandum of its administrator compiled in 1896 (preserved in the Library of Congress), the estate had entirely ceased the practice of leasing land to peasants in the neighboring villages.[101]

    A. I. Cherepov's operation at Cherepovka, Nikolaevskaia Parish, Putivl' District, was begun in 1872 on a holding of 460 *desiatiny* of deep *chernozem* with plans for growing wheat. The grain price depression and the estate's own lack of meadowlands, however, forced the owner to turn to multiple rotations with half of the sown area in timothy, clover and esparto. The latter, it turned out, could be sold locally at big profits, given the general absence of meadowland in peasant allotments in the immedi-

---

[101] For 1900 in *Kratkiia*, 17–19 (Prilepy), 21–22 (Dobroe Pole); *Spisok*, II: 178. Until 1886, the estate of Egor Fedorovich comprised 6,400 *desiatiny* in Dmitriev District, Kursk Province, and in Sevsk District, Orel Province. In 1886, a partition between heirs was effected, with Bogdan (Theofil) Egorovich obtaining the lands at Dobroe Pole (1,100 *desiatiny*) and the Pogrebov farmstead (1,015 *desiatiny*) in Sevsk District. Kondrat and Aleksandr Egorovich gained the balance (4,253 *desiatiny*), which was held jointly. An estate administrator left a detailed account of the business model of the Meiendorf operation centered on the village of Prilepy, Prilepovskaia Parish, Dmitriev District, for the years 1890–1894, analyzing expenditure and income, agricultural regimes, methods and sources of hire, schedule of payments, fines for days missed, and bonuses for conscientious work. Meier, *Opisanie imeniia "Prilepskaia ekonomiia."*

ate environs of the estate. The new orientation allowed Cherepov to expand his own livestock herds and intensify the manuring of an area still sown with grain: very high yields of winter wheat (140–145 *poods*) and spring oats (130 *poods*) per *desiatina* were cited for 1894–95.[102]

The Moscow publishers Sergei Vasilievich and Mikhail Vasil'evich Sabashnikov had bought several small estates in Kostornianskaia Parish, Sudzha District (1,907 *desiatiny*), and in 1890 completed construction[103] of a sugar refinery (729 workers) at Liubimovka that boasted annual output of 866,142 rubles in 1908.[104] The effects of the spread of sugar-beet refining in the area were seen by local observers as particularly profound. Indeed, though our information on estates in the immediate region of the Sabashnikov installation is fragmentary, the inspection tour undertaken by N. A. Chuikov in Kursk Province in 1892 suggested that several of the larger estates had converted to multiple crop rotations mainly in connection with the requirements imposed by the cultivation of sugar-beets. Of particular note were the estate of Sergei Ivanovich Zhekulin at Belyi Kolodez' (1,323 *desiatiny*) and its farmsteads (Sergei Ivanovich leased additional acreage from the Tolmachevy as well), the estate of A. A. Mal'tsev at Sula (422 *desiatiny*) and the holdings of the Evreinovy at Borshchen' (District Marshal of the Nobility Aleksei Vladimirovich Evreinov, 2,230 *desiatiny*; his wife, Antonina Vasil'evna Evreinova, *née* Sabashnikova, 693 *desiatiny*).[105] A 1900 description of Evreinov's Borshchen' estate cites the proximity of the Sabashnikov plant as the prime motivation for cultivation of sugar-beets on a full third of the estate's plowlands.[106] The Zhekulin heirs also owned estates near Sula (Vladimir Ivanovich) and at Maslovka (Aleksandra Ivanovna).

The personal petition of Aleksandra Ivanovna Zhekulina in the police archive for June 1905 regarding recurring incidents of arson on her estate

---

[102] *Opisanie*, 82–84.

[103] *Spisok*, II: 178. Aleksei Vladimirovich Evreinov, brother-in-law of the Sabashnikov brothers, had begun construction of the refinery. Evreinov's in-laws rescued the project from bankruptcy.

[104] Estate size from *Kratkiia*, 59. The Sabashnikovy fail to appear in listings of landowners in *SSSKG, Vyp. IV, Statisticheskiia svedeniia po Sudzhanskomu uyezdu* at 262–309. The refinery was built in 1890 (*Fabrichno-zavodskaia*, No. 7748D). On the Sabashnikovs' capital activities, Anfimov, *Krupnoe*, 269, 281.

[105] Chuikov recorded his observations on the Zhekulin, Mal'tseva and Evreinov estates from his 1893 inspection tour of Kursk Province for the Moscow Agricultural Society in terms that clearly characterize them as model economies. Chuikov, *Kurskaia guberniia*, passim.

[106] *Kratkiia*, 56–57.

and a summary of the subsequent investigation by local authorities are revealing in this same vein. The inquest laid the blame on the estate's steward and the "new order of business" that he had introduced: expansion of direct demesne cultivation, sharp reduction of "privileges" that the peasants of Maslovka had formerly enjoyed (land lease, rights to graze cattle and to collect hay) and an implacable attitude toward safeguarding estate property. The report also noted that the man liked to make passes at peasant wives and daughters who worked on the estate, but the larger issue—that the changeover of estate economy could hardly have been enacted without the direction of the owner—was politely omitted.[107]

One contributor to the Sudzha District Committee on the Needs of Rural Industry (1902) described the situation of the local peasantry in Sudzha District as follows:

The migrant employments available in South Russia for stonemasons and carpenters in former times provided decent wages to several parishes in our district. Earlier these occupations had many negative aspects, mainly because of their lack of organization, the chance character of earnings, and their role in spreading infectious disease. Yet in recent years of industrial crisis and cessation of urban growth, these earnings have almost disappeared, and the population that was accustomed to them has for several years returned from the South having suffered great losses and deprivations. The emigration movement [to Siberia] that had attained considerable development in the 1890s has also ended unsuccessfully: many peasants, finally ruined, have returned, and emigration out of our district has almost entirely ceased. Purchase of land through the Peasant Land Bank has enjoyed no development in the district, mainly because all land that is not held in strong hands has been bought up or rented by the sugar-refining entrepreneurs of neighboring districts. Many of the rest of the private landowners have begun to take up plantation of sugar-beets, and thus, as a result of this more intensive culture, the land that had for a long time been leased to peasants for cash or for half the harvest—and also the pasture and access strips—is now removed from peasant use. In sum, populations of entire villages have been reduced to desperation, forced out of the age-old bases of the natural economy, and, after wandering about unsuccessfully in emigration or in search of earnings outside the province, they are losing their heads. Sucked into a financial *cul-de-sac* by taxes and other rising impositions, the peasants take money in advance for summer labor [*zadatki*] above their strength in several places at one time and in summer run from one employer to another and from these to their own tiny plots, which can feed their families for only an insignificant part of the year... Because of the increasing demand for land, rents are rising and in our district have reached, in certain cases, 21 rubles per *desiatina* for land under spring plantings and 30 rubles under winter sowings.[108]

---

[107] GARF, f. 102, DP OO, op. 233 (II), d. 2550, ch. 44, ll. 72–73 ob., 81–82 ob.

[108] "Doklad G. A. Ganevicha iz Sudzhanskogo uyezda o dolgosrochnom arende," *Trudy mestnykh komitetov*, 694. The agronomist also stated that very similar conditions had been created in the vicinity of the Tereshchenko and Kharitonenko estates bordering on the southern part of the district.

Describing the area in which agrarian disorders broke out in November 1905 (and were to recur in 1906), P. D. Dolgorukov drew much the same conclusion:

> The northern region lies astride the River Reut. It is most thickly covered with private estates, small and large, and among the former serfs there is acute land hunger [*malozemel'e*] that has been sharpened in recent times by the introduction of sugar-beet cultivation for the nearby sugar refineries, which has drawn out of peasant lease-hold much land now within the capitalist economy [of the private estates]. Fairly considerable money wages on sugar-beet plantations somehow have little effect on the prosperity of the local populace, and the absence of any regulation or inspection makes them the breeding ground for various infectious and catarrhal diseases. Land hunger among the peasantry appears most starkly in the level of rents: these have reached 30–35 rubles per *desiatina* for winter field and 22 rubles for spring field. Even if it is true that in recent years our district has had good harvests, such rents, of course, cannot recompense the lessee for his labor and exhibit all the signs of a one-sided monopoly. The richer peasants, mainly through partnerships, have acquired small parcels of private land under the auspices of the Peasant Land Bank for 250–350 rubles per *desiatina*, but in great part only outside the region of sugar-beet cultivation, within which private owners part with their land with the utmost reluctance.[109]

These observations serve to confirm the view, long ago advanced by A. M. Anfimov, that the influence of larger estate economies made itself felt far beyond the bounds of the estate itself. In Kursk Province, competition of well-capitalized landowners with local peasants for the lease of private lands provoked especially sharp local inflation of land rents (not to speak of purchase price) and heavily influenced wages. Local estates in the region of these large producers often evidenced a sudden new interest in intensive modes of cultivation, including sowings of sugar-beet, in response to the proximity of a reliable buyer, as the construction of the Sabashnikov works suggests.

The mass of smaller landowners that made up the bulk of the provincial nobility, the descendants of the officer corps of the sixteenth and seventeenth-century frontier service, resided locally on estates of a size so modest that they did not meet property requirements for direct participation in the Assemblies of the Nobility or the *Zemstvo* and voted for their

---

[109] Dolgorukov, "Agrarnaia volna," No. 1, col. 91–92. During its poll of 1907, correspondents of the Imperial Free Economic Society from Tim District and Ryl'sk District, the latter adjoining Sudzha District on the west, also noted that contraction of land lease to peasants was one of the principal causes of rural disorders. *Trudy IVEO*, No. 3, 1908 g., 58. The Ryl'sk correspondent directly blamed the spread of sugar-beet plantation for the phenomenon.

representatives indirectly.[110] It is of real significance, then, that the grandees who owned the large modernizing estates had little or no personal contact with the locality and, indeed, must very rarely have visited Kursk Province. In their very heterogeneity, these magnates as a body fully reflected the diverse character of the Russian noble elite as a whole at the end of the nineteenth century. They were representatives of princely clans tracing lineages to Riurik (Bariatinskie, Golytsin, Dolgorukov, Kasatkin-Rostovkii) or to Gedemin (Trubetskoi), functionaries of the pre-Petrine military-administrative order (Annenkovy, Levshin), and close associates of Peter I (Sheremet'evy, Golovin, Iusupov). Among them were also the heirs of Russified foreigners who had attained high rank in Imperial military, civil or diplomatic service in subsequent reigns (Biron, Briskorn, Kleinmikhel', Khorvat, Meiendorf, Rebinder, Ribeaupierre), and the descendants of commoners who had gained noble status in recognition of their great wealth, commercial acumen and charitable work (Tereshchenko, Kharitonenko).[111] The landholdings of these clans in Kursk Province were often only a part of far larger family holdings scattered throughout the Empire, holdings that had originated almost entirely in the Petrine and post-Petrine eras, when extensive grants of settled Crown or state (*kazennye*) lands to prominent Imperial servitors and favorites were commonplace. These owners resided permanently in the capitals (the habit of proximity to the seats of power is quite evident from the familiar tone in which their correspondence with the Minister of Internal Affairs was drawn) and supervision of day-to-day operations on their

---

[110] The *Zemstvo* Regulation of 12 June 1890 (*PSZ*, III, ch. 1, No. 6927, 493–511) set the minimum requirement for Kursk Province at between 125–175 *desiatiny* of land, or other real property, including urban holdings, valued at not less than 15,000 rubles. Korelin, "Rossiiskoe dvorianstvo," *ISSSR*, 1971, 5: 56–81. Almost 70% of all gentry holdings in the province (3,140 out of 4,533) fit under the rubric "up to 100 *desiatiny*" (see Chapter I, n. 71). Mid-seventeenth-century muster rolls and inventories (*pistsovye knigi*) for the old Kursk, Belgorod, Oboian, Oskol', Ryl'sk, and Putivl' military districts identify a large number of service clans that found their way "up" into the provincial nobility (and "down" into clans of *odnodvortsy*): Annenkov, Arsen'ev, Bredykhin, Volkov, Goriainov, Kusakov, Levshin, Lukin, Mal'tsev, Stremoukhov, Markov, Tolmachev, Starov, Shchekin, Cherepov and others. Tankov, *Istoricheskaia letopis.* Tom 1, appendices, and Melton, "Serfdom." The canvassers of the 1880s often noted the common ancestry between noble clans of this older lineage and adjoining peasant communities (*odnodvortsy*), often reflected in shared use of pasture and meadow and intermixing of lands.

[111] Assessment of the growth of noble landholding in the region across the era of its transition from military frontier to peaceful interior zone in Vodarskii, *Dvorianskoe zemlevladenie*; Chernikov, *Dvorianskie imeniia tsentral'no-chernozemnogo regiona*.

estates was delegated to small armies of salaried, commonly non-Russian administrators.[112] The interaction of such administrators with neighboring peasant populations in carrying out orders of their distant employers was often cited as a major source of acute local discontent. In this, the administration of the Iusupova estates was especially notorious. To constant pressure on local provincial officials orchestrated by Princess Iusupova and her spouse through Ministry officials, Governor Borzenko had the courage to reply frankly in kind (although already in 1907):

The order that is thus maintained with these measures is, of course, not stable and will survive only until a vast number of troops and a reinforced body of police is found. In the event of removal of the troops, one can expect that the hostility of the peasants will pour out the most unimaginable excesses at any moment. To establish appropriately neighborly relations between the estate and the peasants goes beyond the limits of the competence of the provincial administration. Having in mind the complete removal of occasions and reasons for hostility, I have already indicated the most essential among them—the relations of the estate administration to the surrounding peasant population, which really finds itself in extremely difficult economic straits, almost everywhere living on "beggar's" allotments. I am deeply convinced that these relations are the main source of the constant discord and hostility. I cannot but add here that the Polish element predominates by more than half in the administration of the Rakitnaia estate, that it obviously does not desire restoration of normal relations, and that it conducts itself in an extremely tactless manner. This administration indulges the peasants with all sorts of sops, gladdens them with false promises, then suddenly begins to oppress them, refusing to honor the promises given and taking back the privileges extended. Thus, for example, last year the estate leased the peasants 3,069 *desiatiny* under winter plantings at 12 rubles per *desiatina* and 2,054 *desiatiny* under the spring crop at 8 rubles per *desiatina*. In this year, it is offering to lease 970 *desiatiny* of winter field at 18 rubles and even though the area under spring sowings has not been agreed upon, the price has been set at 14 rubles. This kind of unstable policy, of course, only enrages the peasants and breeds in them an incredible mélange of misunderstandings and animosity, given which any sort of agitation will find a most favorable soil.[113]

---

[112] The grandees' disconnect with reality at times appears directly in the documents: "On retire les dragons de Perewerzevka, district Soudja [sic]. Supplie votre protection pour les laisser ou les remplacer. [Je] suis à Starnberg [Austria] avec Prince Bariatinsky. Avec cœur ému, suivons vos angoisses paternelles. Comtesse Kleinmichel." Telegram from Countess E. P. Kleinmikhel, 6 September 1906, to Minister of Internal Affairs P. A. Stolypin. GARF, f. 102, op. 236 (II), 1906 g., d. 700, ch. 58, l. 270.

[113] Extract from a detailed review of the Rakitnaia situation found in GARF, f. 102, 4-e delo-proisvodstvo, 1907 g., ch. 34.1, ll. 48–50 (Governor V. M. Borzenko to the Department of Police, No. 8783, 5 July 1907). An assessment in a similarly unflattering vein was made during the March conference by Land Captain F. F. Malevinskii of Graivoron District, in whose precinct the estate was located. RGIA, f. 1291, op. 30, 1905 g., d. 4-b, l. 180 ob. (*Zhurnal soveshchatel'nogo zasedaniia 11-go marta 1905 g. v g. Graivorone*).

We have far less information on the estates of the eastern districts, but circumstantial evidence points to a situation that had analogies. Participants in the conferences of Land Captains in Novyi Oskol' and Staryi Oskol' Districts in March 1905 uniformly identified location within their precincts of especially large estates as a powerful irritant in local affairs. Estate operations of Count Sergei Vladimirovich Orlov-Davydov (1849–1905) at Troitskoe (3,776 *desiatiny*), Volotovskaia Parish, and of Prince Ivan Iur'evich Trubetskoi (1841–1915) at Ol'shanka and Khalan' (5,098 *desiatiny*) in Novyi Oskol' *Uyezd* were said to have led to especially poor relations with the nearby peasant communities. In the latter case, the history of ill will went back to the emancipation settlement and the cold-blooded manner in which the young Prince had (illegally) made use of the statutes. His ex-serfs on temporary obligation joined others in the area (including the villagers of Chernianka) in August of 1862 in violently refusing the allotments that the Prince had imposed on them. Military forces had to be called in to restore order.[114] While we have fewer profiles for these estates, the costs of damage were quite high in relation to those of other owners (the average loss among 44 estates that filed was 33,300 rubles) and suggest heavy investment. Losses incurred at Trubetskoi's estate "with distillery and farm" ran to 200,000 rubles;[115] for Orlov-Davydov's heirs, the damage was also estimated as costing 200,000 rubles. For the merchant brothers Shevtsovy, whose estate (1,779 *desiatiny*) and oil-pressing plant were attacked and burned at Chernianka, losses total 225,000 rubles. District Marshal of the Nobility Vladimir Petrovich Miatlev posted the largest single loss in provincial listings for all of 1905 at 334,700 rubles. His estate complex (5,702 *desiatiny*) at *sloboda* Golubina (Prigorodniaia Parish)—dwelling, distillery and state-licensed liquor outlet, water-powered flour mill, brickworks, cooperage and workers' mess hall—was looted and burned during November 3–5 1905. The estate was plagued by arsonists throughout 1906,

---

[114] RGIA, f. 1291, op. 30, 1905 g., d. 4-b, l. 185 (*Zhurnal Novooskol'skago soveshchaniia zemskikh uchastkovykh nachal'nikov 11-go marta 1905 g.*). On the machinations of Prince Trubetskoi (declared illegal by provincial authorities), see Litvak, *Russkaia derevnia*, 208–211; peasant reactions in Ivanov, ed., *Krestianskoe dvizhenie*, 189–190 (No. 62); Tankov, *Krestianskiia volneniia*, 369–371.

[115] The Ministry directory for 1900 listed the Trubetskoi estate at 5,542½ *desiatiny*, out of which 4,397 lay under plowland; only 1,000 *desiatiny* were cultivated by the estate itself in three fields (350 sown with winter rye, 200 with spring wheat, 150 with potatoes). The rest was leased out to the neighboring villagers. The estate ran a distillery, a steam-powered flourmill and four water-powered flourmills. *Kratkiia*, 37–38.

and in October half of the rebuilt structures were again destroyed by fire.[116]

Observers at the March session in Staryi Oskol' District made the same unwittingly prophetic observations with reference to the larger estates in their jurisdictions, especially those in Saltykovskaia and Kladovskaia Parishes, almost all of which were to suffer the depredations of neighboring peasants during 1905 or 1906. Already during 1904, a rash of acts of minor arson had targeted the estates of P. N. Korobkov at Korobkovo and of Nikolai Petrovich Dmitriev at Lukoianovka (Saltykovskaia Parish). Dmitriev's steward had been wounded by a sniper. (About Korobkov, rumors circulated among peasants that he had given all his money to the Japanese and had himself gone into hiding.) Unrest was considered to be likely at the estate of Ivan Nikolovich Tereshchenko at Timiriazevo (5,414 *desiatiny*, formerly of Kleinmikhel') in light of the "extraordinary tactlessness" of estate administration in dealings with the local peasantry.[117]

The crucial importance of the large estates in the mix of local factors that provoked unrest in Kursk Province thus lay in the fact that—faced with the critical situation in private economies throughout the province (and indeed the Central Agricultural Region as a whole) during the late nineteenth century—the owners of the large latifundia adopted an aggressive transition to new strategies for operations on the demesne during the 1890s in order to escape the iron embrace of the old system of patron-client relationships inherited from the past. But these changes had disproportionate effects in greatly magnifying the sense of *unpredictability* and *instability* in micro-economies of specific sub-regions of the province. The influence of this movement on the availability of land resources in the wider locality—resources that were indispensable to peasant communities and most especially to those of former private serfs—had highly negative consequences, as is shown in testimony from the zone of unrest in Sudzha District and elsewhere in the province. It was in locales dominated by operations of such owners that conflicts between villagers and the former masters or their heirs had arrived at a critical juncture even before 1905. This frame of reference goes a long way not only toward making sense of

---

[116] RGIA, f. 1291, op. 122, 1905 g., d. 112 ("So svedeniiami donesennymi Gubernatorami o razmerakh ubytkov, prichinennykh agrarnymi bezporiadkami"), ll. 311–313 (Novyi Oskol' District); ll. 314–314 ob. (Staryi Oskol' District). Miatlev estate size and indication of main facilities in *KGV*, chast' ofitsial'naia, No. 3, 13 ianvaria 1904 g., LXVII.

[117] *Ibid.*, op. 30, 1905 g., d. 4-b, ll. 188 ob.–190 ob. (*Zhurnal Starooskol'skago soveshchaniia zemskikh nachal'nikov 10-go marta 1905 g.*).

the geographical distributions of disturbances among those 287 populated settlements in Kursk Province that participated in rural disturbances, *but also toward an explanation of why the majority of peasant communities, even if to some degree sympathetic to the movement, nevertheless did not participate in the events that we have described at all.*

Rural unrest in Kursk Province during 1905–1906 is separate in time from publication of the Emancipation statutes of 19 February 1861 by only 43 years, not a long span of time in the *longue durée* in which collective social memories alter and mutate. Especially for an older generation in any village community of former serfs, the personal bond between the master and the peasants bound to his estates was a lived experience, an experience passed on over the course of several generations, an experience that expressed a layered accumulation of accommodation, conflict and interdependence that was not always and everywhere wholly negative. It would be an error, I think, to consider that, with the stroke of a pen, social habits formed over two centuries could be made to disappear. To be sure, to the degree that implementation of the emancipation statutes on the ground stood on its head the serf's conception of order—"we are the lord's, but the land is ours" (*my gospodskie, a zemlia nasha*)—it bred incomprehension and a deep and enduring sense of injustice. Yet it was in the very "backwardness" of the majority of private estates that elements of the older reciprocities retained their vitality—and thus a certain aspect of continuity— lasting into the new era. Their heavy reliance on leasing land to peasant neighbors and on exploitation of peasant labor and inventory for working that limited area devoted to demesne cultivation provided critical access to those supplements to household and community resources in which many villages found assurance of a measure of stability and predictability in the year-to-year struggle to subsist and to prosper. A growing sense of the tension inherent in their respective social positions might have been a visible and alarming development in daily discourse, but the relationship of lords and peasants on the land, when it retained a highly personal aspect that drew upon vestiges of older verities, imposed, insensibly perhaps, limits on expressions of peasant discontent. This economic-*cum*-social arrangement and its larger historical frame of reference are severely ruptured precisely in those localities in which just this sense of the predictability and stability of older arrangements broke down—not only within the physical boundaries of the large "modernizing" estates themselves, but also with regard to many of the private holdings in their immediate vicinity.

The vulnerable position of the villages associated in the documents consulted for this work with the incidents of unrest in Kursk Province during 1905–1906 stands as the other half of this fateful equation. In part, as we will see, their situation was attributable to the manner in which the General Statute of 19 February 1861 was drawn and carried out on the ground. The fact that four out of every five rebel settlements in our sample were villages of ex-serfs and their descendants—in a province in which the old state peasantry made up the majority of the population—is a significant indication of the importance of this factor. Beyond this basic frame of reference, however, our analysis will suggest that the issue was even more complex. In the initial chapter of this work, it was evident that, given the limits imposed by emancipation legislation, peasant communities struggled to ensure their subsistence and win some measure of prosperity by recourse to a variety of expedients. Among these, we noted the extension of the area under plowland within the area of the allotment itself, land purchase and land lease, local off-farm employment and the search for wage employment outside the province itself. Based on *overall* indices for mortality, agricultural production, savings and consumption, our opinion was that these expedients had promoted a certain trend toward *general* improvement in peasant life.

Yet the nature and significance of these choices was entirely dependent, first, on the "cooperation" of market forces, not only as these influenced local land rents, wages and commodity prices, but also, at a greater distance, due to the capacity of Russian industry to keep time in absorbing a growing out-migration of persons of working age. In specific rural settlements, moreover, the issue of prosperity, given an uninterrupted natural increase in population, turned on the availability of a physically accessible land fund that offered the possibility of a corresponding extension of agriculture. In the bigger rural villages and densely populated *slobody* that stood in the forefront of the peasant movement in Kursk Province during 1905–1906, however, such recourses had already been exhausted. This resulted, more often than not, in the *attenuation* of the ties to agriculture altogether, and consequently a shift toward industrial and handicraft employment that had altered the character, the perspective and the stability of the rural economy within them. Further, these heavily populated rural centers were quite often home to especially large concentrations of small, nuclear-family households associated with comparatively higher rates of literacy on the one hand and with engagement in off-farm, non-agricultural pursuits on the other. It is to an exploration of this milieu, more than any other identified with emergence of rural unrest in Kursk Province during 1905–1906, that our final chapter is devoted.

CHAPTER V

The Villages That Revolted

In the foregoing chapter, we have seen that when the incidence of agrarian unrest during 1905–1906 is viewed on the level of districts, peasants in all fifteen districts participated in the events of these years, but that when the number of parishes in which unrest occurred is determined, the scale of unrest is somewhat less imposing. Of the 195 *volosti* extant in 1905, 109 recorded disturbances. Then, the corpus of documents consulted for this work contains references to 289 settlements as being associated with incidents of unrest, which, among the 2,916 populated points catalogued by *zemstvo* surveys of the mid-1880s, constitutes 9.9 percent of all settlements in the province.[1] Such restricted participation, in part, reflects the limitations of the sample itself, but a sample twice as large would not alter the picture very much. Rather, it seems evident that a large majority of villagers in Kursk Province stood apart from the events of 1905–1906: I have surmised that the very "survivals" of the older complex of social and

---

[1] District seats of Sudzha and L'gov, in which jail breaks involving persons detained for participation in agrarian disorders were organized, were excluded before analysis as being urban centers. Of the remaining 289 place names, no data for D'iakonovka and Novo-Nikol'skoe in Kostornianskaia Parish, Vasil'evka in Skorodenskaia Parish and Koshary in Belovskaia Parish, appear in the census volume for Sudzha District. In Novyi Oskol' District, the census contained no reference to *khutora*: Sychev or Sytnoe (Chernianskaia) and Soldat or Vysokii (Khalanskaia). A village of Glazovo in Konyshevskaia Parish did not appear among census listings for L'gov District. For Staryi Oskol' District, the village of Luboshevka (Kladovskaia) and *khutor* Godeevka (Viazovskaia) were absent from the listing. *Khutor* Olimpiadskoe on the Tereshchenko estate in Kul'bakinskaia Parish, and *khutor* Kolomok in Snagostskaia Parish, Ryl'sk District, were likewise absent. Lastly, a village of Korsakovo, Vyshe-Ol'khovatskaia Parish, Shchigrov District, was undetected under this name. In total, information on 14 place names was unavailable.

economic reciprocities between lord and peasant, however fraught with chronic tension and intermittent strife, however characterized by economic inefficiencies, managed to ensure a minimal measure of year-to-year predictability and stability in exchanges among opposing social elements, and that this global circumstance played a major role in limiting participation. What features, then, distinguish those rural settlements for which the economic and political conjuncture of 1905 eliminated the last inhibitions to open attacks against the established order? Did militancy reflect merely land hunger? Were there qualitative differences in this milieu—as opposed to the general character of rural districts in Kursk Province—that enable us to draw broader conclusions about the nature of the movement as a whole?

1. Building a Profile of Participating Villages: the Zemstvo Census of 1882–1885

To answer such questions, we built a profile of the villages associated with incidents of unrest, and at the same time composed, for purposes of comparison, more aggregated sets of data for the 195 parishes into which the province was divided in 1905. To this end, we employed detailed, multi-faceted census material on peasant population and economy collected between 1882 and 1886 for the districts of Kursk Province by teams of canvassers of the Statistical Bureau of the Provincial Zemstvo, directed by a member of the Moscow Zemstvo Statistical Bureau, Ippolit Antonovich Verner.[2] In the fifteen district volumes of the census, 275 of the 289 place names to which our sources refer in connection with disturbances were successfully located and line data abstracted. Construction of a profile of villages was not without several problematic moments, these having to do in part with issues previously raised with reference to the police and judicial documents themselves. Especially during November 1905, official sources became notably less precise in their identification of villages "participating" in collective actions, obviously in relation to the

---

[2] Kurskoe gubernskoe *zemstvo*. Statisticheskoe biuro. *SSSKG* (Kursk, 1883–1886). *Vyp.I–XIV*. Verner edited commentaries to the tables and wrote most of the summary volume. The study of Oboian District was conducted, at the invitation of the Oboian District Zemstvo Assembly (resolution of November 1881), by another Moscow Zemstvo Statistical Bureau specialist, A. F. Timofeev. Oboianskoe uyezdnoe *zemstvo*, *Sbornik statisticheskikh svedeniia*. Most unfortunately, this study used somewhat different rubrics.

degree to which the situation in these locales had completely escaped the control of the local authorities. The fact that the location of the estates attacked was always noted in the documents by the name of the village or could be determined by later materials (lists of damage drawn up for the state's program of reparations) greatly aided the fixing of sites of disturbances. The prosecutor of the Kursk Regional Court, from investigations of the November unrest in Novyi Oskol' and Staryi Oskol' Districts, noted that "in almost all cases," attacks were mounted by peasants "from the village immediately adjacent to the estate."[3] Nonetheless, unusually dense documentation preserved in the central historical archives for the events of February 1905 revealed that participation was hardly limited to such villages.[4]

In the second place, use of the census data themselves presented several problems. The *zemstvo* surveys of 1882–1884 in Kursk Province were conducted in answer to an almost complete dearth of reliable information that commonly confronted deputies of the Provincial Zemstvo and without which an estimate of the current situation in the province (area of taxable land, numbers of persons settled in—and the general economic character of—its villages) was impossible. On matters directly within the competence of *zemstvo* institutions—literacy, agronomy, handicraft industries, sanitary conditions and so on—this lack of information was particularly vexing. Discussion during the sessions of 1880–1881 on the necessity of organizing a census led to its authorization at an extraordinary session of the Provincial Zemstvo Assembly in 1882. The survey was to be conducted within a three-year period based on the survey program developed by the Moscow Zemstvo. Vasilii Ivanovich Orlov, senior statistician of the Moscow Provincial Zemstvo, and I. A. Verner, associate member of its Statistical Bureau, were formally invited to direct the first district census (Kursk District). As a result of the further work of the Bureau, of which Verner was named director in 1882, the census of 1882–1884 stands as by far the richest source on the state of the rural economy in Kursk Province during the last quarter of the nineteenth century.

---

[3] Report, Kursk Circuit Court Prosecutor to the prosecutor of the Khar'kov Judicial Chamber, 3 December 1905, RGIA, f. 1405 (Ministerstvo iustitsii, II-oe ugolovnoe otdelenie), op. 108, 1906 g., d. 7006, ll. 1–6 ob.

[4] Outside of the populations of sites directly implicated during the events of 6–21 February 1905, the arrest record shows that large contingents from at least five other villages in the immediate area must also have participated.

Yet publication at the beginning of 1887 of the last, summary volume of the census, *Kursk Province: Results of the Statistical Investigation*,[5] provoked bitter criticism within the Provincial Zemstvo Assembly and personal attacks on Verner himself that appeared in a national journal.[6] Runs of the book, printed by the provincial *zemstvo* press, were impounded, even though the academic council of Moscow University had voted to award Verner the Samarin Prize in honor of his achievement. They remained under seal even eight years later, when efforts were made to gain the release of the book during sessions of the Provincial Zemstvo Assembly in May 1895, which efforts were blocked by Prince N. F. Kasatkin-Rostovskii and Provincial Marshal A. D. Durnovo and their allies.[7] Accusations that the supervisor of the Statistical Bureau had greatly exceeded his mandate to conduct a strictly "evaluative" (*otsenochnyi*) survey were answered easily by reference to the speeches of his main accuser in the 1880–1882 sessions of the Provincial Assembly,[8] to the selection of the Moscow Zemstvo schema of statistical investigation by the Assembly itself, and to the fact that the Assembly had repeatedly approved the content of each of fifteen district volumes—upon which Verner had based his final work—for publication during 1883–1886, at each turn expressing its satisfaction.[9] It was evident, though, that the conservative majority was enraged at the author's starkly negative appraisal of the results of the Great Reforms for the peasant economy in the province, an appraisal in which the parasitical relationship of the estate owners (using the leverage of extraordinarily high land prices and rents) toward their peasant neighbors emerged in particular relief.[10] The deputies could not but be irked as well by the book's digressions on issues of a deeply sensitive nature: the glaring absence of any correspondence between representation in *zemstvo* assemblies and the character of land holding (and the gross inequalities of this scheme of representation due to high property requirements) or the great scale of illegal

---

[5] Verner, ed., *Kurskaia guberniia*.

[6] Roshtok, "Zemstvo i statistika," *Russkii Vestnik*, v. 196 (1888 g.), 137–176.

[7] V. F. Karavaev, "Bibliograficheskii obzor," *Trudy IVEO. 1904.* Tom vtoroi, Kniga 4–5, 6, 238–257.

[8] Roshtok, who was instrumental in launching the whole project, and did himself lead the earliest collection of data in D'iakonovskaia Parish and *sloboda* Iamskaia in Kursk District during 1881—using the same program of collection. The data were later incorporated into the tables of the first volume.

[9] Verner, "Statistika," *Russkaia mysl'*, 1888 g., No. 7, 152–176.

[10] Verner, "Zemlevladenie," *Russkaia mysl'*, 1887, No. 4 (aprel'), 52–73.

seizures of lands of state peasants by the gentry, abetted by local officials, during the General Surveys at the end of the eighteenth century.[11]
The favorable comparison made of the industry and acumen of the ex-
serf population to that of former *odnodvortsy*—ascribed to the latter's
noble origins—stuck in the craw of conservatives long afterward (see
below). Played out in the national journals, this loud incident led to
Verner's dismissal and to the closing of the Statistical Bureau for the
next eight years. It also offers testimony, even for this early date, to the
unrelenting hostility of conservative nobles toward specialists and *zemstvo* employees of undistinguished social origins that was a contentious
issue in *zemstvo* politics in Kursk Province and, conversely, to the
deeply critical views of the existing order in the rural districts that these
specialists often shared.

The household census[12] assembled data based on questionnaires, the
rubrics for which were approved beforehand by the Statistical Bureau.

---

[11] The *General'naia Mezhevanie* was completed in Kursk Province between 1782 and
1797. Verner, *op. cit.* (*Kurskaia guberniia*), 94–95. The enserfment of the free peasantry
and seizure of its lands in the process of the formation of landed estates in Kursk Province in the eighteenth century is treated in Melton, "Serfdom," 27–76. Of special interest
is Melton's point that the mass of minor nobles in Kursk Province emerged from the old
frontier service, while the owners of bigger estates—and especially the aristocratic, absentee owners of large latifundia—were relative newcomers who received their lands
and serfs by grant of the Emperors and Empresses during and after the reign of Peter the
Great. For the events of 1905–1906 in the province, these differences were to exert an
important influence on peasant militancy.

[12] Verner, *op. cit.* (*Kurskaia guberniia*), 1–25. Preparation for a district survey was itself a
whole project that involved collection of sources on several official instances. For the
district scheduled to be surveyed, the associates of the Statistical Bureau drew up a preliminary list of parishes and communes based on data of the Treasury (*kazennaia palata*)
and detailed General Staff maps. This list was checked against tax rolls in the office of
the District Administration and data on private estates abstracted. Preliminary information on soil conditions, harvests, handicrafts, tax levies and arrears, and the general
prosperity of the populace was assembled at various district offices. Based on this collection, the district was divided into sub-regions and teams of canvassers, each headed
by one of the more experienced associates, assigned to each. At the parish administrative
centers in their sub-regions, each team collected data on the numbers of households, total area of allotments, numbers of "industrial" enterprises and numbers of passports
granted for various terms. Armed with this base of data, each team canvassed each
commune in a given parish. This latter phase was conducted in the period between January and March, avoiding both the intensive period of the agricultural calendar and those
periods in which rural roads were almost impassable. Given the three-year term, the Bureau (never more than 36 persons) had to finish the survey of more than 4,300 communes in around 12 months.

Data were collected for population present (*nalichnoe naselenie*)[13] by age and sex. Land resources were documented by area of allotment and purchased land, area of allotment and non-allotment land leased and terms of lease. The numbers of horses and large cattle were recorded, as were those of literate persons and students, and of family members engaged in "industrial" (*promyshlennyi*) pursuits (locally or in migration). The poll also tried to assess the character of conduct of household economy on the allotments—"independently," with outside (*chuzhim*) labor and/or inventory,[14] or renting out one's allotment (that is, abandonment). The survey was conducted by interviewing each householder before the village assembly. Verner's assessment of this method contains some interesting reflections on peasant attitudes:

> Our research is based on a household census of all villages and communes of a district, exactly in accord with the accepted practice of the Moscow Zemstvo and several others that have applied the Moscow program in their statistical work. The long years of the Moscow Zemstvo Statistical Bureau's practice has shown that the best way of collecting information on all householders in a given village or commune is not by visiting each house individually, but by polling each householder individually at the village assembly. Aside from the enormous and quite understandable economy of time, this method ensures more exactness and justice in the data assembled. The distrust with which the peasants greet every government or *zemstvo* agent who comes to the village to collect any kind of information is well known to all. This distrust is based on the unvarying assumption that such official persons come in order to levy on the peasant some new tax. This assumption is so strongly held that it is possible to overcome it only in individual peasants. Starting at the village assembly [*skhod*] with the polling of those peasants whose trust to some degree has been won, one can be sure that, by force of that striving toward equalization that is typical of peasants, the testimony of the others will be honest, since those who have given accurate testimony will not allow inaccuracies from others. We almost never had to correct a householder's error on the basis of his own words—the inaccuracy was always revealed under the pressure of the *skhod*

---

[13] "Present population" (*nalichnoe naselenie*) in the census excluded all persons in military service and those who had resided in another province for more than five years. It *included* members of communes living in other provinces on passports of one year's duration or less (the vast majority), the numbers of which were established before the house census took place and verified in the course of the canvassing.

[14] Here the resort to the hire of non-family labor and/or inventory was viewed *exclusively as a sign of the weakness* of household economy. Verner, ed., *op. cit.* (*Kurskaia guberniia*), 137. This presumption was largely supported by the correlation analyses that appear below, but it stills strikes one as lacking in nuance. Conversely, proponents of the equation of "hired labor" with "capitalist" exploitation routinely ignored the probability that labor-sharing among households that were members of the same kinship group played a role.

and at its insistence. And the assembly in this regard was extremely exact: it did not allow a cow to be registered as a calf; it demanded that beehives be declared empty or a strip of land leased under crops. [15]

The poll of each household head before the *skhod* having been completed and its results inscribed on cards, the Bureau's associates proceeded to aggregation of household data on standardized communal blanks. Aided by ten to twenty of the commune's most knowledgeable residents, the team then sought to compile additional information under a series of rubrics on general conditions in each commune. These examined tenure practice and redistribution, techniques of cultivation and field cultures, area of other communal lands outside the arable proper (forest, meadow and pasture), harvest performance (*sam-skol'ko*), soils and distribution of fields, handicraft establishments, characterization of the communal land situation compared to that following Emancipation, and so on. Communal data were subsequently preserved in district volumes under names of the specific villages: if a village was composed of multiple communes, these appeared with the name of the village followed by the number assigned to each commune. [16]

After aggregation by commune and verification, the original household cards were evidently destroyed at some point thereafter: [17] any possibility of recreating distributions by household for specific villages by allotment size or sown area was forever precluded: only the breakdowns by labor composition and work stock (horses) survived in published volumes. Although budget research had already begun to surface in *zemstvo* statistical practice by this time, such data were not collected. This absence is felt all the more in that the Bureau constructed its conception of land deficit (*malozemel'e*) in the province on calculations of the income/expense of an "average" peasant household without any local data whatsoever. Its observation that an average peasant household of 6.5 persons required an allotment of nine *desiatiny* (about 25 acres, including house plot) to meet its subsistence needs and financial obligations was therefore unsupported. The ethnic

---

[15] "Kurskoe gubernskoe *zemstvo*. Statisticheskii biuro. *SSSKG. Vyp. I. Kurskii uyezd* (Kursk, 1883), 2–3.

[16] Since the unit of analysis imposed by the police reports was the *village name*, the communal data had to be aggregated in our data set in cases where a settlement's population belonged to two or more communes.

[17] Review of the holdings of the State Archive of the Kursk Region in F. I. Lappo and P. P. Piatovskii, eds., *Gosudarstvennyi arkhiv Kurskoi Oblasti. Putevoditel'* (Kursk, Arkhivnyi otdel Upravleniia vnutrennikh del Ispolkoma Kurskogo oblsoveta deputatov trudiashchikhsia, vol. 1 [1958], vol. 2 [1972]) disclosed no reference to any remaining primary materials from this survey.

make-up of the surveyed population was not recorded, even though Ukrainians were well represented in the southern part of the province and were the predominant ethnic group in Putivl' and Graivoron Districts. Due to strict time and funding limits set by the Provincial Zemstvo (the Assembly turned down repeated petitions for time extensions) and the priority assigned to the economic data, the mass of supplementary information collected by the surveys went unpublished in most of the earlier volumes or appeared anecdotally in their pages. This gap was filled only in the last five published volumes for Belgorod, Novyi Oskol', Tim, Korocha and Staryi Oskol' Districts: findings collected on each village were presented in these volumes as a preface to the tables. These districts, however, were all located in the eastern part of the province and, as noted above, were measurably distinct from those in the west and southwest in the level of productivity and prosperity.[18] We are not able, then, to assess in accordance with local testimony any early signs of changes in agricultural practice that were soon to be evident in the western districts of the province in terms of the intensification of cultivation with a more modern inventory.

Furthermore, the questionnaire with which canvassers went into the villages itself changed over time. The polls of 1882 (Kursk and Oboian Districts) were conducted, respectively, using 77 and 112 rubrics. The district censuses during 1883 utilized 125 headings (adding rubrics for household labor composition, for area of types of arable within the allotment, for the physical situation of the allotments and for data on non-allotment leases). Those for 1884 employed 145 rubrics (again adding to information to be collected on non-allotment leasing).[19] As a result, from the 275 villages in the sample for which census information was located, it was necessary at times to exclude 38 of these (from the early 1882 series for Kursk and Oboian Districts) in several analyses due to the absence of the necessary data or to irresolvable discord among rubrics.[20]

---

[18] These same volumes, however, did not contain results for the data collected on the private estates.

[19] In the first volume (Kursk District), information on non-allotment leasehold was collected for (1) the number of households leasing, (2) the total area of plowland leased (in *desiatiny*) and (3) the amount of money spent for leasing hay meadow and pasture. A calculation of leased land per household was then made and entered in the blank. In contrast, the section concerning leasehold in the fourteenth volume (Staryi Oskol' District) contained 28 different rubrics.

[20] In the first release for Kursk District (15 parishes), rubrics for labor composition of the household were not even a part of the programme. These data were tabulated in collection for Oboian District (11 parishes) under households "with no male of working age,"

Even when it reopened in 1895 under the directorship of Ivan Petrovich Belokonskii, the Statistical Bureau was never to be entrusted with a similar mission. Efforts to conduct a second poll on strictly "evaluative" grounds—collections of this sort were successfully completed in a number of *gubernii* of European Russia in the 1890s and 1900s—were cut short after the publication of one volume (Fatezh District) in 1897,[21] and there is thus no possibility of following the movement of various variables over time. With no follow-up surveys, the relative age of data collected twenty years before the events thus presents real problems in key sectors: passport data reviewed in the first chapter of this work, for example, suggest a great expansion in labor migration in the 1890s that would have been confirmed by a later survey. Contraction of the land fund in this same era (shown in the CSC land survey of 1905) cannot be gauged for specific localities.[22] Such lacunae ought not to deter us, however, from using these data to present a picture of the *general* state of rural life in Kursk Province in the era immediately preceding the revolution.

2. Ex-Serfs and the Former State Peasantry

What immediately struck the eye from the analysis of the characteristics of our 275 settlements noted in the documents as being associated with disorders during 1905–1906 was the large weight among them of villages of former private serfs emancipated under the General Statute of 19 February 1861. Fully 198 villages in our sample—72.0 percent—belong to

---

"with 1 worker," "with 2 workers," or "with 3 or more workers." Subsequent volumes adopted a uniform scheme, delimiting households "with no male of working age," "with one worker," "with 2–3 workers," or "with 4 or more workers." Explanation for the unfortunate aggregation "2–3 workers" was absent from the notes to these volumes.

[21] With the failure of the project, Belokonskii (appointed in 1895 at the recommendation of A. A. Chuprov) was dismissed as Director of the Statistical Bureau in June of 1897 and funding for the Bureau was briefly suspended. On the effects of the meddling of the central administration and the obstruction of conservatives in the Provincial Assembly on the work of the Statistical Bureau and its director, see V. F. Karavaev, *op. cit.* "Bibliograficheskii obzor."

[22] To be sure, the study made by the provincial office of the State Treasury on this and other issues—on the basis of responses of parish administrative organs to a questionnaire sent out in late 1906—presented a limited but important range of data by commune. The questionnaire requested numbers of *legally registered* persons and households, which limited its precision. Kurskaia kazennaia palata, *Materialy po krest'ianskomu i chastnomu zemlevladeniiu Kurskoi gubernii, passim.*

this group. Moreover, there were 17 additional villages made up of communes of both state peasants (*gosudarstvennye dushevye*) and ex-serfs holding their lands in communal tenure. "State souls" in such mixed villages commonly ended up under state jurisdiction after the bankruptcy of the former masters. These could very arguably have been listed under settlements of former private serfs and their descendants, but surveys of the mid-1880s did not make sufficiently clear distinctions in this regard. Among those that remain are noted 38 villages (13.8 percent) of former state peasants under communal tenure, 18 settlements of former state peasants under household tenure (*odnodvortsy*) and 4 villages of former state peasants holding their lands under mixed forms of tenure. Roughly nine out of ten villages in the sample held their lands in communal tenure.

This result might seem all the more surprising in that state peasants composed 59 percent of the population of the province. In their vast majority, these latter were descendants of the men who had served in the border garrisons of the Muscovite state during the sixteenth and seventeenth centuries (minor nobles known as *deti boiarskie* or the soldiery that had served under them, the "former servicemen of various services").[23] Certainly, each of these larger groupings had a markedly different experience of the past, which continued to be evident in everyday life even in the last quarter of the nineteenth century. This was especially true for the *odnodvortsy* (or *chetvertniki*). Holding their lands under household tenure, these were all Great Russian peasants, many of whom retained among the family heirlooms the ancient acts (mainly from the seventeenth century) that contained direct evidence of their ancestors' rights to landed estate (*pomest'e*) in service tenure, and they quite commonly viewed themselves as noblemen who had accidentally lost their rights. Their villages retained distinctly military aspects, walled about and located on elevated ground. Legends among them abounded about the time when their ancestors had served the Tsars; the oldest recalled the era when the *odnodvortsy* had owned serfs. Canvassers often observed common genealogical roots of clans of former *odnodvortsy* and clans of much of the minor provincial gentry:[24] such relations were often reflected in intermixing of lands (*cherespolositsa*) and joint use of forest, meadow and other arable land in localities where partition agreements between gentry and peasant representatives of some common ancestor had not been reached. To a certain ex-

---

[23] Distribution of peasants of various juridical standings in Kursk Province in Table 1.1 in Chapter I.

[24] See Chapter IV, n. 109.

tent distinct by dialect, the *odnodvorets* considered it quite beneath his dignity to associate with a *muzhik*—an ex-serf—even if the latter was of equal wealth; intermarriage was quite rare.[25] Verner, however, went on to state his observation (which was to infuriate his noble critics) that "the privileged blood of the *chetvertnik* peasant reveals itself in a certain lack of energy or endurance, in a lesser capacity for heavy physical labor, thanks to which, given equal conditions, the former serf always manages his farm incomparably better. Of course, one notes this distinction only among the well-to-do *chetvertniki*; for the rest, time has exerted its leveling influence, and in those localities in which peasants of different standings live in close proximity this distinction is almost lost, or reveals itself in those spheres of life in which tradition is best able to act."[26]

We have seen in the initial chapter, however, that the terms of the reforms of the 1860s differentiated quite considerably between the two groups in the aims, terms and conditions of the major acts of emancipation and in the manner in which the acts were carried out on the ground. Nowhere was this more evident than in the very different results of the land settlements and their ramifications in the decades that followed. Despite the general tendency of official reporting to attempt to minimize this critical element in the situation in the rural districts during 1905–1906 (see above), there were moments in which the fact had to be faced. After a long indictment of communal forms of tenure so common among peasants in Kursk Province, which he viewed as depriving householders of all motivation for engaging the indispensable technological improvement on the allotments in which their capital was entirely engaged, Governor Borzenko's report to the Ministry of Internal Affairs on reasons for the unrest during 1905 recognized the particular disabilities borne by the former private serfs.

Of course, it is impossible to deny that land hunger [*malozemel'e*] plays a role in the impoverishment of the peasantry. Yet this conception cannot be applied to the whole peasant population of the province. Acute insufficiency of land can be fixed only in relation to individual settlements of former private serfs that were not allotted sufficient land when they went onto redemption. On average, by district, based on data for the quantity of land per allotment household, Kursk Province is divided into two halves—the eastern half, with more land, and the western half, with an insufficiency of land. In the former, toward the beginning of 1887, the average was 10.2 *desiatiny* per allotment household, in the latter 7.4 *desiatiny*. [...] Thus the former private serfs are the most

---

[25] *SSSKG. Vyp. I. Kurskii uyezd*, 31–75; Verner, ed., *Kurskaia guberniia*, 56–57.

[26] *Ibid.* (*Kurskaia guberniia*), 56.

poorly of all supplied with allotments, in particular those sitting on "beggar's" allotments. Among the peasants of Kursk Province, there were 109,554 revision souls who received less than two *desiatiny* per soul at the time of their transfer onto the redemption regime. Of these, 27,442 revision souls received less than one *desiatina* per soul, 36,370 from 1 to 1½ *desiatiny* and 45,642 from 1½ to 2 *desiatiny*. *From the data cited it is evident that there is undoubtedly a major contingent of land-poor peasants in Kursk Province who suffer from an acute need for land. It is worth noting that agrarian disorders spread principally among peasants who were formerly private serfs.*[27]

It is perhaps the periodization schemes that are traditionally employed in the study of the history of late Imperial Russia that make of the Emancipation a watershed event, and there are, of course, weighty reasons for doing so. Yet it is difficult, I think, to assume that in the life of a local society based on constant face-to-face interaction over the course of generations the personal ties of lord and peasant could be severed with the stroke of a pen. "We are the lord's, but the land is ours" (*My gospodskie, a zemlia nasha*): the legislative acts of the Emancipation, as we have already noted, turned this old saying on its head. Lands that had formerly been open to peasant use by custom (not only the "cut-offs"—plowland absorbed into the demesne—but also forest, pasture and meadow) were now closed to the villagers, and redemption dues imposed on the community for the lands that they had received were widely viewed as onerous and unjust. In the larger sense, however, the nostalgia for the days of serfdom that Russian radicals in the 1870s were shocked to find widespread among peasants (especially among the older generations)[28] also testified to a grievance that was perhaps as profound: a loss of the minimal degree of subsistence security and protection that the serf-owner had provided to the community. The liberation of the serfs "from above" to forestall any event that their liberation should be effected "from below" will have therefore taken on the character of a seismic event in the shared socio-historical memory[29] of communities of former serfs that did not merely foster a deep

---

[27] RGIA, f. 1291 (Land Section, Ministry of Internal Affairs), op. 122, 1906 g., d. 123 ("Doneseniia gubernatorov o prichinakh agrarnykh besporiadkov"), ll. 42 ob.–43. Italics mine: these were rare admissions in official reporting. The body of reports filed in response to Durnovo's request republished in N. Karpov, *Krest'ianskskoe dvizhenie* was most unanimous in faulting revolutionary propaganda for the unrest.

[28] Frierson, *Peasant Icons*, 44–45.

[29] Socio-historical memory here in the sense of the formation of "memory" as posited by Maurice Halbwachs as a profoundly "social" phenomenon—inseparable from the association of the individual with other individuals in his family or social group at a defined place and time—in his *Les cadres sociaux de la mémoire* and in the posthumously pub-

sense of injustice over the land issue *per se* (thus the oft-repeated *"zem-litsy by!"*—"If only there were a bit more land!"). The new era also promoted a broad awareness of far less certain prospects of village life, over which presided, as before, a host of elected peasant officeholders among whom corruption and self-enrichment was all too common, now joined by a small army of minor state officials uncomprehending of, hostile to or indifferent to peasant interests. Once again, the geography of the rural disorders in Kursk Province during 1905–1906 would not only show that the historical experience of the two communities—of state peasants and of former serfs—would largely determine their participation or non-participation in collective acts of protest; it would also show that where the interaction of the old master and the adjoining villages of ex-serfs retained a tincture of continuity in its personal, face-to-face component and a year-to-year stability in those reciprocities in the exchange of land and labor that illustrated a regard for peasant subsistence strategies, villagers (whatever their sympathies) generally stayed outside the movement.

3. Correlation Analysis: the Parish Data

If rural disorders were most clearly identified with communes of former private serfs for reasons that are evident from the foregoing chapters, there were still other aspects of the situation that escaped the Governor's attention. Correlation analysis of statistical data from the surveys of the 1880s allowed us to look more closely at characteristics of the milieux in which unrest emerged in rural districts of Kursk Province during 1905–1906. We will compare the structure of peasant economy in the province as a whole (using data aggregated for the 195 parishes) with a profile drawn from the canvasses of those 275 villages noted in the police and judicial documents as being associated with incidents of unrest.

Analysis of the parish data from the *zemstvo* censuses for Kursk Province during the mid-1880s, presented in correlation matrices annexed to

lished *La mémoire collective.* Halbwachs strictly opposed his conception of collective memory to historical treatment of the past, its periodization of the flow of time and its emphasis on change, and did not foresee that historians would become more and more interested in other frames of reference. The implications of Halbwach's conception for the study of history, however, were well understood at the time, as Marc Bloch's review of the 1925 work shows. Bloch, "Mémoire collective," *Revue de Synthèse Historique,* XI (XIV), 1925, Nos. 118–120, 73–83. See also Olick and Robbins, "Social Memory Studies," *Annual Review of Sociology,* 1998, 24: 105–140.

this volume,[30] recalled several aspects of village economy that had long been observed by *zemstvo* statisticians in other provinces of European Russia. In the first place, the initial matrix reveals the more or less close positive interrelationship of the size of the peasant family household, the basic unit of labor and consumption, with measures of the scale of its economy. We attempt to correlate here data collected under identical rubrics for 169 parishes (i.e. less those for Kursk and Oboian Districts) for labor composition of households (households with no male worker of working age, with one male worker, with 2–3 workers, with 4 or more workers) with data for ownership of horses by households (without horses, with one horse, with 2 horses, with 3 horses, with 4 or more horses). The degrees of independence of household economy are also tested against these indices. If one inspects the matrix by category of the number of males of working age per household, the strongest measures of correlation with the categories of supply of horses per household appear to show, in a fairly symmetrical manner, the positive interaction of expansion of the labor component of the household with accumulation of means of production (horse power) and with its capacity to conduct household economy independently. Conversely, the more significant interrelationship of households with a smaller labor component (*malorabochnye*)—but especially of households with a lesser degree of horse power (*malomoshchnye*)—with households renting away their allotments or hiring non-family labor and/or inventory in order to cultivate is also notable.

The coefficients in matrix 2 in the appendix measure the degree of correlation, using the parish data, between the variables employed in the preceding table (labor composition of the household, supply of horses, degree of independence of household economy) and variables for allotment area, non-allotment land leased, numbers of households with persons engaged in "industrial" pursuits, and literacy. For the measures of allotment as well, the larger the labor component in the household is, the more it is more strongly associated with expansion in variables for allotment area and for the quantity of plowland within it (absolutely and in averages per

---

[30] These tables measure the strength of correlation, co-variation or dependence of two variables or two sets of data, the power of such correlation being scored between 1 (perfect positive correlation) and -1 (perfect negative correlation or anti-correlation). The closer the score approaches 0, the more the two variables may be said to be uncorrelated, so that their variation within the data set is unrelated. We have also included a measure of probability that a given score would be in error or produced by chance: a coefficient that is italicized was flagged with a probability (P) of error higher than 0.005 (1 in 200 chances).

household). But here it is of interest to note that, in relation not only to the allotment indicators, but also to the area of non-allotment land leased and number of renters (for which labor component variables remain largely indistinct), the correlation coefficients are strongly differentiated between categories of household by supply of horse power and expand sharply in magnitude from weaker to stronger units. The same picture appears in the variation of the significance of the correlation for the quantitative variables for area of allotment, these being more sharply differentiated by category of household horse power than by categories of labor power, the magnitudes increasing in the direction of households better supplied with work stock.[31] We will return to this problem below, but this finding contrasts with images of "hunger renting" that colors many portrayals of peasant leasehold in Russia[32] in that some added increment not only of labor *but also of inventory* was indispensable to taking on additional acreage.

Coefficients for households with members engaged in industrial pursuits reflect the inverse premise so well known in the literature. The most significant magnitudes of correlation are concentrated across the categories of *malorabochnye* (households without a male worker of working age, or households with only one male worker)—and once again even more strongly for households with no horses or with only a single animal—oriented by virtue of limited supplies of land and/or inventory toward seeking wage employment outside of household agriculture *sensu stricto*. Conversely, much weaker magnitudes of correlation for "stronger" households with these measures of off-farm wage work suggests that to the degree that households in Kursk Province managed to expand the number of workers that the household could bring to bear on farm operations—in conjunction with the accumulation and maintenance of household means of production—"industrial" pursuits lost their original significance. Note that the correlative power for the numbers of males engaged for *local* off-farm earnings is most strongly associated with the smaller household (households with 1 male worker, households with no horses); coefficients for persons engaged in earning *outside the province* are more

---

[31] This finding coincides in principle with observations made variously by Kablukov, *Ob usloviiakh*, 246–273; Kosinskii, *K agrarnomu voprosu*, 198–274; Koval'chenko (for Penza Province), in I. D. Koval'chenko, ed., *Massovye istochniki*, 314–316; Wilbur, "Was Russian Peasant Agriculture Really That Impoverished?," *Journal of Economic History*, 43: 1 (1983), 137–144.

[32] Including I. A. Verner's treatment of this issue from the census returns for Kursk Province.

strongly significant for households with 2–3 male workers of working age and for households with a single horse.[33] Literacy in Kursk Province began to spread most intensively among peasant youth (principally males) after 1861 (see below). It is thus hardly surprising that magnitudes of correlation in matrix 3 clearly indicate more significant association of numbers of literate persons with numbers of smaller, "younger" households—and even more significantly for those with no horse or only one horse. Finally, the considerable magnitude of correlation between numbers of households with members engaged in non-agricultural "industrial" pursuits and numbers of literate persons repeats many of the conclusions gathered by local observers during the mid-1880s and later.[34]

In the introduction to this volume, it was observed that the close association of the size of the peasant family household (its labor component) with its economic activity was one of the principal findings of *zemstvo* statistical studies during the last decades before the October revolution. Since the most immediate aim of a peasant family farm's economy was identified *primarily* with satisfaction of household consumption needs, by means of the application of family labor, the non-capitalist character of the "laboring" (*trudovoi*) peasantry and the family farm remained the dominant feature of rural life in Russia, even considering a massive participation of the peasant sector in national commodity markets. Furthermore, the research of Chernenkov, Kushchenko, Khriashcheva, Rumiantsev and others showed that village society hardly resembled a static order of separate classes, but remained subject to a continuous, multi-directional process of social mobility. The main driver of the process was demographic: expansion of an original nuclear family unit with minor dependents and limited means toward a larger household unit with an enhanced family labor reserves allowed for an expanded scale of farming. Depend-

---

[33] It is inferable from this, though more vaguely than one would like, that off-farm earnings, as a means to occupy excess labor (excess in terms of available household land and inventory) presented quite different choices to small households and big families that, leaving 1–2 workers for the family farm, could release others to search selectively for higher earnings, even outside the province. See the comments of Khriashcheva, ed., in *Materialy……. Novosil'skii uyezd*, 47–67.

[34] Blagoveshchenskii, *Krest'ianskaia gramotnost'*, 1–60 (using survey data from Kursk, Sudzha, Dmitriev, Fatezh, L'gov Districts); *SSSKG, vyp. VI* (Ryl'sk District), 313–319; *SSSKG, vyp. X* (Belgorod District), 190. All commentators were unanimous in finding, logically enough, that literacy rates (and student registration) dropped notably in villages outside a 3–4 *versta* distance from the local school. Verner, *op. cit.* (*Kurskaia guberniia*), 195–228; Belokonskii, ed., *Narodnoe nachal'noe obrazovanie*, 165–177.

ence of smaller units on off-farm wage earnings in the initial phase of this cycle was very common. Large prosperous households, in particular those incorporating three generations and several married working-age couples, often tended to fissure into their constituent nuclear units, not only as a natural issue of the death of the patriarch, but also as the result of intra-family conflicts to which larger, more complex households were increasingly prone. All units were at the mercy, moreover, of the negative effects of short-term global crises (war, famine and epidemics) or specifically household crises (demographic failure, fire or indebtedness). Material disparities between peasant households at any given moment thus spoke largely although not exclusively of the action of simultaneous centripetal leveling and centrifugal differentiating tendencies at work in long-term life cycles of any given sample of households.[35]

Yet even based on the relatively primitive data from the Kursk provincial census, the following question unwillingly arises. Did expansion and activity of peasant households depend not so much on the number of working hands at their disposal (i.e. size of the household) as the decisive factor, as on a totality of various factors, among which the possibilities for the family economy in this or that settlement to accumulate means of production—work stock and land—were just as significant? In comparison with the categories of family size (to which labor composition of the household relates), the greater distinction between the magnitudes namely of variables for supply of means of production (horses) in correlation with those for land supply give us grounds to answer affirmatively. We recall that the specialists of the era were themselves far from unanimous concerning the significance of the demographic principle (i.e. the labor-consumer composition of the household) as opposed to purely economic factors that exerted powerful influences over possibilities and choices of individual households of any size.[36] The availability of a sufficient supply

---

[35] On dynamic studies, see below. Commentary on these issues appears as a central element in many recent studies. Shanin, *The Awkward Class*; E. M. Wilbur, "Peasant Poverty," in Kingston-Mann and Mixter, eds., *Peasant Economy*, 101–127; Worobec, *Peasant Russia*, 76–117; Heinz-Dietrich Löwe, "Differentiation in Russian Peasant Society: Causes and Trends, 1880–1905," in Bartlett, ed., *Land Commune and Peasant Society in Russia. Communal Forms in Imperial and Early Soviet Society*, 165–195.

[36] A. I. Khriashcheva showed that this "multi-directional" process of movement was associated in the closest manner not only with family size, but also with purely economic factors. By the balance of these latter for various households in 1899, moreover, their respective positions at the moment of the census of 1911 could be predicted with a degree of accuracy. Khriashcheva, *Materialy.... Epifanskii uyezd*, especially 166–231. S.

of accessible land and means to buy or lease land at accessible prices and to acquire and maintain the necessary work stock will have been critical.

4. Correlation Analysis: the Village Data

A second analysis of our variables—this time using the data collected for the 275 settlements noted in police and judicial documents as being associated with incidents of unrest in Kursk Province during 1905–1906—will serve as an example in this very same regard. When data on labor composition of households (again without 38 villages for Oboian and Kursk Districts) were once again measured for correlation against data for household accumulation of horse power (matrix 4), the symmetrical character of the coefficients that we observed in the same analysis for the parish data is now nowhere in evidence. On the contrary, the closest association measured for groups of households with no male worker of working age and with one male worker of working age is found in their correlation with the variable "households without horses." Even variables for "households with 2–3 male workers of working age" and "with 3 or more male workers" produce magnitudes of correlation that are strongest for "households with one horse."

In this connection, the clear differentiation observed in the parish data across the categories of household labor composition with regard to capacity to conduct the household economy independently—or with households renting away their allotments or compelled to hire non-family labor and/or inventory—is also lost. The variable "households with one male worker" in the parish data were most closely of all associated with movement of the variable "households conducting their economy independently." The correlative magnitude of this variable in the *village* sample is strongest now with the movement of data for households that hired labor and/or inventory outside the immediate household.

Just so do survey variables for household labor composition and supply of horses act differently in their correlative relationship to variables

---

N. Prokopovich, analyzing correlation coefficients of data from 496 peasant budgets from various regions of the Empire observed that the availability of land and inventory—i.e. of means of production—had notably greater effects on the scale of household economy than the number of working hands or "eaters," and indeed, made the biological growth of the family possible. *Krest'ianskoe khoziaistvo po biudzhetnym*, passim (especially Chapter III, 74–107, and Chapter IV, 108–143).

for area of allotment (matrix 5). Here, the sharp differentiation observed in the parish data across these former categories disappears, at the same time that the quantitative variables for areas of non-allotment lease continue to reflect the same strong association with households better supplied with work stock. Magnitudes in correlation of literacy and of "industrial" pursuits (particularly local occupations)—again most strongly associated with smaller, labor-poor and resource-poor (in terms of horses) households—are notably stronger. In the parish data, numbers of "households with members engaged in industrial pursuits" provoked more robust correlation with the movement of the variable "persons, engaged in migrant occupations." The same variable in the village sample is now most closely allied to "persons engaged in local occupation." Even stronger associations of literacy variables (matrix 6) in the village sample with variables for industrial employment—especially with local occupations—are also noteworthy.

The more generalized pattern of interrelationships brought out in the parish data thus showed a certain symmetry between household size and horse power, and then between horse power and indices of area of land at a household's disposal, either under allotment or leased. The greater the weight of stronger households—by the magnitude of their labor component, but far more notably by their supply of work stock—the more robust was the correlation with households conducting their farming operations autonomously. Furthermore, groups of households least of all supplied with family labor or horsepower were most closely associated with off-farm work generally and with local employment in particular. These latter groupings, in turn, were also more closely correlated to literacy, which, in concert with what we know about the growth of literacy in the province after 1861, seems to us to be an indirect indicator of their youth. In the analysis of the same data for our sample of villages noted in the source materials in connection with the rural disorders of 1905–1906, this interrelationship between the smaller, economically weaker households, off-farm occupations and numbers of literate persons that remained somewhat implicit in the parish materials stood more clearly in the foreground. Together with the loss of symmetry in correlations between the labor component of households and supplies of work stock—especially notable in the association of even households with larger labor components with those least supplied with work stock—these shifts in emphasis pointed toward a measurably different structure of these various elements in the village sample.

5. The Leading Role of the Rural "Towns"

Such significant disparities between analyses of parish data and the village sample are mainly attributable to the fact that, in the chronology of agrarian unrest in Kursk Province during 1905–1906, *the bigger villages in any given zone of unrest and a number of the heavily populated* slobody *in the province as a whole stood at the forefront at every stage in the movement.* In a province in which the average size of a populated point (of the 2,916 populated points counted by the census of the mid-1880s) equaled 650 persons of both sexes, the average size of villages noted in police and judicial documents associated with our sample of incidents of unrest during 1905–1906 equaled 1,214 residents of both sexes.[37] Behind this average stands the fact that revolutionary events in the rural districts began among populations of bigger villages in a locality and either spread to surrounding settlements or remained restricted to these populations. Village populations among which incidents of agrarian unrest were *repeated* both in 1905 and in 1906 were most often those of the bigger settlements. All "repeaters" were populated by former private serfs and their descendants.[38] This tendency is explainable in terms of several factors.

---

[37] There were 180 settlements in 1905 (average size 1,175) and 103 in 1906 (average size 1,416).

[38] From our archival notes, there were 20 settlements—all of them settled by former private serfs and their descendants—that recorded incidents in both 1905 and 1906. Six incidents were noted at *sloboda* Borisovka (formerly of Count D. N. Sheremet'ev; 15,167 persons in 1883; 18,071 in 1897) and three at the village of Rakitnaia (formerly of N. B. Iusupov, 6,623 inhabitants in 1883, 7,920 in 1897). In Dmitriev District, six incidents are noted at Khomutovka (formerly of A. I. Levshin, 954 inhabitants in 1883, 1,015 in 1897), four at Prilepy (formerly of E. F. Meiendorf; 387 persons in 1883; 1,576 in 1897), three at Dobroe Pole (formerly of Meiendorf; 501 inhabitants in 1883; 543 in 1897) and two each at Romanovo (ex-serfs of 7 different owners; 615 persons in 1883; 766 in 1897) and Glamazdino (formerly of P. P. Volkov, son of L. A. Nelidova; 1,095 persons in 1883; 1,209 in 1897). In Novyi Oskol' District, the lone repeater (3 incidents) was *sloboda* Ol'shanka (formerly of Prince Ivan Iurevich Trubetskoi; 3,406 inhabitants in 1884, 3,522 inhabitants in 1897). In Ryl'sk District, there are 3 incidents at the settlement of Snagost'e (formerly of Bariatinskii, 3,277 inhabitants in 1884; 4,131 in 1897). In Staryi Oskol' District, the documents refer to 2 incidents at the village of Lopukhinka (formerly of Isakov; 965 persons in 1884; 1,049 in 1897). In L'gov District, the settlement of Fitizh (formerly of Stremoukhov; 1,119 persons in 1883, 1,605 in 1897) recorded 3 incidents, Peny (*darstvenniki* formerly of Countess Anna Ivanovna Tolstaia (*née* Bariatinskaia); 1,183 persons in 1883; 1,233 in 1897) and Bol'shie Ugony (formerly of Countess Tolstaia by the same; 1,670 persons in 1883; 1,809 in 1897) each registered 2 incidents. In Sudzha District, repeaters in 1905 and 1906, recording single

In the first place, if the situation with regard to land resources among ex-serfs after 1861 was already far more constricted than among former state peasants, as a result both of norms of allotment set forth in the Local Ordinance and of the inordinate and decisive influence of the old masters in the process by which ex-serfs went onto the redemption regime, densely populated settlements were subjected to particularly onerous disabilities. These were evident not only in terms of smaller household allotments *per se* (it is to be recalled that a minimum allotment per male soul under terms of the Emancipation was set at 2 *desiatiny* 2,200 *sazhen* for most of the province). Of equally devastating import was the practice of allocating peasant lands in any number of separate tracts, physically intermixing private acreage with allotment land (*cherespolositsa*), a condition further complicated by the fact that large settlements were commonly constituted out of two or more communes that held lands in the same tracts. For larger villages, furthermore, allotments were often granted in such a manner that many fields were located at distances farther than three *versta* (about 2 miles) from the clustered house plots in the village itself (*dal'nozemel'e*),[39] a distance beyond which the utility of land for regular cultivation was thought to decline sharply.[40]

---

incidents in both years, are the villages of Borshchen' (ex-serfs, 2 different owners; 807 persons in 1883; 936 persons in 1897), Cherkasskaia Konopel'ka (*darstvenniki*, formerly of Shmidt; 438 persons in 1883) and Dar'ino (formerly of Golitsyn; 1,519 inhabitants in 1883, 1,290 in 1897). In Korocha District, single incidents in 1905 and in 1906 are noted for the adjoining *slobody* of Nikol'skaia (formerly of N. B. Iusupov; 1,207 persons in 1884; 1,460 in 1897) and Pentsovka (formerly of Iusupov; 869 persons in 1884; 834 in 1897). One incident in 1905 and one in 1906 were recorded at Kniazhoe-Bogoliubovka, Nikol'skaia Parish, Tim District (formerly of Tomilin, 633 persons in 1885; 756 in 1897).

[39] The number of separate tracts into which the total area of allotment was divided was shown for the 237 villages surveyed after 1882. In 168 of these (average 1,173 inhabitants), allotment land was received in a single tract; for 22 villages (average 1,072 inhabitants) in 2–3 tracts; in 14 settlements (average 1,421 inhabitants) in 4–5 tracts; and in 33 villages (average 1,859 inhabitants) in 6 or more separate tracts. Distance to the furthest fields in the allotment *massif* was indicated for 207 villages: up to 2 miles –: 55 villages (averaging 628 inhabitants); from 2 to 3.3 miles –: 59 settlements (averaging 876 villagers) from 3.3 miles to 6.6 miles –: 71 villages (average 1,450 inhabitants); over 6.6 miles –: 22 (average 2,320 inhabitants). For a fairly striking example, see the review below of the layout for the six communes of the village of Kon'shino, Ol'shanskaia Parish, Novyi Oskol' District.

[40] Detailed review of such conditions in Kursk Province in Sokovnin, *Dlinozemel'e*, later annexed to his report in the Korocha District Committee on the Needs of Rural Industry, *Trudy mestnykh komitetov*, 189–287. Peasant interviewees, especially with respect to

Disabilities of such magnitude created a situation in which, even if villagers were bound to acquit their financial obligations in connection with the allotments, the big rural towns (of both state peasants and of ex-serfs) often displayed a markedly proto-industrial character. In these big centers, a money economy had replaced, to a greater degree, those remaining elements of the natural economy that sustained smaller, outlying villages, and the larger of them were invariably net importers of their grain supplies. These big country "towns" were typically home to numerous small enterprises associated almost exclusively with sale of services and production of small commodities for local consumption, tending here, however, to lose their seasonal character and become fully formed rural industries. At such sites or in their immediate vicinity were located the flourmills, distilleries, sugar-beet refineries, oil-pressing plants and starch works of the large noble-owned estates or, as was the case with villages at the western extremity of Putivl' District, the Konotop Depot of the Moscow–Kiev–Voronezh Railway and its freight sorting yards. Attenuation of the direct ties to agriculture in many of the more densely populated settlements was also reflected not only in comparatively larger percentages of householders renting away their allotments or arranging for their cultivation by hiring labor and/or inventory outside the household unit. Percentages of householders renting non-allotment land ceded their place, in contrast to small villages, to shares of persons engaged in industrial pursuits locally or in migration. *Local* off-farm occupations predominate over those outside the province.

The physical limitations of the land fund available to the largest settlements provoked overcrowding even in the area of the village proper (greatly increasing the dangers of fire that were endemic in rural life) and prompted, in some cases (Tomarovka, Belgorod District), resettlement of part of the population onto *khutora* at a distance from the village center. Since we know that district centers (to say nothing of the town of Kursk), often quite a bit smaller than the bigger rural settlements, had measurably higher crude death rates than adjacent country districts, it is plausible to assume that overcrowding (people, animals and fowl in close proximity), poorer sanitary conditions and heavy traffic of non-residents promoted higher mortality rates associated with transmission of infectious disease

---

regular manuring, echoed Sokovnin's view that the economic utility of lands declined at distances farther out than three *versta* (two miles) from the zone of house plots. Pershin, in his study of the CAR provinces, used Sokovnin's data. Pershin, *Zemel'noe ustroistvo*, 147–277 (178, 200).

that must have distinguished the quality of life in the most populous towns from that of smaller villages in their orbit.

For, secondly, the more heavily populated rural settlements commonly acted as the principal public and commercial spaces in their immediate localities, as administrative and market centers located on or near main roads and rail networks in the province. From these centers, after the harvests, middlemen (*ssipshchiki, prasoli*) fanned out across the countryside to facilitate delivery of grain and livestock to the central bazaar in these same settlements. Others (*korobeiniki, shibai*) set out to trade in the hundreds of small items of manufacture (including books) essential to peasant households. The parish administrative offices, police station, post office and telegraph (and by 1905, the telephone), dispensary and apothecary, the central bazaar, state liquor stalls, shops, warehouses and workshops of quite various types were most heavily concentrated in big centers. Local agricultural fairs were usually organized in the bigger villages in a given locality.[41] The network of banking and credit associations in Kursk Province, though still in its infancy during the era of the revolution, founded their branches in the big settlements, and the installations established by the local *zemstvo* to maintain a public grain reserve or to provide veterinary, sanitary and medical services to peasant clients were likewise located here. Populations of big, heavily populated rural villages therefore resembled more nearly those of "open villages," the "insider" households holding allotments, but now joined by relatively large cohort of "outsiders," persons from other social estates and public formations with quite various views, opinions and attitudes. Newspapers and journals of local and national circulation were sold at the central bazaar and at railway stations and, as the conservative rapporteurs of the Belgorod conference of Land Captains tartly observed in March 1905, these publications did not always hew to an innocent editorial line, but often bore a notably "red" character.[42] Naturally, then, the populations of big rural centers served as a principal source of news, rumor and interpretation for surrounding hamlets.

Even in the mid-1880s, literacy in the larger rural centers was more highly developed than in smaller outlying villages, attaining in certain

---

[41] In 1905 and in 1906, such fairs (at Chernianka, Golovchino, Snagost'e and Slonovka) served as a pretext for large gatherings of local peasants, which turned immediately toward acts of violence.

[42] GARF, f. 1291 (Land Section, MVD), op. 30, 1905 g., d. 4–b, 1. 178 (*Zhurnal Belgorodskago uyezdnago soveshchaniia 9-go marta 1905 g.*).

cases quite impressive scale for the time.[43] Rural schools in Kursk Province, founded at the collective initiative of the peasant commune itself and funded only in part by *zemstvo* subsidies, were invariably located in larger villages in a given locale, together with whatever meager library or adult education services the village teacher (often to supplement extremely modest pay) and his or her clients could organize. As one would expect, increase in rural literacy—we have seen this in the correlation analyses—was largely concentrated in younger age cohorts. Results of the General Census of 1897 for the rural districts of Kursk Province showed that, if the percentage of literates among males aged between 50 and 59 years equaled 15.4 percent, their numbers among the age cohort aged 20–29 grew to 38.4 percent, and among those aged 10–19 to 44.8 percent. This spread of literacy had already begun to find its reflection among peasant girls: in the age cohort aged 10–19, numbers of literate girls already represented a tripling of the number in the next older cohort and attained just over 9 percent of females of the same age.[44] "Conscious youth," the Governor himself noted with some irony, were especially numerous in wealthier "big villages [*slobody*] and districts."[45]

Thirdly, if the *zemstvo* surveys of the mid-1880s had observed among the peasant population of Kursk Province the very significant weight of households without a male of working age or with only one male worker of working age,[46] the numbers of such households were, naturally, larger in absolute terms in larger rural population centers. Of the sample of 275 villages noted in connection with the rural disturbances of 1905–1906, the relevant data were collected for 237, comprising 48,465 households with a population of 301,953 persons of both sexes in the mid-1880s. In villages of less than 1,000 residents (143), this group was already prominent: out

---

[43] Even in the mid-1880s (against a provincial average of male literates at 8.8%), male literates in large settlements range from 32.2% of the male population in the village of Snagost'e (Ryl'sk District) to 16% at Borisovka. This is before the general increase among younger age cohorts recorded in 1897.

[44] Tsentral'nyi statisticheskii komitet, *Pervaia vseobshchaia perepis'*, table XV, 124–127.

[45] GARF, f. 102, 4-oe deloproizvodstvo, 1907 g., d. 108, ch. 21, ll. 4–4 ob.

[46] Data collected under these rubrics in thirteen districts (without Oboian and Kursk Districts) counted 249,802 households with a population of 1,609,009 persons of both sexes. Of these, 14,198 households (5.7%) had no male worker (48,159 persons –: 3.1% of total population; 3.4 persons per household) and 130,231 households (52.1%) had only one male worker (666,973 persons –: 41.5% of the population; 5.1 persons per household). *SSSKG. Vyp. II–XIV* (Kursk, 1884–1886).

of 11,986 households, 6,768 (56.5 percent) belonged to these household categories; in settlements of between 1,000 and 2,000 inhabitants (54), it was a bit larger (6,686 households out of 11,626 or 57.5 percent). In big settlements of over 2,000 residents, however, 15,468 of 24,853 households (61.2 percent) were counted among those without a male of working age or with only one male worker of working age. Such differences find their analogues in clear differentiations between the three groups for precisely those variables that we have seen most closely associated with small nuclear family households in the correlation matrices: the percentages of households with no horses or only a single horse, households with members engaged in off-farm work, and households unable or *choosing* not to work allotments independently, and the incidence of literacy all appear progressively more prevalent from the smaller to the larger. The resort to leasing non-allotment land, the role of non-allotment land in cultivation, and the number of leasing households appeared manifestly more central to the economies of smaller settlements than for those of the largest units, while, conversely, comparison of shares of households leasing non-allotment land and area leased in relationship to total allotment area confirmed that the larger a settlement was, the more a decline of the practice was observable.

The prosperity of the young nuclear family household depended heavily on the ability of the new head of household—commonly its only adult male laborer—to secure a living for his family from a small allotment and from locally available off-farm earnings, often dividing his working time between his own plot and wage employment.[47] The weaker material position of such households in terms of means of production (land, work stock) and a correspondingly limited capacity to draw upon the natural product of their own farm operations meant that the cash component and off-farm employment played an especially crucial role in their budgets. Recall the closer association of the smaller household with "industrial" employment generally and with local off-farm employment in particular that we noted in the correlation matrices. Half-agricultural, half-industrial in their economic profiles, the large, heavily populated rural centers offered a broader range of economic choices in the locality, and such an atmosphere, it would seem, encouraged in its turn a somewhat greater formation of smaller family households. The disturbances of the late spring and summer of 1906 and the central importance of wage, hire and

---

[47] This was a constant finding of budget studies of peasant households. See for example, Chaianov, *Biudzhety krest'ian.*

land lease issues displayed in the clearest fashion the unstable position of such family households.

The economic profile of the big rural settlements, however, pointed to the tendency toward a steady reduction in the importance of agriculture entirely. Higher percentages of households leasing away their allotments or hiring outside labor and/or inventory, the decline in the role of lease-hold, the far stronger association of bigger settlements with non-agricultural occupations: all these suggest that already in the mid-1880s, the capacity of local supplies of land to support the sowings and work stock so indispensable to agricultural pursuits of small family farms—*let alone their further expansion according to the usual schemes of multi-directional mobility*—had attained some sort of natural limit.

Lastly, it is increasingly difficult, in such settings, to speak of that level of knowledge of and frequency of "face-to-face" contact with one's fellow villagers and their affairs which formed the principal parameters of village life in the smaller villages and hamlets that remained the most common form of settlement in Kursk Province. Given the level of distrust, envy and suspicion that conditions of subsistence economies under demo-graphic pressure generated, this lack of anonymity and a long history of habitual everyday contact provided a prudent householder with a means to monitor the behavior of his neighbors, whose names, families and reputa-tions were as familiar to him as his own was to them.[48] Together with widespread endogamy and the effects of extended kinship networks, the efficacy of such vigilance at close range acted, to varying degrees, to blunt the centrifugal tendencies that such tensions exerted on the social fabric of the village and to maintain a structure for intra-village cooperation, soli-darity and the enforcement of community norms. George M. Foster, Jr., however, estimated that such "integrative mechanisms," operated best in small settlements: in villages of up to 1,000 residents, all adults would know each other by sight and by name, but in those of more than 1,500 persons, "the effectiveness of eternal vigilance as a safeguard begins to

---

[48] On the structuring influence of personal reputation on the entire fabric of village social and economic relationships and its central role not only in the resolution of intra-village conflict between householders or in the election of village officials, but in singling out individuals with unusual talent or special knowledge for crucial functions of community life (home curer, storyteller, sorcerer or songstress), see Gromyko, *Traditsionnye normy*, specifically 105–113. The critical role of a peasant's personal reputation in actions be-fore peasant judges or their peers (in parish courts or the village assembly) also treated in Shatkovskaia, *Pravovaia mental'nost'*, 54–73. Reputation as a form of "symbolic capital" in archaic communities in Bourdieu, *Le sens pratique*, 191–207.

break down and the ensuing frustration further strains the integrative mechanisms which maintain social order."[49]

6. Pressures on the Land Commune and Household

This general situation reflected not only the tempo of natural increase in population in absolute terms, but also the processes of household formation itself that kept pace with it. Contemporary agrarian specialists and the legislators that took up preparation of the Law of 18 March 1886[50] considered that the frequency of family partitions—and the fragmentation of peasant holdings that accompanied it—testified to confirmation of the nuclear family as the norm of rural family life in place of the old complex patriarchal household, a process that unfolded mostly without the consent of the village commune.[51] Whether the pace of partitions was actually *increasing* has been a matter of dispute. N. N. Chernenkov insisted that rising numbers of partitions was the natural consequence of population growth and produced evidence to support the view that average family size had actually grown somewhat toward the end of the century.[52] Ippolit Antonovich Verner assembled surveys of "current population" in the populated villages of the province published by the CSC to show a sharp decline between 1862 and 1878 in average family size from 9.4 persons of

---

[49] Foster, "Interpersonal Relations," 174–178. Noting the relationship between settlement size and crowded conditions in arson-prone *gubernii*, one scholar has made the observation that "when communities exceeded 500 persons, the cohesiveness of society was at risk, as was any common definition of norms and relationships." Frierson, *All Russia Is Burning*, 142–143.

[50] "O poriadke razresheniia semeinykh razdelov v sel'skikh obshchestvakh, v kotorykh sushchestvuet obshchinnoe pol'zovanie polevoiu zemleiu," *PSZ*, III: 6 (5578), 116–117.

[51] For Kursk Province, Cathy Frierson counted 69,773 family partitions solely for the period between 1861 and 1882; only 5,283 received approval of the commune. "Peasant Family Divisions and the Commune," in Bartlett, ed., *op. cit.*, 315, table 18.4. Districts dominated by communities of former state peasants often had somewhat higher averages. That the tempo of household formation moderated after 1878 was also noted by compilers of the 1906 study made by the provincial office of the Treasury, which saw rates of household formation fall from 2.9% *per annum* during 1862–1878, to 2.0% in 1878–1885, to 1.3% for 1885–1905. In the same periods, *per annum* rates for the natural increase in population move from 0.4% to 1.5% to 1.6%. Kurskaia kazennaia palata, *Materialy po krest'ianskomu i chastnomu zemlevladeniiu Kurskoi gubernii*, 11.

[52] Chernenkov, *K kharakteristike krest'ianskago khoziaistva*, originally published in 1898 in *Saratovskaia Zemskaia nedelia.*

both sexes per household (174,546 households) to 6.8 persons (257,910). In the era between 1878 and the surveys of 1882–1885 (294,255 households), however, only an additional 36,345 units (14.1 percent) were recorded, revealing a slight further decline to 6.4 persons per household.[53] The ethnologist S. S. Kriukova has recently come to a similar conclusion that the emancipation process released a pent-up pressure for a regularization of family relations that moved in tandem with transition onto redemption regimes, which was not complete in Kursk Province even twenty years after the acts of 1861.[54]

That the incidence of family partition, in the course of a single generation, affected at the very least a quarter of all households and acted with particular force among big, wealthy households—replenishing numbers of small nuclear family units at the bottom of the economic scale—was demonstrated by a number of dynamic studies in the era before 1917. For the interval 1894–1897, Chernenkov found that the percentage of partitioning households in six parishes of Petrovskii District, Saratov Province (of a total number of 7,019 households) was 6.6 percent.[55] The analysis of P. P. Rumiantsev for Viazemskii District, Smolensk Province (12,520 households), showed that in 1900, 21.4 percent of households registered in the 1884 census sixteen years before had undergone family partitions.[56] A. I. Khriashcheva's comparison of the position of 18,106 households registered for 1899 in Epifanskii District, Tula Province, with their position in 1911 (11 years later) noted that 22.6 percent of the 1899 households had gone through partitions. The new households formed as a result of fission constituted 39.0 percent of all households in 1911.[57] The calculations of G. A. Kushchenko for seven villages in Surazhskii District, Chernigov Province—1,477 households registered in the census of 1882—showed at the moment of a second census in 1911 twenty-nine years later, 26.3 percent of the 1882 households had partitioned, and that constituent households resulting from divisions made up 56.7 percent of the 1911 households in these villages.[58] The new households were concen-

---

[53] Verner, *op. cit.* (*Kurskaia guberniia*), 66–71. Data for "districts without the towns" in the General Census of 1897 (328,540 households) showed 6.5 persons. Tsentral'nyi statisticheskii komitet, *Pervaia vseobshchaia perepis'*, table II, 6–9.

[54] Kriukova, *Russkaia krest'ianskaia sem'ia.*

[55] Chernenkov, *op. cit.*, passim.

[56] Rumiantsev, "K voprosu ob evoliutsii," 453–547.

[57] A. Khriashcheva, A., *Materialy....... Epifanskii uyezd.*

[58] Kushchenko, *Krest'ianskoe khoziaistvo.* While Kushchenko deemed his sample "typical" for Surazhskii District in terms of family size and material conditions (land, work

trated largely, though not always, in the lower and poorer groupings by any variable measuring scale of economy.

The reasons adduced to explain this historic shift were several. Disappearance of the close oversight and self-interest of serf-owners after 1861 and unwillingness or inability of the land commune to slow the frequency of family partition meant in effect an absence of external barriers to a practice that, after all, was sanctioned by peasant custom and usage. After reduction in terms of military conscription to six years, moreover, a young draftee's departure was no longer marked in funereal tones, since after demobilization, ex-conscripts returned home still wholly capable of fulfilling roles of husbands and heads of household, but with a broader experience of the larger world outside his village.[59] The working experience of a large part of the younger cohorts of the rural population came more and more commonly to include some term of labor in off-farm wage employment, either locally or in the migration to the provinces of South Russia as agricultural laborers, unskilled factory workers, miners or laborers on the construction sites in one of the big commercial and industrial centers. In his struggle to set his economy on its feet, especially in the big rural centers of Kursk Province, off-farm employment long served the young peasant as an essential part of his working life.

Furthermore, with time, and most frequently in the context of long association with non-agricultural employment—in which connections between literacy and acquisition of higher skills and higher pay did not pass unnoticed[60]—peasants came to prize the ability to read, write and figure. Far less

---

stock), the rate of natural increase in the number of households (+8.0%) and of the population (+23.0%) lagged far behind the recorded increase of households (+34.6%) and of the population (+43.0%) for the district in the same period. In light of these discrepancies, Khriashcheva thought that the number of partitioned households in Kushchenko's study had been strongly underestimated.

[59] It has been cogently argued that military life in the largely peasant armies of Imperial Russia was so little removed from village life that it could hardly act as a "modernizing" influence on peasant conscripts. Bushnell, "Peasants in Uniform," in Eklof and Frank, eds., *The World of the Russian Peasant*, 101–114. Yet the very fact that the recruit was plucked out of his village and posted somewhere else in the Empire in a new setting cannot be minimized in its impact.

[60] M. V. Komarinets, associate of the Statistical Bureau after its reopening in the mid-1890s, wrote the following in 1903, concerning Kursk Province's migrant laborers: "First of all one must make note of the aspiration among migrant workers to literacy. In the periods of his wanderings in search of work, a worker's powers of observation develop and he begins to look at many things with different eyes. It is not difficult for him to see that for the literate worker the possibilities for the application of his labor are

interested in the "cultural" attainments that his well-wishers among educated strata of Russian society might have hoped to impart, the young peasant found the practical improvement that literacy provided in daily life increasingly essential.[61] According to the General Census of 1897, persons under the age of 30 made up the majority (69.5 percent) of literates "in the districts" of Kursk Province: we have already seen that the gains in literacy were particularly notable in this age cohort.[62] The growth of literacy must be in part attributed to the expansion in investment in the system of primary schools. The network of non-religious schools in Kursk Province expanded from 25 in 1863 to 757 during the 1900–1901 school year (including 41 schools directly funded by the Ministry of Popular Education). In 1901, the Consistory was operating 857 parochial and literacy schools. District *zemstvo* funding for non-religious schools rose from 500 rubles in 1863, to 183,583 rubles in 1895–1896, to 311,860 rubles in 1900–1901. *Zemstvo* subsidies, however, constituted only part of the funding: those 101,124 rubles committed by the peasants themselves (for 1901) represented the collective decision of individual village communities to found such schools, to advance a portion of the funding to run them, and to provide certain minimal facilities and services. The educational program was, of course, still wholly inadequate: the course averaged 450 days spread over three winters, schools were overcrowded, textbooks insufficient in number, teachers' pay and working conditions grim. The complete dependence of the school on village elders—and hence on the vicissitudes of village politics—for repairs, firewood, water, security, and transportation on school business was commonly an insupportable obstacle to its proper functioning. Village funds appropriated for the school often had a way of being spent elsewhere or winding up in the elders' pockets.[63] In spite of such obstacles, literacy

---

much broader than for the illiterate, and he commonly notes that a literate worker gets better pay even for the same work. From these circumstances flow this aspiration that, if he himself is not in a position to study reading and writing, then at least his children must study, so that their search for a livelihood will be made easier in the future. M. V. Komarinets, "Otkhozhie promysly", II: 55.

[61] On the clash between educated society's perception of the aims of education and literacy for "civilizing" the countryside and the peasants' own views of their benefits, see Eklof, *Russian Peasant Schools*. Much the same point has been made in a study of the emergence of the penny press and mass popular literature in the late nineteenth century and educated society's mostly negative view of this development. Brooks, *When Russia Learned to Read*.

[62] Tsentral'nyi statisticheskii komitet, *Pervaia vseobshchaia perepis'*, table XV, 124–127.

[63] On the condition of elementary education in Kursk Province at the end of the nineteenth century, see the survey of 643 teachers (438 male, 205 female) in Kursk Province con-

among army conscripts, varying in the range of 9–13 percent in 1874, in 1894–1895 reached 51 percent of all recruits from Ryl'sk District, 41 percent from Novyi Oskol' District, 35 percent from Sudzha District, 32 percent for L'gov District and 21 percent from Tim District. [64]

Yet if the life horizon of younger peasants was necessarily broader than that of their fathers and grandfathers, they remained, until the very end of the *ancien régime*, in full juridical dependence on the head of household, on the financial standing of the household with the commune and on the fiscal calculations of village officials. Conflicts of interest emerged in particular when male members occupied in off-farm employment at a great distance from the village continued to be obligated to give part of their earnings— which they came to view quite naturally as the result of their own personal labor—to household units from which they received little or no economic benefit, but upon which they were entirely dependent for the issuance or renewal of their passports. The position of wives of junior married males under the authority of the in-laws (not infrequently subject to the sexual depredations of other male members of the household) was often particularly onerous. This was especially true if the husband was engaged in work outside the province and was necessarily absent for long periods. Fights between female members of peasant households not related by blood ties are considered a leading cause of partition.[65]

---

ducted in 1896, which suggested that, despite an enormous expansion of demand in peasant communities for the education of their children—increasingly including girls— the school system and its infrastructure (classroom size, heating in winter, student-teacher ratios, availability of textbooks, teachers' pay and so on) remained wholly inadequate. I. P. Belokonskii, ed., *Narodnoe nachal'noe obrazovanie v Kurskoi gubernii* (Kursk, Kurskoe gubernskoe *zemstvo*, 1897).

[64] *Ibid.*; see also I. P. Belokonskii, ed., *Obzor sostoianiia narodnago obrazovaniia.*

[65] Isaev, "Znachenie," *Vestnik Evropy*, 1883, IV, kn. 7, 333–349; Vorontsov, "Semeinye razdely," *Otechestvennye zapiski*, seriia III, 266 (1883), 1: 1–23; 2: 137–161; Shcherbina, "Semeinye razdely," *Russkoe bogatstvo*, 1896 g., No. 6, 199–210; Z. N., "O krest'ianskikh semeinikh razdelakh," *Pravo*, 1901 g., 12: 639–640; Khauke, *Krest'ianskoe zemel'noe pravo*, 219–231. See also Farnsworth, "The Litigious Daughter-in-Law," *SR*, 45: 1 (1986), 49–64; Milogolova, "Semeinye razdely," in *Vestnik Moskovskogo universiteta, VIII (Istoriia)*, 1987, 6: 37–46; Frierson, "Razdel", *RR*, 46 (1987), 35–52; Worobec, *op. cit.*, 76–117; Bezgin, "Semeinye razdely," in *Osobennosti Rossiiskogo zemledeliia i problemy rasseleniia: Materialy XXVI sessii simpoziuma po agrarnoi istorii Vostochnoi Evropy*, 241–245. In relation to the situation in Kursk Province, see Verner, ed., *Kurskaia guberniia*, 77–78, and the observations of M. V. Komarinets on the effects of labor migration on the incidence of partition in "Otkhozhie promysly," II, 42–57. Khriashcheva considered that migration of family laborers—and the role of off-farm labor in the household economy (*promyslovost'*) generally—played

It is thus not so surprising that commentaries on this issue should stress—often in highly negative tones—the appearance among the younger generation of peasants of that striving to arrange their lives according to their own desires and of a growing awareness of personal rights and possibilities: many decried a new spirit of "individualism" among younger villagers for its influence in promoting the "moral decay" of traditional peasant society. Beyond the opprobrium with which official observers sought to paint these phenomena with such a broad brush, however, generational conflict increasingly tended to reflect the sea change in rural life of which the new generation was the bearer. If the modes of domination of the servile era—what was in practice the unrestricted subjection of the person of peasant to a local lord—had been formative both for an older generation of male heads of household that now controlled village politics and for village institutions and their often arbitrary practices,[66] this "past"—as a lived experience in the present—was wholly absent in the lives of those born after the Emancipation. Secondly, in a rural *habitus* in which the inculcation of the sense of self and of community remained an oral tradition—*via* the transmission of village lore, of ritual and ceremonial practice, of an accumulated body of agro-technical wisdom, of the panoply of cultural knowledge and of a dense fabric of social customs and prohibitions, the monopoly that the older generation exercised over this heritage was inseparable from the social reproduction of its authority, particularly over the young.[67] But diffusion of literacy and a growing mobility among younger villagers now gave these latter access to other narratives, other perspectives and bodies of knowledge, other models of behavior, of tastes and of festivity outside this tradition,[68] a broadening of horizons accentuated by growing frequency of contact with non-peasant milieux, either in a local context or as a consequence of movement of a large element of the province's working-age population to sites throughout South Russia in search of wage employment. That generational identities of "children" develop in opposition to those of the generation of the "fathers" was therefore not simply a factor in the social life of the privileged orders of *fin-de-siècle* Russian society as this tension was immortalized in Turgenev's portrait of Evgenii Bazarov. Something

---

a central role in engendering conflicts of interest that led to family partitions in Tula Province. Khriashcheva, *Materialy……. Epifanskii uyezd*, 69–70.

[66] Aleksandrov, *Sel'skaia obshchina*; Hoch, *Serfdom*.

[67] Bourdieu, *op. cit.*, Livre 1, *passim*, especially 87–109.

[68] Frank, "Simple Folk, Savage Customs?"

of this same contest will certainly have unfolded in the peasant milieu between an older generation born in the last decades of the servile era, and a younger generation that had no lived experience of serfdom and the personal character of interactions between lord and peasant, and had grown restive with older, inherited hierarchies of deference and structures of discipline and authority in rural society, rooted in the pre-Emancipation era and substantially preserved in the acts of the 1860s and subsequent legislation.[69] The contest not only engaged a struggle over this inherited "tradition" and the legitimacy of authority for which it acted as the foundation: it also played a direct role in the "land question" itself.

This is not the place to engage the question of the antiquity of rural land commune (*obshchina*), either as an original and unique aspect of the primordial culture of the eastern Slavs, an idea long defended by the Slavophiles, or, as many scholars of the "state school" of historical analysis supposed, as an administrative mechanism that gradually transformed, most definitively in the course of the seventeenth and eighteenth centuries, the customarily loose "neighborly" confederations of independent smallholders settled on the land into appendages of state authority (or, by delegation, of serf-owner control) that aimed principally at the "mobilization" of peasant human and material resources.[70] In the aftermath of the reforms of the 1860s and the lapse of direct oversight of the serf-owners and the Ministry of State Domains, the commune, through

---

[69] For a conception of the generational cohort and its interaction with its inherited sociocultural milieu, see Karl Mannheim's 1928 essay, "The Problem of Generations," in *Essays*. An examination of significant variations in the collective memories of different five-year age cohorts in a sample of 1,410 Americans 18 years old or older is Schuman and Scott, "Generations and Collective Memories," *American Sociological Review*, 54: 3 (1989), 359–381.

[70] The debate is reviewed by Petrovich, "The Peasant," in Wayne S. Vucinich, ed., *The Peasant*, 191–230. For a succinct review of the principal legislative acts during the sixteenth, seventeenth and eighteenth centuries that leans heavily toward the view of the origins of collective authority over community lands and practice of repartition in state policy, see Pushkarev, *Krest'ianskaia pozemel'naia obshchina*. Aleksandra Efimenko's study of the original settlement of the Novgorodian lands (Arkhangel'sk Province), insisted on the absence of fixed communal entities (there was no reference to these where they would be expected to appear—in inventories of the Novgorodian lands of the early sixteenth century) and the gradual evolution of private peasant landholdings up to the mid-seventeenth century, when the Muscovite state began to "organize" peasant life. *Issledovaniia*, 185–382. The complete silence of the Novgorodian inventories (*pistsovye knigi*) on this form of land ownership was also decisive for Sergeevich in the analysis of landholding customs. Sergeevich, *Drevnosti, Tom tretii*, 25 and following.

the agency of the village assembly and its elected officials, continued to play the unavoidably ambiguous role in village life that it had inherited from the servile era. It was the immediate intermediary between the peasant populace and the organs of state power, responsible to these latter for apportionment and collection of taxes, selection of military recruits and acquittal of unremunerated labor obligations and police functions. Within this larger framework, the land commune acted as the guarantor of the community's fiscal solvency, social discipline and moral rectitude within the village, acquitted a wide range of administrative functions associated with day-to-day workings of the village economy (including, but not limited to, setting the agricultural calendar) and joint use of communal lands (forest, pasture, hay meadow), adjudicated minor conflicts between villagers, and commonly exercised its authority to underwrite measures of mutual aid that benefited members struck by sudden catastrophe and that obliged all heads of household to make labor or cash contributions.[71]

What is of interest here is that modern treatments of the Russian peasantry routinely insist that periodic redistribution of arable lands, title to which remained fixed by law in the peasant land commune by the legislative acts of the 1860s, served as one of the principal devices for providing subsistence insurance to all members of the peasant community and was, indeed, one of the defining continuities of collectivist traditions of village life in Russia. It is impossible not to observe, however, that not only did the land commune in Kursk Province exhibit a marked reluctance to intervene in the processes of household fragmentation—let the partitioned units just bear their weight in taxes and redemption dues—but it also did even less to adapt land apportionments to them. During the course of work on the census of 1884–1885, canvassers found (Verner's surprise at the finding is palpable[72]) that, from the era of the general repartitions (korennye peredely) based on "revision souls" of the Tenth Revision of 1858, the land commune in Kursk Province had proved less than eager to carry out such repartitions in order to correlate the size of households with the size of allotments. Twenty-three years after the Emancipation, out of 1,170

---

[71] For recent treatments of the range of these functions, see Mironov, "The Russian Peasant Commune," in Eklof and Frank, eds., *The World of the Russian Peasant*, 7–43; Gromyko, *Traditsionnye normy*, 93–160.

[72] Before 1881, he had served in the Statistical Bureau of the Moscow Provincial Zemstvo and assisted in its survey work in the countryside. Had his experience on this matter been so different?

communes holding lands in repartitional tenure polled in six eastern districts during 1884, only 48 had made the transition to "present souls" (*nalichnye dushi*) by recourse to general repartition. Another 227 practiced partial reshuffling of strips at various intervals to equalize disabilities with regard to soil and distance from house plots: these were carried out based on the old revision souls and left the distribution of acreage by household unchanged. Still 20 others remained in the old allotments by the conjugal pair (*tiaglo*).[73] In both Kursk and Ryl'sk Districts, general repartitions had not been practiced at all since Emancipation.[74]

Why was this so? In the absence of a new "revision," the polling showed, households for whom disposition of allotment land was particularly beneficial ("*mnogodachniki*") in terms of the relationship of household labor to allotment area long rested their arguments against repartition on the heavy weight of redemption dues that they had borne over many years. In many instances, improvements made on allotments by dint of peasants' own labor and expense—this pertained usually to consistent manuring of the households' near strips—worked as a powerful disincentive to the practice. A general apprehension about the larger consequences of such measures was undeniably a factor: the oldest peasant interviewees could often recount in detail the history of long and violent conflicts over repartition within communities of state peasants during 1839–1854 that pitted land-poor householders against those to whom multiple allotments ("*shirokodachniki*") had accrued over time, leading to years of chronic unrest and troubles in the rural districts.[75] Since it was incumbent on those that demanded general repartition to obtain a two-thirds majority in the

---

[73] The 1,170 communes in Novyi Oskol', Tim, Shchigrov, Staryi Oskol', Belgorod and Korocha Districts.

[74] In Ryl'sk District, "there haven't been repartitions [*peredely*] at all since the time of the emancipation of the peasants and partial redistributions or reshufflings [*pereverstki ili "peredvizhki"*] take place only in communes in which the manuring of fields has never been practiced." *SSSKG. Vyp. VI* (Ryl'sk District), XXI. Interviewers in Kursk District found no evidence of full repartitions or even of partial redistributions (*svalki-navalki*) to equalize disabilities of distance or differing soil qualities. *SSSKG. Vyp. I* (Kursk District), 70. As late as 1901, of 284 communities in Kursk District with lands under communal tenure (there were also 193 under household tenure), 205 ascribed their allotments to the old 1858 households; 79 had gone over to "current souls" by full repartition. *Trudy mestnykh komitetov*, 321–322. In Oboian District, matters had progressed a bit further: by 1903, out of 194 communities holding their lands under communal tenure, almost half (96) had made the transition to "current souls." The rest retained their allotments under the old 1858 distributions. *Ibid.*, 530–532.

[75] Verner, *Kurskaia guberniia*, Chapter X, 8–9.

village assembly (*skhod*) for such a measure, the power of such arguments posed real obstacles to its adoption.

The findings of the canvassers of 1884–1885 for communes in Kursk Province on this matter thus anticipate Kachorovskii's later (1906) depiction of a collision of two concepts of "justice" in rural communities: "the right to labor" (*pravo na trud*) in which the right to the means to provide for the subsistence for oneself and one's family expressed itself, and the "right of labor" (*pravo truda*) that embraced the right to the enjoyment of that which one had acquired by dint of one's own personal labor and expense.[76] They also lend credence to the view of the ethnologist M. M. Gromyko that the Russian peasantry's recognition of community rights in the matter of land distribution coexisted in uneasy contradiction with a striving to defend a hereditary right of the household to lands worked by its ancestors, a claim "turned simultaneously against encroachments of the landowner and of excessively zealous partisans of repartition."[77] Enduring ambiguities in attitudes toward property rights, rooted both in peasant custom itself, forged as it was in the era of serfdom[78] and in the body of Imperial statutes, were exacerbated by the marked lack of enthusiasm of local officialdom to disturb the *status quo* in such matters: the reluctance to facilitate initiatives for repartition grew either out of a certain community of interest with existing village elites or simply an unwillingness to engage processes that commonly resulted in lasting acrimony between contending parties well beyond the adoption of the commune's final act.[79] Yet growing demographic pressure, steady inflation of land rents through-

---

[76] Kachorovskii, *Russkaia obshchina*, especially 152–215. This powerful dissonance and its influence on the revolutionary situation in the countryside at the end of the century also found their way into the analysis of Gordon, "Khoziaistvovanie na zemle," in Danilov and Milov, eds., *Mentalitet*, 57–74. See also Leonard, *Agrarian Reform in Russia*, 125–160.

[77] Gromyko, "Sem'ia i obshchina" in Gromyko and Listova, eds., *Russkie*, 7–8.

[78] V. A. Aleksandrov suggested that, if peasant landholding practices had evolved toward the end of the fifteenth century in the direction of household hereditary tenure, the gradual subjugation of the person and the property of the serf to the control of the noble landowners or the state authority, essentially complete around the middle of the seventeenth century, severely limited this development and cemented the place of communal tenure and its repartitional practices in the customary views of landholding in peasant milieux as these survived the Emancipation. Aleksandrov, *Obychnoe pravo*.

[79] *Trudy mestnykh komitetov...* (Kurskii uyezd), 63–71. A penetrating recent analysis of the complex range of issues and conflicts involved in communal decisions on the issue of repartition (including a useful nuancing of Kachorovskii's points, 164–165) is Gautier, *Ruling Peasants: Village and State in Late Imperial Russia*, 132–168.

out Kursk Province and the maturation of a new generation of younger heads of household in the countryside and its weight in the village assemblies meant that this state of affairs could not last indefinitely.

It is therefore not without interest to note the observations of investigators of unrest in Dmitriev District during February 1905 in just this connection:

As has been noted, the peasants in the localities in which the unrest took place are better supplied with land than elsewhere, a situation that has been improved by emigration. The land that remained in the use of the communes had been distributed between householders on the basis of the old "revision souls," but several years ago, peasants with large families [*mnogosemeinye*] succeeded in gaining a repartition of the land (which here, despite the communal order, had never been practiced) on the basis of present-day souls [*nalichnye dushi*]. According to the locals, these repartitions generated conflicts in the communes and discord between the "old souls" and the "new souls." Householders who received significantly less land than they had disposed of earlier were extremely embittered and their complaints about shortage of land were taken up by those who, having got new allotments, had in essence no grounds to complain [...] All such conflicts over land and repartitions, with corrections and alterations in distributions right up until [the adoption of] the commune's final resolution [*prigovor*] deprived the peasants who had received larger allotments of any certainty in the security of their right to the land. The workings of the communal order, which in general does not facilitate reinforcement of firm understandings of private property among the population, in the given case exerted its most negative influence, directing the peasantry's thinking increasingly to the alluring call to seize the lands of the *pomeshchiki* in their own cause.[80]

In his report of January 1906 on causes of the 1905 disorders, the Governor also made note of the fact that "in recent times," a sharp increase in numbers of general repartitions (*korennye peredely*) had been recorded throughout the province, namely in communes of former private serfs that had not agreed to such repartitions since 1861,[81] and this despite the *ukaz* of 8 June 1893 that sought to stem the sudden growth in the frequency of such measures or at the very least to regulate the practice by subjecting all such decisions to administrative oversight and approval.[82] Such periodization crudely correlates with data, reviewed by Ven'iaminov in 1908, sup-

---

[80] *Nachalo pervoi russkoi revoliutsii...*, No. 415, p. 629. The Local Ordinance of February 19, 1861, did indeed award former serfs in Dmitriev District a notably higher range of allotment norms—because of the notably poorer quality of its soils relative to the rest of the province.

[81] RGIA, f. 1291, op. 122, 1906 g., ll. 41–42.

[82] "Ob utverzhdenii pravil o peredelakh mirskoi zemli," *PSZ* III, v. 13, 3 August 1893, No. 9754, 425–427.

plied by parish administrations in 66 unidentified districts selected in different regions of European Russia for 6,830 communes of former state peasants and ex-serfs. Of these, 74 percent had never carried out a general repartition from 1861 (meaning 1858) to "the beginning of the 1880s" and remained in the old partition by revision souls. Polled during 1897–1902, however, fully 86 percent of these same communes had conducted general repartitions based on current male souls, labor composition of the household or numbers of eaters (*edoki*).[83]

Available evidence for Kursk Province did not bear out the usual view that the land commune exercised its repartitional functions *periodically*.[84] Rather, the wave of general repartitions in the 1890s in communes of ex-serfs that had not carried out such operations since the Emancipation— and we know that these constituted a substantial majority—was sooner associated with the unenviable position of the new and restive generation of younger households in such communes and their now decisive capacity to force their will upon the village assembly. The fact that such measures were conducted during or in the wake of an era of elevated death rates (1889–1894) and against a backdrop of the deterioration in terms of leasehold and of the capacity of off-farm employment to absorb an excess of working hands speaks more of their extraordinary—and not periodic— character.[85] I also view such events as indicative of the fact that redistributive mechanisms within the Russian land commune were not accepted as a matter of course, but came down, in the end, to the aggressive, sometimes violent, push-and-shove of village factions and their allies among peasant officeholders and local officials that promoted lasting enmities. Observations of this sort, although impressionistic, suggest that beyond paradigms of the "little community" that are now a dominant *leitmotif* in much of the

---

[83] Ven'iaminov, *Krest'ianskaia obshchina*, 107–154. The author held up the surge of general repartitions as an indication of the vitality of the Russian peasantry's egalitarian proclivities and communal traditions.

[84] See in this connection Christine D. Worobec's findings, "The Post-Emancipation Russian Peasant Land Commune," in Bartlett, ed., *op. cit.*, 86–105.

[85] In contrast, however, atomization of holdings may well have proceeded farther among the *odnodvortsy*, since, with the gradual fading of the older clan tie as the mechanism for apportionment of field allotments, there was no generally accepted means for reapportionment. In Tim District, with the highest concentration of households of *odnodvortsy* in the province, extreme fragmentation of allotment lands was often cited as a factor in the abandonment of fallow and the adoption of continuous cropping. Strips became so small that they could not be cultivated individually: some communities began to petition local officials for permission to go over to communal tenure. *SSSKG. Vyp. XII* (Tim District), Otd. B, "Opisanie volostei Timskogo uyezda," 1–110.

current literature on Russia's village life at the end of the nineteenth century, the reality was perhaps more ambiguous. Collisions between older integrative mechanisms by means of which village communities strove to maintain control over their members and an individualism that had weathered the transformations of the servile era and won a foothold of legitimacy in a younger generation of peasants were increasingly a chronic irritant in rural life.

7. Large Rural Settlements: a Closer Look

The leading role of big rural centers in agrarian unrest in Kursk Province in 1905–1906 and the distinctive combination of greater concentrations of economically weaker nuclear family households, a demonstrably higher level of literacy even in the mid-1880s, and evidence of the decline of agriculture in favor of "industrial" pursuits in the context in which they lived, made up a large part of the backdrop to the disorders. Conversely, the profile of smaller villages and hamlets that tended to follow the lead of their bigger neighbors in disturbances most often presents a picture in reverse, largely more typical for the country districts of Kursk Province as a whole. Data on villages with less than 1,000 residents (143 villages with an average of 543 inhabitants of both sexes) illustrate the fact that the order that obtained at larger sites is stood on its head, so to speak, in the smaller. If in the group of the largest country towns, only 29.8 percent of householders leased non-allotment lands (the area of which, relative to the total area of allotments, constituted 9.7 percent), this contingent of tenants made up over half of all householders (52.6 percent) and area leased by these equaled 27.0 percent of area under allotments. In the biggest centers, 32.5 percent of households were forced—or chose—to work their allotments by hiring non-household labor and/or inventory or to rent away their allotments entirely; in smaller villages, 18.4 percent of households were so registered. The percentage share of households with no horse or a single animal—48.6 percent of households in smaller villages—was progressively higher for settlements of larger size, reaching 62.2 percent in villages with more than 2,000 inhabitants. Far less literate, with far fewer handicraft or small-industrial enterprises (migrant laborers predominated over those employed locally), smaller villages preserved, compared to their larger neighbors, a much closer tie to agriculture.

This general view of a milieu from which revolutionary events in Kursk Province surfaced is most closely approximated by the group of

villages observed in the sources in connection with the zone of disturbances within Novyi Oskol' and Staryi Oskol' Districts during 1–6 November 1905. For half the villages in this zone, even in the mid-1880s, the
average allotment area per *dvor* was well below district averages.[86] This
circumstance was accentuated by the physical position of fields, directly
attributable to land settlements of the emancipation era: allotments of only
thirteen villages lay entirely within two miles of the cluster of house plots;
even in two of these (Petrovskoe, Ezdochnoe), the tract was broken up
into four or more parcels intermixed with holdings of other owners.[87]
Among remaining villages, such problems were more severe: 25 were
fortunate enough to get allotments in single parcels, but of these 14 had to
try to work plots 3 miles or more from their huts.[88] Okuni, Ol'shanka,
Novo-Matveevka, Novaia Bezginka and Kon'shino had allotment lands in
three or more tracts scattered from three to thirteen miles out.[89]

---

[86] In both Novyi Oskol' and Staryi Oskol' Districts, in which former state peasants were
numerous, average allotments were around 9 *desiatiny* per household (8.93, 9.31).
Among the 32 villages noted in the sources in connection with rural unrest in 1905–
1906, 3 had allotments of average size between 1 and 3 *desiatiny* per household
(Maslovka, Sharapovka and Chernianka); 12 possessed allotments averaging between 3
and 6 *desiatiny* (Golubina, Orlik-Nikolaevka, Volkovka, Elizavetenka, Ol'shanka, Petrovskoe, Bol'shoi Khutor, *khutor* Iakovlevka, Lopukhinka, Evgen'evka, *khutor* Malyi
and Troitskaia) and 10 villages held allotments equaling 6–9 *desiatiny* (Nikol'skaia,
khutor Sretenka, Gladkovo, Myshenka, Morkvina, Novaia Bezginka, Volokonovka,
Dubenka, *khutor* Slaviano, *sel'tso* Novo-Matveevka). These were all villages of ex-
serfs.

[87] *SSSKG. Vyp. XI* (Novyi Oskol' District), Ch. 2, pt. 1 ("Statisticheskiia svedeniia ob
ekonomicheskom polozhenii krest'ianskikh obshchin Novooskol'skago uyezda"): Malyi
(Adelaidin), Ezdochnoe, Maslova, Chernianskaia Parish, 130–137; Gladkovo
(Ol'shanskaia Parish, 82–89; Golubina, Sharapovka, kh. Iakovlevka, Prigorodniaia Parish, 114–121; Elizavetenka, Petrovskoe, Volotovskaia Parish, 2–9; *SSSKG. Vyp. XIV*
(Staryi Oskol' District), Ch. I ("Statisticheskiia svedeniia ob ekonomicheskom polozhenii krest'ianskikh obshchin Starooskol'skago uyezda"): Orlik, Orlikovskaia Parish,
82–89; Sretenka, Saltykovskaia Parish, 98–105; Evgen'evka, Kladovskaia Parish, 130–
137; Slaviano, Obukhovskaia Parish, 138–145.

[88] *Ibid., Vyp. XI* (Novyi Oskol' District): Chernianka, Morkvina, Bolshoi Khutor, Chernianskaia Parish, 130–145; Volkovo, Protochnoe, Volkovka, Ol'shanskaia Parish, 82–
89; Nikol'skaia, *sloboda* Troitskaia, Larisovka, Volotovskaia Parish, 2–9; *Vyp. XIV*:
Lopukhinka, Kladovskaia Parish, 2–9; Myshenka-Bogoslovka, Dubenka, Mikhailovka,
Bogoslovskaia Parish, 26–33; Sorokino, Dolgopolianskaia Parish, 34–41; *sloboda* Volokonsk, Obukhovskaia Parish, 138–145.

[89] *Ibid., Vyp. XI* (Novyi Oskol' District): Okuni, Chernianskaia Parish, 130–145;
Ol'shanka, Ol'shanskaia Parish, 74–81; Novo-Matveevka, Ol'shanskaia, 82–89; Novaia
Bezginka, Volotovskaia Parish, 50–57.

At Kon'shino, the situation had reached absurd proportions by the mid-1880s, and a detailed review of the situation is instructive. Among its six communes (128 households of *odnodvortsy*, 122 households of ex-serfs totaling 1,411 inhabitants in 1884; 1,589 in 1897), dispersion of tracts and physical overlapping of allotments was such that villagers had hundreds of lots between half a *desiatina* and 7 *desiatiny* in size scattered through the Kon'shino Tracts up to 4.5 miles from their houses and interspersed with lands of estate owners. The 128 households of state peasants (*odnodvortsy*) at Kon'shino (Kon'shino I) held what looked on paper to be a rather imposing acreage—1,989 *desiatiny* in arable land or 15.5 *desiatiny* per household. Yet these lands were scattered in numerous small bits and pieces (from a quarter of a *desiatina* to seven *desiatiny* in size) throughout the Kon'shino Tracts, a third of a mile to four and a half miles from the village. These parcels were the rest of a larger *massif* of 3,212 *desiatiny* that their ancestors had held, the remainder of which villagers considered to have been illegally seized by neighboring landowners. Local officials had impounded all the old documents and surveys in the 1830s, so an effort to raise a claim in the courts had long been considered futile. However, the inextricable mixing of their plots with lands of nearby estates—and the dues and fines extracted over rights of way—had exhausted their patience by 1884: "The villagers ardently desire a survey," we read, "but the adjoining owner, *materially interested in this interspersing*, obstructs the matter by withholding his agreement. As a result, the peasants have lodged a suit against him."[90] Fifty *desiatiny* of forest, formally ascribed to Kon'shino I, remained under state "management": every year, the commune had to pay to have five *desiatiny* opened for its use. On the main portion of their plowland (1,200 *desiatiny*), the peasants had abandoned crop rotation in favor of continuous sowings without short fallow, as had their neighbors of Kon'shino III and Kon'shino IV. Ex-serfs of these latter (7.3 *desiatiny* per household) had been entirely stripped of meadow land and forest[91] upon transfer onto the redemption regime in 1882–1883.

---

[90] The reluctance of peasant communities to appeal to the Imperial courts had solid foundations. Such cases commonly took 5–10 years and great expense to resolve, and judges appear to have been reluctant to rule against landowners. "Dokladnaia zapiska krest'ianina A. Ia. Vydrina o cherespolositsa," *Trudy mestnykh komitetov*, 656–659. Vydrin regaled the Sudzha District Committee with the account of a suit brought by the villagers of Skorodnoe in 1839 against a nearby landowner, *which had yet to be settled in 1902*.

[91] Peasants of Kon'shino IV burned as their principal fuel manure mixed with rye straw that they got from a local landowner in exchange for labor obligations. This method of

Their allotment lands had been dispersed (respectively) in 50 and 90 small pieces of between half a *desiatina* and 3 *desiatiny* in size throughout the Kon'shino Tracts, from a half of a mile to four and a half miles away from their houses. Even the ex-serfs on "beggar's" allotments of Kon'shino V (1.6 *desiatiny* per household) had had their lands allotted to them in seven parcels of between half a *desiatina* and 3½ *desiatiny* in size, up to two and a half miles from the village.[92] Indications are that attempts to remedy the situation at Kon'shino were still under way twenty years later. At the District Conference of Land Captains in March 1905, it was said that a final survey of the 3rd General Kon'shinskaia Dacha in 1904 had greatly intensified the hostility of villagers toward adjoining landowners because of their sense of having been cheated in both the quantity and quality of lands received.[93]

Among the villages in this region in our sample, this situation was unique only in its severity. Consequences of such disabilities of allotment size and location, however, were reflected differently in the great majority of smaller villages in the substantial role played by the leasing of non-allotment lands—and the unusually prominent signs of a shift away from agriculture toward "industrial" pursuits in many of the larger settlements. Even in the mid-1880s, twenty-two settlements recorded engagement of households in wage labor pursuits that was greater than the average for their districts. Over 40 percent of persons of working age (both sexes) were so engaged in fifteen; particularly high percentage shares are noted for Chernianka, Maslovka, Golubina, Troitskaia, Morkvina (55.7 percent to 46.9 percent) and even for some of the smaller hamlets in the zone of unrest: Elizavetenka, Larisovka, Nikol'skaia and Bol'shoi Khutor (54.3 percent to 47.5 percent). With regard to Chernianka, in which the events of November 1905 began, the canvassers noted with special clarity the manner in which the land settlement had directly forced changes in the occupational orientation of the populace:

---

heating the huts was said to have been widespread in a largely deforested region of the province.

[92] *Ibid.*, *Vyp. XI* (Novyi Oskol' District): Kon'shino (in 1905, Khalanskaia Parish, formerly of Kon'shinskaia, 82–97); see also Part I-B ("Opisanie volostei Novooskol'skago uyezda"), 28–31. Kon'shino VI was made up of former private serfs (of the Achkasovy, Bakeev, Vishniakov, Gutorova) sequestered by the state before 1861: the allotment (1884) averaged 2.4 *desiatiny* per household without meadow or forest.

[93] RGIA, f. 1291, op. 30, 1905 g., d. 4-b, l. 185 (*Zhurnal Novooskol'skago soveshchaniia zemskikh nachal'nikov 11-go marta 1905 g.*).

The character of the population of these four communes is sooner industrial than agricultural. The insignificance of the allotment (2.5–4.2 *desiatiny* per household) and the inconvenience of its location in relation to the settlement long ago forced the inhabitants of Chernianka to turn from agriculture to various kinds of local and itinerant wage earning, like the *kosovitsa*, local agricultural hire and also handicrafts: bootmaking, manufacture of sieves, coopering, woodworking and so on. Of the total number of 464 households counted, only 125 or 28 percent work the allotments with family labor and their own inventory. The rest either work the land with the aid of hire or simply lease the allotment to someone else. The percentage of horseless households among allotment holders here is very high; in all four communes almost 50 percent of householders [...] Literacy has developed quite impressively: there are 374 literates in the four communes or 16 percent of the populace, a very high percentage for such an isolated district as Novyi Oskol'. In general, the inhabitants of Chernianka are quite striking in the degree of their culture relative to other peasants in these parts, a culture formed not only out of industrial activity, but also from the circumstance that Chernianka has long served as one of the main market points of the region.

Over three-quarters of households (76.1 percent) surveyed in Chernianka in 1884 (464 households of ex-serfs, 2,381 inhabitants in 1884; 5,860 persons in 1897[94]) had no male or only one male of working age. Twenty-one percent of males were literate. Despite average allotment at 2.8 *desiatiny* per household, villagers leased only modest additional acreage, being equal to 11.9 percent of the total area under allotments. Moreover, 95.3 percent of its households had no horse or only a single horse. Seven out of ten economies either hired outside labor and/or inventory or simply rented away their allotments. Ninety-seven percent of households had members engaged in off-farm occupations; 55.7 percent of persons of working age were so employed.[95]

At *sloboda* Ol'shanka—ex-serfs formerly of Prince Ivan Iur'evich Trubetskoi (1841–1915), 556 households, 3,406 inhabitants in 1884; 3,522 persons in 1897—the average size of a household allotment was 4.35 *desiatiny*, but leasing of non-allotment lands had virtually ceased. Families with no male of working age or only one male of working age made up 62 percent of all households. Among the males, 27.4 percent were literate. Nine out of ten households had no horse or only a single horse. Almost half hired non-family labor and/or inventory to cultivate or leased out their allotments. Four fifths of households had members engaged in off-farm employment or 40.5 percent of villagers of working

---

[94] The first commune of Chernianka, some 543 households, was not polled due to a fire in 1884 that had destroyed 300 homes. There were thus 1,007 households of former serfs; less than half were polled.

[95] *Ibid.*, Vyp. XI ("Opisanie..."), 102–103.

age.[96] At *sloboda* Golubina (ex-serfs formerly of the Miatlev clan, 291 households, 1,503 inhabitants in 1884; 1,638 in 1897), the average size of the allotment was 3.1 *desiatiny* per household, but here leasehold was also of only modest resort—peasants in Golubina leased an area equal to 7.1 percent of the total area that they had received as allotments. Instead, 93 percent of households had members in off-farm employment, which occupied 51.4 percent of persons of working age. Seventy-three percent of households in the commune had no male of working age or only a single male of working age; 87 percent had no horse or only a single horse and 44.7 percent of families either worked their lands with non-household labor and/or inventory or leased out their allotments.[97] Only 8.2 percent of males at Golubina were literate. Higher rates of literacy were observed, though, at settlements that had decided to support schools, at Kon'shino, Morkvina or Troitskaia (14.2 percent to 11.3 percent among males), where, as in Ol'shanka and Chernianka, village schools had come into existence between 1861 (Troitskaia I) and the mid-1880s.[98]

These large settlements were the first "to raise the red rooster" in the parishes, to be closely followed by surrounding villagers. In this connection, we have already noted the "organizing role" played by the Elets-Valuiki branch of the Southeastern Railway in the first three days of unrest as the axis along which the wave of disorders moved. Almost all villages involved in unrest during 1–3 November had become "railway towns" between 1895 and 1898, though they had long since had in common the fact of their location on the River Oskol', along which the railway right-of-way was built, and the post road that ran between Staryi Oskol' and Novyi Oskol'. But the construction of the railway not only appears to have promoted a certain reorientation of local export strategies among noble landowners—which made Chernianka an even more focal locale—but also brought these country villages along the railway into more immediate contact with each other and with national events.[99] Indeed, a powerful impression must have been created by the national rail strike that took hold in the province after 10 October 1905 and lasted into November. Work at the flour and gristmills

---

[96] *Ibid.*, Vyp. XI, Ol'shanka (Ol'shanskaia Parish, 74–81), "Opisanie...," 143–154.

[97] *Ibid.*, Vyp. XI, Golubina (Prigorodniaia Parish), 114–121.

[98] *Ibid.*, Vyp. XI, Ch. 2-II: "Gramotnost' i shkol'noe delo," 165–227.

[99] M. V. Komarinets, "Vyvoz khlebov," I, 34–47. Sharply increased traffic on the inter-village roads leading to Chernianka forced the county *zemstvo* to invest 60,000 rubles in their improvement and in construction of a dam and four bridges over the Oskol' to ease traffic. "Doklad Predsedatelia Zemskoi Upravy M. D. Orlova ob ustroistve i soderzhanii mestnykh dorog obshchago pol'zovaniia," *Trudy mestnykh komitetov*, 493–494.

along Elets-Valuiki was affected, but more importantly, the capacity of the authorities to move whatever troops were at their disposal was also likely to have been hampered: Cossack and infantry units, from their quarters near Kursk, appear to have begun operations only at night on 4 November. More generally, the entire railway and telegraph link at Chernianka station would have brought both the tidings and the revolutionary act itself into the immediate locality. It can be assumed from subsequent events that such tidings had a receptive audience.

Concrete conditions in other regions or in individual settlements, of course, did not always reflect this general picture. In itself, the presence of settlements of state peasants in our sample of villages, noted in the documents in connection with the disturbances of 1905–1906, masks the more critical situation with regard to the land fund available to communes of former serfs.[100] Yet local conditions and traditions also exerted a strong influence on the qualitative side of the rural profile. In the more populous settlements of Glamazdinskaia and Prilepovskaia Parishes in Dmitriev District, for example, the district's lowest annual harvest averages in the province and a dearth of local wage employment had encouraged especially strong expansion of organized migrant trades, primarily in various specialties in construction. In these locales, trades were conducted through contractors or by highly organized *artely* with their own elected foremen and pay scales that carefully reflected mastery of the trade. Each winter, plenipotentiaries of the *artel* or its agents traveled to the South Russian centers in order to contract ahead of time on terms of hire and wage levels. Literacy among males in the mid-1880s had reached relatively high levels for the time at Vet' (1,142 inhabitants, 21.8 percent of males literate), at Glamazdino (1,095, 17.4 percent literate), at Khomutovka (954, 14.1 percent literate) and at Prilepy (387,[101] 19.1 percent literate) in part

---

[100] Extracting the 38 villages of Oboian and Kursk Districts surveyed in 1882, for which leasehold data were incompatible, the sample contains 35 villages of former state peasants for whom the average area of allotment was 11.28 *desiatiny* and 192 settlements of ex-serfs with an average allotment of a little less than 6 *desiatiny* (5.98). Among state peasants in the sample, 24.1% of all households rented non-allotment land, the area of which made up an additional 6.8% in relation to the total area of allotments. Among the ex-serf villagers in the sample, 45.4% of all households leased non-allotment lands, the area of which, in relation to the area of their allotments, comprised an additional 23.8%. As the size of the ex-serf settlements increased, however, both these indicators tended to decrease, even considering that the average amount of allotment land per household also decreased.

[101] The population figure for Prilepy, in which the General Census of 1897 counted 1,576 persons of both sexes—13 years after the *zemstvo* survey—was the only instance that gave us pause during our review of the census materials.

thanks to a network of schools in these villages.[102] N. A. Dobrotvorskii, who made a special study of off-farm employment based on census interviews of 1882–1883, found that, in Glamazdinskaia Parish, conduct of fieldwork by women of the household during sojourns of male members in the South was increasingly common.[103] Indeed, in his report to Minister Bulygin, General-Adjutant Litvinov drew attention to the fact that, in villages of this sub-region, almost the whole male population, "with the exception of the elderly and children," left the province to work in Odessa, Ekaterinoslav and Kishinev, in the Iusovsk mines and in towns and ports along the Black Sea coast, even as far as Batum.[104]

The village of Sula in Kostornianskaia Parish, Sudzha District, was the largest local center in the vicinity, made up of six communities of state peasants (*dushevye*) on communal tenure with 2,036 inhabitants of both sexes. Literacy, as in the rest of the northern part of the district, was still quite negligible, even though the village supported one of the two schools in the area. If off-farm earnings drew more than a quarter of the population of working age (28.4 percent)—among whom migrant field laborers predominated—the village exhibited an entirely agricultural character. Indeed, as in Kon'shino I, the average area of allotment per household— 13 *desiatiny*—would appear adequate to this pursuit on paper, and leasehold area in relation to allotment area was limited (4.8 percent). However, the villagers of Sula had not been lucky. They had got their allotments in eleven different parcels, from two to four miles from the village proper, and, to make matters worse, these parcels were interspersed with those of private owners Mal'tsev, Zhekulin, Sibilev and Bolychevtsev—whose estates were later to be victimized by peasant unrest. House plots and gardens of Sula II stood on private lands. In order to reach their fields, Sula peasants had to traverse the lands of these owners, a "right" of access that depended on the latter and cost the villagers dearly.[105] The arrival of the Sabashnikovy during the late 1880s in Kostornianskaia Parish and the opening of their sugar-beet refinery in nearby Liubimovka in 1890, how-

---

[102] The school in Khomutovka had been founded and funded by the landowner O. A. Levshina-Shaufus.

[103] Dobrotvorskii, *Promysly*, 47–50; also *SSSKG. Vyp. III* (Dmitriev District), 209–232. In 1883, peasants maintained schools in Prilepy, Dubrovitsy, Sal'noe, Vet', Glamazdino and Khomutovka.

[104] *Nachalo pervoi russkoi revoliutsii....*, 627–628.

[105] *SSSKG. IV* (Sudzha District), 20–31. Out of six communes, five were made up of former private serfs (52 households, 5.4 *desiatiny* per household) that had been sequestered by the state prior to 1861.

ever, transformed the local landscape. Land rents now rose to unheard-of heights, land for sale became scarce and attitudes of local landowners toward any kind of peasant "rights" or "privileges" that might compromise efforts to extend and improve demesne cultivation—among these being use of the access strips for cattle and equipment—began to change sharply.[106] The same *casus belli* will have acted with equal force among settlements noted in the sources as being associated with incidents of unrest in the northern parishes near Sula during 1905–1906. In a district that led the province in terms of its annual harvest averages, these villages as a body tended to retain strong ties to agriculture, as measured by the prominent role of land lease and by much higher shares—compared to the larger villages of Novyi Oskol' District—of householders cultivating autonomously, and less intense development of off-farm employment.[107]

Populated by serfs formerly of the huge Sheremet'ev and Iusupov holdings, the three adjacent villages of Nekliudova (2,126 persons of both sexes in 1884), Nikol'skaia (1,207) and Pentsovka (869) in Nekliudovskaia Parish, Korocha District, participated in incidents of unrest during 1905 and 1906. Each had unusually high percentages of small labor-poor households (range: 64.8 percent to 72.4 percent of all households had no male worker or only one worker) with a weaker base of work stock (89.5—93.9 percent of households had no horse or only one horse). In these, 94–98 percent of all households had members engaged principally in local industry and trades. High levels of rents in the parish, it was noted in the census, made leasehold a prohibitively costly option.[108] Thus, as in Chernianka,

Handicrafts are a much more crucial support for the peasant economy. In the parish, 952 or 86.4 percent of the total number of families have been registered as having members in the trades. The majority of persons in trades belong to the category of

---

[106] "Doklad G. A. Ganevich iz Sudzhanskago uyezda o dolgosrochnoi arende," in *Trudy mestnykh komitetov*, 694–695.

[107] This was typical of the district as a whole. In the southeastern districts of Kursk Province, off-farm employments were already a highly visible aspect of rural economy: in Graivoron District, 759 out of every 1,000 households had members engaged in off-farm employments, in Belgorod District, 756, in Novyi Oskol' District, 734, in Staryi Oskol' District, 716, and in Korocha District, 712. By contrast, in Sudzha District, 559 households out of 1,000 had members so engaged, and in adjoining L'gov District, 510.

[108] Average allotment area per household in the three settlements totaled 2.5 *desiatiny* at Nekliudova, 5.8 *desiatiny* at Nikol'skaia and 4.1 at Pentsovka. Peasants at Nekliudova leased an area equal to 29.5% of total allotment area, at Nikol'skaia—4.4% and at Pentsovka—13.9%.

those locally engaged (77.8 percent), the migrants number only 302 or 22.2 percent of the total number engaged. Of the local trades, handicraft production of wood products is especially developed—wheel-wrighting, coopering, manufacture of carts, cornices and so on. Next come the boot-makers and brick-makers. The census counted 835 handicraftsmen in the parish. All of them take up their trades in time free from field-work. Average wages equal out to 40–60 rubles a year. In recent years, though, wages have significantly declined, because of the general economic crisis, since demand for their product has contracted. Moreover, the costs of the material of production itself—wood—have risen terribly. This circumstance has compelled several craftsmen to quit their trade and look for earnings on the side as agricultural workers and day laborers, and a few have moved away to Stavropol' Province, to the Kuban, since there, "forests are plentiful, and one can work at the trade profitably."[109]

The sensitivity of the economic health of this numerous cohort of handi-craftsmen in the local population both to the effect of local demand in a period of economic instability and to inflation of lumber costs in the con-text of continuing deforestation (worsened by the railway construction boom in the 1890s) gives cause to suggest that its position had declined even further by 1905.[110]

In police and judicial records for 1905–1906, *sloboda* Borisovka, Bo-risovskaia Parish, Graivoron District (15,167 inhabitants in 1884;[111] 18,071 in 1897), ex-serfs formerly of Count D. N. Sheremet'ev appeared in connection with six incidents of unrest in both years, almost entirely aimed at the forest and installations of the former master. In the northern part of the district, *sloboda* Rakitnaia, Rakitianskaia Parish (6,623 inhabi-tants in 1884; 7,920 in 1897), ex-serfs and their descendants formerly of Prince N. B. Iusupov are cited in connection with both the massive tim-bering of private forest during October–November 1905 and multiple incidents during June–July 1906. Yet the orientations of their population, even in the mid-1880s, were starkly different.

Borisovka had always been a small-industrial settlement *par excel-lence*, with its large array of handicraft concerns, among which was an especially large contingent of icon painters, finishers and framers whose

---

[109] *SSSKG. XIII* (Korocha District), Part I-B ("Opisanie otdel'nykh volostei Korochan-skago Uyezda"), 5–7.

[110] Literacy rates follow the size of the village: Nekliudova 15.4%; Nikol'skaia 9.7%; Pentsovka, 2.6%.

[111] At the time of the Emancipation (1862), Borisovka was already a major center, with 16,288 persons, four churches and the Bogoroditsko-Tihkvinskii Convent. Tsentral'nyi statisticheskii komitet. *Spiski naselennykh mest.... Vyp. 20. Kurskaia guberniia*, 37. According to data for 1877, the town had 2,645 households with 17,502 persons. Idem, *Volosti i vazhneishiia seleniia*, 267.

artistry had won them national renown.[112] This orientation was the design of the original grantee (1708) Field Marshal Count Boris Petrovich Sheremet'ev (1652–1719), who himself founded both Borisovka and another big "industrial" village in Kursk Province, Mikhailovka-na-Svape (Dmitriev District), and settled them with his own serfs from outside the province. By the mid-1880s, the land allotment held by Borisovka peasants stood at 3.99 *desiatiny* per household, though this average masks the fact that the allotment tract stretched out to a point some seven miles from the center of settlement. Leased land in relation to the area of allotment was quite negligible (0.9 percent). Over half of all households (55.6 percent) either hired labor or inventory to cultivate or rented out their allotments. Male literacy at 16.0 percent was a bit more than twice the district average (7.5 percent). Almost two out of every three households (64.9 percent) had no male worker or could field only a single male of working age. Nine in ten households had either a single horse or none at all. Eighty-three percent of householders had members engaged in "industrial" occupations, making up 44.8 percent of the village's working-age population. The non-agricultural character of the settlement was even more sharply defined in 1905.[113]

In contrast, like those of the village of Sula, the residents of *sloboda* Rakitnaia in the northern part of Graivoron District remained far more closely engaged with agriculture on the allotments. The lots of Rakitnaia's four communes were considerably larger than those worked by farmers at Borisovka (6.24 *desiatiny* per household), although, again, the fields (the

[112] *Obzor Kurskoi gubernii za 1905 god*, 18–24. It was also home to the precinct (*stan'*) police station, the parish administration, a post office, two schools, a pharmacy and hospital, 54 blacksmiths' forges, 50 wind mills, 44 leather works, 122 stores (*lavki*), a glue factory, a candle-maker, five brick yards and 13 inns (*postoialye dvory*). It hosted the principal annual local agricultural fairs on Palm Sunday, June 24, July 24, September 14, and November 8, and held twice-weekly bazaars. *Ibid.* (*Volosti i vazhneishiia seleniia*), 267. See also Kurskoe gubernskoe *zemstvo*. *Materialy po issledovaniiu kustarnoi*, 309–334, wholly devoted to describing Borisovka's varied artisanal occupations.

[113] Returns of the Borisovskaia Parish Administration for 1905, found in a study by the provincial office of the Treasury, used a total of 3,942 *registered* households with a population of 23,773 persons of both sexes. They reported allotment lands in the four communes of Borisovka at 9,263.18 *desiatiny* (2.35 *desiatiny* per household) with 3,502 households holding 2 *desiatiny* or less. Both the 1,457 households that had no connection with agriculture and high numbers with no horses (2,870) suggest a robustly non-agricultural orientation. Kurskaia kazennaia palata, *Materialy po krest'ianskomu i chastnomu zemlevladeniiu Kurskoi gubernii*, III, Graivoronskii Uyezd.

furthest being four to five and a half miles from the village) were not all at a convenient distance. Dominated by small households (63.9 percent had only one male worker or no male worker), numbers of households leasing out their allotments or cultivating by hiring outside labor and/or inventory were comparatively small (17.5 percent). The cohort with limited work stock was also less numerous than at Borisovka (44.5 percent). A large number (67.6 percent) of households had members engaged in "industrial" occupations in 1884—29.7 percent of working-age males—but two in three of these latter left the province for wage earnings. Moreover, the householders of Rakitnaia actively engaged in leasing non-allotment land (21.5 percent of allotment area in 1884), almost exclusively in dealings with the huge adjacent estate of Princess Iusupova. Rupture of negotiations between the Rakitnaia peasants and Iusupova's administrators on this issue was surely among the causes that provoked unrest in the summer of 1906: the parties finally agreed upon an area of 3,069 *desiatiny* leased under winter sowings and 2,054 *desiatiny* under spring crops for 1906–1907.[114]

The foregoing examples may be replicated at length, but those that we have cited demonstrate that, beyond the general tendencies shown in our statistical analysis, the weight of different elements in combinations of factors that oriented village economies was really too various to extract a single, unambiguous characterization of a revolutionary milieu. Some elements in this mix—Ukrainian-Russian ethnic conflict or even the impact of Old Belief[115]—remain largely invisible in police reporting. Yet the examples serve to reiterate how much village survival strategies were tightly bound up with land lease, agricultural labor, local small-industrial or handicraft occupations and out-migration (short-term or long-term, skilled or unskilled) or, in short, with market forces that—like nature itself—were beyond the capacity of peasant households to predict or control.

---

[114] GARF, f. 102, 4-e deloproisvodstvo, 1907 g., ch. 34.1, ll. 48–50 (Governor V. M. Borzenko to the Department of Police, No. 8783, 5 July 1907). The scale of leasehold here is quite a bit more substantial than that reported for 1884.

[115] The village of Ivanovskoe (Ivanovskaia Parish, L'gov District), peasants of which were the initiators of labor actions on the Bariatinskii estates during May–June 1906, was home to at least one congregation of 100 households of Old Believers, which sent two representatives to speak at the All-Russian Congress of Peasant-Old Believers in Moscow, 22–25 February 1906. Villages in the adjoining Vyshne-Derevenskaia Parish (Cheremushek, Khoroshenki, Kromskie Chermoshki) in this district also sent delegates. *Materialy po voprosam zemel'nomu i krest'ianskomu*, 277–282.

Conclusion

The emergence of a revolutionary situation at the end of the nineteenth century in Kursk Province was ultimately a response to an evident corrosion of the older certainties and inevitabilities of rural life in the face of the accumulated effects of demographic pressures and of long-term economic and cultural processes. Prince Peter Dmitrievich Dolgorukov, writing in early 1906, identified the core problem with "festering wounds of the era of serfdom, which have not yet entirely healed," and there remains a great deal of truth to this assessment. The Emancipation acts of the 1860s represent the central axis of the ambitious attempt by Alexander II and his collaborators to modernize the economic foundations of Russia's Great Power status and to provide for its internal tranquility, "to abolish serfdom from above rather than to await the day when it will begin to abolish itself from below." In their principal aim of regularizing the status of the peasantry as free rural inhabitants with land allotments—legislating, in favor of former private serfs, terms and procedures for a compulsory alienation of significant acreage from the estates of the former serf-owners—the acts were, in the context of the time and the powerful interests at stake, bold and unprecedented, and they resonated powerfully in peasant memories of the "Tsar-Liberator." The manner in which the land issue was resolved on the ground, however, and legislation of the equally critical juridical and institutional provisions that isolated the peasant estate from other Russian subjects and imposed upon it very considerable legal and personal disabilities profoundly influenced both the structure and evolution of socio-economic relationships in the rural districts.

The land settlements envisioned by the emancipation acts as these were played out in Kursk Province, as suggested in the comparative positions of communities of former state peasants and ex-serfs in the mid-

1880s, placed the latter at a significant disadvantage in terms of arable acreage at their disposal. The effect of the acts and their local execution, intended or unintended, was thus to preserve the dependency of sizeable elements of the peasant population on owners of the adjoining private estates, these latter very commonly identifiable as the former serf-owners or their descendants. For communities of liberated serfs in particular, due to disadvantages associated with size, composition and physical dispersion of allotments, a continuing dependency on the old masters as patrons was more vital in terms of subsistence strategies. This was quite evident in the far more important role that leasing of estate land played for such communities. Of perhaps equal importance was a great plethora of rights of access to resources (forest, meadow, pasture, stubble and watering sites) or rights of way over estate land that intervened between peasant fields and their house plots. If at one time such access had been open to peasant use by custom, it now lay in the domain of private property, had to be negotiated with the legal owners and was now subject to cash payments, labor dues and fines for illegal use and trespass. *Yet this enduring dependency, it should be stressed, was in most cases a mutual one and incorporated a history of social interaction that predated the Emancipation.* With limited capital, little expertise and no experience in entrepreneurial practice, most estate owners in Kursk Province (in their majority noble proprietors of small or middle-sized holdings), continued to depend heavily for incomes on cash rents, rents *en nature*, labor dues and the fees and fines extracted in connection with access "privileges" granted to neighboring villagers.

Mutual dependency between peasants and the former masters thus stood upon a kind of fragile community of interest. In annually leasing out the major parts of the demesne to peasant tenants over a single sowing cycle, the great majority of Kursk Province's gentry landowners struggled to guarantee their incomes. That this system of reciprocity was highly exploitative is not the question: it rested squarely, by the landowners' own admission, on the insufficiency of peasant land allotments. Moreover, not only did rents continue to rise steadily with land values toward the end of the nineteenth century, but rents themselves were increasingly converted to fixed cash payments, minimizing the landowners' risks from poor harvests or the desultory performance of their tenants. The conversion of labor obligations and rents *en nature* (parts of the harvest) into cash payments as consideration in lease contract even in old strongholds (Ryl'sk, Putivl', Sudzha *uyezdy*) of *barshchina* labor (the *corvée* of the servile era) thus had the effect of shifting all the risk onto the shoulders of peasant tenants. Notwithstanding the nakedly exploitative features of these arrangements, many of the estates' peasant neighbors, whose household economies rested especially heavily on leasing private acreage reasonably proximate to the village, found this scheme, crucial in its very predictability year after year, to be preferable, in view of the variability of harvests, to formalizing contractual obligations over multi-year periods.

The post-Emancipation order—at the outset therefore the very antithesis of "agrarian capitalism"—thus came to rest upon that dense web of reciprocal interactions between peasant clients and landowner patrons that presents to the historian a composite that drew in part upon a community of interest and in part upon older verities in collective social memory, clothed in the hierarchical customs and patriarchal mores of the servile era and backed in a pinch by the coercive power of the state. By the same token, however, the exploitive character of this system of "patron-client" relationships kept alive a backdrop of bitter tensions and mutual antipathy in rural social relations, expressed in those acts of minor aggression against estate property that were so commonplace in the daily life of the rural districts of Kursk Province, and attracted so much heated commentary from noble participants in Committees on the Needs of Rural Industry during 1902–1903. They also reverberated in those endless rumors of an impending Black Repartition that, as a Land Captain from Staryi Oskol' District noted in March 1905, "have been circulating in the countryside for as long as anyone can remember." At times, peasant dissatisfaction did take on a form and a scale that required movement of troops to restore "order." Yet for all that such phenomena testified to peasants' entrenched sense of grievance over the outcomes wrought by the Great Reforms on the ground, the geography of rural unrest in Kursk Province during 1905–1906 will tell a somewhat different story. *For where this web of "feudal survivals" continued to rest on a persisting history of personal interaction of the lord of the estate with his village neighbors, on real measures of predictability in those concrete benefits gained by both parties in the transactions that gave it meaning and legitimacy, peasants were more likely to remain on the sidelines during 1905–1906.*

From a larger perspective, moreover, the provincial data that we assembled in our initial chapter did not support a view that the rural economy of Kursk Province was in a state of crisis: mortality trends, data for grain production and farm investment actually suggest a certain improvement in the long-term perspective. Despite soaring provincial land values, non-allotment acreage in peasant cultivation, gained by purchase or by lease, continued to expand, if slowly, in the era after Emancipation, in itself an indication of the resiliency of peasant pocketbooks in this period, and though the materials are very meager, savings and consumption data also point in the same direction. The growth in the importance of handicraft and small-industrial employment and their earnings testified not only to a diversification of village economies, but also to an increase in local demand for the goods and services that they produced. Of course, there is no doubt that, under pressures of natural increase in rural population, man:land ratios in the province grew steadily less favorable over time, a trend that contributed to extension of plowland at the expense of pasture, meadow and forest, and acted to severely limit the growth of livestock holdings during the pre-revolutionary decades. Far outstripping the capacity of local off-farm occupations to provide for gainful employment (despite growth in this sector), it also fostered that burgeoning exodus of working-age persons in search of wage work outside the province that, even if these peasant-workers necessarily retained their ties to their home villages, became a sort of *de facto* emigration for a large contingent among them. Land lease, local wage work, the annual migration of working hands to fields, factories, mines and construction sites across South Russia and permanent resettlement (*de facto* or *de jure*) to the peripheries of the Empire all combined to temper the pressure of natural population increase on the land. *Insofar as all such elements in this rural "ecology" continued to function in tandem, and the state and its armed forces stood just over the horizon as the guarantor of "order," the tense and fragile social peace of the post-1861 era was mostly maintained.* It held in spite of extreme variations in harvests, especially rye yields, punctuated by particularly poor harvests in one or both fields in 1881–1882, 1885–1886, 1889, 1891–1893, 1896–1897 and 1905 and periods of crisis mortality, 1882–1884 and 1889–1895. It held despite the more and more evident breakdown of the local structures of authority in the face of sharply increasing levels of crime and lawlessness in the country districts in the pre-revolutionary era. It held despite growing evidence that communal systems of subsistence insurance were unable to cope with either demographic pressure or generational conflicts in village life. And it was largely observed during violent peasant unrest that struck several districts in adjacent Khar'kov and Poltava Provinces in the spring of 1902.

Yet if the "crisis" was not a *systemic* one, there is every indication that at a number of sites, *local* conditions had developed in ways that had placed peasant communities in extremely critical circumstances. These were, again, mainly settlements of former private serfs, those most disadvantaged by the land settlement imposed by Emancipation, though the issue of land allotment *per se*, in our judgment, has to be treated with care. For review of grain production materials suggest that the southwestern districts of Kursk Province, most heavily settled by ex-serfs, most poorly supplied with allotment lands and working somewhat less consistently good soils, were the most productive in the province. It was in this landscape, dominated entirely by communal forms of tenure, that peasant farmers were opting for more intensive methods of cultivation with more modern inventory, even while they retained three-field rotation and traditional grain sowings. Conversely, in eastern and northeastern parts of the province, dominated by former state peasants who had received notably more substantial allotments in the 1860s, the old extensive methods of cultivation were generally preserved, even "intensified": percentages of plowland in arable acreage were measurably higher here than in western districts, the abandonment of rotation in favor of continuous cropping had spread over large expanses of the sown fields already by the mid-1880s, and the old inventory was everywhere predominant. A greater frequency of poor harvests greatly depressed overall averages for these districts during 1885–1913, rates of emigration were comparatively high, and, it bears repeating, the great bulk of tax arrears that went on the books after the crisis of 1891–1892 was concentrated in peasant communities in these districts.

Where the older web of reciprocal interactions over land and labor issues between lord and peasant preserved sufficient vitality and flexibility at the dawn of the twentieth century, such "feudal survivals" acted to deter peasants in the majority of villages in Kursk Province from collective actions during 1905–1906. In contrast, violation of the norms that defined this scheme of socio-economic exchange created an explosive situation. This was the specific predicament of settlements struggling to survive and prosper in zones of influence of the big "modernizing" estates run by an elite of absentee magnates, and their central place in the geography of the rural disorders of 1905–1906.

Very distinct from clans of the rank-and-file nobility of Kursk Province by their vast landholdings, great wealth and close family ties to service at Court or in the upper ranks of Imperial civil, military or diplomatic establishments, owners of the large latifundia were heirs (directly or by intermarriage) to the largesse that Peter the Great and his successors had showered upon their ancestors. Members of an "aristocracy" in the Petrine image, they blended, as a group, ancient Russian and Tatar princely lines, the posterities of both lesser noblemen and commoners of various national origins who had won high honor and distinction in Imperial service, and the heirs of men whose business acumen in the post-Emancipation era had gained them fortune and influence. Armed with extensive capital resources, estate operations run by these magnates proved better able than many of Kursk Province's less fortunate gentry families to devise strategies in order to weather transition from the servile economy, the long depression of grain prices (1875–1895) and ruinous effects of periodic harvest failures. Under the strains of such challenges, the fortunes of many a noble landowner in Kursk Province had been compromised, and not a few had been forced to sell their lands. In the same period, however, operations run by the magnates evidence broad and sustained investment in modern agricultural technologies, imported livestock, structures and on-site processing capacity (large-scale sugar-beet refinery, distillery, flour milling), cadres of full-time and seasonal labor and diversified sowings from selected seed in multiple rotations, realizable in cash in raw or processed form. The aggressive railway construction programs during 1892–1902 more than doubled track miles in the province and tied these huge estates ever closer to national and international markets. On a day-to-day basis, of course, operations were run by corps of salaried administrators who executed directives of their distant employers, the latter residing in the capitals, Moscow, St. Petersburg and Kiev, close to the seats of power and influence.

I have referred to "*zones* of influence," however, because strategies undertaken on the large holdings were felt well outside the bounds of these estates themselves. It was likely that any shift in emphasis (unprecedented rent increases, for example, in Novyi Oskol' District) in operations on especially large holdings, even when broad programs of modernization were not yet contemplated, would have sorely affected nearby peasant villages. Yet modernization schemes on the large latifundia (and construction of processing plants in particular) often moved even more risk-averse owners of small- and middle-sized private estates that adjoined them to increase the scale of demesne cultivation, to invest, however modestly, in work stock and inventory and to reform crop rotation schedules to accommodate, along with traditional grains, sowings of sugar-beet or potatoes that might now be sold locally for cash. Alternatively, a landowner might now as easily lease away demesne plowland to the highest bidder (a local sugar refiner): when large blocks of land were abruptly transferred out of peasant use in this manner (the 46,000-acre estate of Count Sheremet'ev at Borisovka), the result could not fail to have serious consequences. Even when the process was more gradual (the northern parishes of Sudzha District), the end result of the wider transformation was that acreage in peasant leasehold was sharply reduced and could be had only at truly prohibitive rents. Even the access strips and farm roads to and from his own fields, for which he had long paid an annual fee in cash or labor dues, might now triple in price or be plowed under to make way for sugar-beet sowings. Such changes profoundly violated the old order of reciprocities that bound lord and peasant and accelerated the accumulation in these zones of incendiary resentments.

The record thus strongly replicates the considerations that have led James C. Scott and others to situate a principal driver of peasant revolt in the sharp devaluation of those "patron-client" relationships that were crucial to village subsistence strategies. Peasant collective actions in Kursk Province during 1905–1906 would target, in the first instance, the holdings of owners who had not only altered estate operations in ways that directly infringed established patterns of reciprocity with nearby villages, but in doing so had also violated in essential ways the personal, customary and *predictable* character of those mutual interactions that predated the emancipation. Furthermore, peasant militants would attack those gentry networks of authority that dominated local administrative bodies and abetted such violations, not only in attacks on the forces of order, the police and the army, but also in concerted assaults on the holdings of serving and former Land Captains, Marshals of the Nobility and members of their clans. Yet the "peasantry" in Kursk Province hardly showed itself to be a unified social formation in its attitudes toward collective action. The Governor of Kursk Province in his report of January 1906 noted the predominance of communities of former private serfs among those associated in the sources with the disorders. This observation was borne out in our sample, in which such villages made up between seven and eight out of every ten villages so associated, depending on how one defined mixed settlements. This evident divergence between communities of former state peasants and those of ex-serfs and their descendants surely reflects measurable disparities in their respective material conditions, due ultimately to the land settlements of the 1860s, though we have also seen that this disparity had begun to drive regions dominated by the more poorly endowed ex-serf populations toward a new level of virtuosity in managing existing systems of cultivation. What weighed just as much on this divergence, however, was the quite different experience of these communities of the pre-reform epoch and the distinctive collective memories that they drew from this experience. More importantly, while conscious of the size of our sample, peasant collective actions, very destructive in concentrated locales, never drew in the majority of rural communities.

Against the landowners—and against the local structures of authority that fronted for them in maintaining the peasantry in a subaltern position in rural society—acted those elements of the village populations of Kursk Province that found themselves, more than others, at a greater distance from the "traditional" bases (*uklad*) of rural life and its cycles of intra-village mobility. As such, these experienced more harshly the negative features of aspects of demographic and economic forces at work in the rural environment at the turn of the century. Posed especially sharply by the disorders of 1906 during the critical juncture of the agricultural calendar, the issues of local wage work, the exclusivity of local hire and rising rents—which affected the household economic strategies of small family households in particular—emerged and came to the fore. An important role—directly and indirectly—was played by the contingent of migrant workers, which brought back to their home villages that which Litvinov described as "all the negative aspects of factory and city life"—including all sorts of "red" political conceptions—and which, along with many who remained in the villages, militated for, facilitated and not infrequently played a leading role in the unfolding of disturbances. In terms of sites, this characterization pertains above all to populations of large, densely populated half-agricultural, half-industrial rural "towns" and of the mass of younger, nuclear family households that dominated them. These were locations at which disturbances in 1905 or 1906 began and which bulk large among "repeaters" in *both* 1905 and 1906.

The survival strategies of our selection of village communities exhibited high degrees of dependence on land, wage labor and small-commodity markets, even if the weights of one or the other of these strategies varied greatly from village to village and were in fact mutually accommodating. The household census of Kursk Province from the 1880s, however, showed that combinations of three interrelated elements distinguished big rural settlements that played central roles in agrarian unrest during 1905–1906. They exhibited especially prolific development of small-industrial employment, which appears alongside indicators either of real disabilities for cultivation or of a broader attenuation of ties to an agricultural economy as a whole. In circumstances such as these, the "peasant" character of large parts of the populations of such villages is questionable. Furthermore, a notably higher level of literacy was a distinguishing feature of the populations of the big rural towns, which almost invariably maintained the only schools in the area. Finally, the overall impression gained from these analyses was that small, nuclear family householders, quite numerous in absolute terms in the larger rural centers, also made up larger *percentage* shares in their populations. The distinctive cultural atmosphere and diverse occupational settings of prominent country "towns" were closely tied to these factors and acted to magnify their interaction. Such settlements served as commercial hubs and as public spaces for the sub-region that they dominated and as conduits linking this area with the outside world by a thousand threads of trade and means of communication and information.

Conversely, the smaller villages and hamlets in their orbit, in their great majority, retained the characteristics of "closed" or corporate villages, tied more exclusively to the agricultural economy and more uniform both in the absence of village-based small industrial alternatives and in low levels of literacy. For residents of smaller settlements in the zones of unrest, sharp inflation of land rents *or the reduction of acreage available to rent*, combined with disruptions in cycles of out-migration and the downturn in harvests of spring sowings in 1905 (including the principal cash crop, oats) to create an explosive situation. For populations of larger centers, the matter was certainly more complicated. By the measure that they had developed and diversified small industrial employment at the expense of cultivation, the big rural settlements would seem to have been inoculated against downturns in harvest or labor stoppages in South Russia. Yet to the extent that agriculture and migrant labor remained a substantial part of the economies of the heavily populated rural towns—and for almost all of them it did—rising land rents and instability in South Russian labor markets will have had major effects in these as well. Secondly, the small-industrial sector so prominent in large rural towns was almost entirely dependent on local demand, since the development of external markets was still very limited. Thus the economic difficulties in surrounding villages—a prognosis for 1905 yields was obvious by May— exerted inflationary pressure on grain prices (big villages being net importers), while trade in small-industrial and handicraft goods shrank.

Small nuclear family households in our samples were closely associated with those indices of limited economic capacity by which they have been simply relegated to ranks of the "village poor" or assigned a lower rung on the ladder of "biological" development, which, if the householder was lucky, led to a growth of the labor component of the family and the capacity to expand household economy. The correlation analyses of parish data for Kursk Province do point to a sufficiently close connection between labor composition of the household and the quantity of available work stock, and between the quantity of household work stock and area of non-allotment lease. We also saw the close association of labor- and inventory-poor households with wage-earning occupations. Yet high rates of *pre-mortem* family partitions during the second half of the nineteenth century—and the factors adduced to explain them—suggested that, by the novelties of their own life experience, younger generations of peasants found themselves increasingly at odds with their elders and more inclined to seek to establish their own households without waiting for the death of the *bol'shak*. The weight of small family households in profiles of the rural population of Kursk Province—reaching close to two thirds of all households in its biggest settlements—raises the question as to how much household formation at such sites reflect the usual processes of mobility and how much they represent their increasing irrelevance in certain contexts. Analysis of the sample of villages noted in documentary materials in association with agrarian disorders in Kursk Province in 1905–1906 showed that even "normal" associations of family labor composition with work stock indicators and area of non-allotment leasehold were much less in evidence. We have attributed this result to the uncommon weight in the sample of large rural "towns," in which this cohort of small households was often notably larger.

Secondly, we are, at this juncture in the history of rural Russia, quite far along the historical continuum that separated it from the era of the "primordial village." The totality of those socio-economic relationships that fed mobility within peasant society, thanks to or even in spite of conditions fostered by the state acts of the 1860s concerning the status of the peasantry and subsequent amendments, never succeeded in constituting a closed system. Rather, it came to rest in most essential ways on local land and labor markets, movement of grain prices, demand for working hands in the fields, factories, mines and construction sites of South Russia, and the prospects for emigration to peripheral zones within the Empire. From the point of view of peasant communities, a turn for the worse in the terms of these exchanges during the decade prior to the revolution, along with very significant variation in harvest performance, could not remain without profound effects. These instabilities, in turn, placed in ever-higher relief the unresolved conflicts of village politics generally and, in particular, put in question the long-term expectations of that especially large contingent of smaller households that represented the younger generation in the peasant communities. In many contexts—particularly in the big rural towns and densely populated *slobody*—traditional processes of mobility that had long informed such expectations had reached their natural limits. The wave of land repartitions of the 1890s that swept through communes of ex-serfs that had failed to agree to full reapportionments after 1861—and polls of the mid-1880s suggest that such communes were an important majority in Kursk Province—was associated with the advent of a new cohort of younger householders to a deciding position in the village assemblies. That they took place in contexts of sharply rising land values (and concomitant inflation of land rents), extreme variations in harvests and an interval of crisis mortality (1889–1892), however, gave them their extraordinary character. Explosions of mass rural unrest in Kursk Province in 1905 were thus preceded by an era of intense internal ferment within many rural communities that cannot be left without due attention as evidence of powerful conflicts in many villages, conflicts in which the decisive reckoning over issues of land reapportionment bore less of a class than a generational origin. For such conflicts betoken the influence of a new generation of peasants, a generation that had no personal memory of the era of serfdom, its customs and usages, and regarded older patriarchal hierarchies, even in the life of the household, with growing impatience.

Further, this generation lived in an era of an unprecedented erosion of the cultural isolation of village life. The great expansion of railway and telegraph (and by 1905, telephone) networks, the new abundance of the penny press and cheap popular literature and the proliferation of a human traffic in ideas, impressions and tastes between city and countryside that was a by-product of the swelling labor migration could not fail to have an effect, in particular, upon its outlook. By virtue of its experience of military service, wage earning in migration or in the home district, by its greater literacy and oft-decried "spirit of individualism," the life horizon of this younger generation was much broader than that to which its fathers and grandfathers could have pretended. To be sure, the younger peasant clung stubbornly to the essential of their elders' expectations—to become an independent master (*khoziain*) on the land. Yet due to his lowly place in the chain of mobility, due to the concrete cultural and economic conditions adhering in his place of residence and in his more fluid circle of social contact, due to his actual occupations and his increasing distinctive outlook, he had evolved a greater sense than his elders of the precariousness of this expectation in the existing circumstances.

When assessing the backdrop to agrarian unrest of 1905–1906 in Kursk Province, the "land question" had thus to be understood in its three interrelated guises. It related, of course, to the enduring dissatisfactions of the province's peasant masses—and especially of communities of former private serfs that made up at least seven out of every ten villages active in the events of 1905–1906—with conditions established by the Great Reforms. These discontents were kept fresh through endless disputes over land, frequent small acts of resistance or petty aggressions against land-owner property, occasional mass violence, and the peasant's everyday experience of social interaction with "outsiders": local "lords" and petty officials of every rank and venue that brought home to him his subaltern status in rural society. Second, the "land question" remained a focal point of discontent because in the decade prior to the revolution, the terms of exchange in local labor and land lease arrangements turned slowly against peasant communities, but most sharply of all in zones of influence of the large modernizing estates of the absentee magnates. Disruption in cycles of out-migration—especially during the industrial slowdown after 1899—created added instability for that growing segment of the working-age population that now gained its livelihood in wage occupations outside the province.

Yet the "land question" also acted as a central focus of peasant discon-tent at the same time that, in this larger setting, intra-village consensus in many settlements had passed through a harsh, divisive reckoning. The massive character of the migration of working-age males (and increas-ingly females) already testified to the growing incapacity of village sub-sistence arrangements to cope with growing demographic pressure, but a sharpening of struggles over land reapportionment issues in the 1890s appears to have represented a particularly bitter chapter. Where this matter has often been treated as "class" struggle according to variations on the old *bedniak-seredniak-kulak* scheme that attempt to assess the motives of poorer villagers, "middle peasants" and rich *kulaks*, it is quite as likely that these tensions were as much generational in character and expressed the decisive phase of conflict in village politics between a new generation of younger householders and those clans or factions for which the old allotments tied to the Tenth Revision (1858) retained real advantages. For larger rural villages and densely populated *slobody*, moreover, the very limitations of a land fund to be had within a reasonable distance from the area of settlement[1] would long since have acted to limit to or even trans-form the usual patterns of mobility. The "land question" thus acted to

---

[1] In this connection, it is highly questionable whether this specific problem in the context of the most populous rural centers, in its very intractability, would have been susceptible to the reforms envisioned by Stolypin and his collaborators. One recent observer has sug-gested (using data for Tambov *guberniia*) that the size of a commune was a powerful barrier to reordering of land use. Ivanov, "Nekotorye itogi," in *Vekhi minuvshego*, 167 (table 3, Tambov Province conversions by size of commune).

submerge powerful dissensions within village life—including a generational divide—in collective actions against a socially agreed-upon enemy.

If our analysis of the milieux from which rural unrest emerged in Kursk Province during 1905–1906 has emphasized contexts that were not always "traditional" or even "peasant" in character, conceptions of the movement's "autonomy" were likewise proven untenable. The growing intensity of the province's participation in the life of the nation at the end of the century already precluded its isolation. For rural unrest in 1905 emerged out of the mélange of shifting emotions, impressions and expectations fostered by tidings of defeats of Russian arms in the Far East, by government declarations containing vague promises of "reform," by news of the events of 9 January 1905 and of the wave of strikes and demonstrations throughout Russia that followed them, and by the general political turmoil that gathered over Russian society as a whole both before and after proclamation of the Manifesto of 17 October. The broad sweep of these events as they unfolded was brought home to the countryside by letters from the front, newspapers or political tracts, by stories borne back to the villages by peasant-workers returning from near and far, by conversations with students, priests, demobilized soldiers, parish or village elders, or teachers, doctors and other specialists in *zemstvo* employment. The general impression of a crisis of the state order that rural communities sensed in this stream of news and tidings provided the crucial backdrop to the outbreak of unrest itself. Indeed, this circumstance was to distinguish the situation in Kursk Province during 1905 from that, for example, of 1902, when rural disturbances of great violence spread through adjacent Khar'kov and Poltava Provinces. At that time, local officials noted a tense and expectant mood in many villages of Kursk Province, expressed in large illegal meetings at night and in "a more impudent and defiant attitude of the lower classes toward their superiors," but local peasants were soon engaged in bringing in the harvests that would set the record for the pre-1917 era.

By the beginning of 1905, the failure of the autocracy to allay the growing turmoil, and the stripping of the central regions of Russia of armed forces for the war effort in the Far East, fundamentally disabled a crucial actor in the *provincial* equation. State authority backed by military force, as the guarantor of the *status quo*, was for a time effectively absent. To be sure, the glaring ineffectiveness of the authorities in combatting growing rates of crime in the country districts of Kursk Province in the pre-revolutionary era had already significantly lowered its prestige. Now, however, the near-total eclipse of state authority engendered an ever-surer sense of "opportunity" among radically-minded villagers for a reckoning with the landowners that had not existed even in 1902. The "ignition points" were everywhere analogous: peasants at first tested the limits of local officials' capacity to oppose them and, meeting no timely or effective riposte, resolved to act upon their broader aims, the very success of such initial actions inciting a larger neighboring community to adhere to the movement. The crescendo of November in Kursk Province drew, again, upon tidings of strikes and demonstrations in Russia's urban centers and disorders in other locales, both near and far (events in Saratov and Chernigov Provinces). The deliberate temporizing of provincial authorities over the public proclamation of the Manifesto of October 17 and its belated reading out, now in the context of a rising cacophony of government and private partisan manifestoes and declarations, created the certainty that rumor, informed by the old shared dream of Black Repartition, would gain the upper hand. Yet the November–December violence also derived from the on-going failure of provincial authorities to bring force to bear, not just in resolving issues posed by the October general strike, but more broadly against a rising tide of violence in provincial towns and in a number of rural districts.

Deployment of troops in decisive numbers to affected sites began to take effect in late November: provincial authorities slowly recovered the capacity to bring a preponderance of force to bear in the main centers of unrest. The result was visible not only in the cessation of disorders—even if the run-up to the elections for the First State Duma was of equal significance here—but also in a radical change in the tactics of confrontation pursued by peasant communities when unrest resumed in late May 1906. The clear shift away from the paroxysms of looting and arson in 1905 that recalled the *Pugachevshchina* of 1773–1774 toward organized, mainly non-violent disruptions of work schedules on the estates during the agricultural season of 1906—at many of the same sites affected by the unrest of 1905—reflected the changed situation on the ground, but also underscored the stubborn determination of peasant militants to rid the countryside of their enemies. There is no question here that the aims of peasant militants involved a "restoration" of the previous order of reciprocities between social unequals: the movement in Kursk Province, most obviously in 1905, but also during 1906, aimed directly at the destruction of the capacity of the landowners to continue to operate their estates and at the seizure of their lands.

Reactionaries among the landed nobility and, to a less hysterical degree, the Governor of Kursk Province commonly emphasized the importance of "revolutionary propaganda" or "criminal agitation" to the emergence of the peasant movement. How else was one to explain the sudden explosion of violence within the peasant mass, "normally" so docile, obedient to their "superiors" and incapable of managing their own affairs without the guiding hand of their "social betters?" Perhaps imperceptibly for members of the local elites, however, the second half of the nineteenth century had ever more closely linked rural communities even in the agricultural heartland of *fin-de-siècle* Russia to the rest of the Empire by a burgeoning movement of goods, people, news and ideas. This traffic moved by rail, by wire, through the circulation of books and newspapers and through the physical mobility of a steadily growing element of provincial populations between town and country. Due to the force and character of changes in literacy, work experience, residence and the expanding range of its social and intellectual contacts, peasant society itself had grown increasingly familiar with the world outside the village, more heterogeneous in its life experiences, occupations, outlooks and attitudes.

The concrete grievances and aims that drove agrarian disorders, peasants' estimations as to the resolve of their enemies, and the influence of particular aspects of the economic conjuncture at specific sites as these gathered force in the years immediately prior to 1905 were primarily *local* in nature and were refracted largely through the perceptions and folklore broadly common to members of the peasant estate. The documents directly or indirectly testify to the essential role of village assemblies in organizing the disturbances, but also bear witness to peasant communities' equal facility at making common cause with "outsiders" and adopting novel organizational forms in the service of its aims. Yet we may with equal justification point to the key roles played by particular elements of peasant society—including those populations of the big country "towns" and, yes, representatives of Russia's working class—that had lost or shed many of the distinctive characteristics by which one identifies "peasants." In the end, the institutions and aims defining the agrarian movement in Kursk Province in 1905–1906 may have remained those "traditional" to the peasant estate, but the forces arrayed in the movement were quite as often located on the boundary between this older order and an as yet unseen, unknown and unpredictable future. Thus the "land question" that stood at the center of peasant grievances was also as much that surrogate issue that stood in for all of the increasingly intractable social and generational conflicts, the painful adjustments and instabilities brought on by economic modernization and the failure of the state to provide for elementary needs in education, security and an even-handed justice for that 80 percent of Russian subjects who lived and worked in the country districts. In just this sense, the rural disorders that shook the Empire during 1905–1906 expressed the degree to which the processes of the *longue durée* that we have attempted to catalogue in the course of this essay had worked to erode and hollow out the mythologies that had long sustained both the autocracy and the Russian social order under the *ancien régime*, and gave advance warning of the far more momentous events of 1917.

Correlation Tables: Parishes and Villages

Data from Kurskoe gubernskoe zemstvo, Statisticheskoe biuro, *Sbornik statisticheskikh svedenii po Kurskoi gubernii. Vyp. 1 Kurskii uyezd* (M., 1883); *Vyp. II. Statisticheskie svedeniia po L'govskomu uezdu* (Kursk, 1884); *Vyp. III. Statisticheskie svedeniia po Dmitrievskomu uyezdu* (Kursk, 1884); *Vyp. IV. Statisticheskie svedeniia po Sudzhanskomu uyezdu* (Kursk, 1884); *Vyp. V. Statisticheskie svedeniia po Fatezhskomu uyezdu* (Kursk, 1884); *Vyp. VI. Statisticheskie svedeniia po Ryl'skomu uyezdu* (Kursk, 1885); *Vyp. VII. Statisticheskie svedeniia po Putivl'skomu uyezdu* (Kursk, 1885); *Vyp. VIII. Statisticheskie svedeniia po Shchigrovskomu uyezdu* (Kursk, 1885); *Vyp. IX. Statisticheskie svedeniia po Graivoronskomu uyezdu* (Kursk, 1884); *Vyp. X. Statisticheskie svedeniia po Belgorodskomu uyezdu* (Kursk, 1885); *Vyp. XI. Statisticheskie svedeniia po Novooskol'skomu uyezdu* (Kursk, 1886); *Vyp. XII. Statisticheskie svedeniia po Timskomu uyezdu* (Kursk, 1886); *Vyp. XIII. Statisticheskie svedeniia po Korochanskomu uyezdu* (Kursk, 1886); *Vyp. XIV. Statisticheskie svedeniia po Starooskol'skomu uyezdu* (Kursk, 1886). *Sbornik statisticheskikh svedenii po Oboianskomu uyezdu (Kurskoi gubernii),* M., 1882–1883.

Correlation matrix 1: Interaction of variables for household labor composition, household supply of work stock and degree of household autonomy in the conduct of cultivation (based on parish data from the zemstvo census of Kursk Province, 1882–1886).

	1	2	3	4	5	6	7	8	9	10	11	12	13	14	15
1. Number of households	1,00														
2. Households cultivating independently	0,92	1,00													
3. Households cultivating by hiring labor and/or inventory	0,59	0,33	1,00												
4. Households leasing out their allotments	0,37	*0,11*	*0,18*	1,00											
5. Households with no adult male worker	0,82	0,65	0,62	0,65	1,00										
6. Households with 1 adult male worker	0,97	0,85	0,69	0,52	0,85	1,00									
7. Households with 2-3 adult male workers	0,95	0,94	0,53	0,36	0,68	0,86	1,00								
8. Households with 4 or more adult male workers	0,58	*0,67*	*0,17*	*0,13*	0,31	0,39	0,75	1,00							
9. Households without horses	0,67	0,33	0,85	0,58	0,77	0,77	0,56	*0,17*	1,00						
10. Households with 1 horse	0,80	0,75	0,56	*0,18*	0,67	0,78	0,78	0,45	0,56	1,00					
11. Households with 2 horses	0,84	0,94	0,21	*0,08*	0,57	0,81	0,84	0,55	0,23	0,59	1,00				
12. Households with 3 horses	0,71	0,84	*0,05*	*0,10*	0,43	0,61	0,78	0,68	*0,08*	0,31	0,86	1,00			
13. Households with 4 or more horses	0,55	0,66	*0,08*	*0,20*	0,30	0,42	0,60	0,62	*0,00*	*0,11*	0,64	0,88	1,00		
14. Households without large cattle	0,63	0,30	0,80	0,57	0,76	0,76	0,57	0,18	0,96	0,52	0,21	*0,06*	*0,00*	1,00	
15. Average size of settlement	*0,06*	*0,08*	*0,24*	*0,31*	*0,11*	*0,16*	*0,05*	*-0,08*	*0,30*	*0,04*	*-0,10*	*-0,12*	*-0,10*	*0,35*	1,00

Data for Kursk and Oboian District partial. Italics signify coefficient P higher than .005

Correlation matrix 2: Interaction of variables for household labor composition, supply of work stock and degree of autonomy in the conduct of cultivation with variables for allotment and leased acreage, "industrial" employments and literacy (based on parish data from the zemstvo census of Kursk Province, 1882–1886).

	2. Households cultivating independently	3. Households cultivating by hiring labor and/or inventory	4. Households leasing out their allotments	5. Households with no adult male worker	6. Households with 1 adult male worker	7. Households with 2-3 adult male workers	8. Households with 4 or more adult male workers	9. Households without horses	10. Households with 1 horse	11. Households with 2 horses	12. Households with 3 horses	13. Households with 4 or more horses	14. Households without large cattle
16. Total area of allotment land (*desiatiny*)	0,82	0,22	0,33	0,56	0,67	0,85	0,80	0,32	0,55	0,73	0,80	0,74	0,27
17. Average area of allotment, 1 household (*desiatiny*)	0,28	-0,23	0,10	0,01	0,00	0,27	0,59	-0,16	0,00	0,22	0,45	0,51	-0,18
18. Total area of plowland (*desiatiny*)	0,82	0,21	0,32	0,55	0,67	0,85	0,81	0,31	0,55	0,73	0,80	0,74	0,26
19. Average area plowland, 1 household (*desiatiny*)	0,23	-0,17	-0,10	0,00	-0,01	0,26	0,59	-0,16	0,00	0,18	0,39	0,42	-0,16
20. Total area of non-allotment land leased (*desiatiny*)	0,31	-0,14	-0,19	0,09	0,13	0,20	0,12	-0,06	0,00	0,38	0,44	0,48	-0,09

21. % of leased land to area in allotment	-0,28	-0,30	-0,20	-0,36	-0,36	-0,35	-0,33	-0,32	-0,36	-0,19	-0,16	-0,09	-0,31
22. Number of households renting	0,52	0,02	-0,09	0,23	0,36	0,36	0,09	-0,03	0,18	0,62	0,56	0,47	-0,06
23. % renting households to total households	-0,16	-0,33	-0,40	-0,38	-0,35	-0,35	-0,34	-0,46	-0,37	-0,03	-0,01	0,03	-0,47
24. Persons in *local* "industrial" occupations	0,52	0,58	0,45	0,60	0,70	0,58	0,25	0,68	0,56	0,42	0,34	0,23	0,69
25. Persons in *migrant* "industrial" occupations	0,63	0,38	0,31	0,48	0,64	0,67	0,47	0,47	0,66	0,50	0,41	0,30	0,45
26. Number of households with persons in "industrial" occupations	0,76	0,66	0,53	0,73	0,89	0,81	0,43	0,74	0,80	0,63	0,50	0,35	0,75
27. Number of literate persons	0,34	0,52	0,43	0,63	0,59	0,55	0,32	0,66	0,54	0,24	0,10	0,01	0,64
28. % of literate persons in the population	-0,24	0,17	0,37	0,23	0,09	-0,04	-0,13	0,34	0,06	-0,28	-0,35	-0,32	0,35

Data for Kursk and Oboian District partial. Italics signify coefficient P higher than .005

Correlation matrix 3: Interaction of variables for occupation in "industries" and for literacy (based on parish data from the zemstvo census of Kursk Province, 1882–1886).

	24. Persons in *local* "industrial" occupations	25. Persons in *migrant* "industrial" occupations	26. Number of households with persons in "industrial" occupations	27. Number of literate persons	28. % of literate persons in the population
24. Persons in *local* "industrial" occupations	1,00				
25. Persons in *migrant* "industrial" occupattions	0,29	1,00			
26. Number of households with persons in "industrial" occupations	0,77	0,81	1,00		
27. Number of literate persons	0,48	0,38	0,57	1,00	
28. % of literate persons in the population	*0,08*	*0,03*	*0,10*	0,74	1,00

Data for Kursk and Oboian District partial. Italics signify coefficient P higher than .005

Correlation matrix 4: Interaction of variables for household labor composition, household supply of work stock and degree of household autonomy in the conduct of cultivation (based on data for 275 sample villages from the zemstvo census of Kursk Province, 1882–1886).

	1	2	3	4	5	6	7	8	9	10	11	12	13	14	15
1. Number of households	1,00														
2. Households cultivating independently	0,88	1,00													
3. Households cultivating by hiring labor and/or inventory	0,87	0,56	1,00												
4. Households leasing out their allotments	0,77	0,45	0,80	1,00											
5. Households with no adult male worker	0,95	0,73	0,90	0,85	1,00										
6. Households with 1 adult male worker	0,99	0,85	0,89	0,79	0,95	1,00									
7. Households with 2-3 adult male workers	0,98	0,92	0,81	0,71	0,90	0,96	1,00								
8. Households with 4 or more adult male workers	0,77	0,80	0,58	0,47	0,62	0,72	0,83	1,00							
9. Households without horses	0,88	0,56	0,98	0,89	0,93	0,90	0,82	0,57	1,00						
10. Households with 1 horse	0,91	0,87	0,73	0,64	0,85	0,89	0,92	0,72	0,75	1,00					
11. Households with 2 horses	0,74	0,93	0,37	0,26	0,56	0,70	0,78	0,67	0,37	0,67	1,00				
12. Households with 3 horses	0,58	0,81	0,20	0,13	0,39	0,54	0,62	0,65	0,20	0,44	0,90	1,00			
13. Households with 4 or more horses	0,36	0,57	0,06	0,05	0,20	0,33	0,41	0,56	0,06	0,19	0,62	0,81	1,00		
14. Households without large cattle	0,88	0,57	0,96	0,89	0,92	0,90	0,82	0,57	0,99	0,75	0,37	0,20	0,07	1,00	
15. Average size of settlement	0,99	0,91	0,84	0,72	0,92	0,98	0,99	0,82	0,85	0,90	0,77	0,63	0,42	0,84	1,00

Data for Kursk and Oboian District partial. Italics signify coefficient P higher than .005

Correlation matrix 5: Interaction of variables for household labor composition, supply of work stock and degree of autonomy in the conduct of cultivation with variables for allotment and leased acreage, "industrial" employments and literacy (based on data for 275 sample villages from the zemstvo census of Kursk Province, 1882–1886).

	2. Households cultivating independently	3. Households cultivating by hiring labor and/or inventory	4. Households leasing out their allotments	5. Households with no adult male worker	6. Households with 1 adult male worker	7. Households with 2-3 adult male workers	8. Households with 4 or more adult male workers	9. Households without horses	10. Households with 1 horse	11. Households with 2 horses	12. Households with 3 horses	13. Households with 4 or more horses	14. Households without large cattle
16. Total area of allotment land (*desiatiny*)	0,83	0,67	0,61	0,77	0,84	0,88	0,83	0,68	0,76	0,72	0,67	0,52	0,65
17. Average area of allotment, 1 household (*desiatiny*)	0,05	-0,11	-0,04	-0,10	-0,07	0,01	0,27	-0,10	-0,04	0,02	0,20	0,33	-0,10
18. Total area of plowland (*desiatiny*)	0,84	0,65	0,59	0,76	0,83	0,88	0,83	0,66	0,77	0,73	0,69	0,53	0,63
19. Average area plowland, 1 household (*desiatiny*)	0,03	-0,09	-0,04	-0,09	-0,07	0,01	0,25	-0,08	-0,04	0,00	0,15	0,22	-0,08
20. Total area of non-allotment land leased (*desiatiny*)	0,54	0,10	0,01	0,24	0,33	0,39	0,35	0,09	0,27	0,63	0,65	0,55	0,07

21. % of leased land to area in allotment	-0,23	-0,12	-0,12	-0,18	-0,20	-0,22	-0,21	-0,13	-0,21	-0,20	-0,20	-0,15	-0,13
22. Number of households renting	0,67	0,17	0,05	0,35	0,44	0,50	0,39	0,16	0,37	0,78	0,76	0,59	0,14
23. % renting households to total households	-0,27	-0,26	-0,30	-0,32	-0,32	-0,31	-0,29	-0,29	-0,35	-0,17	-0,11	-0,05	-0,28
24. Persons in *local* "industrial" occupations	0,66	0,92	0,82	0,91	0,92	0,86	0,63	0,94	0,79	0,48	0,33	0,21	0,94
25. Persons in *migrant* "industrial" occupations	0,73	0,55	0,42	0,63	0,70	0,75	0,63	0,55	0,76	0,64	0,46	0,18	0,54
26. Number of households with persons in "industrial" occupations	0,81	0,90	0,79	0,94	0,98	0,95	0,72	0,92	0,89	0,64	0,48	0,29	0,91
27. Number of literate persons	0,71	0,85	0,79	0,89	0,89	0,88	0,71	0,87	0,82	0,53	0,37	0,19	0,86
28. % of literate persons in the population	0,33	0,32	0,35	0,40	0,38	0,40	0,34	0,35	0,38	0,28	0,19	0,07	0,33

Data for Kursk and Oboian District partial. Italics signify coefficient P higher than .005

Correlation matrix 6: Interaction of variables for occupation in "industries" and for literacy (based on data for 275 sample villages from the zemstvo census of Kursk Province, 1882–1886).

	24. Persons in *local* "industrial" occupations	25. Persons in *migrant* "industrial" occupations	26. Number of households with persons in "industrial" occupations	27. Number of literate persons	28. % of literate persons in the population
24. Persons in *local* "industrial" occupations	1,00				
25. Persons in *migrant* "industrial" occupations	0,51	1,00			
26. Number of households with persons in "industrial" occupations	0,94	0,74	1,00		
27. Number of literate persons	0,86	0,65	0,90	1,00	
28. % of literate persons in the population	0,34	0,38	0,39	0,63	1,00

Data for Kursk and Oboian District partial. Italics signify coefficient P higher than ,005

Villages Listing

Data for 1897 from *Pervaia vseobshchaia perepis' naseleniia Rossiiskoi imperii 1897 g. Naselennyia mesta Rossiiskoi imperii v 500 i bolee zhitelei c ukazaniem vsego nalichnago v nikh naseleniia i chisla zhitelei preobladaiushchikh veroispovedanii po dannym pervoi vseobshchei perepisi naseleniia 1897 g.* (St. P., 1905), 93–103. Data for 1882–1884 from Kurskoe gubernskoe zemstvo, Statisticheskoe biuro, *Sbornik statisticheskikh svedenii po Kurskoi gubernii. Vyp.1 Kurskii uyezd* (M., 1883); *Vyp. II. Statisticheskie svedeniia po L'govskomu uyezdu* (Kursk, 1884); *Vyp. III. Statisticheskie svedeniia po Dmitrievskomu uyezdu* (Kursk, 1884); *Vyp. IV. Statisticheskie svedeniia po Sudzhanskomu uyezdu* (Kursk, 1884); *Vyp. V. Statisticheskie svedeniia po Fatezhskomu uyezdu* (Kursk, 1884); *Vyp. VI. Statisticheskie svedeniia po Ryl'skomu uyezdu* (Kursk, 1885); *Vyp. VII. Statisticheskie svedeniia po Putivl'skomu uyezdu* (Kursk, 1885); *Vyp. VIII. Statisticheskie svedeniia po Shchigrovskomu uyezdu* (Kursk, 1885); *Vyp. IX. Statisticheskie svedeniia po Graivoronskomu uyezdu* (Kursk, 1884); *Vyp. X. Statisticheskie svedeniia po Belgorodskomu uyezdu* (Kursk, 1885); *Vyp. XI. Statisticheskie svedeniia po Novooskol'skomu uyezdu* (Kursk, 1886); *Vyp. XII. Statisticheskie svedeniia po Timskomu uyezdu* (Kursk, 1886); *Vyp. XIII. Statisticheskie svedeniia po Korochanskomu uyezdu* (Kursk, 1886); *Vyp. XIV. Statisticheskie svedeniia po Starooskol'skomu uyezdu* (Kursk, 1886). *Sbornik statisticheskikh svedenii po Oboianskomu uyezdu (Kurskoi gubernii),* M., 1882–1883.

Dmitriev District

Village	Parish	Population, 1882–1884				Population, 1897			Juridical standing, former owner before 1861
		hhld.	male	female	all	male	female	all	
1 Sal'noe	Prilepovskaia	141	436	394	830	455	458	913	Venevitinov
2 Khal'zovka	Prilepovskaia	61	184	196	380	*no information*			Meiendorf
3 Prilepy	Prilepovskaia	63	183	204	387	790	786	1 576	Meiendorf
4 Iaroslavka	Prilepovskaia	72	236	210	446	242	252	494	Venevitinov
5 Dubrovitsy	Prilepovskaia	139	479	478	957	512	572	1 084	Meiendorf
6 Klintsy	Prilepovskaia	73	211	201	412	232	256	488	Meiendorf
7 Lobki	Prilepovskaia	56	196	174	370	*no information*			Venevitinov
8 Dobroe Pole	Prilepovskaia	65	237	264	501	256	287	543	Meiendorf
9 Aleksino	Prilepovskaia	41	148	127	275	*no information*			Venevitinov
10 Khomutovka	Glamazdinskaia	145	483	471	954	466	549	1 015	Levshin
11 Romanovo (Romanovka)	Glamazdinskaia	116	315	300	615	359	407	766	ex-serfs (7)
12 Glamazdino (-Gremiach'e)	Glamazdinskaia	145	592	503	1 095	562	647	1 209	Volkov (Nelidov)
13 Vet'	Glamazdinskaia	186	570	572	1 142	633	758	1 391	Venevinitov
14 Iudina	Glamazdinskaia	69	207	198	405	*no information*			Litvinov
15 Strekalovka	Glamazdinskaia	51	178	151	329	280	266	546	ex-serfs (4)
16 Kalinovka	Ol'khovskaia	139	454	444	898	446	552	998	Levshin
17 Suchkino	Ol'khovskaia	62	200	182	382	250	289	539	Meiendorf

Village	Parish	Population, 1882–1884				Population, 1897			Juridical standing, former owner before 1861
		hhld.	male	female	all	male	female	all	
18 Kurenki	Ol'khovskaia	99	326	321	647	363	390	753	Denis'ev
19 Prikhodovka	Ol'khovskaia	74	278	238	516	346	353	699	Afanasenko
20 Bogoslovka	Ol'khovskaia	31	101	87	188	*no information*			Denis'ev
21 Zhidenovka	Ol'khovskaia	95	351	307	658	381	437	818	ex-serfs/state souls
22 Khatushi	Staraia-Belitskaia	51	191	170	361	261	254	515	Bobrinskie
23 Staraia Belitsa	Staro-Belitskaia	134	463	424	887	609	672	1 281	ex-serfs/state souls
24 Gladkaia	Kilikinskaia	74	290	277	567	341	363	704	ex-serfs/state souls
25 Luboshevo	Kilikinskaia	116	377	360	737	493	483	976	Artiukhov
26 Zveniachka	Berezovskaia	159	566	544	1 110	594	668	1 262	ex-serfs (5)
27 Ofrosimovka	Berezovskaia	30	102	94	196	*no information*			Ofrosimov
28 Men'shikovo	Berezovskaia	168	535	507	1 042	597	659	1 256	state souls
29 Kozhanovka	Skovorodenskaia	77	260	235	495	241	277	518	ex-serfs/state souls
30 Maleevka	Skovorodenskaia	34	107	108	215	*no information*			ex-serfs (2)
31 Arsen'evka	Skovorodenskaia	33	115	106	221	*no information*			Sagarev
32 Peresvetova Belitsa	Mashkinskaia	121	366	340	706	373	395	768	ex-serfs
33 Sergeevka	Mashkinskaia	51	199	172	371	*no information*			ex-serfs
34 Mikhailovka (Ponashevka)	Mikhailovskaia	654	1 513	1 518	3 031	2 207	2 246	4 453	Sheremet'ev

Sudzha District

#	Settlement	Volost							Owner
35	Maslovka	Kostornianskaia	65	214	210	424	*no information*		Belevtsev
36	Glebovka	Kostornianskaia	27	85	72	157	*no information*		ex-serfs (3)
37	Samsonovka	Kostornianskaia	12	46	45	91	*no information*		Zhekulin
38	Mal'tsevo	Kostornianskaia	139	431	426	857	239	254	493	ex-serfs/state souls
39	Belyi Kolodez'	Kostornianskaia	53	208	206	414	*no information*		ex-serfs/state souls
40	D'iakonovka (*khutor*)	Kostornianskaia	*no information*				*no information*		?
41	Ivanovka	Kostornianskaia	36	115	96	211	*no information*		Zhekulin
42	Borshchen'	Kostornianskaia	135	404	403	807	473	463	936	ex-serfs (2)
43	Liubimovka	Kostornianskaia	74	199	209	408	281	288	569	ex-serfs (3)
44	Blagodatnaia	Kostornianskaia	75	208	206	414	*no information*		ex-serfs (5)
45	Ofrosimovka	Kostornianskaia	32	101	95	196	*no information*		Ofrosimov
46	Novo-Nikol'skoe	Kostornianskaia	*no information*				*no information*		?
47	Izvekova (Nemcha)	Skorodenskaia	28	97	119	216	*no information*		Nelidov
48	Sula	Skorodenskaia	307	1 016	1 020	2 036	1 138	1 202	2 340	state souls
49	Aleksandrovka	Skorodenskaia	48	136	111	247	*no information*		Lukashev
50	Liubostan'	Skorodenskaia	241	925	907	1 832	1 110	1 116	2 226	state souls
51	Vasil'evka (*khutor*)	Skorodenskaia	*no information*				*no information*		?
52	Lipovka (Lipnik)	Skorodenskaia	44	188	161	349	*no information*		ex-serfs (3)
53	Cherkasskaia Konopel'ka	Zamost'ianskaia	73	225	213	438	*no information*		Shmidt (*darstvenniki*)
54	Ozerki	Belovskaia	149	605	579	1 184	570	603	1 173	chetvertniki

	Village	Parish	Population, 1882–1884				Population, 1897			Juridical standing, former owner before 1861
			hhld.	male	female	all	male	female	all	
55	Peschanoe	Belovskaia	291	885	887	1 772	947	973	1 920	ex-serfs/state souls
56	Ganzhevka	Belovskaia	40	141	134	275	*no information*			Sokolov (*darstvenniki*)
57	Ol'gino (*khutor*)	Belovskaia	16	87	67	154	*no information*			ex-serfs
58	Ilek	Belovskaia	220	857	831	1 688	1 023	1 034	2 057	state souls
59	Koshary	Belovskaia	*no information*				*no information*			?
60	Volokonskoe	Bol'she-Soldatskaia	177	551	478	1 029	628	662	1 290	ex-serfs (5)
61	Shcherbachevka	Bol'she-Soldatskaia	130	414	378	792	430	442	872	Tolstoi
62	Bardakovka	Bol'she-Soldatskaia	70	233	237	470	273	280	553	Sukhodolov
63	Nemcha-Shirkovo	Bol'she-Soldatskaia	133	393	405	798	374	433	807	ex-serfs (4)
64	Shagarovka	Bol'she-Soldatskaia	32	119	101	220	*no information*			Evreinov
65	Dar'ino	Novo-Ivanovskaia	232	770	749	1 519	628	662	1 290	Golytsin
66	Nikolaevka	Novo-Ivanovskaia	151	481	490	971	571	610	1 181	Bariatinskii
67	Tolstoi Lug	Novo-Ivanovskaia	182	565	567	1 132	657	698	1 355	Bariatinskii
68	Nikol'skii (*khutor*)	Novo-Ivanovskaia	46	154	151	305	*no information*			Davydov
69	Velikaia Rybnitsa	Miropol'skaia	287	818	758	1 576	949	1 033	1 982	state souls
70	Milaevka	Goptarovskaia	66	218	211	429	*no information*			Stavitskie
71	Demidovka	Goptarovskaia	85	277	277	554	267	301	568	Podol'skie
72	Popovka	Goptarovskaia	39	123	102	225	*no information*			ex-serfs (4)
73	Nadezhevka	Goptarovskaia	31	103	117	220	*no information*			Shabel'skii

No.	Settlement	Volost								Owner / category
74	Kurchaninovka	Martynovskaia	56	164	154	318	*no information*			Mal'tsov
75	Shchegolek	Cherno-Oleshenskaia	149	527	484	1 011	516	560	1 066	chetvertniki
	Novyi Oskol' District									
76	Chernianka	Chernianskaia	464	1 229	1 152	2 381	2 851	3 009	5 860	ex-serfs (5)
77	Adelaidina (Malyi)	Chernianskaia	74	193	214	407	248	256	504	Evreinov
78	Okuni	Chernianskaia	106	366	347	713	392	387	779	state souls
79	Morkvina	Chernianskaia	130	457	427	884	570	547	1 117	ex-serfs (2)
80	Maslovka	Chernianskaia	229	613	599	1 212	489	458	947	Sheremet'ev (*darstvenniki*)
81	Ezdochnoe	Chernianskaia	177	597	562	1 159	532	612	1 144	ex-serfs/state souls
82	Bol'shoi Khutor	Chernianskaia	100	312	275	587	343	327	670	ex-serfs (2)
83	Sychev (*khutor*)	Chernianskaia	*no information*				*no information*			?
84	Sytnoe (*khutor*)	Chernianskaia	*no information*				*no information*			?
85	Ol'shanka	Ol'shanskaia	556	1 768	1 638	3 406	1 724	1 798	3 522	Trubetskoi
86	Volkovo	Ol'shanskaia	185	733	701	1 434	747	712	1 459	*chetvertniki*
87	Protochnoe	Ol'shanskaia	169	604	586	1 190	636	612	1 284	*chetvertniki*/state souls (2)
88	Volkovka	Ol'shanskaia	66	220	240	460	*no information*			Volkov
89	Novomatveevka	Ol'shanskaia	12	46	33	79	*no information*			?
90	Gladkovka	Ol'shanskaia	18	55	48	103	*no information*			Gladkov
91	Nikol'skoe	Volotovskaia	104	336	351	687	369	360	729	Miatlev
92	Troitskaia	Volotovskaia	235	809	808	1 617	708	733	1 441	Trubetskoi

	Village	Parish	Population, 1882–1884				Population, 1897			Juridical standing, former owner before 1861
			hhld.	male	female	all	male	female	all	
93	Novaia Bezginka	Volotovskaia	168	599	582	1 181	433	455	888	ex-serfs (2)
94	Elizavetinka	Volotovskaia	66	223	241	464	*no information*			Bunin (2)
95	Larisovka	Volotovskaia	59	235	226	461	299	271	570	Shidlovskie
96	Petrovskoe	Volotovskaia	43	153	166	319	332	378	710	ex-serfs (4)
97	Kon'shino	Khalanskaia	235	697	714	1 411	770	819	1 589	ex-serfs/*chetvertniki* (6)
98	Gorodishche	Khalanskaia	142	530	518	1 048	550	588	1 138	state souls
99	Kuflievka	Khalanskaia	50	185	170	355	*no information*			Trubetskoi
100	Soldat (*khutor*)	Khalanskaia	*no information*				*no information*			?
101	Vysokii (*khutor*)	Khalanskaia	*no information*				*no information*			?
102	Golubina	Prigorodniaia	291	770	733	1 503	791	847	1 638	Miatlev
103	Sharapovka	Prigorodniaia	120	437	380	817	540	563	1 103	ex-serfs (4)
104	Iakovlevka	Prigorodniaia	49	177	156	333	*no information*			ex-serfs (4)
105	Slonovka	Slonovskaia	554	--	--	3 194	1 781	1 824	3 605	state souls
106	Veliko-Mikhailovka	Veliko-Mikhailovskaia	1 830	5 235	5 039	10 274	5 858	5 995	11 853	state souls
L'gov District										
107	Vyshie Dereven'ki	Vyshederevenskaia	319	970	954	1 924	1 037	1 119	2 156	Tolstoi
108	Ekaterinovka	Vyshederevenskaia	40	130	131	261	*no information*			Tolstoi
109	Liubimirovka	Vyshederevenskaia	70	208	205	413	*no information*			Tolstoi

No.	Settlement	Volost								Owner
110	Bol'shie Ugony	Ugonskaia	297	866	804	1 670	853	956	1 809	Tolstoi
111	Peny	Ugonskaia	201	602	581	1 183	560	673	1 233	Tolstoi (*darstvenniki*)
112	Spasskaia	Bobrikovskaia	110	364	317 –	681	283	293	576	Bydrin/Durnovo
113	Annino (Gusinovka)	Bobrikovskaia	101	354	331	685	357	366	723	Tolstoi
114	Kamenskoe (N-Sergeevskaia)	Bobrikovskaia	340	1 068	1 089	2 157	1 115	1 116	2 231	state souls
115	Iur'evka	Ol'shanskaia	84	212	223	435	238	249	487	ex-serfs (*darstvenniki*)
116	Kozhlia (Kozlia)	Ol'shanskaia	215	623	623	1 246	560	731	1 291	ex-serfs (*darstvenniki*)
117	Zakharkovo	Ol'shanskaia	100	276	278	552	560	413	973	ex-serfs (7)
118	Kochetno	Ol'shanskaia	117	365	361	726	*no information*			ex-serfs (*darstvenniki*)
119	Zagriadnaia	Ol'shanskaia	36	98	97	195	*no information*			Stremoukhov
120	Lukashevka	Kolpakovskaia	44	173	165	338	*no information*			Iarosh
121	Borodina	Kolpakovskaia	79	225	231	456	251	278	529	Iz"edinov
122	Banishchi	Ivanovskaia	543	1 652	1 606	3 258	1 940	2 070	4 010	state souls
123	Ivanovskoe	Ivanovskaia	846	2 470	2 533	5 003	2 609	2 976	5 585	Bariatinskii
124	Gornostaevka	Ivanovskaia	47	143	145	288	*no information*			ex-serfs (3)
125	Zelenino	Ivanovskaia	36	98	97	195	*no information*			ex-serfs (3)
126	Fitizh (Fatezh)	Nizhnederevenskaia	178	580	539	1 119	772	833	1 605	Stremoukhov
127	Karasaevka (Blagodatnoe)	Nizhnederevenskaia	75	222	225	447	232	256	488	Tolstoi
128	Sherekina	Nizhnederevenskaia	100	348	336	684	467	484	951	ex-serfs (2)
129	Kochanovka	Iznoskovskaia	71	233	218	451	*no information*			Gagarin
130	Nadezhdina	Iznoskovskaia	114	335	342	677	349	403	752	Bariatinskii

Village	Parish	Population, 1882–1884				Population, 1897			Juridical standing, former owner before 1861
		hhld.	male	female	all	male	female	all	
131 Shustovo	Shustovskaia	166	552	572	1 124	796	883	1 679	ex-serfs (8)
132 Kudintseva	Shustovskaia	148	455	434	889	784	811	1 595	ex-serfs (2)
133 Voronina	Gorodenskaia	46	140	134	274	no information			ex-serfs/state souls
134 Rechitsa	Gorodenskaia	132	355	363	718	354	409	763	Tolstoi
135 Kotleva	Konyshevskaia	47	150	138	288	no information			ex-serfs
136 Glazovo	Konyshevskaia	no information				no information			?
137 Skrylevka	Sheptukhovskaia	104	303	290	593	382	416	798	ex-serfs
Oboian District									
138 Noven'skoe	Kurasovakaia	224	829	747	1 576	887	875	1 762	state souls
139 Voznesenskoe	Kurasovakaia	143	429	470	899	475	493	968	Ustimovich
140 Orlovka	Kurasovakaia	105	327	340	667	244	251	495	Loiko/Gamalei
141 Vasil'evka	Kurasovakaia	30	105	93	198	no information			Sorokiny
142 Ivnia (Troitskoe)	Kurasovakaia	175	563	551	1 114	666	695	1 361	Kleinmikhel'
143 Kartamysheka	Rybinskaia	109	376	358	734	380	410	790	chetvertniki /state souls
144 Shmireva (Shmerevo)	Rybinskaia	103	338	295	633	353	372	725	state souls
145 Kosinovo (Kasinovo)	Rybinskaia	107	356	332	688	362	393	755	state souls
146 Kopteva	Rybinskaia	81	242	235	477	no information			state souls
147 Rovnia (khutor)	Rybinskaia	11	25	25	50	no information			Bogaevskie

148	Bashkatovo	Rybinskaia	171	564	543	1 107	635	640	1 275	state souls
149	Shevelevo	Rybinskaia	178	602	621	1 223	557	594	1 151	state souls
150	Chekmarevka	Rybinskaia	129	452	436	888	293	290	583	state souls
151	Vyshnyi Reutets	Medvenskaia	347	1 251	1 174	2 425	1 308	1 332	2 640	ex-serfs/state souls (6)
152	Nizhnyi Reutets (Shelkovka)	Medvenskaia	245	885	947	1 832	945	987	1 932	ex-serfs/state souls (3)
153	Gorki	Medvenskaia	13	46	42	88	*no information*			Goriainov
154	Samarino	Pavlovskaia	77	259	281	540	310	334	644	state souls
155	Peschanoe	Pavlovskaia	227	748	728	1 476	788	804	1 592	ex-serfs/state souls (5)
156	Fedchevka	Penskaia	57	202	181	383	243	253	496	Karamzin
157	Studenok	Penskaia	96	274	297	571	*no information*			Kleinmikhel'
158	Rzhavo	Ol'shanskaia	148	451	467	918	680	689	1 369	Kleinmikhel'
159	Lukhanina	Krasnianskaia	140	544	541	1 085	554	616	1 170	state souls
160	Syrtsov (khutor)	Krasnianskaia	54	175	158	333	*no information*			Kleinmikhel'
161	Dmitrievskoe (Ematovo)	Krasnianskaia	110	394	364	758	362	367	729	Kleinmikhel'
162	Pereversevka	Dolzhenkovskaia	59	153	148	301	*no information*			Kleinmikhel'
163	Dolzhenkovo	Dolzhenkovskaia	292	945	888	1 833	1 097	1 082	2 179	state souls
164	Bushmino	Dolzhenkovskaia	113	415	386	801	500	535	1 035	state souls

Putivl' District

165	Cherepovka	Nikolaevskaia	390	1 190	1 205	2 395	1 253	1 297	2 550	ex-serfs (8) Cherepov
166	Gamaleevka	Nikolaevskaia	329	1 011	976	1 987	1 144	1 137	2 281	Cherepov

Village	Parish	Population, 1882–1884				Population, 1897			Juridical standing, former owner before 1861
		hhld.	male	female	all	male	female	all	
167 Glushets	Glushetskaia	369	1 133	1 082	2 215	1 397	1 444	2 841	Ribop'er
168 Peski	Glushetskaia	183	528	488	1 016	710	739	1 449	ex-serfs (11)
169 Starye Viry	Glushetskaia	151	461	441	902	496	502	998	state souls
170 Novye Viry	Glushetskaia	188	650	619	1 269	888	885	1 773	state souls
171 Leont'evskoe	Popovoslobodskaia	188	610	556	1 166	*no information*			Cherepov
172 Popovaia Sloboda (Popova)	Popovoslobodskaia	622	1 859	1 791	3 650	2 485	2 586	5 071	ex-serfs (7)
173 Gvintovo	Popovoslobodskaia	242	738	749	1 487	1 079	1 090	2 169	ex-serfs (5)
174 Bol'shaia Nepliuevka	B.-Nepliuevskaia	726	2 086	2 012	4 098	2 353	2 362	4 715	ex-serfs (12)
175 Pogarich	Beriukovskaia	95	290	290	580	496	502	998	Tolstoi
176 Gruzskoe	Gruzchanskaia	348	1 058	1 034	2 092	1 202	1 331	2 533	Cherepov
177 Zemlianka	Gruzchanskaia	264	852	766	1 618	870	985	1 855	Cherepov
178 Viazovoe	Gruzchanskaia	402	1 300	1 310	2 610	1 435	1 555	2 990	Cherepov
179 Bochechki	Kazachanskaia	591	2 041	2 016	4 057	2 588	2 575	5 163	state souls
180 Kazatskoe (Svechkino)	Kazachanskaia	852	2 738	2 649	5 387	3 125	3 307	6 432	ex-serfs (10)
181 Iur'eva	Volyntsevskaia	98	287	290	577	407	422	829	ex-serfs (9)
182 Shilovka	Burynskaia	130	447	373	820	363	355	718	Apraksin

Graivoron District

183	Borisovka	Borisovskaia	2 744	7 829	7 338	15 167	8 991	9 080	18 071	Sheremet'ev
184	Rakitnaia	Rakitianskaia	1 101	3 332	3 291	6 623	3 936	3 984	7 920	Iusupov
185	Vasil'evka	Rakitianskaia	52	179	151	330	*no information*			ex-serfs
186	Kobel'evka	Rakitianskaia	103	337	309	646	395	387	782	ex-serfs
187	Dunaika	Dorogoshchanskaia	169	527	472	999	431	430	861	ex-serfs
188	Krasnaia Iaruga	Krasno-Iaruzhskaia	458	1 512	1 505	3 017	1 643	1 684	3 327	ex-serfs
189	Markushino	Krasno-Iaruzhskaia	323	1 099	1 064	2 163	1 093	1 106	2 199	ex-serfs
190	Striguny	Strigunovskaia	491	1 557	1 517	3 074	1 605	1 692	3 297	ex-serfs
191	Porubezh	Strigunovskaia	149	470	450	920	468	462	930	ex-serfs
192	Golovchino	Lisichanskaia	658	1 798	1 747	3 545	2 163	2 461	4 624	ex-serfs
193	Sitnoe (Setnoe)	Viazovskaia	189	549	500	1 049	633	620	1 253	ex-serfs

Tim District

194	Kniazhoe (Bogoliubovka)	Nikol'skaia	84	323	310	633	343	413	756	Tomilin
195	Nikol'skoe	Nikol'skaia	170	561	539	1 100	430	475	905	ex-serfs
196	Puzatskie Butyrki	Verkhosemskaia	25	99	93	192	340	377	717	ex-serfs (2)
197	Puzachi	Verkhosemskaia	314	1 130	1 028	2 158	1 066	1 158	2 224	ex-serfs/state souls (5)
198	Protasovka	Afanas'evo-Pakhonskaia	62	230	242	472	235	272	507	ex-serfs (2)
199	Krivets	Mikhel'polskaia	348	1 243	1 292	2 535	1 200	1 332	2 532	ex-serfs/state souls (2)
200	Donskaia Semitsa	Mikhel'polskaia	110	363	340	703	394	440	834	ex-serfs/state souls (2)

Village	Parish	Population, 1882–1884				Population, 1897			Juridical standing, former owner before 1861
		hhld.	male	female	all	male	female	all	
Fatezh District									
201 Konevo	Sergeevskaia	196	617	582	1 199	609	643	1 252	ex-serfs/state souls (4)
202 Linets	Dmitrievskaia	136	432	453	885	366	411	777	Strukov
203 Ponyri	Ponyrovskaia	790	2 874	2 889	5 763	3 234	3 548	6 782	state souls
Staryi Oskol' District									
204 Lopukhinka	Kladovskaia	155	464	501	965	495	554	1 049	Isakov
205 Gushchina	Kladovskaia	156	495	472	967	487	523	1 010	Chervonnyi
206 Bobrik-Evgen'evka	Kladovskaia	16	66	55	121	*no information*			Speshnev
207 Luboshevka	Kladovskaia	*no information*				*no information*			?
208 Kondaurovka	Kladovskaia	41	126	140	266	*no information*			Kondaurovy
209 Timiriazevo (Arkhangel'skoe)	Kladovskaia	135	449	437	886	523	601	1 124	Kleinmikhel'
210 Potseluevka (Lutovinovo)	Kladovskaia	12	43	42	85	*no information*			Lutovinovy
211 Saltykovo	Saltykovskaia	246	977	843	1 820	926	930	1 856	Orlov-Davydov
212 Lukoianovka	Saltykovskaia	213	714	745	1 459	694	890	1 584	Skalon'
213 Korobkovo	Saltykovskaia	115	398	412	810	388	427	815	Korobkovy
214 Sreten'ka (Strechanka)	Saltykovskaia	51	180	171	351	*no information*			Korobkovy
215 Godeevka (*khutor*)	Viazovskaia	*no information*				*no information*			?
216 Chuevo	Viazovskaia	157	666	662	1 328	718	756	1 474	*chetvertniki* /state souls

217	Ukolova	Viazovskaia	105	409	419	828	510	514	1 024	*chetvertniki*
218	Viazovoe	Viazovskaia	267	1 111	1 057	2 168	1 178	1 170	2 348	*chetvertniki /state souls*
219	Orlik (Nikolaevka)	Orlikovskaia	648	1 991	2 011	4 002	1 875	2 135	4 010	Bobrinskie
220	Dubenka	Bogoslovskaia	116	384	381	765	321	305	626	Raevskii
221	Myshenka (Bogoslovka)	Bogoslovskaia	182	643	617	1 260	757	887	1 644	Burnashev
222	Sorokina	Dolgopolianskaia	96	303	329	632	301	332	633	*chetvertniki*
223	Volokonovo (Volokonskoe)	Obukhovskaia	231	848	790	1 638	615	643	1 258	Kochubei
224	Slaviano	Obukhovskaia	85	293	276	569	298	277	575	Trubetskoi
225	Petrovo (*khutor*)	Obukhovskaia	107	342	357	699	*no information*			Orlov-Davydov
Korocha District										
226	Zimoven'ki	Zimovenskaia	240	702	630	1 332	763	754	1 517	Trubetskoi
227	Nizhnee Berezovo	Zimovenskaia	137	460	388	848	440	408	848	ex-serfs/state souls (3)
228	Lomovo	Novoslobodskaia	328	1 035	974	2 009	1 012	1 088	2 100	state souls
229	Zaiach'e	Novoslobodskaia	445	1 478	1 398	2 876	1 323	1 370	2 693	state souls
230	Mazikina	Novoslobodskaia	118	415	365	780	372	362	734	state souls
231	Novaia Sloboda	Novoslobodskaia	451	1 465	1 319	2 776	1 313	1 410	2 723	state souls
232	Alekseevka	Novoslobodskaia	473	1 698	1 583	3 281	1 685	1 624	3 309	state souls
233	Plosskoe	Novoslobodskaia	127	391	364	755	429	406	835	state souls
234	Pestunova	Novoslobodskaia	62	238	228	466	267	237	504	state souls
235	Gorodishche	Novoslobodskaia	55	216	201	417	257	239	496	state souls

Village	Parish	Population, 1882–1884				Population, 1897			Juridical standing, former owner before 1861
		hhld.	male	female	all	male	female	all	
236 Nikol'skaia	Nekliudovskaia	218	632	575	1 207	740	720	1 460	Iusupov
237 Pentsovka	Nekliudovskaia	156	457	412	869	425	409	834	Iusupov
238 Nekliudova	Nekliudovskaia	375	1 114	1 012	2 126	1 175	1 117	2 292	Sheremet'ev
239 Koshlakova	Nekliudovskaia	142	462	446	908	484	533	1 017	*chetvertniki* /state souls
240 Nechaevo	Nechaevskaia	158	514	474	988	526	532	1 058	*chetvertniki*
241 Tiurina	Nechaevskaia	162	491	489	980	518	510	1 028	*chetvertniki*
242 Repnoe	Kupianskaia	165	517	458	975	518	504	1 022	*chetvertniki*
243 Tsepliaeva	Kupianskaia	113	348	332	680	368	417	785	*chetvertniki*
244 Bekhteevka	Prigorodniaia	530	1 860	1 743	3 603	1 953	1 970	3 923	state souls
Ryl'sk District									
245 Ishutina	Volobuevskaia	71	227	200	427	274	279	553	ex-serfs (4)
246 Olimpiadskoe (*khutor*)	Kul'bakinskaia	*no information*				*no information*			?
247 Kul'baki	Kul'bakinskaia	306	1 008	979	1 987	1 124	1 152	2 276	Ribop'er
248 Muzhitskaia	Kul'bakinskaia	217	724	731	1 455	829	888	1 717	Ribop'er
249 Sergeevka	Kul'bakinskaia	71	271	261	532	262	292	554	Ribop'er
250 Snagost'e	Snagostskaia	480	1 633	1 644	3 277	2 001	2 130	4 131	Bariatinski
251 Obukhovka	Snagostskaia	271	831	807	1 638	1 030	1 027	2 057	Bariatinski
252 Liubimovka	Snagostskaia	394	1 338	1 327	2 665	1 604	1 648	3 252	Bariatinski

No.	Name	Volost							Owner
253	Kolomok (*khutor*)	Snagostskaia	*no information*			*no information*			Bariatinski
254	Tetkino	Tetkinskaia	523	1 515	1 523	3 038	2 273	2 354	4 627	Ribop'er
255	Tolpino	Korenevskaia	202	599	537	1 136	558	622	1 180	Polianskii
256	Markino	Markovskaia	233	715	691	1 406	906	896	1 802	ex-serfs
257	Dugina	Bobrovskaia	68	219	221	440	*no information*			ex-serfs
258	Kobylka	Kobylovskaia	548	1 725	1 729	3 454	1 834	1 879	3 713	Ribop'er

Kursk District

No.	Name	Volost							Owner
259	Tsvetovo	Ryshkovskaia	152	601	598	1 199	*no information*			ex-serfs (5)
260	Kamyshenka	Spasskaia	92	317	279	596	282	283	565	?
261	Spasskoe	Spasskaia	162	557	506	1 063	*no information*			ex-serfs (2)
262	Aleksandrovka	Spasskaia	35	116	123	239	*no information*			ex-serfs (2)
263	Gostomlia	Spasskaia	406	1 338	1 252	2 590	1 122	1 177	2 299	*chetvertniki*
264	Pokrovskoe	D'iakonovskaia	127	402	396	798	*no information*			ex-serfs (*darstvenniki*)
265	Nozdriacheva	Kamenevskaia	70	225	203	428	*no information*			*chetvertniki*
266	Mar'ino-Shagarovo	Kamenevskaia	129	391	383	774	346	375	721	Shagarovy
267	Ivanovka-Tsurikovo	Rozhdestvenskaia	30	79	67	146	*no information*			Bugaev
268	Ammosovka	Rozhdestvenskaia	71	237	241	478	*no information*			ex-serfs
269	Vorob'evo	Chermoshenskaia	144	526	539	1 065	594	612	1 206	*chetvertniki*

Village	Parish	Population, 1882–1884				Population, 1897			Juridical standing, former owner before 1861
		hhld.	male	female	all	male	female	all	
Shchigrov District									
270 Ivanovka-Nebol'sino	Khokhlovskaia	24	64	64	128	*no information*			Nebol'sin
271 Nikolaevka	Nikolaevskaia	176	586	608	1 194	491	584	1 075	ex-serfs (Durnovo)
272 Matveevka-Baranovka	Nikolaevskaia	118	427	447	874	*no information*			Bydriny
273 Sergeevka	Nikolaevskaia	38	124	133	257	*no information*			Shchekiny/Derebiny
274 Nizhne-Ozernoe	Ozerenskaia	141	478	499	977	312	424	736	Denis'ev
275 Korsakovo	Vyshe-Ol'khovatskaia	*no information*				*no information*			?
276 Nizhnii Terebuzh	Vyshe-Daimenskaia	68	225	217	442	720	761	1 481	ex-serfs (5) / *chetvertniki* (1)
277 Kazanskoe	Vyshe-Daimenskaia	40	158	154	312	*no information*			Ofrosimov
278 Nizhnii Daimen'	Vyshe-Daimenskaia	152	468	490	958	*no information*			Durnovo, Speshnev, *et al.*
279 Lipovskoe	Lipovskaia	380	1 317	1 342	2 659	2 207	2 246	4 453	ex-serfs (7) / *chetvertniki* (1)
280 Mikhailovskoe	Lipovskaia	210	656	650	1 306	514	611	1 125	ex-serfs (4)
281 Nikol'skoe	Nikol'skaia	145	449	460	909	*no information*			Skariatin
Belgorod District									
282 Naprasnenskoe	Muromskaia	76	262	250	512	335	365	700	Gendrikov (*darstvenniki*)
283 Novaia Tavolzhanka	Shebekinskaia	177	503	458	961	957	805	1 762	Zhukovskii

284	Toplinka (Bogoroditskoe)	Nikol'skaia	126	348	343	691	289	354	643	Seremisovy
285	Sabynino	Sabyninskaia	202	623	588	1 211	649	648	1 297	Volkonskie
286	Nelidovka	Melikhovskaia	51	174	173	347	*no information*			Nelidov
287	Arkad'evka	Melikhovskaia	73	229	228	457	*no information*			Nelidov
288	Bessonovka	Bessonovskaia	296	903	856	1 759	877	861	1 738	Ozerovy
289	Arapovka	Bessonovskaia	133	467	456	923	414	411	825	ex-serfs

Abbreviations

APSR	–	*American Political Science Review*
CSC	–	Tsentral'nyi statisticheskii komitet Ministerstva vnu-trennikh del (Central Statistical Committee of the Ministry of Internal Affairs)
d.	–	the Russian *delo* (matter): a numbered archival folder
EAIVE	–	*Ezhegodnik po agrarnoi istorii vostochnoi Evropy* (Yearbook on the Agrarian History of Eastern Europe)
f.	–	the Russian *fond* or numbered archival repository
GARF	–	Gosudarstvennyi arkhiv Rossisskoi federatsii (State Archive of the Russian Federation)
ISSSR	–	*Istoriia SSSR* (History of the USSR)
IZ	–	*Istoricheskie zapiski* (journal)
JPS	–	*Journal of Peasant Studies*
JSH	–	*Journal of Social History*
JTS	–	*Journal of Theoretical Politics*
KA	–	*Krasnyi arkhiv* (journal)
l.	–	the Russian *list'* or leaf (a page in an archival folder or *delo*). In plural as ll
ob.	–	obverse (of a page in an archival folder or *delo*)
OI	–	*Otechestvennaia istoriia* (History of the Fatherland, journal)
op.	–	the Russian *opis'* or numbered archival service catalogue, containing a listing of numbered *dela* and their titles. Each *fond* can have up to 300 separate catalogues
PSS	–	*Polnoe Sobranie Sochinenii* (Complete Collected

Works)

PSZ	–	*Polnoe Sobranie zakonov Rossiiskoi imperii* (Complete Collection of the Laws of the Russian Empire). Published in three series: Series I (1649–1825); Series II (1825–1881); Series III (1881–1913)
RGIA	–	Rossiiskii gosudarstvennyi istoricheskii arkhiv (Russian State Historical Archive)
RR	–	*Russian Review*
RSKG	–	*Revoliutsionnye sobytiia v Kurskoi gubernii v 1905–1907 gg. Sbornik dokumentov i materialov* (Revolutionary Events in Kursk Province, 1905–1907. Collected Documents and Materials), Kursk, Kurskoe knizhnoe izdatel'stvo, 1955
SR	–	*Slavic Review*
SRI	–	*Statistika Rossiiskoi imperii*
SSSKG	–	*Sbornik statisticheskikh svedeniia po Kurskoi gubernii*
SVRI	–	*Statisticheskii vremennik Rossiiskoi imperii*
Trudy IVEO	–	*Trudy Imperatorskago Vol'nago Ekonomicheskago Obshchestva* (Proceedings of the Imperial Free Economic Society)
VI	–	*Voprosy istorii* (Problems of History, journal)
TS-KhSKGZ	–	*Tekushchaia sel'sko-khoziaistvennaia statistika Kurskago Gubern-skago Zemstva*
VTsSK	–	*Vremennik Tsentral'nago statisticheskago komiteta Ministerstva vnutrennikh del*

Glossary

bol'shak	–	patriarch, head of the extended peasant household (*bol'shukha*).
chernozem	–	literally "black earth": the historically rich and fertile soils of central Russia.
chetvertniki	–	also known as *odnodvortsy*. State peasants whose ancestors formed the corps of minor noble military servitors posted to the frontiers of the Muscovite State in the sixteenth and seventeenth centuries, losing their status after the pacification of the area and creation of a standing army in the Petrine era. They held land in hereditary household tenure by *chet* or *chetvert* (a unit of area). Distinct from "state souls" (*gosudarstvennye dushevye*), composed of descendants of the ordinary soldiery of the frontier era, former ecclesiastical peasants and ex-serfs sequestered by the state (mainly in cases of bankruptcy of their owners). State souls generally held their lands in communal tenure.
darstvenniki	–	former private serfs who, under the Emancipation statutes of 1861, elected to accept "beggar's allotments" (or "quarter allotments") with no redemption payments.
desiatina	–	old Russian measure of land area equal to 2.7 acres.
guberniia	–	province.
khoziain	–	a master, "boss," independent farmer (*khoziaika*).

otkhodniki   –   persons leaving the province in search of earnings (*otkhod:* literally "going away" in reference to migration).

pomeshchik   –   old word for a landowner (*pomest'e:* an estate held in service tenure).

pood   –   Russian measure of weight, equal to 36.07 pounds or 16.4 kilograms.

sloboda   –   settlement, usually larger. The term is also used for an urban suburb.

uyezd   –   administrative subdivision within a province, translated as district. There were 15 districts in Kursk Province (*guberniia*) at the time of the revolution.

ukaz   –   Imperial decree.

versta   –   old Russian measure of distance equal to 3,500 feet.

volost'   –   administrative sub-division within the district, comprising a group of villages, rendered as "canton" or "parish." Their numbers varied over time; in 1905, there were 195 parishes in Kursk Province.

Sources and Literature

Abramov, P. N. "Iz istorii krest'ianskogo dvizheniia 1905–1906 gg. v chernozemnykh guberniiakh" [From the history of the peasant movement of 1905–1906 in the Black Earth provinces]. In *Istoricheskie zapiski* no. 57 (1956): 293–311.

Adamov, V.V., ed. *Voprosy istorii kapitalisticheskoi Rossii. Problema mnogoukladnosti* [Problems of the history of capitalist Russia: the issue of *mnogoukladnost'*]. Sverdlovsk: Ural'skii rabochii, 1972.

Adas, Michael. "'Moral Economy' or 'Contest State?' Elite Demands and the Origins of Peasant Protest in Southeast Asia." *Journal of Social History* 13, no. 4 (Summer, 1980): 521–546.

Afanas'ev, Iurii Nikolaevich, ed. *Sovetskaia istoriografiia* [Soviet Historiography]. Moscow: Rossiiskii gosudarstvennyi gumanitarnyi universitet, 1996.

Agrarnaia dvizhenie v Rossii v 1905–1906 gg. [The agrarian movement in Russia in 1905–1906]. *Trudy Imperatorskago Vol'nago Ekonomicheskago Obshchestva* no. 3 (1908, mai-iiun'), nos. 4–5 (1908, iiul'-oktiabr').

"Agrarnoe dvizhenie v 1905 g. po otchetam Dubasova i Panteleeva" [The peasant movement in 1905 according to the reports of Dubasov and Panteleev]. *Krasnyi arkhiv* 11–12, no. 4–5 (1925): 182–192.

Alavi, Hamza. "Peasants and Revolution." In *The Socialist Register*, 1965, 241–277.

Al'bom portretov chlenov Gosudarstvennoi Dumy [An album of portraits of Members of the State Duma]. Moscow: Vozrozhdenie, 1906.

Aleksandrov, Vadim Aleksandrovich. *Sel'skaia obshchina v Rossii XVII-nachalo XIX v.* [The village commune in Russia from the seventeenth to the beginning of the nineteenth century], Moscow: Nauka, 1976.

———. *Obychnoe pravo krepostnoi derevni Rossii XVIII-nachalo XIX v.* [Customary law in the servile countryside of Russia from the eighteenth to the beginning of the nineteenth century]. Moscow: Nauka, 1984.

Anan'ich, Boris Vasilievich. *Rossiia i mezhdunarodnyi kapital, 1897–1914. Ocherk istorii finansovykh otnoshenii* [Russia and international capital, 1897–1914. An essay in the history of financial relationships]. Leningrad: Nauka, 1970.

———, with Rafael Sholomovich Ganelin, Boris Borisovich Dubentsov, Valentin Semeovich Diakin and S.I. Potolov, *Krizis samoderzhaviia v Rossii, 1894–1917* [Crisis of autocracy in Russia, 1894–1917]. Leningrad: Nauka, 1984.

Anderson, Barbara A. *Internal Migration during Modernization in Late Nineteenth Century Russia*. Princeton: Princeton University Press, 1980.

Anderson, Leslie Elin. *From Quiescence to Rebellion: Peasant Political Activity in Costa Rica and Pre-Revolutionary Nicaragua*. Ann Arbor, Mich.: University of Michigan Press, 1987.

——. "Agrarian Politics and Revolution: Micro and State Perspectives on Structural Determinism." *Journal of Theoretical Politics* 5:4 (1993): 495–522.

——. *The Political Ecology of the Modern Peasant: Calculation and Community*. Baltimore: Johns Hopkins University Press, 1994.

——. "Between Quiescence and Rebellion among the Peasantry: Integrating the Middle Ground." *Journal of Theoretical Politics* 9:4 (October, 1997): 503–532.

Anfimov, Andrei Matveevich. "K voprosu o kharaktere agrarnogo stroia Evropeiskoi Rossii v nachale XX-go veka" [On the question of the character of agrarian relations in European Russia at the beginning of the twentieth century]. *Istoricheskie zapiski* no. 65 (1959): 119–162.

——. "Karlovskoe imenie Meklenburg-Strelitskikh v kontse XIX-nachale XX XX v." [The Karlovsk estate of the Mecklenburg-Strelitskie at the end of the nineteenth and beginning of the twentieth centuries]. In *Materialy po istorii sel'skogo khoziaistva i krest'ianstva SSSR*, sbornik V. Moscow: Izdatel'stvo akademii nauk SSSR, 1962, 348–376.

——. "O melkom tovarnom proizvodstve v sel'skom khoziaistve poreformennoi Rossii" [On small-commodity production in agriculture in post-reform Russia]. *Istoriia SSSR* no.2 (1963, mart-aprel'): 141–159.

——. *Zemel'naia arenda v Rossii v nachale XX-go veka* [Land rent in Russia at the beginning of the twentieth century]. Moscow: Izdatel'stvo akademii nauk SSSR, 1966.

——. *Krupnoe pomeshchich'e khoziaistvo Evropeiskoi Rossii* [Large-scale landowner economy in European Russia], Moscow: Nauka, 1969.

——. *Krest'ianskoe khoziaistvo Evropeiskoi Rossii, 1880–1904* [The peasant economy of European Russia, 1880–1904]. Moscow: Nauka, 1980.

——. *Ekonomicheskoe polozhenie i klassovaia bor'ba krest'ian Evropeiskoi Rossii, 1880–1904* [The economic position and class struggle of the peasants of European Russia, 1880–1904]. Moscow: Nauka, 1984.

——. "O metodike ucheta krest'ianskikh vystuplenii i kolichestva uchastnikov v nikh" [On a method for calculating peasant actions and the number of participants]. In S.L. Tikhvinskii, ed., *Sotsial'no-ekonomicheskoe razvitie Rossii. Sbornik statei k 100-letiiu so dnia rozhdeniia Nikolaia Mikhailovicha Druzhinina*. Moscow: Nauka, 1986, 131–144.

——. "Neokonchennye spory" [Unfinished disputes]. *Voprosy istorii* 1997, no. 5: 49–72; no. 6: 41–84; no. 7: 81–99; no. 9: 82–113.

——, ed. *Krest'ianskoe dvizhenie v Rossii v 1900–1904 gg. Sbornik dokumentov* [The peasant movement in Russia in 1900–1904. Collected documents]. Moscow: Nauka, 1998.

——. *P.A. Stolypin i rossiiskoe krest'ianstvo* [P.A. Stolypin and the Russian peasantry]. Moscow: Institut rossiiskoi istorii RAN, 2002.

Anisimov, V.I. "Svedeniia o nekotorykh sel'skokhoziaistvennykh i remeslennykh shkolakh, nakhodivshikhsia v Kurskoi gubernii" [Information on several agricultural and handicraft schools located in Kursk Province]. In *Tekushchaia sel'skokhoziaistvennaia statistika Kurskago Gubernskago Zemstva. 1903 g.*, I:78–84.

———. "O kustarnoi vystavke, ustraivaemoi gubernskim zemstvom v g. Kurske 10–24 maia 1904 g. i o znachenii eia dlia kustarei Kurskoi gubernii" [On the handicraft exposition held in the City of Kursk on 10–24 May, 1904, and its significance for the artisans of Kursk Province]. In *Tekushchaia sel'skokhoziaistvennaia statistika Kurskago Gubernskago Zemstva. 1903 g.* I:48–49.

Bakhirev, M.V. and M.V. Komarinets. "Obzor deiatel'nosti krest'ianskago banka v Kurskoi gubernii s 1892 po 1901 god" [Review of the activity of the Peasant Bank in Kursk Province from 1892 to 1901]. In *Tekushchaia sel'skokhoziaistvennaia statistika Kurskago Gubernskago Zemstva. 1903 god.* IV:15–36.

Balabanov, Mikhail Solomonovich. *Ocherki po istorii rabochego klassa v Rossii* [Essays on the history of the working class in Russia]. Volume III. Moscow: Ekonomicheskaia zhizn', 1926.

Balzer, Marjorie Mandelstam, ed. *Russian Traditional Culture: Religion, Gender and Customary Law.* Armonk NY: M.E. Sharpe, 1992.

Banfield, Edward C. *The Moral Basis of a Backward Society.* London: Collier-MacMillan, 1958.

Barinova, Ekaterina Petrovna. *Rossiiskoe dvorianstvo v nachale XX veka: sotsio-kul'turnyi portret* [The Russian nobility at the dawn of the twentieth century: a socio-cultural portrait]. Samara: Samarskii universitet, 2006.

Bartlett, Roger, ed. *Land Commune and Peasant Society in Russia. Communal Forms in Imperial and Early Soviet Society.* New York: St. Martin's Press, 1990.

Belokonskii, Ivan Petrovich, ed. *Narodnoe nachal'noe obrazovanie v Kurskoi gubernii* [Popular elementary education in Kursk Province]. Kursk: Tipografiia Kurskago gubernskago zemstvo, 1897.

———, ed. *Obzor sostoianiia narodnago obrazovaniia v Kurskoi gubernii za 5 let* [Review of the state of popular education in Kursk Province over the Past Five Years]. Kursk: Tipografiia Kurskago gubernskago zemstvo, 1902.

———. *Zemskoe dvizhenie* [The zemstvo movement]. Moscow: Zadruga, 1914.

———. *V gody bezpraviia. Dan' vremeni, Ch. II* [In the years of lawlessness. Tribute to time. Part II]. Moscow: Izdatel'stvo Vserossiiskogo obshchestva politkatorzhan i ssylno-poselentsev, 1930.

Bender, I. "Zlatoustovskaia zabastovka" [The Zlatoust' strike]. In Iu. Gessen, ed., *Arkhiv istorii truda v Rossii.* Kniga IV. Petrograd: Izdanie kul'turno-prosvetitel'nogo Otdela Petrogradskogo Gubernskogo Soveta Professional'nykh Soiuzov, 1922, Ch. 2: 50–53.

———. "Iz stachechnogo dvizheniia na Kavkaze v 1903 g." [From the strike movement in the Caucusus in 1903]. In *Arkhiv istorii truda v Rossii*, Kniga V (1922), Ch. 2: 23–27.

———. "K stachechnomu dvizheniiu na Iuge Rossii v 1903 g." In *Arkhiv istorii truda v Rossii*, Kniga VI–VII (1923):183–187.

Bezgin, V.B. "Semeinye razdely v russkoi derevne (konets XIX-nachalo XX vv.)" [Family partitions in the Russian village (end of the nineteenth to the beginning of the twentieth centuries)]. In *Osobennosti Rossiiskogo zemledeliia i problemy rasseleniia: Materialy XXVI sessii simpoziuma po agrarnoi istorii Vostochnoi Evropy.* Tambov: Izdatel'stvo Tambovskogo gosudarstvennogo tekhnicheskogo universiteta, 2000, 241–245.

Blagoveshchenskii, N.A. *Krest'ianskaia gramotnost' i obrazovanie tsentral'nogo raiona Kurskoi gubernii* [Peasant literacy and education in the central region of Kursk Province]. Part I of *Sbornik statisticheskikh svedenii po Kurskoi gubernii. Otdel obshchii. Promysly i gramotnost' krest'ian tsentral'nago raiona Kurskago gubernii.* Kursk: Kurskoe gubernskoe zemstvo, 1885.

Bloch, Marc. *Les Caractères originaux de l'histoire rurale française* [The original characters of French rural history]. Oslo : Institut pour l'Etude comparative des civilizations, 1931.

———. "Mémoire collective, tradition et coutume: á propos d'un livre récent" [Collective memory, tradition and custom: regarding a recent book]. *Revue de Synthèse Historique* XI (XIV), 1925: Nos. 118–120: 73–83.

Bogoslovskii, Mikhail Mikhailovich. "Gosudarstvennye krest'iane pri Nikolaie I" [State peasants during the reign of Nicholas I]. In *Istoriia Rossii v XIX veke*. Tom 1. Saint Petersburg: Granat, 1907, 236–260.

Booth, William James. "A Note on the Idea of the Moral Economy," *American Political Science Review* 87, no. 4 (December, 1993): 949–954.

———. "On the Idea of the Moral Economy." *American Political Science Review* 88, no. 3 (September, 1994): 653–667.

Bortnikov, I. *Iiul'skie dni 1903 na luge Rossii* [The July days of 1903 in South Russia]. Odessa: Oblastnoe izdatel'stvo, 1953.

Boserup, Ester. *The Conditions of Agricultural Growth: The Economics of Agrarian Change under Population Pressure*. Chicago: Aldine Publishing Company, 1965.

Bourdieu, Pierre. *Le sens pratique* [The logic of practice]. Paris: Éditions de minuit, 1980.

Bovykin, V.I. "Dinamika promyshlennogo proizvodstva v Rossii (1896–1910 gg.)" [The dynamic of Russian industrial production [1896–1910]]. *Istoriia SSSR* 1983, no. 3 (mai-iiun'): 20–52.

Brocheux, Pierre. "Moral Economy or Political Economy? The Peasants are Always Rational." *Journal of Asian Studies* XLII, no. 4 (August 1983): 791–803.

Brooks, Jeffrey. *When Russia Learned to Read: Literacy and Popular Literature, 1861–1917*. Evanston, Ill.: Northwestern University Press, 2003.

Bukhovets, O.G. *Sotsial'nye konflikty i krest'ianskaia mental'nost' v Rossiiskoi imperii nachala XX veka: novye materialy, metody, resul'taty* [Social conflict and peasant mentality in the Russian empire at the beginning of the twentieth century: new materials, methods and results]. Moscow: Mosgorarkhiv, 1996.

Buldakov, Vladimir Prokhorovich. *Krasnaia smuta: priroda i posledstviia revoliutsionnogo nasiliia* [Red chaos: the nature and consequences of revolutionary violence]. Moscow: ROSSPEN, 1997.

Burds, Jeffrey. *Peasant Dreams and Market Politics: Labor Migration and the Russian Village, 1861–1905*. Pittsburgh: Pittsburgh University Press, 1998.

Bushnell, John. "Peasant Economy and Peasant Revolution at the Turn of the Century: Neither Immiseration nor Autonomy." *Russian Review* 46, no. 1 (1987): 75–88.

———. "Peasants in Uniform: The Tsarist Army as a Peasant Society." In Ben Eklof and Stephen Frank, eds., *The World of the Russian Peasant: Post-Emancipation Culture and Society*. Boston: Unwin Hyman, 1990, 101–114.

Chaianov, A.V. *Biudzhety krest'ian Starobel'skago uezda. Izdanie Khar'kovskoi Gubernskoi Zemskoi Upravy* [Peasant budgets of Starobe'skii District. A publication of the

Khar'kov Provincial Zemstvo Administration]. Khar'kov: Pechatnia S.P. Iakovleva, 1915.

———. *Organizatsiia krest'ianskogo khoziaistva* [Organization of peasant economy]. Moscow: Tsental'noe tovarishchestvo "Kooperativnoe izdatel'stvo," 1925.

Chelintsev, Aleksandr Nikolaevich. *Opyt izucheniia krest'ianskago sel'skago khoziaistva v tseliakh obosnovaniia obshchestvennoi i kooperativno-agronomicheskoi pomoshchi. Na primere Tambovskoi gubernii* [Results of a study of peasant economy with the aim of organizing public and cooperative-agronomic aid. On the example of Tambov Province]. Khar'kov: Tipografiia "Soiuz," 1919.

Chermenskii, E.D. "I i II Gosudarstvennye Dumy: istoriograficheskii ocherk" [The First and Second State Dumas: An historiographical essay]. In V.P. Naumov, ed., *Aktual'nye problemy sovetskoi istoriografii pervoi russkoi revoliutsii. Sbornik statei.* Moscow: Nauka, 1978, 197–235.

Chernenkov, Nikolai Nikolaevich. *K kharakteristike krest'ianskago khoziaistva* [Toward a characterization of peasant economy]. Vyp. I. Moscow: Tipo-litografiia "Russkago tovarishchestva," 1905.

Chernikov, Sergei Vasil'evich. *Dvorianskie imeniia tsentral'no-chernozemnogo regiona Rossii v pervoi polovine XVIII-go veka* [Gentry estates of the Black Earth region of Russia in the first half of the eighteenth century]. Riazan: P. Tribunskii, 2003.

Chertova, G.I. "Smertnost' naseleniia Rossii v XIX v. po issledovaniiam sovremennikov" [Mortality rates of the population of Russia in the nineteenth century according to the research of contemporaries]. In A.G. Vishnevskii, ed., *Brachnost', rozhdaemost' smertnost' v Rossii i v SSSR.* Moscow: Statistika, 1977, 154–166.

Chugaev, D.A., ed. *Vseobshchaia stachka na Iuge Rossii v 1903 g.* [The general strike in the south of Russia in 1903]. Moscow: Gosudarstvennoe izdatel'stvo politicheskoi literatury, 1938.

Chuikov, N.A. *Kurskaia guberniia v sel'skokhoziaistvennom otnoshenii. Otchet po komandirovke v 1893 g. ot Imperatorskago Moskovskago Obshchestva sel'skago khoziaistva* [Kursk Province in its agricultural aspect. Account of an 1893 inspection of the Moscow Agricultural Society]. Moscow: Skoropechatnia A.A. Levenson, 1894.

Chulos, Chris J. *Converging Worlds: Religion and Community in Peasant Russia, 1861–1917.* DeKalb, Ill.: Northern Illinois University Press, 2003.

Chuprov, Aleksandr Ivanovich and Aleksandr Sergeevich Posnikov, eds. *Vliianie urozhaev i khlebnykh tsen na nekotoryia storony russkago narodnago khoziaistva* [The influence of harvests and grain prices on several aspects of Russia's national economy]. Tom I–II. Saint Petersburg: Tipografiia V.F. Kirshbauma, 1897.

Coale, Ansley J., Barbara A. Anderson and Erna Härm. *Human Fertility in Russia since the Nineteenth Century.* Princeton: Princeton University Press, 1979.

Cole, John Peter, and Frank Clifford German. *A Geography of the USSR.* London: Butterworths, 1961.

Confino, Michael. *Domaines et seigneurs en Russie vers la fin du XVIII-e siècle* [Estates and lords in Russia toward the end of the eighteenth century], Paris: Institut d'Études Slaves de l'Université de Paris, 1963.

———. *Systèmes agraires et progrès agricole: L'Assolement triennal en Russie aux XVIII-e – XIX-e siècles* [Agrarian systems and agricultural progress: the three-field system in Russia during the eighteenth and nineteenth centuries]. Paris: Mouton, 1969.

Cox, Terry. *Peasants, Class and Capitalism: The Rural Research of L.N. Kritsman and His School.* New York: Oxford University Press, 1986.

Czap, Peter, Jr. "Peasant-Class Courts and Peasant Customary Justice in Russia, 1861–1912." *Journal of Social History* 1, no. 2 (Winter, 1967): 149–178.

Danilov, Viktor Petrovich and Teodor Shanin, eds. "Nauchno-issledovatel'nyi proekt 'Krest'ianskaia revoliutsiia v Rossii, 1902–1922 gg.' (Vmesto predisloviia)" [The scholarly research project "Peasant Revolution in Russia, 1902–1922" (in the place of a preface)]. In *Krest'ianskaia revoliutsiia v Rossii, 1902–1922. Dokumenty i issledovaniia. Krest'ianskie vosstaniia v Tambovskoi gubernii v 1919–1921 gg. "Antonovshchina." Dokumenty i materialy.* Tambov: Redaktsionno-izdatel'skii otdel, 1994, 5–6.

———, and Leonid Vasilievich Milov, eds. *Mentalitet i agrarnoe razvitie Rossii (XIX–XX vv.). Materialy mezhdunarodnoi konferentsii. Moskva. 14–15 iiunia 1994 g.* [Mentalité and Russian agrarian development during the 19th and 20th centuries. Materials from the international conference. Moscow, 14–15 June 1994]. Moscow: ROSSPEN, 1996.

Danilova, Liudmila Valerianovna. "Diskussionye problemy teorii dokapitalistichkikh obshchestv" [Discussion questions on the theory of pre-capitalist societies]. In L.V. Danilova, ed., *Problemy istorii dokapitalisticheskikh obshchestv*, Kniga 1. Moscow: Nauka, 1968, 27–66.

Davydov, Mikhail Abramovich. *Ocherki agrarnoi istorii Rossii v kontse XIX—nachale XX vv.* [Outlines of the agrarian history of Russia at the end of the nineteenth and beginning of the twentieth centuries]. Moscow: Izdatel'skii tsentr RGGU, 2003.

Diakin, Valentin Semenovich. "Stolypin i dvorianstvo (proval mestnoi reformy)" [Stolypin and the Gentry (The Failure of local Reform)]. In Nikolai Evgen'evich Nosov, ed., *Problemy krest'ianskogo zemlevladeniia i vnutrennoi politiki Rossii: dooktiabr'skii period. Sbornik statei.* Leningrad: Nauka, 1972, 231–274.

———. *Samoderzhavie, burzhuaziia i dvorianstvo v 1907–1911 gg.* [Autocracy, bourgeoisie and gentry during 1907–1911]. Leningrad: Nauka, 1978.

Dobrotvorskii, Nikolai Aleksandrovich. *Promysly i vnezemledel'cheskie zaniatiia krest'ian tsentral'nago raiona Kurskoi gubernii* [Industries and off-farm occupations of peasants in the central region of Kursk Province]. Part II of: *Sbornik statisticheskikh svedenii po Kurskoi gubernii. Otdel obshchii. Promysly i gramotnost' krest'ian tsentral'nago raiona Kurskago gubernii.* Kursk: Kurskoe gubernskoe zemstvo, 1885.

———. "Saiany." *Vestnik Evropy* 133, no. 5 (1888):179–213.

Dolgorukov, Petr Dmitrievich. "Agrarnaia volna" [The Agrarian Wave]. *Pravo* 1906, no.1 (9 ianvaria), columns 24–36; no.2 (15 ianvaria), columns 90–99.

———. "Agrarnyi vopros s tochki zrenia krupnago zemlevladeniia" [The agrarian question from the point of view of large-scale land ownership], In Petr Dmitrievich Dolgorukov and Ivan Il'ich Petrunkevich, eds., *Agrarnyi vopros: sbornik statei.* Moscow: Tipografiia O.L. Somovoi, 1905, 1–10.

Domar, Evsey, "Were Russian serfs overcharged for their land by the 1861 Emancipation? The history of one historical table." In Evsey Domar, *Capitalism, Socialism and Serfdom.* Essays. Cambridge: Cambridge University Press, 1989, 280–288.

Dorovatorskii, S., and A. Chausnikov, eds. *Ocherki realisticheskago mirovozzreniia. Sbornik statei po filosofii, obshchestvennoi nauki i zhizni* [Essays on a realist world view. A collection of articles on philosophy, social science and life]. Saint Petersburg: Tipografiia Montvida, 1904.

Drozdov, I.G. *Agrarnye volneniia i karatel'nye ekspeditsii v Chernigovskoi gubernii v god*y *pervoi revoliutsii 1905–1906 gg.* [Agrarian unrest and punitive expeditions in Chernigov Province in the years of the first revolution, 1905–1906]. Moscow: Gosudarstvennoe izdatel'stvo, 1925.

Druzhinin, Nikolai Mikhailovich. *Gosudarstvennye krest'iane i reforma P.D. Kiseleva* [State peasants and the reforms of P.D. Kiselev]. Moscow-Leningrad: Izdatel'stvo akademii nauk SSSR, vol, I (1946), vol. II (1958).

———. *Russkaia derevnia na perelome, 1861–1880 gg.* [The Russian village in the time of great change, 1861–1880). Moscow: Nauka, 1978.

Dubrovskii, Sergei Mitrofanovich, *Ocherki russkoi revoliutsii. Vyp. 1. Sel'skoe khoziaistvo* [Outlines of the Russian revolution. First issue: Rural economy]. Moscow: Novaia derevnia, 1922.

———. "Krest'ianskoe dvizhenie nakanune revoliutsii 1905 goda" [The peasant movement on the eve of the 1905 revolution]. *Na agrarnom fronte* no. 10 (1925): 99–112; Nos. 11–12: 107–122.

———. "Krest'ianskoe dvizhenie v gody Stolypinshchina" [The peasant movement during the Stolypin years]. *Na agrarnom fronte* no. 1 (1925): 99–115.

———. "Krest'ianstvo v revoliutsii 1905 g." [The peasantry and the revolution of 1905]. *Istorik-Marksist* No. 1 (1926): 256–279.

———. *Partiia bol'shevikov v rukovodstve krest'ianskim dvizheniem 1905 g. (Tezisy k dokladu)* [The Bol'shevik Party in the leadership of the peasant movement of 1905 (theses for a lecture)]. Moscow: Tipografiia izdatel'stva "Krest'ianskaia gazeta," 1935.

———. *Krest'ianskoe dvizhenie v revoliutsii 1905–1907 gg.* [The peasant movement in the revolution of 1905–1907]. Moscow-Leningrad: Izdatel'stvo akademii nauk SSSR, 1956.

———. *Sel'skoe khoziaistvo i krest'ianstvo v period imperializma* [Rural economy and the peasantry in the period of imperialism]. Moscow: Nauka, 1975.

Edelman, Marc. "Bringing the Moral Economy back into the Study of 21st Century Transnational Peasant Movements." *American Anthropologist* 107, no. 3 (2005): 331–345.

Edelman, Robert. *Proletarian Peasants: the Revolution of 1905 in Russia's Southwest.* Ithaca NY: Cornell University Press, 1987.

Efimenko, Aleksandra, *Issledovaniia narodnoi zhizni. Vypusk pervyi. Obychnoe pravo* [Researches on national life. First issue. Customary law]. Moscow: "Russkaia" tipolitografiia, 1884.

Eklof, Ben, *Russian Peasant Schools: Officialdom, Village Culture and Popular Pedagogy, 1861–1914.* Berkeley-Los Angeles: University of California Press, 1986.

Emel'ianov, N.N. "Pomeshchich'e khoziaistvo kniazei Kurakinikh v Orlovskoi gubernii v 1900–1917 gg." [Estate Economy of the Princes Kurakiny in Orel Province during 1900–1917]. In V.V. Adamov, ed., *Voprosy istorii kapitalisticheskoi Rossii. Problema mnogoukladnosti.* Sverdlovsk: Ural'skii rabochii, 1972, 325–352.

Emets, V.A., and V.V. Shelokhaev. "Tvorcheskii put' K.N. Tarnovskogo" [K.N. Tarnovskii's creative path]. *Istoricheskie zapiski* 118 (1990): 202–231.

Emmons, Terence. *The Russian Landed Nobility and the Peasant Emancipation of 1861.* Cambridge: Cambridge University Press, 1968.

———. *The Formation of Political Parties and the First National Elections in Russia.* Cambridge: Cambridge University Press, 1983.

Evans, Grant. "Sources of Peasant Consciousness in Southeast Asia: A Survey." *Social History* 12, no. 2 (1987): 193–211.

Fafchamps, Marcel. "Networks in Pre-Industrial Societies: Rational Peasants with a Moral Economy." *Economic Development and Social Change* 41, no. 1 (October, 1992): 147–174.

Farnsworth, Beatrice. "The Litigious Daughter-in-Law: Family Relations in Rural Russia in the Second Half of the Nineteenth Century." *Slavic Review* 45, no. 1 (Spring 1986): 49–64.

Fedor, Thomas Stanley. *Patterns of Urban Growth in the Russian Empire during the Nineteenth Century*. Chicago: Department of Geography, University of Chicago, 1975.

Field, Daniel. *The End of Serfdom: Nobility and Bureaucracy, 1855–1861*. Cambridge, Mass.: Harvard University Press, 1976.

——. *Rebels in the Name of the Tsar*. Boston: Houghton-Mifflin, 1978.

George M. Foster Jr. "Interpersonal Relations in Peasant Society." *Human Organization* 19, no. 4 (Winter, 1961): 174–178.

——. "Peasant Society and the Image of Limited Good." *American Anthropology* 67, no. 2 (April, 1965): 293–315.

Frank, Stephen P. "Popular Justice, Community and Culture among the Russian Peasantry, 1870–1900." *Russian Review* 46, no. 3 (July, 1987): 239–265.

——. "'Simple Folk, Savage Customs?' Youth, Sociability and the Dynamics of Culture in Rural Russia, 1856–1914." *Journal of Social History* 25, no. 4 (Summer, 1992): 711–736.

——. "Confronting the Domestic Other: Rural Popular Culture and Its Enemies in Fin-de-Siècle Russia." In Mark D. Steinberg and Stephen P. Frank, eds., *Cultures in Flux: Lower Class Values, Practice and Resistance in Late Imperial* Russia. Princeton: Princeton University Press, 1994, 74–107.

——. *Crime, Cultural Conflict and Justice in Rural Russia, 1856–1914*. Berkeley-Los Angeles: University of California Press, 1999.

Freeze, Gregory L. "The *Soslovie* [Estate] Paradigm and Russian Social History." *American Historical Review* 91 (February 1986): 11–33.

Frierson, Cathy A. "*Razdel*: The Peasant Family Divided." *Russian Review* 46, no. 1 (1987): 35–52.

——. "Peasant Family Divisions and the Commune." In Roger Bartlett, ed., *Land Commune and Peasant Community in Russia*. New York: St. Martin's Press, 1990, 303–320.

——. *Peasant Icons: Representations of Rural People in Late Nineteenth Century Russia*. New York: Oxford University Press, 1993.

——. *All Russia is Burning! A Cultural History of Fire and Arson in Late Imperial Russia*. Seattle: University of Washington Press, 2002.

Gaister, Aron Izraelovich, *Sel'skoe khoziaistvo kapitalisticheskoi Rossii. t. I. Ot reformy 1861 do revoliutsii 1905 g.* [The rural economy of capitalist Russia. Volume I. From the reforms of 1861 to the revolution of 1905]. Moscow-Leningrad: Izdatel'stvo kommunisticheskoi akademii, 1928.

Galai, Shmuel, *The Liberation Movement in Russia, 1900–1905*. Cambridge: Cambridge University Press, 1973).

Ganelin, Rafael Sholomovich. *Rossiiskoe samoderzhevie v 1905 godu: Reformy i revoliutsiia* [The Russian autocracy in 1905: reform and revolution]. Saint Petersburg: Nauka, 1991.

———. "Tvorcheskii put' A. Ia. Avrekha" [The Creative Path of A. Ia. Avrekh]. *Istoriia SSSR* no. 4 (1990): 102–112.

———. *Sovetskie istoriki: o chem oni govorili mezhdu soboi (stranitsi vospominanii o 1940-kh—1970-kh godakh)* [Soviet historians: what they talked about among themselves [pages of recollections from the 1940s to the 1970s]. Saint Petersburg: Nestor-Istoriia, 2004.

Garmiza, V.V. "Rost politicheskii soznaniia russkogo krest'ianstva v period revoliutsii 1905–1907 godov. Vserossiiskii krestíanskii soiuz: Neskol'ko polemicheskikh zametok" [The growth of the political consciousness of the Russian peasantry in the period of the revolution of 1905–1907. The All Russian Peasant Union: Some polemical notes]. *Istoriia SSSR* no. 6 (1986): 135–140.

Gatrell, Peter. *The Tsarist Economy, 1850–1917.* London: B.T. Batsford, 1986.

Gautier, Corinne. *Ruling Peasants: Village and State in Late Imperial Russia.* DeKalb Ill.: Northern Illinois University Press, 2007.

Gefter, Mikhail Iakovlevich, "Iz istorii monopolisticheskogo kapitalizma v Rossii (sakharnyi sindikat)" [From the history of monopoly capitalism in Russia (the sugar syndicate)]. *Istoricheskie zapiski* 38 (1951): 104–153.

———. "Tsarizm i monopolisticheskii kapital v metallurgii luga Rossii do pervoi mirovoi voiny" [Tsarism and Monopoly Capital in the Metallurgy of South Russia up to the First World War]. *Istoricheskie zapiski* 43 (1953): 70–130.

———. "Stranitsa iz istorii marksizma nachala XX veka" [A Page from the History of Marxism at the Beginning of the Twentieth Century]. In M. Ia. Gefter, ed., *Istoricheskaia nauka i nekotorye problemy sovremennosti: stat'i i obsuzhdeniia.* Moscow: Nauka, 1969, 13–44.

———."Mnogoukladnost' – kharakteristike tselogo" [*Mnogoukladnost'* – A characteristic of the whole]. In V.V. Adamov, ed., *Voprosy istorii kapitalisticheskoi Rossii. Problema mnogoukladnosti.* Sverdlovsk: Ural'skii rabochii, 1972, 93–97.

General'nyi shtab. Voenno-topograficheskoe otdelenie. *Spets. karta Evropeiskoi Rossii. Izd. Voenno-topograficheskogo otdela General'nogo Shtaba* [Special Map of European Russia. Published by the Military-Topographical Department of the General Staff]. Saint Petersburg, 1913.

Gerschenkron, Alexander. "Russia: Patterns and Problems of Economic Development, 1861–1958." In *Economic Backwardness in Historical Perspective.* Cambridge, MA: Belknap Press of Harvard University Press, 1962, 119–151.

———. "Agrarian Policies and Industrialization: Russia, 1861–1917." In H.J. Habakkuk and M. Postan, eds., *The Cambridge Economic History of Europe,* v. VI, part II. Cambridge, Cambridge University Press, 1965, 706–800.

Gindin, Iosif Frolovich. *Gosudarstvennyi bank i ekonomicheskaia politika tsarskogo pravitel'stva 1861–1892 gg.* [The State Bank and the economic policy of the tsarist government, 1861–1892]. Moscow: Gosfinizdat, 1960.

———. "Russkaia burzhuaziia v period kapitalizma, ee razvitie i osobennosti" [The Russian bourgeoisie in the capitalist period, its development and peculiarities]. *Istoriia SSSR* no. 2 (1963): 57–80; no 3. (1963): 37–60.

———. "Politika tsarskogo pravitel'stva v otnoshenii promyshlennykh monopolii" [The Tsarist government's policy toward industrial monopolies]. In A.L. Sidorov, ed., *Ob osobennostiakh imperializma v Rossii.* Moscow: Izdatel'stvo akademii nauk SSSR, 1963, 86–123.

——, with L.M. Ivanov, "O neravnomernosti razvitiia Rossiiskogo kapitalizma v nachale XX veka" [On the uneven development of Russian capitalism at the beginning of the twentieth century]. *Voprosy istorii* no. 9 (1965): 125–135.

——."O nekotorykh osobennostiiakh ekonomicheskoi i sotsial'noi struktury rossiiskogo kapitalizma v nachale XX veka" [On several peculiarities of the economic and social structure of Russian capitalism at the dawn of the twentieth century]. *Istoriia SSSR* no. 3 (1966): 48–66.

——. "Sotsial'no-ekonomicheskie itogi razvitiia Rossiiskogo kapitalizma i predposylki revoliutsii v nashei strane" [Socio-economic results of the development of Russian capitalism and the preconditions for revolution in our country]. In I.I. Mints, et al, eds., *Sverzhenie samoderzhaviia: sbornik statei.* Moscow: Nauka, 1970, 39–88

——, with V.V. Timoshenko. "Mnogoukladnost' v sotsial'no-ekonomicheskoi strukture Rossii kontse XIX – nachalo XX veka" [*Mnogoukladnost'* in the socio-economic structure of Russia at the end of the nineteenth and beginning of the twentieth centuries]. *Ekonomicheskie nauki* no. 2 (1982): 61–68.

Glavinskaia, Svetlana Nikolaevna. "Organizatsionno-pravovaia sistema mestnoi politsii v 1907–1917 gg." [The organizational-legal system of local police during 1907–1917]. In G.A. Saltyk, et al, *Politsiia Kurskoi gubernii: istoriia stanovleniia i deiatel'nosti, 1864–1917.* Kursk: Izdatel'stvo Kurskogo gosudarstvennogo universiteta, 2007, 120–237.

Glavnoe Upravlenie Zemleustroistva i Zemledeliia. Otdel Sel'skoi Ekonomii i Sel'sko-khoziaistvennoi Statistiki. *Statisticheskiia svedeniia po zemel'nomu voprosu v Evropeiskoi Rossii* [Statistical Data on the Land Question in European Russia]. Saint Petersburg: Tipografiia V. Kirshbauma, 1906.

Golikov, Andrei Georgevich, and A.P. Korelin, eds. *Rossiia v XIX–XX vekakh. Materialy II nauchnykh chenii pamiati Professora Valeriia Ivanovicha Bovykina* [Russia in the nineteenth and twentieth centuries. Materials of the second scholarly readings in memory of Professor Valeriia Ivanovicha Bovykina]. Moscow: ROSSPEN, 2002.

Gordon, Aleksandr Vladimirovich. "Khoziaistvovanie na zemle – osnova krest'ianskogo mirovospriatiia" [Management on the land: foundation of the peasant world view]. In Viktor Petrovich Danilov and Leonid Vasilievich Milov, eds., *Mentalitet i agrarnoe razvitie Rossii (XIX–XX vv.). Materialy mezhdunarodnoi konferentsii. Moskva. 14–15 iiunia 1994 g.* Moscow: ROSSPEN, 1996, 57–74.

Gorlova, Natal'ia Ivanovna. "Osnovy organizatsii i deiatel'nosti provintsial'noi politsii vo vtoroi polovine XIX veka" [The bases of the organization and operation of the provincial police in the second half of the nineteenth century], in G.A. Saltyk, et al, *Politsiia Kurskoi gubernii: istoriia stanovleniia i deiatel'nosti, 1864–1917.* Kursk: Izdatel'stvo Kurskogo gosudarstvennogo universiteta, 2007, 17–119.

Gorn, V., V. Mech, Chervanin, eds. *Bor'ba obshchestvennykh sil v russkoi revoliutsii. Vyp.III. Krest'ianstvo v revoliutsii* [The struggle of social forces in Russia's revolution. Issue III. The peasant in revolution]. Moscow: Tipo-litografiia "Russkaia," 1907.

Gosudarstvennyi arkhiv Rossiiskoi federatsii. Fond 102 OO. Ministerstva vnutrennikh del. Departament Politsii, Osobyi Otdel. (State Archive of the Russian Federation. Repository 102-OO. Ministry of Internal Affairs. Department of Police. Special Section).

——. Opis' 233 (1-oe otdelenie), 1905 g.

    d. 104, ch. 9: "Sotsialisty-revoliutsionery. Po Kurskoi gubernii" [The socialist-revolutionaries. In Kursk Province]

d. 106, ch. 5: "Svedeniia po guberniiam i oblastiam. Kurskaia guberniia" [Data for the provinces and regions. Kursk Province].

——. Opis' 233 (2-oe otdelenie), 1905 g.

d. 5, ch. 44: "O propaganda sredi naseleniia Imperii. Kurskaia RSDRP" [On propaganda among the populace of the Empire. The Kursk RSDRP]

d. 9, ch. 57: "Svedeniia po guberniiam i oblastiam. Kurskaia guberniia" [Information for the provinces and regions. Kursk Province]

d. 80, ch. 4, pt. 39: "Sotsialisty-revoliutsionery. Kurskaia guberniia" [The socialist-revolutionaries. Kursk Province]

d. 999: "Vserossiskii Krest'ianskii Soiuz" [The All-Russian Peasant Union]

d. 1350, ch. 53: "O bezporiadkakh i demonstratsiiakh. Po Kurskoi gubernii" [On disorders and demonstrations. In Kursk Province]

d. 1800, ch. 13: "O predstavlenii otchetov o sostoianii revoliutsionnago dvizhenii v Imperii. Po Kurskoi gubernii" [On the presentation of reports on the state of the revolutionary movement in the Empire. In Kursk Province]

d. 2500, ch. 44: "O vooruzhennykh napadeniiakh s tsel'iu grabezha i vymogatel'-stva deneg. Po Kurskoi gubernii" [On armed assaults with the aim of theft and extortion of money. In Kursk Province]

d. 2550: "O krest'ianskikh bezporiadkakh (obshchiaia perepiska)" [On peasant disorders (general correspondence)]

d. 2550, ch. 44: "O krest'ianskikh bezporiadkakh. Po Kurskoi gubernii" [On peasant disorders. In Kursk Province].

——. Opis' 234 (1-oe otdelenie), 1906 g.

d. 9, ch. 83: "Po razrabotke sekretnykh svedenii. Po Kurskoi gubernii" [On the processing of secret information. In Kursk Province].

——. Opis' 235 (1-oe otdelenie), 1906 g.

d. 20, ch. 33: "Sotsialisty-revoliutsionery. Kurskaia guberniia" [The socialist-revolutionaries. Kursk Province]

d. 20, ch. 5: "Krest'ianskii Soiuz P. S-R" [The Peasant Union of the Party of SRs]

d. 25, ch. 33: "RSDRP (Kurskii komitet)" [RSDRP. Kursk committee].

——. Opis' 236 (2-oe otdelenie), 1906 g.

d. 9, ch. 83: "Svedeniia po guberniiam i oblastiam. Po Kurskoi gubernii" [Information for the provinces and regions. Kursk Province]

d. 700, ch. 58: "Krest'ianskie bezporiadki. Po Kurskoi gubernii" [On peasant disorders. In Kursk Province].

Gosudarstvennyi arkhiv Rossiiskoi federatsii. Fond 102. Ministerstva vnutrennikh del. Departament Politsii (State Archive of the Russian Federation. Repository 102. Ministry of Internal Affairs. Department of Police).

——. Opis' 99 (4-oe deloproizvodstvo), 1907 g.

d. 34, ch. 1: "Po Kurskoi gubernii. Agrarnoe dvizhenie" [In Kursk Province. The agrarian movement]

d. 108, ch. 21: "O nastroenii Kurskoi gubernii" [On the mood in Kursk Province].

Gosudarstvennaia Duma. *Stenograficheskii otchet. Gosudarstvennaia Duma. Pervyi sozyv* [Stenographic Record. State Duma. First Convocation]. Saint Petersburg, 1906.

Gosudarstvennyi dvorianskii zemel'nyi bank. *Otchet Gosudarstvennago dvorianskago zemel'nago banka za... god.* [Account of the State Bank of the Nobility for the Year ___]. Saint Petersburg: Tipografiia P.P.Soikina, 1889–1908.

Gregory, Paul R. *Russian National Income, 1885–1913*. Cambridge: Cambridge University Press, 1982.

———. *Before Command: An Economic History from Emancipation to the First Five-Year Plan*. Princeton: Princeton University Press, 1994.

———. "Grain Marketings and Peasant Consumption, Russia 1885–1913." *Explorations in Economic History* 17, no. 2 (March 1979): 135–164.

Gromyko Marina Mikhailovna, *Traditsionnye normy povedeniia i formy obshcheniia russkikh krestian XIX veka* [Traditional norms of behavior and forms of social intercourse of Russian peasants during the nineteenth century]. Moscow: Nauka, 1986.

———. "Sem'ia i obshchina v traditsionnoi dukhovnoi kul'ture russkikh krest'ian XVIII–XIX vv.," [Family and Commune in the Traditional Spiritual Culture of Russian Peasants of the Eighteenth and Nineteenth Centuries]. In M.M. Gromyko and T.A. Listova, eds., *Russkie: semeinyi i obshchestvennyi byt*. Moscow: Nauka, 1989, 7–24.

Grosul, Vladislav Iakimovich, ed. *Russkii konservatizm XIX stoletiia: ideologiia i praktika* [Russian conservatism of the nineteenth century: ideology and practice]. Moscow: Progress-Traditsiia, 2000.

Gurko, Vladimir Iosifovich. *Chertyi i siluety proshlogo. Pravitel'stvo i obshchestvennost' v tsarstvovaniie Nikolaia II v izobrazhenii sovremennika*. Moscow, Novoe literaturnoe obozrenie, 2000; first published from the original Russian manuscript as *Features and Figures of the Past. Government and Opinion in the Reign of Nicholas II*. Edited by J. E. Wallace Sterling, Xenia Joukoff Eudin and H. H. Fisher and translated by Laura Matveev. Stanford: Stanford University Press, 1939.

Haimson, Leopold H. "The Problem of Social Identities in Early Twentieth Century Russia." *Slavic Review* 47, no. 1 (Spring 1988): 1–29.

———. "Conclusions: Observations on the Politics of the Russian Countryside, 1905–1914." In *The Politics of Rural Russia, 1905–1914*. Bloomington IN: Indiana University Press, 1979, 261–300.

Halbwachs, Maurice. *Les cadres sociaux de la mémoire* [The social frameworks of memory]. Paris: Librairie Félix Alcan, 1925.

———. *La mémoire collective* [Collective Memory]. Paris : Presses Universitaires, 1950.

Harrison, Mark. "Chayanov and the Economics of the Russian Peasantry." *Journal of Peasant Studies* no. 1 (1974): 389–417.

———. "Resource Allocation and Agrarian Class Formation: The Problem of Social Mobility among Russian Peasant Households, 1880–1930." *Journal of Peasant Studies* no. 1 (1977): 127–161.

———. "The Peasant Mode of Production in the Work of A.V. Chayanov." *Journal of Peasant Studies* no. 4 (1977): 323–336.

Herr, David M. "The Demographic Transition in the Russian Empire and the Soviet Union," *Journal of Social History* 1, no. 3 (Spring, 1968): 193–240.

Hobsbawn, E.J. *Primitive Rebels: Studies in Archaic Forms of Social Movement in the 19th and 20th Centuries*. Manchester: Manchester University Press, 1959.

———, and George Rudé. *Captain Swing*. New York: Pantheon Books, 1968.

Hoch, Stephen L. *Serfdom and Social Control in Russia: Petrovskoe, a Village in Tambov*. Chicago: University of Chicago Press, 1986.

———. "On Good Numbers and Bad: Malthus, Population Trends and Peasant Standard of Living in Late Imperial Russia." *Slavic Review* 53, no.1 (Spring 1994): 41–75.

―――. "Famines, disease and mortality patterns in the parish of Borshevka, Russia, 1830–1912." *Population Studies* 52, no. 3 (November, 1998): 357–368.

―――. "Did Russia's Emancipated Serfs Really Pay Too Much for Too Little Land? Statistical Anomalies and Long Tailed Distributions." *Slavic Review* 63, no. 2 (Summer 2004): 247–274.

Hosking, Geoffrey A. *The Russian Constitutional Experiment: Government and Duma, 1907–1914.* Cambridge: Cambridge University Press, 1973.

―――, and Roberta Thompson Manning. "What Was the United Nobility?" In Leopold H. Haimson, ed., *The Politics of Rural Russia, 1905–1914.* Bloomington IN: Indiana University Press, 1979, 143–183.

Iakovlev, Aleksandr Nikolaevich, ed. *Rossiia v nachale XX-go veka* [Russia at the dawn of the twentieth century]. Moscow: Novyi khronograf, 2002.

Iakushkin, Viacheslav Evgen'evich. *Krest'ianskaia reforma 1861 goda i russkoe obshchestvo* [The peasant reform of 1861 and Russian society]. Moscow: Tipografiia G. Lissnera, 1906.

Ianin, Valentin Lavrent'evich, ed., *Sovetskaia istoriografiia agrarnoi istorii SSSR (do 1917 g.)* [Soviet historiography on the agrarian history of the USSR (to 1917)]. Kishinev: Shtinitsa, 1978.

Isaev, A., "Znachenie semeinykh razdelov krest'ian" [The significance of peasant family partitions]. *Vestnik Evropy* 102, no. IV (1883, iiul'-avgust): 333–349.

Ivanov, Andrei Alekseevich, "Nekotorye itogi Stolypinskoi agrarnoi reformy v derevne chernozemnogo tsentra" [Several results of Stolypin's agrarian reform in the countryside of the Black Earth center], *Vekhi minuvshego: Uchenye zapiski istoricheskogo fakul'teta Lipetskogo gosudarstvennogo pedagogicheskogo universiteta.* Vyp. 1. Lipetsk: LGPU, 1999, 160–172.

Ivanov, Leonid Mikhailovich, ed., *Krest'ianskoe dvizhenie v Rossii v 1861–1869 gg. Sbornik dokumentov* [The peasant movement in Russia in 1861–1869. Collected documents]. Moscow: Mysl', 1964.

―――, ed. *Rabochee dvizhenie v Rossii v 1901–1904 gg. Sbornik dokumentov* [The Workers' Movement in Russia during 1901–1904. A Collection of Documents]. Leningrad: Nauka, 1975.

―――, and Konstantin Nikolaevich Tarnovskii, eds. *Obshchestvenno-ekonomicheskaia struktura Rossii: Problemy mnogoukladnosti* [Russia's socio-economic structure: the problem of *mnogoukladnost'*]. Moscow: Nauka, 1970.

―――. *Problemy sotsial'no-ekonomicheskoi istorii Rossii. Sbornik statei k 85-letiiu so dnia rozhdeniia akademika N.M. Druzhinina* [Problems in the socio-economic history of Russia. Collected essays in honor of the 85th birthday of N.M. Druzhinin]. Moscow: Nauka, 1971.

Ivantsov, D.N., *K kritike russkoi urozhainoi statistiki i opyt analiza nekotorykh offitsial'-nykh i zemskikh tekushchikh dannykh* [Toward a critique of Russian harvest statistics and results of an analysis of several official and zemstvo current data]. Petrograd: Tipografiia V.F. Kirshbauma, 1915.

Izmest'eva, Tamara Fedorovna. *Rossiia v sisteme Evropeiskogo rynka (konets XIX-nachalo XX v.)* [Russia in the European market system (end of the nineteenth – beginning of the twentieth centuries)]. Moscow: Izdatel'stvo Moskovskogo universiteta, 1991.

"Iz istorii bor'by samoderzhavii s agrarnym dvizheniem v 1905–1907 gg.," [From the history of the struggle of the autocracy with the peasant movement during 1905–1907]. *Krasnyi arkhiv* no. 70: 128–160.

Iz istorii Kurskogo kraia. Sbornik dokumentov i materialov. Voronezh: Tsentral'no-chernozemnoe knizhnoe izdatel'stvo, 1965.

Kablukov, N.A., *Ob usloviiakh razvitiia krest'ianskago khoziaistva v Rossii. Ocherki po ekonomii, zemlevladeniia i zemlepol'zovaniia* [On the conditions of development of peasant economy in Russia. Essays on economy, land tenure and land use]. Moscow: I.D. Sytin, 1908.

Kachorovskii, Karl Romanovich. *Russkaia obshchina: vozmozhno li, zhelatel'no li eia sokhranenie i razvitie?* [Is the conservation and development of the Russian commune possible? Or desirable?]. Moscow: Tipografiia "Russkago Tovarishchestvo," 1906.

Kahan, Arcadius. "Government Policies and the Industrialization of Russia," *Journal of Economic History* 27, no. 4 (December, 1967): 460–477.

Karavaev, V.F. "Bibliograficheskii obzor zemskoi statisticheskoi literatury so vremeni uchrezhdenii zemstvo, 1864–1901 gg." [Bibliographical review of zemstvo statistical literature from the time of the institution of the Zemstvo, 1864–1901]. In *Trudy Imperatorskago vol'nago ekonomicheskago obshchestva. 1904.* Tom vtoroi, Kniga 4–6, 238–257.

Karnaukhova, Evfaziia Stepanovna, *Razmeshchenie sel'skogo khoziaistva Rossii v period kapitalizma 1860–1914 gg.* [Territorial distribution of Russian agriculture in the capitalist period, 1860–1914]. Moscow–Leningrad: Izdatel'stvo akademii nauk SSSR, 1951.

Karpov, N., ed. *Krest'ianskskoe dvizhenie v revoliutsii 1905 goda v dokumentakh* [The peasant movement in the 1905 revolution in documents]. Leningrad: Gosudarstvennoe izdatel'stvo, 1926.

Karpov, Sergei Pavlovich, ed. *Problemy istochnikovedeniia i istoriografii: materialy II nauchnykh chtenii pamiati akademika I.D. Koval'chenko* [Problems of source development and historiography. Materials of the second scholarly readings in memory of Academic I.D. Koval'chenko]. Moscow: ROSSPEN, 2000.

Kazarin, A., "Bor'ba za zemliu v Kurskoi gubernii v 1905 godu" [The struggle for the land in Kursk Province in 1905]. In L. Matusevich and A. Kazarin, *1905 god v Kurskoi gubernii.* Kursk: Kurskoe oblastnoe izdatel'stvo, 1941, 55–91.

Kerans, David, *Mind and Labor on the Farm in Black Earth Russia, 1861–1914.* New York–Budapest, Central European University Press, 2001.

Kerblay, Basile, "L'évolution de l'alimentation rurale en Russie (1896–1960)" [The evolution of rural nutrition in Russia (1896–1960)]. *Annales, Economies, Sociétés, Civilisations* 17, no. 5 (1962): 885–913.

Khauke, O.A., *Krest'ianskoe zemel'noe pravo* [Peasant Land Tenure]. Moscow: Tipo-litografiia B. Rikhtera, 1914.

Khriashcheva, Anna Ivanovna, ed. *Materialy dlia otsenki zemel' Tul'skoi gubernii. Opyt vsaimo-otnoshenii elementov krest'ianskogo khoziaistva. Kombinatsionnye tablitsy. Tom I, Vyp. II. Novosil'skii uezd. Podvornaia perepis' 1910 g.* [Materials for a valuation of lands of Tula Province. A test of the interrelationship of the elements of peasant economy. Combination tables. Volume I, Issue II. Novosil'skii District. The household census of 1910]. Tula: Tul'skoe gubernskoe zemstvo. Otsenochnyi otdel, 1915.

———. *Materialy dlia otsenki zemel' Tul'skoi gubernii. Krest'ianskoe khoziaistvo po perepisiam 1899 i 1911 gg: Epifanskii uezd.* Ch. I–II [Materials for a valuation of lands of Tula Province. Peasant economy by the censuses of 1899 and 1911. Epifanskii District, Parts I and II]. Tula: Tul'skoe gubernskoe zemstvo. Otsenochnyi otdel, 1916.

Khromov, Pavel Alekseevich. *Ekonomicheskoe razvitie Rossii v XIX–XX vekakh* [The economic development of Russia in the nineteenth and twentieth centuries]. Moscow: Gosudarstvennoe izdatel'stvo politicheskoi literatury, 1950.

Kir'ianov, Iurii Il'ich. *Perekhod k massovoi politicheskoi bor'be: Rabochii klass nakanune pervoi Rossiiskoi revoliutsii* [Transition toward the mass political struggle: the working class on the eve of the first Russian revolution]. Moscow: Nauka, 1987.

Kiriukhina, E.I., "Vserossiiskii Krest'ianskii soiuz v 1905 g." [The All-Russian Peasant Union in 1905]. *Istoricheskie zapiski* 50 (1955): 95–141.

———. "Mestnye organizatsii Vserossiiskogo Krest'ianskogo soiuza v 1905 godu" [Local organizations of the All-Russian Peasant Union in 1905]. In *Uchenye zapiski. Kirovskii pedagogicheskii institute im. V.I. Lenina. Kafedra Marksizma-Leninizma/Kafedra istorii SSSR*, Vyp. 10, 1956, 83–157.

Kitanina, Taisia Mikhailovna. *Khlebnaia torgovlia Rossii v 1875–1914 gg.* [The Russian grain trade, 1875–1914]. Leningrad: Nauka, 1978.

Klepikov, S.A., *Pitanie russkogo krest'ianstva (Materialy po izucheniiu massovogo potrebleniia, vyp. 2)* [Russian peasant diet (Materials for the Study of Mass Consumption, Issue 2)]. Moscow: Tipografiia "III Internatsionala," 1920.

Kolesnichenko, Diana Alekseevna. *Trudoviki v period pervoi Rossiiskoi revoliutsii.* Moscow: Nauka, 1985.

Komarinets M.V., "Vyvoz khlebov iz Kurskoi gubernii" [Grain export from Kursk Province], *Tekushchaia sel'sko-khoziaistvennaia statistika Kurskago Gubernskago Zemstva. 1903 g.*, I:34–49, II:15–24.

———. "Otkhozhie promysly v Kurskoi gubernii, ikh razmera i znachenie" [Migrant industries in Kursk Province, their scale and significance]. *Tekushchaia sel'skokhoziaistvennaia statistika Kurskago Gubernskago Zemstva. 1903 g.* II: 42–57.

———. "Obzor deiatel'nost' krest'ianskago banka v Kurskoi gubernii v period s 1898 po 1903 god" [Review of the activity of the Peasant Bank in Kursk Province in the period 1898–1903]. In *Tekushchaia sel'skokhoziaistvennaia statistika Kurskago Gubernskago Zemstva. 1903 g.* IV:15–36.

———. "Okladnye sbory s krest'ianskago naseleniia Kurskoi gubernii v period s 1898 po 1903 god" [Tax collections from the peasant population of Kursk Province in the period 1898–1903]. In *Tekushchaia sel'skokhoziaistvennaia statistika Kurskago Gubernskago Zemstva. 1904 god.* III:34–41.

Komissiia pri Kurskom gubispolkome po organizatsii prazdnovaniia 20-letiia revoliutsii 1905 goda. *1905 god v Kurskoi gubernii. Sbornik statei* [The year 1905 in Kursk Province. Collected essays]. Kursk: Ispartotdel Kurskogo gubkoma RKP(b), 1925.

Kondrashin, V.V. "Golod v krest'ianskom mentalitete" [Hunger in peasant mentality]. In *Mentalitet i agrarnoe razvitie Rossii (XIX–XX vv). Materialy mezhdunarodnoi konferentsii, Moskva 14–15 iiunia 1994 g.* Moscow: ROSSPEN, 1996, 115–123.

———, "Krest'ianskaia revoliutsiia na Povol'zhe" [Peasant revolution in the Volga Region]. *Istoricheskie zapiski* 4 (2000): 179–186.

Korelin, Avenir Pavlovich. "Rossiiskoe dvorianstvo i ego soslovnaia organizatsiia, 1861–1904 gg." [The Russian nobility and its social organization, 1861–1904]. *Istoriia SSSR* 5 (1971, sentiabr'-oktiabr'): 56–81.

———. "Rossiia sel'skaia na rubezhe XIX–XX vv." [Village Russia at the turn of the nineteenth to the twentieth centuries]. In A.N. Iakovlev, ed., *Rossiia v nachale XX veka*. Moscow: Novyi khronograf, 2002, 224–233.

———, ed. *Rossiia sel'skaia XIX-nachalo XX veka (Pamiati Andreia Matveevicha Anfimova)* [Village Russia at the end of the nineteenth and beginning of the twentieth centuries (In memory of Andrei Matveevich Anfimov)]. Moscow: ROSSPEN, 2004.

———, and S.V. Tiutiukin, eds., *Pervaia revoliutsiia v Rossii: Vzgliad cherez stoletiia* [The First Russian Revolution: A view across a century]. Moscow: Pamiatniki istoricheskoi mysli, 2005.

———. "Istoki Rossiiskoi revoliutsionnoi dramy" [Sources of the Russian revolutionary drama]. In A.P. Korelin and S.V. Tiutiukin, eds., *Pervaia revoliutsiia v Rossii: Vzgliad cherez stoletiia*. Moscow: Pamiatniki istoricheskoi mysli, 2005, 21–76.

Korf, P.L. "Poezdka v neurozhainyia mestnosti Kurskoi gubernii. Doklad prezidenta Obshchestva Barona P.L. Korf obshchemu sobraniiu 29-go aprelia 1892 g." [Tour of the famine localities of Kursk Province. Report of the President of the Society Baron P.L. Korf at the General Assembly of 29 April 1892]. In *Trudy Imperatorskago vol'nago ekonomicheskago obshchestva*, 1892, tom vtoroi, razdel 1, 109–120.

Kornilov, A.A., A.S. Lappo-Danilevskii, V.I. Semevskii and I.M. Strakhovskii, eds. *Krest'ianskii stroi. Sbornik statei.* [The peasant order. Collected essays] Tom 1. Saint Petersburg: Beseda, 1905.

Koroleva, Nadezhda Georg'evna. *Zemstvo na perelome, 1905–1907 gg.* [The zemstvo at the crossroads, 1905–1907]. Moscow: Institut rossiiskoi istorii RAN, 1995.

Kosinskii, Vladimir Andreevich. *K agrarnomu voprosu. Vyp. I. Krest'ianskoe i pomeshchich'e khoziaistvo* [On the agrarian question. Issue I. Peasant and landowner economy]. Odessa: Tipografiia "Ekonomicheskaia," 1906.

Kots, E. *Krest'ianskie dvizheniia v Rossii: Ot Pugachevshchiny do revoliutsii 1905 g.* [The peasant movement in Russia. From the Pugachev revolts to the revolution of 1905]. Petrograd: Seiatel', 1924.

Koval'chenko, Ivan Dmitrievich. "Ob izuchenii melkotovarnogo uklada v Rossii XIX veka" [On the study of the small-commodity order in Russia of the nineteenth century]. *Istoriia SSSR* no.1 (1962, ianvar'-fevral'): 74–93.

———. *Russkoe krepostnoe krest'ianstvo v pervoi polovine XIX veka* [Russian serfs in the first half of the nineteenth century]. Moscow: Izdatel'stvo Moskovskogo gosudarstvennogo universiteta, 1967.

———. "V.I. Lenin o kharaktere agrarnogo stroia kapitalisticheskoi Rossii" [V.I. Lenin on the character of the agrarian order of capitalist Russia]. *Voprosy istorii* no. 3 (1970): 30–51.

———. "Sootnoshenie krest'ianskogo i pomeshchich'ego khoziaistv v zemledel'cheskom proizvodstve kapitalisticheskoi Rossii" [Correlation of peasant and landowner economies in the agricultural production of capitalist Russia]. In *Problemy sotsial'no-ekonomicheskoi istorii Rossii: Sbornik statei.* Moscow: Nauka, 1971, 171–194.

———, with Leonid Vasil'evich Milov, *Vserossiiskii agrarnyi rynok XVIII—nachalo XX veka: opyt kolichestvennogo analiza* [The All-Russian agrarian market of the eight-

eenth to the beginning of the twentieth centuries. Results of a quantitative analysis].
Moscow: Izdatel'stvo Moskovskogo gosudarstvennogo universiteta, 1974.

——, ed., *Massovye istochniki po sotsial'no-ekonomicheskoi istorii Rossii perioda kapi-talizma* [Mass sources for the socio-economic history of Russia in the capitalist era].
Moscow: Izdatel'stvo Moskovskogo gosudarstvennogo universiteta, 1979.

——, with Natalia Borisovna Selunskaia, Boris Moiseevich Litvakov, *Sotsial'no-ekonomicheskii stroi pomeshchichego khoziaistva Evropeiskoi Rossii v epokhu kapital-izma: istochniki i metody izucheniia* [The socio-economic structure of landowner economy of European Russia in the capitalist epoch: sources and methods of study].
Moscow: Nauka, 1982.

——. "O burzhuaznom kharaktere krest'ianskogo khoziaistva Evropeiskoi Rossii v kontse XIX—nachale XX veka (Po budzhetnym dannym srednochernozemnykh gu-bernii)" [On the bourgeois character of peasant economy in European Russia at the end of the nineteenth and beginning of the twentieth century (based on budget data from the middle Black Earth provinces)]. *Istoriia SSSR* no. 5 (1983): 50–81.

——, with Tatiana Leonidovna Moiseenko, N.B. Selunskaia, *Sotsial'no-ekonomicheskii stroi krest'ianskogo khoziaistva v Evropeiskoi Rossii v epokhu kapitalizma: istochniki i metody izucheniia* [The socio-economic structure of peasant economy of European Russia in the capitalist epoch: sources and methods of study]. Moscow: Izdatel'stvo Moskovskogo gosudarstvennogo universiteta, 1988.

Kovan'ko, Petr. *Reforma 19 fevralia 1861 goda i eia posledstviia s finansovoi tochki zrenia. Vykupnaia operatsiia: 1861 g. – 1907 g.* [The Reform of 19 February 1861 and its consequences from the financial point of view. The redemption operation, 1861–1907]. Kiev: Tipografiia universiteta Sv. Vladimira, 1914.

Krasin, Iurii Andreevich. *Lenin, revoliutsiia, sovremennost': Problemy leninskoi kon-septsii sotsialisticheskoi revoliutsii* [Lenin, revolution and the modern era: issues of the Leninist conception of socialist revolution]. Moscow: Nauka, 1967.

"Krest'ianskoe dvizhenie v tsentral'noi polose v 1905 g." [The peasant movement in the central region in 1905]. *Krasnyi arkhiv* 73, no. 6 (1935): 127–169.

Kritsman, L.N. "K voprosu o klassovom rassloenii sovremennoi derevni" [On class differ-entiation in the contemporary village]. *Na agrarnom fronte* no. 2 (1925, fevral'): 47–55; no. 7–8 (1925, iiul'-avgust): 3–37; no. 9 (1925, sentiabr'): 23–32; no. 10 (1925, oktiabr'): 17–46.

Kriukova, S.S., *Russkaia krest'ianskaia sem'ia vo vtoroi polovine XIX veka* [The Russian peasant family in the second half of the nineteenth century]. Moscow: Institut etnologii i antrpologii im. Miklukho-Maklaia RAN, 1994.

Kropotkin, G.M., "Praviashchaia biurokratiia i 'novyi stroi' rossiiskoi gosudarstvennosti posle Manifesta 17 oktiabria 1905 goda" [The ruling bureaucracy and the "new struc-ture"of the Russian state order after the Manifesto of 17 October 1905]. *Otechestven-naia istoriia* no. 1 (2006, ianvaria): 24–42.

Kurenyshev, Andrei Aleksandrovich, *Vserossiiskii Krest'ianskii soiuz, 1905–1930 gg.: Mify i real'nost'* [The All-Russian Peasant Union, 1905–1930. Myths and reality].
Moscow: AIRO-XX; Saint Petersburg: Dmitrii Bulanin, 2004.

Kurlov, Pavel Grigor'evich. *Konets russkogo tsarizma. Vospominaniia byvshego Ko-mandira Korpusa Zhandarmov* [The end of Russian tsarism. Recollections of a former Commander of the corps of gendarmes]. Moscow–Petrograd: Gosizdat, 1923.

Kurskaia kazennaia palata. *Materialy po krest'ianskomu i chastnomu zemlevladeniiu Kurskoi gubernii. Izdanie Kurskoi kazennoi palaty* [Materials on peasant and private landholding in Kursk Province. A publication of the Kursk Treasury Office]. Kursk: 1908–1909.

Kurskaia gubernskaia zemskaia uprava. *Otchet Kurskoi gubernskoi zemskoi upravy po vzaimnomu strakhovaniiu ot ognia za (1893–1913) god* [Account of the Kursk provincial zemstvo administration on mutual fire insurance for the year (1893–1913)]. Kursk, 1894–1914.

Kurskii gubernskii statisticheskii komitet. *Pamiatnaia kniga Kurskoi gubernii za 1894 god* [Notebook for Kursk Province, 1894]. Kursk, 1894.

Kurskii kalendar'. Spravochnaia i adresnaia kniga za 1912 g. [Kursk calendar. Reference and address book for 1912]. Kursk, 1912.

Kurskoe gubernskoe upravlenie. *Obzor Kurskoi gubernii za... god. Prilozhenie k vsepoddaneishemu otchetu* [Review of Kursk Province for the year ____. Annex to the most humble account (to the monarch)]. Kursk: 1882–1916.

Kurskoe gubernskoe zemstvo. *Materialy po issledovaniiu kustarnoi promyshlennosti v Kurskoi gubernii. Vypusk I. Opisanie kustarnykh promyslov po otdel'nym uezdam.* [Materials for the study of artisanal industry in Kursk Province. Issue I. Description of artisanal industries in the individual Districts]. Kursk: Kurskoe gubernskoe zemstvo, 1904.

Kurskoe gubernskoe zemstvo. Statisticheskoe biuro (Ippolit Antonovich Verner, ed.). *Sbornik statisticheskikh svedenii po Kurskoi gubernii* [Collected statistical materials for Kursk Province]. Vyp. I–XIV. Kursk: Tipografiia Kurskago gubernskago zemstva, 1883–1886. Subtitled:

Vyp. I (Kurskii uezd). Kursk, 1883.

Vyp. II. Statisticheskie svedeniia po L'govskomu uezdu [Issue II. Statistical data for L'gov District]. Kursk, 1884.

Vyp. III. Statisticheskie svedeniia po Dmitrievskomu uezdu [Issue III. Statistical data for Dmitriev District]. Kursk, 1884.

Vyp. IV. Statisticheskie svedeniia po Sudzhanskomu uezdu [Issue IV. Statistical data for L'gov District]. Kursk, 1884.

Vyp. V. Statisticheskie svedeniia po Fatezhskomu uezdu [Issue V. Statistical data for Fatezh District]. Kursk 1884.

Vyp. VI. Statisticheskiia svedeniia po Ryl'skomu uezdu [Issue VI. Statistical data for Ryl'sk District]. Kursk, 1884.

Vyp. VII. Statisticheskiia svedeniia po Putivl'skomu uezdu [Issue VII. Statistical data for Putivl' District]. Kursk, 1884.

Otdel obshchii. Promysly i gramotnost' krest'ian tsentral'nago raiona Kurskago gubernii [General section. Peasant industries and literacy in the central region of Kursk Province]. Ch. I: Blagoveshchenskii, N.A. *Krest'ianskaia gramotnost' i obrazovanie tsentral'nogo raiona Kurskoi guberniia* [Peasant literacy and education in the central region of Kursk Province]; Ch. II: Dobrotvorskii, N.A. *Promysly i vnezemledel'cheskie zaniatiia krest'ian tsentral'nago raiona Kurskoi guberniia* [Industries and off-farm occupations of peasants in the central region of Kursk Province]. Kursk, 1885.

Vyp. VIII. Statisticheskie svedeniia po Shchigrovskomu uezdu [Issue VIII. Statistical data for Shchigrov District]. Kursk, 1885.

Vyp. IX. Statisticheskiia svedeniia po Graivoronskomu uezdu [Issue IX. Statistical data for Graivoron District]. Kursk, 1885.

Vyp. X. Statisticheskie svedeniia po Belgorodskomu uezdu [Issue X. Statistical data for Belgorod District]. Kursk, 1885.

Vyp. XI. Statisticheskiia svedeniia po Novooskol'skomu uezdu [Issue XI. Statistical data for Novyi Oskol' District]. Kursk, 1885.

Vyp. XII. Statisticheskie svedeniia po Timskomu uezdu [Issue XII. Statistical data for Tim District]. Kursk, 1886.

Vyp. *XIII. Statisticheskiia svedeniia po Korochanskomu uezdu* [Issue XIII. Statistical data for Tim District]. Kursk, 1886.

Vyp. XIV. Statisticheskie svedeniia po Starooskol'skomu uezdu [Issue XIV. Statistical data for Staryi Oskol' District]. Kursk, 1886.

———. *Kurskaia guberniia. Statisticheskii obzor. 1896 g. Izdanie Kurskago Gubernskago Zemstva* [Kursk Province. A statistical review. 1896. A publication of the Kursk Provincial Zemstvo]. I.P. Belokonskii, ed. Kursk: Tipografiia Kurskago gubernskago zemstvo, 1897.

———. *Narodnoe nachal'noe obrazovanie v Kurskoi gubernii* [Popular elementary education in Kursk Province]. I.P. Belokonskii, ed. Kursk: Tipografiia Kurskago gubernskago zemstvo, 1897.

———. *Tekushchaia sel'skokhoziaistvennaia statistika Kurskago Gubernskago Zemstva za* (1897–1907) *god* [Current agricultural statistics of the Kursk Provincial Zemstvo for the year ____]. Quarterly. Kursk, Tipografiia Kurskago gubernskago zemstvo, 1898–1907.

Kurskie Gubernskie Vedomosti.

Kushchenko, Georgii Aleksandrovich. *Krest'ianskoe khoziaistvo v Surazhskom uezde, Chernigovskoi gubernii, po dvum perepisiam 1882 i 1911 gg.* [Peasant economy in Surazhskii District, Chernigov Province, according to two censuses of 1882 and 1911]. Chernigov: Chernigovskoe gubernskoe zemstvo, 1916.

Kuznetsov, I.V. "Ob ukladakh i mnogoukladnosti v Rossii" [Of social contexts and multi contextuality in Russia]. *Voprosy istorii* no. 7 (1974, iiul'): 20–32.

Landsberger, Henry A., ed. *Latin American Peasant Movements*. Ithaca NY: Cornell University Press, 1970).

———, ed. *Rural Protest: Peasant Movements and Change*. London–New York: MacMillan, 1974.

Lappo-Danilevskii, A. "Ocherk istorii obrazovaniia glavneishikh razriadov krest'ianskogo naseleniia v Rossii" [Essay on the history of the formation of the principal categories of the peasant population of Russia]. In *Krest'ianskii stroi. Sbornik statei*. Saint Petersburg: Beseda, 1905, 1–156.

Lenin, Vladimir Il'ich. *Polnoe sobranie sochinenii* [Complete Collected Works], 5th edition, 55 volumes. Moscow: Gosudarstvennoe izdatel'stvo politicheskoi literatury, 1958–1965.

Leonard, Carol S. *Agrarian Reform in Russia: The Road from Serfdom*. New York, Cambridge University Press, 2011.

Leont'ev, A. *Volostnoi sud i iuridicheskie obychai krest'ian* [The volost' court and peasant juridical customs]. Saint Petersburg: Tipografiia M. Merkusheva, 1895.

Leshchenko, N.N. "Itogi statisticheskogo izucheniia krest'ianskogo dvizheniia na Ukraine v period revoliutsii 1905–1907 gg." [Results of a statistical analysis of the peasant movement in the Ukraine in the period of the revolution of 1905–1907]. In V.L. Ianin, ed., *Sovetskaia istoriografiia agrarnoi istorii SSSR (do 1917 g.)*. Kishinev: Izdatel'stvo "Shtinitsa," 1978, 47–59.

Lewin, Moshe. "Customary Law and Russian Rural Society in the Post-Reform Era." *Russian Review* 44, no. 2 (January, 1985): 1–19 (and following).

Lewis, Oscar M. *Life in a Mexican Village: Tepoztlán Re-Studied*. Urbana IL: University of Illinois Press, 1951.

Liashchenko, Petr Ivanovich. *Istoriia narodnogo khoziaistvo SSSR*, vol. II [History of the national economy of the USSR]. Moscow: Gosudarstvennoe izdatel'stvo politicheskoi literatury, 1948.

Littlejohn, Gary. "The Peasantry and the Russian Revolution." *Economy and Society* 2, no. 1 (February 1973): 112–125.

Litvak, Boris Grigor'evich. *Russkaia derevnia v reforme 1861 goda: Chernozemnyi tsentr, 1861–1895 gg.* [The Russian countryside in the reform of 1861: the black earth center]. Moscow: Nauka, 1972.

———. *Opyt izuchenie krest'ianskogo dvizheniia v Rossii v XIX veke* [Method for the study of the peasant movement in Russia in the nineteenth century]. Moscow: Nauka, 1967.

Liuboshits, L.I. *Voprosy marksistsko-leninskoi teorii agrarnykh krizisov* [Problems of Marxist-Leninist theory on agrarian crises]. Moscow: Gosudarstvennoe izdatel'stvo politicheskoi literatury, 1949.

Lositskii, Aleksei Emel'ianovich. "Proizvodstvo khlebov i ego otnoshenii k potrebleniiu i sbytu: torgovlia polevymi proizvedeniiami i tseny na nikh" [Production of grain and its relation to consumption and marketing: the commerce in field products and their prices]. In *Kurskaia guberniia. Statisticheskii obzor, 1896 g.* (Kursk: Kurskoe gubernskoe zemstvo, 1896), 300–367

———. *Vykupnaia operatsiia* [The Redemption Operation]. Saint Petersburg: Tipografiia aktsionernago obshchestva "Slovo,"1906.

Löwe, Heinz-Dietrich. "Differentiation in Russian Peasant Society: Causes and Trends, 1880–1905." In Roger Bartlett, ed., *Land Commune and Peasant Society in Russia. Communal Forms in Imperial and Early Soviet Society*. New York: St. Martin's Press, 1990, 165–195.

Macey, David A.J. "The Peasantry, the Agrarian Problem and the evolution of 1905–1907." *Columbia Essays in International Affairs* VII (1971): 1–35.

———. *Government and Peasant in Russia, 1861–1906: The Prehistory of the Stolypin Reforms*. DeKalb, IL: Northern Illinois University Press, 1987.

Magagna, Victor V. *Communities of Grain: Rural Rebellion in Comparative Perspective*. Ithaca, NY: Cornell University Press, 1991.

Makarov, Nikolai Pavlovich. *Krest'ianskoe khoziaistvo i ego evoliutsiia* [Peasant economy and its evolution]. Moscow: Tipografiia N. Zheludkovoi, 1920.

Maklakov, Vasilii Alekseevich. *Pervaia gosudarstvennaia duma: vospominaniia sovremennika* [The First State Duma: recollections of a contemporary]. Paris, n.p., 1939.

Maliavskii A. D. "Krest'ianskoe dvizhenie v Kurskoi gubernii v revoliutsii 1905–1907 gg." [The peasant movement in Kursk Province in the revolution of 1905–1907]. In *Kraevedcheskie zapiski*, vyp. I (Kursk, Kurskoe knizhnoe izdatel'stvo, 1959), 3–69 (and annex).

Malysheva, Ol'ga Geral'dovna. *Dumskaia monarkhiia: rozhdenie, stanovlenie, krakh. Chast' 1: Vlast' i zarozhdenie Gosudarstvennoi dumy* [The Duma monarchy: birth, formation, collapse. Part 1: the state and the emergence of the State Duma]. Moscow: Izdatel'stvo RAGS, 2004.

Mandel, James I. "Paternalistic Authority in the Russian Countryside, 1856–1906." Ph.D. dissertation, Columbia University, 1978.

Mannheim, Karl. "The Problem of Generations," in Paul Kecskemeti, ed., *Essays on the Sociology of Knowledge.* New York: Oxford University Press, 1952, 276–320.

Manning, Roberta Thompson. *The Crisis of the Old Order in Russia: Gentry and Government.* Princeton: Princeton University Press, 1982.

Maress, Lev Nikolaevich. "Pishcha narodnykh mass v Rossii" [Nutrition of the popular masses in Russia]. *Russkaia mysl'* X (1893): 45–67 and XI (1893): 60–75.

———. "Proizvodstvo i potreblenie khleba v krest'ianskom khoziaistve" [Production and consumption of grain in the peasant economy] in Aleksandr Ivanovich Chuprov and Aleksandr Sergeevich Posnikov, eds., *Vliianie urozhaev i khlebnykh tsen na nekotoryia storony russkago narodnago* khoziaistva. Saint Petersburg: Tipografiia V.F. Kirshbauma, 1897, Tom I, 1–96.

Markwick, Roger D. "Catalyst of historiography, Marxism and dissidence: the Sector of Methodology of the Institute of History, Soviet Academy of Sciences, 1964–68." *Europe–Asia Studies* 46, no. 4 (July 1994): 579–596.

———. *Rewriting History in Soviet Russia: The Politics of Revisionist Historiography, 1956–1974.* New York: Palgrave, 2001.

Martov, L., P. Maslov and A. Potresov, eds. *Obshchestvennoe dvizhenie v Rossii v nachale XX-ogo veka* [The public movement in Russia at the beginning of the twentieth century], Tom II. Saint Petersburg: Tipografiia "Obshchestvennia Pol'za," 1910.

Mashkin, (Aleksei Stepanovich). "Byt krest'ian Kurskoi gubernii, Oboianskago uezda" [Peasant life in Oboian District, Kursk Province]. *Etnograficheskii sbornik* vyp. V. Saint Petersburg: Tipografiia V. Bezobrazova i Ko., 1862, otd. I, (6th essay), 13–119.

Maslov, Petr. *Agrarnyi vopros v Rossii* [The agrarian question in Russia]. Saint Petersburg: Tipografiia "Obshchestvennia Pol'za," Tom I, 1905; Tom II, 1908.

———. "Krest'ianskoe dvizhenie 1905–1907 g." [The Peasant Movement of 1905–1907]. In *Obshchestvennoe dvizhenie v Rossii v nachale XX-ogo veka,* Tom II, Chast' 2. Saint Petersburg: Tipografiia "Obshchestvennia Pol'za," 1910, 203–282.

Materialy po voprosam zemel'nomu i krest'ianskomu. Vserossiiskii s"ezd krest'ian-staroobriadtsev v Moskve 22–25 fevralia 1906 goda [Materials on the land and peasant questions. All-Russian Congress of Peasant Old Believers in Moscow February 22–25, 1906]. Moscow: Tipo-litografiia I.N. Kushereva, 1906.

Materialy Vysochaishe utverzhdennoi 16-go noiabria 1901 g. Kommissii po issledovaniiu voprosa o dvizhenii s 1861 g. po 1900 g. blagosostoianiia sel'skago naseleniia sredne-zemledel'cheskikh gubernii, sravnitel'no s drugimi mestnostiami Evropeiskoi Rossii [Materials of the Commission ordered by His Majesty on November 16, 1901, for a study of the question of trends in the prosperity of the rural populace of the Central Agricultural provinces from 1861 to 1900, compared to other localities of European Russia]. Chast' I. Saint Petersburg: Tipografiia P.P. Soikina, 1903.

Matusevich, L., and A. Kazarin, *1905 god v Kurskoi gubernii* [1905 in Kursk Province]. Kursk: Kurskoe oblastnoe izdatel'stvo, 1941.

McKay, John. *Pioneers for Profit: Foreign Entrepreneurs and Russian Industrialization, 1855–1913.* Chicago: University of Chicago Press, 1970.

Meier, Viktor Iakovlevich. *Opisanie imeniia "Prilepskaia ekonomiia" brat'ev Baronov Meiendorf sost. Glavno-upravliaiushchim V. Ia. Meier* [A description of the estate "Prilepskaia Economy" of the Meiendorf Brothers, compiled by Chief Manager V. Ia. Meier]. Moscow: Pechatnia A.I. Snegirovoi, 1896.

Melton, Herman Edgar, Jr. "Serfdom and the Peasant Economy in Russia, 1780–1861." Ph.D. dissertation, Columbia University, 1984.

Migdal, Joel S. *Peasants, Politics and Revolution: Pressures toward Political and Social Change in the Third World*. Princeton: Princeton University Press, 1974.

Mikhailov, Iosif Antonov. "K voprosu o prokormlenii skota v 1897/8 khoziaistvennom godu" [On the problem of feeding cattle during the 1897–1898 economic year]. In *Kurskaia guberniia. Statisticheskii obzor, 1896 g.* Kursk, 1896, 273–283.

Milogolova, I.N. "Semeinye razdely v russkoi poreformennoi derevne (po materialov tsentral'nykh gubernii)" [Family partition in the Russian post-Reform village (according to materials of the central provinces)]. *Vestnik Moskovskogo universiteta, seriia VIII (Istoriia)* no. 6 (1987): 37–46.

Minarik, Liudmila Petrovna. "Sistema pomeshchich'ego khoziaistva v Rakitianskom imenii Iusupovykh, 1900–1913 gg." [The system of landowner economy on the Rakitnaia estate of the Iusupovy, 1900–1913]. In A.A. Novosel'skii, ed., *Materialy po istorii sel'skogo khoziaistva i krest'ianstva SSSR*, sbornik V. Moscow: Izdatel'stvo akademii nauk SSSR, 1962, 377–397.

———. "Kharakteristika krupneishikh zemlevladel'tsev Rossii kontse XIX-nachala XX v." [A profile of Russia's large-scale landowners at the end of the nineteenth and beginning of the twentieth century] in *Ezhegodnik po agrarnoi istorii vostochnoi Evropy. 1963 g.* Vilnius: Mintis, 1963, 693–708.

———. "Ob urovne razvitiia kapitalistichekogo zemledeliia v krupnom pomeshchich'em khoziaistve Evropeiskoi Rossii kontse XIX-nachala XX v." [On the level of capitalist agriculture in large-scale landowner economies at the end of the nineteenth and beginning of the twentieth century]. In *Ezhegodnik po agrarnoi istorii vostochnoi Evropy. 1964 g.* Kishinev: Kartia Moldoveniaske, 1966, 615–626.

———. *Ekonomicheskaia kharakteristika krupneishikh zemel'nykh sobstvennikov Rossii kontsa XIX-nachala XX v. Zemlevladenie, zemlepolzovanie, sistema khoziaistva* [An economic profile of Russia's large-scale landowners at the end of the nineteenth and beginning of the twentieth century: land ownership, land use, system of economy]. Moscow: Sovetskaia Rossiia, 1971.

———. "O sviaziakh krupneishikh zemel'nykh sobstvennikov s promyshlennost'iu k nachalu XX v." [On the connections of large-scale landowners with industry toward the beginning of the twentieth century]. In *Ezhegodnik po agrarnoi istorii vostochnoi Evropy. 1971 g.* Vilnius: Mintis, 1974, 307–318.

Ministerstvo iustitsii. *Svod statisticheskikh dannykh po delam ugolovnym, proizvodivshchimsia v...god v sudebnykh uchrezhdeniiakh, deistvuiushchikh na osnovanii ustavov Aleksandra II* [Digest of statistical data on criminal cases conducted in the year ____ in the judicial institutions acting on the basis of the statutes of Aleksandr II]. Annual. Saint Petersburg: Izdatel'stvo Ministerstva iustitsii, 1876–1916.

Ministerstvo finansov. *Ministerstvo finansov, 1802–1902* [The Ministry of Finances, 1802–1902], Ch. 1–2, Saint Petersburg: Ekspeditsii zagotovleniia gosudarstvennykh bumag, 1902.

———. *Ezhegodnik Ministerstva finansov za...god* [Yearbook of the Ministry of Finances for the Year ____.] Annual. Saint Petersburg: Tipografiia redaktsii periodicheskikh izdanii Ministerstva finansov, 1869–1916.

———. Departament okladnykh sborov. *Svod svedenii o postuplenii i vzimanii kazennykh, zemskikh i obshchestvennykh sborov za (1891–1906)* [Digest of data on the receipt and levy of state, zemstvo and public taxes for the year (1891–1906)]. Saint Petersburg: Tipografiia P.P. Soikina, 1902, 1903, 1906, 1909.

———. Departament torgovli i manufaktur. *Materialy po statistike khlebnoi torgovli* [Materials on the statistics of the grain trade]. Vyp. II: *Tseny rzhi po guberniiam i uezdam Evropeiskoi Rossii za 1889–1898 gg.* [The prices of rye in the provinces and districts of European Russia for 1889–1898], Vyp. III: *Tseny ovsa po guberniiam i uezdam Evropeiskoi Rossii za 1889–1898 gg.* [The prices of oats in the provinces and districts of European Russia for 1889–1898]. Saint Petersburg, 1899.

———. Departament torgovli i manufaktur. *Svod tovarnykh tsen na glavnykh russkikh i inostrannykh rynkov za (1903–1905) god. Materialy dlia torgovopromyshlennoi statistike.* Saint Petersburg: Tipografiia V. Kirshbauma, 1904–1906.

———. Departament zheleznodorozhnykh del. *Materialy k peresmotru torgovago dogovora s Germaniei i drugimi inostranymi gosudartvami. Perevozki po russkim zheleznym dorogam. Ch. 1. Raspredelenie khlebnykh gruzov po guberniiam i oblastiam i po portam i pogranichnym punktam* [Materials toward the review of the trade treaty with Germany and other foreign states. Transit on Russian railways. Part 1. Distribution of grain freight by province and region and by port and frontier points]. Saint Petersburg: Tipografiia redaktsii periodicheskikh izdanii Ministerstva finansov, 1914.

———. Departament zheleznodorozhnykh del. *Statisticheskiia dannyia ob otpravlenii i pribytii prodovol'stvennykh gruzov po russkim zheleznym dorogam s raspredeleniem po guberniiam i oblastiam za 1912, 1913 i 1914 gg.* [Statistical data on departure and arrival of foodstuffs on Russian railways with distribution by provinces and regions for 1912, 1913 and 1914]. Petrograd: Tipografiia redaktsii periodicheskikh izdanii Ministerstva finansov, 1916.

Ministerstvo Putei Soobshcheniia. Otdel statistiki i kartografii. *Statisticheskii sbornik Ministerstva Putei Soobshcheniia. Svedeniia o dvizhenii tovarov po zheleznym dorogam i vodnym putiam za* (1885–1913) *god* [Statistical digest of the Ministry of Ways. Data on the movement of goods by railway and waterways for the year (1885–1913)]. Annual. Saint Petersburg: Tipografiia Ministerstva putei soobshcheniia, 1886–1914.

Ministerstvo vnutrennikh del. Veterinarnoe upravlenie. *Otchet Veterinarnago Upravleniia Ministerstva Vnutrennikh Del za (1887–1913) god* [Account of the Veterinary Administration of the Ministry of Internal Affairs for the year ____] Annual. Saint Petersburg, 1890–1916.

Ministerstvo torgovli i promyshlennosti (Vasilii Egorovich Varzar, ed.), *Spisok fabrik i zavodov Rossiiskoi imperii* [List of factories and works of the Russian Empire]. I–II. Saint Petersburg: Tipografiia V. Kirshbauma, 1912.

Ministerstvo zemledeliia i gosudarstvennykh imushchestv. Departament Zemledeliia. *(...) god v sel'skokhoziaistvennom otnoshenii po otvetam poluchennym ot khoziaev* [The year ____ in its agricultural aspects according to the responses received from farmers]. Annual. Saint Petersburg: Tipografiia V. Kirshbauma, 1882–1918.

———. *Opisaniia otdel'nykh russkikh khoziaistv. Vyp. III. Kurskaia guberniia* [Descriptions of individual Russian economies. Issue III: Kursk Province]. Saint Petersburg: Tipografiia V. Kirshbauma, 1897.

———. *Kratkiia spravochnyia svedeniia o nekotorykh russkikh khoziaistvakh* [Brief informational description of several Russian economies]. No. 1. Saint Petersburg: Tipografiia V. Kirshbauma, 1900. Additional information in the last (4th) number.

———. *Pochvennaia karta Evropeiskoi Rossii, sostavlennaia po pochinu i planu Prof. V.V. Dokuchaeva, Prof. N.M. Sibirtsevym, G.I. Tanfil'evym i A.P. Ferkhminym, pod nabliudeniem Uchenago Komiteta Ministerstva Zemledeliia i Gos. Imushchestva. Izdanie Departamenta Zemledeliia* [Map of the soils of European Russia, compiled at the initiative and plan of Prof. V.V. Dokuchaev, by Professor N.M. Sibirtsev, G.I. Tanfil'ev and A.P. Ferkhmin under the supervision of the Scholarly Committee of the Ministry of Agriculture and State Property. A Publication of the Department of Agriculture]. Saint Petersburg: 1901.

———. *Sel'skokhoziaistvennyia statisticheskiia svedeniia po materialam, poluchennym ot khoziaev, Tom X: Rasprostranennost' navoznago udobrennia v Rossii.* [Statistical data for agriculture based on materials received from farmers. Volume X: The prevalence of manure fertilization in Russia]. Saint Petersburg: Tipografiia V. Kirshbauma, 1901.

———. *Sel'skokhoziaistvennyia statisticheskiia svedeniia po materialam, poluchennym ot khoziaev, Tom XI: Primenenie i rasprostranenie v Rossii sel'skokhoziaistvennykh mashin i orudii.* [Statistical data for agriculture based on materials received from farmers. Volume XI: Application and diffusion in Russia of agricultural machines and tools]. Saint Petersburg: Tipografiia V. Kirshbauma, 1903.

———. *Sel'skokhoziaistvennyia statisticheskiia svedeniia po materialam, poluchennym ot khoziaev. Tom XII: Sostoianiia travoseianiia v Rossii* [Statistical data for agriculture based on materials received from farmers. Volume XII: The condition of fodder cultivation in Russia]. Saint Petersburg: Tipografiia V. Kirshbauma, 1905.

Mironov, Boris Nikolaevich. "Traditsionnoe demograficheskoe povedenie krest'ian v XIX-nachale XX v." [Traditional peasant demographic behavior in the nineteenth and early twentieth centuries]. In A.G. Vishnevskii, ed., *Brachnost', rozhdaemost' smertnost' v Rossii i v SSSR*. Moscow: Statistika, 1977, 83–104.

———. *Khlebnye tseny v Rossii za dva stoletii (XVIII-XIX vv.)* [Grain prices in Russia over two centuries (18th–19th centuries)]. Leningrad: Nauka, 1985.

———. "The Russian Peasant Commune after the Reforms of the 1860s." In Ben Eklof and Stephen Frank, eds., *The World of the Russian Peasant: Post-Emancipation Culture and Society*. Boston: Unwin Hyman, 1990, 7–43.

Mixter, Timothy R. "Peasant Collective Action in Saratov Province, 1902–1906." In Rex A. Wade and Scott J. Seregny, eds., *Politics and Society in Provincial Russia: Saratov, 1590–1917*. Columbus OH: Ohio State University Press, 1989, 191–232.

———. "The Hiring Market as Workers' Turf: Migrant Agricultural Laborers and the Mobilization of Collective Action in the Steppe Grainbelt of European Russia, 1853–1913." In E. Kingston-Mann and T.R. Mixter, eds. *Peasant Economy, Culture, and Politics of European Russia 1800–1921*. Princeton: Princeton University Press, 1991, 294–340.

Moise, Edwin E. "The Moral Economy Dispute." *Bulletin of Concerned Asian Scholars*, 1, no. 14 (1982): 72–77.

Moiseev, S. Ia. "Kerosin." In *Tekushchaia sel'skokhoziaistvennaia statistika Kurskago gubernskago zemstva za 1904 god.* II, otd. 1, 23–60.

Moore, Barrington, Jr. *Social Origins of Dictatorship and Democracy: Lord and Peasant in the Making of the Modern World.* Boston: Beacon Press, 1966.

———. *Injustice: The Social Bases of Obedience and Revolt.* Armonk, NY: M.E. Sharpe, Inc., 1978.

Morokhovets, Evgenii Andreevich. *Krest'ianskoe dvizhenie i sotsial-demokratiia v pervoi russkoi revoliutsii* [The peasant movement and Social Democracy in the First Russian Revolution]. Moscow: Gosudarstvennoe izdatel'stvo, 1926.

Naumov, V.P., ed. *Aktual'nye problemy sovetskoi istoriografii pervoi russkoi revoliutsii. Sbornik statei* [Current problems of Soviet historiography on the First Russsian Revolution. A collection of essays]. Moscow: Nauka, 1978.

Nekrich, Aleksandr Moiseevich. *Otreshis' ot strakha: Vospominaniia istorika* [Renounce Fear: Recollections of an Historian]. London: Overseas Publications Interchange, Ltd., 1979.

Nifontov, Aleksandr Sergeevich. *Zernovoe proizvodstvo Rossii vo vtoroi polovine deviatnadtsotogo veka po materialam ezhegodnoi statistiki urozhaev Evropeiskoi Rossii* [Grain production in Russia in the second half of the nineteenth century according to materials of the annual harvests statistics for European Russia]. Moscow: Nauka, 1974.

———, and Zlatoustovskii, B.V., eds. *Krest'ianskoe dvizhenie v Rossii v 1880–1889 gg. Sbornik dokumentov* [The peasant movement in Russia in 1880–1889. Collected documents]. Moscow: Izdatel'stvo sotsial'no-ekonomicheskoi literatury, 1960.

Noonan, Norma C., and Carol Nechemias, eds., *Encyclopedia of Russian Women's Movements.* Westport, Conn., Greenwood Press, 2001, 64–65.

Novosel'skii, Aleksei Andreevich, ed., *Materialy po istorii sel'skogo khoziaistva i krest'ianstva SSSR* sbornik V [Materials on the history of rural economy and the peasantry of the USSR]. Moscow: Izdatel'stvo akademii nauk SSSR, 1962.

Novosel'skii, Sergei Aleksandrovich. "K voprosu o ponizhenii smertnosti i rozhdaemosti v Rossii" [On the question of the decline of mortality and fertility in Russia]. *Vestnik obshchestvennoi gigieni, sudebnoi i prakticheskoi meditsiny* no. 4 (1914): 339–352.

———. *Smertnost' i prodolzhitel'nost' zhizni v Rossii* [Mortality and life expectancy in Russia]. Petrograd: Tipografiia Ministerstva Vnutrennikh del, 1916.

Oboianskoe uyezdnoe zemstvo. *Sbornik statisticheskikh svedenii po Oboianskomu uezdu Kurskoi gubernii* [Collected statistical materials for Oboian District, Kursk Province]. Moscow: Tipografiia S.V. Gurianova, 1882–1883.

Obshchii tarifnyi s"ezd predstavitelei russkikh zheleznykh dorog. *Statisticheskiia dannyia o dvizhenii khlebnykh gruzov po russkim nepreryvno mezhdu soboiu sviazannym zheleznym dorogam, sostavlennym po guberniiam* [Statistical data on the movement of grain traffic for directly interconnected Russian railroads, compiled by province]. Vyp. I–IV. Saint Petersburg: Skoropechtnia P.O. Iablonskago, 1896.

Ocherk deiatel'nosti Sudzhanskago uezdnago zemstva po razvitiiu kustarnykh promyslov i opisanie nekotorykh iz nikh [An essay on the activity of the Sudzha District Zemstvo in the development of artisanal industries and the description of several of these], Vyp. 1–2. Kursk: Tipografiia Kurskago gubernskago zemstvo, 1902–1903.

"Ocherk deiatel'nosti gos. sberegatel'nykh kass v Kurskoi gubernii" [Essay on activities of state savings banks in Kursk Province]. In *Tekushchaia sel'sko-khoziaistvennaia statistika Kurskago Gubernskago Zemstva za 1904 god.* I, otd. 1, 9–24.

Oganovskii, N.P., *Zakonomernost' agrarnoi evoliutsii. II. Ocherki po istorii zemel'nykh otnoshenii v Rossii* [The regularity of agrarian development. II. Essays on the history of landed relations in Russia]. Saratov: Elektro-tipo-litografiia B.L. Rabinovicha, 1911.

Olick, Jeffrey K., and Joyce Robbins. "Social Memory Studies: From 'Collective Memory' to the Historical Sociology of Mnemonic Practices." *Annual Review of Sociology* 24 (1998): 105–140.

Olsen, Mancur. *The Logic of Collective Action.* Cambridge, Mass.: Harvard University Press, 1965.

Osobennosti agrarnogo stroia Rossii v period imperializma. Materialy sessii Nauchnogo soveta po probleme "Istoricheskie predposylki Velikoi Oktiabr'skoi sotsialisticheskoi revoliutsii." Mai 1960 g. [Peculiarities of the Russian agrarian order in the period of imperialism. Materials of the Scholarly Council session on the problem "Historical Preconditions for the Great October Socialist Revolution." May, 1960]. Moscow: Izdatel'stvo akademii nauk SSSR, 1962.

Pavlovsky, George. *Agricultural Russia on the Eve of the Revolution.* New York: Howard Fertig, 1968.

Paxson, Margaret. *Solovyovo: The Story of Memory in a Russian Village.* Washington, D.C.: Woodrow Wilson Center Press, 2005.

Pereselencheskoe upravlenie. *Itogi pereselencheskago dvizheniia za vremia c 1896 po 1909 gg. vkliuchitel'no* [Results of the emigration movement in the period 1896 to 1909 inclusive]. N. Turchaninov, ed. Saint Petersburg: Izdatel'stvo pereselencheskago upravleniia, 1910.

———. *Itogi pereselencheskago dvizheniia za vremia c 1910 po 1914 gg. vkliuchitel'no* [Results of the emigration movement in the period 1910 to 1914 inclusive]. N. Turchaninov, ed. Petrograd: Izdatel'stvo pereselencheskago upravleniia, 1916.

Peretz, Michael G. "Moral and Political Economies in Rural Southeast Asia: A Review Article." *Comparative Studies in Society and History* 25, no. 4 (October, 1983): 731–739.

Perrie, Maureen. "The Russian Peasant Movement of 1905–1907: Its Social Composition and Revolutionary Significance." *Past and Present* no. 57 (1972): 123–155.

———. "Folklore as Evidence of Peasant *Mentalité*: Social Attitudes and Values in Russian Popular Culture." *Russian Review* 48, no. 3 (April, 1989): 119–143.

Pershin, Pavel Nikolaevich. *Zemel'noe ustroistvo dorevoliutsionnoi derevni. Tom I.* [Land tenure systems in the pre-revolutionary countryside. Volume I]. Moscow–Voronezh: Gosudarstvennyi nauchno-issledovatel'skii institute zemleustroistva i pereseleniia, 1928.

———. *Agrarnaia revoliutsiia v Rossii. Tom I. Ot reformy k revoliutsii* [Agrarian revolution in Russia. Volume I. From reform to revolution]. Moscow: Nauka, 1966.

Peshekhonov, Aleksei Vasilievich. "Iz teorii i praktiki krest'ianskogo khoziaistva" [From the theory and practice of peasant economy]. *Russkoe bogatstvo,* no. 9 (1902, sentiabr'): 161–193; no. 10 (1902, oktiabr'): 71–119.

———. *Agrarnaia problema v sviazi s krest'ianskim dvizheniem* [The agrarian problem in connection with the peasant movement]. Saint Petersburg: Russkoe bogatstvo, 1906.

Petrov, Iurii Aleksandrovich. "1905 god: Prolog grazhdanskoi voiny" [1905: Prologue to civil war]. In A.N. Iakovlev, ed., *Rossiia v nachale XX-go veka*. Moscow: Novyi khronograf, 2002, 354–395.

Petrovich, Michael B. "The Peasant in Nineteenth Century Historiography." In Wayne S. Vucinich, ed., *The Peasant in Nineteenth-Century Russia*. Stanford: Stanford University Press, 1968, 191–230.

Piaskovskii, A.V. *Revoliutsiia 1905–1907 gg. v Rossii* [The revolution of 1905–1907 in Russia]. Moscow: Nauka, 1966.

Pirumova, Natalia Mikhailovna. *Zemskoe liberal'noe dvizhenie. Sotsial'nye korni i evoliutsiia do nachala XX veka* [The zemstvo liberal movement. Social roots and evolution to the beginning of the twentieth century]. Moscow: Nauka, 1977.

Plekhanov, G.V. "Nashi raznoglasiia" [Our Disagreements], Sochineniia II. Moscow–Petrograd: Institut Karla Marksa i Fridrich Engelsa, 1923, 199–232.

Pokrovskii, V.I. "Vliianie kolebanii urozhaev i khlebnykh tsen na estestvennoe dvizhenie naseleniia" [The influence of fluctuations of harvests and grain prices on natural population movement]. In A.I. Chuprov and A.S Posnikov, eds., *Vliianie urozhaev i khlebnykh tsen na nekotoryia storony russkago narodnago khoziaistva*. Tom II. Saint Petersburg: Tipografiia V.F. Kirshbauma, 1897, 171–370

Polikarpov, Vladimir Vasilievich. "'Novoe napravlenie' 50–70-kh gg: posledniaia diskussiia sovetskikh istorikov" [The "new direction" of the 1950s and 1960s: the last discussion of Soviet historians]. In Iu. N. Afanas'ev, ed., *Sovetskaia istoriografiia*. Moscow: Rossiiskii gosudarstvennyi gumanitarnyi universitet, 1996, 349–400.

Popkin, Samuel L. *The Rational Peasant: The Political Economy of Rural Society in Vietnam*. Berkeley and Los Angeles: University of California Press, 1979.

Popov, Konstantin Andreevich and Ia. Rezvushkin. *O pererastanii burzhuazno-demokraticheskoi revoliutsii v proletarskuiu. Uchenie Lenina i ego kritiki* [On the merging of the bourgeois-democratic revolution into the proletarian one. The teaching of Lenin and its critics]. Moscow: Gosudarstvennoe izdatel'stvo, 1929.

Prilutskii, Aleksandr Mikhailovich. *Istoricheskii opyt preobrazovaniia sela: krest'ianskoe khoziaistvo Kurskoi guberniia v 1906–1916 gg.* [The historical experience of the transformation of the countryside: peasant economy in Kursk Province, 1906–1916]. Kursk: Kurskii intitut sotsial'nogo preobrazovaniia MGSU, 2003.

Prokopovich, Sergei Nikolaevich. *Agrarnyi krizis i meropriatiia pravitel'stva* [The agrarian crisis and the government's legislative measures]. Moscow: Izdanie Sabashnikovykh, 1912.

———. *Krest'ianskoe khoziaistvo po biudzhethym i dinamicheskim issledovaniiam,* [Peasant economy according to the budget and dynamic studies]. Berlin: Kooperativnaia mysl', 1924.

Protokoly delegatskago soveshchaniia Vserossiiskago Krest'ianskago Soiuza 6–10 noiabria 1905 g. v Moskve [Protocols of the delegate congress of the All-Russian Peasant Union 6–10 November 1905]. Moscow: Novoe tovarishchestvo, 1906.

Pushkarev, Sergei Germanovich. *Krest'ianskaia pozemel'naia obshchina v Rossii* [The peasant land commune in Russia]. Newtonville, Mass.: Oriental Research Partners, 1976.

Pushkareva, Irina Mikhailovna. "Pervaia Pobeda Revoliutsii" [The first victory of the revolution]. In A.P. Korelin and S.V. Tiutiukin, eds., *Pervaia revoliutsiia v Rossii:*

Vzgliad cherez stoletiia. Moscow: Pamiatniki istoricheskoi mysli, 2005, Ch. 5, 280–350.

———. "1905 god: revoliutsionnyi shturm ili 'perestroika' gosudarstvennoi vlasti?" [1905: revolutionary assault or a "remaking" of state power?]. In A.G. Golikov and A.P. Korelin, eds., *Rossiia v XIX–XX vekakh. Materialy II nauchnykh chenii pamiati Professora Valeriia Ivanovicha* Bovykina. Moscow: ROSSPEN, 2002, 276–289.

Raleigh, Donald J. "Translator's Introduction" to Eduard Nikolaevich Burdzhalov. *Russia's Second Revolution: The February 1917 Uprising in Petrograd*. Bloomington, IN, Indiana University Press, 1987, ix–xxii.

Rashin, Adol'f Grigor'evich. *Naselenie Rossii za 100 let* [The Population of Russia over 100 Years], Moscow: Gosudarstvennyi statisticheskoe izdatel'stvo, 1956.

———. *Formirovanie rabochego klassa Rossii* [The formation of the Russian working class]. Moscow: Izdatel'stvo sotsial'no-ekonomicheskoi literatury, 1958.

Redfield, Robert. *Little Community; Peasant Society and Culture*. Chicago: University of Chicago Press, 1956.

Reiber, Alfred J. *Merchants and Entrepreneurs in Imperial Russia*. Chapel Hill NC, University of North Carolina Press, 1982.

Reichman, Henry, *Railwaymen and Revolution: Russia, 1905*. Berkeley–Los Angeles: University of California Press, 1987.

Revel, Jacques. "Microanalysis and the Construction of the Social." In Jacques Revel and Lynn Hunt, eds., *Histories: French Constructions of the Past*. New York: The New Press, 1998, 492–502.

Revoliutsiia 1905–1907 gg. v Rossii. Dokumenty i materialy. [The revolution of 1905–1907 in Russia. Documents and materials], 18 volumes. Moscow: Izdatel'stvo akademii nauk SSSR, 1955–1969.

Revoliutsionnye sobytiia 1905–1907 gg. v Kurskoi gubernii. Sbornik dokumentov i materialov [Revolutionary events of 1905–1907 in Kursk Province. Collected documents and materials]. Kursk: Kurskoe knizhnoe izdatel'stvo, 1955.

Revoliutsionnoe dvizhenie v Voronezhskoi gubernii 1905–1907 gg. Sbornik dokumentov i materialov [The revolutionary movement in Voronezh Province, 1905–1907. Collected documents and materials]. Voronezh: Voronezhskoe knizhnoe izdatel'stvo, 1955.

Rexheuser, R. *Dumawahlen und Lokale Gesellschaft. Studien zur Sozialgeschicht der russischen Rechten vor 1917* [The duma elections and local society. Studies in the social history of the Russian right before 1917]. Cologne–Vienna: Böhlau Verlag, 1980.

Rittikh, A.A., ed. *Vysochaishe uchrezhdennoe Osoboe Soveshchanie o nuzhdakh sel'skokhoziaistvennoi promyshlennosti. Svod trudov mestnykh komitetov po 49 Evropeiskoi Rossii. Krest'ianskii pravoporiadok* [Special commission ordered by His Majesty on the needs of rural industry. Digest of the proceedings of the local committees of the 49 provinces of European Russia. Peasant legal status]. Saint Petersburg: Tipografiia V. Kirshbauma, 1904.

Robinson, Geroid Tanquary. *Rural Russia under the Old Regime: A History of the Landlord-Peasant World and a Prologue to the Peasant Revolution of 1917*. New York: The MacMillan Company, 1932.

"'Rodstvennye poriadki' v zemstvo: Pis'mo is N-skago uyezda, Kurskoi gub." [The "clan order" in the zemstvo: a letter from "N" District, Kursk Province]. *Russkoe bogatstvo* no. 2 (1898, fevral'): 212–223.

Rossiiskii gosudarstvennyi istoricheskii arkhiv. Fond 1291. Ministerstva vnutrennikh del. Zemskii Otdel. [Russian State Historical Archive. Repository 1291. Ministry of Internal Affairs. Land Section].

———. Opis' 30 (1-oe deloproisvodstvo). 1905 g.

    d. 4-b: "Po tsikuliaru za No. 4 o zemskikh nachalnikov" [On Circular No. 4 on the Land Captains]

    d. 4-v: "O sobranii zemskikh nachal'nikov svedenii o sovremennom sostoianii i proiavleniiakh obshchestv i zhizni krest'ian" [On information collected by the Land Captains on the current conditions behavior of communes and peasant life].

———. Opis' 50 (3-oe deloproisvodstvo). 1906 g.

    d. 5, ch. X: "O vydache po zakonu 15 marta 1906 g. ssudy postradavshim ot agrarnykh bezporiadkov zemledeltsam Vitebskoi, Voronezhskoi, Ekaterinoslavskoi i Kurskoi gubernii" [Of the grant of loans under the Law of 15 March 1906 to those landowners damaged by peasant disorders in Vitebsk, Voronezh, Ekaterinoslav and Kursk Provinces].

———. Opis' 122 (kantselariia). 1905 g.

    d. 34-a: "Komandirovka Ego Prevokhoditel'stva Ia.Ia. Litvinova dlia rukovodstva deistviami vremennykh uezdnykh kommisii, uchrezhdennykh na osnovanii Ukaza 10 aprelia 1905 goda" [The inspection tour of His Excellency Ia. Ia. Litvinov for leading the work of the Temporary District Commissions instituted on the basis of the Decree of 10 April 1905]

    d. 34-b: "Materialy otnosiashchiesia do poezdki Ego Prevokhoditel'stva Ia.Ia. Litvinova dlia rukovodstva deistviami vremennykh uezdnykh kommisii, uchrezhdennykh na osnovanii Ukaza 10 aprelia 1905 goda" [Materials related to the inspection tour of His Excellency Ia. Ia. Litvinov for leading the work of the Temporary District Commissions instituted on the basis of the Decree of 10 April 1905]

    d. 34-v: "Ob obrazovaniia vremennykh uezdnykh kommisii, uchrezhdennykh na osnovanii Ukaza 10 aprelia 1905 goda" [On formation of the Temporary District Commissions instituted on the basis of the Decree of 10 April 1905]

    d.112: "So svedeniiami, donesennymi Gubernatorami o razmerakh ubytkov, prichinennykh agrarnymi bezporiadkami" [With information reported by the Governors on the size of losses inflicted by peasant disorders]

    d. 123: "Doneseniia Gubernatorov o prichinakh agrarnykh besporiadkov" [Reports of the Governors on the reasons for peasant disorders].

Rossiiskii gosudarstvennyi istoricheskii arkhiv. Fond 1405. Ministerstva iustitsii. 2-oe ugolovnoe otdelenie (Russian State Historical Archive. Repository 1405. Ministry of Justice. Second Criminal Division).

———. Opis' 107 (1905 g.)

    d. 7371: "O krest'ianskikh bezporiadkakh v s. Dugine, Ryl'skago uezda (krazha solomy na Peretseluevskoi ferme)" [On peasant disorders in the village of Dugino, Ryl'sk District (theft of straw at the Peretseluev farm)].

———. Opis' 108 (1906 g.)

    d. 2622–2628, inclusive: "Krest'ianskie besporiadki v Kurskoi, Orlovskoi i Chernigovskoi guberniiakh, fevral'-mart, 1905 g." Tom I–VII. [Peasant disorders in Kursl, Orel and Chernigov Provinces, February–March, 1905]

    d. 2705: "O krest'ianskikh bezporiadkakh v Novooskol'skom u. osen'iu 1905 g." [On peasant disorders in Novyi Oskol' District in autumn, 1905]

d. 2724: "O krest'ianskikh bezporiadkakh v Graivoronskom u. vesnoiu 1906 g." [On peasant disorders in Graivoron District in spring, 1906].

———. Opis' 194 (1908 g.)

d. 102: "O krest'ianskikh bezporiadkakh v Kurskoi gubernii" [On peasant disorders in Kursk Province]

d. 137: "O krest'ianskikh bezporiadkakh v Graivoronskom uezde, Kurskoi guber-nii, osen'iu 1905 g." [On peasant disorders in Graivoron District, Kursk Province, autumn, 1905]

d. 200: "O krest'ianskikh bezporiadkakh v Kurskoi gubernii vesnoi 1906 g." [On peasant disorders in Kursk Province in spring, 1906].

Roshtok, A.I. "Zemstvo i statistika" [The zemstvo and statistics]. *Russkii Vestnik*, 196 (Mai, 1888): 137–176.

Rotberg, Robert I., and Theodore K. Rabb, eds. *Hunger and History: The Impact of Changing Food Production and Consumption Patterns on Society.* London–New York: Cambridge University Press, 1985.

Rubenshtein, N.L. "O melkotovarnom proizvodstve i razvitii kapitalizm v Rossii" [Of small-commodity production and the development of capitalism in Russia]. *Istoriia SSSR* no.4 (1962, iiul'-avgust): 66–86.

Rumiantsev, P.P. "K voprosu ob evoliutsii russkogo krest'ianstva" [On the question of the evolution of the Russian peasantry]. In S. Dorovatorskii and A. Chausnikov, eds., *Ocherki realisticheskago mirovozzreniia. Sbornik statei po filosofii, obshchestvennoi nauki i zhizni.* Saint Petersburg: Tipografiia Montvida, 1904, 453–549.

Ryndziunskii, P.G. "O melkotovarnom uklade v Rossii XIX veka" [The small-commodity milieu in Russia of the nineteenth century] *Istoriia SSSR* no. 2 (1961, mart-aprel'): 48–69.

———. "Voprosy izucheniia melkotovarnogo uklada v Rossii XIX v." [Problems of the study of the small-commodity milieu in Russia of the nineteenth century]. *Istoriia SSSR* no.4 (1963, iiul'-avgust): 95–119.

Sakharov, Andrei Nikolaevich, "Vvedenie" [Introduction]. In A.N. Iakovlev, ed., *Rossiia v nachale XX-go veka.* Moscow: Novyi khronograf, 2002, 5–72.

Saltyk, Galina Aleksandrovna. "Es-Ry tsentral'nogo chernozem'ia v 1905–1907 gody" [SRs of the Central Black Earth Region in 1905–1907]. *Otechestvennaia istoriia* 1 no. (2004): 55–69.

———, with N.I. Gorlova, S.N. Glavinskaia and A.A. Beloborodova. *Politsiia Kurskoi guberniia: istoriia stanovleniia i deiatel'nosti (1864–1917).* [The police of Kursk Province: the history of its establishment and activity, 1864–1917]. Kursk: Izdatel'stvo Kurskogo gosudarstvennago universiteta, 2007.

Savel'ev, P.I. *Agrarnye otnosheniia i klassovaia bor'ba v Srednem Povolzhe v period kapitalizma, 1861–1905 gg.: uchebnoe posobie k spetskursu* [Agrarian relations and class struggle in the Middle Volga Region in the capitalist era, 1861–1905: A Textbook for the special course]. Kuibyshev: Kuibyshevskii gosudarstvennyi universitet, 1987.

———. "Put' agrarnogo razvitiia Rossii v diskussiiakh sovetskikh istorikov" [The Path of Russia's agrarian development in the discussions of Soviet historians]. In A.P. Korelin, ed., *Rossiia sel'skaia XIX-nachalo XX veka (Pamiati Andreia Matveevicha Anfimova).* Moscow: ROSSPEN, 2004, 25–53.

Sazonov, V.M. "O kreditnikh tovarishchestvakh" [On Credit Partnerships]. In *Tekushchaia sel'skokhoziaistvennaia statistika Kurskago Gubernskago Zemsiva 1903 g.* I, 59–71.

Schuman, Howard, and Jacqueline Scott. "Generations and Collective Memories." *American Sociological Review* 54, no. 3 (June, 1989): 359–381.

Scott, James C., *The Moral Economy of the Peasant: Rebellion and Subsistence in Southeast Asia.* New Haven: Yale University Press, 1976.

———. "Protest and profanation: agrarian revolt and the little tradition." *Theory and Society* IV (1977), No. 1: 1–38; No. 2: 211–246.

———. "Hegemony and the peasantry." *Politics and Society* 7, no. 3 (1977): 267–296.

———. "Revolution in the revolution: peasants and commissars." *Theory and Society* VII, nos. 1–2 (1979): 97–134.

———, with Benedict J. Tria Kerkvliet, eds., *Weapons of the Weak: Everyday Forms of Peasant Resistance in South-East Asia.* London–Totowa, NJ: Frank Cass, 1986.

———. *Domination and the Arts of Resistance: Hidden Transcripts.* New Haven: Yale University Press, 1990).

Semevskii, Vasilii Ivanovich. *Krest'iane v tsarstvovanie Ekateriny II* [The peasantry during the reign of Catherine II]. Tom II.. Saint Petersburg: Tipografiia M.M. Stasiulevicha, 1901.

———. "Pamiati V.E. Iakushkin, 1856–1912" [In Memory of V.E. Iakushkin, 1856–1912]. *Golos minuvshego* no. 1 (1913): 271–276.

Senchakova, Larisa Timofeevna. "Opublikovannye dokumenty po istorii krest'ianskogo dvizheniia 1905–1907 gg." [Published documents on the history of the peasant movement of 1905–1907]. *Istoriia SSSR* no.2 (1979, mart-avrel'): 68–86.

———. *Krest'ianskoe dvizhenie v revoliutsii 1905–1907 gg.* [The peasant movement of 1905–1907]. Moscow: Nauka, 1989.

Seregny, Scott J., *Russian Teachers and Peasant Revolution: The Politics of Education in 1905.* Bloomington, IN: Indiana University Press, 1989.

Sergeevich, Vasilii Ivanovich. *Drevnosti russkago prava. Tom tretii. Zemlevladenie, tiaglo, poriadok oblozheniia* [Antiquities of Russian law. Volume Three: Land tenure, taxes, order of imposition]. Saint Petersburg: Tipografiia M.M. Stasiulevich, 1903.

Sevost'ianov Grigorii Nikolaevich, ed., *Akademik P.V. Volobuev: neopublikovannye raboty, vospominaniia, stat'i* [Academic P.V. Volobuev: Unpublished works, recollections, articles]. Moscow: Nauka, 2000.

S"ezd sovetov predstaviteli promyshlennosti i torgovli. *Fabrichno-zavodskaia predpriiatiia Rossiiskoi imperii*, vyp. II. Saint Petersburg, 1914.

Shanin, Teodor. "Socio-Economic Mobility and the Rural History of Russia, 1905–1930." *Soviet Studies* (1971): 222–235.

———. *The Awkward Class: the Political Sociology of the Peasantry in a Developing Society (Russia, 1905–1930).* Oxford: Clarendon Press, 1972.

———. "The Nature and Logic of Peasant Economy." *Journal of Peasant Studies* no. 1 (1973, October): 63–80.

———. *The Roots of Otherness: Russia's Turn of the Century. Volume 1: Russia as a "Developing Society."* New Haven: Yale University Press, 1986.

Shapkarin, Anatolii Vasil'evich, ed. *Krest'ianskoe dvizhenie v Rossii v 1890–1899 gg. Sbornik dokumentov* [The peasant movement in Russia in 1890–1899. Collected documents]. Moscow: Izdatel'stvo sotsial'no-ekonomicheskoi literatury, 1959.

Shatkovskaia, Tat'ianaVladimirovna. *Pravovaia mental'nost' rossiiskikh krest'ian vtoroi poloviny XIX veka: Opyt iuridicheskoi antropometrii* [The legal mentality of Russian peasants of the second half of the nineteenth century: an experiment in juridical anthropometry]. Rostov-na-Donu: Rostovskii gosudarstvennyi ekonomicheskii universitet, 2000.

Shcherbina, Fedor Andreevich. "Semeinye razdely u krest'ian Voronezhskoi gubernii" [Family partitions among peasants of Voronezh Province]. *Russkoe bogatstvo* no. 6 (1896, iiun'): 199–210.

———. *Svodnyi sbornik po 12 uyezdam Voronezhskoi gubernii. Statisticheskie materialy podvornoi perepisi po gubernii* [Summary collection for the twelve districts of Voronezh Province. Statistical materials from the provincial household census]. Voronezh: Voronezhskoe gubernskoe zemstvo, 1897.

———. *Krest'ianskie biudzhety* [Peasant Budgets]. Voronezh: Tipografiia V.I. Isaeva, 1900.

Shelokhaev, Valentin Valentinovich, and Nadeazhda Ivanovna Kanishcheva, "Dolgorukov, Petr Dmitrievich (1866–1951)." In A.A. Kara-Murza, ed., *Pervodumtsy. Sbornik pamiati deputatov Pervoi Gosudarstvennoi Dumy* [*Pervodumtsy*: A collection in memory of the deputies of the First State Duma]. Moscow: Prem'er Press, 2006, 99–117.

———, eds. *Gosudarsvennia Duma Rossiiskoi imperii, 1906–1917 gg.* [The State Duma of the Russian Empire, 1906–1917]. Moscow: ROSSPEN, 2008.

Shestakov, Andrei Vasil'evich. *Kapitalizatsiia sel'skogo khoziaistva Rossii* [The capitalization of Russian agriculture]. Moscow: Gosudarstvennoe izdatel'stvo, 1924.

———. *Krest'ianstvo v revoliutsii 1905 goda* [The peasantry in the Revolution of 1905]. Moscow: Gosudarstvennoe izdatel'stvo, 1930.

Sidel'nikov, Stepan Mikhailovich. *Obrazovanie i deiatel'nost' pervoi Gosudarstvennoi Dumy* [Formation and activity of the first State Duma]. Moscow: Izdatel'stvo Moskovskogo universiteta, 1962.

Sidorova, Liubov' Alekseevna. *Ottepel' v istoricheskoi nauke: Sovetskaia istoriografiia pervogo posle-stalinskogo desiatiletiia* [The "thaw" in historical science: Soviet historiography in the first post-Stalin decade]. Moscow: Pamiatniki istoricheskoi mysli, 1997.

———. "Innovatsiia v otechestvennoi istorigrafii: opyt rubezha 50-kh–60-kh godov" [Innovation in National Historiography: The Experience of the 1950s and 1960s]. In Sergei Pavlovich Karpov, ed., *Problemy istochnikovedeniia i istoriografii: materialy II nauchnykh chtenii pamiati akademika I.D. Koval'chenko*. Moscow: ROSSPEN, 2000, 401–409.

Simms, James Y., Jr. "The Crisis of Russian Agriculture at the End of the Nineteenth Century: A Different View." *Slavic Review* 36, no. 3 (September 1977): 377–398.

Simonova, Marlena Sergeevna. "Krest'ianskii Pozemel'nyi Bank v sisteme obshchei agrarnoi politike samoderzhanviia (1895-3.XI.1905 g.)" [The Peasant Land Bank in the system of the general agrarian policy of the autocracy (1895 to November 3, 1905)]. In *Ezhegodnik po agrarnoi istorii vostochnoi Evropy. 1966 g.* Tallin: Redaktsionno-izdatel'skii sovet Akademii nauk Estonskoi SSR, 1971, 471–484.

———. "Krest'ianskoe dvizhenie 1905–1907 gg. v sovetskoi istoriografii" [The peasant movement of 1905–1907 in Soviet historiography]. *Istoricheskie zapiski* no. 95 (1975): 204–253.

——. *Krizis agrarnoi politiki tsarizma nakanune pervoi russkoi revoliutsii* [The crisis of Tsarist agrarian policy on the eve of the first Russian revolution]. Moscow: Nauka, 1987.

Smith, Robert E.F., and David Christian. *Bread and Salt: A Social History of Food and Drink in Russia*. Cambridge: Cambridge University Press, 1984.

Sobranie uzakonenii i rasporiazhenii pravitel'stva, izdavaemoe pri Pravitel'stvuiushem Senate [Collected acts and instructions of the government, published by the Ruling Senate], 1893 g. Tom II. Saint Petersburg: Senatskaia tipografiia, 1893.

Sokovnin, P.N., *Dlinozemel'e i cherezpolosnost' krest'ianskikh nadelov v Kurskoi gubernii* ["Longlandedness" and intermixing of peasant allotments in Kursk Province]. Kursk: Kurskoe gubernskoe zemstvo, 1902.

Solomon, Susan G. *The Soviet Agrarian Debate: A Controversy in Social Science, 1923–1929*. Boulder CO: Westview Press, 1977.

Stanziani, Alessandro. *L'Economie en révolution: Le cas russe, 1870–1930* [An economy in revolution: the Russian case, 1870–1930]. Paris: Albin Michel, 1998.

Stepynin, Vasilii Aleksandrovich, ed. *Khronika revoliutsionnykh sobytii v derevne Voronezhskoi gubernii, 1861–1917 gg.* [A chronicle of revolutionary events in the countryside of Voronezh Province, 1861–1917]. Voronezh: Izdatel'stvo Voronezhskoi universiteta 1977.

——. *Krest'ianstvo chernozemnogo tsentra v revoliutsii 1905–1907 godov* [The peasantry of the Black Earth center in the revolution of 1905–1907]. Voronezh: Izdatel'stvo Voronezhskoi universiteta, 1991.

Struve, Petr Berngardovich. *Kriticheskie zametki po voprosu ob ekonomicheskom razvitii v Rossii* [Critical notes on the question of the economic development of Russia]. Vyp. 1. Saint Petersburg: Tipografiia I.N. Skorokhodova, 1894.

Tankov, Anatolii Alekseevich. "Krest'ianskiia volneniia v Kurskoi gubernii v 1862 godu" [Peasant disturbances in Kursk Province in 1862]. *Istoricheskii vestnik* XLI (1890): 343–379.

——. *Istoricheskaia letopis' Kurskago dvorianstvo. Sostavil chlen' Imperatorskago Akheograficheskago Instituta Anatolii Alekseevich Tankov. Izdanie Kurskago gubernskago dvorianskago sobraniia.* [Historical chronicle of the Kursk nobility. Compiled by member of the Imperial Archeographical Institute Anatolii Alekseevich Tankov. A publication of the Kursk Provincial Assembly of the Nobility]. Tom 1. Moscow: Tipografiia "Pechatnik," 1913.

Tarnovskii, Konstantin Nikolaevich. "Problemy agrarnoi istorii Rossii perioda imperializma v sovetskoi istoriografii (1917-nachalo 1930-x godov)" [Problems of agrarian history of the period of imperialism in Soviet historiography (1917 to the Beginning of the 1930s)]. *Istoricheskie zapiski* no. 78 (1965): 31–62.

——. "Problemy agrarnoi istorii Rossii perioda imperializma v sovetskoi istoriografii (konets 1930-x – pervaia polovina 1950-x godov)" [Problems of agrarian history of the period of imperialism in Soviet historiography (End of the 1930s to the first half of the 1950s)]. *Istoricheskie zapiski* 83 (1969): 196–221.

——. "Problemy agrarnoi istorii Rossii perioda imperializma v sovetskoi istoriografii (diskussiia nachala 1960-kh godov)" [Problems of agrarian history of the period of imperialism in Soviet historiography (the debates of the 1960s)]. In L.M. Ivanov, ed., *Problemy sotsial'no-ekonomicheskoi istorii Rossia. Sbornik statei k 85-letiiu so dnia rozhdeniia akademika N.M. Druzhinina*. Moscow: Nauka, 1971, 264–311.

Thompson, E.P. "The Moral Economy of the English Crowd in the Eighteenth Century." *Past and Present* 50, no. 1 (1971): 76–136.

Tikhonov, Boris Vasil'evich. *Pereselenie v Rossii vo vtoroi polovine XIX veka* [Resettlement in Russia during the second half of the nineteenth century]. Moscow: Nauka, 1978.

Tikhvinskii, Sergei Leonidovich, ed. *Sotsial'no-ekonomicheskoe razvitie Rossii. Sbornik statei k 100-letiiu so dnia rozhdeniia Nikolaia Mikhailovicha Druzhinina* [The socio-economic development of Russia. Collected essays in honor of the centenary of the birth of Nikolai Mikhailovich Druzhinin]. Moscow: Nauka, 1986.

Tiukavkin, Viktor Grigor'evich, with Ernst Mikhailovich Shchagin. *Krest'ianstvo Rossii v period trekh revoliutsii* [The Russian peasantry in the era of the three revolutions]. Moscow: Prosveshchenie, 1987.

Tropin, Vladimir Ivanovich. *Bor'ba bol'shevikov za rukovodstvo krest'ianskim dvizheniem v 1905 g.* [The struggle of the Bol'sheviks for the leadership of the peasant movement of 1905]. Moscow: Izdatel'stvo Moskovskogo universiteta, 1970.

Tsamutali, Aleksei Nikolaevich, ed. *Konstantin Nikolaevich Tarnovskii: Istorik i ego vremia. Istoriografiia, vospominaniia, issledovaniia* [Konstantin Nikolaevich Tvardovskii: The historian and his time. Historiography, recollections, research]. Saint Petersburg: Blits, 2002.

Tsentral'nyi statisticheskii komitet Ministerstva vnutrennikh del. *Dvizhenie naseleniia v Evropeiskoi Rossii za...god* [Movement of the population of European Russia in the year _____]. Published annually. Saint Petersburg, 1872–1916. Data for 1867–1878 in issues of *Statisticheskii vremennik Rossiiskoi imperii* [Statistical Annals of the Russian Empire], Seriia II, vyp. 8, 12, 13, 14, 17, 18, 20, 21, 22, 23, 24 and 25; for 1879–1884, Seriia III, vyp. 3, 7, 20, 21, 23, 24 and 25. The 25th number (1890) provided retrospective district breakdowns for 1876–1878; for the years 1885–1910, the digests appear in *Statistika rossiiskoi imperii* [Statistics of the Russian Empire], volumes XI, XII, XVIII, XXI, XXIV, XXXIII, XXXIV, XXXVIII, XLI, XLV, XLVII, XLVIII, L, LVI, LVIII, LXII, LXIII, LXVI, LXX, LXXIV, LXXXIV, LXXXV, LXXXVII, LXXXVIII, XCI, XCIII. Saint Petersburg, 1890–1916.

———. *Goroda Rossi v 1910 godu.* Saint Petersburg: Tipo-litografiia N.L. Nyrkina, 1914.

———. *Naselennyia mesta Rossiiskoi imperii v 500 i bolee zhitelei s ukazaniem vsego nalichnnago v nikh naseleniia i chisla zhitelei preobladaiushchikh veroispovedanii, po dannym pervoi vseobshchei perepisi naseleniia 1897 g.* [Populated places of the Russian Empire with 500 or more inhabitants with reference to all of their current population and the number of inhabitants of the predominant religious faiths in accordance with the data of the First General Census of Population of 1897]. Saint Petersburg: Tipografiia "Obshchestvennia pol'za," 1905.

———. *Obshchii svod po Imperii resul'tatov razrabotki dannykh pervoi vseobshchei perepisi Rossiiskoi imperii proizvedennoi 28 ianvaria 1897 g.* [Aggregate digest for the Empire of the results of the processing of data of the First General Census of the Russian Empire conducted on January 28, 1897]. Tom I. Saint Petersburg: Tipo-litografiia N.L. Nyrkina, 1906.

———. *Pervaia vseobshchaia perepis' naseleniia Rossiiskoi imperii 1897 g. Vyp. XX. Kurskaia guberniia* [The First General Census of the population of the Russian Empire of 1897. Issue 20: Kursk Province]. Saint Petersburg: Tipografiia aktsionernago obshchestva "Slovo," 1904.

————. *Spiski naselennykh mest Rossiiskoi imperii, sostavlenniya i izdavaemya Tsentral'-nago statisticheskago komiteta Vyp. 20. Kurskaia guberniia po svedeniiam 1862 goda* [Lists of populated places of the Russian Empire, compiled and published by the Central Statistical Committee. Issue 20. Kursk Province according to information from 1862]. Saint Petersburg: Tipografiia Karla Vul'fa, 1868.

————. *Statisticheskii Ezhegodnik Rossii. 1911 god* [Statistical Yearbook of Russia. 1911]. Saint Petersburg, 1912.

————. *Statisticheskii vremennik Rossiiskoi imperii* [Statistical annals of the Russian Empire], Seriia III, vyp. 5 (1885): *Ponizhenie vykupnago platezha po ukazu 28 dekabria 1881 g.*, Reduction of Redemption Payment by the decree of December 28, 1881. G. Ershov, compiler.

————. *Statisticheskii vremennik Rossiiskoi imperii* [Statistical annals of the Russian Empire], Seriia III, vyp. 11 (1886): *Materialy Tsentral'nago statisticheskago komiteta Ministerstva vnutrennikh del po spetsial'nomu ponizheniiu vykupnykh platezhei.* [Materials of the Central Statistical Committee of the Ministry of Internal Affairs on the special reduction of redemption payments.]

————. *Statistika pozemel'noi sobstvennosti naselennykh mest Evropeiskoi Rossii. Vypusk I. Gubernii tsentral'noi zemledel'cheskoi oblasti* [Statistics of land ownerships in the populated places of European Russia. Issue I: Provinces of the Central Agricultural Region]. Saint Petersburg: Tipografiia Ministerstva vnutrennikh del, 1880.

————. *Statistika Rossiiskoi imperii. Tom XXII (1899). Glavneishiia dannyia pozemel'noi statistiki po obsledovaniiu 1887 goda. Vyp. XX. Kurskaia guberniia.* [Statistics of the Russian Empire. Volume XXII. Principal data for land statistics according to the investigation of 1887. Issue XX: Kursk Province.]

————. *Statistika Rossiiskoi imperii. Tom XX (1891): Voenno-konskaia perepis' 1888 goda; Tom XXXVII (1896): Voenno-konskaia perepis' 1893 goda; Tom LV (1902): Voenno-konskaia perepis' 1900 goda.* [Statistics of the Russian Empire. The military horse census of the year ____].

————. *Statistika Rossiiskoi imperii. Tom LXXIX (1913). Sel'skokhoziaistvenniia mashiny i orudiia v Evropeiskoi Rossii v 1910 godu.* [Statistics of the Russian Empite. Volume LXXIX. Agricultural machines and tools in European Russia in 1910].

————. *Statistika Rossiiskoi imperii. Urozhai (1888–1913) goda v Evropeiskoi Rossii* [Statistics of the Russian Empire. Harvest for the year ____ in European Russia]. Published annually. Saint Petersburg, 1890–1913.

————. *Statistika zemlevladeniia 1905 g. Vyp. 37: Kurskaia guberniia* [Statistics of Land Ownership for 1905. Issue 37: Kursk Province]. Saint Petersburg: Tipo-litografiia N.L. Nyrkina, 1906.

————. *Urozhai (1883–1887) goda v Evropeiskoi Rossii* [Harvests for the year ____ in European Russia]. Published annually. Saint Petersburg, 1884–1888.

————. *Volosti i vazhneishie seleniia Evropeiskoi Rossii. Vyp. I. Gubernii tsentra'noi zemledel'cheskoi oblasti* [Parishes and principal settlements of European Russia. Issue I. Provinces of the Central Agricultural Region]. Saint Petersburg: Tipografiia Ministerstva vnutrennikh del, 1880.

————. *Vremennik Tsentral'nago Statisticheskago Komiteta Ministerstva vnutrennikh del* [Annals of the Central Statistical Committee of the Ministry of Internal Affairs], Seriia III, vyp. 4 (1884): *Raspredelenie zemel' po ugod'iam i pakhatnykh po raznago roda posevam v Evropeiskoi Rossii (Po dannym obsledovaniia, proizvedennago osen'iu*

1881 goda) [Distribution of lands by arable type and by various crops sown (based on data of the investigation conducted in the autumn of 1881)].

———. *Vremennik tsentral'nago statisticheskago komiteta Ministerstva vnutrennikh del* [Annals of the Central Statistical Committee of the Ministry of Internal Affairs], No. 2 (1888): *O zadolzhennosti zemlevladeniia v sviazi s statisticheskimi dannymi o pritoke kapitalov k pomestnomu zemlevladeniiu so vremeni osvobozhdeniia krest'ian.* On the indebtedness of landholding in connection with the flow of capital to gentry landholding from the time of the Emancipation. I.I. Kaufman, ed.

———. *Vremennik Tsentral'nago statisticheskago komiteta Ministerstva vnutrennikh del* [Annals of the Central Statistical Committee of the Ministry of Internal Affairs], No. 9 (1889): *Svedeniia o chisle sotskikh i desiatskikh v 1888 godu.* [Data on the numbers of hundredsmen and thousandsmen in 1888].

———. *Vremennik tsentral'nago statisticheskago komiteta Ministerstva vnutrennikh del* [Annals of the Central Statistical Committee of the Ministry of Internal Affairs], No. 50 (1901): *Svedeniia o kolichestve skota v 1900 godu (po dannym volostnykh pravlenii i uezdnoi politsii).* Information on numbers of cattle in 1900 (according to the data of parish administrations and the district police].

———. *Vzaimnoe zemskoe strakhovanie, 1866–1876. Izdanie Tsentral'nago statisticheskago komiteta Ministerstva vnutrennikh del* [Zemstvo mutual insurance, 1866–1876. Publication of the Central Statistical Committee of the Ministry of Internal Affairs]. Saint Petersburg: Tipografiia Trenke i Fiusno, 1884.

———. "Vzaimnoe strakhovanie ot ognia gubernskoe, zemskoe i gorodskoe, 1889–1892 gg." [Provincial, zemstvo and urban mutual fire insurance, 1889–1892]. *Vremennik Tsentral'nago statisticheskago komiteta Ministerstva vnutrennikh Del* no. 27 (1893): 18–33.

"Tsirkuliar' predsedatelia Soveta ministrov P. A. Stolypina ot 15 sentiabria 1906 g. general-gubernatoram, gubernatoram i gradonachal'nikam." *Krasnyi arkhiv* 32 no. 1 (1929): 162–182.

Tvardovskaia, Valentina Aleksandrovna. "Tsarstvovanie Aleksandra III" [The Reign of Alexander III]. In Vladislav Iakimovich Grosul, ed., *Russkii konservatizm XIX stoletiia: ideologiia i praktika.* Moscow: Progress-Traditsiia, 2000, 276–360.

Upravlenie delami Osobogo soveshchaniia dlia obsuzhdeniia i ob"edineniia meropriatii po prodovol'stvennomu delu. *Proizvodstvo, perevozki i potreblenie khlebov v Rossii, 1909–1913 gg. Vyp. 1. Rozh', Pshenitsa, Iachmen', Oves* [Production, transport and consumption of grain in Russia, 1909–1913. Issue 1: Rye, wheat, barley, oats]. Petrograd: Gosudarstvennaia tipografiia, 1916.

Urlanis, Boris Tsesarevich. *Rozhdaemost' i prodolzhitel'nost' zhizni v SSSR* [Fertility and life expectancy in the USSR]. Moscow: Gosstatizdat, 1963.

V.Sh. "Trudovaia gruppa v gosudarstvennoi Dume" [The Labor Group in the State Duma], brochure, no date, no publisher, probably late May, 1905, 16.

Vainshtein, A.L. "Iz istorii predrevoliutsionnoi statistiki zhivodnovodstva" [From the history of pre-revolutionary statistics on animal husbandry]. *Ocherki po istorii statistiki SSSR* no. 3 (1960): 86–115.

Vdovin, Vitalii Aleksandrovich. *Krest'ianskii Pozemel'nyi Bank: 1883–1895 gg.* [The Peasant Land Bank, 1883–1895]. Moscow: Gosfinizdat, 1959.

Ven'iaminov, P. *Krest'ianskaia obshchina: chto ona takoe, k chemu idet, chto daet i chto mozhet dat' Rossii* [The peasant commune: What it is, toward what it heads, what it provides and what it might provide Russia]. Saint Petersburg: "Trudovoi soiuz," 1908.

Verner, Andrew M. *The Crisis of Russian Autocracy: Nicholas II and the 1905 Revolution.* Princeton: Princeton University Press, 1990.

Verner, Ippolit Antonovich, ed. *Kurskaia guberniia. Itogi statisticheskago issledovaniia* [Kursk Province. Results of the statistical investigation]. Kursk: Tipografiia Kurskago Gubernskago Zemstva, 1887.

——. "Zemlevladenie i zemledelie v Kurskoi gubernii" [Land tenure and agriculture in Kursk Province] *Russkaia mysl'* no. 4 (1887, aprel'): 52–73.

——. "Statistika pered sudom Kurskago zemstva" [Statistics before the judgment of the Kursk zemstvo] *Russkaia mysl'* no. 7 (1888): 152–176.

Veselovskii, Boris Borisovich. *Krest'ianskii vopros i krest'ianskoe dvizhenie (1902–1906)* [The Peasant Question and the Peasant Movement (1902–1906)]. Saint Petersburg: Elektropechatnia tovarishchestvo "Delo," 1907.

——. *Zemstvo za sorok let* [The zemstvo over forty years]. Volumes I–IV. Saint Petersburg: Izdatel'stvo O.N. Popovoi, 1909–1911.

Vishnevskii, A.G., ed. *Brachnost', rozhdaemost' i smertnost' v Rossii i v SSSR* [Nuptuality, fertility and mortality in Russia and the USSR]. Moscow: Statistika, 1977.

Vitte, Sergei Iulevich. *Zemstvo i samoderzhavie. Konfidentsial'naia zapiska Ministra finansov Stats-Sekretaria S. Iu. Witte* [Zemstvo and autocracy: confidential memoire of the Minister of Finances S. Iu. Witte]. Stuttgart: Verlag und Druck von J.H.W. Dietz Hachf., 1901.

——. *Vospominaniia* [Memoirs]. 3 volumes. Moscow: Izdatel'stvo sotsial'no-ekonomicheskoi literatury, 1960.

Vodarskii, Iaroslav Evgen'evich. *Dvorianskoe zemlevladenie v Rossii v XVII-pervoi polovine XIX v.* [Gentry landholding in Russia from the seventeenth century to the first half of the nineteenth century]. Moscow: Nauka, 1988.

Volin, Lazar. *A Century of Russian Agriculture.* Cambridge, Mass.: Harvard University Press, 1970.

Von Laue, Theodore. *Sergei Witte and the Industrialization of Russia.* New York: Columbia University Press, 1963.

Vronskii, Oleg Genrikhovich. *Krest'ianskaia obshchina na rubezhe XIX–XX vek: struktura upravleniia, pozemel'nye otnosheniia, pravoporiadok* [The peasant commune at the turn of the nineteenth century: structure of administration, landed relationships, juridical order]. Moscow: Moskovskii gosudarstvennyi pedagogicheskii universitet, 1999.

——. *Gosudarstvennaia vlast' i krest'ianskaia obshchina v gody "velikikh potriasenii" 1905–1917* [State power and the peasant commune during the years of the "great shocks," 1905–1917]. Tula: Tul'skii poligrafist, 2000.

Vucinich, Wayne S., ed. *The Peasant in Nineteenth-Century Russia.* Stanford: Stanford University Press, 1968.

V.V. "Semeinye razdely i krest'ianskoe khoziaistvo" [Family partitions and peasant economy]. *Otechestvennye zapiski* III, t. 266, no. 1 (1883, ianvar'): 1–23; no. 2 (1883, fevral'): 137–161.

Vysochaishe uchrezhdennoe Osoboe Soveshchanie o nuzhdakh sel'skokhoziaistvennoi promyshlennosti. *Trudy mestnykh komitetov o nuzhdakh sel'skolhoziaistvennoi promyshlennosti. XIX. Kurskaia guberniia* [Proceedings of the local committees on the needs of rural industry. Issue XIX: Kursk Province]. Saint Petersburg: Tipografiia V. Kirshbauma, 1903.

Wheatcroft, Stephen G. "Crises and the Condition of the Peasantry in Late Imperial Russia." In Esther Kingston-Mann and Timothy Mixter, eds. *Peasant Economy, Culture and Politics of European Russia, 1800–1921*. Princeton: Princeton University Press, 1991, 128–172.

Whelan, Heidi W. *Alexander III and the State Council: Bureaucracy and Counterreform in Late Imperial Russia*. New Brunswick NJ: Rutgers University Press, 1982.

Wilbur, Elvira M.W. "The Peasant Economy, Landlords, and Revolution in Voronezh: A Call for a Reappraisal of the Nature of the Russian Revolutionary Crisis at the Turn of the Century." Ph.D dissertation, University of Michigan, 1977.

———. "Was Russian Peasant Agriculture Really That Impoverished? Evidence from a Case Study from the 'Impoverished Center' at the End of the Nineteenth Century." *Journal of Economic History* 43, no. 1 (March 1983): 137–144.

———. "Peasant Poverty in Theory and Practice: A View from Russia's 'Impoverished Center' at the End of the Nineteenth Century." In Kingston-Mann, E. and Mixter, T., eds. *Peasant Economy, Culture, and Politics of European Russia 1800–1921*. Princeton: Princeton University Press, 1991, 101–127.

Wisclo, Francis William. "The Land Captain Reform of 1889 and the Reassertion of Unrestricted Autocratic Authority." *Russian History* 15, nos. 2–4 (1988): 285–326.

———. *Reforming Rural Russia: State, Local and National Politics, 1855–1914*. Princeton: Princeton University Press, 1990.

Wolf, Eric R. *Peasant Wars of the Twentieth Century*. New York: Harper & Row, 1969.

Worobec, Christine D. "The Post-Emancipation Russian Peasant Commune in Orel Province, 1861–1890," in Roger Bartlett, ed., *Land Commune and Peasant Community in Russia*. New York: St. Martin's Press, 1990, 86–105.

———. *Peasant Russia: Family and Community in the Post-Emancipation Period*. Princeton: Princeton University Press, 1991.

———. "Death Ritual among Russian and Ukrainian Peasant: Linkages between the Living and the Dead." In Stephen P. Frank and Mark D. Steinberg, eds., *Cultures in Flux: Lower Class Values, Practices and Resistance in Late Imperial Russia*. Princeton: Princeton University Press, 1994, 11–33.

Yaney, George L. *The Systematization of Russian Government: Social Evolution in the Domestic Administration of Imperial Russia, 1711–1905*. Urbana IL: University of Illinois Press, 1973.

Zaionchkovskii, Petr Andreevich. *Provedenie v zhizn' krest'ianskoi reformy 1861 g.* [Implementation of the peasant reform of 1861]. Moscow: Gosudarstvennoe izdatel'stvo sotsial'no-ekonomicheskoi literatury, 1958.

———. "Podgotovka i priniatie zakona 24 noiabria 1866 g. o gosudarstvennykh krest'ianakh" [Preparation and adoption of the Law of 24 November 1866 on the state peasants]. *Istoriia SSSR* no. 4 (1958, iiul'-avgust): 103–113.

———. *Otmena krepostnogo prava v Rossii* [The abolition of serfdom in Russia]. Moscow: Gosudarstvennoe izdatel'stvo politicheskoi literatury, 1968.

———. *Rossiiskoe samoderzhavie v kontse XIX stoletiia: Politicheskaia reaktsiia 80-kh nachala 90-kh godov* [The Russian autocracy at the end of the nineteenth century: the political reaction of the 1880s and beginning of the 1890s]. Moscow: Mysl', 1970.

————. *Pravitel'stvennyi apparat samoderzhavnoi Rossii v XIX v.* [The state apparatus of autocratic Russia in the nineteenth century]. Moscow: Mysl', 1978.

Zaitsev, V. "K voprosu o chislennosti naseleniia v Rossii v period 1871–1915 gg." [On the question population numbers in Russia during the period 1871–1915]. In *Vliianie neurozhaev na narodnoe khoziaistvo Rossii. Pod obshchei redaktsiei V.G. Gromana.* Chast' vtoraia. Moscow : Rossiiskaia assotsiatsiia nauchno-issledovatel'skikh institutov obshchestvennykh naukov, 1927, 60–93.

Zak, Aleksandr N. *Krest'ianskii Pozemel'nyi Bank, 1883–1910* [The Peasant Land Bank, 1883–1910]. Moscow: Skoropechatnia A.A. Levensona, 1911.

Zakharova, Larisa Georg'evna. *Zemskaia kontrreforma 1890 g.* [The zemstvo counterreform of 1890]. Moscow: Izdatel'stvo Moskovskogo universiteta 1968.

————. *Samoderzhavie i otmena krepostnogo prava v Rossii, 1856–1861* [Autocracy and the abolition of serfdom in Russia, 1856–1861]. Moscow: Izdatel'stvo Moskovskogo universiteta, 1984.

Zhurnal Vysochaishe utverzhdennoi 16-go noiabria 1901 g. Kommissii po issledovaniiu voprosa o dvizhenii s 1861 g. po 1900 g. blagosostoianiia sel'skago naseleniia srednezemledel'cheskikh gubernii, sravnitel'no s drugimi mestnostiami Evropeiskoi Rossii. Zasedaniia 10, 19, 20 i 24-go oktiabria 1903 g. [Journal of the Commission ordered by His Majesty on November 16, 1901, for a study of the question of trends in the prosperity of the rural populace of the Central Agricultural provinces from 1861 to 1900, compared to other localities of European Russia. Sessions of 10, 19, 20 and 24 October, 1903]. Saint Petersburg: Tipografiia P.P. Soikina, n.d.

Z.N. "O krest'ianskikh semeinikh razdelakh" [On peasant family partitions]. *Pravo* no.12 (1901 18 marta): col. 639–640.

Index

Oboian District